THE WRITER'S HANDBOOK

The *Writer's* Handbook

Edited by

SYLVIA K. BURACK

Editor, The Writer

Publishers THE WRITER, INC. Boston

"Plot and Character in Suspense Fiction," by Joan Aiken. Copyright © 1988, by Joan Aiken Enterprises, Ltd.

"Always a Storyteller," by Mary Higgins Clark, Copyright © 1987, by Mares Enterprises, Inc.

"Dick Francis: An Interview" is reprinted by permission of the author from *Writers' Monthly* (England)

"Grilling Ed McBain," by Evan Hunter, Copyright © 1989, by Hui Corp., published by permission of the author, c/o John Farquharson, Ltd.

"How Much of That Story Is True?" by David Huddle, reprinted from *The New York Times Book Review* (October 7, 1990), by permission of the author.

"Getting Started," by John Irving, Copyright © 1991 by John Irving. Originally published in *Publishers Weekly* (January 24, 1991).

"Inside a Poem," Copyright © 1989 by Eve Merriam.

"Ballad of the Boneless Chicken" and "Euphonica Jarre" from *The New Kid on the Block* by Jack Prelutsky. Copyright © 1984 by Jack Prelutsky. Reprinted by permission of Greenwillow Books, a division of William Morrow & Co.

"I Wave Good-bye When Butter Flies" from *Something Big Has Been Here* by Jack Prelutsky. Copyright © 1990 by Jack Prelutsky. Reprinted by permission of Greenwillow Books, a division of William Morrow & Co.

Library of Congress Catalog Card Number: 36-28596
ISBN: 0-87116-165-6

Printed in The United States of America

CONTENTS

BACKGROUND FOR WRITERS

HOW TO WRITE—TECHNIQUES

GENERAL FICTION

WHERE TO SELL

BACKGROUND FOR WRITERS

1

RECREATING REALITY: MAKING IT HAPPEN FOR YOUR READER

BY URSULA K. LE GUIN

I DON'T KNOW HOW MANY TIMES I READ OR WAS TOLD, "Write what you know. Write about what you know."

And it is certainly good advice.

On the common sense level, it keeps you from looking foolish. For instance, when I was a very young writer, I wanted very much to put an Englishman in the story I was writing. But I didn't know any Englishmen, didn't really know how the English talk, except in movies; all I knew was that there were lots of people who *did* know—including the population of England. And if they read my story, they'd notice every mistake I made. I had read stories by English writers who had characters from Brooklyn saying things like "Aw, shucks, podner, I reckon 'tain't so," and I knew that a story can never recover from what you might call the Shock of Ignorance. So, until I really knew some Englishmen, I'd better stick to American characters.

If you take it in its deepest meaning, "Write about what you know" means write from your heart, from your own real being, your own thoughts and emotions. It means what Socrates meant when he said, "Know yourself." If you don't know who you are and what you know, if you haven't worked to find out what you yourself truly feel and think, then your work will probably be imitation work, borrowed from other writers. It may be brilliant, full of meanings and ambiguities and symbols and all that stuff they teach in literature courses, but it won't be the real goods. It won't wash. There won't be any wear in it, and the colors will run. . . .

See, I know quite a lot about doing the wash. I know what you can put in the dryer and what you have to line-dry, and what happens to rayon if the water's too hot. Doing the wash has been a notable part of my life experience. I could write plenty about it.

So I can draw on it for a metaphor. Or if a character in a story is doing the wash, I can describe what she does (or, less probably, what he does) without having to do any research on it—at least, if my washerwoman is modern American. If she lives in Borneo, or in 1877, then I know only part of what doing the wash involves for her. I may well have to go read up on it—literally go to the library to find out how to do the laundry.

And this is where the advice about writing what you know begins to get a little tight at the seams. How much does any of us really know?

Writers who start out young often feel they really don't know *anything;* but those who begin writing later in life know that you can only get so much into a few decades. Most of us have not wrangled cattle, piloted a jet, been a midwife, managed an insurance office, nursed in a burn ward, or visited Saskatchewan; none of us has done all those things. Even if we've traveled, changed jobs, changed spouses, had adventures, there's no way we can experience everything, and if we tried, we'd be so busy rushing about "getting experience" that we'd never write anything.

"Write what you know" doesn't mean you have to know a lot. It just tells you to take what you have, take who you are, and *use it.* Don't try to use secondhand feeling; use yourself. Stake your claim, however small it may seem, and dig your own gold mine.

Artist-writers are miners, digging deeper and deeper to get to the true gold—to find out what it is they really know about themselves, about their life, about other people, about life.

But their shovel, their pick, the tool they use, *is their writing.* Writing itself, writing fiction or poetry, is a learning device—a means of knowledge, self-knowledge, knowledge of life.

So how can you write what you know, if you use your writing to find out what you know?

If you truly limited yourself to "what you know," you would have to write only about people of your gender, living during your lifetime in places where you have lived, doing and thinking and feeling just what you do, think, and feel.

Is that so bad? Well, it rules out fantasy, romance, historical novels, and science fiction, but still, don't most real novelists write from their own experience? Isn't that what Jane Austen did? Isn't that what Dickens and Tolstoy and Woolf did?

I don't think so. Jane Austen was never a man, Dickens never was a

4

hunted murderer, Tolstoy didn't fight in the Napoleonic Wars, and Virginia Woolf was not a spaniel. Yet they wrote about those experiences. In using what they knew, using *everything* they knew about their own incredibly intensely lived/thought/felt lives, they also used their imagination.

Aha, what is this stray sock that's come up as the wash goes round? Is it a red one? Will it turn everything else pink? Yes, it will! Once you get the imagination in, all the colors of everything change. And the color never fades.

Jane Austen couldn't experience what it was to be a man. All she—a shy, unmarried woman—could do was watch the men who came into her narrow, limited life—father, brothers, brothers-in-law, clergymen—listen to them, think about them, and imagine her way into their minds and hearts, until she knew what a certain kind of man would think and feel, would say and wouldn't say—knew it with the knowledge of the imagination. And so created proud, stubborn, honorable, lovable Mr. Darcy, a real man, a true man.

What distinguishes imagination from wishful thinking is truthfulness. Heroes in romances aren't meant to be true men, but dream-men—boytoys. Women in novels by men all too often are mere objects of desire or of terrified hatred, stereotypes: sexpots, witches, the fair maiden, the bad mother, etc. Here both knowledge and imagination have failed.

If fiction is to be truthful about what human beings really are and do, we have to define knowledge as a goal of the imagination. After all, when I go down to the library and find out about doing the laundry in Borneo or in 1877, I'm not learning through experience, but through the imagination: I read, and recreate the reality in my mind till I know it. That's what writing, fact or fiction, is for. What I "know" comes to me maybe from experience, maybe from hearsay, maybe from books or other arts. What matters is what I make of it—what I do with it.

Let's say that there is something you know, an experience, a fact: When you were a kid, Mrs. Brown next door put so much bleach in the wash that her family's clothes disintegrated. This event has stuck in your mind ever since. Did she mean to pour in a gallon of Clorox? Did she know she was doing it? Did she think about it beforehand? You don't *know,* but you begin to *imagine* how it happened . . . and a story begins to grow around that memory and those imaginings.

So the fact becomes a nucleus of a story. Maybe it's one small event in the story, maybe it's the climax, depending on how you imagine it. That's the imagination using knowledge to create deeper knowledge. And the story is how you arrive at and how you tell that new understanding.

But then a very upsetting thing can happen when other people read your story. They say, Oh, wow, this is great, but listen, there's this one part that I just don't believe. It's where she pours a whole gallon of Clorox into the washing machine. It just isn't convincing.

Hey! you say. But that's the true part! It happened! I was there!

And your reader looks at you and says, So what? You have to make it happen for me. You have to make *me* be there.

That is the trick hidden in "write what you know." Just knowing isn't enough. You "know it for a fact"—but your job as a writer is to "make it true." The writer makes it *seem* true (so that the reader won't question it), and also finds out the *truth* of it (so that telling matters).

A gallon of Clorox in the wash is the fact.

Making it seem true is imagining the scene: the way the Clorox gurgled out of the heavy plastic jug, the way the white, white shirts tore and shredded away from the clothesline as the wind tugged them. . . .

Finding the truth in it is imagining what Mrs. Brown thought and felt: how she picked up her husband's overalls from the floor where he'd dropped them and looked at the oily filth ground into them, while she heard him in the other room turning the pages of his porn magazine. . . .

If we look at "writing what you know" in this way, we can even put fantasy and science fiction back in the tub. The whole wash has turned rainbow-colored anyhow. If Dickens can kill Nancy (in *Oliver Twist*), Virginia Woolf can be a spaniel (in *Flush*), and Tolstoy can be Napoleon (in *War and Peace*), and yet all of them are writing from real knowledge given them by the imagination, then you and I can be tentacled purple dweebdorks from the Planet Fsrxki. If we think about the dweebdorks, if we listen to them, feel what they feel, get into their purple skins, if we *know* them, if we even know how dweebdorks do their laundry . . . then we can show our readers that they, too, can be dweebdorks for as long as the story lasts, and that, though it never happened and never will, it matters—it is true.

6

2

Everything You Need to Know About Writing Successfully— in Ten Minutes

By Stephen King

I. *The First Introduction*

THAT'S RIGHT. I know it sounds like an ad for some sleazy writers' school, but I really am going to tell you everything you need to pursue a successful and financially rewarding career writing fiction, and I really am going to do it in ten minutes, which is exactly how long it took me to learn. It will actually take you twenty minutes or so to read this essay, however, because I have to tell you a story, and then I have to write a *second* introduction. But these, I argue, should not count in the ten minutes.

II. *The Story, or, How Stephen King Learned to Write*

When I was a sophomore in high school, I did a sophomoric thing which got me in a pot of fairly hot water, as sophomoric didoes often do. I wrote and published a small satiric newspaper called *The Village Vomit*. In this little paper I lampooned a number of teachers at Lisbon (Maine) High School, where I was under instruction. These were not very gentle lampoons; they ranged from the scatological to the downright cruel.

Eventually, a copy of this little newspaper found its way into the hands of a faculty member, and since I had been unwise enough to put my name on it (a fault, some critics would argue, of which I have still not been entirely cured), I was brought into the office. The sophisticated satirist had by that time reverted to what he really was: a fourteen-year-old kid who was shaking in his boots and wondering if he was going to get a suspension . . . what we called "a three-day vacation" in those dim days of 1964.

I wasn't suspended. I was forced to make a number of apologies—they were warranted, but they still tasted like dog-dirt in my mouth—

and spent a week in detention hall. And the guidance counselor arranged what he no doubt thought of as a more constructive channel for my talents. This was a job—contingent upon the editor's approval—writing sports for the Lisbon *Enterprise,* a twelve-page weekly of the sort with which any small-town resident will be familiar. This editor was the man who taught me everything I know about writing in ten minutes. His name was John Gould—not the famed New England humorist or the novelist who wrote *The Greenleaf Fires,* but a relative of both, I believe.

He told me he needed a sports writer and we could "try each other out," if I wanted.

I told him I knew more about advanced algebra than I did sports.

Gould nodded and said, "You'll learn."

I said I would at least try to learn. Gould gave me a huge roll of yellow paper and promised me a wage of ½¢ per word. The first two pieces I wrote had to do with a high school basketball game in which a member of my school team broke the Lisbon High scoring record. One of these pieces was straight reportage. The second was a feature article.

I brought them to Gould the day after the game, so he'd have them for the paper, which came out Fridays. He read the straight piece, made two minor corrections, and spiked it. Then he started in on the feature piece with a large black pen and taught me all I ever needed to know about my craft. I wish I still had the piece—it deserves to be framed, editorial corrections and all—but I can remember pretty well how it looked when he had finished with it. Here's an example:

> Last night, in the ~~well-loved~~
> gymnasium ~~of~~ Lisbon High School, partisans
> and Jay Hills fans alike were stunned by
> an athletic performance unequalled in school
> history: Bob Ransom~~, known as "Bullet" Bob~~
> ~~for both his size and accuracy~~, scored
> thirty-seven points. He did it with grace
> and speed...and he did it with an odd courtesy
> as well, committing only two personal fouls
> in his ~~knight-like~~ quest for a record which
> has eluded Lisbon ~~thinclads~~ *is basketball team* since 1953...

When Gould finished marking up my copy in the manner I have indicated above, he looked up and must have seen something on my face. I think *he* must have thought it was horror, but it was not: it was revelation.

"I only took out the bad parts, you know," he said. "Most of it's pretty good."

"I know," I said, meaning both things: yes, most of it was good, and yes, he had only taken out the bad parts. "I won't do it again."

"If that's true," he said, "you'll never have to work again. You can do *this* for a living." Then he threw back his head and laughed.

And he was right: I *am* doing this for a living, and as long as I can keep on, I don't expect ever to have to work again.

III. *The Second Introduction*

All of what follows has been said before. If you are interested enough in writing to be a purchaser of this magazine, you will have either heard or read all (or almost all) of it before. Thousands of writing courses are taught across the United States each year; seminars are convened; guest lecturers talk, then answer questions, then drink as many gin and tonics as their expense-fees will allow, and it all boils down to what follows.

I am going to tell you these things again because often people will only listen—really *listen*—to someone who makes a lot of money doing the thing he's talking about. This is sad but true. And I told you the story above not to make myself sound like a character out of a Horatio Alger novel but to make a point: I saw, I listened, and *I learned*. Until that day in John Gould's little office, I had been writing first drafts of stories which might run 2,500 words. The second drafts were apt to run 3,300 words. Following that day, my 2,500-word first drafts became 2,200-word second drafts. And two years after that, I sold the first one.

So here it is, with all the bark stripped off. It'll take ten minutes to read, and you can apply it right away . . . if you *listen*.

IV. *Everything You Need to Know About Writing Successfully*

1. *Be talented*

This, of course, is the killer. What is talent? I can hear someone shouting, and here we are, ready to get into a discussion right up there with "What is the meaning of life?" for weighty pronouncements and total uselessness. For the purposes of the beginning writer, talent may as well be defined as eventual success—publication and money. If you wrote something for which someone sent you a check, if you cashed the check and it didn't bounce, and if you then paid the light bill with the money, I consider you talented.

Now some of you are really hollering. Some of you are calling me one crass money-fixated creep. And some of you are calling me *bad* names. *Are you calling Harold Robbins talented?* someone in one of the Great English Departments of America is screeching. *V. C. Andrews? Theodore Dreiser? Or what about you, you dyslexic moron?*

Nonsense. Worse than nonsense, off the subject. We're not talking about good or bad here. I'm interested in telling you how to get your stuff published, not in critical judgments of who's good or bad. As a rule the critical judgments come after the check's been spent, anyway. I have my own opinions, but most times I keep them to myself. People who are published steadily and are paid for what they are writing may be either saints or trollops, but they are clearly reaching a great many someones who want what they have. Ergo, they are communicating. Ergo, they are talented. The biggest part of writing successfully is being talented, and in the context of marketing, the only bad writer is one who doesn't get paid. If you're not talented, you won't succeed. And if you're not succeeding, you should know when to quit.

When is that? I don't know. It's different for each writer. Not after six rejection slips, certainly, nor after sixty. But after six hundred? Maybe. After six thousand? My friend, after six thousand pinks, it's time you tried painting or possibly computer programming.

Further, almost every aspiring writer knows when he is getting warmer—you start getting little jotted notes on your rejection slips, or personal letters . . . maybe a commiserating phone call. It's lonely out there in the cold, but there *are* encouraging voices . . . unless there is nothing in your words which warrants encouragement. I think you owe it to yourself to skip as much of the self-illusion as possible. If your eyes are open, you'll know which way to go . . . or when to turn back.

2. *Be neat.*

Type. Double-space. Use a nice heavy white paper, never that erasable onion-skin stuff. If you've marked up your manuscript a lot, do another draft.

10

3. *Be self-critical*

If you *haven't* marked up your manuscript a lot, you did a lazy job. Only God gets things right the first time. Don't be a slob.

4. *Remove every extraneous word*

You want to get up on a soapbox and preach? Fine. Get one and try your local park. You want to write for money? Get to the point. And if you remove all the excess garbage and discover you can't find the point, tear up what you wrote and start all over again . . . or try something new.

5. *Never look at a reference book while doing a first draft*

You want to write a story? Fine. Put away your dictionary, your encyclopedias, your World Almanac, and your thesaurus. Better yet, throw your thesaurus into the wastebasket. The only things creepier than a thesaurus are those little paperbacks college students too lazy to read the assigned novels buy around exam time. Any word you have to hunt for in a thesaurus is the wrong word. There are no exceptions to this rule. You think you might have misspelled a word? O.K., so here is your choice: either look it up in the dictionary, thereby making sure you have it right—and breaking your train of thought and the writer's trance in the bargain—or just spell it phonetically and correct it later. Why not? Did you think it was going to go somewhere? And if you need to know the largest city in Brazil and you find you don't have it in your head, why not write in Miami, or Cleveland? You can check it . . . but *later*. When you sit down to write, *write*. Don't do anything else except go to the bathroom, and only do that if it absolutely cannot be put off.

6. *Know the markets*

Only a dimwit would send a story about giant vampire bats surrounding a high school to *McCall's*. Only a dimwit would send a tender story about a mother and daughter making up their differences on Christmas Eve to *Playboy* . . . but people do it all the time. I'm not exaggerating; I have seen such stories in the slush piles of the actual magazines. If you write a good story, why send it out in an ignorant fashion? Would you send your kid out in a snowstorm dressed in Bermuda shorts and a tank top? If you like science fiction, read the magazines. If you want to write confessions stories, read the magazines. And so on. It isn't just a matter of knowing what's right for the present story; you can begin to catch on, after awhile, to overall rhythms, editorial likes and dislikes, a magazine's entire slant. Sometimes your reading can influence the *next story,* and create a sale.

7. *Write to entertain*

Does this mean you can't write "serious fiction"? It does not. Somewhere along the line pernicious critics have invested the American reading and writing public with the idea that entertaining fiction and serious ideas do not overlap. This would have surprised Charles Dickens, not to mention Jane Austen, John Steinbeck, William Faulkner, Bernard Malamud, and hundreds of others. But your serious ideas must always serve your story, not the other way around. I repeat: if you want to preach, get a soapbox.

8. *Ask yourself frequently, "Am I having fun?"*

The answer needn't always be yes. But if it's always no, it's time for a new project or a new career.

9. *How to evaluate criticism*

Show your piece to a number of people—ten, let us say. Listen carefully to what they tell you. Smile and nod a lot. Then review what was said very carefully. If your critics are all telling you the same thing about some facet of your story—a plot twist that doesn't work, a character who rings false, stilted narrative, or half a dozen other possibles—change that facet. It doesn't matter if you really liked that twist or that character; if a lot of people are telling you something is wrong with your piece, it *is.* If seven or eight of them are hitting on that same thing, I'd still suggest changing it. But if everyone—or even most everyone—is criticizing something different, you can safely disregard what all of them say.

10. *Observe all rules for proper submission*

Return postage, self-addressed envelope, all of that.

11. *An agent? Forget it. For now*

Agents get 10% of monies earned by their clients. 10% of nothing is nothing. Agents also have to pay the rent. Beginning writers do not contribute to that or any other necessity of life. Flog your stories around yourself. If you've done a novel, send around query letters to publishers, one by one, and follow up with sample chapters and/or the manuscript complete. And remember Stephen King's First Rule of Writers and Agents, learned by bitter personal experience: You don't need one until you're making enough for someone to steal . . . and if you're making that much, you'll be able to take your pick of good agents.

12. *If it's bad, kill it*

When it comes to people, mercy killing is against the law. When it comes to fiction, it *is* the law.

That's everything you need to know. And if you listened, you can write everything and anything you want. Now I believe I will wish you a pleasant day and sign off.

My ten minutes are up.

3

KEEPING A JOURNAL

BY BARBARA ABERCROMBIE

FOR MY THIRTEENTH BIRTHDAY, my parents gave me a five-year diary. The pages were dated, so I always felt guilty if I skipped a day, or frustrated when I had a lot to report and not enough space to write it all down. For the most part, I filled it with descriptions of teenage boys—what they looked like and things they said and did—followed by rows of exclamation points. I gave up on the diary when I was about sixteen. Years later in a creative writing class I began keeping a journal, which sounded more serious than writing a diary.

Whether you call yours a diary, a journal, or simply a notebook, this daily record can be one of your most important tools as a writer. It's your camera, a place to record raw material for future fiction, poems, or articles: details of daily life, overheard dialogue, descriptions of landscapes, rooms, faces, weather, behavior. It can be as personal or as impersonal as you want it to be. There are no rules to keeping a journal.

If you've just begun to write, keeping a journal can be a way to establish the habit of writing regularly, though the words "habit" and "regularly" may seem contradictory to anything creative. When you're inspired, you create, and inspiration, as we all know, has no regular habits. Inspiration is the spark, the pressure to give form to chaos, and to put experience or dreams into words. Unless you're a saint or a genius, it's rare to wake up every day feeling inspired. However, when you force yourself to write in a journal regularly, even fifteen minutes a day, the act of writing can lead to inspiration.

Keeping a journal can help you learn about yourself, find out what you think and feel. Use it to discover what you really want and need to write about and the pattern of your highs and lows.

Your journal is a place to find your voice and tone, the true rhythm of your writing. When we begin writing, most of us sound self-consciously literary and stiff, or chatty and sometimes a bit hysterical, with ex-

14

clamation points and capitalized or underlined words. Your journal can be a place to experiment. Try writing an entry in the third person, using the present tense, or from the point of view of your dog or cat. A journal is a private place to take risks.

In *A Writer's Diary* Virginia Woolf asks herself what kind of a diary she'd like to write, and answers: "I should like it to resemble some deep old desk, or capacious hold-all, in which one flings a mass of odds and ends without looking them through." *Without looking them through—* that's important. Try not to censor yourself. Fill your journal with odds and ends, quotes, a running list of the books you read, a record of anything that reflects your inner life and thoughts. Include pictures and clippings that spark your imagination, poems and song lyrics that move you. Write letters in it that you never mail.

There are no rules, but follow this advice: Guard your journal's privacy. Don't let anyone read it. If you want to share a journal entry, copy it out first. Otherwise you may find yourself censoring what you put in it or writing for an audience. Three-ring lined notebooks of about one hundred pages make ideal journals; undated pages give you a greater sense of freedom. (Date them as you make your entries.)

If you feel stuck or overwhelmed when you look at all those blank pages, here is an exercise to get you started: Think about the instant you woke up this morning. Did an alarm clock wake you? Music from a clock radio, another person, your own internal clock? What was your immediate thought or feeling? A dream you'd just had, a physical sensation, joy, dread, a gray blur? Whatever it was, begin writing about it on the first page. Write down *anything* that comes into your head, and continue to write for five minutes. Don't let your pen or pencil stop moving. Memories may surface, maybe something that has nothing to do with waking up this morning. This is called automatic writing (also free writing, stream-of-consciousness, and right-brain writing). It's a useful exercise whenever you're stuck or can't get started.

Now, taking your time about it, write about the first thirty minutes of your morning. Record all your sensory impressions. Did you hear voices, TV music, traffic, birds, or an appliance running? Did you touch skin, water, a pet, something soft, or something rough? Did you taste toothpaste, a cigarette, medicine, food, coffee? Did you smell soap, bacon cooking, smog, perfume? Did you look out your window? What does the wall opposite your bed look like? Describe the way your sheets

15

and blankets look in the morning. Include just the details without commenting on your observations.

In Thornton Wilder's classic play, *Our Town*, there's a powerful and moving moment at the end when Emily returns from the dead to say goodbye to the things she'd taken for granted when she was alive: clocks ticking, her mother's sunflowers, freshly ironed dresses, food and coffee. "Do any human beings ever realize life while they live it?— every, every minute?" she asks.

Realizing life is what writing is all about. Good writing comes from paying attention. Tomorrow in your journal try writing again about the first thirty minutes of your day, but this time make a conscious effort from the moment you wake up to pay attention. Pretend you're Emily returning from the dead for one more look at your life. Pretend you're five years old. Pretend you're from another planet. Pretend whatever is necessary to help you see your own life with fresh eyes and take nothing for granted. The emotional impact of Emily's speech is based on specific and ordinary details of daily life.

May Sarton's published journals about her struggle to grow as a writer and human being weave their spell in part by her faithful rendering of daily life: the seasons, the quirks of an old house, beloved pets, working in a garden, preparing meals. See how simply she begins *Journal of a Solitude:* "September 15th. Begin here. It is raining. I look out on the maple, where a few leaves have turned yellow, and listen to Punch, the parrot, talking to himself and to the rain ticking gently against the windows." In her journals you also find the raw material that she later transforms into her fiction and poems.

To make or break a habit, it's been said, takes twenty-one days. Here are twenty-one suggestions to get you started writing in your journal every day until doing so becomes a habit:

1. What three things in life sustain you emotionally and spiritually?
2. Using all five senses, describe the place you're writing in.
3. How do you feel today? If you come up with a word that can describe food, it's not a feeling. How does this emotion make your body feel?
4. What ten things give you joy?
5. List five things you want. List five things you need.
6. Describe yourself in the third person.

7. What's the best thing that's happened this week? The worst?

8. What is the weather like today? The color of the sky? Is there wind? How does the weather smell? Taste?

9. Write a letter to someone famous, alive or dead.

10. Write a letter to someone you love. Include a request, a regret, and an appreciation.

11. Find a quotation that moves you and copy it down in your journal. Why does it move you?

12. Write a memory from your childhood. Begin with the words, I remember . . .

13. What three goals do you have for the coming year?

14. What do you want to be doing next year at this time? In five years?

15. What's keeping you from doing it right now?

16. Have an imaginary conversation with someone about something that's troubling you.

17. If you could change one thing about yourself, what would it be?

18. Describe a recent dream. If you can't remember one, make one up.

19. Describe something beautiful you saw yesterday. Something ugly.

20. Write about the best meal you had this week. The worst.

21. What are you wearing right now? Describe your clothes in detail to someone from another century.

4

WAITING FOR THE TENTH

BY WILLIAM RAINBOLT

MR. G. RAPPED ON THE DOOR OF THE CLASSROOM and leaned inside. He nodded toward me and asked the history teacher, "Can I see Bill for just a moment?"

I had known Mr. G. for two years, since my sophomore year in high school. He had made us read *Silas Marner,* but I didn't hold that against him, because he also had encouraged me to write. Once, Mr. G. had assigned everyone else in his English class to produce an essay about a football game, but he told me to describe an empty football stadium an hour after a game: "Go there by yourself and just walk around, and *get to know it,*" he said. It was the first time I realized a place could be a character.

But I didn't think anyone could really enroll in a lifelong course called "Writing." For two years, Mr. G. had been encouraging me to join the staff of the school newspaper, or the literary magazine, or do anything else that made me write, but I usually just smiled away this notion. I thought I had to be a coach or doctor or something equally sensible.

Now Mr. G. looked straight at me as we stood in the hallway. He had a thin, ruddy face with clear blue eyes and a wry smile. He wasn't yet thirty, but I thought he was much older.

"You're going to be the sports editor for the school paper," he said firmly. This time it wasn't a question. I was a senior, and he must have felt time was running out for both of us.

I'll never understand how epiphany works, but the instant he said that to me I knew that I had no choice—not because he had ordered me, but because he was right. Graham Greene says a person can grow up in the blink of an eye, and though I didn't become adult in that one instant, I realize now that in a deserted hallway of a Texas high school in the Fall of 1963 my life changed.

Mr. G. is on my list. It's a secret list, nine names written on a yellow slip of paper that is never far away from me. Nine people who have

18

changed me in some way, nine artists who helped create my life as a writer. Nine people, other than my family and my wife, who cared enough to say or do something for me. All writers need such a narrow list, one that has nothing to do with *influences*—a list of Faulkners, Flauberts, and Fitzgeralds—but has everything to do with *inspirations,* a list of names few people would recognize.

But I haven't added anyone to my list in twelve years, and I wonder if I ever will. I've added a lot of names to my roll of influences, but no one has dramatically changed my writer's self in these past twelve years. Will anyone else ever divert my life again, redefine it? Is this what being an adult writer means, that I'm on my own now, beyond the power of someone else to teach me something I myself cannot even imagine yet?

Six years after Mr. G. spoke to me in the hallway, I sat in another classroom, but this time I was not daydreaming about football glory (it never came) or the senior prom (Linda turned me down). No, it was 1969, and I was nauseated with fear.

I had joined the Navy for the sole purpose of avoiding the draft and, hence, Vietnam. Then, in one of those mischievous acts of irony that life enjoys, I found myself assigned to 48 weeks of intensive Russian language training—*me,* so insecure about foreign languages that I had failed college Spanish twice. (I'd assumed I was going to fail, so I didn't go to class.) I had been at the Russian language school for six weeks, waiting for the inevitable dismissal and then for assignment to Vietnam, because that's what was happening to many enlistees who flunked out of their designated schools. I knew I would fail, and this time maybe die for it. *At least,* I was telling myself then, *I'll get good material to write about. I'll be able to leave a legacy written from the flimsy deck of some river patrol boat before it goes up in flames.*

Andre S. rapped on the door, coughed and shrugged his bony left shoulder as he always did, and motioned to me. He was the director of my language program, a fidgety, wiry little man. He and his staff of ten were all emigrés; most of them had fought their way out of Stalinist Russia. They cried when we watched Russian films of Chekhov stories, and so did I.

"What's wrong with you?" Andre snapped as we sat in his office a few minutes later.

"I can't do it. I'll never learn Russian," I whispered, my voice wavering.

"*Nyet!* You *will* learn this language!"

Tears burned my eyes.

He opened the text and workbook, scooted his chair next to mine, and made me tell him everything I'd learned in six weeks. It was more than I'd imagined. He kept saying, "yes, yes, *da.*" I amazed even myself.

Two hours later he sent me back to class, and I couldn't wait to start the six hours of homework. Seven months later I graduated and spent the rest of my tour peacefully as a translator.

He's on the list.

Not all of the nine are teachers—but four of them are. Two others are editors: a young one who gave me my first job—I was seventeen—even after the newspaper's publisher had declared a hiring freeze (my desk was hidden behind three filing cabinets, and I was not to come out between two and four in the afternoon, when the aged publisher usually shuffled through the newsroom); and the other a seasoned, patient pro who let me make mistakes and do childish things, eventually appointing me to be one of the youngest sports editors in Texas at the time because he believed in me. Then there's a minister and his wife (they might be disappointed in me now). I won't describe the ninth. I know at least one of the nine is dead. I know where one of the others is, but the remaining seven are mysteries.

Mysteries, as far as what they're doing now. But there's no mystery about what they each did for me at one point when our lives met. They all gave me something, shaped me, pushed me, changed me. They probably didn't even realize what was happening, and I didn't either at the time.

But it was twelve years ago that I added that last name.

I sit in my own classroom now, teaching and talking about writing, looking at the door and remembering Mr. G. and Andre searching for me. I remember the young editor fidgeting in his creaky chair and shaking his head over my fifth attempt to write a straight news story about a music concert riot; I think I got it right on the sixth try, after his obscenity decibel level had reached what other reporters later claimed was a record height. I see and hear all the people on the list although the doorway is empty, the newsroom has long been rearranged and computerized. Sometimes I talk out loud to the nine.

I can't help but wish they would come back just once and speak to me again—any one of the nine, or all to return as ghosts. And even more, I wish I could write down a tenth name.

20

5

WHY IT'S HARDER TO FIND AN AGENT THAN A PUBLISHER

BY EDWARD NOVAK

IF YOU'VE NEVER TRIED TO SECURE the services of a literary agent, you should be forewarned that at times you'll feel as if you are searching for the Holy Grail. Getting published for the first time is no picnic—unless you are a former President of the United States or have slept with Elvis's ghost and can prove it. However, finding an agent who will consider your idea for a novel or nonfiction book, read your manuscript or proposal, answer all your questions, provide encouragement and expertise, and, yes, sell your book, will not only save you time and money, but you will have gained a valuable, much-needed ally in the swirling, shark-infested waters of publishing.

Why do you need an agent? If you are an unpublished author, here's why: One of the duties of my first job in publishing was to read unsolicited manuscripts sent to Macmillan directly from writers. These manuscripts came in all shapes and sizes, but my directive was the same: Unless you saw another *Gone With the Wind,* forget about it. In my two years in that job, I saw a number of admirable manuscripts, but not one unagented manuscript I read caught the fancy of an editor. You see, editors are extremely busy people: They meet with the sales department, the marketing department, the art department, the publicity department, and the editorial department every week. They meet with agents every day. And, in the evenings and on weekends, they squeeze in time to read manuscripts. Every time I meet an editor for the first time, their first complaint is how little time they get to read *published* books, which is something the rest of the world takes for granted.

Which manuscript do you think they are going to spend time considering seriously: the one sent in over the transom and read by an inexperienced, underpaid reader or the one recommended by an experienced agent?

21

Put another way: The editor's job, redefined over the years, is to publish writers, not discover them. For better or worse, editors simply have come to rely on agents to discover the next Hemingway, Fitzgerald or Welty and bring them to publishers.

If you are already a published author, here's a good reason for you to get an agent: Imagine how much more productive you would be if you didn't have to oversee the details of getting published; it can take weeks or even months to sell an idea to a publisher and negotiate the contract. Wouldn't you rather be writing than worrying?

How do you get an agent, how do they do business, and what can an agent specifically do for you?

The easiest way to get an agent is through the personal recommendation of a close friend, relative or another writer who has or knows an agent. When I first set up shop as an agent, I depended upon referrals from authors I had worked with in my days as an editor; they either became clients or sent authors my way. If you were looking for a lawyer or an accountant, wouldn't you ask your friends first whom they use and if they're happy with them? That's the easy way.

Step #1: Do a little research. Go to your local library or bookstore and find a copy of one of the dozens of books (such as the grandfather of reference tools, *The Literary Marketplace*—or *LMP* as we call it) that have lists of reputable agents, the kind of books and/or clients these agents are looking for, and their requirements for submission.

Step #2: After you've narrowed down the list of agents to ones who meet your criteria, write a letter describing your book idea and your background and inquire if they would be interested in it (be sure to include a stamped, self-addressed envelope!). I would advise against trying to describe your book over the telephone; a letter doesn't betray nervousness or forget to mention anything or put any sort of pressure on you. This letter will be very important, so spend some time and thought on it—a strong letter stating your case gives you a chance to include all your thoughts cogently and allows the agent to judge your writing. I always tell writers to state why thousands of people would be willing to spend $18.95 to read their book when they can just as easily spend the same amount of money on someone else's book. You don't have to do that exactly, but keep it in the back of your mind as you compose your letter.

Do not get discouraged if you do not receive an answer from every agent. I cannot speak for every agency, but we respond to every query that includes an SASE, and we are not all that different from a lot of other agencies. Do not be surprised if some tell you they are not looking for new clients. To provide a professional level of service to their current clients, agents must devote most of their time to them.

Step #3: Keep it up. While many publishers no longer consider unagented work, almost every good agent will consider yours if he or she finds it well written and intriguing. If one agent turns your manuscript down, keep trying. There are any number of reasons for an agent to turn down perfectly good books, some having nothing to do with the quality of your work. We don't all think alike or like the same kinds of books, so maybe the second, third, or tenth agent *will* like your book and take it on. Persistence works! I always like to tell people about one of my clients who had written a fine novel in the seventies and got precious little encouragement. She put the novel away in her closet for fifteen years before finally getting up the nerve to show it to an agent—she showed it to me and I sold it to the second editor who read it. This is a story with a happy ending, but I always think about what this author would have accomplished had she been more persistent from the beginning.

[A few words on multiple submissions: Many agents will not consider multiple submissions because they do not want to spend the time reading an entire manuscript only to discover the author decided on another agent two days earlier. If you are going to submit your work to a number of agents at one time, make sure you inform the agents that it is a multiple submission, and be prepared for some very quick rejections. On the other side of the coin, if you have a strong idea—more likely for a nonfiction book than a novel—you may very well get quicker answers from agents who know they are in a competitive situation. And no, agents do *not* hate each other—some of my best friends are agents!]

A fourth suggestion, which will work for some writers but not all, would be to attend a writers' conference. First of all, this will give your writing exposure to professionals who can critique it and work with you; secondly, agents (like me) and editors attend conferences throughout the year looking for new talent. Though it is often difficult to develop any kind of relationship with an agent at a conference, many published authors got their starts at such conferences.

What kind of manuscripts are agents looking for? In one word:

salable. Few agents I know really specialize in any one type of book, and most will work with both nonfiction and fiction. (I would venture to guess that most agents deal more in nonfiction than fiction.) In nonfiction, we look for subjects of timely nature, written by authors who have solid credentials in their field. If you want to write your autobiography, you had better either be mentioned regularly in *People* magazine or have lived a secret, incredible life. If you want to write a piece of investigative journalism, it helps if you actually are a reporter. Demonstrated expertise cannot be understated. With novels, however, agents simply look for good writing mixed with a good sense of storytelling— and novelists can be *anyone* with talent.

Most agents I know will not consider magazine articles, poetry or children's books. Major magazines solicit or commission most of the pieces they publish. Poetry can be submitted to literary journals directly by the author; book publishers, however, will consider publishing collections of only the most accomplished and published poets. More agents nowadays are considering children's books because publishers are paying larger advances for them, but these agents are still in the minority. You should definitely consult the *LMP* about which agents will consider this kind of work.

I have two pieces of advice for writers looking for subjects: 1) Go to a bookstore and see what is being published. If you see twenty books on a subject, it's a good bet that the market is saturated. For instance, 1990 saw an explosion in the publication of books dealing with the environment; after a while, publishers simply stopped considering new books on this subject, no matter how good their prospects were. 2) Write about something you know about and believe in or care enough about to do the necessary research. If you want to write a novel about soldiering experiences during the Vietnam War, you had better have been there; on the other hand, which science fiction novelist has actually been to Mars or Venus?

Finally, what can you expect from an agent who decides to take on your book? Well, perhaps to become the most important person in your writing life. Years ago, editors such as Maxwell Perkins and publishers such as Bennett Cerf dominated the industry and were the bedrocks of an author's career. Not any more. Certainly, there are many wonderful editors and heady publishers in the business today, but with the rapid and deep changes that have taken place in publishing—takeovers and mergers and "consolidations"—many editors of major firms frequently change jobs and houses before they are able to form close relationships with the authors. Time and time again, I've seen an editor sign up a book and, two months later, announce he or she has landed a new job with another publisher. Nowadays, it is not unusual for an author to write, say, four books and have four or more different editors. The one constant in an author's career is his or her agent.

The most important thing an agent can do for you is to find a publisher for your book and negotiate contract terms and an advance on royalties for you. As a writer, what you want to worry about is your writing; your agent will sweat the details of the business of writing. Successful agents know the industry and will know not to send a first novel to a publisher that specializes in how-to books. A good agent will know not only which publisher is appropriate for your book, but which editor at a particular house is more inclined to consider your book seriously, since editors, unlike agents, tend to specialize in subjects. There are such things as business editors, political editors, fiction editors, and cookbook editors.

Agents can also provide ideas and criticism. Many agents reading a client's new novel, for instance, will suggest changes before submitting it to a publisher. Would you rather have your book submitted to a publisher knowing it was not quite right? Sometimes an agent will read an article in a magazine or newspaper that suggests a book idea and will give the idea to a client who will then write the book. And over the years, we see more books being written by celebrities, but do you think Tip O'Neill took nine months out of his busy schedule to write his memoirs? No, an agent convinced him to get the book done, introduced him to a writer who collaborated with the former Speaker of the House, and negotiated the package with Random House. O'Neill and his collaborator worked together intermittently for a couple of months, and the writer then produced a manuscript, which became a huge bestseller. Without the agent's role in this, the book never would have been published.

Agents also administer the life of a publishing contract, which means this: We keep track of and make sure the publisher pays the advance on time; we also track royalty payments and the issuance of statements. We oversee the selling of various foreign and subsidiary rights to a book: Do you want your book translated and sold in Spain or Japan?

how about getting it excerpted in a magazine or newspaper? recorded on audio cassette? or made into a movie? Literary agents handle all these matters for their authors.

All this is the good news. Agents, quite simply, make an author's life easier and their work more commercially viable in return for a commission on all the deals they handle. These commissions usually range from 10–15 percent on domestic sales and licenses and 15–20 percent on all foreign transactions, which often involve "subagents" in other countries who share the commission.

Then there's the bad news, which you saw in the title of this piece. It's tough to get an agent. The arithmetic is against authors. I personally receive roughly thirty query letters a week from writers who have not been referred to me by close friends, relatives or other writers asking me to consider their books. Of this number, I will ask to see anywhere from two to four manuscripts, and, typically, I take on only one manuscript every two months. This does not mean that everything I reject is bad; actually some of it is good, but even good may not be good enough for publishers. And I'm sure the math works the same for most successful agents. Look at it another way: If only one book were published in this country every year, no matter the subject or the quality, it would sell millions and millions of copies. Actually, about fifty thousand books are published here every year, and for every one of those published, I'd bet there are one hundred that are not.

What this means in practical terms for you and for me is that the struggle to get published is often reduced merely to getting a publisher to sit down and seriously consider your book. And oftentimes, alas, talent simply isn't enough. You *will* need an advocate to give you a fighting chance.

So, in closing and recognizing the self-service I am about to perform, I'll just echo the first piece of sound advice given every writer in this country for the last fifty years: Do everything you can to get an agent, because it's a lot harder to get a publisher!

6

A Writer's Education

By Rick DeMarinis

I wasn't raised in a family of book readers. My mother worked in a fish cannery, and my stepfather drove a bread truck. There were a few books in the house—a library copy of *Forever Amber* no one had bothered to return, some mildewed paperbacks with racy covers, an ancient encyclopedia, and, amazingly, a beautiful, gold-embossed, wonderfully illustrated copy of the Koran! (My mother was Lutheran, my stepfather Baptist, and I, at sixteen, was a fallen-away Catholic.) This small and exotic collection of books didn't make much sense, but it contained an essential message for a young aspiring writer: don't expect things to make sense. Expect surprise.

In high school English class, we were introduced to something called, with unmistakable reverence, Literature. I hated it. I remember having to read novels such as *Silas Marner.* But the nebulous minds of sixteen-year-old California kids were hardly prepared for such fare. We traded copies of Mickey Spillane out in the parking lot, away from the snooping eyes of teachers. A novel about gang warfare called *The Amboy Dukes* was hugely popular with us. We saw reading as an extension of our internal lives, and could not make the great leap to the world of George Eliot.

Something happens to people destined for a life of writing that has nothing to do with Literature. It happens early in life, and is probably the psychological equivalent of scarlet fever. It has to do with pain. In answer to the question, "How does one become a writer?" Ernest Hemingway is said to have replied, "Have a lousy childhood." I believe this, but I also know that people who have had wonderful childhoods— on the surface at least—have become, in spite of this handicap, first-rate writers. Even so, something happened to them. Maybe *birth* happened to them and that was disaster enough. Someone sensitive to his or her surroundings, sensitive in the sense of always being aware, of noticing the details, and of being affected imaginatively by the force of these impressions—i.e., a person destined to be an artist—will find trauma waiting around every corner. A childhood doesn't have to be lousy to be traumatizing. As Flannery O'Connor said, ". . . anybody who has survived his childhood has enough information about life to last him the rest of his days."

Then something else happens. We find that words can be an escape from the pain of social impotence. Words became, for me, a bright mantle of power. I discovered that pressing a #2 pencil into a sheet of clean white paper was a sensual experience. And as that pencil moved, a world was created. What power *that* was! Creating fictional worlds is a natural refuge for the powerless, since it *confers* power. There, on the clean white page, all power is restored. My English teachers (except for that one fine teacher all of us seem to encounter, that mythic "helper" who appears just at the right time with the right kind of encouragement) had no perceivable passion for words. It was as if the Literature we were asked to read were made of rarefied ideas breathed directly onto the page by pure mind from the slopes of Olympus. It was the rock solid clatter and bang of our raucous and flexible language that moved me like small earthquakes. Rarefied ideas were a vapor that would be condensed in college and graduate school much later on. Besides, at sixteen I had no apparatus for absorbing serious ideas, and surely none for expressing them. Writing was a physical exercise, as pleasureful as bench pressing heavy weights, but not as socially acceptable. There was something shameful about a strong, healthy boy spending long hours in his room *writing stories*. And so writing, like all suspect activities, had to be done in secret. But how lovely it was, putting down those blocks of words until I and my perplexing, misperceived world were redefined on *my* terms. I became a middleweight boxer, on his way to the championship, when a beautiful girl (who looked remarkably like Jean Simmons in one of her Christian epics) convinced me that boxing was brutal and inhuman—hours before my title fight! Or I became a jet fighter pilot, touring MIG alley in Korea with a vengeance unknown to modern warfare, or a professional quarterback playing in the NFL title game against a team who had dropped me from their roster.

My English teachers and I regarded each other through the wrong ends of our private telescopes. We shied away from each other, and yet they gave me an occasional B or A for my awkward but imaginatively untethered "essays" that twisted the world out of its expected shapes. This habit of twisting the world persisted. If you twist hard and long, it surrenders its truths. George Eliot knew that. All writers know that. Too often, English teachers, even college English teachers, don't know that or they don't see it as the central mission of fiction writing.

Is the writer therefore anti-intellectual? Not necessarily. The intellect, however, wants to be "right." It wants answers and it wants certainty. A writer operates in a different atmosphere, an atmosphere charged with uncertainty and surprise. I heard E. L. Doctorow say, in a recent speech, that the writer, *as* a writer, is someone who places equal value on the objects of his experience. The latest cosmological theory is of no more intrinsic importance than the way sunlight passes through a Japanese fan. This democracy of the objects of experience is a necessary state of mind for the writer. It opens the gates and lets a whole world in where things won't necessarily make sense. For example, you might find your mother in such a world, just home from the cannery and smelling like fish—your mother who quit school at fourteen—sitting at the kitchen table reading a gold-embossed, illustrated edition of the Koran.

7

WHAT WRITING HAS
TAUGHT ME—THREE LESSONS

BY KATHERINE PATERSON

SOMEWHERE IN THE MIDDLE OF WRITING my tenth novel, it occurred to me that I had been at this business for twenty-five years. Since the book was moving along about as rapidly as a centipede with corns, I was not in the mood to celebrate the silver anniversary of my life as writer—not published writer, mind you, just writer. The silver anniversary of publication will be a few more years coming. But now the book is in the mail at last, and I am wracking my brain for lessons gleaned along the quarter-century journey. They seem pitifully few, but here they are:

1. *One idea doth not a novel make.* In answer to the often-asked question, Where did you get the idea for this book? I have at long last come to realize that a novel is not born of a single idea. The stories I've tried to write from one idea, no matter how terrific an idea, have sputtered out and died by chapter three. For me, novels have invariably come from a complex of ideas that in the beginning seemed to bear no relation to each other, but in the unconscious began mysteriously to merge and grow. Ideas for a novel are like the strong guy lines of a spider web. Without them the silken web cannot be spun.

The ideas that came together for *Park's Quest* were a long time in process. I had wanted for years to set a story on the Virginia farm where my father grew up and where I had spent many summers of my childhood. Once I even tried setting a short story there which never quite jelled. In one of those flashes that writers are prone to, I saw a scrawny Oriental-looking girl standing in the dark hall of that farmhouse. It was a child I didn't know, and I had no idea what she was

30

doing there, so I tucked her away until I had the other strands for her story.

The second came when my husband and I happened to visit old friends the day after they returned from the dedication of the Viet Nam memorial. Their eldest son had been killed during the war, and it was evident that the memorial and the services surrounding its dedication had been a time of real healing for their whole family. I went to visit the memorial myself soon afterwards and felt something of that power that all its visitors seem to experience. But still I was not ready to begin a novel.

The final strand began as an almost off-hand remark made by a speaker at the National Women's Conference to prevent Nuclear War in 1984. She warned those of us concerned about the nuclear threat that we could not simply frighten our friends and neighbors into responsibility: People who are frightened tend simply to deny the fact that any danger exists. "I think what we must do," she said, "is to ask the question of Parzival."

A shiver went through my body. I didn't know what the question of Parzival was, but I knew I had to find out. And, of course, when I found Wolfram's Medieval romance, which climaxes in Parzival's powerful question, "Dear Uncle, what aileth thee?" I found why my story would tie together our ancestral farm and the Viet Nam War. For surely for all Americans, not just for those who went to war, that conflict is "the wound that will not heal" and will never heal until we ask ourselves Parzival's question.

2. *My target audience is me.* Since I write primarily for children, people often ask me for what age child a book is intended. I have trouble answering the question, partly because I know very little about developmental psychology, but mostly because I know that people, even people of the same age, vary enormously in their interests and abilities. To try to "target an audience," as we writers for children are urged to do, would be impossible for me. I decided years ago it was not my job to decide who could or would read my books. If the publisher needs to suggest age or grade level designations in the catalogue, fine, but I will simply try to tell a story as well and as truly as I can. It would then be up to each reader to decide if my story was for him or her.

I suppose this truth came home to me after *Bridge to Terabithia* was published. I had written the book after a year during which I had had surgery for cancer and our youngest son's best friend had been killed by lightning. I wrote the book because I could neither bring back the little girl my son had loved nor could I seem to comfort him. In order to keep going, I needed, somehow, to make sense for myself of senseless tragedy. I truly thought that no one whose name was not Paterson would understand the book. I was very much in doubt that my editor would even want to publish it. Over the years the book has not only sold millions of copies and been published in at least seventeen languages, it is the book that prompts readers of all ages to write me and pour out the pain of their own lives. I keep learning that if I am willing to go deep into my own heart, I am able, miraculously, to touch other people at the core.

But that is because I do have a reader I must try to satisfy—that is the reader I am and the reader I was as a child. I know this reader in a way that I can never know a generic target out there somewhere. This reader demands honesty and emotional depth. She yearns for a clear, rhythmically pleasing language. She wants a world she can see, taste, smell, feel, and hear. And above all she wants characters who will make her laugh and cry and bind her to themselves in a fierce friendship, as together they move through a story that pulls her powerfully from the first word to the last.

O.K. So she's a fussy reader. I've never fully satisfied her, but I would love to spend the next twenty-five years trying.

3. *A novel can be finished.* Some years ago I was having lunch in a crowded restaurant with a writer friend who has been at this business a lot longer than I. I was moaning that I was stuck—that this book I had poured two years of my life into was going nowhere. "This is my seventh novel! All these years and I haven't learned anything!" I cried out, eliciting a few stares from the diners at the next table.

"Yes, you have," my friend said. "You've learned one thing. You've learned that a novel *can* be finished." I cling to that knowledge every time I hit the invariable stone wall in the middle of a novel. I have finished nine of them now. I can finish another. And when it is done, given time and several sturdy guy lines, I may even be able to begin weaving yet another. There is always the hope that within the next twenty-five years I will be able to fully please my reader.

8

Six Myths That Haunt Writers

By Kenneth T. Henson

AMONG THE MANY THINGS I have learned in conducting writers workshops on campuses across the country is that there are several false ideas, myths, that haunt most writers and often impede and/or block beginners. The following are six of these myths—and some suggestions for dealing with them.

1. *I'm not sure I have what it takes.*

I have found that on each campus, coast to coast, there is a superstar writer who, I am assured, has only to put his fingers to the keyboard or pen to paper and, presto, words, sentences, and paragraphs—publishable ones—flow. And, it is thought, these creations are effortless.

These tales are as ridiculous as ghost stories, but more damaging, since most people *believe* them. And like ghost stories, their purpose is to frighten.

If I were a beginning writer and believed that writing comes so effortlessly to some, I would be totally discouraged.

You admit that you, too, have heard of such a superwriter? You may even know such a person by name. Well, don't believe it. It's probably the creation of a person who doesn't intend to write and therefore would prefer that you don't either. The next time someone mentions this super-person, think of Ernest Hemingway, who wrote the last chapter of *Farewell to Arms* 119 times. Or think of the following definitions of writing: "Writing is 10 per cent inspiration and 90 per cent perspiration" and "Successful writing is the ability to apply the seat of the pants to the seat of the chair." Contrary to the myth, all writers perspire; some even sweat!

33

2. *I don't have time to write.*

You have heard this many times, and if you're like most of us, you have even said it yourself: "If only I had time to write." Ironically, most would-be writers have more time to write than most successful writers do. Some writers even have 24 hours a day to do as they please. But they represent only a small fraction of all writers. The vast majority of writers are free lancers who have either part-time or full-time jobs and pick up a few extra dollars, a little prestige, and a lot of personal satisfaction through writing articles.

The reason behind the bold statement that you have more time than most successful writers have to write is that, probably like you, most of them must earn a living some other way. Yet, these individuals have allotted themselves some time for writing: they took it away from their other activities. Good writers don't *make* time, and they don't *find* time. Rather, they reassign part of their time to writing. And that part of their lives is usually some of their leisure time.

I don't suggest that you stop golfing or fishing or jogging or watching TV, but if you are to be a successful writer, you must give up part of the time you spend (or waste) in the coffee room or bar and you must also give up the idea that you are too tired to write or that watching a mediocre TV show relaxes you. Writing is far more relaxing to most of us who return from our work emotionally drained; it provides an outlet for frustrations, a far more effective release than our more passive attempts to escape from them.

The next time you hear people say, "I don't have time to write" or "I would write for publication if I had time," observe how those persons are spending their time at that moment. If writing is really important to you, replace the activities that are less important with writing. Let your friends and family know that this is your writing time and that you're not to be disturbed. Then tell yourself the same thing. Disciplined people have much more time than do undisciplined people.

3. *I don't have anything worth writing about.*

We've all heard this for years. A significant percentage of aspiring writers really believe that they don't know anything that is worthy of publication. If you are one of them, you're not learning from your experiences: either you don't make mistakes or you don't adjust your behavior to avoid repeating them.

The truth is that you possess a lot of knowledge that would be valuable to others. And you have the abilities that successful writers have to research the topics you wish to write about. I don't know any successful writers who don't feel that they need to research their topics. Start with the subjects that are most familiar, then enrich your knowledge of these subjects by periodic trips to the library, or by interviewing people, or by conducting surveys on these topics.

4. *The editors will reject my manuscript because my name isn't familiar to them.*

Of all the excuses that would-be writers give for not writing, none is weaker than, "If my name were James Michener or Stephen King, editors would listen to me."

But these people don't consider the fact that the Micheners and Kings didn't always have famous names; they started as unknowns and made their names known through talent and hard work. And they would probably be first to say that they have to keep earning their recognition through hard work. Of course, these writers have unusual talent, but you can be equally sure that they work hard and continue to do so to sharpen their skills, research their topics meticulously, and to create and invent new, fresh ways to express their ideas.

There's no guarantee that any of us can earn similar status and acclaim, but we can improve our expertise in our areas of interest and improve our communication skills.

5. *My vocabulary and writing skills are too limited.*

Many people equate jargon, unfamiliar words, complex sentence structure, and long paragraphs with good writing. Actually, though a good vocabulary is a great asset to writers, so are dictionaries and thesauruses, for those who know how to use them and who are willing to take the time to do so. Jargon and long sentences and unnecessarily complex paragraphs harm writing more than they help it.

The sooner you replace words like *utilize* and *prioritize* with words like *use* and *rank,* the faster your writing will improve. Remember, your job is to communicate. Don't try to impress the editor. Editors know what their readers want, and readers seldom demand jargon and complexity.

6. *In my field there are few opportunities to publish.*

If your area of specialization has few professional journals (actually, some fields have only one or two), you may feel trapped, knowing that this uneven supply/demand ratio drives up the competition for these journals.

You might deal with this by searching for more general journals that cover your field, or journals whose editors often welcome articles written by experts in outside but related fields. For example, a biologist or botanist might turn to wildlife magazines, U.S. or state departments of conservation publications, forestry magazines, hunting and fishing publications, or magazines for campers and hikers.

Again, you could consider writing for other audiences, expanding your areas of expertise by taking courses in other disciplines, reading widely, and doing research in other fields to help you develop a broader range of subjects to write about.

Some fields have more journals than others, and some writers are luckier (and more talented) than others. But for those who are willing to work hard at their craft, writing offers a way to reach many professional and personal goals.

9

SURVIVING REJECTION

BY CAROL DIGGORY SHIELDS

MY HUSBAND COLLECTS DEAD AND DYING CARS. My sons collect bugs and baseball cards, among other things. My own hobby is collecting rejection slips. In seven years of writing, I've put together a pretty impressive collection, ranging from the common anonymous three-by-five preprinted card, to the much rarer personally signed, sincere regrets.

Like gathering bugs, collecting rejection slips is not a hobby for the faint-hearted. One becomes an expert in the fine art of cushioning the blow by reading through envelopes, of speculating on the possible meaning of return address and postmark, and of opening suspicious envelopes gingerly.

Looking through my collection, I've come to the conclusion that I pass through a variety of emotional stages as I write, and am rejected, and write, and am rejected again. It also occurs to me that these stages are not unlike the five stages of grief.

You have produced this precious manuscript—witty yet profound, bold yet subtle, simple yet elegant. In short, the manuscript the publishing world has been waiting for. So you do your research, and after careful comparison of qualifications, average advances and royalties, select *the* publisher to whom to submit your gem.

You compose a cover letter that takes longer to write than your story did, you spend twenty-seven dollars on heavyweight, archival-quality bond paper and typewriter ribbons, and shop for a week for the perfect envelope. You send it off, sealed with a kiss, certified, insured, return receipt requested, SASE enclosed, and you tell your family to stay off the phone because you're expecting an important call from New York in a couple of days. You tell people that you are (modest pause) a writer. You wonder what to wear for the photograph on the jacket of your book.

37

Of course miracles happen. I'm sure there are at least seven people on the face of the earth who have had their first manuscript, sent to their first publisher, accepted, just like that.

But in most cases, you wait. And wait. And wait, checking the mail four times a day for several months, until you get an envelope back, usually looking as if it's been run over by a truck. Inside is your manuscript, with a note clipped to its limp pages: "Thank you for giving us the opportunity to consider your manuscript. However, we do not feel that . . ."

Stage one: *Denial*. This cannot be true! The publishers mixed up your manuscript with somebody else's. It never got read. The editor you sent it to suffered a fit of temporary insanity. Someone, somewhere, made a *big* mistake. Everyone in your family comforts you. You wouldn't want a publisher with such obvious lack of judgment or taste to handle your work, anyhow.

So on to Publisher B on your list. Won't Publisher A be stunned when Publisher B comes out with your mega-hit! Dusted off and spruced up, off it goes again. But hey, you're becoming more professional already. You check the mail only twice a day this time around.

Somewhere around Publisher J, the next stage kicks in. The stage known as *Anger*. What is it with these mufflegrubbingsonofabunching New York publishers? Who do they think they are? You start to feel angry at anyone from New York.

Anger is the stage at which it's tempting to stop writing. Many's the time I've been tempted, during this period, to gather up all my work and throw it into the flames. Who cares? Let it burn! Unfortunately, all my work is now on floppy disks, and there's nothing romantic about watching manuscripts melt.

Of course, you can't stay angry forever. So, if you're still in the game, anger carries you on to the next stage, known as *Bargaining*. Magic hasn't worked. Threats haven't worked. Maybe a little wheeling and dealing will get you in the publisher's door?

Time to call that cousin whose brother-in-law has a friend who works in the mailroom at HarperCollins. Your thoughts turn to bribery. At this point you'd sell your soul, or your mother, or the kids, if there were any takers, for a single short story in *The New Yorker*. This is the point at which many join writers' organizations. Maybe if you can touch an author for luck, meet an editor face to face. . . .

This is the time for gimmicks. Maybe if I have my manuscript delivered by carrier pigeon? My own gimmick at this stage was sending out manuscripts in astrobrite envelopes of fuchsia, purple, or lime green, and enclosing return envelopes that were . . . black.

This can be a lot of fun. It can be a period of professional growth, of reaching out to the other authors, comparing notes, getting excited about what you're doing. And also of finding out that bargaining doesn't work.

And then on to the longest, the hardest, and probably the most important stage. It's known as *Depression.* But maybe a better term would be *Reality,* the reality that publishers are not rejecting your work out of stupidity, or vengeance, or because of the color of your envelopes, but the realization that the only thing that's going to get you into print is writing. Good, solid, plain old writing.

This is the unglamorous, shoulder-to-the-wheel, nose-to-the-keyboard period when you realize the awful truth that the first manuscript you wrote, that precious gem, was only practice.

I once had an art professor who said that the measure of a great artist was not in the successful, finished work of art produced, but in how much was thrown away. This is the time of throwing away. Of tossing out that witty, beautifully turned phrase that doesn't add a thing to the story. Of trashing that ingenious plot you've never been able to put into the right words.

This is the time when you stop telling people that you are a writer. It's also the period when, if you've come this far and you're still writing, you realize you're not doing it for fame, for the money, or even for an audience. You're writing because it brings you great joy. Publication would be nice, publication would be heavenly. But there's nothing like writing a good sentence.

The final stage of grief, as defined by Elisabeth Kubler-Ross, is appropriately named. It's called *Acceptance.* I reached this stage on an autumn morning at 8:17 a.m., give or take a few minutes, when my agent called to tell me that E. P. Dutton was buying my book.

Happy ending? Well, happy beginning. There's acceptance, and there's acceptance—my acceptance into that great and mysterious world of The Published, and my own acceptance of rejection as part of a writer's life. A grudging admission that maybe the R-word forced me, kicking and screaming all the way, into becoming a better writer.

I'd like to think I can relegate my collection of rejections to the attic now, but unless I'm Danielle Steel (and last time I checked, I wasn't), I know those cards and letters will keep coming in. I'll never, ever like them. But I know I can survive them.

10

COMMON QUESTIONS ABOUT COPYRIGHTS

BY HOWARD ZAHAROFF

TO BE A GOOD WRITER, YOU MUST UNDERSTAND THE BASICS OF WRITING. To be a published writer, you must understand the basics of manuscript submission and the editorial process.

And to be a successful writer, the owner of a portfolio of published manuscripts, you must also understand the basics of copyright law. As a lawyer who practices in the field, I promise that this isn't too hard. Let me prove it by answering a dozen questions that free lancers often ask.

Before doing so, a few comments. First, the answers I give are based on U.S. law. International issues are mostly ignored. Second, my focus is mainly on works first published or created after March 1, 1989, the last major revision of the Copyright Act (which I refer to below as the "Act"). Third, although the Copyright Office cannot provide legal advice, its Circulars and Public Information Office (call 202/479-0700) provide guidance on many of the following issues. (Start with Circular 1, "Copyright Basics.") There are also many excellent books available, such as Ellen Kozak's *Every Writer's Guide to Copyright & Publishing Law* (Owl, 1990).

1. *What can be copyrighted?* Copyright protects nearly every original piece you write (or draw, compose, choreograph, videotape, sculpt, etc.): not just your novel, article, story or poem, but the software program you create, the advertisements and greeting cards you published, and the love letters you wrote in high school. But copyright does not protect your ideas, only the way you *express* them.

2. *What protection does copyright provide?* A "copyright" is really a bundle of rights. The copyright owner (whom we'll call the "proprietor") controls not only the right to copy the work, but also the rights

to prepare "derivative works" (i.e., adaptations, translations, and other modifications), to perform or display the work publicly, and to make the "first sale" of each copy of the work.

3. *What is the duration of copyright protection, and is it renewable?* For works created or first published after 1977, copyright generally lasts 50 years after the death of the author. However, for anonymous or pseudonymous works, or works made "for hire" (see below), the term expires 100 years from creation or 75 years from publication. There are no renewals. (For works published before 1978, the term is 28 years, with right to renew for 47 additional years. See Circular 15, "Renewal of Copyright.")

4. *How do you obtain a copyright?* Copyright protection arises *automatically* as soon as you put your ideas into tangible form. Thus, once on paper, canvas, video, or computer disk, your creation is protected by law.

5. *Is a copyright notice required for protection?* No. Until recently a notice was required on all *published* copies of a work. ("Published" simply means distributed to the public; it does not require printing in a periodical or book.) However, on March 1, 1989, the United States joined the international copyright treaty known as the Berne Convention and removed this requirement for works published after that date.

Still, including a copyright notice alerts everyone to your claim and prevents an infringer from pleading "innocence" (that is, that he had no idea your work was copyrighted). Thus, good reasons remain for including notices on all published copies of your work, and for insisting that your publisher do so.

If you are concerned that your *unpublished* work may be used or copied without permission (e.g., you are circulating copies of your most timely and accomplished piece within your newly formed writers group), you can't lose by including a notice.

6. *What should my copyright notice say?* A proper notice has three elements:

• The international copyright symbol © or the word "Copyright." Most publishers use both. (The abbreviation "Copr" is also acceptable.)

42

- The year in which the work is first published. (For unpublished works, you may omit a date.)
- Your name, or a recognizable abbreviation (e.g., International Business Machines Corporation may use "IBM").

In general, notices should be displayed prominently at the beginning of your work, although any reasonable location is acceptable. If your piece will appear in a magazine, anthology, or other collective work, a single notice in the publisher's name will preserve most of your rights. However, including a separate copyright notice in your own name will clarify that only you, *not* the publisher, has the right to authorize further uses of your work.

7. *Must I register my work with the Copyright Office?* Although registration is not required for copyright protection, it is a precondition to suing for infringement of the copyrights in any work first published in the U.S. (and in the unpublished works of U.S. citizens and residents), and enables you to recover both attorneys' fees and "statutory damages" (i.e. damages of up to $100,000, determined by the judge, which the proprietor may elect to recover from the infringer in lieu of proving and recovering actual losses).

You can register your copyrights at any time during the term of copyright. However, registration within three months of publication generally preserves your rights to all infringement remedies, including statutory damages, while registration within five years of publication provides special benefits in legal proceedings.

8. *How do you register a work?* Copyright Office Form TX is the basic form for nondramatic literary works. Form PA is used to register works of the performing arts, including plays and movies. These one-page forms cost $20 to file and are fairly easy to complete (but only if you read the accompanying instructions!). Adjunct Form GR/CP allows writers to reduce costs by making a single registration for all works published in periodicals within a 12-month period. (You can order forms and circulars over the Hotline, 202/707-9100).

When you apply you must submit one copy of the work, if un-published, and two copies of the "best edition" of the work, if published. (Only one copy of the best edition is required for contributions to collective works.) The "best edition" is the published edition of highest quality, determined by paper quality, binding, and other factors listed by the Copyright Office (see Circular R7b). For example, if the work was published in both hard and soft covers, the hard cover is normally the best edition.

9. *Should I register my work?* In most cases, no. If your work was published, your publisher may have registered it. If not, failure to register costs you mainly the option for *immediate* relief and statutory damages. Moreover, infringement is the exception and, where it occurs, often can be settled without lawsuits or registration. Besides, most writers earn too little to justify the cost of registration (certainly for articles, poems, and other short works).

10. *What is "public domain" and how can you find out what's there?* Works that are not protected by copyright are said to be in the "public domain"—i.e., freely usable by the public, without the need to get permission or pay a fee. This includes works in which copyright has expired or been lost, works for which copyright is not available, and works dedicated to the public. Although there are many exceptions, *in general* the following are in the public domain:

- Works published more than 75 years ago.
- Works published more than 28 years ago, if the copyright was not renewed.
- Works published without a proper copyright notice before 1978.
- Works published without a proper notice between January 1, 1978 and February 28, 1989 (although the Act enables the proprietor to correct this failure).
- Works created by employees of the Federal government as part of their duties.

For a fee the Copyright Office will examine the status of a work. (See Circular 22, "How to Investigate the Copyright Status of a Work.")

11. *What is fair use?* The Act allows the limited use of others' works for research, teaching, news reporting, criticism, and similar purposes. These permitted uses are called "fair use," although the Act never defines that term. Rather, it lists factors to consider, including the purpose and character of the use (e.g., for-profit vs. teaching), the nature of the work (e.g., a science text vs. a poem), the amount and substantiality of the use, and its effect on the market for the work.

Here are some basic rules that should help you stay on the right side of the law (and help you recognize when someone's use of your work doesn't).

• **Copying for noncommercial (e.g., educational) purposes is given wider scope than copying for commercial use.** For example, in general you may quote less of the published writings of a politician in a television docudrama than a history professor may quote in journal articles.

• **Copying factual material gets more latitude than copying fiction.** Fiction contains more of the "originality" protected by the Act: characters and events, sometimes even time and place, derive from the writer's imagination. Facts cannot be copyrighted.

• **Parody is a permissible use, as long as it does not appropriate too much of the original.**

• **Copying from unpublished works without permission is usually considered unfair.** This was illustrated in a 1989 case concerning an unauthorized biography of Scientologist/SF writer L. Ron Hubbard. Referring to an earlier case, in which Random House was enjoined from publishing an unauthorized biography of J. D. Salinger because it infringed copyrights in his unpublished letters, the court wrote that "unpublished works normally enjoy complete protection" from unauthorized publication. (However, legislation is being considered that would expand the application of fair use to unpublished works.)

• **The Act permits certain uses of copyrighted works by libraries, archives, educators, charitable organizations, and others.** See sections 108–110 of the Act and Circular 21.

These rules are complex. Therefore, if you intend to copy more than a negligible amount from another person's work without permission, write to the publisher or copyright owner. Don't take a chance.

12. *What is a "work made for hire," and who owns the rights to these works?* The creator of a work generally owns the copyrights. There is an exception, however, for "works made for hire." Here it is the party who commissions and pays for the work, rather than the actual creator, who owns the copyrights. So when is a work "for hire"?

First, unless expressly excluded by contract, all works created by employees within the scope of their employment are "for hire." (This will normally not include works created on your own time that are unrelated to your employment.) So if you are employed by a newspaper, or hired by a software publisher to write documentation, your employer owns the copyrights in the works you've been paid to create. If you use copies of these works at your next job, you are infringing on your former employer's copyrights.

Second, certain specified categories of works (including translations, compilations, and parts of audiovisual works) are considered "for hire" if they have been specially commissioned and a signed document identifies them as "for hire." Therefore, *if you are not an employee and you haven't agreed in writing that your work is "for hire" (or otherwise assigned your rights), you will generally continue to own the copyrights in your work* even if others paid you to create it (although they will have the right to use your work for the express purposes for which they paid you).

You may wonder about the division of rights when your article, story, or poem is published in a magazine (or other collective work) and there is no written agreement. The Act supplies the answer: The publisher acquires only the right to publish your piece as part of that collective work, of any revision of that work, and of any later collective work in the same series. You retain all other rights, so you are free to revise or remarket your piece.

The above is a *general* discussion of the copyright law as it applies to freelancers. Myriad qualifications and exceptions are not included here. Before making any important copyright decisions consult a knowledge-able copyright lawyer, the Copyright Office, or a trusted publisher or agent with an up-to-date understanding of the law.

11

THE WRITER'S EYE

BY RANDALL SILVIS

A PART of every successful writer is, and must be, amoral. Detached. Unfeeling. As nonjudgmental as a tape recorder or camera. It is this capacity to stare at pain or ugliness without flinching, at beauty without swooning, at flattery and truth without succumbing to the lure of either, which provides the mortar, the observable details, to strengthen a story and make it a cohesive unit. This capacity I call the writer's eye.

As a child, I was and still am fascinated by the peaks and valleys of people's lives. I was blessed—or cursed—with what was often referred to as "morbid curiosity." At the scene of a funeral, I would be the one trying to inch a bit closer to the coffin, one ear turned to the dry intonations droning from the minister; the other to the papery rustle of leaves overhead. I would take note of how the mourners were standing, where they held their hands, if there were any clouds in the sky, who wept and who did not even pretend to weep, which shoes were most brilliantly shined, the color of the casket, the scent of smoke from someone's backyard barbecue, a killdeer whistling in the distance.

This is how I would remember and record the day, the event. In the details themselves, unbiased, unvarnished and pure, was every nuance of emotion such a tragedy produced. The same held true for weddings and baptisms, for joyous moments as well as sad. Almost instinctively I seemed to know that every abstraction had an observable form: To remark that my neighbor, a tired and lonely man, was drunk again, said nothing; to say that he was standing by the side of the road, motionless but for his gentle, oblivious swaying even as the cars zipped by and blasted their horns at him, his head down, eyes half-closed, hands shoved deep in his pockets as he sang a mumbled "Meet Me Tonight in Dreamland," said it all.

The writer's eye discriminates. It does not and cannot record every detail in a particular scene, only the most telling ones. It is microscopic

47

in focus, telescopic in intent. If, for example, you wish to depict a woman who is trying to look poised despite her nervousness, does it deepen the depiction to say that she wears a two-carat diamond ring on her left hand? Probably not. But if she is shown sitting very straight, knees and feet together, a pleasant smile on her lips as her right hand unconsciously and repeatedly pulls at and twists the diamond ring on her left? These details are in and of themselves emotionally pallid, but in sum, they add to a colorful, revealing whole. In such a description, the word *nervous* need never be uttered. Yet the conclusion is inescapable, and all the more acute because the reader has not been informed of the woman's uneasiness but has witnessed it for himself.

In my novel *Excelsior* (Henry Holt, October, 1987), one of the most important scenes is a moment of closeness between an inept father and his six-year-old son. The scene takes place in a YMCA locker room minutes after the father accidentally knocked the terrified boy, who cannot swim, into the pool. Bloomhardt, the father, despises himself for his own incompetence, and believes that his son does, too. But during a rare moment of openness, six-year-old Timmy admits *his* feelings of frustration and failure. At this point, it would have been quick and easy to state simply that Bloomhardt was relieved, grateful that his son did not despise him, and was filled with a fervent, though awkward, desire to reassure the boy. Instead, I chose to show his state of mind as evidenced in observable details:

Bloomhardt blinked, his eyes warm with tears. He leaned sideways and kissed his son's damp head. . . . He faced his open locker again, reached for a sock and pulled it on. He smiled to himself.

Bloomhardt's actions are elemental and, on their own, nearly empty of emotional value. But in the context of this passage and in relation to the man's and boy's characters as defined prior to this scene, these details are all that are needed to show the beginnings of a mutual tenderness, trust, and love.

The writer's eye is not merely one sense, but every power of observation the writer possesses. It not only sees, but also smells, tastes, feels, and hears. It also senses which details will paint the brightest picture, which will hint at an unseen quality, which will allow the reader to see beneath the surface of a character to the ice and fire of emotion within.

Think of each phrase of description, each detail, as a dot of color on a Seurat landscape. Individually, each dot is meaningless, it reveals nothing, neither laughter nor sorrow. But if you choose your dots carefully and arrange them on the canvas in their proper places, you might, with luck and practice, compose a scene to take the breath away.

❧ 12

Don't Sabotage Your Chances of Getting Published

By Wendy Corsi Staub

As a Manhattan book editor who has also done free-lance reading for the fiction department of a respected national magazine, I have often seen more than two hundred unsolicited submissions in a single week. Going through them can become grueling work, and time doesn't allow me to read each and every manuscript word for word. I've had to train myself to recognize the merit of a submission after reading only a few paragraphs—but sometimes, I don't even get that far. The cover letter can be a dead giveaway that the author is not a professional, and while many successful writers have been discovered in the slush pile, sheer volume can stack the odds against having that happen to you. There are two things you can do to improve your chances immensely: Send only quality work that you have polished and rewritten until it's the best you can do, and send it in a professional manner.

Following are ten basic tips that address the most common mistakes new writers make when submitting their work:

1. *Don't* address your submission: "To whom it may concern," "Dear Editor," "Dear Sir" (*many* editors are women!), or "Dear . . . (an editor whose name you found in a 1987 market listing—and who, chances are, is long gone)." Instead, take the time to find out who handles the type of material you're submitting. Check the masthead in the current issue of the magazine for correct names and titles, or call the publishing house and ask for the editorial department, where the assistant who answers the phone will tell you whom to address.

2. *Don't* try to catch the editor's eye by using colored paper, decorations, non-traditional typeset, and the like. Such trappings *will* catch

the editor's eye, all right—and alert him or her that you're an amateur. Instead, use good quality, white, 8½ × 11 paper, and make sure the type is plain, clear, and dark.

3. *Don't* count on impressing an editor with a business card that reads, "John Doe, Freelance Writer." Anyone can have one printed, and it doesn't make him a professional. If you have your heart set on getting a business card, it's best to use only your name, address, and phone number, and avoid pretentious titles.

4. *Don't* send loose stamps, and never send cash for postage. Unfortunately, things can easily get separated in the mailroom or on a crowded desk, and the editor ends up with addressed envelopes without postage, or stray stamps and dollar bills. Affix all postage to the addressed envelope, and make sure there's enough to accommodate the weight of your manuscript. If you don't want it back, specify that the envelope is for reply only, and the manuscript can be destroyed.

5. *Don't* staple or bind your manuscript. This is inconvenient for the editor, who usually finds it easier to flip loose pages. Paper clip short stories and article submissions, and put a rubber band around thicker manuscripts.

6. *Do* put your name on every manuscript page, and type your full name and address on the cover letter, SASE, first manuscript page, and any clips, photos, illustrations, or other material you're including. Never send anything that can't be replaced, such as original documents or the only copy of a photo.

7. *Do* mention that you were encouraged to submit again, if that's the case. If the editor himself wrote you a personal reply on a rejection, asking to see more, you can include a photocopy of the letter to remind him. If another editor at the same magazine or publishing house made the request, mention his name; and if it was a scribbled comment on a rejection slip, say that, too. Many a puzzled editor has received a letter that begins, "Here is the new story you asked for . . ." when in reality, the editor himself never heard of you. By the same token, don't assume that your name is fresh in the editor's mind even if he *did* respond personally in the past. Always include such basic information as your address, publishing credits, and past submissions as if you're starting

from scratch. Never say, "I told you all about myself when I submitted a short story three years ago . . ."

8. *Do* include publishing credits, but be aware of what they say about you. If your experience is limited to over fifty stories published in confession magazines, and now you're trying to sell a nonfiction, self-help book, don't list each and every confession credit. That can cause the editor to categorize you, and label you a specific genre writer with narrow capabilities. Instead, mention some of the publications you've appeared in, but focus on your qualifications for writing the kind of piece you're trying to sell now. Don't expect to impress an editor by mentioning that you've written several novels unless you've actually published them, or are under contract. Anyone (well, *almost* anyone) can fill a stack of pages with words; it's getting a publishing house to *buy* your work that shows your merit.

9. *Do* keep your cover letter professional and to the point. If you have never been published before, don't emphasize your lack of experience by telling the editor that your mother (husband, wife, kids, neighbors, bridge club, classmates) is convinced you are the next Stephen King. Don't tell the editor how nervous you are about submitting, or that you'll be so disappointed if you're rejected. Stick to, "Dear _____/ Enclosed for your consideration is (title), (word count) . . . /I appreciate your time . . . /SASE included . . ./ Thank you, Sincerely . . ." All it takes is a paragraph or two to cover that. It's best not to attempt wit or creativity in your cover letter, since it's difficult to do that well, and when it's not well done, it can hurt your chances of getting an objective read.

10. *Do* mention the rights (First American, Serial, etc.) you are offering. *Never* mention money. It's an enormous turnoff for an editor to read a cover letter that concludes, "I will accept payment of your usual rate, $2,500, made out to me in the form of a cashier's check." While many magazines list their pay rates in *The Writer, The Writer's Handbook,* or on their tip sheets, the editor will discuss payment only when offering a contract, so don't jump the gun.

While the saying goes, "Rules were made to be broken," it's wise not to break these if you're serious about getting published. Editors realize how frustrating it is for writers to adhere to such a strict set of submission guidelines. They are aware that writers feel as if there are rules only on *their* end, while editors don't have to adhere to any set procedure or time frame when responding. But there are *thousands* of talented, hopeful *you's,* and only *one* frazzled, overworked *me* . . . so do everything you can to make it easier on both of us!

13

WRITER'S GAMBIT

BY SCOTT D. YOST

CHESS OPENINGS AND FICTION HAVE MORE IN COMMON than you might think. In fact, if you learn the rules of good opening play for chess and apply them diligently to your writing, you'll end up with winning stories and novels. Just take a look at these chess maxims and their fiction analogues.

• *Grab the center.* The two most common (and best) first moves in chess involve taking a central pawn and putting it right smack in the middle of the board. You should do this in your writing, too: *Begin your story in the middle.* Get to the heart of the matter. Open with a bang. A good chess player doesn't fool around with side pawns at the beginning—there'll be time for those less important pawns in the middle of the game. And a good writer hooks the reader from the first page. Later, you can use flashbacks or dialogue to fill in background material. Time is precious in both a game of chess and a good story. So don't waste it.

• *Get the pieces out fast.* "Pieces" in chess are anything other than pawns—knights, rooks, bishops, the queen, and the king. They are your army, what you play the game with. As soon as you've moved a few pawns and cleared lanes of passage for the pieces, *get the pieces out*. In fiction, your "pieces" are your main characters—and you should introduce them early and get them out quickly, doing whatever it is they'll be doing.

• *Make moves that threaten something.* When you move a piece, always think: *Attack!* Cause problems for your opponent; make moves that hinder his or her opening. When writing, pretend your protagonists are opponents in a chess game: give them problems. Put obstacles in their way. Make each new event apply additional pressure to your protagonist. In chess and in stories, don't be afraid of conflict. Good stories are tales of struggle.

- *Don't bring the queen out too early.* The queen is the most powerful piece on the board. It should be used when the time is right, not before. Get your opponent on the ropes with deft moves of the minor pieces *and then* bring out the queen. Keep this strategy in mind when you write also. Hinder your protagonist, and make his or her goal difficult to attain. Then, when their situation can't get any worse, make it worse. Knock the characters down and hold them there; *then start kicking them.* That is: Bring out the queen—the Big Problem—to menace them, making a solution appear impossible. Set the stage with other events, but save that knockout punch for the end, when it can be most effective.

- *Make each move accomplish several things.* Each chess move should have more than one purpose: ideally it opens lines of attack, gets a piece out, influences the center, attacks the opponent, and fortifies your defenses. All in one move.

Each passage of writing should also do as much as it can. A description, for instance, should not only describe, but progress the plot and characterize as well. Dialogue can perform several functions—characterize, give exposition (though be careful here), move the story, etc.

- *Castle.* Castling is a special move that allows a player to tuck the king away safely, keeping it free from attack until it's needed at the end of the game. When writing, don't reveal your strategy. The solution to the protagonist's problem should be there, on the board and in plain sight, but safely tucked away. Then, when the time is right, use it to help you win the game.

So next time you sit down to write fiction, remember your chess: grab the center, get the pieces out.

14

THE AUTHOR/AGENT RELATIONSHIP

BY JONATHAN DOLGER

IT USED TO BE TRUE, WHEN I FIRST STARTED working in publishing, that the hardest thing to accomplish was finding a publisher. In those days, publishers still accepted unsolicited manuscripts from authors, and they were read by the editorial staff on a weekly basis. There were fewer agents, and contact between the writer and the editor was on a one-to-one basis, simpler than is currently the case.

With the increasing growth and consolidation of publishing companies, publishing has become a more bureaucratic process. Editors' choices are subjected to a review process that includes looking at "profit and loss statements," input from the marketing and sales staff, etc. Rarely can an editor make the final decision on whether or not to publish a manuscript. Instead, we have judgment by consensus, with editors functioning as *de facto* lobbyists.

It's not productive or helpful for the author to worry about these matters. The "gentlemen's business" has become a real business, and that's not so bad. It has produced, from a variety of viewpoints, a collective approach to publishing, which when it works, can be very successful.

The result of this is that many agents have taken over what used to be seen as part of the editorial side of publishing: i.e., reading and evaluating new work. Agents are not magicians, so it would be unreasonable to expect that if an agent agrees to represent you, you will automatically find a publisher. No one can force an editor to buy a book: There has to be reaction to and interaction with the material itself.

What an agent can do, if your work is accepted for publication, is not only make sure that you get the best possible contract, but also continue to protect your interests with the publisher throughout the entire publication process. This is extremely important, since with so many editors changing from one house to another, it is not at all uncommon to have several editors work on your manuscript. Indeed, a client of mine recently had five different editors at the same house, beginning with the one who acquired the book and ending with the one to whom the book was assigned at the time of actual publication.

Now that I've stated just how important an agent can be for a writer, let me also say that a beginning writer can, and should, begin to establish a career before finding an agent. Magazines and newspapers are still the best places for a beginning writer to get published. Don't confine yourself to the few "brand-name" publications, as they may have many of the same problems as book publishers when it comes to screening and reading unsolicited material. It is possible to begin to build your reputation on a local and regional level, develop contacts, and have a good body of work published, at which point you will be in a better position to approach a potential publisher or agent. I recently attended a writers' conference where there were 450 writers, and many of them began their professional careers in just this manner. A good source book here is *The International Directory of Little Magazines and Small Presses,* published by Dustbooks (P.O. Box 100, Paradise, CA 95967).

If you have already reached the point in your professional career where you think you should have an agent, your next hurdle will be to find the right agent and agency for you. You may have contacts who can personally recommend you to some literary agents. If this isn't the case, there are a number of reliable source books that list literary agents and their requirements, including *Literary Market Place* and *The Writer's Handbook.* Most agencies can easily tell you what kind of material they represent and what types of manuscripts you should submit for their consideration. For example, my agency represents adult trade fiction and nonfiction, as well as illustrated books. We do not accept unsolicited manuscripts, but will consider query letters with sample material, and an SASE. So if you are an author of science fiction or children's books, my agency would not be the best choice for you. In general, you should also be aware that most agencies will not charge a reading fee, so double-check any offers to "evaluate" your material for a price.

Once you find the right agency for you, it's time to consider the question of author/agent contracts. Should authors have contracts with agents, and what happens if things don't work out and you want to break the contract? Some agencies insist on having a contract with every client. Generally, the contract will specify what happens if either the author or the agent wants to end the relationship, but if no such language exists, you should ask that it be inserted into the agreement. The contract between you and any agent should not make you liable for work, or options on your work that continue after the agreement is terminated. There are exceptions to this rule: For example, if an agent sells something before the official termination date of a client's agreement, the agent is entitled to the agreed-upon percentage of proceeds from that sale.

One of the main benefits of a writer's contract with an agent (and the reason many authors request such a contract) is that it makes the agent/client relationship clearer and more professional. There should be little reason for disputes if both parties know the responsibilities of the other, what rights are being negotiated, and what percentages the agent charges (percentages vary with the number of services offered—i.e., sales to foreign publishers, sales of film/television rights, etc.—but usually range between 10% and 20% of the author's gross receipts). A simple letter of agreement spelling out these terms should be sufficient. You don't need to sign away your soul on a document that is more convoluted than the tax information provided *gratis* by the IRS.

One of the most important functions an agent performs before sending your material out to publishers is to make sure that it is in the most intelligible and marketable shape. There is a difference between fiction and nonfiction, and I will address these areas separately.

For a nonfiction book by an unpublished author, the publisher can reasonably expect an outline or proposal, and two or three sample chapters that will give him some sense of how the writer will deal with the chosen subject. It doesn't matter whether it's a self-help book or a sociological study of environmental hazards; what these pages must demonstrate is the tone the book will take. To this exent, the agent acts as a "pre-editor," making sure that the ideas are clearly articulated and presented and that the author clearly has a point of view and knows how to communicate it. Also included should be some information about the author: background, other published articles, education. Equally important, the agent can help the author focus the proposal for its potential market.

The agent will want to know—just as the publisher will—what competition there might be. Are there similar books in the field that have been or are about to be published? If so, does this one have a special handle that will distinguish it from the others? Are there other markets that the publisher should consider with this book—special premium sales, professional groups, etc.—that will give the book added appeal? Has the book been endorsed or recommended by someone prominent in the field? Does the author have personal contacts with other professionals who would help him obtain information that might not be readily available to others? The proposal should be fifty to seventy-five pages of material that is as good as the author and agent can make it. The agent will add his own perspective and information when the material is sent out to the publisher, but this will serve only to highlight the information in the proposal. The author's voice must be heard on its own.

The handling of fiction is often quite different. In the current diminished and very competitive marketplace, it is rare to sell a novel by an unpublished or even published writer on the basis of a few sample chapters and a synopsis. Most publishers want to see a complete manuscript before making a decision to take on a writer. There are exceptions—mostly in "category" books such as romances or male adventure stories—but these novels are written to a specific formula and therefore are not judged by the same standards and criteria. Also, fiction is a *subjective* art: One editor's taste and sensitivity will vary from another's. Only from reading a completed manuscript can an editor judge what a writer is trying to accomplish.

Here again, the agent can help the author by trying to be sure that the pacing is right, the characters well developed, and that the author makes the reader care and sympathize with his story, but there is less involvement by the agent on this level than with a nonfiction proposal. To a certain extent, the agent's view is also subjective; the agent must take into account that his or her reactions may be personal and that an editor might have a different response.

Once an agent has decided to take you on as a client, whether for fiction or nonfiction, there are several ways to submit your manuscript for publication.

The traditional method has been to choose one publishing house and editor at a time and let them consider the book on an exclusive basis. If there is no sale, you move on to the second, third, or fourth choice.

However, because time is so limited and the publishing process so much more complicated by the many editorial committees that often control selection at a publishing house, the agent may want to submit that material to a number of publishers at the same time. Another obvious reason for multiple submissions is that if the book's subject matter is timely (for example, a current political topic), you want to get the widest amount of exposure as quickly as possible. Some publishers used to be offended by the practice of multiple submissions or auctions, but I don't believe that is a valid viewpoint for the current publishing climate. I try to find the best match between editor, author, and publisher and hope that it works. If it doesn't, I will try a few other houses, but if I still haven't been successful, I will make a limited number of multiple submissions, informing each prospective buyer that other publishers are looking at the material at the same time.

Apart from making the best deal and negotiating the most favorable terms for a client, it is the agent's responsibility to know the publishing network—to make the selection and determination of which editor and house are right for your book. As your link to the publishing community, the agent should shepherd you through the publishing process, looking out for your best interests, but also helping you see the publisher's side of any dispute or disagreement. This requires experience, knowledge, intuition, and often just good diplomatic sense. It has been my experience that authors often do not act in their own best interests when they act alone; they require the objective help of an agent.

Negotiating contracts can vary as much as contracts vary from publisher to publisher. The business points, such as advances and royalties, may be similar, but there are many subtleties in such areas of negotiation as subsidiary rights, warranty, and out-of-print clauses that only an experienced agent can handle. A good agent will also be aware of recent changes in publishing agreements, such as those resulting from the united European market, which make it even more imperative to have an agent's solid, professional advice.

Having your work accepted for representation by an agent and obtaining a publishing contract may seem like the end of a road well-traveled, but in truth it's only the beginning. When the sale is concluded, the publishing process begins. Along the way, there are many decisions that will have to be made regarding editorial changes, book

design, promotion, and publicity. In the current publishing climate, even
the most sophisticated writer can feel like a new arrival in Oz, where
the direction of the Yellow Brick Road has changed, and the Wizard has
a boss! In these uncertain times, the good counsel of your literary agent
means that you won't travel alone and there'll be someone to help you
read the map.

15

CRITICISM: CAN YOU TAKE IT?

BY LANCE E. WILCOX

WE WRITERS OFTEN FANCY OURSELVES THE loneliest of lone wolves. We delight to picture ourselves hidden away in our dusty garret or our remote New Hampshire cabin, giving birth to our works in sublime isolation. But this is curious when you consider that the business we're about is furiously social. We're trying to communicate. In our splendid solitude, we write and rewrite, polish and repolish, all in hopes of breaking through that solitude into the lives and minds of other people. Because writing is so social, it makes sense now and then to gather up our papers, leave our garret, and seek out other people's reactions to our work before even thinking of sending it to an editor. How best can we go about doing this?

Whenever you seek others' reactions to your work, your attitude toward your writing is especially important. Don't hand your manuscript to your reader and cry, "Here it is! Unworthy, presumptuous trash, I know! Tear it to pieces!" This sounds like humility, but it's really manipulation. It's a desperate and dishonest plea for mercy, and mercy is precisely what you don't need.

What you want to cultivate is a poised, matter-of-fact objectivity about yourself and your work. You already know, if you think about it, that everything you've ever written, and ever will write, could be better. There is always room for improvement. And once you get this firmly in your head, you won't be tempted to ask (a hopeful quaver in your voice), "Is it. . . . O.K.?" but simply, "How does this work for you? What do you like and dislike? What parts catch your attention or give you trouble?" Then, when your reader does point out strengths and weaknesses, you won't be devastated. In fact, you'll probably face the task of rewriting with more confidence and energy than usual.

You're not obliged to get an expert's opinion. What you're after is a sample audience—not a brilliant, scholarly, authoritative critic, but just people who like to read, who are reasonably bright, and who won't either coddle or attack you. You're not seeking The Indisputable Truth about your piece, but simply how it works. Where is it interesting? Where is it confusing? Do your readers feel as if they're skiing down the slopes or trudging uphill through the sand?

You may, in fact, have to help your readers here. They may feel pressured to play English teacher, and you don't need that. All you ask is that they report their real felt reactions in as clear and honest a manner as possible. When your reader tells you, "I was really enjoying it up to this point, but right around here somewhere I started to bog down," or, "Edward intrigued me, but I never really knew what he wanted," that's when you know where to put your efforts in revision.

Your readers also at first may offer reactions that are vague, global, impressionistic. This isn't a bad place to start, but you will want to press them further. Try to draw them out on their reactions. Point to specific passages you yourself aren't sure about and get their reactions to those. Try to get them to pinpoint, as precisely as possible, what in your draft attracted them or turned them off, and why.

You will find as you do this striking differences among your acquaintances as to how much they actually help you. Some are nitpickers. Others are incapable of anything but diffuse, unhelpful praise. But still others will prove level-headed, frank, at once encouraging and incisive, and adept at saying just how they felt paragraph by paragraph as they were reading. Keep them around!

Finally—and this should go without saying—*never, under any circumstances, defend your work to your readers.* If your work bored them, it bored them. Don't try to convince them that, dullards as they are, they simply failed to see how fascinating it really is. If something on Page Three confused them, it confused them. Don't insult them by pointing out the perfectly lucid explanation on Page Two that they must have overlooked. When you're actually discussing your work, you're on a fact-finding mission. What did these words do for them or to them? You want to see the work through *their* eyes, not bully them into seeing it through yours.

So then, you've sought, listened to, and taken note of the reactions of a few capable readers to the draft you worked on so carefully. Now what? Well, first you curl up, whimper a bit, and lick your wounds. Secretly, we always hope we've written the loveliest sonnet since Yeats, the suavest essay since E. B. White, the truest story since Hemingway—and we haven't, and every time it's a disappointment.

Then dust yourself off, roll up your sleeves, and start back to work, rewriting again what you've already labored over so long. You needn't take all your readers' suggestions, but you should probably take most of them. As a rule, whatever flaws they report are really there—as you'd see for yourself if you were to file the piece away for six months and read it then. But the final responsibility is always yours and yours alone.

For the beginner, nothing makes real the sense of an audience . . . like an audience. For the pro, it's Continuing Education. But perhaps best of all, it continually reminds you that you're really not alone. You can hide in an igloo at the North Pole, and your readers are all huddled in there with you. Sometimes they may terrify you. But if you genuinely wish to do well by them—that is, to provide them good reading matter—you'll find, after all, that they're ready and able to help.

How To Write—Techniques
GENERAL FICTION

16

GETTING STARTED

BY JOHN IRVING

IT IS USEFUL WHEN YOU BEGIN A NOVEL to invoke certain guidelines if not actual rules that have given you aid and comfort during the periods of tribulation that marked the beginnings of your Novels Past. You are never, of course, so given to imperatives as when you don't know what you're doing and, therefore, haven't begun. This helps to explain an obvious contradiction in most book reviews: a notable absence of any understanding of the examined work in tandem with a flood of imperatives regarding what the work ought to have been. First novelists, especially, are afflicted with the need to give advice—witness Tom Wolfe's advice to us all, regarding our proper subject matter (lest we end up bantering among ourselves, like so many poets). But I digress—a common weakness with all beginnings.

Beginnings are important. Here is a useful rule for beginning: Know the story—as much of the story as you can possibly know, if not the whole story—before you commit yourself to the first paragraph. Know the story—the whole story, if possible—before you fall in love with your first *sentence,* not to mention your first chapter. If you don't know the story before you begin the story, what kind of a storyteller are you? Just an ordinary kind, just a mediocre kind—making it up as you go along, like a common liar. Or else, to begin a novel without an ending fixed in your mind's eye, you must be very clear, and so full of confidence in the voice that tells the story that the story itself hardly matters. In my own case, I am much more plodding; confidence comes from knowing the story that lies ahead—not in the limited powers of the voice that tells it. This calls for patience and for plotting.

And most of all, when beginning, be humble; remember that your first, blank page has this in common with all other blank pages: It has not read your previous works. Don't be enthralled by the sound of your own voice; write with a purpose; have a plan. Know the story, *then* begin the story. Here endeth the lesson.

The authority in the storyteller's voice derives from foreknowledge. In my opinion, a novel is written with predestination—a novel being defined as a *narrative; a good* narrative has a *plot.* If you're not interested in plot, why write a novel? Because plot provides momentum, plot is what makes a novel better on page three hundred than it was on page thirty—*if* it's a good novel. A good novel, by definition, keeps getting better. Plot is what draws the reader in—plot *and* the development of characters who are worthy of the reader's emotional interest. Here endeth another lesson.

Is this advice for everyone? Of course not! "Plot" isn't what compels many novelists to write, or some readers to read. But if you choose to write a novel without a plot, I would hope three things for you: that your prose is gorgeous, that your insights into the human condition are inspirational, and that your book is short. I am directing my remarks, of course, to those writers (and readers) of *long* novels.

Would a film director begin to shoot a picture without a screenplay? I would never begin a novel without knowing the whole story; but even then, the choices for how to begin are not simple. *You* may know exactly where the story begins, but choosing where you want the *reader* to begin the story is another matter. And here cometh another lesson for the writer of long novels: Think of the reader. Who is this reader? I think of the reader as far more intelligent than I am, but a child—a kind of hyperactive prodigy, a reading wizard. Interest this child and he will put up with anything—he will understand everything, too. But fail to seize and hold this child's attention, *at the beginning,* and he will never come back to you. This is your reader: paradoxically, a genius with the concentration span of a rabbit.

I am amazed that mere consideration of the reader, nowadays, often marks a writer as "commercial"—as opposed to "literary." To the snotty charge that Dickens wrote what the public wanted, Chesterton replied, "Dickens *wanted* what the public wanted!" Let us quickly clear up this name-calling regarding "commercial" and "literary": It is for artistic reasons, in addition to financial wisdom, that *any* author would prefer keeping a reader's attention to losing it.

Three obvious but painstaking components either succeed in making a novel "literary," or they fail and make it a mess: namely, the crafts-manlike quality of the storytelling (of course, in my opinion, a novel should be a story worth telling); the true-to-life quality of the characters (I also expect the characters to be skillfully developed); and the meticulous exactitude of the language (discernible in every sentence and seeming to be spoken by an unmistakable voice).

What makes a novel "commercial" is that a lot of people buy it and finish it and tell other people to read it; both "literary" novels and failed, messy novels can be commercially successful *or* unsuccessful. The part about the reader *finishing* a novel is important for the book's commercial success; both good reviews and the author's pre-existent popularity can put a book on the bestseller lists, but what keeps a book on the list for a long time is that a lot of those first readers actually finish the book and tell their friends that they simply must read it. We don't tell our friends that they simply must read a book we're unable to finish.

In my own judgment, as a reader, the faults of most novels are the sentences—either they're unambitious or they're so unclear that they need to be rewritten. And what's wrong with the rest of the novels I don't finish is that the stories aren't good enough to merit writing a novel in the first place.

One of the pleasures of reading a novel is anticipation. Would a playwright *not* bother to anticipate what the audience is anticipating? The reader of a novel also enjoys the feeling that he can anticipate where the story is going; however, if the reader actually does anticipate the story, he is bored. The reader must be able to anticipate, but the reader must also guess wrong. How can an author make a reader anticipate—not to mention make a reader guess wrong—if the author himself doesn't *know* where the story is going? A good beginning will suggest knowledge of the whole story; it will give a strong hint regarding where the whole story is headed—yet a good beginning must be misleading, too.

Therefore, where to begin? Begin where the reader will be invited to do the most anticipating of the story, but where the reader will be the most compelled to guess wrong. If anticipation is a pleasure, so is surprise.

My last rule is informed by a remark of the late John Cheever—from his journals—that he was "forced to consider [his] prose by the ignobility of some of [his] material." My advice is to consider—from the beginning—that *all* of your material suffers from ignobility. Therefore, *always* consider your prose!

In the past, I have deliberately loaded my first sentences with all these admonitions in mind. The first sentence of *The World According to Garp:* "Garp's mother, Jenny Fields, was arrested in Boston in 1942 for wounding a man in a movie theater." (The sentence is a shameless tease; "wounded" is deliberately unclear—we want to know *how* the man was "wounded"—and that the person "arrested" was somebody's *mother* surely suggests a lurid tale.) The first sentence of *The Hotel New Hampshire:* "The summer my father bought the bear, none of us was born—we weren't even conceived: not Frank, the oldest; not Franny, the loudest; not me, the next; and not the youngest of us, Lilly and Egg." (Well, what is shameless about this is that *anybody* bought a bear—the rest of the sentence is simply an economical means of introducing the members of a large family. In fact, this family is so large, it is cumbersome; therefore, a few of them will die deaths of convenience rather early in the novel.) The first sentence of *The Cider House Rules:* "In the hospital of the orphanage—the boys' division of St. Cloud's, Maine—two nurses were in charge of naming the new babies and checking that their little penises were healing from the obligatory circumcision." (This beginning operates on the assumption that orphanages are emotionally engaging to everyone; also, how people are named is always interesting, and the matter of "obligatory circumcision" suggests either religion or eccentricity—or both. Besides, I always wanted to put "penises" in an opening sentence; the word, I suppose, sends a signal that this novel is *not* for everyone.) And the first sentence of *A Prayer for Owen Meany:* "I am doomed to remember a boy with a wrecked voice—not because of his voice, or because he was the instrument of my mother's death, but because he is the reason I believe in God; I am a Christian because of Owen Meany." (When in doubt, or wherever possible, tell the whole story of the novel in the first sentence.)

All of those first sentences were not simply the first sentences I ended up with; they were, with one exception, the first sentence of those books that I wrote. (In the case of *Garp,* the *first* first sentence was the sentence that is now the last sentence of the book: "But in the world according to Garp, we are all terminal cases.")

In the case of the novel I am now writing, I have narrowed the possible beginning to three choices; I haven't made up my mind among these choices—so it is still possible that a fourth alternative will present itself, and be chosen, but I doubt it. I think I shall proceed with something very close to one of these.

1. "A widow for one year, Ruth Cole was forty-six; a novelist for twenty years (counting from 1970, when her first book was published), she'd been famous only a little longer than she'd been a widow—in fact, in Mrs. Cole's mind, her husband's death and her literary success were so closely associated that her grief overshadowed any enjoyment she could take from the world's newfound appreciation of her work."

This is a plain, old-fashioned beginning: It holds back more than it tells, and I like that. The character is a woman of some achievement; we may therefore expect her to be a character of some complexity, and—as she is a recent widow—we can be assured that we enter her life at a vulnerable moment. This beginning continues to build on our impression of Mrs. Cole *at this moment:*

"Furthermore, she'd always perceived any recognition of her writing—both when the praise had been spotty and now that it was profuse—as nothing more than a seductive invasion of her privacy; that such sudden and so much attention should come to her at a time when she most sought to be alone (and most needed to grow accustomed to being alone) was simply annoying. Fame, to Mrs. Cole, was merely a trivial vexation among the more painful torments of her loneliness. She wanted her husband alive again, she wanted him back; for it was only in her life with him that she'd been afforded the greatest privacy, not to mention an intimacy she'd never taken for granted."

We stand on solid ground with this beginning; we already know a lot about Mrs. Cole and her situation. We may be interested in such a woman, at such a time in her life, but there is no hook; the beginning is *too* plain—it lacks even a hint of anything sensational.

Try again.

2. "Dr. Daruwalla had upsetting news for the famous actor, Inspector Dutt; not sure of the degree to which Inspector Dutt would be distressed, Dr. Daruwalla was impelled by cowardice to give the movie star the bad news in a public place—young Dutt's extraordinary poise in public was renowned; the doctor felt he could rely on the actor to keep his composure."

This, of course, is the beginning of a novel by Ruth Cole; it is one of *her* beginnings. Mrs. Cole continues in a tone of voice that promises us she will, occasionally, be funny. "Not everyone in Bombay would have thought of a private club as a 'public place,' but Dr. Daruwalla believed that the choice was both private and public enough for the particular crisis at hand." And the second paragraph provides the "hook" I feel is missing from my first beginning.

> "That morning when Dr. Daruwalla arrived at the Duckworth Sports and Eating Club, he thought it was unremarkable to see a vulture high in the sky above the golf course; he did not consider the bird of death as an omen attached to the unwelcome burden of the news he carried. The club was in Mahalaxmi, not far from Malabar Hill; everyone in Bombay knew why the vultures were attracted to Malabar Hill. When a corpse was placed in the Towers of Silence, the vultures—from thirty miles outside Bombay—could scent the ripening remains."

This is certainly a more mysterious beginning than my first—not to mention more foreign. The language (that is, Mrs. Cole's) is more lush and dense than my own—this beginning is altogether more exotic. But pity the poor reader when he discovers that this is *not* the novel he is reading—rather, it is a novel *within* the novel he is reading. Won't the poor reader feel misled too much? (To mislead is divine, to *trick* is another matter!) However, I am aware that I will never get the reader to read Mrs. Cole's Indian novel as closely as I want him to *if* the reader knows it is merely a novel within a novel; by beginning with Mrs. Cole's novel, I make the reader read it closely. What a choice! And so I come, cautiously in the middle, to the third possibility.

> 3. "*Son of the Circus,* the seventh novel by the American novelist Ruth Cole, was first published in the United States in September, 1989; the excitement was mitigated for the author by the unexpected death of her husband—he died in his sleep beside his wife, in a hotel in New York City; they had just begun the promotion tour."

This is not yet quite the blend I want—between what is plain and old-fashioned, and what is exotic—but this comes close to satisfying me, *provided that* I begin the so-called Indian novel quickly, before the reader becomes *too* involved in poor Mrs. Cole's widowhood (not to mention the bad timing of her husband's demise). And that last line— "they had just begun the promotion tour"—hints at a tone of voice that will prevail both in Ruth Cole's fiction and in my telling of her actual story; any consideration of one's prose must include a consideration of the tone of voice.

But what I miss (from Mrs. Cole's beginning) is greater than the kind of purity gained by the third possibility. Both the first and third beginnings tell the reader what *has* happened to Ruth Cole; Mrs. Cole, on the other hand, tells us what Dr. Daruwalla is *going to* do—he's going to give an actor named Inspector Dutt some bad news. What *is* this news? I want to know. And Dr. Daruwalla may be so used to vultures that *he* does "not consider the bird of death as an omen," but we readers know better: Of *course* the vulture is an omen! *Anyone* knows that! Therefore, at this writing, I am inclined to begin my novel with Mrs. Cole's first chapter, or part of it. If Mrs. Cole's story is good enough, the reader will forgive me for my trick.

Even as I write, a fourth opportunity presents itself to me: Instead of starting with Mrs. Cole's novel or with Mrs. Cole, it is possible to begin with someone else reading her novel—perhaps her former lover.

"At that moment, the German stopped reading; he was a golfer himself, he did not find dead-golfer jokes amusing, and he was overwhelmed by the density of the description—the pace of this novel was unbearably slow for him, not to mention how little interested he was in India. He was not much of a reader, especially not of novels, and he despaired that he was less than halfway through the first chapter of a very long novel and already he was bored. (The last book he'd read was about golf.) But special interests, none of them literary, would compel him to keep reading the novel he'd momentarily put aside.

"He knew the author; that is, he had briefly been her lover, many years ago, and he was vain enough to imagine that in her novel he would find some trace of himself—that was what he was reading for. Once he penetrated the story—past the dead golfer—he would find much more than he'd bargained for; his imagination simply wasn't up to the task he'd set for himself, but he didn't know that as he sat fingering the German translation and smiling boorishly at the author photograph, which he found faintly arousing."

And by the time you read this, I may be considering a fifth possibility. Anyway, once the beginning is locked in place, it is time to invite similar scrutiny of the next chapter and then the next. With any luck, you will hear from me (and Mrs. Cole) in about four years.

§ 17

THE ESSENCE OF STORYTELLING: DRAMATIZE, DRAMATIZE

BY ELIZABETH FORSYTHE HAILEY

DRAMATIZE, DRAMATIZE" IS THE ADVICE Henry James gave to writers of fiction.

His advice was reinforced in my own case by marriage to a novel-hating playwright who is not only my first audience but also my first editor. I knew when I started my first novel I would have to find a form that would engage and hold his attention—which is why I chose in *A Woman of Independent Means* to show the life of a woman from childhood to old age through the letters she writes, leaving the audience to imagine what her correspondents say to her in reply.

One of the keys to dramatizing is enlisting the imagination of your audience, forcing them to do some of the work and in effect making them accomplices in the conspiracy that is fiction.

Drama is the essence of storytelling. Wanting to know what happens next is what keeps a viewer in his seat or a reader turning the pages of a novel. But telling a story—like starting a fire—requires friction, two different elements striking against each other. Like natural combustion, the dramatic conflict that ignites a work of fiction requires antagonists.

In *A Woman of Independent Means* the main antagonist—the arch villain, if you will—is time. My heroine Bess, a character based on my own grandmother, was a woman with an extraordinary appetite for life. She wanted to see and do it all, and a single lifetime was not nearly long enough. She asked that her epitaph read "to be continued."

This central conflict was heightened when I adapted the novel into a one-person stage play. Thanks to a tour-de-force display of acting by stage and film star Barbara Rush, the audience was able to witness a lifetime in the space of two hours. Without benefit of makeup or costume changes, relying only on the most subtle adjustments in speech and movement, she was able to transform herself from a young

72

girl of eighteen into a frail old woman facing death. The message of the book—to show how quickly even a long, full life passes—was translated into heightened dramatic terms on the stage.

The experience of adapting my first novel into my first stage play continues to serve me well when I return to the novel form.

I had no problem finding points of conflict and dramatizing them in my novel *Joanna's Husband and David's Wife*. It's the chronicle of a marriage over twenty-five years from a dual perspective—the point of view of both husband and wife.

Joanna starts a diary the day she meets David, determined to have a complete record of her relationship with the man she plans to marry. On their twenty-fourth anniversary, she returns to her parents, leaving the diary to her daughter, who has fallen in love for the first time. The diary is her way of showing her daughter what marriage is like (my characters have learned the secret of dramatizing: show, don't tell). But David discovers the journal first and decides to add his side of the story before their daughter reads it.

The device of the diary—and David's later discovery of it—allowed me to make use of two techniques that reinforce dramatic conflict: passage of time and point of view. The narrative spine of the novel is from Joanna's point of view—her diary entries. But David, looking back at an event, often remembers it differently—and there are times when he has no memory at all of what Joanna is describing. Using two points of view and locating them at different moments in time not only allows the characters to express hidden conflicts (those hidden from each other as well as those hidden from the reader), but encourages them to keep secrets. Sometimes what is unsaid between them can be more explosive than what is said.

However, in transforming *Joanna's Husband and David's Wife* into a two-character stage play, I had to write some of the novel's unwritten scenes, exploring the conflicts anew and allowing the characters to confront each other in the same time frame.

With my novel *Home Free*, my heroine took shape in my head a full year before I could come up with a story for her. I wanted to write about a middle-aged woman from a conventional, middle-class background who finds herself alone (I wasn't sure in the beginning whether her husband would die or desert her for another woman) and is forced to redefine her ideas about home and family.

I had some vague idea that she would sell the house she had shared with her husband and, instead of finding another permanent residence, would become a housesitter for friends who traveled a lot or divided their lives among houses in different places. My idea was to make her a member (at least through marriage) of the moviemaking community— work that keeps people on the move. I saw her becoming involved in the lives of the different families for whom she served as a housesitter.

But even though I made a lot of notes on possible characters and situations, I knew in my heart of hearts I did not have the makings of a novel: The elements of conflict were missing. At best what I had was a book of interrelated short stories with my main character serving as a connecting device. But that was not what I wanted to write. My heroine, Kate Hart, was real and full to me, and I wanted to write a novel in which her actions would be focal.

Then three years ago at Thanksgiving I read a magazine piece on a homeless family in Los Angeles. The faces in the accompanying photographs seared my consciousness. There was a husband, a wife, a son, a daughter, even a dog—the all-American family—but they were living in their car. The article describing their ever more desperate plight changed all my comfortable assumptions about why and how people found themselves living on the street. Suddenly I saw my heroine opening the front door of the house where she now lived alone to a fictional family very much like the one whose faces now confronted me in the magazine. And I knew I had found the missing half of my novel. My heroine, who had a home but no family, was going to get involved with a family who had no home.

The story fell into place very quickly. I saw it in scenes, like a film, and used a device screenwriters often employ when constructing a movie script. I took a pack of index cards and, allotting one card for each scene, made notes of what I imagined happening between characters. The test of whether a scene deserved to be written was the strength of the potential conflict at the core of it.

I have a tendency in my first draft to spend too much time establishing characters and setting before zeroing in on the central conflict. But using the index card system forces a novelist to think in terms of scenes rather than endless chunks of prose.

When I first started plotting *Home Free,* I planned to show my two main characters in their separate settings before bringing them together. I wrote on my first index card: "Christmas Eve. Kate and her husband fight. He leaves." And on my second card: "Christmas Eve. Homeless man panhandles outside supermarket to buy presents for his family." Staring at my third index card, wondering how they would meet, I realized I had started the book too soon. The point of the novel was to make their two very separate worlds collide, and the sooner that happened, the more compelling and original my novel would be. So I put aside my first two index cards and started over. Notes for my new opening read: "Kate sees homeless man's car stall in front of her house as her husband walks out the door." Those two abandoned index cards saved me hundreds of unnecessary words.

Index cards are a terrific way to construct anything—novel, screenplay, magazine article, possibly even a poem (though I've never tried it)—much less cumbersome and rigid than a prose outline. You can shift scenes around or delete them with ease, and whenever a random idea occurs to you—a line of description, a scrap of dialogue—you can jot it down where you think it might fit.

The novel is such an open-ended form (running anywhere from several hundred pages to several thousand), it does not encourage disciplined dramatic construction. In contrast, the length of a play or film (with some well-known exceptions) is pretty much decided by the patience of the audience, and usually takes place within a two- or three-hour time frame. Also, economics can dictate the number of characters and settings.

But the novel is wide open—choices of scenes, characters, points of view limited only by the imagination of the novelist. The intoxicating possibilities of so much freedom can easily overpower a latent sense of dramatic economy. The task of the novelist is to practice from within the discipline imposed on the playwright from without.

It is not a coincidence that a lot of best-selling authors—Sidney Sheldon is a notable example—began by writing for the screen. They developed the craft of storytelling by learning how to construct scenes—scenes that would advance the action by entangling the characters in conflict.

In plotting your novel, try to see it as a film or play. Watch the story unfold before your eyes. Listen as your characters talk and argue.

My friend, the late Tommy Thompson, was a distinguished journalist and author of such nonfiction bestsellers as *Blood and Money* and *Serpentine* when he embarked on his first novel. Several chapters into it, he found himself for the first time in his life paralyzed by a massive case of writer's block. He had churned out hundreds of thousands of words under unrelenting deadline pressure as a journalist, but he was not prepared for the terror that comes from facing a blank page when the story is taking place only inside your own head.

Fortunately, he had a very wise editor who said to him, "Just because you're writing fiction doesn't mean you've stopped being a reporter. What you have to do is what you always do when you cover a story. Look at what's going on, listen to what people are saying, and report it—report all of it. The only difference is that the story you're reporting now is taking place in your imagination. But the process is the same."

I can imagine no better advice for a writer of fiction, whether novelist, playwright, or screenwriter. First see the scene, then report it. From that point on, you're home free.

Home free. Good title.

18

EMOTION IN FICTION

BY ROSAMUNDE PILCHER

I WAS, AS A CHILD, extremely emotional. Almost anything or anybody could make me cry. I wept copiously as I listened to Paul Robeson singing "Ol' Man River." Soggy with sentiment, I begged my Scottish mother to oblige me with a rendering of "Loch Lomond," swearing that I wouldn't blub. But when she got to the bit, "But me and my true love will never meet again," my good resolutions went with the wind and the tears poured down.

There were books as well. A dreadful Victorian drama for children called *A Peep Behind the Scenes.* I have no recollection of the plot, but I know that almost everybody, in some way or another, died. Mother had tuberculosis, and a saint-like child who crossed the road in order to pick buttercups in a field was squashed flat beneath the wheels of a passing cart. When I found myself with an empty afternoon and no one to play with, I would find myself drawn, with hideous inevitability, to the bookshelf, and the dismal book. Sitting on the floor, I would turn the pages, scarcely able to see the print for weeping.

In other words, I, like an awful lot of other people, enjoyed a good cry.

The poem, "The Raggle, Taggle Gypsies" had the same effect on me, and, oddly enough, so did Beatrix Potter's "Pigling Bland." I say "oddly enough," because Beatrix Potter was always marvelously un-sentimental and thoroughly practical about the seamy side of life. Jemima Puddleduck, laying her eggs in the wrong places, was deemed a simpleton. Squirrel Nutkin, teasing the owl, got his deserts and lost his tail. And right and proper, too. But Pigling Bland was different. He and his little girlfriend Pig Wig finally escaped the dreadful fate of being sent to market, and sent off on their own, running as fast as they could.

> They came to the river, they came to the stream,
> They crossed it, hand in hand,

Then over the hills and far away,
She danced with Pigling Bland.

It made me cry, not because it was sad, but because it was beautiful. I still think it is beautiful, and I still get a lump in my throat when I read it aloud to my grandchildren.

The most subtle form of arousing emotion is to slip the reader, with little or no warning, from laughter to tears. James Thurber wrote a piece entitled "The Dog That Bit People." It was about an Airedale called Muggs. He didn't simply bite people, but terrified the life out of deliverymen and was regularly reported to the police. Told in Thurber's laconic style, it was marvelously funny.

But in the last paragraph, Muggs dies, quite suddenly, in the night. He is duly buried, in a grave alongside a lonely road. Mother wants a marble headstone erected, but finally settles for a smooth board, on which Thurber wrote, with an indelible pencil, "Cave Canem," and his mother was pleased with the simple classic dignity of the old Latin epitaph.

All right; so the death of any faithful animal is a sure-fire tear-jerker, but it still gets to me, every time I read it.

Emotion, conveyed by the written word, is a delicate business. Like humor, it cannot be pushed, or it slips into sentimentality. Hemingway, that master of reported speech, could wring the heart by the bare bones of his painful dialogue. He never stressed the fact that he was telling you something that went beyond ordinary feelings, and yet you read the mundane, oft-used words, and hear his voices, and recognize the poignancy of the frailty of man, and there comes the lump in the throat and the sting of incipient tears.

Some years ago, I wrote a three-act play, with a single set; not a very accomplished piece of work, but it was produced by our local repertory theater, and for a few weeks I enjoyed a mild local fame. For the first time in my life, I was invited to open fetes, judge competitions, and hand out prizes for various contests. I found none of this too daunting. But then I was approached by a woman famous for her good works, and asked if I would make an appeal on radio to raise funds for her pet project—a training center for young mothers (scarcely more than schoolgirls) unfit to care for their unwanted babies. Touched by the plight of these little families, I agreed. Only then was I told that not only would I have to deliver the appeal, but would have to write the message myself.

It was the first time that I had been faced with a situation in which I deliberately had to drag emotion out of the bag. For without emotion, I should not touch hearts, and if I didn't touch hearts, I would not touch pockets. I engaged the help of a bright girl who was involved in the project, and for two days we sat at our typewriters, finally bashing out five minutes' worth of heartbreak, sentiment, and crying need. I duly read this out over the radio one Sunday morning, and by the end of the week the center was about a hundred and fifty pounds to the good. It wasn't much, and it wasn't enough. They struggled on for a month or two, and then closed down. We had tried, but it hadn't worked.

Much more recently, the very opposite occurred. In Dundee, Scotland, a small boy was desperately ill. Specialized neurosurgery was required, but the Dundee Royal Infirmary did not have the necessary equipment. In Boston, Massachusetts, however, the equipment was available, and this was flown, in some urgency, to Scotland. The two neurosurgeons had never used the device before, but they operated, with total skill, and the small boy's life was saved.

The story appeared the next day in our local paper, *The Dundee Courier and Advertiser.* A plain, factual account of what had taken place. We learned that the reason the equipment had had to be borrowed was that the Infirmary could not afford the £60,000 necessary to purchase it. With some idea of expressing my gratitude and admiration for the two doctors, I put five pounds in an envelope and posted it to the Infirmary. So did just about everyone else, who, that morning, took the paper. A fund had to be hastily set up, without an appeal ever having been launched, and within the next two weeks, the £60,000 target had been achieved. Which proves that if you've got a good story to tell, you don't need to play your sobbing violin at the same time.

Sadness, bravery, beauty, all touch our heart strings. Great happiness can be deeply touching, else why do we sometimes weep at weddings, or that moment when an old gentleman heaves himself to his feet at his Golden Wedding party and raises his champagne glass to his wife?

My novel *The Shell Seekers* covered a span of fifty years, and because of this, the varying ages of the characters, and the intrusion of two terrible wars, I found myself writing, more than once, about death. The demise of an elderly person I do not, in fact, find particularly sad. A

79

shock and a loss, certainly, to be followed by a period of grieving, but death is part of life, and just about the only thing we can all be certain of.

However, the death of the young officer, Richard Lomax, killed on Omaha Beach, with all his life ahead of him, I found quite agonizing to set down. And worse was endeavoring to describe the reactions of Penelope Keeling, who when told of his tragic end, knew that their brief love was finished, and that the rest of her life would have to be lived without him. Struggling, as she struggled, for words, I gave her only the most banal of sentences to utter. And then cheated, and instead let her recall the final passage of the Louis MacNeice poem which they had both known and loved.

> . . . the die is cast
> There will be time to audit
> The accounts later, there will be sunlight later,
> And the equation will come out at last.

Cheating, perhaps. But it seemed to me to say it all.

To sum up, an analysis of what touches the writer is what will eventually get through to the reader. Understated, underplayed, unexaggerated, and yet totally sincere. There has to be rapport, a chime of instant recognition, clear as a bell. If you don't produce tears, you will at least kindle understanding, identification, and so forge a bond with the reader. And, at the end of the day, perhaps this is what writing is all about.

19

A Canyon, An Egret, and A Book

By Tony Hillerman

On page 185 of *A Thief of Time*, readers encounter a snowy egret, flushed from his roosting place in the San Juan River Canyon by a Navajo Tribal Policeman. The policeman is fictional. But the canyon is real and so is the startled egret. Therein lies a tale of how a novel evolved and how a silent, empty place can stimulate the human imagination.

It happened because of one of those odd confluences of needs that sometimes occur. I needed locations, and inspiration, for a book that was trying to take shape in my head. Specifically, I needed an Anasazi cliff dwelling in an isolated place. There I intended to have a pot hunter murder an anthropologist. That was to be the pivotal point in a story about those "thieves of time" who loot ancient ruins. Since the anthropologist, the pot hunter, and the crime would be pure fiction, it would seem logical that the cliff dwelling could be fictional as well. But logic doesn't apply when I am trying to write a novel. For some reason I need almost to memorize the landscape I write about.

Meanwhile, two other coinciding needs had developed. Dan Murphy of the U.S. Park Service was feeling a need to show me—a skeptic—that the San Juan River Canyon above Lake Powell was as awe-inspiring as he had been claiming. And Charles DeLorme of Wild River Expeditions at Bluff, Utah, needed two people to go along on a raft trip he was organizing. He needed someone to explain to his paying guests the geology, flora and fauna of the canyon they would be seeing and someone to tell them campfire stories about the mythology, culture, and history of the Navajos, whose territory the river invades. Thus Murphy and I signed on to float down the San Juan as natural historian and yarn spinner, respectively.

About three miles into the journey, we pulled our rafts onto the north shore and inspected an unexcavated mound where some nine hundred years of drifted dust buried an Anasazi ruin. Above it, footholds cut into the stone mark the path they used to reach the mesa top. A mile farther along, we made another stop and examined what is, in effect, an Anasazi mural. Here petroglyphs were cut through the dark manganese oxide ("desert varnish") stains on the sandstone face of the cliff—forming rows and rows of figures. Some I could identify. One was obviously a snowy egret. Others are abstract representations of the reptiles, birds and animals that still inhabit the canyon (or, like the Big Horn Sheep, have vanished with the Anasazis). But many of the forms are humanoid shapes with great square shoulders cut into the stone representing (anthropologists believe) the kachina spirits. Stripes are cut over their heads indicating whatever one's imagination suggests—perhaps speech, or song, or rank, or magical power.

My own imagination was trying to deal with this remarkable mural cliff through the eyes of two fictional characters. One is Lieutenant Joe Leaphorn of the Navajo Tribal Police, whom I've used for years and know as one knows a dear old friend. No problem with Joe. I know how his mind works. But the other character was a still nebulous stranger— my murder victim. I had decided to make him a contract archaeologist working for the U.S. Park Service. This character was a male, and existed only as about 45 words on paper on my desk. He was to be a specialist in something yet to be decided, and he was supposed to be dead by the end of the first chapter—the victim of the murder on which the plot of this book would turn.

As I stared at figures cut into this cliff, I found myself thinking of the artists who carved it. They would have used tools of sharpened antlers and flint. It would have been a hard, hot job on a summer day like this. I thought of their scarred and callused hands. That led me to remember that hands of a woman archaeologist I know—a beautiful, graceful young woman who rarely is seen without at least one finger bandaged. Suddenly, I found myself thinking of my murder victim as a woman. She had the scarred, callused hands of digging archaeologists and a Phi Beta Kappa mind. She was a working class woman—an oddity in this field. Thus under this cliff where Anasazi artists toiled a thousand years ago, what had been a one-dimensional character changed gender in my mind and developed a personality, with a memory of family, with a failed marriage, an admiration for an older man she wants to impress, and a love of the abstract art she sees on this cliff. It's a shame she was to die so soon. On the Navajo side of the river the stone walls of a small

Anasazi cliff dwelling are visible, high under the arched roof of the wall on a small side canyon. We drifted past that canyon's mouth. On the opposite side of the river a massive sandstone overhang shelters another ruin—some of its walls still intact all the way to the natural stone roof.

The raft crew calls this place "River House." Its most prominent feature is a roundish stone tower that looks a little like a silo and must have been used for storage of grain or other foodstuff.

It was cool on the earthen floor of River House, and quiet—a good place to sit and think bookish thoughts. This ruin has never been officially excavated by a research team. But it has been tentatively probed by pot hunters. They have left shallow holes in the hummock of earth that must have been this family's trash heap and is, therefore, a likely place for Anasazi burials. It has also been vandalized. The raft crew told me that the vandal is a member of an unpopular Navajo family that had moved across the river from the reservation. They described him as a boy with severe emotional problems.

And so, while I sat looking at the damage this boy has done, a possible first chapter took shape! A Navajo boy, a neurotic loner, would be a witness to my intended murder. I convert him from a vandal per se into a would-be artist who paints pictographs on cliffs. My Navajo policeman knows by their nature that they must be of Navajo origin, finds the boy, solves the crime. But this River House is too visible to be an appropriate scene for my crime. My setting needs isolation. Murphy told me that the ruins downstream and up a canyon on the Navajo side of the river were much better.

From River House, an old trail leads a half mile downstream to the mouth of Comb Wash and up to traces of an old road that climbs Comb Ridge, a barrier of solid rock. The road was cut by the Mormons Brigham Young had sent to establish an outpost on the San Juan where Bluff is now located. For me it was an ordeal to huff and puff up the traces of that old exploit, even burdened with nothing heavier than a canteen.

The road leads past a circular mound that must cover the remains of an unusually large ceremonial kiva and to an impressive long view over the Bluff Valley and the sandstone wilderness that surrounds it. The climb also brought to mind the sort of iron-willed men and women who were the ancestors of Bluff.

Thus *A Thief of Time* took another of its quirky turns. I decided I would try to work in just such a Mormon as a character—an elderly man, if possible. Not many months before, the home of a prominent citizen of this Southern Utah canyon country had been raided by the federals. The man's collection of artifacts had been seized, and he'd been accused of dealing in illegal Anasazi pots. For my purposes, that was perfect material for the sort of red herring subplot I'm always looking for.

Beside the river below this high edge of Comb Ridge, there still stands the stone foundation of a water wheel used to grind grain into flour, and above this old mill stand the roofless ruins of a one-room building. Murphy told me this structure was built as a trading post, that its owner was shot to death in a dispute with two Navajo customers— who then fled across the San Juan and vanished.

That story stuck in my memory. I found myself looking for a spot where two men—probably poor swimmers—could have crossed without drowning. Could my fictional neurotic young Navajo swim? Such bootless mental exercises explain why writers of fiction have reputations for blank expressions and absent-mindedness. This train of thought was occupying my imagination when our approaching raft caused the snowy egret to rise out of a clump of tamarisk and seep willows on a sandbar just ahead of our raft. He flew slowly, no more than six feet above the water, a graceful shape gleaming white against the dark, shadowed cliffs ahead. And then he disappeared around a river bend. I remembered the petroglyph egret. A thousand years ago, I think, the Anasazi artist saw an identical bird and was impressed enough to preserve him in stone.

Since childhood I have been impressed by birds—an idle, amateur student of crow migrations, of how mocking birds tease cats, of the kaleidoscope patterns that snow geese use to form their first dawn flights from water, of the concentrated patience of the heron waiting for the minnow to move nearer. Here was just one egret, no mate, no companions. Are snowy egrets, I wondered, like swans and wolves, among those species that mate only once, and for life? What holds this great bird in such a lonely, empty place?

By the time we were rolling out our sleeping bags and building our evening fire, things were coming clear about my book. The egret would have his place in it somehow, and the thoughts of his solitary presence seemed to be turning the tale of action I had intended into a novel of character. I found myself trying to attach the same perpetual monogamy I had imagined for the egret to one of the characters. I tried it first on the victim. (By now she had become Dr. Eleanor Friedman-Bernal to me, with the hyphenated Bernal to drop as soon as her divorce became final.) It didn't work. She was the wrong type. I turned from that to collecting the sort of impressions she would collect as she arrived at this place. She would make the trip secretively and at night, since her dig would be illegal. She would have the sort of nervousness that law-abiding people feel when they are knowingly breaking the law. Still, she would be stirred by this evening as I was. Violet-green swallows and "nighthawks" are out, patrolling the twilight for insects. A beaver, looking old and tired, swims slowly up the river keeping out the current and paying no attention to me. I hear the song of frogs and, as the rising moon lights the tops of the cliffs, a coyote and his partner begin exchanging coyote talk high above us on Nokaito Bench. Battalions of bats flash through the firelight making their high-pitched little calls. I make notes of all of this, using reality to spare my imagination. I still had a lot of work to do on this plot.

While not a drop of rain had fallen here, a substantial flash flood had roared down the wash. The bottom is muddy and the potholes still hold water. In these the eggs of Leopard Frogs had hatched, and the new generation (about thumbnail size) was everywhere ahop. Such frogs are exactly the sort of specific details I look for, hoping they will make fictional landscapes seem real. I would remember these frogs.

For a collector of such odds and ends as Leopard Frogs, Dan Murphy is a perfect guide. He had come to show me a specific cliff dwelling. But en route he showed me the trap door lid under which a wolf spider was lurking, a Navajo pictograph in which a man on foot is shooting an arrow at a big-hatted horseman who is shooting a pistol at him; "Baseball Man," an unusual Anasazi pictograph that depicts—larger than life—a figure that seems to be holding a big reddish chest protector, like a home plate umpire. But the cliff dwelling at the end of this long walk was the prize.

Reaching it involved climbing out of the wash bottom onto a broad stone shelf, which led to a second level of cliffs and past another of those petroglyph murals, decorated with beautifully preserved depictions of the little humpbacked flute player anthropologists call Kokopela.

Anthropologists believe Kokopela was the Anasazi fertility figure, and he may be seen carved into cliffs and painted on lava rocks throughout Anasazi country. At the moment I was thinking of his flute. Specifically I was considering how eerie it would seem if my fore-doomed anthropologist, aware of the presence of these figures, hears the piping of his music in the canyon darkness. But how? Can I make my neurotic Navajo a musician? That seems strained. I dismissed the idea. It refused to go away.

The flute player notion was still with me when we reached the ruins Murphy had thought would be exactly right for my purposes. They were far better than anything I could have imagined. Behind a curve in the towering sandstone wall of the mesa, nature had formed a cavernous amphitheater some fifty feet deep, sixty feet wide, and perhaps seventy feet from floor to ceiling. A seep high up the face of the cliff produced enough water to cause a green curtain of moss and ivy to thrive beneath it and to feed a shallow basin perhaps ten or twelve feet across on the stone floor of the alcove. Behind this pool on a ledge some twelve feet above the alcove floor an Anasazi family had built its stone home. The centuries had done their damage, but the walls of the small structure were mostly intact. Up the cliff at the edge of the alcove a ladder of footholds had been cut into the stone. They lead to a shelf high above. There another stone structure still stands, probably built as the family's desperate last defense if danger came and trapped them.

The pool had produced its own swarm of the inevitable Leopard Frogs. Watching them raised many questions in my mind: Were those drought-resistant frogs here when the Anasazi family occupied the house behind me? How would it have felt to have lived in this lonely place as the tag end of a dying culture? What was this danger so fierce that it caused these people to build their tiny little fort?

I imagine the family huddled behind the walls above. I make it night. A dark night. Something has frightened them into scurrying up the footholds, listening. Hearing what? The Anasazis become Eleanor Friedman-Bernal, already uneasy by the illegality of her dig here, and now hiding, terrified. What does she hear? I think of Kokopela's flute—music from a spirit vanished a thousand years. Crazy, I think. And while I am into the craziness, I try again to do something with the neurotic

Navajo. I change him to a neurotic local Mormon boy whose only relief from some mental illness is music. But what is he doing here? Hiding out after committing some crime I will dream up later. What else would Eleanor hear? The frogs, perhaps, hopping about on the fringes of the pool. I try to look at the frogs through the eyes of a mentally ill boy hiding here. The majestic snowy egret reinserts itself into this daydreaming, and with it, my speculation about its loneliness and its faithfulness. An idea comes, and another.

Gradually, my Navajo Tribal Policeman became a widower, and the framework for my tale became the makings of a novel.

It took another trip down the San Juan Canyon, and up Chinle Wash, before I could complete it all. This time I went during what the Navajos called "the Season when the Thunder Sleeps." In this rainless time, the potholes in the wash were dry, and so was the pool under the ruins. The frogs had vanished; the snowy egret had vanished, too. But the ruins of the trading post on the shelf above the river were there and I visited them again because now they were firmly planted in my mind. How could a crime that had destroyed a family leave a memory that would destroy a man today? I began to see how it could happen.

And thus the San Juan Canyon generated another story.

20

"Where Do You Get Your Ideas?"

By Elizabeth Peters

ONE OF THE QUESTIONS most often asked of writers by readers and interviewers is, "Where do you get your ideas?" I used to sputter and roll my eyes when this query was put to me; there was in it the implication that ideas were physical objects, like avocados, and all one had to do was go to the proper store in order to pick up a supply.

However, my prejudice began to diminish when I started thinking seriously about the question. It is not a silly question. I thought it was silly only because I didn't know the answer. I still don't know the answer, but I have arrived at some answers—the sources from which I derive many of my ideas. I can't answer for other writers, but perhaps some of these will work for you.

First, let's define the term: An idea is not a plot. This distinction may seem so obvious that it isn't worth mentioning, but many of the earnest souls who offer me "plots" or "ideas" ("You write the book, and we'll split the royalties") don't know the difference. What I call an idea is not a plot. An idea is the germ from which a plot may one day develop if it is properly nurtured and tended. For me, the "idea" has two distinct stages.

It begins with a "one-liner"—a single sentence or a visual image, characterized by brevity and vividness. Since an idea is not an avocado, you can't simply go out and get one. In fact, the technique of finding a usable idea is more akin to birdwatching than to chasing butterflies: There are ideas all over the place, the trick is to recognize one of the elusive creatures when it flits past. I'm not being whimsical. It is certainly possible to search actively for an idea, but unless you know one when you see one, there is no point in looking.

The most obvious source of inspiration is your own hobby or profession or job specialty. My training is in archaeology and history, so I derive a good many plot ideas from those fields. The archaeology themes have been particularly prominent in my Elizabeth Peabody novels.

My hobbies—cats, needlework and gardening—have also provided me with ideas. Once when I was absorbed with collecting and embroidering samplers, I thought vaguely, "I wonder if I could use a sampler as a clue in a book?" This idea ended up as *House of Many Shadows*. I usually have an animal, or three or four, in my books, but cats have played seminal roles in the inspiration of ideas. "How about a ghost cat, who shows up in the nick of time to save the heroine?" That one turned out to be *Witch*.

Ideas don't always come from nonfiction reading. Sometimes irritation spawns a plot idea—when I read a book with a smashing twist that doesn't quite come off, prompting me to mutter, "I would have done that differently. . . ." And I do. Sometimes admiration of a particular book prompts not imitation so much as emulation. *Sons of the Wolf,* one of my early Gothics, was inspired by Wilkie Collins's *The Woman in White*. I took his two heroines, one dark and homely and competent, the other beautiful and blond and fragile. . . . Or so she seemed. It surprised me as much as it did some of my readers when the fragile blond came to the rescue in a moment of crisis, but her development was probably the result of my unconscious resentment of Victorian assumptions about women, which affected even so sensitive and gifted a writer as Collins. I turned his stereotype around to produce different characters and a different plot.

When you are looking for a plot idea, it is helpful, therefore, to read as widely as possible. I got one idea from the *Smithsonian Magazine,* not from an article but from a reader's letter that described a black rainbow. I had never heard of such a thing, but the image was so evocative I knew I had to use it.

Since I am by nature and by training a reader, I derive most of my ideas from books. However, visual images can also be useful. The most obvious visual image is physical—a handsome old house, a quaint village, a medieval town. The dark closes of old Edinburgh, the triple-layered church of San Clemente in Rome, a country inn in Western Maryland—these and other locations have inspired books of mine.

Other images from which I have derived ideas are also physical, but they are one step removed from reality. They are, in fact, misinterpretations of what I actually see. (Being absent-minded and/or nearsighted helps here.) The commonest misinterpretation, with which most of us are familiar, occurs when we wake in the night and see some familiar object in the room transformed by shadows and moonlight. A robe hanging on the bedpost becomes a dangling body or a looming spectre. A rocking chair appears to have an occupant, misshapen and frightening. My most recent stimulus of this nature came when I was driving alone a narrow country road and saw a bundle of trash lying in a ditch. (At least I hope it was a bundle of trash.) The shape suggested a human body, and all at once I had a mental image of a skeleton, dressed in a pair of overalls, sprawled by the road. The exigencies of the plot that I developed from this image demanded a female rather than a male skeleton, and the overalls turned into a calico dress.

Once you learn to spot ideas, you see them all over the place— remarks overheard on planes or buses, unusual signs in shop windows, street names, those one- or two-line fillers newspapers sometimes insert to fill out a column. Then there are satires and take-offs. Hundreds of ideas there! Having once attended a Romance Writers Convention, I knew I had to do a book about such a group. Nothing personal—I plan eventually to satirize cat shows, sci-fi conventions, and my own professional society meetings.

One purely mechanical technique you may want to develop is to write down or clip anything that seems to have potential, and file it away. I have a file bulging with cryptic notes. A few examples: a scribbled description of a mourning gown once worn by the Empress of Austria. It is a fantastic outfit, all black without a speck of color, featuring a face mask of black lace. What am I going to do with this? I don't know yet. But I have a hunch that one day a lady dressed in this fashion will make a marvelous ghost. In my file, there is also an eerie story told me by a local antique dealer about one of her customers; a notation on nuncupative wills; notes on an article on early American gravestones; and a list of terms for groups of animals (a kindle of kittens, a shrewdness of apes) from a book published in 1614. (Goodness, what a mess; I must clean this file out!)

Another file, labeled "miscellaneous," contains newspaper clippings. I keep separate files for clippings on archaeology, the supernatural, and crime. In the miscellaneous file I find, among many others, articles with the following headlines: "Twins May Have One Mind in Two Bodies"; "Switzerland's Dying Language (Romansh)"; and my personal favorite, "The Tree That Ate Roger Williams." Sooner or later I'll get a book out of one of these—maybe all of them.

But—I hear you, the reader, complain—it's a long way from your one-liner to a finished book. True, I told you that in the beginning, remember? An idea is not a plot. A "one-liner" may not even turn out to be an idea! For me, the second stage of the process loosely termed "getting an idea" is to encourage the initial image or brief sentence to develop into something a little more substantial. It's a difficult process to describe or define; perhaps an example will demonstrate what I mean.

Legend in Green Velvet started with a visual image—a view of a steep winding street in the Old Town of Edinburgh. The "idea" that popped into my mind was a single sentence: "What a super setting for a heroine to be chased in." (Grammar never concerns me at such moments.) But I was getting tired of reading and writing books about pursued heroines. Mulling this over, I thought, "How about having the heroine do the chasing for a change?"

Then I turned to my most useful source—books. I started reading about Edinburgh and its history. Before long I came across the old story of Mary, Queen of Scots' illegitimate baby, who was carried off and adopted by one of her ladies-in-waiting. If the story were true (I doubted it, but that wasn't important), Mary was not only an ancestress of the present British royal house, she was also an ancestress of a Scottish noble family. How about one of those close physical resemblances, between a young man (hero or villain, I hadn't decided which) and a Prominent Royal Personage?

I needed more. For one thing, if I decided to make my young man the hero, I needed villains. My reading turned up another intriguing story—that of the Scottish students who swiped the Stone of Scone from Westminster Abbey. The memory of a delightful conversation with an Edinburgh taxi driver who treated me to a fiery lecture on Scottish rights reinforced the idea of using a Scottish Nationalist group in my book. But I couldn't bring myself to make the Nationalists real villains. From what I knew of them, they were an amiable lot. They would, however, provide a useful red herring, and my heroine could safely pursue one of them, since he would not be inclined to harm her.

I still needed villians—genuine, wicked, evil villains. Back to the history books and eventually another piece of the plot. The ancient regalia of Scotland—vanished, during one of the periods of warfare.

By this time my original one-line idea of a heroine chasing a villain through the streets of Edinburgh had developed, not into a plot as yet, but into the skeleton of a plot. I had a heroine, a hero who bore an uncanny resemblance to a Royal Personage, and two sets of villains who were interested in the same treasure for different reasons. The Nationalists wanted the lost royal regalia for its symbolic importance; the genuine villains planned to steal it and sell it. I had strengthened and encouraged my original idea to a point where, or from which, it could be developed into a genuine plot.

There is another technique I often employ when engaged in this second stage of idea development. It is almost the exact antithesis of the active, reading-research method; one might call it a variety of free association. First, it is necessary to find an ambiance in which your mind is free to wander as it will. For me, the ideal situation is a form of mild physical activity (I never engage in strenuous physical activity) that requires minimal mental effort. Walking is ideal. Some types of housework, such as ironing, necessitate a blank mind. (If I thought about what I was doing, I wouldn't do it.) Total relaxation, flat on my back, doesn't work, because when I am relaxed I promptly go to sleep. But as I walk or push the iron across the fabric, a goodly portion of my mind takes off on a tack of its own. With a little encouragement I can turn that detached section down the track I want it to follow. "What about that girl chasing a man up a flight of stairs in Edinburgh? Why the dickens would she do that? Why do people chase people? Did she think he was someone she knew? Did she see him drop his wallet or his handkerchief?"

These methods work for me. They may not work for you, but something else will, if you experiment. And the most encouraging thing about writing is that, as with any other talent, your skill will improve with practice.

21

Novel Ideas

By Barbara Taylor Bradford
An Interview by Billie Figg

Timing

A finger on the public pulse is vital. When I wrote *A Woman of Substance* twelve years ago, I was obsessed by an urge to write about strong women. It was what felt important then and the character Emma Harte was the right woman at the right time.

Since then many surrogate Emmas have been created, not just by me, but by other authors, too. I had kicked off the decade of the "matriarchal dynastic saga."

In 1988 I was about to embark on a novel about a woman who creates a great shipping empire when a new book landed on my desk for comment.

To my dismay I saw it was yet another "woman of substance" story. Everyone was writing about women heading great businesses. It simply wasn't new any more.

That's when I decided that strong women books were over and it was time to write about a man.

The fact that *The Women in His Life* was number one on the bestseller lists for five weeks shows that readers feel as I do. A good hero is *in*.

And it demonstrates that if you are going to produce bestsellers on a regular basis, you've got to feel along with the public. Call it a sixth sense, if you like. The point is: Have *you* got it?

Motivation

A burning desire to write novels must be paramount. If you don't feel driven, I would say forget it. I was writing stories in childhood, usually about an imaginary friend named Sally who shared my games and tea-parties because I was an only child.

By the time I was sixteen I knew I wanted to be a novelist, but realized I wasn't ready. It was thirty years before I was!

Creating characters

Creating believable characters is the hardest part. That was what I had to get to grips with and, if you're serious about novel writing, so will you. You will be a close people watcher, observant of mannerisms, susceptible to inner reactions, a bit of a psychologist and emotionally able to get under their skin.

I always start my novels with the character. For instance, faced with the switch from dominant heroine to powerful hero, the crucial question was: What kind of man should he be?

I thought hard about it. Then one day as I was passing my favorite house set on a corner in London's Mayfair, it suddenly struck me—he's a tycoon and that's where he lives. As I walked on, it came in a rush. He has to be top of the pile, successful on a Gargantuan scale, because he must be larger than life to live on paper.

He has to be special, too. I couldn't write about a struggle to succeed, as that's not interesting enough now. He has to have a conflict within himself.

Imagination

You have to indulge a lively imagination. For instance, when my husband Bob and I were in Berlin a few years ago, we were walking down the Unter den Linden looking at the Brandenburg Gate when I suddenly had a sense of déjà vu. I felt I had stood at the same place—before—during the war.

I really did hear the metallic click of jackboots, the voice of Hitler screaming and crowds applauding. It was like a bit of film unrolled in my head with the sound-track running.

And I saw a woman's face. She had big, luminous eyes, pale, blonde hair and was standing in a reception room under chandeliers, wearing a white, satin gown with diamond necklace and earrings.

Her image stayed in my mind's eye when I got home to New York, but it wasn't until two years later when I was determinedly discarding matriarchal dynastic sagas that this image came back very strongly.

By this time, I had built up the personality of my tycoon, Maximilian West. So it was easy to work out his childhood trauma.

94

I thought: He's a German Jew who escaped, but was wrenched from his mother and never saw her again. And that's who that woman is, his mother.

Suddenly the character sprang to life and from him the plot. The conflict arose from the fact that he always goes after women who remind him of his mother. He's the little boy lost.

How did he become a tycoon? It occurred to me that as a child growing up in England, he determines he is not going to be a victim ever again, but a victor trampling over the graves of those who persecuted him and his family. So he builds a citadel of power and wealth.

That's how my stories shape up. Character first, then plot, welded together by a healthy dose of imagination.

Research

Sound research gives a novel reality. A lot of people can string words together, but you are not a novelist unless you are able to tell monumental lies around invented people and make them seem believable.

That's what I failed to do in my earliest attempts in the Sixties. I set tales in exotic places I hardly knew—and my fibs failed to convince even me. Result: I scrapped them.

It wasn't until I wrote about Yorkshire, where I was born and bred, that my fairy tales rang true and *A Woman of Substance* was born. The strength of *The Women in His Life* is that I have related personal lives to political reality and researched it carefully.

Curiosity

Getting the atmosphere accurate takes a strong streak of curiosity. I had always been fascinated by Nazi Germany, so it was a coincidence that twenty-eight years ago I married a man who escaped as a child from East Berlin to France, never to see his family again.

Not that this book is my husband's story. But, of course, his background enhanced my interest in how Hitler's evil regime held power.

Now I had to understand the climate of those times. I read about thirty books including diaries of the era and looked at pictures showing the chilling theatrical effects the Nazis created with giant columns topped by floodlit eagles down the Unter den Linden boulevard. I got hold of prewar maps and walked the rebuilt streets, trying to sense the daily life in Berlin in those days.

That's how deeply you have to immerse yourself in your subject.

95

A sense of drama

Character, plot, and research work only with a sense of drama. Mine was sharpened as a cub reporter on the *Yorkshire Evening Post*. The police beat and the coroners' courts showed me plenty of drama in everyday situations.

You've only to read the papers to pick up ideas. Nothing is more dramatic than real life. And watching television, going to the cinema or reading books and plays shows you how to present a story and what makes it click.

Organization and a quick eye

You need to be organized with memories and papers. I've trained myself so that I can tell you what's in a room in the flash of an eye—and then keep a mental note of it to put in my computer.

As for research, three quarters has to be thrown away and the vital information filed. My desk has just a typewriter, telephone, pens, photo of Bob, yellow notepad and immediate research. I can't stand stuff around me—mistakes lurk in mess.

Tenacity

So now it's down to tenacity, a must for any novelist. If you can't stick at things, try stories, not books. Sometimes, though, a promise to someone will keep your nose to the grindstone.

That's what finally got me through over six hundred pages and two years' hard slog to the end of *A Woman of Substance*. I had interested an agent and vanity would not let me fail.

Even if you can't get taken on professionally—and remember, I had years of journalistic work to show—it might help if someone you trust declares confidence in your idea. Your pride is then on the line.

Writer's block

Writer's block is no excuse for giving up. I admit that at the start of a book I might not know what I'm going to say. But if the going gets tough, I always put something down—even if it's rubbish!

By the time I have been to a bookstore, done some more research or had a hair-do, I feel refreshed and at least I've something to polish up.

Relationships

Finally, never forget, relationships are what the reader cares about.

To get them on the page in a way that reads true, you have to know and feel what they are made of.

I treasure my friends—most of them date from thirty or more years ago. I see them regularly between novels or when I'm on promotion tours for the books or the television mini-series my husband makes of them.

But you can't be a social butterfly *and* a successful novelist: I have to cut off from people when I'm writing, which can mean months locked in my Manhattan room with just Gemmy, my dog, for company.

But that's what I want to do. In the depressed Thirties, when my father was out of work, my mother went back to nursing to enable me to go to a private school. I still remember what she used to say to me: "Never waste your gifts. Pursue your dreams."

22

BREAKING THE RULES

BY JOHN LUTZ

YOU'VE PROBABLY HEARD OR READ IT: The rule is there are no rules, and that's the only reliable rule for writing good fiction.

However, over the years and from countless creative writing classes, panels, and seminars, there has evolved what is known as the conventional wisdom. Beginning writers pay close attention to the various pearls of advice dropped by those established in the fields of writing or teaching fiction. Many of the pearls are false.

Writing is a uniquely individualistic endeavor, not for the most part mystical, and to a large degree teachable and learnable. But since it is, more than most activities, individual and personal, there are dangers in embracing what seems to be the soundest advice.

When aspiring writers attend seminars or read instructional books or articles, they should select very carefully what methods might work for their particular way of writing, then experiment with them before adopting them. Professional writers understand the difficulties involved in learning to write, and almost all of them are empathetic and really do want to share what they know to help others hone their craft or make that first sale. But advice given with wholehearted sincerity by established pros can sometimes harm more than it helps, in the way of strong medicine wrongly prescribed. I'm not saying it's always, or even usually, wise to reject the conventional wisdom, but I *am* saying you should always question it. Be extremely selective before incorporating it into your personal and distinctive method of writing.

The first piece of advice offered, even crammed down throats, in creative writing classes is to WRITE ABOUT WHAT YOU KNOW.

Wrong. Don't write about things of which you are entirely ignorant, but don't hesitate to build on scant knowledge and explore unknown territory. The fact is that no one "knows" enough about enough subjects to write expertly on the many elements that make up most stories or novels. Probably you'll exhaust your expertise long before you learn how to write effectively. The trick is to learn to research in a way that complements your writing and to select which facts to use to capture the essence of the subject. Not so much the hard facts, but the nuances, the mood and character. In some instances, the reader will sense and share your pleasure of discovery when you've explored and chosen what's useful and representative and incorporated it in your fiction.

It's possible to know *too* much about a subject. For instance, I learned recently that many Revolutionary War battles weren't fought mainly at a distance with muskets and bayonets, but fought at close quarters with knives, hatchets and weapons known as spontoons. A spontoon is a sort of combination spearhead and axe head fitted to a staff about six feet long. Revolutionary War officers carried them rather than firearms because George Washington didn't want his field commanders concentrating on loading the inaccurate and time-consuming powder weapons of the era rather than paying attention to strategy and the ebb and flow of battle. However, the spontoon hardly fits the average reader's concept of Revolutionary War skirmishes, so were I writing fiction set in that period, I'd deliberately leave out that morsel of fact and probably arm my officers with muskets. Let's leave spontoons to the historians.

ALL GOOD FICTION IS ROOTED IN REALITY.

This is true only up to a point. Reader concept of reality is as important as the reality itself. We write fiction, not travelogues or instructional manuals. Your streets are not made to seem real because you've made sure the traffic is flowing in the right direction, or the street signs are spelled correctly, or the addresses match genuine house numbers, etc. Fictional streets are made real when your character bruises a heel stepping on a sharp stone, or stumbles over a raised section of concrete, or is made uncomfortable on sunbaked concrete by heat radiating through thin soles; when on a certain level the reader *feels* what the character feels.

It's a mistake to rely heavily on trying to create plausibility by impressing readers with a deluge of details and facts. You might educate them right out of suspension of disbelief. Of course, essential, widely known facts should be portrayed accurately so a glaring inaccuracy (a mountain in Florida, a subway system in St. Louis) won't puncture the

99

illusion you're trying to create, but they have little do to with the actual creation of the illusion.

Using reality is fine unless carried to the extreme of emphasizing irrelevant or esoteric details rather than writing to engage the reader emotionally. That's what fiction's really about: engaging the reader's emotions. If you do everything else wrong but manage that, you've succeeded. Fiction isn't about facts, and sometimes facts need to be ignored, twisted, or embellished. Like Mark Twain's prematurely reported death, the importance of truth in fiction is greatly exaggerated.

CREATE AN OUTLINE BEFORE YOU BEGIN TO WRITE.

Here's another piece of conventional wisdom that can be a mistake. Most writers need some kind of map to lend their story sure-footedness and direction, but a rigid outline can lead to rigid, mechanical writing. It can be constricting as well as defining. I think it's best to keep the work fluid as long as possible, not close doors in the mind even before you sit down and begin writing. My own method is to work from a loose and free-flowing synopsis that provides general direction but at the same time leaves room for improvisation; maybe a clever new plot twist, expansion of the role of a previously minor character who's evolved surprisingly well, exploration of a subplot that's taken on life and interest, or a romance that's created more heat than anticipated. We cannot, and should not, know *everything* before we write the first word. If nothing else, that would take some of the fun out of writing.

KNOW THE ENDING OF A STORY BEFORE YOU WRITE THE BEGINNING.

Now, while I find this one to be generally true, and certainly true in my case, I know a few writers who begin without the slightest idea of the tail of their tale. Possibly this has to do with the way story concept takes root in their minds. Some writers seem to start with an interesting slant, startling incident or powerful theme, then charge ahead and somehow find not only direction, but a powerful and meaningful ending. Or they begin with some sense of direction, maybe even an outline, but project the ending only in simple or vague terms. That's fine if it works for them.

Each writer possesses a unique creative process, often not thoroughly understood even by the writer.

This rule is definitely one you should experiment with. Begin at least one story without any ideas as to how you'll end it. See what happens, the better to know thyself.

REVISE, REVISE, REVISE.

Again, this is true of me. But I've observed that there are writers who write "long" and writers who write "short" and then add (not pad) as well as cut and tighten. I fall into the "short" category unfortunately, and the more I embellish and revise the better the result. A well-known science fiction writer often told me he didn't revise at all, which I doubted until I went to his home and watched him sit at his typewriter and in a burst of creativity reel out one excellent page after another. Go figure. The point is, had he been following the conventional and usually correct advice to revise his work extensively, he'd probably still be unsold.

BASE YOUR CHARACTERS ON PEOPLE YOU KNOW.

This one can get you into serious trouble. While it will be easier to remember your characters' eye and hair color and little eccentricities, you should also take into account that your fictional characters must fit the requirements of your novel or story.

If you populate your fictional world with non-fiction people, it could cause you problems in character delineation and motivation. Your real Aunt Millie (the one you know so well) might indeed have done something your fictional Aunt Tillie does, though in the case of Aunt Tillie it might be totally out of character in the eyes of your readers, who've never met Millie.

The "real" person might in a number of ways get in the way of his or her fictional counterpart, might even behave in some fashion during the course of your writing that alters your perception of him or her. And the fact that someone does something in real life doesn't mean such behavior has been qualified to occur in fiction. Real people don't always behave logically, but fictional people almost always do. I've heard even professional writers complain, when an editor objected to a character behaving implausibly, that no revision was necessary because the real person on whom the fictional person was modeled actually behaved that way, so it *must* be in character. This often prompts the editor, who has heard this before, to sharpen a blue pencil.

CHOOSE A SUCCESSFUL WRITER WHOSE WORK YOU ENJOY AND ADMIRE, AND COPY HIS OR HER STYLE.

I've heard this dubious piece of advice a lot lately, and I'm sure it works for some. But then some people like eggplant. It seems to me that this game is supposed to be about originality. Publishers won't pay real money for imitation books or stories. Following this advice is rather like a singer or actress building her career on imitating Madonna. Lots of performers can do that, but there's still only one Madonna, and she tends to get the bookings.

Maybe you can imitate someone else's work long enough and exhaustively enough so that somehow your own style finally emerges. On the other hand, maybe your own style will be suppressed.

If I were you, I'd think hard about this one.

STUDY MAGAZINES SO YOU KNOW WHAT KIND OF FICTION THEY PUBLISH.

Well, if you were to read issue after issue of a magazine and then write a story almost exactly like most of the stories that had appeared in it, your story would probably be rejected for not being fresh. No editor wants to buy a story that reads too much like every other story. So much familiarity breeds rejection. Study the magazines again and in each story you'd probably find some unique angle or strength, something arresting, that made it different from all the others. That is why it was published.

A better approach might be to read a magazine to learn what it *doesn't* publish. Try to determine editorial taboos, then avoid them, and write the story *you* want to write. It will automatically fall within the parameters of what the editor's looking for, and at the same time be fresh.

As an example, one of the leading mystery magazines seldom publishes stories that feature diseases, denigration of the old, or subject matter that might even remotely risk legal action. Nor will you find in its pages graphic violence or sex (though a certain measure of subtle eroticism is acceptable), or stories involving spouse murder. These taboos, shaped by taste as well as marketing considerations, are for the most part reasonable and easy enough to avoid, and they leave a wide range of subjects for good fiction.

These are only a few of the maxims launched the beginner's way when he or she seeks advice. Also heard are: "Set aside a certain amount of time each day to write." "Show your work to a friend whose judgment you trust before you submit it for publication." "Read some poorly written but strongly plotted 'formula' fiction so you can clearly see how it's constructed." And so on. There are many such standard pieces of advice floating around writers' conferences and creative writing classes. All of them are wrong at least some of the time.

While writers do have much in common, the odds on finding two who are alike are longer than with snowflakes. There are writers who require silence and writers who work with the radio blaring. Some who demand solitude and some who forge successful careers working in the company and din of a growing family. Some can't work without cigars or cigarettes in their mouths, or cups of coffee at hand, or cats in their laps. Some write in longhand, some type, some use word processors. Probably somewhere there is one who uses mud and a sharp stick.

Despite the established rules of creativity and marketability, writing remains an intensely personal and unique exercise, as mysterious as the labyrinth of the human mind. That might very well be why we write.

Before you wrap yourself too tightly in the security of the rules, ask yourself if a measure of daring might not be more valuable than any of them.

23

Writing the Short Magazine Story

By Marjorie Franco

SHORT STORIES COME IN VARIOUS LENGTHS, but in today's market, many of the major magazines prefer stories of two to three thousand words. Within that limited space, the writer must deal with the usual requirements of character, setting, plot and theme, or a point to be made, but with a sense of economy that rules out unnecessary words and at the same time conveys more than can be said in words.

When I get an idea for a story I let it stay in my head for a while. If it is fleeting, if it fails to grow and eventually demand my attention enough so that I begin to take notes, I forget it and go on to something else. But if it remains there and persistently accrues details pertaining to character and dialogue, I finally sit down and write. Just getting that first paragraph, even that first sentence, on paper, is a relief, for it is making concrete what had heretofore been a jumble of sometimes imprecise thoughts.

My idea for "The Best of Friends" (*Good Housekeeping*, May 1991) came from a real-life situation. A young woman agrees to share an apartment with a young man she has just met. He needs someone to pay half the rent; she needs a place to stay. To give them a mutual interest, I put a rented piano in the apartment, which they also share with the understanding that each will have allotted practice time.

Many of us write too long, and we can't count on an editor to show us how to tighten, clarify, and cut. This we must try to do for ourselves, even though deleting a descriptive passage, or, in some cases, an entire scene, can be not only painful but downright depressing. "That's my favorite part, I worked hard on it," our subjective self might protest. "Sorry," our objective self replies, not unkindly, "it has to go."

Beginning writers, as well as those of long experience, need to view their manuscripts with a critical eye before sending them out. In "The Best of Friends," the original opening didn't move quickly enough, and

I had to cut at least half a page to where the real beginning was. Instead of explaining about my character's former boyfriend (an extra character I didn't need), whom she wasn't sure she wanted to marry, and relating the questions in her mind concerning marriage, I began with this simple statement. "For a change of scene and a new job, Marlena came to Chicago."

What do I know about this character, and how do I present her in a situation that will interest the reader? Since long descriptions and rambling dialogue are out of the question, characters are revealed through details, or else they reveal themselves through dialogue. In the second paragraph, Marlena asks her friend, Lisa, who is soon to be married, "What's it like, falling in love?" Lisa explains that she didn't actually fall in love, but that love crept up on her until "the time came when I knew this was it." But Marlena doesn't think that is possible, at least not for her.

By the time she meets Roy at a party, the reader already knows that Marlena has given up on marriage because she has never managed to fall in love. The first thing Roy says to her is, "Are you looking for an apartment?" Then, a few lines later, "Look, I have this place, and my roommate, Steve, got married, and well—I need someone to share the rent."

Though it is not uncommon for an unmarried man and woman to live together, the arrangement between Marlena and Roy is, as he puts it, "strictly business—privacy guaranteed."

At this point, about two pages into the story, I have the characters, the setting, and a situation from which the plot will develop.

But what is the problem? A story needs conflict, tension between characters and a resolution unpredictable enough to keep the reader reading. In some stories, the problem, or conflict, is presented in the opening line. In others, the story opens with a minor problem, or situation, from which the real conflict develops. Such is the case with Marlena and her relationship with Roy.

It's not a complicated plot, and shouldn't be for this length. The story takes place over three months, long enough for Marlena and Roy to become friends, to value each other's presence and, most important, to practice their music on the piano. Roy plays Scott Joplin's Ragtime, Marlena plays Mozart.

During this time, Marlena doesn't realize the true nature of her

105

feelings, or that Roy's position in her life is advancing beyond friendship to something more personal—this in spite of the fact that both date other people. Her unrecognized feelings are expressed through her compulsion to learn Roy's music, Ragtime, which she practices in secret, thus creating conflict between her feelings and her predetermined attitude. When Roy says "I'm never getting married," she replies with all sincerity, "Neither am I."

The realization comes after a brief separation and the discovery that each has secretly learned to play the other's kind of music, which becomes a symbol of their falling in love.

It's helpful for beginning writers to know at the outset how long a period of time their stories will cover. By its very nature the short story does not lend itself to long time spans, although such a thing is not unheard of.

I knew when I began writing "The Best of Friends" that a three-month time span would be necessary to allow for the developing relationship. But many stories take place in a much shorter period. In another story of mine, "Path Through the Snow" (St. Anthony Messenger), the time span is less than half an hour, during which (as the editor describes in his notes) "grace comes to a depressed, grieving husband during a bus conversation with an eccentric woman."

As an example of how real life informs our fiction, I first got the idea for this story a long time ago, but had no clear idea of how to write it until a friend, whose wife died suddenly, had to deal with his loss. Although the character of Grady is not based on my friend, I did use a few real-life details which my imagination could not have provided. For example, the way he calls out "Hello!" into the empty house when he comes in after work; and his refusal to let anyone else inside, not even his best friend, for fear of disturbing the perfect order.

In this story the problem is presented in the opening line. "After his wife's death, Grady began taking the bus to work every day." He has a car but he can't bring himself to drive it, "maybe because Amy's last breath had been drawn in a car that was rear-ended at an intersection not three blocks from their house."

On his way home from work, while the bus is stopped at a corner, Grady sees from his window an elderly woman running to catch the bus. She makes it, and sits down next to him. The plot, and the forward

106

movement of the story, involves the progress of the bus on its route toward his stop, and his encounter with this woman who, eccentric though she is, shows real understanding of his plight.

Prior to that meeting he has felt isolated in his situation. In order for the reader to understand, there are several brief flashbacks interspersed in the forward movement, which touch on Grady's relationship with his wife, his friends, and his parents. "His friends had said, 'I know how you're feeling,' but they didn't know, because after saying it, they could go home to their own, uninterrupted lives. How could they really understand what his life had become? No one close to him could, not even his parents. They still had each other."

At first, Grady wants nothing to do with the woman sitting next to him. He is annoyed at her attempts to engage him in conversation. But she persists. The dialogue is essential in developing the plot and, therefore, the story, and his view of her changes progressively.

"Foolish old woman," he thinks, when she makes a fuss over her absurd hat. Then he feels alarm when he learns that she has just gone to the funeral of a woman she'd never met. He considers getting off the bus, which is impractical, then hopes she won't speak again. But, of course, she does. She talks about her son, and in so doing, seems unaware of his neglect of her, which is obvious to Grady, making him hostile toward the son, sympathetic toward her.

In this mood, he asks, "How often do you do that—go to funerals?"

"Oh, two or three times a week. I meet a lot of nice people that way." She laughed. "I've always been the sociable type."

When the conversation turns to her husband, who has recently died, and to whom she was married for forty-nine years, Grady is struck by the emotional connection between them. What happens next might be described in psychological terms as reality orientation. I describe it thus:

" 'Forty-nine years,' he repeated with awe, trying to imagine the scope of her memories." He tells her that he and his wife had been married for only ten years. And then "she looked at him directly, openly, as if she knew exactly what he was talking about—everything, and in detail." At first sorry, he is then glad he has spoken, "for he knew she understood what his friends did not."

Before she gets off the bus, Grady tells her how alone he is. " 'You're young,' she said, 'It won't always be so.' 'Perhaps,' he said, unconvinced. But he felt a trickle of warmth, and it began to soothe him. 'Perhaps,' he repeated, softly, hoping to sustain the feeling."

At length, when Grady gets off the bus at his stop and walks through the fresh snow, there is indication that he is ready to make the first step in getting on with his life.

Although these two stories are quite different in mood and subject matter, they are similar in several ways. Both are of the same length—two to three thousand words. Both have a simple plot and a resolution that effects an important change in the character. And in both I have tried to make the characters likable, but certainly not perfect, in the hope that readers will relate to them.

Who are these readers, and how do we get in touch with them? It's a good idea to study the magazines that use fiction of this length and try to determine if your story is suitable, or if it can be made to be suitable. I had a market in mind for the first story I've discussed here, but not for the second. I wrote that second story anyway.

If an idea for a story becomes persistent, I sit down and write, whether or not I have a particular market in mind. I can worry about that later. At the moment the story is demanding to be told, I believe it is worthwhile for me to respond to that creative urge, for it can lead to unforeseen pleasure, including the bringing to life of something totally new and completely my own.

24

What You Need to Know About Fiction Writing: Questions and Answers

By Sidney Sheldon

Q. *Could you suggest any test that new writers might use to tell if a plot idea is substantial enough for a novel? Have you ever discarded a plot, and if so why? Could you describe it?*

A. I think the only test of whether an idea is substantial enough for a novel is how much of it excites the writer, and how strong one's imagination is. Using this criteria, one can write a novel about almost anything.

Q. *Do you have favorite themes or types of characters to write about, and why?*

A. I like to write about themes that are larger than life—people in desperate trouble, headline events that take place around the world. It's fun for me, and I think it's fun for my readers.

Q. *Writers often get so involved with their research for a novel, they keep putting off the actual writing. How do you know when it's time to stop researching and begin the novel? Also, how much of your book is planned before you begin the research?*

A. When I write a novel, I begin with a character and no plot. For example: I will decide to write about a criminal attorney, or an ambassador, or a psychiatrist. That is really all I start with. The plot unfolds as I dictate the first draft to a secretary. Incidentally, this is not a practice I recommend to a beginning writer because it can lead to a lot of blind alleys. I would suggest that you plot out your book before you begin to write.

I do extensive research for my novels, and when I have all the answers I need, I incorporate the research into the book.

Q. *What is the role of minor characters in your writing?*

A. There should be no minor characters in a novel. Every character should be interesting, exciting, and colorful.

Q. *Describe the sorts of changes that you make in a novel from draft to draft.*

A. I spend from a year to a year and a half writing my novels. When the first draft is typed, I go to page one and do a complete rewrite, throwing out 100 to 200 pages at a time, eliminating characters, creating new characters, etc. When that version has been typed, I go to page one and start all over again. I will do up to a dozen complete rewrites until the book is as good as I know how to make it. At that point, I send it in to my publisher.

Q. *In your opinion, what makes a good book editor?*

A. I think a good book editor should be completely in tune with his material. For example, a poetry editor should not work on an Elmore Leonard book.

Q. *How do you feel about the need for isolation in the life of a writer? How does it affect personal relationships? Professional activities other than writing?*

A. Some writers can work in the middle of a New Year's Eve celebration. Others have to be alone to write. It depends on the individual. Personally, I lock myself up in an office. Since my office is at home, I'm available to my family during the day.

Q. *Do you ever become emotionally involved with your characters? Does it adversely affect or help you in creating true-to-life fictional characters?*

A. If there is any one reason for the success of my books, I think it is because my characters are very real to me and, therefore, very real to my readers. As I write, I feel every emotion the characters are experi-

110

encing. If I am writing a scene where someone is angry, I feel anger; if they are in pain, I feel pain. In *Rage of Angels,* I let a little boy die, and I got a blitz of letters from my readers. One woman wrote to me and gave me her telephone number. "Call me," she wrote. "I can't sleep, knowing that you let John die." It got so bad that when I produced the miniseries, I let him live.

Q. *Do you have any unique characteristics or flaws as a writer?*

A. I consider myself a storyteller. I am sure I have a lot of flaws. One of them is that I am less good at description than I am at keeping the action moving.

Q. *How do you feel about beginning writers showing their works-in-progress to friends or family?*

A. I think it's fine for beginning writers to show their works-in-progress to friends or family if these people are sympathetic. If they are negative, I would find some new friends.

Q. *Do you consider writing a need? a compulsion? a job? a joy?*

A. I consider writing the most exciting thing in my life. Most of my writer friends hate writing; they love "having written." I love the actual act of creating.

Q. *What early reading did you do that has stayed with you and influenced your writing throughout your life?*

A. I read a great deal when I was young. Some of the authors, I'm afraid, no longer are with us, but among the ones I recall very fondly: Booth Tarkington, Somerset Maugham, Robert Benchley, Thomas Wolfe, George Bernard Shaw, Daphne du Maurier.

Q. *When did you realize that writing was going to be your profession? Was there a definitive moment?*

A. I am fortunate in that I knew I wanted to be a writer when I was ten years old. At ten, I sold my first poem to a children's magazine, and I kept writing from then on.

25

WHY I WRITE NOVELS

BY T. ALAN BROUGHTON

ONE OF THE REASONS I KEEP WRITING NOVELS is to try to find out why I do it. The vexations are so daunting: all those years of struggling through versions that may go dead at any moment, a concentration so absorbing that family and friends become less real than imagined characters and their plights, a world of publishing that remainders one's efforts in such a short time that each new novel is a "first" novel. What kind of fool would accept a job with such a description?

One answer is in the process itself. Writing can be a journey of discovery to learn whether the right words will be found to reveal what I did not know I knew. This involves a tension between the knowledge I want to hold on to and a new understanding the work will reveal to me. If I am to defeat my own ignorance, I must be as open to the work as I am to my own raw experience.

Reader and writer meet, if all goes well. The writer hopes the reader will be unaware of all the discarded novels one book represents, but certainly a reader aware of craft and technique stands very close to the writer. Much of writing is in revision, a process in which I am struggling to see the work for itself, and when all the things I have learned are helpful. But even though I need to know how to construct the illusions that dramatize character, or how to manipulate point of view, I am also trying to reach that confusing, chaotic part of the mind that is in all of us, but which I want to hear because it can speak with the wider voice of the species.

That area is not limited to the more narrow, daily self, and fortunately it remains largely untutored. Because of this, it can offer us new and unbiased approaches. We all have that area of the mind and must deal with it. But an artist seems driven by talent and obsessive persistence to make things with its help, hoping to share them with others.

If I take my third novel, *The Horsemaster,* and try to recall how it happened, I can tell you about incidents that helped to start it and about some landscapes that I felt needed a story, but why I should want to write about horses and abandoned daughters and familial relationships, I know only vaguely. I think most stories or novels originate in something so deeply personal that the writer can never fully know why that image or incident insists on words. But if that connection has been effectively explored, the image or symbol is the private doorway of re-entry to the magic garden of the species.

When I was a child visiting a farm belonging to relatives in Canada, horses always fascinated me. But once I saw how dangerous they could be when I watched my father being dragged by a runaway team, the reins tangling his arms, the disk harrow nearly running over him as he struggled for control. Much later, the occurrence that started my novel was narrated to me in a letter from my father. Both of these incidents were violent, and I know that writing stories has often been a way for me to circumscribe violence I find hard to understand or accept.

In a first draft, I have only an inkling. I make some notes. Perhaps a character, a name. I pause, take a deep breath. Look again. I cannot make a clear diagram or outline. All is dim. If I could make that outline, I probably would not proceed. Without the excitement of discovery, why bother? Am I saying I really don't know what the book will be, or am I saying I prevent myself from knowing so that I can keep working every day for the year or so that the first draft will take me? What I do know is that I have a faith in the mind's form—maybe a sense that the book is all there in the mind, but it will be paid out to me only from slowly unraveling, tangled skeins. And part of the problem is that sometimes what I am being given is false matter, a test by that surly gnome far below to see how determined I am to find the secrets out. The only way to find the form that is embedded in the material is to let it grow, then look—pruning, redirecting, finding out what really made it grow.

There is a farm at the bottom of the hill near our summer place in the Adirondack Mountains of New York State. It was owned for a while by wealthy visitors who bought some Percheron horses. All this was a hobby for them, but for their hired hand it was a return to the best times of his youth—a time when he and his father had worked with draft horses.

When the summer people divorced each other and then their farm,

113

the caretaker bought the horses and rented one of the fields. One night after a party on a nearby estate, some rowdies decided it would be fun to ride the horses. The horses were not happy; they had never been subjected to the indignity of carrying men on their backs. They panicked and broke out into the highway where they were hit by a passing truck. The handyman had to shoot them. That is the incident my father described to me and it appears in the middle of *The Horsemaster,* although it is transformed by the necessities of imagined characters, plot, and altered landscape.

After I heard about the incident, I could not stop thinking of the horses and a man who cared for horses as much as he cared for anything. I found a name for the horseman—Lewis Beede. I gave him a cabin. I found him a job caring for someone else's horses. I decided that he was single but not unattached, that he was middle-aged and about to learn what that entailed. I made him forty-five because I was forty-three and figured I'd finish the novel when I was forty-five. Lewis and I could arrive together.

I thought I was ready to start. But for the first time in anything I'd written, I knew I had to know something else.

Facts. I could describe horses, but how could I pretend to know them? Research, or the gathering of facts for a specific piece of writing, can be dangerous for a writer. After all, the book was not about horses, but living in a world in which horses also lived—the difference between facts as knowledge and facts as experience. But what a writer must know is the vocabulary. I had better be able to pretend to be as knowledgeable as Lewis.

I read veterinary texts. I read books on raising and breeding draft horses. I read texts on farm machinery, a book on the language of horses, and even one on the magic and folklore of horses. Whenever I saw horses, I would stop the car and watch them, or I trudged to the fence and tried to talk to them. I promised myself a trip north where friends were raising horses, but I never made it. I began writing instead. I was losing Lewis in all that information. I decided that I would send portions of the book to horse people when I finished it. I did, and I passed inspection, even in the descriptions of a birth and copulation, neither of which I had observed.

It pleased me after the book came out that my uncle in Canada who had spent much of his life farming and on whose farm I had met some horses in my childhood, said, "I couldn't but wonder how you learned so much about horses and their care, things like the pitman shaft of mowing machines." Or that a reviewer in *The Evener,* a draft horse journal, said, "There is a detailed description of breeding a Percheron stud to a mare that might be as useful as any found in a veterinary guide."

Now, after the book is done and my obsession with that world is over, I dread a conversation with my uncle in which he will be puzzled to discover I no longer know any of that. It's gone, learned and held onto for as long as I needed it, knowledge as illusory as the world it was used for. I want these worlds to seem real and possible, but I don't raise and breed horses, only characters. Fiction depends on our willingness to listen to illusions in order to hear truths, and art is a world of permissible lies. But a good liar gets his facts straight.

I began writing the novel in September, 1979. I write every day when working on a first draft and am very nervous or unhappy to miss a day. The people, places, events gradually become as real as, if not more real than the lives around me. I dream about them. I have to run home halfway through jogging to get a snippet of conversation down or note the direction the next scene must go. But I am hardly ever more than a day or so ahead in my mind. I like to stop when I can vaguely hear the next words coming. I finished the first draft five months later, a very short time for me.

What followed were four complete revisions, innumerable revisions of certain passages here and there that remained stubborn to the end. There were alterations when my editor read and commented. At no point in all of this was there—or is there now—a sense of completion. Maybe more certainty—that is, I became more and more sure what the characters could do, what the world would do to them—but there is no end to what I could tell you about them, have them do or reveal. I left them finally with mingled regret and weariness. I'd never see them again or enter their lives with such intimacy, and that was a kind of death, but I had tired of them.

The hardest part for me is that perilous strait between the wish and the reality. I am often too soft-hearted, and in the end of the first version of the book I gave Lewis back his woman Annie, his daughter Miriam, a new horse farm, and just about everything he might have wanted, even if not in quite the way he would have liked to obtain it.

In a letter of complaint to my editor, I wrote:

I have been working hard every day. I am only just beginning to separate myself from the characters sufficiently to see them. In my daily life, I am always struggling to control angers or frustrations, to treat the people around me with the kindness and understanding they deserve. Even in my writing I want to give my characters harmonious lives. I want them to find blessings, and bless each other.

But what I want in my life has little to do with what must happen in a book. A good novel shows that rub between what we want and what we are—what we are going to get whether we want it or not. If the book is to suggest the wholeness of this man's specific life, the final destination cannot be what I desire for Lewis any more than what he desires for himself.

Working through this book again in the last weeks, I have sensed how hard it is both to love a character and be totally objective. Thank God we can't do that in life!

But this isn't the first novel I've blundered through, so I know that a year from this fall I'll look at it (as I have with all the others) and say, "Damn it, what a book this could have been."

The novel was published, but it is not finished and never will be. I wonder if someday I will feel pleasure in picking up that book and reading a paragraph or two rather than merely seeing all the ways it should be revised. At this point *The Horsemaster* seems to have been merely a good way of learning a little more about how to make a novel.

26

BEGINNINGS

BY PHYLLIS A. WHITNEY

BEGINNINGS ARE FUN. BEGINNINGS ARE A HEADACHE.

By the time you sit down to write, you have some notion of where you're going. Your ideas are still fresh and carry a magical glimmer—just out of reach. You can almost taste how wonderful *this* story will be, once you get it down on paper.

You don't want to think about "rules." There are no restrictions, so let the adventure begin! You sit at your keyboard (typewriter to me) and plunge in. Then, suddenly you are writing reams of exposition—because the reader can't possibly understand what you're writing about until you have explained all those details about your characters and the past action that led up to the opening of the story. Before you reach Page Three, you know how boring and confusing all this is going to be. The headaches have started.

A long time ago someone told you that you need to hook your readers in the first paragraph. Or at least on the first page. But you aren't hooking anyone. You are driven to explain, and you put in a lot of narrative material that nobody cares about—but which *is* or will be necessary somewhere along the way. A dilemma.

Perhaps one solution is simply to go ahead and get it all down on paper and out of your system. Once you have all the exposition behind you, you can then go back and pick out what is most interesting and vital. The rest can be worked in gradually as you develop the story. When these matters have been decided, you can write your opening paragraph more effectively and pull your readers in with less confusion.

I'm sure some writers can get into their stories quickly and competently, but I know that my best openings are written after several tries. *The Turquoise Mask* is a novel that readers have written to say they liked. It was also one for which the beginning gave me a great deal of trouble. I never really solved the problem. The first paragraph wasn't so bad:

I had set out my "arguments" carefully on the drawing table. Every item was significant and to be considered soberly if I was to make a right decision. To act meant stepping into something completely unknown and facing what I had been warned against, while not to act meant continued loneliness and the frustration of never knowing the truth.

In the next paragraph, I worked in the necessary background information about the setting, time of year, and where my heroine is going that frightens her. After that, the story bogs down while she examines various objects connected with the past. There is too much thinking and weighing, too much explanation, and a total lack of action. It was really a pretty slow opening.

I believe I did much better in the paragraph for *Feather on the Moon*:

I held the telephone tensely as I listened. The woman from the Center sounded compassionate, kind, considerate—all those good things that I'd needed so desperately in the past. Only now I dreaded the opening of old wounds. Seven years had gone by since Debbie was three, and the chances of finding my lost daughter grew slimmer all the time.

I don't hesitate to claim that this is a good opening. It's not someone sitting around thinking. Something is happening and about to happen, and the main problem of the novel is immediately presented. It took me any number of attempts to produce an opening that seems simple. Unfortunately, not all stories lend themselves to quick, dramatic treatment.

There's one good time-tested "rule" to follow for story openings: *Tell the reader who, what, where, when, and why, and do it as quickly as possible.*

Information that orients readers can be woven into many types of beginnings, and working this out is part of the fun and the challenge of getting a novel started. Another rule is not to start too far back in the story line. Though this isn't always good advice. Under certain circumstances starting close to the climax can defeat you because of the amount of information you may need to present. For the novel I am now writing (still no title) I tried five or six starts before I realized that I was beginning too far along in the story. Too many characters needed to be introduced, and too much exposition was necessary before the reader

118

could understand what was happening. Though the situation should have carried real emotion, no feeling was coming through. Nothing worked until I realized that this novel called for a prologue. Not a flashback, which would still require too much explanation, but the need to go back in time twelve years in order to show *firsthand* what had happened.

Now the characters would play the scene onstage, and the reader could experience what had happened earlier, along with my heroine. When I wrote the first chapter (which was set twelve years later) the scene carried the emotion I wanted because of the reader's knowledge of the past. Characters and incidents that had been confusing were now easily understood. I bridged what might be an interest gap for the reader by leaving the prologue at a point of suspense.

There's no one sure way. In contrast, I did something totally different in *The Winter People*. I began with a tense scene for the *middle* of the book:

I was asleep, and then I was awake, listening.
I could hear the snow hissing at the windows, hear the storm behind it and the rushing sound the wind made through the pine trees. But the sound that wakened me was inside the house. A key had been slipped into a lock . . .

And we're on our way. But we *are* in the middle of the story, and there's no way to make the reader understand what has gone before. So I went into a flashback and told the whole story up to the moment when my heroine hears that key in the lock. The flashback lasted for half the book—and no one even seemed to notice.

It's interesting to break the "rules" when you can manage it successfully. But first it's necessary to understand and respect those rules to be sure you know what you're doing.

Flashbacks can be useful, but they are always tricky. If you have interested your readers in what is happening *now*, they won't thank you for taking them away from an interesting scene and putting them into the past, where they couldn't care less about what's happening. So two devices are necessary. The situation first established must be suspenseful, yet the past scene to which you flash back needs to be equally compelling, so that readers will be beguiled into following it. When you return from the flashback, you must again take your readers from a scene in which they've become interested and return them to the present. This is a little easier because they already know what is happening.

The one absolute must for flashbacks is to make it clear when you are moving into the past, and just as clear when you return to the present. Those past perfect "hads" are useful in going back: "Mary *had* always known that when Dick *had* . . ." etc. But then you should drop "had" and continue as if the action were taking place now.

There are various means of returning to the present. Sometimes an object, a sound—anything at all that was in the present scene—is picked up when you return to remind readers that you are shifting to the present. The threatening sound of a car approaching down the road pulls the reader back into a moment of peril. Of course it doesn't have to be peril—it might be the fragrance of Grandma's apple pie baking in the oven that returns readers to a situation that had held their interest in the first place. Even the simple word "now" can often lead us back to the present. Watch in your reading for how skilled writers handle these matters.

In *The Winter People* I went back many weeks earlier and told the whole story up to the place I've quoted above, where a key turns in a lock. Then I continued with what happened next, as if there'd been no flashback. I don't recommend this type of flashback, and I knew I was taking a chance. The fact that readers never seemed to notice let me know that it worked.

Sometimes the beginning of a story can last for chapters, instead of a few pages. For a while you may lead your readers along with curiosity. There are interesting unanswered questions, bits of tantalizing action. You are still introducing your characters and making the situation clear. There's no set pattern about how long this phase of your novel will last. The beginning is over when your main character decides to *take action* on whatever problem started off the story. Then you move into the middle of the book, and for the sake of reader interest, the sooner the better.

In *Feather on the Moon,* this happens in the first chapter, when my main character decides to go to British Columbia to discover whether the child she's just learned about on the telephone is her lost daughter. And we are into the body of the story in the next chapter with her arrival in Victoria, B.C.

I used a flashback within the first chapter so I could show the scene where the child was taken. In the early draft, I didn't present the flashback scene until well into the chapter. As a result, though the reader knew in general what had happened, the first pages lacked emotion. When I used the kidnap flashback earlier, I was better able to involve my readers in the deep emotion my main character was feeling. Before the flashback, she is looking at a photograph of her three-year-old child while she remembers. When we return from the flashback, she is still looking at the picture, and readers know where they are.

In *Feather on the Moon,* it was easy to have my heroine decide quickly on action she must take, but this isn't always simple to manage. In the novel I'm now working on, this decision to "stand and fight" can't happen until five chapters into the book.

There are, of course, many ways to start a story. If you begin with description—scenery—it should include something to arrest the reader right away. Sometimes focusing on some small object can be effective. Even something as prosaic as a door-knob, lovingly described, can arouse curiosity and capture attention. Almost any object that has significance for the main character can give you an opening that will be interesting to develop.

One of the most difficult things for me as a writer of a particular type of mystery novel is to devise a threat of danger as soon as possible. Sometimes this can be managed by giving the reader straight-out information in the opening paragraph, a method I used in *Vermilion:*

The first step that would take me to Arizona began at the time of Jed Phillips' murder.
Jed was my father, and for most of my life I had loved and resented him . . .

This is intriguing enough to make the reader sit still for some explanation. There is the promise of danger, and of something about to happen—soon.

In *The Stone Bull,* I opened with my heroine in a state of fear, though the scene is a quiet one:

Tonight I am alone for almost the first time since my marriage. I sit here in our bedroom at the Mountain House, with all the lamps burning, and I am afraid.

In a few lines, I skip a space and go into a flashback that begins with a hook: "Am I to blame for my sister's death?" Readers are caught, both by the woman sitting by a window afraid and by the flashback sentence concerning her sister.

Some of these story openings were easily developed, but mostly I've found my way by trial and error. Sometimes I may have whole chapters written before I understand fully what must be done in my opening paragraphs.

Probably the least effective means of opening a story is to start with dialogue. There are always exceptions, but until readers know who is talking, they are hearing strangers, and it's hard to get them involved.

Make an action opening personal as soon as possible. Impersonal action, however busy and possibly violent, doesn't necessarily catch and hold a reader. Even if you open with a car chase, a football game, or an earthquake, you may not hold the reader's attention. You need to have some personal, human connection before the reader will care.

Perhaps the best and safest beginning is for the writer to present immediately *someone interesting doing something interesting*. Usually, this means introducing a viewpoint character whose thoughts and feelings readers can get into right away:

Louise was very careful about where she set each seashell. She knew all too well that one mistake could bring on the very disaster she feared.

I made that up this minute, and *I* am hooked! What on earth is Louise doing with those seashells? This is a good exercise when you are merely stirring ideas around and trying to get started. Make yourself curious, and you'll make your reader curious as well.

When I was teaching writing classes, students would often come to me concerned because they couldn't decide where to start a story. Should it be here, or there, or somewhere else? I would say, "Try all three. How can you know what will work until you try it?" Words for a writer are never carved in marble. They can be thrown away with no cause for alarm, and only by experimenting can you find your way.

Beginnings really are fun, and once you look at the possibilities, the headaches diminish, and the fascinating landscape of your story comes into view. The opening has pulled *you* into it as well as the reader.

27

WRITE THE STORY <u>YOU</u> WANT TO TELL

BY SUSAN ISAACS

SO THERE I WAS, at a "Meet the Author" luncheon in Detroit, my speech about how I became a writer finished, the question-and-answer segment concluded, when this ferociously determined woman with shoulder pads bulldozed a couple of innocent bystanders, came up beside me and announced: "Susan, you give me *such* confidence!" I smiled and began work on a modest thank you, but she cut me off: "If *you* can do it, anybody can."

Condescending? Sure. But also correct. If I could do it, so could she . . . or, if not, her neighbor . . . or you.

Of course, any literate person can write, but writing that *lives* is a gift; the earth is not teeming with billions of potential novelists, waiting only for time and a typewriter. Writing is a talent you're either born with or have acquired by the time you're eight or nine years old. Where does the gift come from? I don't know. How do you know if you have it? Only one way: you write.

This takes enormous courage. We all have successful writer dreams: exchanging bon mots with Johnny Carson, delivering our Nobel address. You will always be great in these dreams, but let me tell you: The reality of actually writing will wake you up. Nothing I've written is as clever, brilliant (or as well received) as my original conception of it. Deep down I think we all sense this disparity, this abyss between our dreams and our talents, so actually sitting down and writing an entire novel takes guts.

I used to think: Who am *I* to be a writer? Writers don't wear makeup. And they're gaunt, haunted-looking, like Virginia Woolf or Joyce Carol Oates or Joan Didion. Or else, writers are incessantly witty, urbane— even glamorous. Well, all that is nonsense, pure stereotype. A writer can look like Christie Brinkley or a troll. As for sophistication, a writer is not necessarily someone who can get a good table at Elaine's. In fact, life in the fast lane probably does more to destroy talent than nurture it; look at F. Scott Fitzgerald, Truman Capote. Further, a writer is not someone who touts his or her genius or vulnerability. Nor is he or she someone who goes from writer's conference to writer's conference, year after year, working over the same fifteen pages of exquisitely refined prose.

A writer can be *anyone*—pretty or not, a sophisticate or a creep. As for writing, like making chicken soup or making love, it is an idiosyncratic act. There is no one right way to do it. I can only tell you how I do it.

Writing is a job, and I go to work every morning: nine o'clock, five days a week. I quit about noon when I'm working on a novel (creating a universe being somewhat fatiguing), although I might edit the two or three pages I've written the rest of the day, or go to the library: What did most women do about birth control in 1940? How did the OSS screen potential agents?

(Writing a screenplay is less taxing, and by the time production rolls around I am so familiar with my characters that I can, on occasion, write whole scenes on the set while electricians drag cables over my sneakers and the grips look over my shoulder and critique my dialogue.)

But back to the beginning writer. When I decided to start my first novel, which was to be *Compromising Positions,* I thought about taking a fiction workshop. Lucky for me, I couldn't get a baby-sitter at the time the New School's best course was being offered. So instead I bought a copy of John Braine's *Writing A Novel.*

Like the Montessori method of tying a shoelace, the book broke a complicated task into a lot of idiot steps, so that the job didn't seem overwhelming. *Make an outline of no more than four pages*: When I began all I knew was I had a housewife-detective who lived on Long Island. When I finished, I not only knew who'd done it, I knew where, how, and why. In writing those few pages, putting down ideas that had probably been whizzing around my unconscious for months or years, I discovered that my heroine, Judith Singer, and the homicide lieutenant were soulmates, while her husband . . . Well, you get the point. *Draw up a list of characters*: I did, and suddenly Judith's best friend, an ex-Southern belle with an earthy sense of humor, jumped up and winked at me. The victim? I considered who most deserved to die: a periodontist.

You know that old platitude: *write about what you know.* Well, it's not a bad idea. You can use what you know—computers, mahjongg, Harlem, or parakeets—either as the core of the novel or as a background. And write about what you care about. I care about people, character. For me, writing a novel is fashioning an intimate biography.

In *Compromising Positions,* I used my home, suburban Long Island, as the setting, and bestowed my then-job, housewife, on my heroine. In *Close Relations,* I drew on Brooklyn and Queens, the world I grew up in, the world of New York City ethnics. I also took my (brief) experience as a political speech-writer, as well as my passion for New York Democratic politics and gave them to Marcia Green. In *Almost Paradise,* I wrote about show business (this was before I became a screenwriter) and celebrity. Wasn't that writing about what I didn't know? Well, in America show business *is* everybody's business. And celebrity? I took my own minor exposure to it, my twelve-city book tour for *Close Relations,* and puffed it up: being on a TV talk show; being recognized by an effusive reader in the ladies' room; having mere acquaintances feel my sex life—to say nothing of my tax return—is their property.

By the time it came to writing *Shining Through,* I was secure enough in my proficiency as a novelist, in my imaginative ability, to write about what I didn't know: speaking German, being a spy in World War II. But what I *did* know was what it's like to look at the rich and powerful through the eyes of someone who was neither. Linda Voss, my heroine, like me, started as an outsider. Like Linda, I worked as a secretary and knew what it was like to be thought of as something more than a typewriter—but less than a human being. (Later when Linda became a spy, her "cover" was a cook. Listen, I was still writing about what I know. I was a housewife. I know from pot roast. I just transferred it to Germany and made it sauerbraten.)

In other words, in *Shining Through,* I was writing about *people.* I was writing about love—real and unrequited—and passion, honor, deceit, friendship, patriotism, courage, terror. In other words, having lived for over forty years, I *was* writing about what I knew.

Another suggestion: *write for yourself.* I was among the blessed. I never went to a writers' conference, never took a fiction workshop. I learned to write for *me,* not for a teacher, a critic, an editor or even that amorphous, intimidating mass, the "audience." I never allowed myself to worry: What will my mother think? The minute you write to please

125

someone, or not to offend someone, or to take big bucks, or to be taken seriously, you're gazing outward, not inward, and you're doomed to lose sight of what is unique and true in you.

So then, what does it take to be a novelist? Well, a gift for writing. A willingness to sit alone in a room for one or three or ten years, telling yourself a story. Then you must be able to *become your toughest critic*. Ask yourself the blunt questions: What is there about this protagonist that would make someone else besides me, the creator, care about his or her fate? What propels the novel, what will drive the reader to turn the page? This may be the most difficult task of all. With all four of my novels, there were days I was embarrassed—no, mortified—at the drivel I was passing off as fiction; and there were days that I was jolted by the force of my own brilliance. You will discover, after many readings, that the truth lies somewhere in that broad range in between.

If you want to write, expect criticism, some of it personal. If you write about sex, someone will inevitably tell you that you have a dirty mind. If you are a woman and you write about something other than glitz or, on the other hand, quiet, domestic lives, you run the risk of being criticized for *chutzpah* or naiveté. ("Serious" American female novelists are almost all experts at literary petit point; the big canvas is left to the men with their broad strokes.) Don't be afraid of what They say. *Write*. Don't write the story you think they want to listen to. Write the story you want to tell.

I know, it seems overwhelming. But then again maybe that nagging thought—if *she* can do it, I can too—is really a good, honest gut feeling about your own talent. Do you think it's worth taking the chance to discover the truth?

28

DIALOGUE—THE FIZZ IN FICTION

BY PETER LOVESEY

DIALOGUE OUGHT TO FIZZ like champagne. It should be the guarantee that our writing doesn't go flat.

As a child deciding what to read, I would flick through books to see how much the characters talked. I wasn't attracted by pages dense with prose. I was impatient to get on with the story. A page of dialogue with its lines of different length was more engaging than solid text. Still is, both to read and write. And dialogue also appealed to me because it gave me a direct link with the characters in a book. I wasn't conscious of the writer at work, as I was in descriptive sections. I heard the words of the characters and they came alive. I would sometimes skip sections of description; dialogue, never.

So let's brighten up this page with the opening lines of Gregory Mcdonald's *Fletch*:

"What's your name?"
"Fletch."
"What's your full name?"
"Fletcher."
"What's your first name?"
"Irwin."
"What?"
"Irwin. Irwin Fletcher. People call me Fletch."
"Irwin Fletcher, I have a proposition to make to you. I will give you a thousand dollars just for listening to it. If you decide to reject the proposition, you take the thousand dollars, go away, and never tell anyone we talked. Fair enough?"
"Is it criminal? I mean, what you want me to do?"
"Of course."
"Fair enough. For a thousand bucks I can listen. What do you want me to do?"
"I want you to murder me."

For me, that opening has the rhythm and power of poetry. It is tense, sonorous writing that conveys vital information and ends with a surprise. The writer gives it conviction with naturalistic touches. It is believable as speech.

I used this example because it is pure dialogue. It could be a film script, or the speech bubbles in a cartoon strip. It dispenses with all of the props conventionally used to support direct speech. The identity of the one character we need to know is contained in the first lines, so the writer doesn't need to have *Fletch said* at the beginning or end of any of the lines.

Of course the to and fro of dialogue isn't usually so clear. We need to identify the speakers at some point; they won't necessarily supply their names in the words they speak. But as soon as we add explanatory words, we are dealing in artifice as much as art. The *he/she said* that we tag on is just a device to help the reader distinguish between the speakers. It should be unobtrusive.

The common variations of *he said* are so familiar that they, too, can do their work almost unnoticed: *he remarked/commented/asked/inquired/answered/responded*. But beware. It's a short step to words that may appear strained when you use them: *he questioned/interposed/interrogated/enunciated/averred*. Such words can distract from the dialogue. So, also, can the group often used to portray speech in animal terms: *he snapped/growled/barked/whimpered/yelped/howled/squawked*.

All of us use such words occasionally for color. The danger is that color can clash. My own preference is to stay with the simple *said* in most cases. If the dialogue is sufficiently interesting, the reader can stand the repetition. Occasionally, variations seem appropriate. Fine— but they shouldn't distract. Brilliant writers from Jane Austen to Raymond Carver have been content for the most part to settle for the stark *he/she said*.

The same principle can be applied to the adverbs writers often tag on to the *he said*. Used with discretion, they are effective. It's easy, however, to overdo it, to emulate the writer of the Tom Swift stories. We have all come across writing in which every *he said* is followed by an adverb—and sometimes a redundant adverb: *"I'm sorry," she said apologetically./ "I wonder," he said thoughtfully.*

It *is* a problem, particularly when you want the reader to be conscious of the characters and their response to the things being said. It can be helpful to study the techniques of writers you admire. Graham Greene, one of my favorites, makes regular use of the construction *he said with . . .* The examples that follow are from *The Human Factor*:

> *. . . he said with his habitual guilty grin.*
> *. . . he said with formal politeness.*
> *. . . he said with a sharp note of accusation.*

Raymond Chandler's solution in *The Big Sleep* is frequently to give a short sentence describing some gesture or facial expression of the speaker:

> *Sudden panic flamed all over her face.*
> *His mouth became a hard white grimace.*

In giving these examples, I have over-simplified. Writers as skillful as Greene and Chandler employ a variety of techniques. My point is that if you analyze successful authors' methods of presenting dialogue, you may well be inspired to try different techniques of your own, for nowhere else in the writing of fiction does it come down so obviously to the nuts and bolts. Make yourself aware of well-tested methods and adapt them to your own creative output.

Let's turn from the externals to the dialogue itself. The English thriller-writer, Len Deighton, once wrote that he didn't want to be so famous that people recognized him. "I like to be able to listen to conversations without people turning around to look at me over their shoulders. I want to be the man behind you in the fish shop." All writers should be eavesdroppers. We dignify it by saying that we have to cultivate an ear for dialogue, but it comes down to listening to other people's conversations. If our characters are to talk like real people, the speech-patterns must be in our heads. When we come to write conversations down, it's sensible to speak them aloud and see how they compare with what we overheard in the fish shop or on the train.

What you end up with is not quite what you heard in the fish shop. Anyone who has tape-recorded and then transcribed a conversation knows how banal most of it appears. You have to delete the ums and ers, the tedious repetitions of "you know" and "as I say." A few may stay in, but many would be tedious unless used for some special

129

purpose. You compress and select. You are in charge—up to a point. Here we enter controversial territory.

Almost all novelists, as they write their books, have experienced the phenomenon of having a character grow and develop in an unplanned way. "The characters have their own lives and their own logic, and you have to act accordingly," is the way Isaac Bashevis Singer expressed it. This mysterious process is often at work when you compose dialogue. A character almost demands to say something. And quite frequently this can reveal new possibilities to the writer. Not all writers are comfortable when it happens. Jorge Luis Borges put it this way: "Many of the characters are fools and they are always playing tricks on me and treating me badly." However, it can be worth submitting to the treatment, if only in a draft, just in case serendipity hands you a pearl.

Time for some more of the real thing, from *The Silent Salesman,* by Michael Z. Lewin:

As I opened the door, I saw a girl sitting behind my desk. Late teens, with slightly reddish-brown hair, dark brown eyes, and freckles. She looked vaguely familiar. I took two steps inside and stumbled over a knapsack that I hadn't left in the middle of the floor.

I hadn't left it anywhere; it wasn't mine.

"This yours, Miss?"

She nodded. Then she opened the middle drawer of my desk. "Hey, there's nothing in here," she said. "Why don't you keep anything in it?"

"Because when I'm out working I leave the office open. To offer a moment's rest for strays and waifs and the occasional client. Which might you be?"

She smiled at me until she saw that I wasn't smiling. "I don't think I'm any of those categories. Do you?"

"Look here, young lady, it's hot. I've had a hard day—"

She stood up with a sense of urgency. "Don't you really recognize me?"

I frowned. She did look . . .

"Daddy!" she said.

"Oh my God," I said. It takes a wise father to know his own child.

"I recognized *you!* And all I've had is a picture from more than twelve years ago."

"My God," I said. "My God."

Leaving aside what I called the nuts and bolts, let's concentrate on the effectiveness of the dialogue. First, the voices sound right: the Private Eye, suave, capable of handling most emergencies, but getting a severe jolt here; and his daughter, casually playful until she senses that this reunion isn't working out exactly as she planned. Dialogue works best when there is disharmony between characters. By disharmony I

130

don't necessarily mean conflict. I mean the friction between two points of view.

In the extract you have just read, the story is written in the first person, from the point of view of the man. Yet Michael Lewin makes us conscious of the girl's unease *(She smiled at me until she saw that I wasn't smiling)* swiftly turning to alarm *(She stood up with a sense of urgency),* and we are engaged by her vulnerability in this situation as much as her father's. They are two people with different expectations.

There ought to be friction of some sort in most dialogue. Even in situations where characters have an identity of interest—say, a love scene—you don't want them echoing each other's words. They are individuals with their own perceptions, and the more conscious we are of their different personalities, the more effective will the scene become. So it is essential to *know* the characters, their hopes and hang-ups, before you attempt to give them speech.

The pace and rhythm of dialogue must be a matter of judgment. We've looked at examples of tense dialogue using short speeches. Difficulties can arise when you need a longer piece of exposition. Crime writers like me usually face this problem in the last chapter of a book, when everything has to be explained. A protracted speech calls for an effort of concentration that the reader isn't always prepared to give at that stage, so we have to devise ways of breaking up those long speeches. Occasionally writers will divide a long speech into paragraphs, but that is the least satisfactory remedy. It is preferable to have another character interrupt the speaker with some question or comment, and to prevent this becoming too obvious a device you might change the pace for a few lines with a staccato exchange:

". . . and left the gun in his hand."
"And a note in his pocket."
"Yes."
"Why?"
"Why the note?"
"The gun."

Such an exchange may seem artificial as you write it. However, it's worth noting that in real conversations people rarely allow anyone to talk on for very long, and when an interruption comes, the original speaker can be thrown for a moment. The floundering before order is restored provides a convenient pause for the reader.

131

The need to be realistic, to make people sound believable as they speak, has to be reconciled with your wish as a writer to move the story in a particular direction. As I have said, it can be helpful sometimes to let the characters take over, particularly when their voices demand to be heard. But ultimately dialogue must be controlled by the writer. It is not conversation, but the semblance of conversation. It is a distillation of what might have been said in real life, selected and shaped to a degree that the reader shouldn't begin to suspect.

The quotations from *Fletch,* by Gregory Mcdonald, and from *The Silent Salesman,* by Michael Z. Lewin, are reprinted here by permission of the authors.

29

WRITING THE NOVEL SYNOPSIS

BY MARGARET CHITTENDEN

MANY NOVELISTS SAY THAT A SYNOPSIS is their most important selling tool. My own feeling is that *good writing* is the writer's most important selling tool, but certainly a well-thought-out, well-constructed synopsis comes a close second.

In recent years, publishing houses have pulled in their economic belts; they don't have the number of first readers they used to have—college graduates who sat all day reading through what was called the "slush pile" or the "manuscripts that come in over the transom," more professionally known as unsolicited manuscripts. A synopsis saves an editor's time. It lets the editor know you have the ability to organize and plot a complete novel. If the story is not suitable for the particular publishing house, the editor will recognize that fact immediately. On the other hand, if the story does seem suitable and the synopsis is well written, the editor will often encourage the writer to complete the book and submit it, thus turning an unsolicited manuscript into a solicited one.

Some publishers will even go to contract with an author on the basis of a novel proposal, which consists of a synopsis and three sample chapters, usually the *first* three chapters. Other publishers want to see a completed book from a beginning writer before going to contract, but almost all publishers will ask for a synopsis first. The reason for this is that often others in the company besides the editor must be consulted before a novel is purchased. Those on the editorial board will probably read only the synopsis and will base their approval or lack of it on that reading alone. Obviously, then, it is essential to know how to write a good synopsis.

What exactly is a synopsis? The dictionary definition is "a statement giving a brief, general review or condensation; a summary, as of a story."

Many new writers are horrified at the very idea of writing a summary of a novel. It's not possible, they say, to condense a story of 60,000 to 100,000 words into six pages, or ten pages, or twenty—depending upon a particular editor's requirements.

If you agree with that statement, remember that your unconscious mind is ticking away, recording everything. When you say or think, "I can't write a synopsis," or "I hate writing a synopsis," it makes sure that those statements are true for the rest of your life. So, try to get into the habit of repeating every morning and every evening, with conviction, "There is nothing easier than writing a synopsis."

It's true.

Before writing a novel, you need to know what it's about. And that's all a synopsis is—a summary of what the novel is about. Even if editors didn't want to see a synopsis before considering a novel, it would be necessary for you to write a synopsis, simply because its the best possible thing to have on hand when you start writing your novel. A synopsis is your guide, your security blanket, your map, your chronology. Without a synopsis, a plan, the writer is in danger of being like the character in a Stephen Leacock story who "flung himself from the room, flung himself upon his horse and rode madly off in all directions."

I cannot tell you precisely how to write your synopsis; I can only tell you how I write mine and hope it will be helpful. Remember, different writers have different methods. This is just my approach.

First of all, I don't even think of starting a synopsis until I have a whole lot of notes on characters, plot, settings, occupations, conflicts, story situations, et cetera, et cetera.

I make notes in a notebook of all these story elements. In a box, I gather brochures, maps, articles about the occupations I've chosen, newspaper clippings, books that deal with the subjects I'm covering. In the notebook, I write down everything that comes to me in connection with my story, without worrying how I'm going to use it. Sometimes these notes are in the form of memos to myself. "How about having a scene at his home in France." Or notes on characters. Or it might be a whole page of dialogue—or notes about the weather, or local flora and fauna.

Layer by layer, bit by bit, the story grows. As the plot grows, the characters start coming to life. As the characters grow, they affect the plot. It's a symbiotic relationship, and it cannot be rushed. As I collect all this material, a story line begins to emerge, and I start making notes for this on the left side of the pages. By the time my notebook is pretty well filled, I have a fair idea of the whole story line. I'm ready to write the *first* synopsis. (I'll explain that in a little while.)

I always start writing the first synopsis first thing in the morning, so that I can finish it in one day. I try to write at white heat, writing straight through, without referring to my notes, because by now everything is in my head. I aim to write fast, without stopping to think, "How am I going to get these people out of this situation?" or "How will I fill this black hole?" The idea is to get the story down. This part is *not* carved in granite. I can change the whole thing later if I find it necessary.

I usually start with a little background on one or two of the main characters. Like this in my latest novel, *The Scent of Magic* (Harlequin Superromance):

Casey (Cassandra) Templeton is twenty-seven years old, red-haired, green-eyed, petite. The only child of a somewhat flamboyant preacher, Casey had grown up in Illinois, in poverty—and occasionally as an object of ridicule, always feeling different from other people. After graduating from high school, she moved to Seattle to get away from her father, a rigid disciplinarian.

Casey owns "The Second Time Around," a fashion store in Seattle's historic Pioneer Square area that specializes in cast-off designer clothing, vintage clothing, and antique jewelry. To advertise her business, she often dresses in vintage clothing, which makes her look somewhat eccentric.

After a little more of this, I go directly to:

The Scent of Magic begins when Casey is poking around at a huge antique fair in Seattle's Kingdome, looking for fashions of a hundred years ago.

When she comes across a stall run by an elderly lady with an unusual accent, she is enchanted by the stall's antique objects, though few of them are suitable for her shop. The old lady, who introduces herself as Inga, seems mysteriously interested in Casey, asking her some very personal questions. Finally she shows Casey a beautiful antique perfume bottle of amber-colored Saracenic glass, made in Mesopotamia. The small amount of perfume left inside has the most lingering, seductive aroma Casey has ever smelled. Casey hands the bottle back reluctantly, telling the woman she probably can't afford it. The woman says she is not permitted to sell it—it has to be a gift, and she would like to give it to Casey. It is a magic perfume, she says, guaranteed to bring the wearer her heart's desire.

135

I go on from there, bringing in other characters and settings as needed.

When I'm actually writing the novel, I keep a calendar that shows exactly where the story is, but when I'm writing the first synopsis I'm more interested in just getting everything down and organizing it later. I write very simply and as if I were *telling* someone the story. I write down everything I know about the story. *Everything.* I include the ending, of course. I'm sure you know that you must always let the editor know how the story turns out. Not just, everybody lives happily ever after, but *precisely* how they are going to solve their difficulties, in summary form, of course. I've seen a lot of synopses that leave the ending vague, and it's not a good idea to do that.

When I have the first synopsis written I read through all my notes and put in anything I've left out. I want to have as much detail in it as I know about the story.

Other writers have disagreed with me on this, but I find it helps to put in bits of dialogue occasionally as they occur to me, because this brings characters to life and makes reading more interesting. It also breaks up the pages a bit. I don't do much, just something like: Casey tells her friend Skip she's still not sure she should see Michel again, adding wistfully that it had been fun while it lasted.

"That's what you need, fun," Skip assures her. "Trouble with you is, your father's walking around in your head telling you if it's fun it can't be good for you. You need livening up, Casey. Maybe Michel's the guy to do it for you."

Casey reminds him she's dating Justin.

"Uhuh," says Skip, who doesn't like Justin.

When I'm quite sure I have everything in the first synopsis, I go through it and arrange it in chronological order, grateful for word processing; then I print it out. This is *my* synopsis. This is not to be shown to any editor. This is often fifty to a hundred-and-fifty pages of sprawling story.

On the hard copy I've printed out, I mark where I think chapter endings will come. Again, this is just for *my* information. Then I look at each chapter and ask myself, "What is the purpose of this chapter? Where is the conflict in this chapter? Who is present in this chapter? Whose viewpoint are we in? And so on. If necessary, I make changes in the synopsis so that I can answer these questions. Then I start cutting

136

and editing and revising and polishing until I have 20 to 30 fairly tight pages that contain only what the editor absolutely must know in order to evaluate this story. This is the *editor's* synopsis, and it's the one I send out with sample chapters.

Some editors want a short synopsis, six pages or so; others want a long one. I usually send 20 to 30 pages double-spaced, and so far that's been acceptable. It is not divided up in any way. It is merely a summary of the whole story. Traditionally, a synopsis is written in present tense. Some writers say you should single space, but I think double space is easier for the editor to read.

One final note. Even though I've put in all this work on a synopsis, as I write the novel, things change. I do not stick slavishly to the synopsis. I just go blithely ahead and write it the way that seems best now. No editor has ever said to me, hey, you changed this story from the synopsis. Sometimes the change is slight, sometimes I introduce a whole other character with a subplot that wasn't in the original synopsis. Often I change characters' names and the color of their hair or eyes. In *The Scent of Magic,* I changed the whole ending. The editor didn't seem to mind. However, I only make changes that I think are an improvement on the original story.

So—there it is. I hope you will develop a positive attitude toward synopsis writing. I was one of those who thought I hated writing the synopsis. And I'm a hard-headed Englishwoman. If I can change my attitudes, anyone can.

30

REWRITING YOUR NOVEL

BY S. L. STEBEL

LET'S SUPPOSE YOU'RE ONE OF THOSE HAPPY FEW who have filled enough intimidatingly blank pages to flesh out a book, and have actually been able to write those magical words: THE END!

The novel may have ended. That's the good news. But is it finished? Alas, more than likely not.

How to know? Fortunately, there are some simple yet effective procedures that I've developed to help a writer determine, first, whether a novel meets the standards deeming it "publishable," and second, whether it has achieved all the possibilities inherent in the material.

It's important to let the book "settle" for a time. Put it away—out of sight, out of mind—long enough to enable you, when you pick it up again, to read it "cold," giving you a reasonably fresh and objective look. Do not despair if you then discover that your story line is murky, that your beginning, which seemed lively enough at the time you wrote it, soon slacks off, and that your ending seems to be overly abrupt and (dare you admit it?) not quite as powerful as you had intended.

What has gone wrong? The guideposts of your outline (assuming that you had one) seem to have disappeared underneath an avalanche of words; your scenes sprawl randomly and without point; your characters wander like underutilized actors in search of a drama in which they may act out their parts.

But no doubt there are also scenes you do not even recall writing that have sprung brilliantly to life, and one or more characters that have become so vivid and uniquely individual they surprise even you. (Let's hope one of them is your protagonist!) Keep those wonderful moments ready at hand; they are products of your writing partner—your unconscious—and are key clues to the solving of any problems your novel may have.

But wait. Don't start rewriting yet. Instead, write a glowing review of

138

the novel you had hoped you were writing. Putting modesty aside, imagine that you're the leading reviewer of the most influential book reviewing publication in the country, and you're going to do your utmost to convince readers that they must go out and buy your novel immediately!

"Let's not mince words," you may write. "This is a stunning novel, written by (your name here), a master of his/her craft, who has produced as enthralling, if not profound, work that keeps the reader engrossed from first page to last."

O.K. so far: You've tantalized your audience. But in order to get them to rush out to the bookstore, you first have to give them a reason, and that involves telling them who and what your book is about. Seems easy enough. . . .

"The protagonist," you continue enthusiastically, "with a *dominant attribute* (i.e., *ambitious* young priest, *melancholy* Dane, *risk-taking* wife, *greedy* stock manipulator, *frightened* soldier), encounters *another character with a dominant attribute* (see examples above), who offers a fatal temptation. In a momentary lapse, for reasons buried deep within his psyche, the protagonist steps from the straight and narrow and in a series of harrowing events discovers (blank) about life and (blank) about him/herself."

Pause a moment here. Have you found it easy to describe a dominant trait about each of your characters? If not, why not? Could it be they're not well enough defined, even in your own mind? If so, it's imperative for you to learn more about them. Do a little creative snooping into each character's history. You may discover hidden motivations that can surprise you, that must surprise you before you can surprise your readers.

And how clearly have you been able to describe the basic conflict? How determined is your protagonist to achieve some goal? What, or who, stands in his/her way? Does *every* character you've created contribute to the dramatic action? If not, what are they doing in your story?

If those questions prove difficult to answer, try listing all the emotional and historical baggage your leading characters carry. I'll bet you'll find some things you didn't expect. Now chart your main characters' emotional journeys from the beginning to the end of your novel. Examine the result: Do your leading characters grow and develop?

One way readers know they've been told a story is by seeing that a

139

character has changed, or has at least been enlightened in some important, revelatory way. In any relationship story (is there any other kind?), the characters should change or enlighten each other.

What about the dramatic action? As you continue writing your review, do you find it easy to sketch the narrative line (sometimes called plot) in a gripping way, yet clearly enough for a reasonably intelligent person to understand it?

If the story line—even in an episodic, metaphorical novel—does not possess some kind of interior logic, or if the events, sparse as they may be, only "happen," without any motivation except the author's recognition of the need for some kind of "action," it may be necessary to take a more practical, hands-on approach. To do this effectively, there is nothing better than borrowing from the past and taking a "classical" approach to the material.

A very useful technique is to break your novel down arbitrarily into three acts. (It may be a book of many acts, unnatural and otherwise, but for the purpose of this exercise, assume there are only three.) We'll further assume, in the interests of simplification, that Act One states the problem, Act Two complicates the problem, Act Three resolves the problem.

Next, do a "step" outline. We'll take it for granted that each of your chapters deals with a separate event. But it can be extraordinarily helpful simply to write a sentence for every time something actually happens in your novel. That can be a *physical* happening—one character murders another, or merely enters or leaves a room—or it can be an *emotional* happening, in which, for example, one character professes love for another, threatens another, or breaks down and weeps.

Though in this step outline you may write a sentence when one character newly engages another character in dialogue for the first time (not mere conversation), you may not write another sentence, no matter how long they talk or how many pages of exquisite descriptive prose goes on, unless something *else* happens: a sudden lie, say, or an unexpected idea in the mind of one of the characters that has the potential for action (i.e., a mental vow for revenge). If you find that there are a great number of pages for which you are not able to add another sentence to your step outline, you'd better investigate: Has your material become static, and in all likelihood, boring?

When you've finished this step outline, examine it, then revise it, and keep revising it until you have a story line that moves, clearly and dramatically, in a slowly ascending scale of intensity. Obscurity is not a virtue. Neither is ambiguity, unless deliberate. The author should always know what is going on, even if at some point the object will be to keep the characters and/or readers in the dark.

This brings us to what I believe is the underlying purpose of the writing process: a search for the thematic statement. The thematic statement can, and should, be simple. "Oh, what a tangled web we weave when first we practice to deceive." "Love can transform the most savage beast." "Revenge, at first though sweet, bitter ere long back on itself recoils." A writer can ring as many changes on a theme as are within his or her inventive powers. He can rebut the theme, reinforce it, complicate it, but he must never deviate from it. If in writing your review, you find yourself saying that your novel is about this, and it is also about that, and it may well be also about another thing, be assured that your thematic statements will contradict rather than reinforce one another, leaving readers frustrated and confused.

Once you've discovered and clarified your thematic statement, you'll be able to approach the actual rewriting of your text with the kind of assurance that will convince your readers that they are in the hands of a confident and skilled writer. "Author" is (or should be) short for authoritative.

The Greeks, especially Aristotle, had a word for it. Their attitude toward the writing of drama—in which I include all forms of fiction—is worthy of emulation. Every line you write, they believed, should do one of three things (or, in the best of all possible worlds, all three things simultaneously): (1) define character (2) create atmosphere (3) advance the action.

All else is redundant. It may be writing for the sake of writing, a form of intellectual pretension that may delude some into believing they're in the presence of artistry. Or it may be misguided hope on the author's part that the reader will fill in the gaps, supply the missing motivations.

With this approach, however, your novel will become coherent, its underlying theme, or subtext, suddenly all of a piece. Knowing your theme will make rewriting a delight and give you the freedom to be as inventive as you're capable of being. Try it. You have everything to gain, and nothing to lose.

141

§ 31

THE CHALLENGE OF THE SHORT SHORT STORY

BY ISOBEL STEWART

MOST ADVICE THAT APPLIES TO WRITING the short story applies to the short short—but even more so!

Though many short stories can stand a little skillful editing and pruning, trying to cut a longer story down to a short short is not likely to be successful. You have to think "short short" right from the start. I'm sure that you, like me, have many ideas in your notebook that really don't have enough in them to make a full-length short story. Good ideas, yes, but when you're being clear-sighted and honest with yourself, you have to admit that you'd be committing the unforgivable sin of padding if you tried to use them for a story of 3,500 to 5,000 words. But have another look at these ideas, and consider whether their very simplicity doesn't lend itself to the short short story, anything from 1,000 to 2,000 words.

Once you've hit on an idea suitable for a short short, there are a few specific guidelines that I find helpful.

Keep it simple.

Not too many characters, an uncomplicated plot, and no long conversations. People have to say what they want to say as concisely as possible. Try reading your conversations aloud—I find it helps in judging whether they sound natural or stilted.

Your first sentence and your last sentence, important in any short story, are even more important in the short short. I find I spend quite a lot of time on getting these right.

I find, too, that in a short short, it's wise to observe the classic unities of time, place, and action. You can't afford flashbacks, you can't afford to move your people around too much, and most of all, you can't afford to get involved in action that needs a great deal of description. Not in a short short.

You don't have a wide canvas on which to portray your characters and their problems, so you have to make your people come to life with a swift stroke or two, a spoken phrase, a fleeting bit of action that pinpoints their salient characteristics.

And if the concept of getting your reader's attention in your opening sentence applies to a short story of ordinary length, it applies even more to a short short, in which you cannot waste a single word.

I've used these two opening sentences in recent short shorts published in *Good Housekeeping* ("Lessons in Love"):

"You can go to cooking classes," Caroline said briskly, "and I'll go to auto maintenance."

This tells the reader a fair bit about Caroline right away: She's brisk and efficient, an organizer, and she has strong views on the sharing in modern marriages. I would hope the reader would be intrigued enough to read on and find out the effect of the cooking classes and the auto maintenance on Caroline and Tim's relationship.

And another opening, this one from "A Sister for Cheryl":

Linda hadn't expected it to be easy, becoming stepmother to a girl of seventeen.

Here, I hoped to establish the situation right away and to raise some interest in the question of whether it was in fact easy or not. In this story, Linda's problem is not with her stepdaughter, but with her own hitherto easy-to-manage daughter. In a longer story, the conflict could be developed gradually between Linda and her daughter, between the two girls, between the stepfather and daughter. In a short short, you have to indicate the problem immediately, briefly, and clearly—but not baldly.

In "A Sister for Cheryl," a short conversation between Linda and her husband can reveal their concern, their previous efforts, and what they plan to do. One or two brief incidents—the daughter's refusal to help her mother unpack her bundles; the stepsister's warm and willing acceptance of the new relationship and pleasure in helping—these actions should be enough to suggest that things are getting worse.

Short as the short short is, it must fulfill the essentials of the longer short story, which, very broadly speaking, can be described as Problem—Conflict—Solution. But in a short short, I would go for a simple

143

and straightforward problem, for example, the relationships in a new family situation: A young widow with two children learning that she must not overprotect her children, and, at the same time, learning to overcome her own reserve in a new relationship. A farming community in the grip of drought and a little girl who has the faith to go to a prayer service for rain, taking her umbrella with her.

Of course, all these simple approaches have to be fleshed out, but you have to do it deftly, with a sure touch, avoiding any obvious techniques.

I once wrote a short short which had a rather clever—I thought!—bit of "business" in it. The fiction editor of *Good Housekeeping* pointed out that the essential story was fine, but spoiled by the unnecessary complications I had introduced. She was, of course, right. I rewrote the story, and it was much better.

Dialogue is important in any short story, but particularly in a short short in which every word must count. I have always found that in writing dialogue, it is a great help to read it aloud. Does it sound easy and natural? Do people actually talk that way? If it is at all stilted and forced, try again.

For me, a sure sign that a story is going well is when I find my fictional people having conversations in my head. Sometimes I hear myself saying out loud the words I want to use in the story, and when it comes to the actual writing, my face wears the appropriate expression. If the characters should be frowning, I frown; if someone says something coolly, my expression is cool.

Long, involved thought processes expressed in conversation are out in the short short. You must condense such exchanges of ideas in a few words. In my story, "The Girl Called Samantha" (*Good Housekeeping*, August 1990), a little girl had to indicate to her next-door neighbor not only information essential to the story, but an impression.

Steve asks Samantha if her mother will be looking for her.

Samantha shook her head. "No, she'll be busy for a while." She sighed. "She works at home on a computer, you see. So I can stay."

I wanted to convey to the reader—as Samantha wanted to convey to Steve—the impression of a child whose mother seems more concerned with her computer and her career than with her child. But I couldn't afford to use too many words to do this. Samantha's explanations had to be short; I couldn't go into a detailed description of her mother working at home.

But do remember that your readers are smart enough to fill in the gaps in conversation, and the short cuts. In real life, we leave out a word or two, we condense, we are casual. People in stories are more natural if they do the same, if they say "I can't do that" instead of "I cannot do that."

And in dialogue, in the short short, if you have a choice of two words, go for the shorter one. In most cases, it has more punch, more impact, and it keeps the story flowing.

What I have to watch out for in writing a short short is keeping this flow. When you have to keep a story to the bare bones, there's a very real danger of having it become jerky.

When I write a short short, what do I want to do?

I want to take a common, everyday situation about ordinary people, and turn it into a story with real emotion, a story readers can relate to. I want to write about life and love, about living and loving, as it happens to me, to you, to the woman next door.

At the same time, in any short story, I want to give an indication of what has happened before the story begins—its background—and hint at what is going to happen after my story ends.

In other words, I want to compress yesterday, today, and tomorrow into my story. And the shorter the story, the less space and time I have to do this in. The challenge of a short short is to ask yourself, when you have finished, how well you have succeeded in this aim.

The catchword and the watchword for the short short could well be ECONOMY. Be economical in every way—with your idea, with your characters, with what they say, and with what they do.

I've always felt that writing a short story, as compared to a full-length novel, is something of a challenge.

Think of the short short as even more of a challenge!

32

THE MAJOR ROLE OF MINOR CHARACTERS IN FICTION

By Hans Ostrom

AFTER READING AN EARLY DRAFT of a novel I had submitted, my editor—as I expected—commented on several areas that needed improvement. One of her responses to the novel surprised me, however. She said that she had had some difficulty with several of the minor characters. In her view, I had not depicted these characters vividly enough, and when a significant amount of time had elapsed between appearances of some secondary characters, she found that her sense of those characters had become cloudy.

To be sure, the remarks about the novel's minor characters came toward the end of the editor's written evaluation, after she had commented on larger elements of the novel. I do not want to imply that a concern for minor characters should outweigh a concern for the plot, primary characters, threads of suspense, setting, and other crucial aspects of a novel.

Ironically, however, because novelists must focus so intently on these obvious concerns, minor characters may not receive the attention they deserve, especially in early drafts. And poorly conceived minor characters can weaken a novel substantially. As a newcomer to writing novels, I realized after reading my editor's letter that concentrating on the major areas of my novels did not mean that I could afford to neglect minor characters. I also realized that, perhaps unconsciously, I had made the mistake of equating "minor" with "incidental."

Revising the manuscript in response to my editor's concerns was not difficult, but my interest in the topic of minor characters did not stop there. I thought further about the essential ways in which minor characters contribute to novels in general, and I offer my observations here in hopes that they might help other new novelists.

Perhaps the most obvious function of minor characters is in advancing the plot. In basic terms, the plot consists of events in which the main character(s) take part. Nonetheless, minor characters can often play major roles in constructing the plot.

In mystery novels, they can provide a crucial bit of information to the sleuth, or they can become unwitting obstacles to the success of either a detective or a criminal, or they can trigger a memory on the part of a detective that will allow him or her to solve a puzzle or to take the right action. In mainstream novels, the contribution of minor characters to the plot can be just as important but in an even greater variety of ways. Virtually any element of crisis or resolution can be enhanced by a minor character.

Charles Dickens's novels remain an excellent example of this potential; even though ideas about "the novel" have evolved since his era, the range of ways in which he used minor characters to contribute to intricate plots still offers a model to novelists for what it is possible to do with minor characters. Compared with many contemporary novels, Dickens's works may sometimes seem crowded or "overpopulated" with minor characters, and yet the portraits and functions of those characters are always painstakingly precise. Dickens is beyond imitation, but he may be the best example of how seriously a novelist must take lesser characters. His works reinforce the platitude about a chain being as strong only as its weakest link: A minor character, even one with a bit part, can be the most important link in a chain of events that constitutes the plot of your novel.

A second major contribution minor characters can make to a novel is to enhance the development of the main character(s). We learn much about main characters *only* from main characters—from seeing them in action or from listening to their interior voices. However, we can learn as much about them from the way they behave in encounters with secondary characters. Even when such brief encounters are not crucial to the plot (and they often are), they show us how the main character functions in "ordinary life." Furthermore, the whole concept of "round" or "three-dimensional" characters depends on the existence of "flat," "two-dimensional" characters who allow primary characters to stand in relief. As in motion pictures, such characters literally "support" the major roles in novels.

Another way of describing this function of minor characters is to say that they add texture to a novel. In fact, one of the discoveries I made in

147

my transition from writing short fiction to writing novels is that novel writing allows me more latitude to work to enrich the texture of my fiction. Generally speaking, one can employ a larger cast of characters in a novel than one can in a short story. This situation makes for more freedom, but it also asks the writer to think more extensively about what to *do* with the freedom and, more specifically, what to do with additional minor characters in the cast.

Minor characters can also contribute to the development of suspense, either in a scene or in a whole novel. Consider one example from a classic of the suspense genre, Dashiell Hammett's *The Maltese Falcon*. In Chapter 16, when "the black bird" suddenly falls into the hands of Sam Spade, it is delivered by a mysterious, dying stranger:

> The corridor door opened. Spade shut his mouth. Effie Perine jumped down from the desk, but a man opened the connecting door before she could reach it. . . . The tall man stood in the doorway and there was nothing to show that he saw Spade. He said, "You know—" and then the liquid bubbling came up in his throat and submerged whatever else he said. He put his other hand over the hand that held the ellipsoid. Holding himself stiffly straight, not putting his hands out to break his fall, he fell forward as a tree falls.

The scene itself is suspenseful, for as readers we sense the mixture of confusion and terror that Spade and his secretary feel when the dying man appears at their door. Moreover, in relation to the entire plot, the appearance of this minor character adds enormously to the suspense. Who is he? How did he get the Maltese Falcon? Who killed him? Will Spade be accused of killing him? What should Spade do now? To a great extent, suspense is uncertainty, and Hammett uses a minor character to dump a truck load of uncertainty on Sam Spade's doorstep.

Minor characters can contribute to suspense not just in mystery and action fiction but in virtually every kind. Rust Hills, in *Writing in General and Short Story in Particular,* applies the idea of suspense to all good fiction, saying that it "can function in literature as subtly and effectively as it does in music." Minor characters are one important source of such subtlety and effectiveness. In James Joyce's classic story "Araby," for example, the minor character of the uncle is an enormous problem for the main character, the boy who wants to go to the bazaar to buy something for the girl he worships. In coming home late and generally being difficult, the uncle delays the boy's departure, adding to the suspense of the story (will the boy make it to the bazaar or not?)

and to the sense of disillusionment and disappointed desire that Joyce creates.

Still another way minor characters can be useful to fiction writers is to help evoke a sense of place and atmosphere. Whether it's Conan Doyle's London, Raymond Chandler's Los Angeles, William Faulkner's Mississippi, or Ann Beattie's New York, our sense of place depends on the people in the place. Authors can use minor characters to help convey the flavor of a region or a city quickly and convincingly. Fog and gaslights add to our sense of Holmes's London, but Mrs. Hudson, cabbies, bobbies, and a legion of other minor characters contribute as much, if not more, to our mental picture of the fictional London Conan Doyle creates.

Finally, minor characters can be interesting in and of themselves. A quick sketch of a minor character can (and should) be vivid and entertaining—should stand on its own in some way. Moreover, like all characters, minor ones grow in surprising ways, demanding more attention from the author during revisions, competing for greater roles as novels or stories take shape. In my own novel, a bartender (of all people) who I thought would be almost incidental became more crucial to the plot and to the sleuth (a sheriff) than I had ever imagined. He became more of a confidante and a representative of sorts of the ordinary people in the rural county. Such "independence" on the part of minor characters may be even more likely to occur in novels than in short stories.

These, then, are several significant roles minor characters can play in fiction. In addition, there are some rules of thumb a writer should keep in mind during the revision process:

1. Beware of stereotyping. Because minor characters *are* minor, and because authors cannot afford to spend more than a few sentences describing them, a stereotype can be tempting. A waiter or a cop or a librarian need not be a stock character. Don't call Central Casting; instead, draw on your own experience and your notebook for a not-so-typical sketch.

2. Beware of the time lapses between appearances that minor characters make. If the interval between appearances is substantial (several chapters, for instance), it is even more necessary for the first appearance to be striking. As mystery novelist Lillian O'Donnell has remarked, "Clue: If I have to go back into the early pages of a first draft

149

to find out a character's name, that character is not real." O'Donnell's observation applies to mainstream fiction as well, of course, and one might add that if a reader's memory of a minor character's first appearance is fuzzy, how well is that character really functioning in the novel?

3. Give minor characters memorable but not outlandish names, and make sure the names and initials of your minor characters are sufficiently different to avoid confusing the reader. Don't make your reader wonder which character was Ron Ryan and which was Bryan Ray. Most of us are unconsciously attracted to a very narrow range of names, and we need to broaden that range in our fiction.

4. Don't be afraid to eliminate a minor character entirely. The fact that minor characters can themselves be interesting cuts both ways because a minor character can upstage a major one without contributing to plot, character development, suspense, or atmosphere. He or she may be engaging without being genuinely functional.

Ask yourself whether the character ought to appear at all. (If you are moving from short fiction to a novel, you may find that the comparative freedom of the novel creates a greater temptation to clutter the stage with characters; the clutter springs not so much from the number of characters as from the purposelessness of characters.) Such characters need not disappear forever. They may turn out to be useful in other stories and novels, and may even become main characters in other works.

Ultimately, the nature of minor characters in fiction is something of a paradox: although such characters are by definition secondary and often two-dimensional, they add depth to various elements of stories and novels.

33

FROM RAW MATERIAL TO STORY

BY MAYA SONENBERG

IDEAS FOR STORIES STRIKE FROM ANYWHERE, spring from anything—dreams, newspaper articles, paintings, relatives' lives, the words of a song, the encyclopedia—and then we set out to transform them into fiction. "Write what you know," we've all been told. But we know things in so many ways, from so many sources, and any one of these can start a train of thought that ends with a story.

We limit ourselves by thinking that "what we know" means only what we've lived intimately, daily, for it can also mean what we've read, what we've been told, what we've observed in the woods, on Main Street, in museums. We limit ourselves, too, by thinking that these germs of stories must already contain a compelling plot and fully rounded characters; the raw material of fiction can as easily be image, idea, metaphor, language—plot and characters growing only as necessary from these sources. The less we limit ourselves, the more chance we have of finding the trigger for what may be a fantastic story.

How do we transform these scraps of experience—all kinds of experience—into fiction? For the art resides not in the experience itself but in what we do with that raw material. Often personal experience serves as the catalyst for a story. The place you live can spark the imagination. A quirky aunt who forgets to wash behind her ears; lives in an empty apartment because she's given all her furniture to refugees; does cartwheels down Fifth Avenue; and is also an unrivalled success as a trial lawyer can inspire a story about a young nephew who discovers the evils of conformity and the importance of independent thinking.

This material is immediate. Making a story from it seems easy enough, but the first draft may be little more than a journal entry, a memoir, or a character sketch instead of a full-fledged story. We've all faced the criticism—or realized ourselves—that a character, setting, or image is vague, dead, unconvincing. It does no good to tell ourselves, "But it really happened that way. She's really like that." Instead, it may help to think of this as a problem of transformation, or really lack of transformation. Close your eyes and you see Aunt Edith so clearly that the words "crazy, quirky, and successful" seem to describe her perfectly. She's so real to you that you don't need to create her with words; you can't see the fictional character for the actual person, and such lack of vision makes your story murky and keeps you from using language accurately. This, I think, is why writing fiction based on auto-biographical material can be so deceptively easy and so hard to do well.

It takes special care to make the transformation from life to art successfully. The first step may simply be to pretend you've never met Aunt Edith. After you've convinced yourself of this, reread your story. Is she clear to you? Do you feel you've been introduced to a new person? If not, this is the time to cut out the hackneyed words and the too-broad images, the outlines you can fill in as you read because you know Aunt Edith but that fail to create a picture for anyone else. Replace them with specific description and action—old advice, I know, but especially important to remember when writing about things and people we're close to. Don't just say Aunt Edith was a bit strange; describe her doing pirouettes on the escalators in Bloomingdale's.

My story "Quarry Games" grew out of visits to an abandoned quarry near the ocean. In part, I simply wanted to describe a place I loved. I also wanted to write about sensing the past, the way I could imagine so clearly how other people had walked and worked there. In the story, a young girl uses the quarry as a springboard for her imagination and brings to life everything she sees, only to have an older boy disparage these fantasies until she abandons them. But if readers can see neither the actual quarry nor the girl's inventions, they will not find the loss of her imagination compelling. Early versions of this story were bland, threadbare. I was taking for granted that everyone already found old quarries intriguing and knew which games could be invented there. I needed to forget my own reactions to the place and imagine the girl's—from inside.

Personal experience is just one example of raw material that needs to be transformed to become a story. While all fiction writing demands the exactitude I've described, stories that arise from other sources present other opportunities and problems. You may find an idea in a newspaper, a book, or a conversation you overhear on the bus. The problem here is to write something new, to transform something that already exists in language. I once gave students a newspaper article about a Czechoslovak family who escaped to Austria in a hot air balloon and asked them to turn it into fiction. "Don't tell the whole story," I suggested. "First, figure out what intrigues you most about the account." The seven-year-old son's fear as he steps into the balloon? The way the earth looks from above on a moonlit night? The father's sorrow at leaving his own parents behind? The idea of pursuit? The workings of the balloon? The surprise of the Austrian border guards when the balloon lands? This decision made, point of view, voice, tense, time frame, start to fall into place.

With a story you've heard hundreds of times before—a myth, fairy tale, or history book standard—you can start by choosing a different point of view, perhaps that of the character you feel has been slighted in the original, and see where that takes you. Tell "Rapunzel" in the witch's voice. Describe the assassination of Abraham Lincoln through the eyes of John Wilkes Booth. In "Ariadne in Exile" I decided to retell the story of Theseus and the Minotaur through the Minotaur's sister and found I was writing a story about a woman abandoned on an island and haunted by her memories.

Of course, more unusual things can serve as sources and subjects for fiction—a visual image, a painting, for example. In "Nature Morte," I tried to bring a cubist baby to life. As a cubist painting depicts its subject from many points of view at once, I approached my cubist baby through the voices of a number of characters—mother, doctor, school-yard friend, and the baby himself—in order to create a verbal equivalent of a visual experience.

Day-to-day images also trigger stories of all types. You see a bowl sitting on a table with the light from a lamp throwing its interior into shadow, and this image refuses to let you alone. "Who owns that bowl?" you ask yourself. "Is it whole or cracked? New or old? What color is it? Where was it purchased? Who made it? Was it a gift? What does it hold?" In inventing answers to these questions, you're starting a story—perhaps a story about the bowl's owner, the bowl's maker, or the bowl itself, passing from hand to hand, affecting lives.

Sometimes we start making up a story when a phrase buzzes in our ear, the way a mosquito hovers in the dark as we try to sleep. The phrase can be a bit of conversation that leads us to invent the speaker, a sentence whose music makes us think of water kissing the side of a ship, or a metaphor waiting to be given flesh. What if that sound of kissing becomes a real kiss between two passengers on the ship? What if two map-makers carry on a love affair the way they make and read maps, the way the imagination relates to "reality"—recreating, inter-preting, inventing, failing to communicate? In "Cartographies," I ex-plored these metaphors in trying to answer that question. What triggered these meditations on maps, map-makers, and imagination that ended in a love story? The title of a poem by Adrienne Rich—"Cartographies of Silence." Just a few words can be raw material if we work out the ramifications: Just what is a map of silence and how can it be expressed as a relationship between people?

Questions often goad us into writing, but they are not always ques-tions about characters, places, or events. They can also question ab-stract ideas. What is the nature of loneliness? What if immortality were a reality? In the stories we write, characters can ask these questions. Characters' lives can represent possible answers. Or, the form of the story can embody both questions and answers. If you decide there are twelve varieties of loneliness, you might write a work in a dozen sections, exploring in each a different facet of that emotion. I started the story "Dioramas" when I asked myself about the different ways one might relate to nature. In "Cartographies," my mapmakers end by finding a peace and wholeness in nature, but in "Dioramas" I wanted to explore less romantic ways of relating to landscape. What if someone preferred an industrial park to a national park? What would it be like to feel beholden to a place, tied to it against one's will? To fear a place? To be seduced by countryside? To be cursed by a location? To be obsessed with a landscape? To be literally absorbed by land? To simply be bored? Eventually I chose seven settings and peopled each with a different couple whose relationship mirrored the relationship between them and the land. These questions may be only the framework I use to build the piece, no longer visible, but still necessary to the construction. In this way, writing fiction can be a dialogue *with*—though not neces-sarily *about*—yourself, one story acting as the impetus for the next, a give-and-take on whatever images, characters, metaphors intrigue you.

Writing fiction based on material that at first seems distant does not mean avoiding the things you care about, but expands the range of those materials. Learn to pounce on whatever starts you thinking about a new story, however unlikely (for me it's very often a visual image), and you've found your catalyst.

Still, it's only a catalyst, a moment of inspiration that needs to be shaped by imagination and verbal ingenuity. What prevents writing about personal experience from being a diary? What prevents writing about current events from being an essay? Or an idea from being philosophy? The boundary lines—thank goodness—are rarely clear, but one distinction may be this: With fiction, the experience or idea resides *in* language and form, in image, voice, character, scene, and is inseparable from these things rather than explained by them. Fiction is language the way an ice sculpture is ice; dissolve the ice surface to search for supports, disregard the verbal surface to find another meaning, and the whole thing disappears. With language, we create a fictional equivalent, a parallel or not-so-parallel universe, rather than describing the one that already exists.

Fiction may be far indeed from the event or image that triggered it. In revisiting a setting I've used in a story, I'm always surprised by how different it is from what I've described, how much more space there is, simply how physical it is. By now, I should expect this to happen, but I always sit up with a jolt, gasp at the beauty or ugliness that didn't make it to the page, and realize again that writing fiction is not a process of holding a mirror to the world and transcribing what one sees, but a process of transformation by language and into language, a creation rather than a *re*creation, an experience of great and terrible freedom more than anything else. It matters little that the granite quarry I described doesn't match the one I see; that day exploring ledges by the ocean was only the trigger for a story, not its reason for being.

34

LET FICTION CHANGE YOUR LIFE

BY LYNNE SHARON SCHWARTZ

THE LURE OF USING our own experiences in fiction is almost irresistible—not only for beginners but for seasoned pros as well. What could be more natural, or more inevitable? To tell what has shaped us, to cast the incidents of our lives in the form of narrative, with ourselves as heroes and heroines, is instinctive: It shows itself as soon as children acquire language. And personal experience is a vital source of fiction, one might even say the only source: what else *can* we write of but what we have seen, felt, thought, done, and as a result, imagined? As readers, we're touched most deeply by stories that possess, in Henry James's phrase, the sense of "felt life," stories the author has cared about and lived with and presented in all their intensity; the others lie stone cold on the page. Indeed, a corollary to the old saw, "write what you know," could be, "write what you care about."

But if all of the above is true, then fiction might be no more than faintly disguised autobiography, an indulgent exercise in self-expression. Fiction would be a sorry, impoverished thing indeed, deprived of the rich and incomparable offerings of the imagination and the unconscious, with their enigmatic leaps and turns. Thankfully this isn't so.

How do we make use of the tremendous stores of material our lives provide, and at the same time avoid boring our readers by being that most tedious of companions—the kind we all know and dread—who talks only of himself, by himself, and for himself?

The lamest excuse beginning fiction writers give in response to criticism is, plaintively, "But that's what really happened." Who cares, I'm tempted to ask. To put it more tactfully: If you want to write fiction that others will love to read, you have to be willing to sacrifice parts of your life. Or if that sounds rather extreme, let's call it giving up "the way it really happened" in favor of a greater truth. For a story, in some unaccountable fashion, makes its own demands, like a child outgrowing the confines of the parental home. When you're willing to let the story's life take precedence over your own and go its way, you've taken the first step to becoming a successful writer.

Once you've embarked on that journey, the urge to tell what happened is slowly transformed into the desire to give events pattern and significance, to construct a *thing*, almost like a free-standing sculpture whose shape and contours are clear to all, with the power to delight, or amuse, or provoke, or disturb. Above all, to draw in an entrance. In its final form, while the construction may have been inspired by happenings in the writer's own life and may still contain their germ, it has taken on its own life. It has, sometimes in most surprising ways, gone beyond the writer's experience.

This doesn't mean you can't allow your deepest concerns into your fiction—quite the contrary. Look at the work of Jane Austen, who has left us the most witty, thorough, and painstaking account of nineteenth-century courtship and marriage rites in the middle classes; no sociological study could be more informative, not to mention enchanting. Little is known of Austen's personal life; we cannot say for certain who were her suitors or why she did not marry; we cannot point to episodes in her novels and trace their origins. What we do know is that she scrutinized the mating game in all its aspects, with a unique blend of irony, skepticism, and mellow acceptance. In other words, Austen managed to put her individual sensibility into her work in a far more profound way than by merely drawing on actual events.

As a humbler example, since it's what I know best, I'll use my own novel, *Rough Strife*, which also happens to be about a marriage. The story follows some twenty years in the life of a couple, Caroline and Ivan, who meet in Rome then return to the United States to live in Boston, Connecticut, and finally New York City—settings I chose because I knew them and felt on "safe" territory. During the time I was writing *Rough Strife*, a spate of novels appeared in which married women, weary and disgusted with the inequities of family life, were cutting loose to find independence and adventure. Something about the ease and abruptness of their flights from home bothered me; much as I sympathized with the problem of constraint, the solution seemed oversimplified. I was determined to write about a heroine who stayed to see it through, to learn where that route could lead. At the same time I, too, was determined not, fashionably, to abandon my marriage, a fact that surely influenced the book.

I suppose I planned, in some imprecise way, to have Caroline and Ivan face many of the issues my husband and I faced. But in the end the couple bypassed me to lead their own lives. Caroline, for example, surprised me by having a difficult time conceiving their first child. A mathematics professor, she has an affair with a graduate student, which leads to an abortion; later on, her second child with Ivan turns out to be hyperactive. Why, I wondered as I wrote, did I invent all that? Why did it invent itself, might be more accurate. Well, I wanted to illustrate the enormous effects that bearing and raising children have on a marriage, and those events heighten the illustration. They apply pressure and create tension. They arose from the imagination, wisely, I think, to serve the story.

At still another point the characters escaped me, quite against my will. I was writing a scene of a marital quarrel, with some rather acidic repartee. No one could have been more alarmed than I when Ivan suddenly turned violent, pushing Caroline to the floor. It was not at all what I had intended—not with these characters, anyway, civilized people, incapable of such behavior. In shock and horror, I watched a rape scene unfold. How much more shocking that it was coming from my own pen! And Caroline's reaction was equally horrifying. Instead of being indignant and repelled, she thinks she invited it in some way. She even feels sorry for Ivan in his guilt and remorse! The whole incident contradicted my beliefs as well as my experience—in real life I would have shaken them both to their senses. But this was not real life. This was the utter mystery and excitement of fiction, where characters rebel and demand their own errors and their own destiny, and we had best not stand in their way.

In the end, I had a novel about a couple whose story barely resembled my own. The only autobiographical elements left were a certain analytical turn of mind and a sense of the complex, ambiguous accommodations involved in living with another person. Whatever my original aims, I had written about the gradual process of accepting the results of one's uneducated choices. With the benefit of several years' hindsight, I can see that this notion of process, not the details of the plot, is what makes the book personal as well as, I hope, universal.

The same shifts occur in writing stories, only on a smaller scale. How well I remember lying awake one entire night with a gray spot jiggling before my eyes—something the doctors call a "floater," I later learned. It didn't let me sleep, and as the hours passed, I slipped into a miserable, unreasonable state of mind, berating myself for all the mistakes of my past, wondering what it all meant, if anything. . . . Anyone who's spent a sleepless night recently will know what I mean. The experience was so powerful and disturbing that naturally I wanted to write about it. The result was a story, "Acquainted With the Night," whose main character turned out to be a male architect ten years older than I. Why, I can't say. He too lies awake, victim of a floater, examining and agonizing over his past, which, needless to say, has nothing in common with my own. (I took the opportunity to give him a life full of moral crisis, without the straints I might have felt about detailing mine.) Again, the common and personal element, as well as the universal one, is simply the insomniac's painful and—in the light of day—distorted trip, a trip almost every reader has taken at one time or another.

The path leading to a newer story was more circuitous. Several years ago, a fire forced my husband and me out of the apartment building where we had lived for twenty years and raised our two daughters. Besides the shock and pain of losing our home, we and our fellow-tenants were outraged at the behavior of the landlord, Columbia University, in the aftermath of the fire. A lengthy court case ensued, with the tenants ranged against the power and willfulness of a large institution. Two years later I completed a book about the fire, the legal proceedings, and the social implications of institutions as landlords. Since I had written mainly fiction till then, I was prepared when friends asked why I hadn't turned my experience into a novel—what an ideal story it seemed, full of drama and conflict. My answer was, first, that the truth was topically urgent and needed to be told precisely as it happened; and second, that the story (plus the research it would entail) really didn't interest me as a novelist. I had been writing long enough to know that real estate practices, demographics, and the nature of bureaucracy were not my subjects.

Some time later, though, probably under the influence of many newspaper and magazine articles about homelessness in New York City, an imaginary family moved into my mind. Little by little their features became clear: they were newcomers from the Virgin Islands, the father was an electrician but temporarily working at a lunch counter, they were black, they were very proper and conventional, there were three young children. . . . They too had been forced out of their apartment by a fire, but unlike my family, they had had to accept the city's offer of a welfare hotel, a dismal and dangerous environment. The father, a proud man, found that intolerable, but with so little money what could he do? I became obsessed with the family until their story virtually wrote itself—"The Last Frontier," in which George and Louise Madison and their children move onto the stage set of a situation comedy, contrasting the whitewashed TV image of family life with their own reality.

None of the details about the Madisons corresponded to my own life—none, that is, except their condition of homelessness, and the resulting anger, frustration, and bewilderment. In those feelings that give the story its life, we were identical. One might say it is autobiographical in the deepest sense.

The ability I've been discussing—giving up the facts for the broader reaches of the imagination—may sound daunting, but it comes with experience, and with the confidence and willingness to let the story take control. For almost always, at some point in the arduous process, the inner voice will whisper, "What if . . . instead of . . . ?" The secret is to listen, and to yield.

But that's not the only way. Some fiction gets written backwards, so to speak. In the case of *Balancing Acts* (my first novel, though it was published second), I was on the third draft and puzzled over why it wouldn't come right, when I finally grasped what the book was about and what its connection was to me.

I had begun it after a friend told me about her ten-year-old daughter's strong attachment to an elderly man, a volunteer teacher in her school. The man had just died, and the child was suffering the sort of grief—for the loss of a close friend—that most of us don't know till later in life. The story stayed with me—I didn't know why; one often doesn't—and I constructed a novel around it, with background and details far different from those of my own life. I couldn't help but notice, though, that the man in my novel had much in common with my father, and the thirteen-year-old heroine, with me. Not circumstantial matters in common, but affinities of temperament and attitude. Only on that third draft, when I realized that book was a particular emotional struggle on my part, connected with my aging father, could I rewrite it with coherence and conscious design. Plot, setting, and characters all remained the same, but I had found the autobiographical impulse at the core and could work outwards, using its energy.

Giving the imagination free reign, or conversely, locating the fertile source of a story, is exhilarating as well as productive. But it has its negative side (doesn't everything?). The upshot of letting fiction change the events of your life is losing parts of your past. It's not an overstatement to confess that looking over my work, I occasionally note bits that sound familiar, yet I can't quite remember whether they happened or whether I made them up. Did the neighbors down the street when I was nine years old really shout those awful things out the window, or did I imagine it? Or exaggerate it? Did that man in the boat really look at me in that seductive way? Was the path behind the country houses really as dark and lush with greenery as I wrote? And were my grandmother's glasses of tea with lumps of sugar as wonderful as I've made out? The line between memory and invention blurs; I can't say for sure what happened, and I have the sinking feeling that I've erased parts of my life in order to write stories over them. I may have given up more than I expected, becoming a writer. The only relief for such doubts is to go back and write some more. Because in the end, as the Roman poet said, life is short, but art is long.

35

How Much of That Story Is True?

By David Huddle

How much of that story is true?" is what I'm likely to be asked after I've given a public reading. It's a naïve question, one that irks most writers of fiction. A friend of mine sometimes fires back from the podium, "Would you even dream of asking an actor, 'How much of your own personal experience did you use to play that role?' "

But the autobiographical question interests me. My own response to it recently has been "84 percent," "79 percent," or something like that. I'm not fooling around; I mean to be estimating as exactly as I can the literal truth of the story. What's peculiar is that the interrogation stops there; my percentage answers almost always satisfy both the questioner and the rest of the audience. I never get the seemingly inevitable follow-up, "Which parts are true and which aren't?" I can't explain such audience behavior; it seems to me that if someone is bold enough to ask the first question, surely that person or somebody else ought to have the nerve to ask the second.

I'd be ready to try to answer that one, too, as sincerely as I could, because that's the one that interests me most of all. Thirty years of reading serious fiction and twenty years of trying to write it haven't cured me of my own naïve curiosity about what's true and what isn't in a good story. When I read "A Good Man Is Hard to Find," I wonder if Flannery O'Connor ever read a newspaper account of a criminal like the Misfit, who killed off a whole family. When I read "Goodbye, My Brother," I wonder if John Cheever ever swatted his brother in the head with something like a piece of seawater-soaked driftwood. When I read "For Esmé, With Love and Squalor," I wonder if J. D. Salinger ever had an intense conversation over tea with an English schoolgirl and her little brother.

Not only do I wonder about these possibilities, I also enjoy speculating about them. I'd be willing to bet a fair amount of money that

162

Raymond Carver once had a wild conversation about love with some people who were drinking and sitting around a kitchen table. Part of my reading pleasure comes from guessing about the actual experience upon which the author might have based the parts of his or her story.

So I'm ready to try to answer a reader—or listener—who might be similarly wondering about something in a story of mine. Perhaps perversely, in the eyes of most of my brother and sister fiction writers, I feel honored, rather than bemused, by my audience's curiosity.

But in most cases, providing an answer would be a tough assignment for me. When I start writing a story, it's usually based on something I lived through, but as I'm writing it, I quickly forget what actually happened. That kind of truth is useful to me only as a starting point in my thinking about a story. Even though I begin with personal experience, I'm tinkering with it from the first words I set down. When I finish writing—finish the last of the 10 to 25 or 30 drafts that it takes for me to feel I've done all I can for my story—my memory of the truth of what happened has been clouded by my many alterations of it.

But not only would I be willing to try to pick the facts line by line out of my fiction, I'd also be interested in what the project might yield.

I'd be up for such a tedious project because I think I'd probably learn something from it. I think my benefit would be similar to what a tennis player gains from watching a slow-motion video of his or her strokes. I wish I had had a chance to sit down with O'Connor, Cheever, or J. D. Salinger to examine a passage of one of their stories and to discuss what was remembered and what was imagined in terms of their sentences' diction and syntax; I'm certain I'd have learned a great deal about the mix of memory, imagination, language and epistemology in the individual writer's composition process. I'm pretty sure I'd have felt that I was approaching the beating pulse of that writer's art.

My fiction writing colleagues who resent being asked about the truth of their stories suspect that their achievement is being insulted. I can see their point: If the author admits that the story is mostly true, then the questioner feels that there really wasn't much to the writing. The author simply recorded some history he or she happened to stumble into. If the author says that the story is entirely imagined, then the questioner feels that there's really not much to that piece of writing. The writer just made it all up: Heads, you lose; tails, I win.

There is a level at which I'm impatient with these distinctions anyway. At some writers' conference in the future, I'll be the guy who stands up and makes a shaky-voiced speech about how autobiographical writers use immense amounts of imagination and make-it-up-from-scratch writers use memory in every paragraph, and so what are we arguing about anyway? Aren't we all in the business of trying to make a good story out of whatever materials we can find? What I think is that the bias against memory-writers and in favor of imagination-writers is held almost entirely by a few critics and literary snobs, and that fiction writers and ordinary readers understand perfectly well that what matters is the quality of the story, not which brain cell produced it. If I weren't so aggravated over the anti-memory bias, I'd shut up and sit down.

The reader's understanding of a story can be enhanced by a useful biographical fact: that Flannery O'Connor was Roman Catholic; that Hemingway was wounded in war; that Raymond Carver and John Cheever had drinking troubles; that Jayne Anne Phillips's brother served in Vietnam; that Andre Dubus served as a Marine officer; that Eudora Welty has lived most of her life in Jackson, Mississippi; that Toni Cade Bambara grew up in New York City; that John Updike worked for *The New Yorker;* that James Alan McPherson and John Casey have degrees from Harvard Law School; that John Gardner rode motorcycles and played the French horn; that John Irving is serious about wrestling and cooking; that Harold Brodkey was an adopted child; that Stephen King was a high school English teacher—these are facts that enhance the intelligence and the pleasure with which we read these authors' books.

Characters, as far as I'm concerned, never take on lives that are wholly separate from the author; an author is most deeply revealed through his or her most compelling and fully developed characters. When Flaubert says, *"Madame Bovary, c'est moi,"* he means what he says. Furthermore, I think that personal dimension is the main force that moves most of us to read fiction: Intimate human company is what we want when we curl up with a novel or a book of stories. When we say, "I'm reading Flaubert," we mean what we say. The more highly developed our sensibility, the more highly refined our taste in narrative will be, but at a primary level, one of us reads Harold Brodkey for the same reason another reads Stephen King: We wish to spend time in the

164

company of the grown-up adopted child or the former high school English teacher.

In choosing to work "close to the bone"—to make narrative out of personal experience—the autobiographical fiction writer risks working "person to person," risks exposing the most essential aspects of himself or herself. Irony is possible, but trickery isn't. Personally vulnerable to the scrutiny of anyone who picks up the book, the autobiographical fiction writer offers a reader company that is, for better or for worse, sincere and intimate.

In spite of what we know instinctively about reading fiction, writers and critics alike speak of literary art as if the relationship between reader and author had no bearing on the act of reading. A friend of mine is willing to tell me personally that her stories are somewhat autobiographical, but she says that if asked about it publicly, she would deny it. She says, "It's none of their business."

She's right, of course. Story writers have to protect themselves from readers who are only idly or pruriently curious about the truth of their work. Who would be surprised that the author of a best-selling literary novel that contains some brilliant and bold writing about sex must take an unlisted phone number because of the abusive calls she receives? Sometimes a book provokes readers to feel such intimacy with the author that they leap to the conclusion that they're entitled to impose on that author. I can see why my friend thinks the autobiographical truth of her stories is not the business of strangers.

On the one hand, "How much of that story is true?" is a profoundly antiliterary question, to which it isn't surprising that someone who has given his or her life over to the practice of writing might respond with hostility. On the other hand, it's a doggedly human question; the fiction writer who attempts to answer it sincerely is likely to have the rare and perhaps illuminating experience of discussing his or her art in the most basic—most purely human—terms.

Most serious writers of fiction don't think much about their readers when they're actually writing, but they do think about how much of themselves they're giving to their art. Mere technique won't produce stories a writer wants to live with. An esthetic axiom (as applicable to high literature as it is to country music) is that the more of yourself you're able to give your art, the stronger your art will be. So most writers try to locate and use subject matter that brings forth their most passionate feelings, most rigorous thought, most lyric sentences, and most complex vision.

The autobiographical fiction writer chooses as subject matter material from his or her own life because that material brings forth his or her best writing. This is an instinctive, necessary choice, because finally what the serious fiction writer—of whatever inclination—aims to do is to make art that embodies his or her best self. That author wants a reader to be caught up in what happens in the story, to be engaged by the characters, to be pleased by the sound of the language and by its imagery, to be stimulated by the story's thematic concerns, and to be satisfied by the story's form. These are the means by which that writer hopes to deliver over this "best self" to the reader. This best self embodies everything the writer knows and feels about human aspiration; it is the dearest truth the writer has been able to purchase with his or her esthetic resources.

Foolishly or not, I believe that revealing the exact nature of the material I've used for my stories will not harm me, my family or my friends, and will not provoke my enemies to take me to court. Why am I so willing to talk? Because to anyone who's seriously curious, I think I can demonstrate something I deeply believe, that autobiographical fiction is the highest form of narrative art. So how much of my story is true? That's a terrific question, sir. Let's sit down right over here and have a look at a paragraph or two. I hope you've got plenty of time.

36

SHORT FICTION IS SALABLE

BY HELENE LEWIS COFFER

IN 1965, I SOLD MY FIRST SHORT STORY to *Good Housekeeping.* "A Saint on Earth" had a serious theme, a love story, five well-developed characters, and an O. Henry ending. The tale was told in twenty-five pages (about 6,250 words).

Over the years, I've had to tailor my storytelling to the incredible shrinking magazine fiction market.

Two of my recent stories in *Good Housekeeping* are excellent examples. "A Delicate Affair" was written in sixteen pages; "Along Came Love" in eight. Both were cut further before publication.

Today, I wouldn't write "Saint" as a short story. I might as well try to sell an elephant in a flea market. Yet, to be salable today, a short story must have the same basic elements: appealing characters, interesting situation, conflict, suspense, and a believable resolution, preferably one that tugs the heart. Above all, something important must happen, something that literally changes the life of the protagonist. Otherwise, your story will be dismissed as "slight." The problem is packaging these elements in fewer pages. So much to say, so little space.

Before I put a word on paper, I have thought about the people and the situation until I know a great deal more than I am going to tell. Someone said that a story is like an iceberg; seven-eighths is below the surface. That has never been truer than it is today.

First, I must be selective. The plot can't be overly complex. I must use a smaller cast and resist the temptation to develop a character who interests me but doesn't enhance the plot.

In "A Delicate Affair," the heroine is a young woman from Mexico who is learning English from a young Anglo teacher. As I start writing, I know her family, her reasons for coming to America, her goals, and all about any love interest in her life. Since I teach evening English classes in the Amnesty program, I don't have to dream up this background.

But if I tell all this upfront, the story will never get off the ground. So I start in the classroom:

Connie Cortez arrived for her evening English class at exactly eight o'clock. As she slipped into her seat, she glanced around the room. At the last session, six students had received their 40-hour certificates. Not one had returned.
Connie sighed. Teacher would be cross.

With this introduction, we launch directly into the relationship developing between student and teacher. Background will be slipped into the continuing story.

We learn that Connie, coached by her American Aunt Rosalia, is a star student, but shy, and sensitive to her classmates' feelings. This comes in brief bursts of exposition punctuated by dialogue:

Connie glanced at the serious faces and found herself wishing Mr. O'Neal could understand how hard it was for most of these young people to get to class at all.
The teacher had written sentences on the board, leaving blanks. He pointed to the first sentence.
"Who can read this for me and supply the correct preposition?" he asked. "Anyone. Connie?"
Connie read, "The light is *above* the door."
"Right. Next sentence?"
The class was silent, still ill at ease with oral recitation. So Connie read the sentence.
"Someone else besides Connie," prompted Mr. O'Neal.
Connie flushed. She was small and slim, with black hair and dark brown eyes, fresh and neat. She was beautiful, and completely unaware of it.

Before this scene is over, Connie has observed that her teacher is not as fluent in Spanish as he appears; he is using his dictionary to write out his speeches before delivering them. She nerves herself to do the same in defense of her classmates. The ensuing dialogue establishes the teacher's character:

Connie took a deep breath, and began, "I see that you feel it much when the students do not return after forty hours," she recited. "It is hard for them to come. They work . . . ."
"Well, so do I work," David O'Neal burst out. "I teach school all day, and believe me, I don't spend my evenings doing this for the money. I'm here because I know people come to America for a better life. My ancestors came from Ireland to keep from starving in the potato famine. Usually, the first generation is handicapped by lack of education, *especially* if they don't know the language . . . ."

The dialogue continues, with Connie trying to explain the special circumstances of her immigrant classmates, and her teacher asking questions. David—and the reader—are learning considerably more about Connie.

By now, I hope to have provoked the reader's interest sufficiently so that he will stay with me while I provide some background. I do this in flashback; Connie is thinking about the drastic changes in her life as she drives home.

From here, the story can proceed without interruption. Connie gets pressure from home to marry a family friend, older than she but handsome, kind . . . and wealthy. Meanwhile, the reader can't miss Connie's burgeoning attraction to her teacher, and suspects it may be mutual. But David doesn't make a move.

Do I tell the reader why? No, indeed. Here's an element of suspense that needs to be maintained until the last moment.

The closing three pages of the story are almost entirely in dialogue, conducted between Connie and David as he drives her home from the class's final session. Near the end, the burning question is answered in these few lines:

> David said, "Connie, I'm twenty-six, not wealthy but gainfully employed, and single. And I'm not your teacher any more."
> Only the last sentence had impact for Connie. She felt tears tears gathering behind her eyes.
> She whispered, "I am going to miss you . . ."

Each story presents its own problems in management, but some techniques always help. From my newspaper training comes a tip for tight writing: use strong verbs, avoid meaningless modifiers. One editor instructed reporters tempted to use *quite, very* or *rather* to write *damn* instead. This word he would be sure to notice and eliminate.

Compare these two sentences:

The sidewalk was very hot.

The sidewalked *sizzled*.

Once I've started a story, I usually write steadily, not interrupting the flow. After I've done the rough draft, the real work begins. As I go back through it, I test every line for excess verbiage. I may redraft a passage many times before I'm satisfied.

For me, dialogue falls into place more naturally than exposition. Listen to a couple of people engaged in conversation. On occasion, there may be an impassioned speech of some length. But most of the time, sentences are short, and not necessarily complete. I write dialogue that way.

Still, first efforts can often be improved. As I reread, I "listen." Does it sound natural, while conveying the character's exact meaning? Does it suggest his *feelings?* I've been known to start up out of bed after "hearing" a sentence that struck a false note. "He wouldn't say that," I mutter, as I dash to the typewriter.

It pays to let the story cool before you send it off. As a less desirable legacy from my newspaper days, I have a tendency to be a fast and impatient writer. I've sent a story out, read my copy a week later, spotted a weakness and wished I had it back.

For illustrations of how you can pack a lot of information into a little dialogue, I'll quote from "Along Came Love." As the story opens, Shelley is resigning from her job as a magazine editor to work on a small-town paper. The surprised editor asks:

"What's changed your mind about having a magazine career? Some man in Oklahoma?"

"Some man here. He's married," said Shelley flatly. "Only he never got around to telling me . . ."

That's all the reader needs to know about the dead affair, and we can get on with the story.

In Oklahoma, Shelley is teamed with a taciturn photographer. They work well together. But months pass before Shelley realizes that she has recovered fully from her blighted romance. The Moment of Truth comes when her teammate reports a job offer from a national magazine.

Shelley was aware of a sudden sinking in her chest. "I suppose you can't turn this offer down."

"I haven't decided," said Will. "How about you? When you get over whatever you came here to get over, will you go back?"

She was surprised he knew. "Was it so obvious?" she asked.

"I've been there, too, Shelley; it gives you insight. Have you made any plans? We're a good team . . ."

"Businesswise, you mean?"

"So far."

"So far! Will, we've been together all summer, and you've never even kissed me!"

"And I won't, so long as I see someone else in your eyes."

Shelley lifted her face. "Take a good look," she said.

As they say in movie-making, time for the clinch and fade-out.

To sum up:

1. Keep plots simple. Eliminate nonessential characters and sub-plots.
2. Start in the Here-and-Now.
3. Work in necessary background briefly and simply. Keep the story moving. Too long a flashback can slow it down.
4. Don't tell everything you know. Leave an element of suspense.
5. Let dialogue save space. Don't describe a character's feelings if you can *show* them in his speech.
6. Set the finished story aside for a while, then read it again. Do you believe every word of it?

I must believe in my story as I read it that final time. The conclusion should bring tears to my eyes. If I can stay detached, it probably means the story won't sell. If I've written a worthy story, I'm lost again in a world of my own making.

And how sweet it is.

37

THE MISSING PIECE SYNDROME

BY RICHARD MARTIN STERN

NO PROFESSIONAL WRITER I KNOW will challenge the need for discipline. It is the *sine qua non* of the trade, craft, business, call it what you will, of setting thoughts and ideas down on paper and selling them. A writer's place is at his desk facing his typewriter or word processor, *not* finding reasons why today he cannot write. And yet. . .

I speak here only of and for writers of fiction. Writers who deal with facts have, or should have, the facts in front of them before they sit down to write. The fortunate ones can wrestle with those facts, arrange and rearrange them, in effect play with their material as with the pieces of a jigsaw puzzle until the picture finally becomes whole and clear and ready to be presented as effectively as the writer can manage.

Fiction writers are in a somewhat different situation. We deal not with facts but with dreams and smoke and mirrors, and these *on occasion* refuse to fit together in a way that will make the illusion you are attempting to create, the illusion of reality, even inevitability in your tale, come off.

It is always possible that somewhere along the way your hand has slipped, and the picture you have presented of this character or that has thrown your entire story out of whack. Reading and rereading and frequently rereading again can usually turn up the cause of this aberration. You can then stifle the guilty character's propensity for taking center stage and shove him or her back into his proper niche in the story.

Or you may have made the mistake (all too easy to make) of putting certain scenes in the wrong sequence, thereby destroying the effect of building suspense, and what you intended to be a crashing climax fizzles like a wet match because you have told too much too soon.

It is also possible that in the delicately tangled web of your narrative you have overlooked a complete contradiction and, say, had Character A behaving on the basis of knowledge he could *not yet have had*. It does happen. You might even have already killed off a character you now bring on stage to catch your reader's attention with his brilliant performance.

These, of course, are only a few of the possible flaws in your tale that have brought you to the discouraging but unavoidable conclusion that the story as written will not wash. To return to the jigsaw analogy, what I am talking about is the *missing* piece syndrome, the missing twist of plot, the character emphasis, the single, cohesive fact of feeling or force that can bring the entire story into sharp focus. In short, you do not yet have the handle, and this is when discipline, that *sine qua non* of writing, as I said, simply does no good at all.

This is one of the most discouraging of times for a writer. You *know* something is wrong, badly, basically, damnably wrong, but you don't know what it is. Reading and rereading what you've written turns up nothing but emptiness. You sit and stare at the machine and the blank page or screen. You go over and over the entire story as it first appeared in your mind—that shining, whole, flawless concept—and you realize that it does not even vaguely resemble what you have put down on paper, but you don't know why.

All of the characters are there, and the situations, the conflicts, the interplay of emotions and even the drama, carefully contrived. But the whole picture is askew, out of focus, whopperjawed, simply *not right*.

If you plow on, you tell yourself, it will all come out the way it should. If at first you don't succeed . . . But there also comes to mind the conclusion W. C. Fields put to that dictum: "Give up; stop making a fool of yourself." And sometimes W. C. Fields was right; a small voice tells you so, and *sometimes* you had better listen to that small voice, because if you do not, you are headed for nothing but disaster.

In every successful story there is something—and I will not even try to put a name to it because it is too nebulous, no more than a feeling—that binds the story into a whole, brings it alive, draws the reader into it page after page and in the end lets him put the tale down, satisfied.

Without that feeling, that binder, that whatever it may be called, there is nothing. And until you have found that essential force and have it firmly in mind, you will do well to throw discipline out of the window and wait for something within you, perhaps your unconscious, to come up with what is needed.

Only then, after balancing conscience against reality, is apparent sloth not only justified, it is mandatory.

I have recently begun the third complete revision of a new 135,000-word novel, and it has struck me with stunning force that I do not yet have the handle; in short, I do not know yet what the hell I am doing. I will now do nothing until the answer appears out of nowhere, as it will, bright and clear and good, tying everything together, bringing the story off the paper and into reality, making the entire tale *alive*.

Then, and only then, will I be able to proceed with confidence.

38

Too Good To Be True: The Flawless Character

By Mary Tannen

My mother once bought a new table that came with a card printed on buff-colored heavy stock explaining that the table had been "distressed" with artful gouges and well-placed worm holes to give it a patina of age. We (her four children) thought this was hilariously funny and said that if we had only known she wanted distressed furniture we would have been happy to oblige and that clearly we had misinterpreted her screams of anguish every time we left a soda bottle on the coffee table or ran a toy car up the leg of the Duncan Phyfe chair.

The very phrase "character flaw" makes me think of that distressed table, as if characters were naturally shiny new and perfect and needed only the addition of a flaw or two, artfully placed, to make them more realistic. To me, a personality, whether actual or fictional, is not solid but liquid, not liquid but airborne, as changeable as light. What looks like a flaw might turn out to be a virtue. Virtue might, under certain circumstances, prove to be a fault.

When my daughter was reading *Billy Budd* and having a hard time with it, she came storming into my room to protest, and seeing the book I was working on in galleys, took it into her room to read. She brought it back the next day and announced that it was "better than *Billy Budd*."

"Better than *Billy Budd*!" I could see it emblazoned across the book jacket. Actually, my novel isn't better than *Billy Budd*, but the style was a lot more congenial to my daughter. She was appalled by Melville's heavy symbolism, by the way Billy Budd was the representation of an idea, not an actual man.

Billy Budd had no flaws, physical or moral (except for his stutter). He was illiterate, of noble but unknown birth, untainted by the corrupting influence of either family or literature. He was a myth, "Apollo with his portmanteau"! Melville never intended to create a realistic character. Billy Budd was Adam before the fall.

Sometimes when reading over a draft of a fiction piece I am working on, I realize that one of my major characters is suspiciously lacking in flaws. She is usually a person like me, but she is lacking in defects as well as in color and definition. When this happens in a piece of fiction I'm writing, it is a sign that I am identifying too closely with her. Just as I try to show my good and hide my bad, I am protecting this fictional person.

Recently I discovered a trick that helped me correct this. I was working with a character, Yolanda, a woman my age who ran a bookstore. Yolanda was nice. She was good. A nice good woman, and very bland. I couldn't get a grip on her or who she was. I went to my local swimming pool to do a few laps and take my mind off my troubles, when I saw a woman I'd seen many times before but don't know very well—a tall skinny woman with short elfin hair and wide-awake eyes. I decided to steal this woman's body and give it to Yolanda.

It worked miracles because now Yolanda was no longer me. She was this woman I didn't know very well. She began to exhibit all kinds of personality traits. She was allergic to almost everything and purchased her meals at the New Age Take-Out Kitchen. This explained why she was so thin. She spent lonely nights watching the families in the apartments across the street. The strange thing was that although Yolanda had many more weaknesses than she did before I discovered she wasn't me, I liked her better.

Another way to break the spell of the flawless character is to elicit the opinion of another character in the novel or story, one who dislikes, resents, or holds a grudge against the paragon of virtue. In *Second Sight,* I had a perfectly lovable older woman, Lavinia, who refused to believe that her philandering husband, Nestor, had left her for good. Instead of selling the house and investing the proceeds in order to live off the income, she managed on very little so that she could keep the house intact for Nestor's return.

Nestor (who had flaws to spare) had another version of the story. Lavinia's loyalty enraged him. He saw it as a ploy to make him feel guilty and remain tied to her. Indeed, at the end when Nestor asked Lavinia to take him back, Lavinia realized she no longer wanted to return to her old life with Nestor. She wondered if perhaps instead of being noble and true all those years, she hadn't actually been taking out a genteel and subtle revenge.

A character without flaws has nowhere to go. He can't change or grow. In Philip Roth's *The Counterlife,* the novelist Zuckerman, who used himself as a character in his books, was writing about his younger brother Henry. Because Zuckerman had given all the faults to himself-as-character, he had doomed his brother-as-character to a life of virtue. Henry had always been the good son, the good husband, father, dentist. Writing about Henry at thirty-nine, Zuckerman imagined him as the suffocating prisoner of his perfect but shallow life. The only way Henry could break the pattern was to escape altogether, leave his family and practice in New Jersey and begin anew in Israel. Zuckerman went to visit Henry in his kibbutz on the West Bank and found that his younger brother had simply exchanged one slavish system for another. He was still the good brother. He could change the scene, but he couldn't change himself because he was a character without flaws.

I realize I have been using the term "flaw" as if it could mean anything from nail-biting to one of the Seven Deadly Sins. I think of a flaw as a personality trait I wouldn't confess to, except on a dark and stormy night to a stranger passing through. And then there are the flaws we hide from ourselves, or lack the insight to see, but which help determine the course of our lives.

When I'm writing, the flaws that interest me are not the ones I assign ("Q kicks small dogs"), but those that emerge in the course of the story. Take Yolanda, who tries to be good, to be virtuous, to do no harm to others: I was amazed to discover, somewhere near the end of the first draft, that she had used someone, a man, a friend, to get over a wound suffered long ago, and in using him had hurt him. Yolanda didn't see how she could hurt this friend whom she considered much more powerful and attractive than she. The more I work on that novel, the more I see that Yolanda's major flaw is her modesty. She lets people down because she cannot conceive that she means as much to them as they do to her.

In *Second Sight,* the opposite was true: a character's flaw proved to be her saving grace. Delia, the widowed mother of a twelve-year-old son, lacked all marketable skills. She lived on welfare and whatever she could make telling fortunes over the phone. Everyone, but especially

177

Delia's career-minded sister Cass, faulted her for not taking her life in hand and finding a way out of the dead-end life of poverty she and her son had fallen into.

But Delia operated on another level from her more rational friends and relatives. She was watching for signs and portents, for signals that the time was right. She refused to force the unfolding of her life.

Delia did manage finally to bring about a change for herself and her son, to the amazement of the others, who began to see a glimmer of wisdom in her otherworldliness. Cass, however, could never accept that Delia's passivity had enabled her to recognize and receive love when it came her way. Cass would continue to take charge of her life, as Delia said, captaining it as if it were a ship, but never allowing for the influence of wind or tide or current.

People, fictional and real, are not perfect, like fresh-from-the-factory tables. They come with their faults built in, mingled and confused with their virtues. Whenever I find I am dealing with a character without flaws, and I am not intending a twentieth-century rewrite of *Billy Budd,* I take it as a sign that I have not done my work. I have not imagined my character fully, have not considered her through the eyes of the other characters. Finally, I have not cut the umbilical cord. I am protecting her, shielding her, and, at the same time, imprisoning her in her own virtue. It is time to let her go so she can fail and change and grow.

39

NAMES THAT FIT YOUR CHARACTERS

BY VEDA BOYD JONES

DO YOU WANT TO CREATE unforgettable characters? Give them unforgettable names—not unfamiliar names but those that fit your characters' personalities. Here are some ways to help you accomplish this
when you write your next piece of fiction. It may make the difference
between weak and convincing characterization.

1) Don't give different characters names that are similar or even start
with the same letter. If Vanessa, Valerie, and Viola are the names of
major female characters, readers will be confused. We don't pronounce
names as we read silently. After reading them the first few times, we
recognize them and continue down the page. If a reader has to go back
two pages to figure out who did what, the reader isn't going to finish the
story or book.

2) Don't use first and last names with the same number of syllables.
We can all think of celebrities with the same syllable names—Bob
Hope, Mae West, Johnny Carson, Engelbert Humperdinck. However,
these names are not very melodic. Varying the syllables can add a
poetic sound to your characters' names—Tom Sawyer, David Copperfield, Scarlett O'Hara, Winston Smith, Atticus Finch.

3) Match the name to the character's traits. Don't go for melodrama
and name the villain Mr. Doowrong, but give a strong character a strong
name, a weaker character a weaker name. Which is stronger—Rhett
Butler or Ashley Wilkes? The sounds suggest a sense of character. By
the same token, don't give a romance hero a "soft" name like Kenny,
which just doesn't have the strength of Colt or Taylor or Ben.

The connotation of a name should also match the character, so you
wouldn't give a nondescript or weak character a last name like Stone,
which certainly implies a hard, strong person, male or female. Conversely, don't give a strong person a last name like Willow, which is
wispy and delicate, and bends and bows.

4) When your main character bears a family name and his father also plays a major role in the story, give one of them a nickname. For example, if Warren Delderfield, Jr. is the stronger of the two, call him Warren and give his father a nickname or have him called by his middle name.

5) Be aware of changing fashion in names. Historical novels can have a Veronica or Beulah or Calvin or Oliver. A contemporary story would more likely have a Jennifer or Amy, Travis or Josh.

6) If your character comes from a foreign country, give him or her a name that at least indicates that general part of the world. If a character is French, however, you don't have to name him Pierre. Look in any name-your-baby book to find the country of origin.

Different sections of our country often use different types of names. For a story set in Tennessee, for example, you can throw in a Betty-Sue, Della Kay, Joe Bob, or other double names, but those names wouldn't be appropriate for a story set in Maine.

7) It is not necessary to name a minor character—for instance, a postman who may appear only once and have no relation to the other characters or to the story itself. It will only add clutter to the story to name him Mr. Wellington. Readers will try to remember that name, believing that if the person is important enough to be named, he will show up later in the story.

Will a badly named character keep your manuscript from selling? It's hard to say. Another writer received author copies of her story in a children's magazine and wailed, "They changed the name of the little boy! I named him after my friend."

Obviously the editor bought the story. She simply wielded her editorial privilege to edit, and the boy's name changed. Why? Maybe that name had been used in a story two issues before, or was it just because the editor didn't like the name?

So what's in a name? Quite a lot, actually. Give it some thought: Write a character profile, then see if your character will dictate his or her own name. At the very least, your character will veto certain names you may have chosen before you wrote the profile. Be sure the name fits.

40

MAKING YOUR READER FEEL: YOUR STORY'S HIDDEN POWER

BY MARION DANE BAUER

WHY DO PEOPLE, YOUNG OR OLD, read stories? For entertainment, for escape, to gather information about other people, places, cultures, times, to find meaning that can be applied to our own lives. These are the answers fiction writers give when I ask them why they read stories, why does anyone? But the most important reason for reading stories is seldom mentioned.

People read fiction in order to *feel,* to have strong feelings in a context of safety. The thrill of danger without the threat of harm. Cleansing tears, but without loss. Even laughter, dignity intact.

And you, the fiction writer, must be the one to satisfy this unarticulated but very real need in readers. How can you guarantee that will happen? Through the strong feelings of your central character, one who is individual, fully rounded, and involved in a conflict important to him or her.

Nothing could be more obvious than that the main character of your story must be an individual, not a mob. If you tell me that five hundred people were left homeless by the ravages of a hurricane, I will respond because my attention is caught by struggle, but my response will be abstract and brief. I don't know those people, and thus I don't feel their hurricane.

If you narrow that down to one victim of the storm, with a name and perhaps a face but without any emotional history, and if you tell me how she struggled against the hurricane, you will catch my attention on a deeper level. Human interest newspaper and television stories achieve that all the time. But you won't hold me for very long.

If, however, you go farther and let me know your character, her history and her hidden terrors, the hopes and dreams she brought into the confrontation with the hurricane, you will have not only my attention, but my empathy as well. You will be satisfying my deep need for safe, vicarious feeling.

Your story begins, then, with somebody who has a problem he must struggle to resolve or who wants something he must struggle to get. The somebody (character) and the struggle (plot) are inseparable. The problem doesn't have to be as large as a hurricane; in fact, it probably won't be life threatening in any way. Many of the most interesting story problems occur entirely on an inner, psychological level. But the key is, whatever the problem, it must be important to your main character. In other words, your main character must have strong feelings about the conflict he is involved in.

And in order to have strong feelings (and therefore to elicit strong feelings in the reader), your main character must *be* somebody. Stick figures evoke little emotion, no matter what contortions they go through. To elicit empathy, your character must give the illusion of being like us . . . complex, even contradictory, someone with preferences and prejudices, hopes and fears, someone with a history upon which the story is based.

How do you create such a person and bring your character to life? You begin with the richest and most mysterious source of all . . . yourself.

Your self-knowledge will be your primary source for every character, particularly every central, perceiving character you create. If you are going to write a story from the perspective of a murderer, you must look into yourself and find that place where you, too, given the right personal history or circumstances, could be capable of murder. To write about greed or fear, passion or loss, you must first touch those qualities in yourself.

You may find that the deepest feelings, the ones that set off your strongest stories, are the ones you yourself don't yet understand. That is often the case for me. And in fact, I decide which story I am going to write, which character I am going to explore, far more on the basis of what I *feel* when I am sifting through story ideas than on what I *understand* about my reasons for responding to one idea over another.

The most important question I find I must answer is not, why do I care? Rather it is, do I care passionately enough to continue exploring this character and her problem for the months or even years it will take me to complete the novel? My strong feelings will not only hold me throughout the story, but they will, ultimately, give me an opportunity to draw an emotional response from the reader. Lack of such feelings in me will leave my main character—and consequently my reader—emotionally flat.

However, while your own feelings are the richest resource you have for creating good fiction, your feelings alone will not be enough to guarantee a reader's response. In fact, the strength of your own emotion, if you are too close to it as you write, can keep you from knowing whether you are touching the reader or not. Good fiction, fiction capable of drawing response from the reader, is neither a therapeutic exercise for the writer nor a vehicle for emotional flashing. And it is the hard lessons of craft that can keep it from being either.

The core of your character's struggle will come out of the mysterious jumble of your own psyche, that place where you yourself may still be struggling in your own life. But you will need to assemble the flesh and bones from the most accessible regions of your imagination.

First, begin, very consciously, to distance your main character from yourself. Preserve the core of feeling related to your central story problem, but give your character a history, or pieces of a history, different from your own. Change the gender or create life circumstances for your character that separate her from you. Make him much older or younger than you are or modify the superficial manifestations of the problem he faces. If you are, for instance, drawing energy for a story from a long-standing battle you have had with a childhood friend, alter the conflict so that it is with a sister or change the occasion for it entirely, while retaining the feelings the conflict generates in you.

How much distance you will need will depend upon many factors, one of which is how vulnerable you feel to the story issue you have taken on, how much distance you have already established within yourself. I have found that the more crucial the issues are to me, the more distance I need, and some distancing mechanisms give me more freedom and perspective than others. Sometimes I can give myself the most freedom of all by making my perceiving character male (since I am female); two of my strongest novels are perceived through the eyes of a young boy.

Most writers' first work of fiction is intensely and sometimes even embarrassingly autobiographical, which is natural enough. But few first stories are published, because there is a kind of blindness in most autobiography, a self-indulgence, that fails entirely to evoke reader response. The more I write, the deeper I reach into my own core to locate the energy for my stories, but the smaller are the fragments of my own life or history that make their way onto the page.

The first question I am usually asked by my readers, young or old, is, did that really happen? And the fact is that only one of my books, *On My Honor,* is based on an actual event—and that even occurred to a childhood friend of mine, not to me. *On My Honor* is the story of two boys who go swimming in a forbidden river, and one of them drowns. The boy who is left is so terrified and feels so guilty, knowing he was doing something he wasn't supposed to do, that he goes home after the accident and tells no one of the other boy's death. The last half of the book involves the working out of his guilt as the survivor.

The remembered incident began to work in me as a story for reasons I don't fully understand. I know only that I have a strong emotional response to the issue of survivor guilt that made the story *feel* important to me. I could easily have created the incident itself, because none of it came from my own experience. I had never gone swimming in that river or been involved in a serious accident or witnessed a death. I had to imagine my way into my main character's thoughts and feelings. And in order to do that, I reached deeply into that place in myself where my own unexplained survivor guilt resides, and used it to bring to life a character created from my imagination. (No, I did not try to reproduce the boy actually involved in the original incident, because his reality would have gotten in the way of my attempt to inhabit him with my own feelings.)

But I don't always find that core immediately. Sometimes my early ideas of a character are all surface, and sometimes they remain surface through the first, or even several, drafts. That happened with Steve, the main character in my novel *Rain of Fire*. After about the third draft a friend read the manuscript and told me that by the end of the story she liked Celestino, the story's villain, better than she liked Steve. Naturally, I sat down to figure out where I had gone wrong.

What I discovered was that I had given Steve a lot of my own life's surfaces, more than usual, in fact, because I had put him in my own childhood setting and time. But perhaps because he was the first male I had used as a central character, he shared none of my inner reality. Knowing that I needed to give him some of my own substance, I decided to make him a liar. Not a vicious liar, but the liar every storyteller is, the kind for whom a good story, any good story, can be far more attractive than mere truth. And once I invested that emotional part of myself in my character, Steve sprang to life.

The difference between melodrama, which brings amused tolerance, embarrassment or even disdain, and drama, which the reader feels, is not mysterious at all. If the action of your story is imposed upon flat figures, you will have melodrama. If it rises out of grounded, believable, complex characters, characters whom you both feel and stand apart from, you will have drama. You will have a story that lives, that produces the purging of pity and fear which Aristotle spoke of.

If you want your readers to feel—and if you want them to read, you must want them to feel—start with what you yourself feel most strongly. But don't end there. Shape and control and distance your feelings through craft. Work with them as though they were diamonds to be mined and cut—which is exactly what they are. And if you do this, your readers will give you the greatest compliment of all. They will tell you that your story made them laugh or cry or shiver with terror or sigh with relief.

And you will have readers—first, that most important of readers, an editor—who will be waiting anxiously for your next story.

SPECIALIZED FICTION

41

Having Something to Say

By Patricia D. Cornwell

I REMEMBER TAKING LITERATURE AND CREATIVE WRITING CLASSES AT Davidson College in North Carolina and being struck by a frustrating dilemma. It seemed that the best stories were told by the worst writers and the best writers had nothing to say. I have decided by now that this is a common problem, if not THE problem.

The sad reality is, talent does count. You cannot muscle your way to the top simply by doing enough research and spending twelve hours a day in your office. An example is my tennis ability. My pipe dream when I was a child was to play at Forest Hills. I practiced six hours a day, watched matches on TV, and kept *The Inner Game of Tennis* on the table by my bed. The highest I was ever ranked, I think, was fourteenth in North Carolina. The only way I was ever going to make it to Forest Hills was to sit in the stands.

Though you can improve your writing skills, just as you can improve your tennis skills, you cannot learn the inner poetry and descriptive brilliance that extraordinarily gifted writers seem to conjure up without trying. But instead of dwelling on the unsurprising revelation that few of us are geniuses, I'd rather assume that most of us fall into the category of the *good writer who has nothing to say.*

Your voice

I decided to write crime novels not because I liked to read them but because I had been a crime reporter for *The Charlotte Observer*. Beyond that, I cannot fully explain my fascination with violence, but I suspect it has to do with my fear of it.

In my college days, I think I imitated whomever I was reading at the time. This is fine when you are in your formative stages as a writer. But in order for you to write successfully, you must discover your voice and your story. Your voice is what you sound like when you no longer are consciously trying to imitate someone else. Perhaps your voice is dry and quite funny, like Sue Grafton's. Or it may be melancholy and richly poetic, like Pat Conroy's. When you really tap into your own voice, you are discovering a layer of yourself that is not necessarily apparent in the personality other people see when they meet you. For example, my writing is dark, filled with nightscapes and fear. Isolation and a sense of loss whisper throughout my prose like something perpetually stirring in the wind. It is not uncommon for people to meet me and find it incongruous that I write the sort of books I do.

Finding your voice requires endless writing, and you may discover your voice at the same time you discover your story.

Your story

What draws you in? When you read the newspaper in the morning, what do you look at first? Sports, comics, crime stories, or politics? My eye has always caught crime stories first, and that's been true for as long as I can remember. Ask yourself other questions, as well. Or maybe you already know your story. Maybe you're a lawyer like Scott Turow or know as much about horse racing as Dick Francis. Maybe you fought in Vietnam or work in law enforcement. Maybe your life has been a series of tragic romances—or no romances—and that's the song you want to sing.

Whatever your story is, if you write enough, certain themes will reappear. Watch for them. Don't be afraid to face them. Writing is an intensely psychological experience, or it should be, and the words don't have to be born of wounds, but they might be. My story is violence. I finally figured that out after years of failed manuscripts. My story is people who carry on in a world that is hard and cold and sharp around the edges. My story is not Southern or "clever" or derivative. It is an eyewitness account, the framework starkly wrought from what I see, the flesh and soul nurtured by my own experience and personality. I've done and continue to do a lot of research. Could I redesign my life, I would have been a chief medical examiner with a law degree who somehow found time to write novels featuring a chief medical examiner with a law degree. Then I would have discovered that my true gift was writing and could have lived off my intellectual investments for the rest of my literary life. But had I been a forensic pathologist with a law degree, I would have been far too busy and burned out to feel creative after hours. The truth is, I am a former journalist who majored in English in college. I hated chemistry and math, did not want to touch a computer, and was indifferent toward biology. By the time I was twenty-five I'd never been to a funeral because I was afraid of death.

I began work on my first murder mystery in the fall of 1984. A physician I knew recommended that I interview a medical examiner since forensic medicine is so important in modern criminal investigation. I was fortunate enough to get an appointment at the Office of the Chief Medical Examiner in Richmond, Virginia. I spent three hours talking with Dr. Marcella Fierro, the deputy chief. I was utterly fascinated, and I was horrified by how ignorant I was. I thought, "How can you write crime novels when you don't even understand what these people are talking about?"

I began to discover that subjects I had fled from in college not only fascinated me now, but I had an aptitude for them. Without realizing it, I had just embarked upon a grim and peculiar journey that, oddly, would lead me to my voice and story.

Authentic credibility

If you are interested in a particular field or intend to address a particular subject, you must learn something about it. Being a master at stringing words together or describing sunsets is not enough. If your story lacks credibility and authenticity, no one will care how exquisite your metaphors are.

For example, if your knowledge of journalism is limited to what you read in the paper or see in movies, don't decide to create a protagonist who is a journalist. Or if you do, start educating yourself. Get someone to introduce you to a journalist. Ask him if you can ride with him on his beat one day. Or see if you can do any sort of volunteer work in the newsroom on your day off from your regular profession.

For me, it is essential to experience directly what I'm writing about (within reason). I want to know what it looks like, feels like, smells like, sounds like. Writers are pests. We drive everybody crazy with our cries for help when we're getting started, and I've decided that you might just get what you want if you abandon any notion of entitlement. Don't think some harried reporter is going to be thrilled about having you ride shotgun while he rushes around on his beat. A lot of cops or other experts would get tired of you, too. Forget a medical examiner warming up to the idea of your hanging around the morgue. If you're determined to master a subject, apply the same rules that work in good business: You give me something, I give you something.

What would you like to master? Is there something you can do to help? Let's say you want to create a protagonist who is a gardener, yet you live in a fourteenth-story apartment in Manhattan. Find a greenhouse and go to work or volunteer. Expose yourself, somehow, to whatever it is you wish to understand. But never forget—if you want, you also must give. The irony is that when you're P. D. James, everybody wants you doing research at their facility when you no longer need it. When you're just getting started, you have to pay your dues because nobody cares.

I wanted to understand police work better, so I signed on as a volunteer police officer in Richmond City. I dressed in uniform. I took dog bite reports, directed traffic, and worked parades. I gave the city hundreds of hours of my time, but I got something extremely valuable in return. I know how to drive an unmarked car, get free coffee at 7-Elevens, talk on the radio and light flares. I've been to numerous homicide scenes and I know homicide detectives because I've ridden with them on their four to midnight shifts more times than I can count.

I know how Pete Marino, the homicide detective in my series, thinks. To learn how Dr. Scarpetta thinks, I went to work for the medical examiners. At first I assisted in technical writing. Eventually, I became their computer analyst. Though I work only as a consultant for them now, I was down there constantly for more than six years. I would place myself on the extreme end of the spectrum. Not everyone could or would throw himself into research to this extent. Most writers have other professions. Moderation for all things, but if you have a passion for westerns, at least go ride a horse.

Seeking advice
In the early days, I used to have friends read chapters as I wrote them. I wrote letters to P. D. James. I did everything most fledgling writers do, and now I know why. I thought I wanted advice. What I really wanted was assurance. What I got was a lot of confusion.

If it works better for you to discuss constantly a current project with someone, then do it. I can't. If meeting with groups of aspiring writers and commiserating and sharing ideas works for you, do it. I can't. In the first place, I feel that my ideas are private. I'm not going to tell you about this great plot I've devised. That places a burden on you to keep my secret, and the more I talk about my great plot, the more I relieve the tension necessary to drive me into my office. I have about concluded that the more someone talks about a book, the less he's working on it.

Writing is solitary. You can't write unless you are willing to spend a lot of time alone. I'm not saying you should never meet with groups or go to conventions. Much depends on your personality type. Some writers like crowds and derive much from panel discussions. Others, like me, choose to confide in a friend, but in the main, figure it out on their own. I believe trial and error is the best teacher, and that you can learn most about what makes a novel or story work by reading the best authors.

$\S$ 42

LIVING WITH SERIES CHARACTERS

BY JAMES MELVILLE

WHEN I DECIDED SOME FIFTEEN YEARS AGO to send Superintendent Tetsuo Otani to investigate reports of odd goings-on at a Buddhist temple in an out-of-the-way part of Hyogo prefecture in western Japan, I never supposed that he, his wife Hanae, and Inspectors "Ninja" Noguchi and Jiro Kimura would still be the daily companions of my imagination today. That much may easily be inferred by anyone who glances through *The Wages of Zen,* which was published in 1979. In that first book, I made two thumping mistakes that could serve as awful warnings to any writer creating a character who might develop a will of his or her own and refuse to fade away after the words "The End" are typed.

First, I made Otani much too old for his and my own good, by suggesting that he was approaching retirement age. Worse, I fixed him in historical time by stating that he had seen brief service in the Imperial Japanese Navy as a very young and junior intelligence officer at the end of World War II. Assuming therefore that he was 19 years old in 1945, Tetsuo Otani was well into his fifties when he made his debut, an age when senior Japanese police officers do as a matter of fact retire. Moral: If you want to begin a series without making trouble for yourself, either create a young hero or heroine with reasonable career prospects, or avoid being too specific about dates.

My problem was that in addition to writing my first murder mystery, I wanted to describe and try to communicate to fellow westerners some of my own fascination with various aspects of Japanese society and culture as they were when I encountered them during the sixties, when I lived for seven years in Kyoto. Moreover, I've been trying in an amateurish sort of way to record the changing face of modern Japan ever since. Well and good: All the pundits agree that one should write about what one knows, but it does mean that Otani has had to age to the point at which he's distinctly long in the tooth for a working police officer.

Needless to say, there are plenty of detective Methuselahs in the mystery field, compared with whom Otani is a mere stripling. Already retired from the Belgian police when first sighted, Poirot must have been nudging his centennial by the time Agatha Christie eventually pulled the plug on him. The great Nero Wolfe was a game old survivor, too, while (admittedly at the hands of Hollywood writers) Sherlock Holmes himself was still going strong in the mid-nineteen-forties, nearly sixty years after he first captivated Victorian readers.

There's no point in getting upset about this. I can testify from personal experience that mystery fans and even critics are tolerant souls, more than willing to suspend their disbelief and grant generous extra time to characters they approve of. My novels have sometimes been praised and sometimes panned, but no reviewer has complained that both Otani and Noguchi should have been pensioned off by now, or that the indefatigably randy Kimura really can't go on being a playboy for much longer. I'm not about to tempt providence, but there may perhaps be just a little life still left in my team.

Certainly I have no intention of killing any of them, as Conan Doyle killed Sherlock Holmes, and Nicholas Freeling terminated Van der Valk. Look what happened to them: Both characters demanded to be resuscitated. Besides, I'm much too fond of Otani & Co. to see any of the inner circle off, even though the Chief is becoming more and more crusty and contrary as we grow old together.

Like any other long-term relationship, the one between a durable fictional character and his creator has its ups and downs, and any author contemplating putting one or more into several books needs to be aware of the delights and pitfalls ahead. As it seems to me, these balance out pretty evenly. First, I'll consider the advantages for the author.

The first and most important of these from the severely practical point of view is that publishers of mysteries and thrillers like series characters. All other things being equal, they are more likely to accept a first novel featuring a strong central character if there is the prospect of more appearances to come. In my own case, it was made clear to me (with urbane, iron-hand-in-velvet-glove courtesy) that *The Wages of Zen* would be accepted for publication only on the understanding that

Otani would take center stage in at least three further books. After all these years, I still sometimes break out into a cold sweat when I remember my euphoria as I accepted the obligation, and the pure panic that supervened an hour later when the cold reality of what I'd let myself in for dawned on me. In the event I instinctively adapted the excellent advice given to alcoholics, by persuading myself that I could surely write *one* more book, and then perhaps one after that . . . and who knows how many more?

Readers of crime fiction like series characters, too. At least, I do, and I think I belong to the majority. We enjoy a judicious mixture of the familiar and the unfamiliar. I sigh with pleasure every time Nero Wolfe opens his pre-prandial bottle of beer after coming down from his morning session in the plant rooms, and I settle back with satisfaction when Perry Mason lumbers to his feet and starts working his courtroom magic for the umpteenth time. Such repetitive formulae, like the much-loved catch-phrases of an established comic, would, however, soon stale if new material weren't also forthcoming every time.

The most successful serial characters are people with whom a majority of readers can in some respect or degree identify; and that means they must be fallible and imperfect. Even Sherlock Holmes was a delightfully *flawed* superman, after all. His weaknesses were appealingly human (and we must remember that in Victorian times the drug habit that would damn him nowadays was viewed rather differently). The writer who creates a paragon as a serial character will soon find that there's no scope for development as book follows book. The protagonist who is exactly the same in the fourth novel as the first is going to disappoint readers. He or she must be seen to change and grow, to face dilemmas, problems, frustrations, and temptations that we can imagine cropping up in our own lives. In short, the series character must be credible and command both sympathy and a degree of affection; which also means that a character can be moderately naughty and self-indulgent, but shouldn't be in thrall to any wildly aberrant vices.

A well-established series character offers both opportunity and challenge to an author. When I embark on a new Otani book, it is often on the basis of a newspaper cutting sent to me by one of a number of kindly friends in Japan. Not always: My novel *The Bogus Buddha* had its origins in an eye-catching headline in the London *Financial Times*. "Japanese Fund Manager Buried in Concrete," it announced baldly, and I immediately asked myself how Otani and his associates would cope with that. Because I now know them so well, after a comparatively short period of reflection I had the basis of a plot to work on. My regular characters, therefore, act as pegs for me to hang ideas on; between books they are always there in the wings, made up and in costume, waiting patiently to walk on. However, I would stress again that, while many a well-loved film or stage actor can get away with playing himself or herself over and over again, when it comes to crafting a novel, a writer should try to keep his characters moving and show new sides to them from time to time.

Thus, Otani has from the outset been a Rotarian and a mystery fan, but only after several years did I discover that he is really quite serious about *bonsai,* or that he has an unlikely crony in the person of a trendy author and TV personality. Hanae and he have become grandparents, and their daughter Akiko has had quite an eventful married life. I often fill in details of my characters' biographies by references to past events, and one recent book *(A Haiku for Hanae)* is based on an account of a twenty-year-old case.

At this point, a little more needs to be said about conveying information in novels whose principal purpose is to entertain. In my capacity as a reviewer, all too often I come across authors who undoubtedly write about what they know, but who lecture me. Their narratives frequently grind to a shuddering halt while they supply great blocks of unadulterated information. Professional journalists trying their hands at thriller writing are particularly liable to offend in this way, and it simply won't do. Any passage that doesn't either help the story along or serve to round out a character should be excised ruthlessly. The reader should ingest information almost unconsciously *while* enjoying the story.

I was faced with a particular problem in this context while writing *A Haiku for Hanae,* and anyone who wants to decide whether or not I managed to solve it should read the chapter in which Otani calls on the eccentric lawyer Mori. I might want to use Mori again in another book, because it goes without saying that minor series characters can come and go. I was rather sorry to part with the chilly martinet Inspector Sakamoto at the end of *The Death Ceremony,* but his erudite successor Inspector Hara is fun to work with. Another occasional character, Hanae's formidable sister Michiko Yanagida, seems to be demanding a

194

lot more of the limelight these days, while I'm expecting great things of female detective Junko Migishima.

If a series is to be successful over a long period, the right ratio of familiarity to novelty must be achieved with reasonable consistency. One must always respect readers and never take their good will or loyalty for granted. Above all, therefore, the author must be ever alert for signs of boredom or listlessness in himself. If and when they are manifest, it's time to think seriously about abandoning a series or at least trying something completely different for a while in order to put a bit of fizz back into the creative juices; because if the author's bored you can bet your life his readers will be. I've taken time off from Otani to write two political thrillers (*The Imperial Way* and *A Tarnished Phoenix*), and an invitation to write three new lighthearted Miss Seeton tales around some of the late Heron Carvic's English village cozy characters was very welcome. I enjoyed being "Hampton Charles" for a year or so, and while I'm currently once more mentally in Japan, I won't necessarily stay there.

43

Horror Fiction: Time for Some New-Fangled Fangs

By Graham Masterton

ABOUT SIX OR SEVEN YEARS AGO, horror started to become a very popular genre for new, young authors just starting out on a writing career.

This was partly because of the huge and obvious success of Stephen King, and partly because a new young generation of writers was coming of age, a generation brought up on horror comics, TV's *Twilight Zone,* and even books by me. They had a comprehensive reading background and a natural interest in horror.

But it was also because the horror market was rapidly expanding. Publishers were demanding more and more horror titles, and quite simply it was easier for a new writer to get his or her work published in the horror genre than almost any other.

So long as the fiction market in general and the horror genre in particular were expanding, this was fine, and in those six or seven years, many excellent new authors found their way into print. Only a couple of years ago, almost every major publisher had a horror list, and in almost every case that I know of, that list was administered by a young, enthusiastic, and dedicated editor. It was New Author Heaven.

But when recession struck the publishing industry, those horror lists were among the first casualties. Within a dramatically short space of time, opportunities for new horror writers have been considerably reduced, and it is now much harder for a new horror writer to get started in the genre, harder . . . but by no means impossible. More demanding, yes . . . but *because* it's more demanding, much more rewarding, too.

In fact, I can let you into a secret: If you have real faith in your writing skill and a deep and genuine interest in the development of yourself as a horror writer and horror fiction in general, it may even be a *better* time than ever before. But, you must be prepared to accept the challenge of a much tougher market, and be prepared to commit yourself to a considerable amount of preparation, writing, rewriting, and polishing. More than anything else, though, you must be prepared to stretch your imagination to the utmost. To succeed in horror fiction today, you must not only write skillfully, but you must come up with some *very* new ideas.

If you can invent a totally novel and unexpected terror, and present it with style and quality, then you have the chance not only of breaking into the horror market, but breaking into it at a time when it is much less flooded with other horror books . . . giving *your* book a better chance of standing out.

If there was ever a chance of your becoming the next Stephen King, it's now.

You see, one of the effects of a quickly expanding market was that publishers tended to bring out far too much category horror, much of it deficient in invention and quality of writing. Even some of the very best horror writers seemed to run short of new ideas and began to regurgitate themes that had lost much of their surprise, their shock value . . . and thus all of their *terror,* too.

Quite apart from the problems of recession, horror fiction began to show signs of creative exhaustion, the same kind of tiredness that, thirty years ago, affected the western. In particular, many leading writers seemed to forget that readers buy horror to be scared half to death and started to indulge in political and philosophical waffle along with the horror. There's nobody like a well-established horror writer for indulging in political and philosophical waffle.

An infallible sign of literary arthritis in *any* genre is when the books start getting thicker and thicker and thicker . . . as if length and verbosity can somehow make up for a fundamentally thin idea.

Publishers frequently send me new horror manuscripts to read, for the purpose of giving endorsements. In the past two years, I have seen nothing but the old, old stories. Vampires, werewolves. More vampires, more werewolves. Mutant babies. Children with unusual psychic powers. Children with *usual* psychic powers. *Exorcist III* asks, "Dare you climb these steps again?" and the answer is yes, we dare, but who cares? We know what's up there and it doesn't frighten us any more.

Even the recent books by the market leader, Stephen King (*The Dark Half* and *Misery*) have, quite simply, lost their power to scare. Whereas, after rereading some of *'Salem's Lot* the other day, I still believe that it's frightening.

Clive Barker has become (by his own admission) more of a "fantasist" than a horror writer and the splatter-punk brigade (John Skipp and Craig Spector) are straining harder to think of new ways of being disgusting, to the point where the suspension of disbelief becomes stretched beyond breaking-point. A novel that you can't believe in is no longer frightening, by definition.

So what is a new horror writer supposed to do? He or she is faced with the very difficult task of creating a story that goes beyond the bounds of acceptable taste, as well as, with the seemingly impossible task of creating a totally new terror—totally new, but believable, too.

How can this be done? Well, in my opinion, by rethinking the entire framework of modern horror fiction, by rejecting the patterns and devices and themes developed over the past two decades by Stephen King and John Farris and Rick McCammon (*They Thirst,* et al.) and, yes, by me, too. The way I see it, the future of modern horror fiction lies in far greater believability, and in the development of stories that are far less gimmicky and outré—stories that come closer to the quirks of real human psychology.

Stories, too, that are well-written, soundly constructed, and obey the fundamental principles of good novel-craft. That is: that they have engaging and three-dimensional characters, an interesting and credible setting, a strong forward movement, a heart-clutching beginning, a sound middle, and a huge mind-expanding climax. Easy, *ja?*

We have all tried to stretch the boundaries of the supernatural as far as we can. One of the most implausible stories that I recently attempted was *Walkers,* a novel in which the inmates of an asylum for the dangerously insane had escaped from captivity by disappearing into the walls. They traveled *inside* the bricks and out through the ground, and made good their getaway.

Of course, the basic notion of *Walkers* was utterly wacky. We all know Newton's Law that two objects cannot occupy the same space at the same time, which is one of the reasons that we have traffic accidents and bump into other shoppers in the supermarket. But I worked hard to develop a locale and an atmosphere that would make the reader want to believe that such a thing *could* happen. And that's the difference: *want* to believe.

It's comparatively easy to create a horror scenario in which the reader *doesn't* want to believe that such hideous events can take place. But it requires much more skill and much more thought to create a horror scenario in which the reader is actually working *with* you, rather than against you, a horror scenario in which the reader actively helps you to frighten them.

Enlisting the reader's support requires acute observation, writing discipline, and a strong empathy with other people's feelings. It requires not only believability, but a certain degree of *likability*. Your characters have to be not only real people, but *enjoyable* real people, people your readers wish they could spend some time with, whether they get involved in the Horror Beyond The Grave or not.

It also requires a fast, strongly constructed plot; a plot that trots; a plot that never allows your reader to get ahead of it. Sometimes, if your characters are really strong, you can get away with a certain amount of predictability. But you shouldn't take the risk. A horror novel should be a novel of sudden shocks and surprises, right to the end. It's better to make an unexpected change in your story line (unexpected even for *you*, the author) than allow your reader to guess what's going to happen next. The worst response a horror writer can hear is "I *knew* that would happen."

So let's take a look at all the demands that I've made. First, you need a startling new premise: an idea that's fundamentally frightening, but which nobody has ever thought of before. Here's a paragraph from *Walkers* that might give you a taste:

A little farther away, a *face* had emerged from the floor, too. A man's face, with a heavy forehead and a strong jaw, and a fixed triumphant grin. It looked as if it had been smothered in dry cement. There were powdery wrinkles and cracks around its mouth. Its eye sockets were totally black—*black,* like night, no whites at all, as if the inside of its head were empty. But it was alive, there was no question about that. It had risen straight out of the concrete floor, in the way that a swimmer emerges from the dust-covered surface of a lake.

It was alive and it was grinning at him and it was gleefully trying to drag him under the surface of the concrete, too.

No vampires, no werewolves. Something different. But something that can appear at any moment and threaten your hero or heroine with total fear.

It can be very fruitful to delve into occult archives to learn what demons and devils and odd monsters frightened people in the past. Many of the olden-day demons were created out of very strong and primitive fears—fears to which people can still be remarkably sensitive, even today. I used legendary Red Indian demons in *The Manitou* and *Charnel House*; Mexican demons in *The Pariah*; and stories about the real Scottish witch Isabel Gowdie in the third and last of my Night Warriors triology *Night Plague*. I altered many of the mythical details of their malevolent powers in order to suit my stories, and in some cases I changed their names. But they were all characterized by their elemental threat to human stability and human security; and this elemental threat was worth analyzing and translating into modern terms.

Demons and ghouls were created by the earliest storytellers as a way of giving shape and meaning to their most deeply seated anxieties and superstitions. Because they were the imaginary embodiment of such very basic terrors as fear of the dark, fear of inanimate objects changing into vicious creatures, fear of one's own reflection in a mirror, fear of children, they have a lasting potency that you can adapt and exploit, even today. Alternatively, you can use a modern artifact as a demon: a car *(Christine)* or a motorcycle, or a building, or a subway train. But I must warn you: Demonic possession of inanimate objects recently reached a nadir with a British horror-flick entitled *I Bought A Vampire Motorcycle,* and you will probably find it hard to have any similar ideas taken seriously after that.

Personally, I believe that a strong social theme has always been essential to a good horror novel (though beware waffle). In *The Burning,* a novel of fiery reincarnation, I attempted to deal with the issues of materialism, prejudice, and personal responsibility. So my characters had to deal with their own conscience and their own part in a larger society, as well as with horrific and supernatural terrors.

In his interview for horror-anthologist Stanley Wiater's collection of interviews, *Dark Dreamers,* David Morrell (author of *Rambo*) very correctly said that "when you're talking about a breakthrough book, it's not so much the field you're working in, it's the 'canvas.' I hate to use that overworked word, but it's one we all understand. The scope and breadth of a book."

He added (and I really can't put it better): "Most horror novels tend to be inbred: They rely on the ideas and concepts of others who have gone before them. Of course, a horror writer must be aware of the history of the genre. But to sell a lot of copies, a horror writer also has to find a large idea and head toward uncharted territory, announcing, in effect, that this book is *different* from other horror fiction."

The challenge to new horror writers is enormous. But it's a challenge that you *must* address if you're going to make your mark. When I wrote *The Manitou* in 1974, the horror market was Dennis Wheatley and me. Jim Herbert hadn't yet written *The Rats*; and Stephen King was unheard of. But now, many years later, a whole new generation of writers has emerged who were brought up on King and Straub and McCammon and me . . . and instead of being a field of four or five horror writers, as it was then, it's literally a field of thousands.

The next Stephen King will have to be a writer so innovative and striking that his (or her) talent spans many fields of thought and social relevance and be twenty times better than Stephen King—much more stunning than *'Salem's Lot* ever was. I really can't wait for this to emerge. That new writer could be you.

I discussed the necessity for characters who are both likable and real. The problem with many horror manuscripts that I've read recently is that the hero or heroines have been weak or corrupt or plain obnoxious or (even worse) unbelievable. I can understand why horror writers bring such characters into their stories. They have difficulty in dealing with the extremity of the threat their characters have to face. They don't attempt to imagine *how it actually feels* to witness a loved one having her head cut off in front of them, or *how it actually feels* to see a roaring demon emerging from their root-cellar.

Just because their fictitious threats are wild and imaginary doesn't mean that their characters should be wild and imaginary. In fact, totally the opposite. The more real the characters' response, the more frightening the threat turns out to be.

I can understand that, nervous of failure, many writers try to distance themselves from the raw emotions that any horrific or supernatural crisis would evoke. Have you ever witnessed a serious traffic accident? Have you tried to describe how you really felt about it? You should recognize that a horror novel will work well only if the characters react in a credible, true-to-life manner. So many horror movies flop because teenage girls keep screaming whenever a monster appears. Watch the newsreels. Watch the way people really behave when they're desperately frightened. They don't scream. The way they really act is far more disturbing than the way so many writers make their characters act.

The characters in a horror novel should be as detailed and believable as the characters in any other novel. I've read so many horror novels in which the protagonists have no parents, no wives, no children, no job, even. They seem to be rootless, floating dummies, just waiting to have something Horrible inflicted on them. Just remember: Their *raison d'être* isn't to be victims in your novel; they have their own *raison d'être*. And if you have a struggle making them believe in your horrific threat, and in making them respond to it, then so much the better. You will end up with a far more convincing story.

Make sure that even your minor characters are real. Bob Tuggey, a McDonald's grillman who witnesses the first ghastly immolation in *The Burning,* was described in three dimensions, even though his part in the novel was comparatively small:

. . .balding and overweight and by far the oldest employee at McDonald's Rosecrans Street. When his left eye looked west, his right eye looked nor-norwest. . . . He had drifted through one menial government clerkship after another, black coffee, brown offices. He had started to drink, a bottle of Ricard a day, often more. Days of milk-white clouds and aniseed.

Make sure that your locations are real. Choose somewhere you know, or visit somewhere specially. I set *Walkers* in Milwaukee, which is an energetic city of varied weather and distinctive character, but which also suited the blue-coller personality of the hero. In contrast, I set *The Burning* in La Jolla, which was a perfect setting for the fashionable upwardly mobile restaurant owner who was the protagonist of *that* novel. Each setting in its own way was fascinating to discover and describe, and added to the depth of the novel.

Out of a strong combination of believability and daring imagination, I believe the next generation of horror fiction will eventually be born. The challenge is enormous; the creative task is very great. However, I am looking forward with considerable relish to the day when the advance manuscript arrives through the mail that will tell me somebody has given horror fiction the sharp new teeth it needs.

202

44

WRITING THE HISTORICAL NOVEL

BY JANICE YOUNG BROOKS

SOMERSET MAUGHAM IS SUPPOSED TO HAVE SAID, "There are three rules for writing a novel; unfortunately, no one knows what they are." Well, I think there's one primary rule for historical novels and about 119 other rules that need to be broken as often as they're observed.

The one rule is this: The historical novel must be first, last, and throughout, A GOOD NOVEL.

That sounds obvious, but historical novels present a special challenge. They have two plots: the what-really-happened plot and the plot that comes from your imagination. If your plot cannot be interwoven with historical reality and still remain the primary focus, you don't have a novel; you have a history book with fictional flourishes. Think about *Gone With the Wind*. It is *not* a story about the Civil War. It's a novel about a fascinating woman and the man she loves and eventually loses. It happens to take place during the Civil War, but it is *about* Scarlett and Rhett.

I speak from experience. My first book was about the War of the Roses. I had a good story, good characters, and an excellent romantic conflict, but I didn't keep all of that center front because I also had a huge amount of research about the period that I couldn't resist using. The result was boring. Only rarely did the characters manage to break free of all those facts and do something on their own.

How do you avoid the problem? Start with people in conflict. Don't even consider the setting until you know what they're like and what their problem is. My novel *Glory* was a good example. I've always loved *The Rainmaker* story: the uptight old maid who meets and falls in love with an outrageous, flamboyant man who opens her eyes. But in *The Rainmaker*, Lizzie stays at home when forced to choose between following him into the unknown and sticking with the boy next door. But what if Lizzie had changed her mind the next day? Every time I watch the movie and Burt Lancaster says, "Are ya coming with me, Lizzie?" I wonder what he'd do if she said, "Well, yes, I guess so." That was the premise of the story I wanted to write: The Lizzie-type character takes off after him, burning all her bridges, and when she catches up with him, she finds out that he didn't really want her to. At that point, I started thinking, *where* and *when?* I knew I wanted her to catch up with him in some remote spot, so she couldn't just get her feelings hurt and get the next bus home as soon as she discovered the truth.

I wanted to draw on my long-time interest in the Yukon Gold Rush, but all I knew about it was that it took place sometime in the 1800s; that it was cold, involved a lot of real eccentrics, and that eggs cost a dollar apiece. But that was all I needed to be sure the Yukon was where I wanted my heroine to follow the hero. The library supplied everything else—later.

How do you decide when and where to set your novel if you have a mishmash of information about the Yukon Gold Rush in the back of your mind? My advice may seem strange: Pick a time and place you know nothing about. There are two good reasons for this: First, if you choose a place you've studied all your life, your perspective will be far too detailed and/or academic. The temptation to put it all into your story will be overwhelming. But if you choose a place totally unfamiliar to you, certain facts and events will leap out of your research and make you think, "Isn't this fascinating!" Those are exactly the facts that will interest your reader, too. Trust your instinct. Before you start to write, you will, of course, come to know a great deal more about your subject than you need, but your fresh-eyed "Isn't that fascinating" attitude will come across to your readers.

Setting is important. Getting the feel of a different time and place into your novel is the reason you write and others read historical novels. But it mustn't be taken too far. Think of your historical setting as a stage set. It must be appropriate; it must be interesting, but it can't be so elaborate or colorful that readers are distracted by it.

There's another aspect to setting that relates to marketing. If you try to get an edge by coming up with a time and place never used before, you may well find that there's a good reason it hasn't been done before: (1) There's not enough information about it to give you the kind of facts you need. (2) Its culture is so far removed from ours that a realistic treatment would be incomprehensible or distasteful to today's readers. Or (3) it's just plain boring. Some things are.

All right. You've got your characters, conflict, time and place, and you're ready to begin. The next question is the one I'm asked most often: "How do you do your research?" The key is to start simply. When you've decided where you want to set your book, or the event you want it to hinge on, go to the library and find the most basic book on the period. The children's department is an excellent place to begin. Books for young people on the subject will give you a clear, concise, simplified overview of the place you're interested in.

Work from the general to the specific, and always consider how the facts you are learning can relate to your main character. In this way, your story will unfold as you do your research. I'm often asked if I write my plot first or do my research first. The answer is, "Both." Each should grow out of the other; otherwise, you're going to have research imposed on your story, or a story that bends and twists in unconvincing ways to fit the research. If they develop together, they will intertwine into a cohesive book.

I keep two sets of notes, one chronological, the other topical. For my novel about the Revolutionary War, one set of pages, with the year at the top of each page, listed the events of the American Revolution. I also included on them the basic fictional "facts" of my story—when people were born, got married, died, etc. On a separate set, I kept notes on such things as fashion, food, customs, holidays, furniture, slang expressions of the day, common names in use at the time, hairstyles, weapons, and modes of transportation. I also have maps and make floor plans to keep characters from turning right to the kitchen in Chapter 1 and left in Chapter 24. I try to find information about plant, animal, and bird life, though I seldom use more than a few words about these details.

My chronology included succinct notes: "October 1781—Battle of Yorktown." And in the topic notes I listed detailed facts about the event. For example: At the ceremony marking Cornwallis's surrender at Yorktown, the Continental Army played "Yankee Doodle" and the British Army played, "The World Turned Upside Down." The bare-bones chronology keeps you from getting lost in a welter of auxiliary facts, and can save you from having a minor character turn up at a party several years after he dies.

Take down everything you think might be useful, but don't get the idea that because it's interesting and you recorded it, you have to use it in your novel. So what if your story takes place at the same time as the

San Francisco earthquake and you'd love to write about it? Don't send your characters off to visit San Francisco at just that time to experience the earthquake unless their going has something vital to do with the story you're telling.

What if you can't find a fact you need? First, consider whether you *really* need it. I used to agonize over how people lighted things. Being part of the lighter generation, I don't understand flint and steel. But I finally learned just to say, "He lighted the candle." Period. Nobody really cares how he did it. But if you really need a fact and can't find it in the library, try state historical societies and chambers of commerce. When I had almost finished my Revolutionary War novel, I saw something on the news about a storm in South Carolina, with pictures of palm trees bowing under snow. I was sick! I had an important scene with snow in *North* Carolina, but I had never heard of snow in a place with palm trees. Did North Carolina have snow or palm trees or both?

I called the Wilmington, North Carolina, Chamber of Commerce and asked about the weather. Yes, they did have a flurry of snow every four or five years. They sent me a packet of material with complete weather information—times of sunrise and sunset, average rainfall, temperatures, tides.

What do you do if your sources disagree on "facts"? I don't have an easy answer to that, except to say, they will. History is just old gossip, and no two historians see events the same way. There may even be disagreement on such seemingly indisputable facts as dates. Judge the relative authenticity of the sources, and, if you can, get a "third opinion."

Should you visit the place you intend to write about to do your own "on-site" research? If it's practical, by all means do so. But if you can't, don't despair. It just means you'll have to work harder to get the feeling of place across. And remember, you can go only to the *place,* not the *time.*

Another source of information are experts in local history, who are usually eager to share their expertise. But don't go to them knowing nothing and expect them to tell you all you need to know. Do your homework first—lots of it—so you can ask intelligent, specific questions.

Don't wait until you have all this detail before you start to write; you could make a life's work of preparing and never get to the writing.

206

Research is a continuing process. If, for example, you find an intriguing item for Chapter 2 when you're nearly finished with your book, go back and put it in.

So now you're ready to start: You have a detailed plot outline and stacks of notes. How do you work all that research into your novel? You don't. The factual details are useful only if you use them sparingly. The key is to keep your characters center stage and the research in the background.

I'm drawn to details of daily nuisances. I like the image of a knight dressed in rich parade garb, carrying a tall lance, but the scene really comes alive when the lance gets caught in the laundry on a line strung above a narrow street, and he ends up with a petticoat on the tip of the lance and an irate housewife in pursuit. This sort of homey realism does much to make readers feel that they're really living the story, not just reading something a writer has made up.

Now a few odds and ends: Get clear in your mind exactly the kind of novel you are writing. Is it a historical romance, with emphasis on a single relationship, or a family saga chronicling many years of many generations? Or is it a bodice-ripper? The style would be different for each. Keep the "voice" consistent. And don't worry about length. Every book is written a single page at a time, whether there are going to be 220 pages or 820.

Keep in mind that the rules, or someone else's advice, can help you only so far. There are exceptions to every rule, some notable. But a new author who breaks the rules takes extra risks. Sometimes they pay off; most often they don't. All that remains for me is to encourage you to give it a try. I'm a writer of historical novels, but I'm also an avid reader, and I can never find enough good ones.

45

Writing "True" Crime: Getting Forensic Facts Right

By Steven Scarborough

THE STORY READS LIKE THIS: Mitch Sharp, the skillful detective, solves the "Casino Slasher Case" by tracing cloth fibers and a drop of saliva found at the murder scene to the stealthy criminal.

What's wrong with the facts in this scenario? This simply can't be done. The evidence is scientifically dubious. When is a case plausible, and when does it stretch reality? A writer can know only by examining the type of forensic evidence necessary for the events of the story and then by doing the appropriate research.

Fingerprints

Fingerprints are the most conclusive form of forensic evidence; they are the only type of evidence that does not require corroborative proof. Though the probability of finding that elusive fingerprint or that single strand of hair is low, it can be woven into your story if you include the proper background. Fingerprint processing of a toenail and an eyeball of a murder victim in the *Red Dragon* is not only technically correct, but it also lends a gritty credence to Thomas Harris's novel.

Fingerprints command the most attention in court, and they should get equal billing in your crime story. In a city of about 300,000, fingerprints lead to the identification, arrest, or conviction of nearly one person every day.

While fingerprints are readily retrieved from glass, shiny metal, and paper, they are difficult to recover from fabric, textured objects, or finished furniture. Surface to surface, the methods of recovery differ, so the writer should know the proper processes for recovering incriminating fingerprints. It will make a story both interesting and accurate.

In *Presumed Innocent,* Scott Turow gives us an impressive account of

208

the questioning of a fingerprint witness in court. His only lapse is in describing blue fingerprints developed on glass with ninhydrin powder. Ninhydrin, a liquid chemical brushed on paper, produces a purplish fingerprint. The common graphite powder method is used on slick surfaces such as glass.

A dramatic punch to your story might be to recover prints from one of your victims, and it can be done. Iodine fumes are blown over the body with a small glass tube and a silver plate is pressed against the skin to lift the print. However, at this time prints can be recovered only within two hours from a live person and within about twelve hours from a deceased one.

Is your antagonist trying to incriminate someone else? Maybe he has considered forging a fingerprint? Forget it; his attempts are sure to be futile. It is nearly impossible to recreate an accurate die of someone's fingerprint. A cast can be made, provided he has a willing or dead hand to cast. Yet, even then the resulting print will be reversed or backward if transferred to an object.

A fingerprint expert cannot testify to how long a fingerprint will last on an object. General rules suggest that a fingerprint will last days, not weeks, outside in the weather; weeks but not months in a residence; and a month would not be long for a fingerprint left on a mirror, especially if encased in a drawer or a safe. Fingerprints have been chemically recovered years later on the pages of a book.

When tracing someone from latent fingerprints, the investigator must have the suspect's name and fingerprint record on file to make a positive match. Lawrence Block captures the essence of fingerprints in *The Burglar Who Painted Like Mondrian*:

> . . . you can't really run a check on a single print unless you've already got a suspect. You need a whole set of prints, which we wouldn't have, even if whoever it was left prints, which they probably didn't. And they'd have to have been fingerprinted anyway for a check to reveal them.

Historically, fingerprints have been filed using a ten-print classification system; without recovering latent fingerprints of all ten fingers, a person could not be identified. In the 1980s, the AFIS (Automated Fingerprint Identification System) computer was introduced, enabling jurisdictions with access to the computer to link a single latent fingerprint to a suspect previously fingerprinted. Writers should remember that AFIS computers cost over a million dollars, and your quaint Vermont village will not have one. The well-connected fictional investigator should know someone at a large agency or the FBI for a record check.

Body Fluids

Fingerprints may be the most positive form of identification, but what if your perpetrator does not leave any? In the absence of fingerprints, body fluids are a common type of evidence found at a crime scene. If an intact sample of adequate size is recovered, body fluids can be analyzed to obtain a DNA genetic profile that can be compared with the suspect's or examined for blood type.

Blood, semen, and saliva are all excellent media for determining a DNA match. DNA (deoxyribonucleic acid) is the blueprint of a person's genetic makeup and is absolutely unique for each individual.

Contrary to common belief, hair will not reveal a person's DNA pattern. Have your victim yank out a clump of hair with the skin cells to make a DNA match.

The equipment necessary to analyze DNA is highly specialized and costly. Again, if your story is set in a quaint village, it may not be feasible to run a DNA check. It also may take months to get results from one of the few laboratories that do DNA analysis. This need not be a negative; think of the desperation, the agony, of waiting for results while your killer still stalks.

Body fluids can be analyzed by the local crime lab to help your detective. An important factor associated with body fluids, including blood types, is secretor status. A secretor puts out, i.e., secretes, his ABO blood type into peripheral body fluids such as semen, perspiration, etc. It is possible for your fictional serial rapist to avoid any link to his body fluids by being one of the 15 per cent that are non-secretors.

What does blood type tell the investigator? Normally a blood type places a person in a broad portion of the general population. A community might have 45 per cent of its members with O blood, 40 per cent with A blood, and so on. Therefore, if standard ABO typing is done, the results are of little value because of the large population with that blood type.

Additional blood grouping techniques, specifically enzyme and protein analyses, enable the forensic chemist to assign a suspect to a narrower population. Your fictional crime lab should not give your detective a match on blood from the crime scene. They can limit only the number of people in your town that have that type of enzyme blood group.

The special equipment needed for thorough blood analysis is costly, and it is probable that numerous crimes go unsolved because sufficient testing is either too expensive or neglected.

Other evidence

Hair can be of forensic value. Strands found at the scene of the crime can be compared to a suspect's for similarities in color, shape, and texture, but it is difficult to determine race or even sex. An author can write that some of the suspects were eliminated because analysis concluded that their hair was not similar or consistent with the hair found at the crime scene.

Footwear prints, recovered by photography, fall into the class category. Except for the exceptional case, shoeprints can only be said to be made by the same type of shoe. Footwear, or any class type evidence (hair, fiber, ABO blood type) by itself would normally not be enough to convict your suspect in a court of law.

Handwriting cases rarely get into court. A handwriting expert renders an opinion after examining several varying factors such as letter height ratio and slant. If the writing is similar, then degrees of match probability are reported.

Criminals usually disguise their writing. It is unlikely that a kidnapper's ransom note, written in block letters will lead to the identity of your brutish villain. Words in blood dribbled on a wall may provide a strong clue and add color to your story, but they will not enable a handwriting examiner to point to your murderer.

Striations on a bullet are unique, much like the ridges of a fingerprint. Therefore, a bullet can be traced to a gun using the scratches or lands and grooves imprinted on it by the barrel of a gun. Unfortunately, if the barrel is damaged or changed, or if the bullet is mangled, the examination will be inconclusive. Careful scrutiny is necessary before including a firearms match in your murder mystery.

Thomas Harris was very skillful in weaving his forensic research throughout his novel. FBI Agent Will Graham explores the gamut of forensic evidence from fingerprints to blood typing to bite marks. *The Red Dragon* could be used as a forensic model for crime writers.

The increasing sophistication of today's readers is a two-edged sword: Readers are no longer satisfied with, "He was the only one tall enough who had a motive." A writer trying to add more realism to a story need not shy away from scientific evidence, but he must check his forensic facts for accuracy. Credibility is the key to a successful crime novel. Just as a character's action may lead the reader to say, "He wouldn't do that," an erroneous forensic fact can turn off the reader. Do your research well, and you will be rewarded by readers clamoring to pick up your latest authentic crime story.

46

SCIENCE FICTION WRITING AT LENGTH

BY ROGER ZELAZNY

IN THIS BOLD NEW AGE OF LITERARY EXPERIMENT and scientific breakthrough, how do the old rules apply? In science fiction the answer requires some knowledge of the field itself.

Science fiction is an interesting literary phenomenon not only because it has evolved rapidly through a great number of forms during the past 60 years—space opera, the "hard" sf tale, social sf, experimental sf, a fusion of all of the above—but because every one of these forms is itself alive and well today. Fashions come and go. New scientific gimmickry may come into prominence and be overworked, the social focus may shift from the middle or upper class of a hypothetical society to its underside. The introspective may for a time become more fashionable an emphasis than the external. But the field has grown to the point at which it can support all of these categories today, so that a writer need not indulge in archaeology to find good examples of any sort of science-fiction story told in any fashion. And all of them are still fair game for series development. Writers of science fiction should be aware of the variety of forms available, and, in considering a possible series, should select the type closest to their interests and abilities.

The sequel, the trilogy, the series, or whatever represents a continuation of a story from one novel to another—all of these have become particularly prominent in science fiction in recent years. They have come into being for a variety of reasons, in a variety of forms, and represent a mixed bag of results.

First, it should be noted that this is not a new phenomenon. For an interesting, well-written story as well as a reasonably authentic picture of the British publishing scene of over a century ago, I recommend George Gissing's *New Grub Street,* a novel by a man intimately acquainted with the Victorian marketplace, where the "three-volume novel" was the publisher's mainstay. Readers who enjoy a certain group of characters are likely to come back for more of the same. And with a series, the appearance of each successive volume gives a boost to the sales of the previous novels. So there is a definite commercial incentive for their production.

Not all series were originally intended as series, though. Often an author will write a novel that sells well beyond expectation and leaves a sufficient number of characters alive at its conclusion for an editor to see future possibilities and suggest, "Couldn't you do something more with these people/that idea/this place?"

But my longest series—novels dealing with Amber and its royal family—came about in a somewhat different manner from this. When I began to write the first novel in that series, *Nine Princes in Amber,* I had no idea where it was headed. There was actually a point at which I thought it would be a single book. I forget where I was in its telling when I realized that I had more story than I'd at first thought, and that a sequel would probably be required for its completion. So a series was born. When the second volume failed to resolve things, I decided simply to keep going till I came to the end. And it took five volumes to do it.

With my Dilvish series, on the other hand, I intentionally created a situation from which I could generate fresh stories whenever the need arose. I did this so I would never be caught short of material if I needed to produce a story in a hurry.

The stories of my nameless detective, collected in *My Name is Legion,* came about in a similar fashion.

My novel *Madwand* was written at editorial request because its predecessor, *Changeling,* had been well-received.

These are all valid means, all valid ways of going about the business. Valid, because they worked.

I have been told that the difference between a series and a serial lies in the serial's being a single, continued story, carried out through a number of volumes—as I did with Amber—whereas a series is tied together by continuing characters of a common setting, but generally possesses brand-new plots for each successive story. This is often the case in the mystery field. It is certainly a consideration in plotting. Are you setting out to write, say, a trilogy, requiring you to conceive and execute a big, three-part story with appropriate build-up and climax for each part? Or are you attempting to create characters sufficiently interesting that there may be an indefinite demand for their adventures?

Both require that build-up and a climax in each book—the rhythm of the novel—but the serial needs an overall crescendo as well. The most common distinction between serial and series, however, lies in characterization. Characters are supposed to develop, or at least change, in a story. If they're pretty much the same coming out as going in, the entire action seems, in a sense, wasted. In a series, though, you don't want the characters to change too much unless you're willing to risk losing those readers who liked them just as they were in the first place, and only want more of the same. In its worst form, such a story represents comic-book-type heroes who revert to precisely the same situation and attitude after each adventure. There are tricks, though, for providing excitement and maintaining interest in the series without creating such a blatant flatness of character. Sherlock Holmes, for example, remained pretty much the same throughout his adventures, but a) he was seen through the eyes of another (Dr. Watson), one who was constantly amazed by his intellectual prowess and who talked about it at length; b) the magician's trick of misdirection drew part of the reader's attention from the protagonist to the puzzle that he faced; and c) there was a process of "slow revelation," allowing the reader a few new tidbits about the protagonist every now and then. These are all useful tricks to bear in mind to keep a continuing character from seeming too flat through a long series of tales.

And whenever we're talking of fiction at length, another practical consideration involves the amount of material to be used. If we're thinking in terms of a quarter-million-word story, rather than one of 85,000 words, how are we to maintain the pace and hold reader interest, while achieving the length, without "padding?" The answer is in the second step of plotting.

After the writer has worked out what is to happen in a story, he must consider how it is to be told. Using the point of view of a single character is rewarding in that it provides constant opportunity for characterization in depth; on the other hand, it is often inappropriate when dealing with a "broad canvas" story. A writer might consider using third-person viewpoint, with subplots featuring a number of point-of-view characters, maintaining suspense by separating these

215

characters and then following and departing from them at crucial moments—in effect, telling several stories, a piece at a time, all of them fitting together into the greater whole. William Gibson's *Mona Lisa Overdrive* is an excellent example of this technique, as it is when used by writers as diverse as J. R. R. Tolkien and Edgar Rice Burroughs. This presupposes a single, long story spaced out over a number of books.

Another method, found in the mystery area, is to use the same character in a sequence of totally different stories, as I did with my futuristic detective in *My Name Is Legion*. I could still bring him back—same character, same world, same methods of operation—in a new story which could stand independent of the earlier ones. Unlike Dilvish, there was not a continuing thread, a kind of "overstory" lurking in the background—one which finally got told in a novel *(The Changing Land)*. In such a case, it is easier to find some new wine with which to fill such a bottle than to nurture a fresh grape crop. Knowing when to quit may well be the hardest part of such an enterprise.

I feel that once an entertainment ceases to be fun, you should stop. I've seen too many good stories dragged out beyond the point of no return just for the earnings. Don't do it. There are plenty more stories waiting to be written in the place where that first, good impulse arose. If it isn't there, don't be persuaded to force it. Quit entertaining and go write something new and different.

47

ALWAYS A STORYTELLER

BY MARY HIGGINS CLARK

THERE'S A THEORY that our lives are set in seven-year cycles. Vaguely, I remember that the basis for that belief is that in seven years every cell in our bodies has replaced itself. In case that's mountain-folk legend, I hasten to apologize to the more learned in the scientific fields. Recently I reread an article on suspense writing that I wrote just seven years ago to see what I've learned since.

My conclusion is that the more you know, the more you don't know. I've written four books, short stories, a novella, and film treatments since then, and I'm not sure I've gained any greater insight into this wondrous, complex and tantalizing field we call writing.

However, we must start somewhere, so let's go with the basics. How do you know that you are supposed to be a writer? The first necessity is that utter yearning to communicate, that sense that "I have something to say"; reading a book and knowing, *knowing* that you can write one like it; the sense that no matter how well ordered your life is, how thoroughly you delight in your family and friends and home and job, something is missing. Something so absolutely necessary that you are constantly swallowing ashes. You want to write. You must write.

These are the people who just might make it. That yearning is usually accompanied by talent, real talent, often native, undisciplined, unfocused talent, but certainly it's there. The degree of yearning separates the *real* potential writer from the truism that everyone has one story in them. How many times are professional writers approached at seminars or parties with the suggestion, "I've got a great story to tell. You jot it down for me, and we'll split the royalties."

Face the yearning. At some point, you'll have to or else eventually go to that great beyond unfulfilled. My mother always told me that my grandmother, struggling to raise her nine children and an orphaned niece, used to say, "Oh, how I'd love to write a book." On her deathbed, she was still regretting that she'd never tried.

Now you've acknowledged that you've simply got to try. Where do you begin? Most of us have a sense of what we want to write. If you don't, a terrific clue is to analyze what you like to *read*. I hadn't the faintest idea that I could write suspense, but after my first book was published, a biographical novel about George Washington that was read by the favored few, I knew that if I tried again, I'd really want to look forward to that lovely mailing from the publisher known as a royalty statement. I cast about for a story idea and looked at the bookshelf. I was astonished to realize that ninety percent of the books I'd read in the last couple of years had been mysteries. I did further soul-digging and began naming my favorite authors: Mary Roberts Rinehart, Josephine Tey, Agatha Christie, Charlotte Armstrong, and on and on. That was the clue that helped me decide to try a suspense novel. The one I launched was *Where Are the Children?* It's in its forty-second printing right now.

Footnote, just so I don't forget. Judith Guest's first novel was turned down by two publishers. She then looked at her bookshelf and realized that many of the books she read were published by Viking Press. She sent her manuscript to them. Months later she received a telegram. "Viking Press is honored to publish *Ordinary People*." The point is that the books you like to read give you a clue to what you may write best. The publisher of the books you read may turn out to be the best potential publisher for you.

Back to the beginning. Having determined whether you want to begin the writing adventure in the field of suspense or romance or science fiction; mainstream novels or books for children or adolescents; or poetry or articles, the next step is to treat yourself to several subscriptions. *The Writer* is the best at-home companion for the aspiring and/or achieving writer I can suggest.

I sold my first short story on my own. It went to forty magazines over the course of six years before it found a home. Which leads to the next question the new writer invariably asks. "How do I get an agent?" It's the chicken-and-egg query. In my case, in 1956 a young agent read the story and phoned me, saying, "I'd like to represent you." We were together thirty years until she retired two years ago. I'm still with her agency and the terrific people she put in her place. The point is, I think it's a lot easier to get an agent after you've proven yourself, even if your success is a modest one. That story brought me one hundred dollars. But remember. No story or book should ever sit in your drawer. If you get it back from one editor, send it out to the next. And don't sit in never-never land waiting for that one to sell. Start on the next project.

O.K. You have the determination; you know what you want to write; you're gathering the tools. I think it's fundamental to set aside time every day. Even one hour a day creates a habit. When my children were young, I used to get up at five and work from five until seven. I have the whole day to write now and don't get up that early, but I'm tempted to start setting the alarm again. There is something exhilarating about the world being quiet and you're somehow alone in it knowing that the phone won't ring or someone won't stop by. On the other hand, maybe you work best at night. Take that extra hour after everyone else in the family has been tucked in and use it to work on the story or poem or novel. No matter how tired you are when you start, I promise you that the sense of accomplishment of seeing even a page or two completed will make your dreams blissful.

I urge you to join some kind of writing group. Writing is one of the most isolated professions in the world. Your family can be marvelously supportive, but it's not the same. One of two things happen. They see the rejection slips and urge you not to keep banging your head against a wall. "Give it up, dear. It's just too tough to break into that field." Or they think that every word you write is gospel and expect a massive best seller any minute. Your local college or library may have writing courses available. Sign up for one of them. Don't worry about the fact that you'll inevitably miss three or four classes during the semester. You'll make the other ten or twelve. Listening to a professional, getting to know people who are in the field or aspiring to it is balm to the soul. When you begin having contact with others who share your need, you'll experience the feeling Stanley must have had when he said, "Dr. Livingston, I presume."

Be aware that there is probably an organization in your general area you should join: mystery writers, science writers, poets, among others. They're waiting for you. After that first story sold, I joined the Mystery Writers of America. I still remember my first meeting. I didn't know a soul. I was in awe of the name writers around me. Many of my best friends today I met at MWA meetings. And oh the joy of talking shop! Besides that, at these professional organizations you get to meet editors and agents who otherwise would be behind closed doors.

That's how it should be in the beginning. The determination. The quest to know what to write. The studying of the craft. The fellowship of other writers. And then in the quiet of that study or the space you cleared for yourself in the corner of the kitchen or bedroom, begin to write. Always remember that what you are is a storyteller. No matter how elegant your prose, how descriptive your passages, how insightful your eye, unless you tell a story people want to hear, you're not going to make it. A story has a beginning and a middle and an end. It tells about people we all know and identify with. It tells of their hopes and dreams and failures and triumphs. It tells of the twists of fate that bestow fortune on one person and rob another who is equally deserving. It makes us laugh and mourn and hope for the people whose lives we are sharing. It leaves us with a sense of catharsis, of emotion well spent. Isaac Bashevis Singer is a dedicated mystery reader. Several years ago at the Mystery Writers annual banquet, he received the award as Mystery Reader of the Year. This great writer offered simple yet profound advice. It was that the writer must think of himself or herself primarily as a storyteller. Every book or story should figuratively begin with the words "Once upon a time." Because it is as true now as it was in the long ago days of wandering minstrels, that when these words are uttered, the room becomes quiet, everyone draws closer to the fire, and the magic begins.

48

DICK FRANCIS: AN INTERVIEW

Q. *Did your journalistic training provide a good background to novel writing?*

A. Journalism was a wonderful school for book writing. Newspapers will never print an unnecessary word because they're always pushed for space. I used to think I was a pretty good editor and, in the end, it annoyed me intensely if I took my article up to Fleet Street and the sub found an unwanted word.

Q. *Why didn't you write your first thriller until five years after your autobiography?*

A. Writing for the *Sunday Express* was quite hard and I didn't think I had a story to tell. But as we passed the book stands in a railway station once I suddenly said to my wife, "I'm going to write one of those thrillers one day."

Some time later, the carpets were wearing out and we had two sons to educate. Although I had a good job on the newspaper, it wasn't as lucrative as being a successful jockey had been. Mary said, "Well, you always said you were going to write a novel. Now's the time." So I sat down and wrote *Dead Cert,* which took about a year.

Q. *Do you carry a notebook around and jot down ideas?*

A. Before I go to bed, I sometimes put a note down about something. But my wife Mary and I have quite good memories. Mary especially. I'm always asking her to reel off what happened at such and such an event.

Mary also takes photos of things like telephone kiosks and buses. These help to describe the scene when I am writing a story.

Q. *How do you plan your books? Do you know how they will end when you start?*

A. I have a good idea of the main crime upon which I'm basing the story. But I create many sub-plots as I go along. I often describe things I hadn't thought of before or introduce new characters.

I do only one draft. I hear of people doing two or three but I couldn't possibly do that. I write it all in longhand in a notebook and then put it onto a word processor. My procedure hasn't changed in the past 25 years. Even when I wrote the racing articles, I only ever did one draft.

Q. *As you write one chapter, then, you can't know what will happen in the next.*

A. That's right. I can't really be sure. But when I'm halfway through a chapter, I know I've got to start warming it up. I try to finish at an exciting spot, so that the reader can't put the book down and starts the next chapter.

Q. *There's a good balance in the scenes between action pieces—full of shocks and climaxes—and descriptive pieces. How do you create this?*

A. I don't know. I suppose it comes from experience. I like to grab the reader on the first page. It's rather like riding a race. You keep your high moments until the last furlong and then you produce your horse to win. When you're jumping the big fences, you're placing your horse to meet that fence. When you're writing your story, you're placing your words so that the reader will be excited at the right moment and, then, easing off after you've jumped the fence.

Q. *All your novels are written in the first person. Are there any limitations with this?*

A. I write in the first person because that's how I like to describe things. I had great difficulty in writing the Lester Piggott biography because I had to write in the third person.

I think this is one of the reasons no films have been made of the books, although options have been taken on them all. As they're written in the first person, a lot of each book describes what's in the hero's mind. It would be difficult to portray on screen.

Q. *Do you identify with your heroes?*

A. Probably, yes, though I'm not as tough and brave as my main characters are. They usually have some cross to bear but I try to make them compassionate and likeable, with a sense of humor and a lively eye. I wouldn't want to write about a miserable, depressing character. I get on well with people myself and I try to make my hero do the same.

My heroes aren't like James Bond superstars throughout. I try to make them human and make them develop in the book.

Q. *Do you ever get writer's block?*

A. Not really. Nowadays I do most of my writing in Florida, sitting on the balcony looking out to sea. I spend hours looking at the ocean, thinking. Often I've got a character in a certain position and I don't know how I'm going to get him out of it. I think out all the pros and cons of one way and then another and, eventually, find the right one.

ᔚ 49

MEANWHILE, BACK AT THE RANCH . . .

By Warren Kiefer

A FULL-SCALE NOVEL ABOUT THE WEST is as different from a formula Western as a satellite view of the Great Plains is from a county roadmap. Although elements of "formula" writing may be used in both, the dynamics are significantly altered. But it is the formula Western and its perpetuation of the Western myth that people generally mean when they speak of Western fiction.

A "formula" Western is as structured as a sonnet, and as stately as a minuet, and any writer who breaks the rules does so at his peril. Simplicity and violent action are what matter. Humor and sex are rarely allowed, and only on the periphery of the story.

One theme, justice, is central to the plot, although there are endless variations on the righting of wrongs which include certain classic, immutable elements readers of the genre have come to expect and rely on.

Most of us are familiar with these elements, if not from the books themselves, from films and television screenplays that follow similar patterns. Good and evil, black and white, right and wrong must be clear from the start.

The hero must be single, rootless, and reluctant to be drawn into conflict. He is embarrassed about his deadly skills and tries to hide them, while the villain can brag or show off as long as he is absolutely villainous. His greed, sadism, lust or avarice should be as obvious as a sandwich board.

At the beginning, the reader of the formula Western only has to know who wants what and why he can't get it, while evil must appear to be winning. By the middle of the story, reader interest may shift to the question of who's doing what to whom, and how long can they stand it.

Everyone knows what must happen at the end, but nobody knows exactly how it will happen; this is the kind of suspense that invites the reader to gallop along behind.

The climax comes only after the clamor for the hero's services has peaked, and not one page earlier, when even his friends are beginning to doubt his courage. He then shows us what we suspected all along, that heroes shoot only when provoked, but are fearless, tough, and implacable even when outnumbered.

Other characters adhere to certain rules or standards, too. Wives and daughters are chaste and virtuous while dance hall girls can be "loose," but not mean or vindictive. The town drunk, gambler, or any other non-combatant can betray the hero, but only out of fear or weakness. Never for money, which only interests villains.

In the past, if blacks appeared at all, they were cast as servants, Chinese were cooks or laundrymen, and the Native American Indian passed successively from his original role as Bloodthirsty Savage to Noble Redman to Tragic Victim, all of which have mercifully bitten the dust over recent years.

But with the elimination of old racial (and racist) stereotypes, Native Americans have become as invisible as blacks in the formula Western. Action, not opinion, moves this kind of story, and dialogue works only when it complements that action. The format is visual and visceral rather than verbal, with images as precisely circumscribed as those of a fairy tale.

The prose must be lean, fast and sinewy as the hero, but with more obvious direction and control. Stylistic no-nos include such avoidable sins as intransitive or compound verbs, the passive voice, and un-wieldy dependent clauses; a list that would find a place in any chapter on clear, concise writing.

Above all, the formula Western is a commentary on universal justice and on the time-honored principle of virtue triumphant as wrongs are redressed. Although its tested structure is fairly rigid and unforgiving, it is not necessarily confining.

This may sound a little like painting by the numbers, but it doesn't have to be. Within limits, one may write anything. But to tamper with those limits is to court disaster.

How does a writer go about it then, if he wants to break the pattern? How can he write about a kindly cattle thief, an Indian policeman, a black cowboy or a near-sighted hero who drinks too much? How does he escape the old restrictive clichés to write what he believes to be a story closer to historic truth?

He abandons the formula Western entirely and writes a novel about the historic West. Only in that way is he free to create a gallery of offbeat, even eccentric characters who would never be allowed inside the Western myth. Here he can deal with sex as well as violence, and may even attempt the subtlest nuances of character without necessarily losing his reader.

Such unlimited creative freedom, however, like the wide open spaces the writer writes about, is attended by high risk. What he is attempting flies in the face of the Western myth, and he will not be easily forgiven if he fails. He must be very good and extraordinarily careful not to fall between two stools.

Verisimilitude is the hallmark of the Western novel, and a sloppily researched fact or an off-pitch line of dialogue can shatter a reader's trust. The novelist who abandons all pretense of formula writing is saying, "I will not lie." The West was a challenge, and maybe some men did fight for justice, but mainly it was a hostile, desolate place, full of danger, dirt, and disease, with greed, violence, and corruption as common as they are today. Spectacular scenery abounded, but little civilized comfort reached people except where the railroads passed, in themselves a mixed blessing. The Great Plains swarmed with buffalo, and the forests teemed with deer, but few towns boasted potable water, plumbing, street lights, or any reliable public transportation.

The historic West, as opposed to the mythic West, is exciting territory for the novelist. By abandoning the safe confines of the traditional form, he gains plenty of creative elbow room. He can be funny, bawdy, original, and clever, as well as historically accurate. But in order to make it to the end of his chosen literary trail, he will probably need as much stamina and luck as the best of his characters.

Unlike the familiar terrain of the formula Western, this strange and difficult frontier must be explored with no maps. The writer is now free to gallop ahead of a prairie fire, cross the Rockies in winter, and shoot the rapids in the Grand Canyon. But he must never forget that in his special private wilderness he is the only guide the reader can follow.

What is often the hardest task for the writer—research in depth— begins long before he starts to write. For example, when I chose turn-of-the century New Mexico for *Outlaw*, I already knew a lot about the people and politics of the place, having gone to school there. But twenty more years of research were needed for a cumulative laying up of facts.

A general interest in the period gave me a working knowledge of everything from railroad timetables and sexual mores, to the state of the art in medicine and mining. I learned about horses and jails and military meals, about oil, wars, and tropical diseases. About trolley lines and rodeos, and women's skirt hems and Gatling guns.

I read or studied hundreds of books, documents, letters, diaries, military manuals, court records, and newspapers. I pored over old photographs and even looked up a few surviving people who had been young in those days, and who remembered.

To avoid historical anomalies, every writer should acquire a feel for the workaday lives of ordinary people, the tensions between competing groups, the dreams and scams and prejudices of the time. And once he's done all that, he must find the best voice to use in telling his story.

Mark Twain once said, "I only write about what I know and then blame it on somebody else in case they catch me out." He was being facetious, but what I'm sure he meant was that every author has to find the right voice, one that is both authoritative and unique, and which the reader implicitly trusts.

For *Outlaw*, I invented eighty-nine-year-old Lee Oliver Garland, a cowboy with scant education and total recall, who began life as an orphan, became successively a cattle rustler, soldier, banker, oil millionaire, and ambassador to Mexico.

Lee Garland's story is the story of New Mexico, our third youngest state, and much of 20th-century America as well. Shards of the mythic West survive in his tale, but he soon takes it far beyond anything in formula fiction. Lee is a decent man who is faster than most with a gun. He is bigger than life, as a Western hero should be, but he is also truer to life, as no mythic hero can ever be.

Lee's own view of his exploits and crimes is succinct. He tells us:

"I wasn't no hero, even if the army did give me a medal, and I wasn't no villain, even though I did commit a murder."

I knew all about the mythic West and formula writing before I began *Outlaw*, having written scripts for Western films and television. But my involvement with Garland was an entirely new experience. I knew his was the right voice, yet two or three hundred pages into the story, I nearly abandoned it, thinking I had been too ambitious. But Garland was no quitter and gave me no sleep until I resumed the writing. Since then, the critical and commercial success of the book more than justified his persistence.

As fast with his tongue as with his Colt, Garland could never have been squeezed into any kind of formula fiction, and I was glad I had not tried to do it. But he tells it better than I do. Trying to reassure a frightened woman during an attack by Pancho Villa's bandits, he brags about his marksmanship:

"Where are you from, ma'am?"
"P-p-port Huron, Michigan."
"Back there, maybe my name ain't a household word yet, but around these parts it is. You heard of Kit Carson? Jesse James? Billy the Kid?"
She nods, tiny tears of fear watering her eyes.
"You might say I'm in the same category."
"But they're all dead," she says, with that stubborn kind of logic some females got a talent for.

His view of his own actions is summed up thus:

"Sometimes there's principles more important than the law . . . It ain't easy for a man to know where he stands anymore. Today everything's more complicated, watered down, lacks salt."

On blacks:

"A colored man's got as much right to be what he wants as me, but nobody admits that. If he's lazy like me, they call him no-account and say what do you expect? If he's smart and hardworking and educated, they say he don't know his place."

On Indians:

"We pass some Apache . . . poor as mice, walking along barefoot . . . they don't go near the ranches or towns because some folks will shoot an Apache same as a coyote. . . . It's hard to believe these was the people gave the white man the hardest run for his money. They never surrendered, never signed no treaty and never stayed put on no reservation. The poor devils kept their pride, but they sure didn't keep much else . . . you got no right to expect gratitude from an Indian."

And on love for his wife:

"As many years as we was together, we never got everything said we had to say to each other . . . She showed me when you love somebody enough, you never really lose them."

This is the same Lee Garland who earlier in the story hunts down the man who has murdered his friend Cody, wounds him and stands over him with a gun, thinking:

"I feel no pity for him . . . mocking my weakness, so goddamn cocksure I lack the guts to shoot him. . . . Who cares about Cody, he says? . . . There's only one answer to that and I got it . . . I fire the last shot into Sorenson's face while he's looking at me, and pull the trigger on the empty chambers until Mountain takes the gun away."

I did not plan to have Garland fight in the Battle of San Juan Hill, but after he joined Roosevelt's Rough Riders to avoid jail, I could not keep him off the battlefield:

"Our infantry starts up the other slope, their blue shirts against the green grass in the sun. Little pinpoints of fire pick at them from the Spanish trenches, and they look pitiful and disorganized, scrambling around, spread out, holding their rifles across their chests, slipping in the grass. There don't seem to be very many, not nearly enough for what they're trying to do.

"I'm thinking there's been a terrible mistake here. Somebody gave the wrong order and the poor dumb bastards don't know it. It ain't heroic or gallant or brave, just pathetic. The only thing you can admire is the stubborn way they keep going, slipping and sliding and falling. I want to call out to them to come back, not even try it."

He says about our victory in the Spanish American War:

"As wars go, it wasn't much. A couple of battles and the surrender of a third-rate power to an army of scarecrows. There was more mistakes than glory and more misery than action. None of us asks if it was worth it. Wars never are, I guess, to the men that fight them."

On his son's death during the 1918 influenza epidemic:

"I couldn't deal with it, just plain couldn't. Couldn't believe it, couldn't accept it and couldn't understand it . . . Like he forgot his manners and just left us. Like he didn't know how much we loved him and how much our own happiness depended on his staying around. . . . I spent days locked in the library with my Colt in my lap, drunk a lot and feeling sorry for myself, cocking and uncocking

229

that old revolver as I tapped the barrel against my teeth. Until one day I looked up and saw how Caroline was suffering, and realized I was the only one could help her."

In that way, Lee told his own story for me, as surely as if he had elbowed me aside while I wrote. It is a Western all the way, but as far removed from traditional mythology and formula writing as a story can be.

His was not an easy voice to catch at the beginning, and I was never sure I could sustain him throughout a rambling account of his long and exciting life. But I did not have to, really. He helped me get away with it. Like a lot of fascinating old geezers I've known, once I got him talking it was hard to shut him up.

50

THE POLICE PROCEDURAL

BY ERIC WRIGHT

IF YOU WRITE THE KIND OF NOVELS that are called "police procedurals," one of the comments you will get most frequently is "You must do a lot of research." It is a natural assumption that you cannot write about the inside of a police station without being thoroughly soaked in the day-to-day routines of the cops. It isn't true, but before I talk about my experience in this area, let me deal with the general question of research or my own attitude toward it.

One of the pieces of advice I have developed since I started writing crime novels is this: Do your research last.

I am against spending a minute longer than necessary on research, and if you do all your research before you start you will probably do ten times as much as you need, because you do not know what is necessary until you have finished the book. So let me say it again: Leave your research to the end.

If this sounds bizarre (and I've had screams of outrage from research addicts on this one), remember you are writing a novel, not a documentary, and you are not accountable for the absolute accuracy or completeness of your factual information so much as for its plausibility. Write it so that it sounds right—then check the facts. And this is the place to restate the old maxim that if the truth is implausible, you can't use it.

The important thing is that you don't become a bag-lady (of either sex), a bag-lady of literature. We've all met them. I came across them first in graduate school where they carried shopping bags and small suitcases full of notes they were accumulating for a thesis. If you said anything remotely touching on their interests, they made a little note and popped the card into the shopping bag for the day they would begin writing. Sadly, in too many cases, that day never came.

When I started to publish and as a consequence was invited to speak in public, I always saw one of these bag-ladies in the audience, usually in the back row. They were the ones with the questions about how much research I had to undertake to write a book. They themselves had been "researching" a mystery novel for three years and were wondering when they should plan to begin the next stage.

Of course, if you are setting your novel in Ulan Bator in February, say, you will need to know the temperature and how much daylight there is. But chances are you already know these things or why would you set it there? Almost certainly, you have done the bare minimum of research necessary to get going, long before you started to plan. Georges Simenon is said to have set a novel in Cambridge, England, because he changed trains there one afternoon and did not wish to waste the experience. Too many people would not dream of writing about Cambridge without at least a year's study.

I want to apply this point about research to all fiction before I speak about police procedurals. I think if I were writing a novel about eighteenth-century England, I would write it out of my hazy notion of what life was like before the Industrial Revolution; then, if the fiction worked, I would "research" it. I have just finished a novel that takes place on a film set. I have never been on a film set, and in this case, I deliberately resisted all offers to visit a set until I had the book done. When I was finished, I asked a friend, a film producer, to check it, not for accuracy, but for plausibility. I didn't want to know if he would advise making a film my way, but, rather, if it was conceivable that a film might be made something like this. He said it was.

Of course, there were a number of technical points I had no idea about, things that were crucial to the plot: What happens to the exposed film at the end of the day? Who keeps the record of script changes on the set? (My ignorance was total.) But these things I guessed at, or made up, and he corrected them in a few minutes. The point is, if I had tried to research them ahead of time, I might have spent weeks doing it, and most of all, I would have wasted most of the research because I didn't know what I would need until all the details of the plot emerged. By doing the research afterward, I do only as much as I need. I could guess or make up the technical points because I have seen them or something like them in hundreds of movies and dozens of books whose plots involve movie-making. And, to come to the point, exactly the same is true of police procedurals.

My decision to write a police procedural came by a process of elimination: It was the only subgenre that would allow me to do what I wanted with the characters. I am in no way fascinated by police routine. When I wrote my first novel with a police inspector as hero, I had never been inside a Toronto police station, or spoken to a senior police officer. I have now. But in the beginning I wanted to know most of all if I could write a book like that. I wanted to spend as little time as possible doing things that might be a waste of time if it turned out I had no talent for the main task. So I devised a plot that allowed me to avoid the whole question of procedure: My murder took place in Montreal, but my story is about that part of the investigation that takes place in Toronto, the victim's hometown.

When I had finished, I found an agent. A few weeks later my agent sold the book, and then I did some research. It took me about an hour down at police headquarters to ask them the dozen or so questions that I had to have answers to, questions about pay and ranks and the vacations that Toronto police are entitled to, and the book was published.

Every succeeding book has raised three or four more questions to which I have found the answers afterward, and now, seven books later, I have a fairly good idea of police procedure in Toronto, at least, but I don't think I write better as a result.

And whenever I speak in public, invariably someone in the audience comments admiringly on the enormous amount of research I must have done to get the details of police procedure straight.

Why did I choose the procedural at all, if I have such an aversion to unnecessary work? The answer is that I wanted to write a realistic novel, created as far as possible out of my own experience of people, an experience largely confined to middle-class urban Canada. I wanted to tell stories about people I have known, about situations I have experienced, and for me, the crime novel is just that, a way of telling stories (and getting them published).

One of the stories I wanted to tell was about the life and times of a typical middle-class Canadian in mid-life (no research required here), and to continue that story through a series of novels. Having decided on that, the decision to make the hero a cop was already made for me. Private eyes rarely have a domestic life that includes children.

Having decided, or better, having long known what kind of hero you want to figure in your procedural—his age, the stage of his career, his family, his habits—the next thing is to decide fairly early if you are going to have a Horatio for your Hamlet. Nicholas Freeling's hero, Van der Valk, talks to himself, but Reginald Hill now has three policemen talking to each other. The results are equally superb. My guess is that more of us than not find it convenient for the hero to have someone to talk to, and it's nice to know that police always investigate a homicide in pairs.

Think long and hard about the relationship of the hero to his (usually) junior colleague. Should the junior be younger or older? A comic figure? Will he have his own kind of savvy, or be like Dr. Watson, as thick as two planks?

My first supporting cop was a domesticated old sergeant who treats my hero (in his late forties) like the young master. This worked very well for me for four books, but then it was time for him to retire. (In my books, people age from book to book, another decision you will have to make.) I gave my hero a new assistant, a young Yugoslavian plainclothes constable from the drug squad. I wasn't sure that these two would get along because the new man was a bit puppyish, but it turned out that he admired my hero extravagantly. Then for my recent book, *A Sensitive Case,* I found yet another sidekick, another old, nearly retired sergeant. I had a story I wanted to tell, quite apart from the murder, and it was a story that could be told only through such a man. I don't believe he will be back, but my young Yugoslavian has already returned.

A word of warning here. Like most writers, I stumbled into my stories and characters, but even if I had foreseen all my problems, I do not think I would have planned much more carefully. I am pretty sure it would have been a mistake to plan a series, because it would have affected the writing of each book, not for the better. I assume that every book is going to be the last in the series, and I tell the reader everything I know about my people. There always seems to be more when I come to the next book.

Make up your mind about your hero's private life. My hero is uxorious: His wife is just as bright as he is and better educated, which may cause him some problems one day, because he takes his job home too much. His sons create their own problems, and his father is a cantankerous old misanthrope. You see what I mean? There are times when I forget that I'm writing a crime novel as I watch the stresses produced by my hero's marriage—and reviewers have chided me for it.

The most important other character is the killer. Perhaps the chief thing I have discovered is that it is both easier to write the novel and more interesting if the villain is understandable, if not likable. I have done it both ways, but if my villain is a nasty piece of work, then I have difficulty spending much time with him. Abnormal psychology doesn't fascinate me as I know it does some very good writers. I also think that if you spend much time with him and do a thorough job of bringing him to life, then it is difficult to conceal the fact that he is the villain. What I prefer is a comprehensible homicide committed by someone who has a good deal of my sympathy. Then I can give the character some weight and substance.

The important thing about minor characters, in my experience, is to treat them as if they are major, to stay with them, think them through until they could carry a major role without boring the reader. Even if they have only a dozen lines, they must speak out of a fully realized character, or their language will be generalized and uninteresting. (It surprises me how often they unexpectedly reappear in the course of the rewriting, so I like to know them well.)

Finally, something has to be said about plot. You will have to make up your mind what kind of plot you prefer. The classic British mystery relies on a brilliant puzzle and a brilliant criminal and a slightly more brilliant detective, and the effect is of a giant game. This is not my way: I never liked this kind of novel much, and I am not ingenious enough to write one. When I look over my books I see that I have generally looked for a nearly accidental murder, often concealed by a piece of luck, and my hero employs a mixture of intuition, character analysis, and a bit of luck himself to solve them. I prefer that my crimes and their solutions be as plausible, as close to what my neighbors might perpetrate, as possible.

And here the writing begins. I never plot beyond this, because I do not know what is going to happen. If I did, I might not write it, because a huge part of the pleasure for me is wondering how my hero will solve it. I know where he must end, but I have no idea how he is going to get there.

They call my novels "low-key." That suits me. I am not trying to write about the extraordinary, or even about the unusual, but to make the ordinary interesting.

51

GRILLING ED McBAIN

BY EVAN HUNTER

Evan Hunter: I'm often asked why I chose to use the name Ed McBain on my crime fiction. I always respond that when I first started writing the 87th Precinct novels . . .

Ed McBain: I thought *I* was the one who wrote the 87th Precinct novels.

EH: The point is . . .

McB: The point is, *we* chose the McBain pseudonym because we didn't want to mislead people.

EH: Mislead them how?

McB: Into believing they were buying a mainstream novel, and then opening the book to find a man with an ax sticking out of his head.

EH: Yes. But in addition to that, mysteries back then were considered the stepchildren of literature, and . . .

McB: They still are, in many respects.

EH: You surely don't believe that.

McB: I believe that a grudging amount of respect is given to a good mystery writer. But if you want to win either the Pulitzer Prize or the National Book Award, stay far away from corpses among the petunias.

EH: You've been writing about corpses among the petunias . . .

McB: Other places, too. Not only in flower beds.

EH: For thirty-three years now. You've remarked that you begin work at nine in the morning and quit at five in the . . .

McB: Don't you?

236

EH: Exactly.

McB: Just like an *honest* job.

EH: But I wonder if you can share with us how you manage such a regimen. It must require a great deal of discipline.

McB: No. Discipline has nothing whatever to do with it. Discipline implies someone standing over you with a whip, *forcing* you to do the job. If you have to be *forced* to write, then it's time to look for another job. If you don't *love* every minute of it, even the donkey work of endless revisions, then quit.

EH: Do you make endless revisions?

McB: Not endless, no. One of the most important things about writing is to know when something is finished.

EH: When is it finished?

McB: When it works.

EH: But how many revisions *do* you make?

McB: As many as are required to make the thing *work*. A good piece of fiction *works*. You can read it backward and forward, or from the middle toward both ends, and it will *work*. If a scene isn't working, if a passage of dialogue isn't working . . .

EH: What do you mean by working?

McB: Serving the purpose for which it was intended. Is it supposed to make my hair stand on end? If my hair isn't standing on end, the scene isn't working. Is it supposed to make me cry? Then there had better be tears on my cheeks when I finish it.

EH: Do you make these revisions as you go along, or do you save them all up for the end?

McB: I usually spend the first few hours each morning rewriting what I wrote the day before. Then, every five chapters or so, I'll reread from the beginning and rewrite where necessary. Happily, nothing is engraved in stone until the book is published. You can go back over it again and again until it works.

237

EH: There's that word again.

McB: It's a word I like.

EH: How do you start a mystery novel?

McB: How do *you* start a mainstream novel?

EH: With a theme, usually.

McB: I start with a corpse, usually. Or with someone about to become a corpse.

EH: Actually, though, that's starting with a theme, isn't it?

McB: Yes, in that murder is the theme of most mysteries. Even mysteries that start out with blackmail as the theme, or kidnapping, or arson, eventually get around to murder.

EH: How do you mean?

McB: Well, take a Private Eye novel, for example. When you're writing this sort of book, it's not necessary to discover a body on page one. In fact, most private eyes—in fiction *and* in real life—aren't hired to investigate murders.

EH: Why are they hired?

McB: Oh, for any number of reasons. Someone is missing, someone is unfaithful, someone is stealing, someone is preparing a will, or inheriting money, or settling his son's gambling debts, or what-have-you. But hardly any of these reasons for employment have anything to do with murder. In fact, the odd thing about private-eye fiction is that the presence of the p.i. on the scene is usually what *causes* a murder. Had the p.i. not been hired, there'd have been no body.

EH: What about other categories of mystery fiction?

McB: Such as?

EH: Well, Man on the Run, for example. Is it necessary to start with a body in this type of story?

McB: That depends on why the guy is running, doesn't it?

EH: Why *would* he be running?

McB: Because he did something.

EH: Like what?

McB: Anything but murder. If he's done murder, you can hardly ever recover this guy; he's already beyond the pale, so forget him as a hero. I would also forget rape, kidnapping, terrorism, child abuse, and arson as crimes to consider for your hero. But if he's committed a less serious crime—such as running off with a few thousand dollars of the bank's money—then the police are after him, and he must run. And running, he meets a lot of different people, one of whom he usually falls in love with, and experiences a great many things that influence his life and cause him to change—for the better, we hope.

EH: That's what fiction is all about, isn't it? Change?

McB: I like to think so.

EH: But surely there are dead bodies in a Man-on-the-Run novel.

McB: Oh, sure. Along the way. I'm merely saying that in this sub-genre of Man on the Run, it isn't essential to *start* with a corpse.

EH: Are there other sub-genres?

McB: Of Man on the Run? Sure. We were talking about a man who'd actually *done* something. But we can also have a man who'd done absolutely *nothing*.

EH: Then why would he be running?

McB: Because the something he didn't do is usually murder. And that's where we *do* need a corpse. Immediately. For the police to find. So that they can accuse our man and come looking for him, which prompts him to flee, fly, *flew* in order to solve the murder and clear his name while of course falling in love with someone along the way.

EH: A Man on the Run can also be a person who *knows* something, isn't that so?

McB: Yes. Where the body is buried, or who caused the body to become a body, or even who's about to *become* a body. Dangerous knowledge of this sort can cause a person to become a man who knows too much and who must flee north by northwest in order to escape becoming a body himself.

EH: On the other hand, it isn't necessary that he *really* be in possession of dangerous knowledge, is it?

McB: No. As a matter of fact, he can know absolutely nothing. In which case, he merely *appears* to know something which the bad guys think he actually *does* know.

EH: And this semblance of knowledge becomes even more dangerous to him than the knowledge itself would have been because he doesn't even know *why* someone wants him dead.

McB: In either case, a body is the essential element that sets the plot spinning.

EH: A body, or a substitute for one. The body doesn't have to be an *actual* stiff, does it?

McB: No, it can be what Alfred Hitchcock called the MacGuffin. I prefer the real thing, but there are many successful thrillers that utilize to great effect a substitute corpse.

EH: Can you give us some examples?

McB: Well, the classic Woman-in-Jeopardy story, for example, may very well be *Wait Until Dark,* where a *blind* woman unknowingly carries through customs a doll in which the bad guys have planted dope. They want the dope back. So they come after her.

EH: That's a woman in jeopardy, all right.

McB: In spades.

EH: A gender reversal of Man on the Run.

McB: Which all Woman-in-Jeopardy stories are. In this case, the substitute corpse is a doll—a graven lifeless image of a human being. The woman doesn't *know* where the body is buried, but they think she does. Without the doll—that is, without the corpse—there'd be no reason to stalk and terrify this woman, and there'd be no thriller.

EH: And in much the same way that our Man on the Run learns and changes from *his* hair-raising escapes, so does our Woman in Jeopardy become stronger and wiser by the end of *her* ordeal.

McB: Leaving the reader or the viewer feeling immensely satisfied.

EH: Let's get back to the way you begin one of your mysteries.

McB: With a corpse, yes. Well, actually, before the corpse, there's a title.

EH: I find titles difficult.

McB: I find them easy. I look for resonance. A title that suggests many different things. For example, the title *Ice* seemed to offer limitless possibilities for development. Ice, of course, is what water becomes when it freezes. So the title dictated that the novel be set during the wintertime, when there is ice and snow . . . ah. Snow. Snow is another name for cocaine. So, all right, there'll be cocaine in the plot. But in underworld jargon, to ice someone means to kill him. And ice also means diamonds. And, further, ice is the name for a box-office scam in which tickets to hit shows are sold for exorbitant prices. The title had resonance.

EH: A lot of people had trouble with one of my titles.

McB: Which one?

EH: *Love, Dad.*

McB: That's because it's a terrible title, very difficult to say. You have to say "My new book is called Love Comma Dad." Otherwise, no one will know what you're talking about.

EH: Most people thought the title was *Dear Dad*.

McB: Why?

EH: I don't know why. Actually, I thought *Love, Dad* was a wonderful title.

McB: You should have called it *No Drums, No Bugles*.

EH: Why?

McB: Were there any drums or bugles in it?

EH: No.

McB: There you go.

EH: Tell me where *you* go after you've got your title and your corpse.

McB: I write the first chapter. Or the first two or three chapters. As far as my imagination will carry me until it gives out.

EH: Then what?

McB: I'll outline the next few chapters ahead.

EH: Not the whole book?

McB: No.

EH: Why not?

McB: Because in mystery fiction, the reader never knows what's going to happen next. It helps if the *writer* doesn't quite know, either. If what happens is as much a surprise to him as it is to the reader.

EH: Isn't that dangerous?

McB: *If it doesn't work, you can always go back and change it.*

EH: As I understand it, then, you keep outlining as you go along.

McB: Yes. Whenever I feel a need to move things along in a certain direction. Which, by the way, may change the moment the characters *get* there and discover things I didn't know they'd discover.

EH: I always love the moment.

McB: Which moment?

EH: When the characters do just what the hell they *want* to do.

McB: When they come alive, yes.

EH: That's when you know you've got a book. That's when you know these aren't just words on paper.

McB: A lot of writers talk about how *awful* it is to be a writer. All the suffering, all the pain. Doesn't anyone find *joy* in it?

EH: I do.

McB: So do I.

EH: You once said . . . or *we* once said . . .

McB: *We* once said . . .

EH: . . . when asked which qualities we considered essential for a writer of fiction today . . .

McB: Yes, I remember.

EH: We said . . . a head and a heart.

McB: Yes. The head to give the work direction, the heart to give it feeling.

EH: Would you change that in any way now?

McB: I would say only please, please, please don't forget the heart.

52

PLOT AND CHARACTER IN SUSPENSE FICTION

BY JOAN AIKEN

WHICH CAME FIRST, the chicken or the egg? Does plot arise from character, or character from plot? The question is in many ways an artificial one; most writers have felt, at one time or another, the heady excitement of knowing that a whole story, or at least its basic elements—plot, character, and development all tangled together—is struggling to emerge from the dark.

But if this does not happen?

"What is character," says Henry James in *The Art of Fiction* (1884), "but the determination of incident? What is incident but the illustration of character?" And the Old Master goes on to add (several pages later), "The story and the novel, the idea and the form, are the needle and the thread, and I never heard of a guild of tailors who recommended the use of the thread without the needle, or the needle without the thread."

Perfectly true, and you have to have both before you can begin. But, suppose you have only half of the combination?

Characters are generally the problem. *Plots* come a dime a dozen, they are easy to pick up. We read them every day in the papers. A mother, even after several years, remains positive that the death of her teenage son, classified as suicide, was not so; but whenever she pushes her inquiries about it, other unexplained deaths take place. The pet poodle of a notorious Chicago mobster is stolen. The CIA sets up a spurious marine engineering firm in an effort to salvage a sunken Soviet submarine. A middle-aged woman demands a daily love poem from her browbeaten husband. A descendant of one of the twenty-one victims of the Boston Molasses Disaster is still seeking compensation. A convention of magicians plans to meet in an Indian town, but the citizens raise strong objections. . . .

Any of these incidents, all culled from the daily press, might trigger a

244

story, might produce that wonderful effervescent sensation, familiar to every writer (it really is like the working of yeast in one's mind), when different elements begin to ferment together and create something new. The best plots, of course, instantly create their own characters. That wife, that domineering wife, compelling her husband to produce a new love lyric every evening: we know at once what she would be like. And the cowardly put-upon husband, submitting to this tyranny, trudging off to the library for new rhymes and new verse forms, until the climactic moment when he rebels, and supplies you with the start of your story. Or the grieving, brooding mother, worrying on and on about her son's death, gradually acquiring little bits of information. It would be very easy to tell her story.

But if you have the plot without the characters?

There's nothing so frustrating for the reader as a potentially interesting, intricate story, full of turns and twists, in which the characters are so flat, machine-made, and lifeless that they form a total barrier to following the course of the narrative, because it is impossible to remember who is who. Is Miranda the actress or the secretary? Was it Wilmost whose car was stolen, or Harris? Is Casavecchia the gangster or the millionaire? Why *does* Kate hate Henry?

In murder mysteries and procedural detective novels, character portrayal is not so important. The reader won't expect great depth among the victims and suspects, while the detective probably has a number of well-established peculiarities, built up over a series of books: he is Spanish, wears elegant grey silk suits, and carries his exclamation point upside down; or he is very fat and drinks a pint of beer on every page; or he is a rabbi; or she is female, karate-trained, and has a huge wardrobe, which is just as well, since the vicissitudes of her job frequently reduce her clothes to tatters. We know all these and love them as old friends.

The problem of character arises most particularly—and can be a real handicap—in suspense novels.

Suspense novels are deservedly popular, but very hard to define. They are not murder mysteries. They are not just straight novels, because something nasty and frightening is bound to happen. That is the promise to the reader. They are not spy stories, and they are certainly not procedurals. One of the very best suspense novels ever written, *A Dram of Poison,* by Charlotte Armstrong, had no murder in it at all, not even any death (except a natural one in the first chapter, setting off the whole course of events), but it possesses more riveting tension than any other story I can recall.

In a suspense novel, the element of character matters very much indeed. The hero/heroine is pitted, not against organized crime or international terrorism, but against a personal enemy, a personal problem; the conflict is on an individual, adversarial level. And so, if either hero or hero's enemy is not a flesh-and-blood, fully rounded, recognizable entity, the tension slackens, the credulity drops.

In *A Dram of Poison,* all the mischief is caused in the first place by the arrival of the hero's sister, one of those terrible, self-satisfied, know-it-all characters (plainly Charlotte Armstrong wrote the story in the white heat of having recently encountered one of them) who can always interpret other people's motives and give them some disagreeable psychological twist. By her confident assertions, she soon has the heroine paralyzed with self-distrust and the hero downright suicidal. Then, in between the breathless excitement of trying to find what he did with that wretched little bottle of poison he had meant to swallow, the reader has the fearful pleasure of knowing that, in the end, odious Sister Ethel is bound to receive her comeuppance.

Charlotte Armstrong was particularly skilled at villains; the frightful parasitical pair of sisters who, in *Mask of Evil,* (originally published as *The Albatross*) come and prey on the two central characters are particularly memorable, with their sweet saintly selfishness. The sense of being *invaded,* taken over, in their own home, by repulsive aliens, was particularly well conveyed in that story.

The suspense novel is often a closed-world plot. The hero/heroine must battle it out against the adversary in a situation that, for some reason, allows for no appeal to outside help. There must be valid reasons for this. If not a snowstorm, with all phone lines down, then the villain has bruited it around that the hero is hysterical, unbalanced, alcoholic, a drug abuser, or just traumatized by recent grief so no call for help will be heeded or believed.

Ursula Curtiss had a particular gift for these enclosed-world situations, and she had a masterly touch with villains as well. It is an interesting exercise to compare some of her stories with others, for she was a very fertile creator of creepy domestic-suspense plots. Many of her ideas were brilliant, but some of them succeeded far better than

246

others. Why? Because of the characters with which they were ani-
mated. *Voice Out of Darkness,* which has a fine snowy Connecticut
setting and an excellent basic idea—harking back to the long-ago question of whether the heroine did or did not push her very unpleasant
adoptive sister under the ice when they were both eleven—yet somehow fails to come off because it is peopled with rather stock characters:
two handsome young men, two pretty girls, and some recognizable
small-town citizens, the drunk writer, the gossipy lady. Her novel, *The
Stairway,* however, is pure gold from the first page to the last. Why?
Because of its villainness, the repulsive Cora. Judged dispassionately,
the plot is simple and only just credible. Madeline, the heroine, is
married to Stephen, an intolerable man whom she is about to divorce, a
monster of tyranny who terrifies her small son. But Stephen falls
downstairs and breaks his neck. Cora, the humble cousin, the poor
relation, by pretending to believe that Madeline pushed him, gradually
assumes more and more dominance over the household and seems all
set to stay for the rest of her life. Madeline, in a bind because *she*
believes that *Cora* pushed Stephen, feels that she can't betray her and is
helpless. All this, given a moment's cool thought, seems hard to swallow. Why had Madeline married the horrendous Stephen in the first
place? Why should she submit to Cora for a single moment? But Cora is
made so *real,* with her greediness, her anxious, reproachful air, her
dreadful clothes, her fondness for eating candy out of a paper bag and
rustling the sheets of the newspaper, that all she does and says is
instantly, completely credible.

Playwright Edward Albee once observed that the test he had for the
solidity of his characters was to imagine them in some situation other
than the play he had in mind and see if they would continue to behave in
a real manner. The character of Cora would be credible and recognizable whether we saw her in a hospital ward, a supermarket, or a
graveyard.

The Stairway was an early Curtiss novel, but one of her later ones,
The Poisoned Orchard, contains the same terrifying claustrophobic,
inturned quality, again because of its hateful and convincing villainness,
the heroine's cousin Fen, and her accomplice, the cleaning lady, Mrs.
List. This sinister pair have Sarah the heroine hog-tied, especially
clowning, ugly, self-assured Fen, who continually manages to force her
much nicer, much better-looking cousin into the unenviable role of

247

straight man refusing to laugh at Fen's jokes. The relationship between the two is beautifully and most credibly realized, so that the reader is prepared to swallow the fact that Fen and her evil ally seem to be omniscient and omnipresent, able to anticipate Sarah's efforts to combat their plots almost before she can make a move. And what is it all about? We hardly know. A wicked deed, way back in Fen's past, that is catching up with her. And anyway, what can they *do* to Sarah? It hardly matters. The point is that they are menacing, and that she is more and more at their mercy. Fen is a wholly convincing monster, the more so because she is quick-witted and amusing, as well as being unprincipled. *Fear* is the essential ingredient of a suspense novel, and fear can be achieved only if the reader thoroughly sympathizes with the main character and thoroughly believes in the villain.

If the villain is less convincing, then the main character must be made more so.

Dick Francis, the English writer of deservedly best-selling mysteries with horse-racing backgrounds, wrote an interesting early novel, *Nerve,* in which all the jockeys on the turf were being persecuted by a well-known TV personality who secretly spread malicious gossip about them, prevented their getting to races on time, and had their horses doped. Why does he do this? Because he, son of a famous racehorse owner, is terrified of horses, and therefore psychotically jealous of all who succeed in the horsey world.

What a preposterous theme it sounds, set down in cold blood. And the villainous TV star, Maurice Kemp-Lore, somewhat sketchily depicted, only just makes his murderous obsession credible to the reader. What does give the book immediate life, great energy and plausibility, so that it moves at a rattling pace and carries the reader along, completely hooked by the story, is the treatment of the hero. As always in Dick Francis novels, the hero tells the story in the first person; in common with other Francis heroes he is an odd man out, who has fallen into the racing world by a series of accidents. Descended from a family of professional musicians, he is the only non-musical one; despised by his kin, he has had to justify himself in some other direction. The contrast between the hero's elegant relations conducting Beethoven at the London Festival Hall, while he gallops through the mud at Ascot, is bizarre enough to be convincing, so that we are passionately on the hero's side as he struggles to combat what he begins to recognize as a sinister plot against his whole *raison d'être*. The villain remains shadowy, but the hero, in this case, carries enough weight to sustain the story.

Given a satisfactory plot, it should not be too hard to equip it with characters. But what if the boot is on the other foot?

Some writers are compulsive character collectors. Wherever they go, they watch, listen, record, jot down notes and descriptions: the fat woman in the black-striped dress at the rail station with two elegant little pig-tailed girls, also in black-and white striped outfits, hanging on her arms. The lanky, unshaven six-foot male in the subway, with a shock of red hair and gold rings in his ears. The professional portrait painter, met at a party, who has produced a portrait every two months for the last twenty years, and has a photographic eye for a face. The woman who, though courteous and well-mannered, is an obsessive corrector, so that she can never hear a sentence spoken without chipping in to put the speaker right—politely, but *oh*, so firmly. . .

Character collecting is an excellent habit, because sooner or later some of these characters will start to move.

You have a whole cast of characters, but no plot. So: Make extensive notes about them—their preferences, dislikes, habits, childhood history. Like Edward Albee, set them in different environments, confront them with crises. What would the woman in the black-striped dress do if she were in charge of forty school children on a sinking cruise liner? Make them encounter each other. Suppose the portrait painter were sitting in a subway train, drawing lightning sketches, and the man with red hair and gold earrings, unaccountably angry at being drawn, grabs the sketchbook and gets out at the next stop? A character may suddenly get up and walk away, pulling a skein of plot behind him. Suppose they then meet by chance, somewhere else?

Imagine Jane Austen saying to herself, "Now, let's tell a story about a sensible practical sister and a self-indulgent, overemotional sister. What sort of men shall they fall in love with?"

Suppose in writing *Sense and Sensibility,* she turned her story the other way round. Suppose sensible Elinor had fallen in love with handsome, romantic Willoughby, and susceptible Marianne had been bowled over by reliable, prosaic Edward? But, no, it won't work. Marianne could never have fallen for Edward, not in a thousand years. Jane Austen, even at a young age (she was twenty-two), had her characters and plot inextricably twined together, one growing out of the other; there is no separating them. But it is fun to probe and investigate and reconsider; fun, after all, is what writing is all about. Jane Austen took huge pleasure in writing *Sense and Sensibility*. The fact is evident; she knew these characters entirely before she put pen to paper.

What is the best way of displaying your characters?

There are, of course, hundreds, but the worst way is to describe them flatly.

My recent novel, *Blackground,* has the theme of two characters who marry in romantic haste, and then, on a winter honeymoon in Venice where they are, as it were, suspended together in a vacuum, they discover that they had in fact met long ago and aren't at all the people each thinks the other to be. To make this as much of a shock as I intended, both of them and, hopefully, for the reader, I had to be familiar with their life stories right back to childhood. In order not to a) begin too early or b) bore the reader with too much flashback, I make Character A tell his story to Character B on the honeymoon, while hers is disclosed to the reader in snatches throughout the narrative.

Michael Gilbert, a writer of several different kinds of mysteries, whose characters are always remarkably individual and three-dimensional, adopts a very swift and vivid method of displaying his quite large cast of characters in his suspense novel *The Night of the Twelfth* (about sadistic murders in a boys' school). Sometimes a whole chapter is divided into blocks of conversation, often only about half a page—between A and B, between B and C, between C and A, between A and D—these fast-moving dialogues equally convey character and advance the action.

Sometimes you know your character *too* well; you could write volumes about his quirks and complications. But how do you get all this across to the reader without being pompous, or overexplicit?

How about portraying this person as seen through the eyes of another narrator, quite a simple soul (like Nelly Dean, the housekeeper in *Wuthering Heights,* who tells much of the story), or even a child? *What Maisie Knew,* by Henry James, can be an example to us all.

"Try to be one of those people on whom nothing is lost," said Henry James.

Perfect advice for a writer!

250

53

FREE-FORM PLOTTING THE MYSTERY NOVEL

BY MARCIA MULLER

PLOTTING THE MODERN MYSTERY NOVEL is a complex task that bears as little resemblance to so-called formula writing as Miss Jane Marple does to Lew Archer. One of the questions most often asked by aspiring mystery writers (frequently in tones of frustration, after being outfoxed by one of their favorite authors) is, "How on earth do you complicate your plots and still get them to hang together?"

Unhappily for those who seek instant solutions, there is no one sure-fire method of plotting. The techniques vary from writer to writer along a continuum that stretches from detailed, extensive outlining to what I call winging it (writing with no planning whatsoever). Writers adopt the type of plotting that best suits their working styles and personalities. Some hit on the appropriate type immediately, others gradually make their way toward it through experimentation—plus hard work and practice. There are no major shortcuts, but there are *little* shortcuts. Tiny ones, actually. What I'm about to tell you about plotting is only my highly individualized technique; all, some, or none of my suggestions may help.

I've learned my craft the hard way. In the past fifteen years I've made every attempt to "reinvent the wheel," especially where plotting is concerned. I began by making detailed character sketches, outlines, and time charts, a method distilled down to a lengthy storyline synopsis. I've tried winging it, with unsatisfying results. What I've finally settled into is a technique that I call "free-form plotting"; as the term implies, its key ingredient is flexibility.

Before we go on, however, let's discuss the concept of plot. If someone were to ask you what a novel's plot is, you'd probably say "the story." But if you examine a given *plot,* you'll see it's somewhat different from the *story.* The story is linear; it is the events that happen,

251

both on and off scene. The plot is the *structure* you impose on those events. You select which to include, in what order, and how to tell each one. You shape your plot from the raw material—the story.

Here's an example of a crime story, simplified for our purposes:

1. Killer meets victim; they interact.
2. Killer murders victim.
3. Murder is discovered; detective enters case.
4. Detective investigates.
5. Detective solves murder; killer is apprehended.

Taking the raw material of this particular story, you could plot in a number of ways. You could tell it in a linear fashion, from step one to step five (although that's not likely to be surprising or dramatic). You could start with the discovery of the murder, continue through to the killer's apprehension, explaining in flashback or dialogue what went on in steps one and two. You could start with the actual murder, masking the identity of the killer. The steps may be ordered any whichway, depending on what kind of book you want to write. It is up to you to decide how this simple story is told; the question we are addressing here is how you make and follow through on your decision.

What I like about free-form plotting is that it allows me to defer the decision, feeling my way as I write. It saves me from becoming locked into an inflexible plot outline that may, in the end, not suit my purposes. I can start a novel with a minimal idea of where I'm going, develop some ideas and characters, experiment with them, keep what fits, discard what doesn't. An example of this is how I plotted my most recent Sharon McCone novel, *There's Something in a Sunday.*

When I started I had in mind a beginning situation, a few characters, a background, a theme, and a hazy idea of the ending. The situation has Sharon McCone being hired to follow a man who came to San Francisco every Saturday night and stayed through the early morning hours on Monday. The characters were the man, Frank Wilkonson; Sharon's client; a woman the man was looking for; and a married couple who were friends of the woman's. The background was dual: neighborhood activism and the plight of San Francisco's homeless people. The theme was the relationships between men and women, and how they go awry. And the ending—well, I won't reveal everything.

When I start a mystery novel, I like to set the situation in the first one or two chapters. In this case, it was Sharon following Wilkonson, observing his eccentric Sunday activities, and wondering if the client had told her the entire truth about his interest in Wilkonson. Because she observed Wilkonson's movements closely for nearly twenty-four hours, she feels that she knows him—and so did I, although he had not as yet uttered a single word of dialogue. In these two chapters, I had developed his character in some depth, and had begun to consider him a real person. As he developed, I began to think differently about Wilkonson and what I intended to do with him later on.

I employed the rule of flexibility very early. When I read my first two chapters, I found something was wrong: Taken together, they moved too slowly. So I broke them up, inserting a flashback chapter between them, in which I introduced the client, Rudy Goldring, and showed how Sharon had come to spend her Sunday tailing Wilkonson. By the time I finished the scene, both Goldring and the derelict who served as "doorman" at his office building had come alive for me, and I began to see new ways they could be used in the plot.

My next step was to introduce the supporting characters: the people at All Souls Legal Cooperative, where Sharon works. Again, something was wrong with the scene I'd planned. I was tired of writing about the co-op in the same old way. If I had to write the scene with Sharon sitting in her boss's office discussing the case one more time. . . . My solution was to introduce a new attorney and an assistant for Sharon, to give more prominence to an old character, the secretary, and to create personal problems for the boss, whose previous life had been placid. Now I had a situation that I was eager to write about, and a fast-developing personal subplot that (because the life of Sharon and the people at All Souls is an ongoing story from novel to novel) didn't necessarily have to be wrapped up at the end.

Of course, what happened in the scene at All Souls required going back and making minor adjustments in the first three chapters; the new attorney, for instance, was now the person who had handed Sharon the Goldring assignment, rather than her boss. This is a time-consuming necessity of free-form plotting but, as we'll see later, it has its advantages.

At this point I was ready to establish my other characters. And, while

253

a lot had happened and a number of questions about Wilkonson and Goldring had been raised, I needed something more dramatic—the murder.

At the scene of the crime I was able to introduce another of the main characters, an unnamed woman who appeared suddenly and then vanished. In the next few chapters, as Sharon followed up on the case for reasons of personal satisfaction, I brought in the other characters who would figure prominently: the married couple, Wilkonson's wife, and his employer.

Most of these characters had turned out differently from what I'd first envisioned. A character "taking over" the story is a phenomenon that writers often discuss. No one knows exactly why or how this happens, but I suspect it has to do with the writer's being relaxed and "into" the story. As you sit at the keyboard, new ideas start to flow. Characters take on fuller identities as you allow them to speak and act and interact with one another. When this happens to me, I simply go along with whatever is developing; often I write pages and pages of dialogue or action, then pare them down or toss them out entirely. It's easier to cut or eliminate your prose than to go back and add material later. By setting down these free-flowing scenes on paper, you will avail yourself of the opportunity to create something that may vastly improve your novel. And (impossible in real life) you can always rip up the pages or hit the delete key.

One example of this phenomenon is the development of the married couple that I've mentioned—Vicky and Gerry Cushman. Originally, I'd seen them in a strictly functional sense, as friends of the woman who appears at the murder scene and then vanishes—the pivotal character in the plot. But, as Vicky began to take shape, what emerged was not the coolly efficient neighborhood activist I'd planned, but a woman with severe emotional problems. And in response to this development, her husband Gerry emerged as a selfish man who exacerbated her problems. I had created an unexpected conflict that wove nicely into the theme of the novel—and I was able to use it to further complicate my plot.

At this point—the end of your primary development stage—you can take full advantage of free-form plotting. You have your characters in all their individuality and richness; you have a situation that is ripe for additional complication; you have an idea of where you're going. Now is the time to find out exactly where that is—and how you're going to get there.

The way I accomplish this is to read what I have on paper. Then I play the game of "what if." The game is a question-and-answer process: "What if such-and-such happened? How would that work?"

In *Sunday,* I reached this point just as Frank Wilkonson disappeared. He had gone to an abandoned windmill in Golden Gate Park; Sharon was following him, but lost him in the darkness and fog; Wilkonson never returned to his car. This was an unplanned development; the setting of the windmill had occurred to me while driving by it one day, and it seemed a perfect place for an eerie, late-night scene. The scene wrote easily, but at its conclusion I had to admit I had no idea why Wilkonson had gone there or where he'd gone afterwards. Time for "what if. . . ."

Why did he? I asked myself. The obvious answer was that he planned to meet someone there. Sometimes the obvious choice is the best. But who? I could think of one character who would have reason to be there, but no reason to meet Wilkonson. But what if he was asked to contact Frank? By whom? I knew who that might be. But then, why hadn't Sharon seen Frank meet the other person? What if Wilkonson had. . .?

By the end of this question-and-answer session I found myself in possession of a new plot twist: an eventual second murder and a killer who hadn't even been on my list of primary suspects. Because of my accidental choice of a setting and the manner in which I wrote the scene, my plot had taken on greater complication—and greater mystery.

A few chapters later I was faced with another situation calling for "what if." Sharon had finally located the woman from the murder scene. The woman had ties to all the major characters, but they were as yet nebulous. In a few cases, they were nebulous even to *me.* So I considered the connections among all six of these people. What if the client was an old friend of the woman? What if they had once been lovers? No, friends was better. But what if she had had a lover? What if it was Frank? Or Gerry? Or Frank's boss? Or. . .? Because the characters were well established at this time, I was able to come up with a logical answer.

As I've said, free-form plotting requires constant readjustments of scenes and details to make them consistent with one another. This is laborious at times, often necessitating extensive rewriting. But I'm convinced that it is also extremely beneficial. As you rewrite, you are forced to pay great attention to detail, to polish your prose, to reexamine your logic.

Logic is crucial to a mystery novel. If it is flawed, the whole plot—no matter how original your premise, fascinating your characters, or vivid your settings—simply falls apart. I advise frequent rewriting and rereading. Check every detail; make sure every place is described properly, especially if the action depends on the lay of the land. As I was preparing the final draft of an earlier McCone novel, *Eye of the Storm,* I found that I'd handled a description of a boathouse in two different ways. In the early chapters, it had been a building on pilings over the water; later on, it had a concrete foundation and boat wells. Since near the end something happened in one of those wells, the initial description made no sense whatsoever!

This may sound like an incredible error, but, believe me, things like this happen to professionals, too. When I discovered it, I had read the manuscript numerous times. A friend and frequent collaborator had read it twice. Neither of us had caught the discrepancy. So check your copy. Recheck. Publishing houses have copyeditors to catch the little things, but the big things are your responsibility.

There you have the basics of free-form plotting. Develop a general situation, background, theme, characters, and ending. Set the situation. Allow your characters to act and interact with one another. When the primary development stage is complete, complicate by playing "what if." Write some more. Be flexible; play "what if" again and again. Rewrite, reread. Check, recheck. And as you write, take advantage of the surprising things that develop—they will often point the way to a truly baffling plot!

54

THINK OF THE READER

By Piers Anthony

I AM KNOWN AS A WRITER of popular fantasy and science fiction, though my output is not limited to that. Thus my view is that of a genre writer who is trying to understand more general principles.

Back when I was struggling to break into print, I took a correspondence course in writing. The instructors knew a great deal about writing, but little about science fiction. No matter, they said; the fundamentals of good writing apply to all genres, and they could help me. They were only half right: the fundamentals do apply, but you do have to know the genre—any genre—in order to write successfully for it. I studied my market on my own, and in the end I made it on my own. From this I derive a principle: There is virtue in being ornery. I continue to be ornery and continue to score in ways the critics seem unable to fathom.

A writer *should* study his market, and study general principles; both are essential. He should also forge his own way, contributing such limited originality as the market will tolerate. There is plenty of excellent instruction elsewhere on such things. I am concerned here with a more subtle yet vital aspect of writing than most: the writer's liaison with the reader. This can make or break a piece of writing, yet few seem to grasp its significance. This is one of my many differences with critics, so I will use them as a straw man to help make my point.

I picture a gathering of the elite of the genre, who are there to determine the critic's choice of the best works of science fiction and fantasy of all time. That is, the List that will be graven on granite for the edification of the lesser aspirants. In the genre these would be Samuel Delany's *Dhalgren,* Brian Aldiss' *Report on Probability A,* and Russell Hoban's *Riddley Walker,* and the finest writer of all time would be J. G. Ballard, despite his one failure with *Empire of the Sun.*

Have you read any of these? Have you even heard of them? No,

257

except that you did like the motion picture based on the last? Well, the critics have an answer for you: You are an ignorant lout whose library card and book store privileges should be suspended until your tastes improve.

Yet any ordinary person who tries to read such books will wonder just what world such critics live in. The answer is, of course, a different world. They are like the poet Shelley's Ozymandias, whose colossal ruin lies in the barren sand. "Look on my works, ye mighty, and despair." Yet his works are completely forgotten.

I am in the world of commercial writing, which means it is readable and enjoyable, and the only accolade it is likely to receive from critics is a mock award for WHO KILLED SCIENCE FICTION? (I was in a five-way tie for runner-up on that one last year, but there's hope for the future.)

But I maintain that the essence of literature lies in its assimilation by the ordinary folk, and that readability is the first, not the last criterion for its merit. Therefore I address the subject of writing, regardless of genre, from this perspective. What makes it readable? To hell with formal rules of writing; they are guidelines in the absence of talent and should be honored only so long as they do not interfere. If it's clear and interesting and relates to the needs of the reader, it will score. I like to tell audiences that they may love or hate what I write, but they will be moved by it. Then I prove it. The only person to fall asleep during one of my recent readings was a senior editor. Well, there are limits, and even I can't squeeze much blood from a stone. I am successful in part because I make connections with my readers that bypass the editors as well as the critics.

How do I do it? Well, there are little tricks, and one big secret. All of them are so simple that it's a wonder they aren't practiced by every writer. But they are not, and indeed critics condemn them, and editors try to excise them from my manuscripts. I have had many an inter-necine battle with editors, and finally left a major publisher because of this. I understand I am known as a difficult writer to work with, though no editor says it to my face. I can't imagine why!

All the tricks can be subsumed under one guideline: *Think of the reader*. Do it at every stage. Every paragraph, every word. If you are writing fantasy, don't use a word like "subsumed" because the reader won't understand it. It's a lovely word, but unless your readership consists of intellectuals or folk interested in precise usage—such as those who are presumed to read a book like this one—forgo your private pleasure, and speak more plainly. "All the tricks add up to this." I can with ease overreach the horizons of my readers, but I do my damnedest not to. Any writer who thinks he's smart when he baffles his readers, whether by using foreign phrases or obscure terminology, is the opposite.

When you refer to a character or situation that has not been mentioned for some pages, refresh the matter for the reader, so that he won't have to leaf back interminably to find out what you're talking about. Don't say, "The List is foolish." Huh? What list? Say "The List of the critics' top genre novels I parodied above is foolish." Editors seem to hate this; they blue-pencil it out as redundancy. But it enables the reader to check in with your concept without pausing, and that's what counts. Never let your reader stumble; lead him by the hand—and do it without patronizing him.

When you introduce a new character, don't just throw him at the reader unprepared. Have him introduced by a familiar character, if you possibly can. In my forthcoming mainstream novel *Firefly*, I start with one character, who later meets another, and then I follow the other character. That one meets a third, and I follow the third. In the course of 150,000 words, the only character the reader meets cold is the first one. Thus the reader can proceed smoothly throughout, never tripping. It was a job to arrange some of the handoffs, but that *is* my job as a writer: to do the busy-work for the reader. Some of the concepts in this novel are mind-stretching, but the little tricks smooth the way.

When I do a series—and I've done ten so far—I try to make each novel stand by itself, so that the reader who comes to it new does not have to struggle with an ongoing and confusing situation. Yes, this means repeating and summarizing some material, and it is a challenge to do that without boring those who have read the prior novels. But it means, for example, that a reader can start with my tenth Xanth novel and read backwards toward the first, and enjoy them all. Xanth has many readers, and this is part of the reason: It is easy to get into, and it does not demand more than the reader cares to give. Perhaps no other series shows a greater dichotomy between the contempt of critics and the devotion of readers. I do know my market, and it is not the critics. I suspect the same is true for most commercial writers.

Science fiction is fantastic stuff. Little of it is truly believable, and less is meant to be. It represents a flight of fancy for the mind, far removed from the dullness of mundane affairs. Yet even there, human values are paramount. There needs to be respect for every situation and every character, no matter how far out. Every thing is real on its own terms, and every one is alive, even when the thing is as outrageous as a night mare who is a female horse carrying bad dreams and the one is the Incarnation of Death itself, complete with scythe. Can a robot have feelings? Yes, and they are similar to those of a human being. For in the tacit symbolism of the genre as I practice it, a humanoid robot may be a man whose color, religion, or language differs from those of the culture into which he is thrust, and his feelings are those any of us would experience if similarly thrust. The essence of the genre is human, even when it is alien.

I am in an ongoing situation that illustrates the way that even the most fantastic and/or humorous fiction can relate to serious life. A twelve-year-old girl walking home from school was struck by a drunk driver and spent three months in a coma, barely responsive to any outside stimulus. At her mother's behest, I wrote her a letter, for she was one of my readers. I talked about the magic land of Xanth, and the sister realm of Elfquest by another author, and the value of children to those who love them, and I joked about the loathsome shot the nurse would give the Monster Under the Bed if she saw him. I spoke of the character with her name who would be in a future Xanth novel, an elf girl or maybe an ogre girl.

The child's mother read the letter to her, and it brought a great widening of her eyes, and her first smile since the accident. She became responsive, though able to move only her eyes, one big toe, and her fingers. She started to indicate YES or NO to verbal questions by looking to placards with those words printed on them. She made her preference emphatically clear: an elf girl, not an ogre girl!

It is my hope that she is now on the way to recovery, though there is of course a long way to go. It was fantasy that made the connection to reality, her response to my interest and my teasing. I think that fantasy needs no more justification than this. I, as writer, was able to relate to her, my reader, and she responded to me. The rest will be mostly in the province of medicine, but the human spark was vital to the turning point.

And here is the secret I am working toward: Writing and reading are one on one, writer to reader and back again, and the rest of the universe doesn't matter. The writer must know his readers, not the details of their lives, which are myriad, but their hearts and dreams. He must relate. He must care.

When I write to you, it is as if we are in a privacy booth, and we are sharing things that neither of us would confess elsewhere. We love, we hurt, we laugh, we fear, we cry, we wonder, we are embarrassed— together. We *feel,* linked. We share our joy and our shame, and yes, I feel your tears on my face as you feel mine on yours. We may be of different sexes and other generations, or we may match—but we relate to each other more intimately than any two others, dream to dream, our emotions mixed and tangled—for that time while the book that is our connection is open. When it closes we are cut off from each other, and we are strangers again, and we regret that, but we remember our sharing, and we cherish it. We were true friends, for a while. How precious was that while!

55

WHAT MAKES A GOOD HISTORICAL NOVEL?

BY JILL M. MORGAN

WHAT INGREDIENTS COMBINE TO CREATE a marketable historical novel?

Setting, certainly. Exciting plot, absolutely. Detailed background information, probably. All these are part and parcel of historical novels, but sometimes they get in the way of the most important element—interesting characters.

You might be thinking that you've heard this same advice as a guideline for writing other kinds of novels—and you'd be right. Character development is the most important ingredient in any novel. An interesting setting cannot carry the story alone. If the reader doesn't care what happens to the protagonist and antagonist, the rest of the novel is so much literary exercise and travelogue.

How does a writer make the reader care?

First, don't confuse *care* with *like*. It isn't necessary for the reader to like the main characters of your novel; you might want the reader actually to dislike them. But you do want them to care.

What works best is to write the plot around the character, not the character around the plot. Bringing the protagonist of your novel to an interesting city so that you, the clever writer, can show off your accomplishments in recording the historical details of that place, does not work. Bringing the protagonist to this same city does work, if observing the historic buildings, for instance, is a natural extension of the character's interest.

The same rule applies to death scenes. Historical novels are full of them. If you're going to write any death scenes in your historical, make sure that you have given the reader sufficient reason to be affected by whether or not the character lives or dies. Nothing is more boring than reading a death scene that doesn't cause the reader one flutter of distress. Why kill a character if it won't make your readers weep?

Moving down the scale of importance, the next element in creating this magic mix is plot. Yes, plot—even in a historical. Especially in a historical. Too many writers feel that fitting the characters into real historical events will be enough to carry the story. It never is.

Like so many related genres—suspense, mystery, and even horror—the historical moves on a swift river of tension. It is a balance that teeters over the edge, and then pulls back. It races forward in a fast-paced plot that winds and twists, and falls back upon itself to linger long enough for the exhausted reader to draw one quick breath. Then on it goes. It's how the characters react to the drama of the plot that creates this tension. A well-crafted historical novel is as exciting as any thriller.

The character is greater than the plot; the plot is greater than the setting. At its best, each segment blends and complements the other. The plot should never outshine the character, and the setting should never outshine the plot. Look at it this way: The reader doesn't want to read a book about Ireland. He or she wants to read a book about a no-longer-young woman named Moira, who was past the age of youthful fancy when Dougal O'Shay asked for her hand. That this event happens to take place in Ireland is the lovely drapery of a backdrop, or setting, and not the theme of the novel.

Readers of historical novels love to learn new facts and anecdotes about the people and the period. Writing a historical is a wonderful opportunity to sprinkle the details of history like seasoning into the rich stew of your novel. Too little, and it will be bland; too much, and you will have an indigestible mixture. A dash of history can enrich a scene or spoil it.

Because readers of historical fiction are sticklers for accurate details, writers of this genre must check the accuracy of all verifiable dates, names, and places. Your readers will be the first to tell you if you're wrong, and if you don't respect the facts as sacrosanct, you'll lose your readers. Historical authenticity is what historical fiction writers must try to achieve, so take the time to do it right. If you convince readers with a few authentic facts, they'll be more likely to suspend their doubts over the long sweep of the novel.

Facts are introduced into fiction to hook readers into believing the

263

story. This technique, like character development, works in every genre. It is as important a tactic in suspense, western, and mystery novels as it is in historical fiction. Facts legitimize the fiction. They persuade the reader to believe.

One question frequently asked is whether you have to go to the exotic places you want to write about. While I think it would be pleasant to visit every city or country you want to write about, the answer is definitely no. You're a reader as well as a writer. So just keep in mind: Have library card, will travel.

If you're writing a novel based in Scotland—notice, I didn't say about Scotland—check out the wide variety of books on Celtic Scotland, the Highland people, the Picts, ancient Scotland, and other books tracing the history of its people and the geological formation of the land. Libraries have many good books on these subjects, as well as glossy photos and captions for quick information.

Pick out a few examples of books on the flowers and the horticulture of the area. It's easy to write about heather when you have a color illustration sitting right in front of you. Using the authentic name of the flower or tree gives your reader the sense of the place. In writing a historical, conveying a sense of the place is more than half the battle.

You might also find such details in unusual reference sources. A book about the Loch Ness monster might have photographs and explicit description of vegetation and ground cover on the surrounding hillsides—which could come in handy for a scene based in the rustic Scottish countryside.

It's rewarding to browse through several kinds of books written about the particular country. A biography can be a good source for the flavor of a country, written in the voice of one of its inhabitants. Or try books on geology, sociology, religion, law, and travelers' guidebooks. You don't have to read them cover to cover; scan them for details.

A sometimes overlooked, but wonderful source of information for writers of historical fiction is the children's section of the local library. Children's books are short, to the point, and illustrated. They highlight important details such as those all-too-illusive dates and facts you've been searching for, and they're not dry reading.

Leaf through these reference books quickly for arresting details. If something piques your interest, it might attract a reader's attention, too. Jot it down. Keep going until you've compiled a tidy stack of note cards, with book title, author, publisher, and page number for each notation.

It's frustrating to find the perfect opportunity to use one of these details and not have the slightest idea where you found it. You might want to check it again for some thoughts it triggered—the color of a flower, or a haunting image. When you have made all the reference notes you will need for later checking, put them into a drawer and forget about them. The few that made the strongest impression will surface when you need them; the rest will sink. This may sound peculiar, after all the work you've done, but it allows you to write your novel without forcing it into a framework of facts.

A novel should be the work of your imagination. Historical notes are only present to accent its free-flowing development. If you jot down all the pertinent facts and then build your story around these details, you'll have a good basis for a textbook, but a very dull novel.

What sets historical novels apart from other genre fiction? In a historical, the setting often takes on the quality of an additional character of the novel. It may exist as strongly in the reader's imagination as do the protagonist or antagonist. The sense of place bonds the reader to the words, and the words to the characters, and the characters to the action. It is within this rarefied atmosphere of setting that the flavor of the novel comes through.

How do you add flavor to your writing?

Dialogue. Become a careful listener. Be attuned to that nuance in sentence structure that denotes the particular speech pattern of a region. Flavor in dialogue is far more than the dialect of that area. It is how the words of a character's sentences are strung together. And what choice of words? Plain? Fancy? It is through dialogue that writers convey the rhythm of the setting. Like a pulse, it reflects the heart and spirit of the characters, the setting, and the plot.

What is the catalyst that can blend all the above elements into a marketable historical novel?

Interest. To sustain the effort it requires to produce such a book, the writer must be genuinely fascinated by the characters, plot, place, and mood of the historical. The foreign names, story, and setting of the novel must become as much a part of the writer's life as his or her own family history and hometown. The true success lies in making what was strange and far away become familiar and understandable.

Shape the manuscript into its final form, and when you've done so, the novel will be ready to go to market.

56

CHARACTERIZATION AND STORY

BY L. R. WRIGHT

THE BULLETIN BOARD IN MY OFFICE is studded with pieces of paper bearing aphorisms. Most are typed on index cards, the authors' names noted at the bottom. But some are scrawled on paper torn from whatever lay handy, written in ink now faded, and of these, a few lack attribution. One of these unintentionally orphaned maxims reads as follows: "It's the way we are that makes things happen to us."

The relationship between character and story is so close as to render the two indistinguishable: Each story must seem inevitable, given its characters. Writers are often asked where their stories come from, and my answer is, from our characters. The better defined we make our characters—the better we know them—the stronger the stories they tell.

But where do these people come from?

They emerge, gradually, from a conglomeration of memory, observation, and imagination. Some emerge easily, and some only with great difficulty.

Each of my novels, except one, evolved from a visual image of somebody doing something. *Among Friends,* for example, began as an image of a woman in an alley, at night, staring at something lying on the ground. When I started to write it, I knew absolutely nothing about this character, except that she was female. I began work on the novel by describing the picture that had lodged itself in my head. The character then began to come to life. (More accurately, by describing the scene in the alley, I began creating that character.) She developed into a woman in her late fifties who lives alone and works as a secretary-receptionist for a small news magazine. Because of the kind of person she is— reserved, proud, solitary—she doesn't ask for help when the underpinnings of her life give way. And because she is also frightened, and possesses an extravagant imagination, she conjures up a terrifying hallucination upon which to focus her fraying powers of concentration.

266

Although the following lines were written as the first paragraphs of the first draft of the book (there were at least three rewrites), in the completed novel they don't appear until page 132, at the beginning of Emily's crisis:

A few minutes later Emily stood immobile in a dark downtown lane, her concentration fixed on something lying on the ground. The blank surface of the lane looked wet and slick, and it shone dully in the light from the streetlamp at the end of the lane. Huddled against a brick wall, away from the light, an old man lay on his stomach with his knees pulled up; like a baby asleep in its crib. His right cheek was cuddled into the pavement, and his left hand clutched an empty wine bottle. His grey hair stood up in spikes and his eyes were tightly closed. A white shirt collar poked up from the old grey coat in which he was wrapped. He wore hiking boots and a pair of dark pants.

Emily turned slowly, holding her purse in both hands. She sighed, a soft, barely perceptible sound, and walked back toward the street. . . .

Any other night, she was sure, if her eye had been caught by something moving and glinting in a late night downtown lane, she would not have entered it but walked on. She couldn't understand what had possessed her to go in there. She remembered a feeling of detachment, and a sensation that she was invisible, or at least invincible.

Emily was a character who came easily.

Karl Alberg, though—that's another story. Alberg is the Royal Canadian Mounted Police staff sergeant in my three mystery novels, and perhaps it's because he was so difficult to "get" that I am especially fond of him.

Initially, I didn't know that my fourth novel, *The Suspect,* was going to be a mystery, even though it opens with the murder of one octogenarian by another. I had expected that once I'd written the crime (the visual image with which the book opens) and created the criminal, I would become immersed in a long flashback that would reveal the reasons for the murder, and this flashback, I thought, would constitute the book. But I became so caught up in the deed and its effects upon George, the elderly murderer, that momentum swept me along until the next thing that had to happen was a police investigation.

So I needed a policeman.

It was easy enough to decide upon his physical characteristics, his age, his marital status; but as hard as I tried, I simply could not make the man real.

Finally, somewhat desperate, I took him out of the book. I wrote about him in all manner of situations: in the middle of a funeral; grocery shopping; in conversations with people I know—fictional and real. All this is a painful, laborious attempt to breathe life into him. Nothing worked. He remained stiff, awkward, utterly unbelievable, until . . . One morning I armed him with pruning implements and dispatched him into his overgrown backyard to cut back the greenery. Then, who knows why, he suddenly became authentic.

It is because of the kinds of people George and Alberg are that *The Suspect* develops as it does. George feels no guilt about trying to evade punishment for his crime, because he knows that his suffering for earlier "crimes" far outweighs anything the law can do to him. Alberg grows, reluctantly, to admire George even as he suspects him; but he can't stand the thought of anybody—including George—getting away with murder.

A Chill Rain in January is the only one of my novels that didn't begin for me with a visual image and some sense of a central character, however vague and fuzzy.

I became curious about people who lack a conscience, who are incapable of distinguishing between right and wrong; sociopaths. For them, I thought, life must be complicated and hazardous—rather like trying to walk when lacking a sense of balance. They are also very dangerous people, because they are impervious to guilt. Psychiatrists differ about what causes this condition. Some think it is learned behavior, and others believe it is the result of a physiological abnormality, a chemical imbalance in the brain. I opted for the latter. My sociopath would be born that way.

For a while I struggled with a male character, because the books say that sociopaths are almost always male. But I soon decided that it would be more interesting if the character were female. A great deal of anger attends this condition, and a female sociopath would have to place stronger controls on her anger than would a male.

The process of creating her was different from anything I'd experienced before, since I had no picture in my head to get me going. I began by recalling events in my childhood that I associated with the emergence of my own sense of morality, and I described them, in the first person, as if I were another person, a child incapable of understanding "morality." Some of this work survived to become a part of the novel. Here's how it developed:

One day when I was very young, I scissored away some of the fur on my cat's back. In my memory, the cat (whose name was Myrtle)

268

screeched and howled, tore herself from my grasp, ran out the door, and was never seen again. (My mother assures me that Myrtle, although she avoided me for a few days, didn't run away.) I remember a feeling of absolute amazement as it dawned on me that I had done something that caused another creature anguish, and that it was something I had had no right to do. I used this incident to create an imaginary one:

. . . The cat screamed and bashed around among the burning leaves and finally rolled out of the flames: it looked as if it had smoke coming out of it. It got to its feet and fled drunkenly across the park. . . .

Zoe's mother looked as if she felt dizzy or something. She kept staring at Zoe and saying her name, over and over again, as though she couldn't believe Zoe was really standing there, as if Zoe had just suddenly appeared, out of no-where. . . .

"What did you do?" said Zoe's mother.

"I put Myrtle in the fire."

"But why? How could you do such a terrible thing?" She was staring at Zoe and hanging on to her purse with both hands. The purse had a couple of new scratches on it—places where the leather had been made less brown. Zoe thought Myrtle had probably done that, with her stupid claws.

"I don't know. She made me angry."

Her mother turned around so that her back was to Zoe, and then she turned the rest of the way around, so that she was looking straight at her again. "Didn't you hear it screech? Don't you know how much it must hurt?"

"But—it wasn't me," said Zoe.

"But you just said—you just said, I heard you, 'I put Myrtle in the fire.' You just told me that."

"Yes," said Zoe. "I mean, it wasn't me that hurt."

Again, it is what Zoe *is* that generates the story. When she feels threatened, the only "right" thing to do is the thing most likely to re-establish order in her world. The cost to others is irrelevant to her.

Situations of crisis, danger, dread, or distress are not hard to imagine; we've all survived a few. And it's amazing what's stored in our memories just waiting to be used—not the events themselves, but the ways in which we experienced them.

When I was about eight years old, I was attacked by a guard dog chained up behind a warehouse. He and I were friends, I thought. But on that day I approached him while he was eating, and that turned out to be a big mistake. Thirty years later I wrote a novel called *The Favorite,* in which a little girl gets beaten up by one of her schoolmates. While writing that scene, I used "sense memories" from the day the dog attacked me:

. . . she stood feeling small on the playground, blood running slowly from her nose, a bruise on the side of her head, ragged with dust, hair full of it, tangled and wild. . . .

Sarah aimed herself toward the sidewalk and started to move her feet, one after the other. She knew her body must be broken into hundreds of pieces. It wasn't falling apart because of her skin. She was grateful to her skin. It would have been awful if her whole body had fallen apart right there on the public sidewalk.

She struggled up the street and past the neighbors' houses and if she saw anybody she knew, she didn't remember it later. . . .

She walked up to her front door and hoped Muriel would know what to do about something like this. She knew her father would know what to do, but he was at work, and so was her mother. She put her hand out to take hold of the doorknob and saw that her hand was shaking, her whole body was shaking, she thought her skin wouldn't be able to hold in all the broken pieces if it kept on being shaken around like that and she opened the door and started to scream.

If you allow yourself time to develop characters who are concrete and substantive, you can, by making use of your own personal memories as well as your imagination, put these characters into any imaginary situation, into confrontations with any other fictional people, and discover, as you write, how they must react.

It is these stage-managed collisions—character with character, character with life events—that produce for me the best and often the most unexpected results in storytelling; the thing that everyone calls plot.

ॐ 57

CREATING A CREDIBLE ALIEN

BY JERRY L. STERN

AS SCIENTISTS HAVE EXPANDED OUR KNOWLEDGE of physics, biology, and astronomy, writing science fiction has become more difficult. An alien character that would have been believable fifty years ago might now be rejected as either impossible or unreasonable. Modern fans of science fiction have far more expertise in the sciences than the fans of those early years. They love searching stories for scientific errors, and they are very good at finding them!

These modern science fiction readers won't tolerate a bug-eyed monster as the bad guy from outer space. They won't watch the hero of a story be ripped to shreds by an alien character who talks like a human, stalks like a hunter, pounces like a cat, screams like a banshee, or sniffs out your hero like a bloodhound. How terrestrial. How boring. If you can't do better than that, write a werewolf story instead, and set it in London in 1880.

Building a truly alien character is difficult. It takes a lot of work, a lot of thought, to design an alien's physical characteristics, home planet environment, and language. But without taking that time, a writer may create only an alien costume, or a man in a creature suit. That alien shell would behave exactly like a human. If the alien in your story behaves like a human, then *make it a human!* Your story gains nothing by the addition of an anthropomorphic alien. Science fiction readers can tell the difference between good and bad aliens, and they will tell you quite emphatically when you've made a mistake.

Science fiction fans constantly play "the game." Their part of the game is to find all of an author's science errors. An author's job in the game is slightly more difficult. The author must decide on the basic characteristics of a story. Are the characters performing on a oddball planet? Is the hero reptilian, or is the story about the consequences of a new invention? The game will allow nearly any combination of these factors as starting points. Once that initial premise has been established, however, every other detail in that story must be consistent not only with all the details of that premise, *but also with the reasonable extrapolations of those ideas, within the limits of current scientific knowledge.*

But you can write science fiction if you don't know every last fact about the science of the nineties. There is a method. Limit your science to the minimum necessary for your plot, and the logical extrapolations of that scientific premise. It may not be necessary to use an alien in every story. If your story really *needs* an alien for plot reasons, here are some things to consider while developing the concepts needed for building a believable alien. . . .

Biochemistry

Does the alien have our basic body biochemistry? Does it use the carbon-based system of converting sugars and water and oxygen to carbon dioxide? Then it must breathe oxygen and come from a planet that has photosynthesis, or an equivalent, to cycle that process backward. That limits its livable temperature range basically to that of liquid water. A "hot" alien, from a desert planet, where the temperature is always above 250 degrees, couldn't share our body chemistry no matter how strange its anatomy. If you choose a different chemical basis for life, be sure it is theoretically possible, or the readers will say, "Ahhh! Another inconsistency! Bad science!" Bad alien, too.

Physics

Maybe you would like to write "hard" science fiction. The "hard" applies to the science involved. It's easy to determine if a piece of science fiction writing is classified as "hard." If there is a lot of mathematics involved in proving a premise, that's hard. Unless you have a lot of science background, you might want to leave such subjects to the experts. For example, the subject of living on a neutron star has been explored by the science fiction novelist Robert L. Forward, who is also a consultant on scientific matters such as solar sails, deep space exploration, and anti-matter. His novel *Dragon's Egg* speculates how life might evolve on a neutron star, and how we could communicate with it.

Without going quite to a neutron star, you can still describe a strange environment. Think about how a heavy gravity planet would affect the development of a culture. Or maybe, how would living in the zero gravity environment of an interplanetary trading ship be different from the life on a ship limited not to space, but bound to an ocean.

Anatomy

How many arms does an alien need to work on a space-faring vessel? How many joints should there be in an arm? Or should your alien have arms? Should it be he or she? Or maybe there is a realistic story reason to use three sexes, or some other system that could only evolve under conditions that would have to be scientifically explained.

These are just some of your choices in building an alien body. You are not necessarily limited to what would look familiar or reasonable on Earth. Anything that can be explained as a reasonable evolutionary development is fair play.

Say, for the sake of a thought experiment, that you've devised an alien. We'll call this one a *he,* although we suspect some quirky adaptive bits in his biology. He comes from a planet under a sun similar to our own, although his planet is just slightly warmer than the Earth, and has considerably stronger gravity. But the creatures on his planet have evolved shaped like barrels, with five double-jointed arms and matching legs and feet, each with five smaller appendages that we'll call fingers and toes for lack of better terms.

Psychology

If something that grew up on a heavy gravity planet came to Earth, and saw the skyline of New York, what would be its reaction? In three gravities, a skyscraper could not be built with the methods and materials used on Earth.

Science fiction fans will carry this analysis much further. If you jump off a building, the factor that determines how badly you will be injured is not the height of the building; it is the speed that you're traveling when you hit the ground. On Earth, that speed is always the same for a given height off the ground. The higher the gravity, the more quickly a falling object increases in speed. On a heavy gravity planet, a drop of only a few inches would be fatal. Our alien is probably afraid of heights.

If you think that's a minor point in developing the cultural codes of a

273

civilization, take a look at Hal Clement's novel, *Mission of Gravity*. Clement's planet Mesklin is a great example of a strange planetary environment, a flattened spheroid with variable gravity and a day of seventeen and three-quarter minutes. The gravity is strongest at the poles of the planet, where the aliens each weigh over 900 pounds. At the equator of their planet, the Mesklinites have a weight of only a few pounds each, and are understandably worried about the strong winds carrying them away.

Clement's Mesklinite aliens are sailors and explorers on a sea of liquid methane. Certainly humans could not live in such cold, so the cultures of humans and Mesklinites will have very different structures.

Culture, personality, and language

Culture and personality are the most important parts of alien characterizations. Given a background of the basic premise of the story and descriptions of the environment, chemistry, and anatomy of an alien, as a science fiction author you must develop a feel for what an alien's social culture could be like. What reasonable personality could develop from these starting points? After the third chapter, creatures that merely look strange will no longer hold the attention of a science fiction reader. There must be an *alien persona* resident in an alien, matching what should reasonably have evolved in such a creature.

Next decision: Will the alien be able to learn our language fairly well, or just a pidgin dialect? It may become difficult to convince your readers of the intelligence of an alien that has only a limited vocabulary; it may become impossible to express ideas through that alien that relate to real concerns of fully developed characters.

You'll have to watch your language when talking to aliens. The verbal shortcuts that we have developed may not be understandable. Sure, we can assume that once they learn English they will understand some of our expressions, but will symbols make any sense at all? *We* may understand "dropping pennies into a piggy bank," but our five-sided alien will not understand why we place coins in livestock.

Just as some English might not be understandable to your alien, some of his language may not be translatable into English. You'll need to make up an alien language. Fortunately, you won't need an entire vocabulary and grammar, but you will need words for the basic concepts of the alien society, including names and titles of aliens. Words for those concepts that are not translatable will be useful, as will terms of respect and admiration. Don't go overboard on language, though. The more details present in a fictional language, the more likely it is for a fan to find an inconsistency and tear your work apart. So, before you throw in alien language words, decide if those concepts really cannot be said in English.

When designing your alien's language, look out for pronunciation and phonemes. If your alien has a different mouth structure from ours, the phonemes he uses, or cannot use, will be different from ours. Could an alien with a bird beak say, "*Friend* or *Foe*"? An alien language does not need to be verbal, but look out! A tonal or sung language, or a language based on body movement, will be difficult to convert into words; don't approach it casually. Your readers will not appreciate being unable to pronounce character names or alien terms. If necessary, invent a subtle way to sneak in an explanation of pronunciation, maybe as an aside comment of a human character.

Human body language is a set of visual codes. Our alien is five-sided. When he nods his head, does it mean yes? Think about it. Isn't nodding or shaking your head side to side the same motion to this creature? So his body language will not be based on anything we could understand easily. Any gestures he makes will have to be explained, or translated into our own visual codes, at least the first time each gesture is made.

To see how an expert creates aliens and language and social structures, read C. J. Cherryh's novel, *Cuckoo's Egg*. Cherryh does the best aliens in the science fiction genre. She has managed to incorporate enough alien concepts to make the aliens come alive and not seem to the reader like costumed humans, and yet she has not made the aliens so strange that communication is lost.

An alien and a human must have something in common if there is to be any competition or friendship or even hate beyond pure xenophobia. There must be enough jointly held concepts to keep a conversation moving, a joint exploration traveling, or a colonial trader running from planet to planet.

Just because you've created a creature that, to human eyes, appears strange, don't assume that you've created an alien being. Even a bug-eyed monster can become a believable alien. Just use some empathy, a touch of psychological strangeness, and some good extrapolation from a purely biological description of the alien to the planet, evolution, and culture that created it. As a writer, build up a picture for yourself of the kinds of events that could trigger your alien character's responses, and you'll soon have an alien writing his own action and dialogue for you. Once that happens, writing science fiction is like any other fiction. Just let the characters do what they must, and hang on for the ride through space and time.

58

WRITING THE REALISTIC WESTERN NOVEL

BY RICHARD S. WHEELER

THE TRADITIONAL WESTERN NOVEL has always been hedged about with more conventions than any other category, with the possible exception of women's romances. The publishers of hardcover library westerns have allowed a certain freedom recently, but the mass market houses that spin out the novels that fill the paperback racks have essentially the same requirements as ever.

These conventions dictate that the story occur some time between the Civil War and the 1890s, roughly when the frontier vanished; also that those westerns be about loners in armed conflict—for example, the young rancher just starting out who must fight off the predatory cattle king. With very few exceptions over the years, the central figure in westerns had to be male, as in the gunman-type story. These male protagonists had to be of heroic and mythic stature. Their character is commanding: They rarely wonder what course of action is wisest or dither about what to do. Usually, they are hardy and strong, skilled in various martial arts, from gunmanship to brawling. As is true of all mythic characters, they don't grow or change as a result of their trials, but triumph because of their innate superiority over their antagonists.

Very few traditional western heroes are married. The women that do appear are portrayed as secondary figures. There is no substantial love interest, although love is not totally forbidden. But emotions are largely taboo: The mythic western heroes are poker-faced and stoic and avoid anything resembling rage, tears, shame, tenderness or laughter, and it's especially important that they not express gentle or poetic feelings. They are born leaders who never seem to suffer dissent or rebellion of their allies, and who enjoy the unquestioning obedience of women.

Another convention of the classic western is that characters are shown only in the depiction of action. Readers must never be made privy to the hero's private torments or doubts, or his rejoicing or dreams, lest the flow of action be interrupted. As a result, we rarely see a fully rounded western hero.

I have described here the classic Louis L'Amour western hero and story, and because of his awesome success, few publishers have ever deviated from the formula. L'Amour, who dominated the field for so many years, was both an asset and liability to the western story. At one point in the early 1980s, he was virtually the only author of single-title (not series) westerns being published, and he kept the category alive at a time when publishers had largely abandoned it. But if he was the rescuer of the category, he was also unwittingly responsible for keeping it in a straitjacket. His very success at writing the mythic, romantic western ensured that the mass market houses would not deviate from stories about a frontier west that never really existed. And sad to say, I believe his influence narrowed down the western market, driving away women readers, and especially better-educated readers who might have enjoyed a story about real, flawed mortals wrestling with the terrible dangers of a real frontier and wilderness. His influence was so profound that in his later years the type of western story accepted by publishers narrowed more than ever. As a result, gifted earlier authors who wrote of the west in broader strokes—Ernest Haycox in particular—would have found their manuscripts unwelcome. Haycox's women—the wives, sweethearts, or allies of his heroes—were much too feisty to fit into the L'Amour tradition.

As much as I have loved the western story all my life, I found these ironclad rules daunting. When I began writing westerns in the mid-seventies, I yearned to tell a more realistic story, about real people challenging the awesome difficulties posed by the wild west. A person of ordinary courage promised to be a better protagonist than the mythic type whose victory is foreordained. There seemed to me a much better possibility of suspense, or story tension, cowardice and honor, skill and clumsiness, moral certitude, and occasional weakness. Such a protagonist can fail; he could grow or shrink, but certainly not remain the same by the end of the story.

In the course of my extensive research, I discovered something else: The real historical west offers far better material, more colorful and fantastic, than the wildest imaginings of the romantic western novelists. For a brief, unique period in the 19th century, the great western expansion into unknown lands fraught with dangers captured the imagination of the country—indeed, of the world. There had never been anything like it, and never will be again. Far from being exhausted and arid as a result of innumerable western novels, films, and TV series, the *real* frontier west is virtually untouched, virginal material available to any novelist. The traditional mythic western has used this material only as backdrop, or stage setting, while focusing on its real theme, male pecking-order struggles between loners on a lawless land, where the social rules didn't apply. But the real west was rarely like that. The real stories and characters are much wilder, more violent, more astonishing than anything on the paperback racks.

When I set out to write westerns, I had one additional goal: to appeal to a more educated, literate readership. That meant doing two things: using a rich vocabulary, on a level with any serious novel, along with effective metaphors and other figures of speech. Here I butted against a style common in traditional westerns, which are written in the most basic, pedestrian language.

My second purpose was to deepen my characters, work within their heads, in a way that didn't slow the story. One way to do this is to make the characters' calculations a part of the plot itself.

I've had the good fortune to have editors who have permitted me to write nontraditional westerns and have encouraged me to reach toward literary quality. I set my two western series in the 1840s and 1850s, which I find much richer than the post-Civil War era. The result of all this has been a number of novels that are about as far removed from the usual category western as possible. In one, the hero is a Harvard-educated Boston Brahmin. In another, there's a venal sheriff too fat to ride a horse, so he covers his county in a buggy. In another, the hero is a former mountain man, now a trader to the Blackfeet, who'd been a classics professor at Amherst. In one of my series, the hero is an Irish doctor pressed temporarily into being a sheriff. In another series, Skye's West, the hero is a former British sailor who jumped ship and is now a boozy guide with an older Crow wife and younger Shoshone wife and a singularly evil horse. In one of my novels, the heroine is a clever con artist who matches wits with a rascal. In yet another, the hero is a farmer who's clawed a fortune in gold out of a Montana gulch, only to lose it to road agents. Is he brave? No, he falls to the ground, weeping, but is later redeemed by other values.

One could scarcely imagine western heroes, or situations, farther removed from the L'Amour approach. And yet they are succeeding, some of them handsomely. And more important, they are being read by people who otherwise don't read westerns. I've written traditional stories, too, most recently one that reworks the *Shane* theme about the man familiar with weapons but who doesn't wish to use them again—in this case a young banker. But the nontraditional story is my joy.

All of which is to say that it is possible to market western stories that buck the category tradition. Much of the work of Elmer Kelton and Will Henry lies outside the stock category approach. Likewise, some of Jack Schaefer's work and the western stories of Doug Jones and Ben Capps, whose work has inspired and influenced me.

Change is in the air. It began, actually, with Larry McMurtry's great Pulitzer-Prize-winning novel, *Lonesome Dove,* back in 1985. That novel is a watershed in western fiction, and well worth close study; it is a model of what can be accomplished in a nontraditional western novel. Others worth study are Will Henry's *I, Tom Horn,* Jack Schaefer's *Monte Walsh,* and Elmer Kelton's *The Good Old Boys.* All of these transcend the realm of the category story. They can be considered literature, and are delightful, realistic expressions of frontier life.

In spite of the recent suspension or reduction of several western lines, the frontier story is not in danger of extinction. Both Bantam and Zebra continue publishing this category. The present turmoil is really an opportunity for writers to write and publish new forms of westerns, stories that will appeal to the broad national audiences that the old *Saturday Evening Post* attracted with serialized westerns enjoyed by people in all walks of life. A bold novelist willing to research and write about the *real* frontier, use realistic heroes and story lines instead of mythic ones, and add literary graces to the genre, can capture a new market for himself and his publishers. The historical frontier is a new frontier.

59

THE MYSTERY IS IN THE WRITING

BY WILLIAM MURRAY

WE TEND IN THIS COUNTRY TO PIGEONHOLE and compartmentalize everyone and everything, which saves us the trouble of thinking. I don't consider myself an author of mysteries per se. I chose the mystery genre only because it seemed to me to be the only way I could find an immediate audience for myself and my stories. It also made it easier for publishers to launch them into an increasingly precarious market.

Being identified as a genre author has its drawbacks (one tends not to be taken seriously by the highbrows), but the best way to handle the situation is simply to write the best books one is capable of and wait for the critics to catch up. They are usually well behind the reading public in these matters. One could argue, for instance, that Haydn was a genre composer, as was Verdi in his early operatic years, since they both composed in established forms and for a particular audience. The safest approach is to tell a good dramatic story as well as possible and not worry about genres and whether, in the publishing jargon of the day, it will turn out to be "the breakthrough" book.

I'm not primarily a reader of mysteries, but it seems to me that there are two kinds of detective stories. One is the pure whodunit, which is constructed like an elaborate puzzle and in which the primary interest centers on the old question of Who Killed Cock Robin. The great practitioners in the field, most notably Agatha Christie, have ennobled the form and become stars in the process. The second kind consists of the novels of such writers as Dashiell Hammett, Raymond Chandler, Ross Macdonald, and Ross Thomas, which illuminate the darker corners of an entire society and portray a particular world. The latter are the writers who, in my opinion, have used the genre as a legitimate literary form and who can be considered artists as well as storytellers.

The world I deal with in my novels is the circumscribed one of the racetrack, with its large floating population of horsemen, grifters, speculators, aristocrats, pimps, prostitutes, addicts, gypsies, and hustlers of all varieties. Its great appeal to me is that of an ambience I understand and which I think of as a metaphor for life itself. One of its great fascinations derives from the fact that it is a world of new beginnings. No matter how disastrous events have proved, there is always tomorrow. Or, as an old racetrack adage goes, "Nobody ever committed suicide who had a good two-year-old in the barn." What could be more appealing to a novelist than that?

The reviewers of my books seem to be pretty much in agreement on one aspect of my writing—an ability to create vivid and believable characters. I think this may be because I always begin with the people in my stories, never with the story itself. I detest outlines, mainly because I find the idea constricting. I generally have only a vague idea of what my story will be about and what might eventually happen, but nothing more. Once I have this concept, then I start thinking about the characters in the piece, because I know that ultimately it is they who will dictate the outcome of events. Very often, in fact, characters I haven't even envisioned or who appeared as minor ones suddenly take on a life of their own and become major players.

In my book, *I'm Getting Killed Right Here,* a minor female character named May Potter becomes, by the end of the story, a major one, with a history and a life all of her own, one that I hadn't conceived at all when I sat down to write. For some mysterious reason, I gave her a scar on her neck. It wasn't until three-quarters of the way through the novel that the reason for the scar became clear to me and turned into a plot revelation. I don't pretend to understand this process of creation, but it is the reason I keep writing. Every novel becomes an adventure and a process of discovery.

These stories are all told by my narrator and alter ego, Shifty Lou Anderson. When I first decided to write them, I knew only that I wanted a narrator who was not a private eye or a cop. I also wanted one who was an artist in a profession that paid poorly, so that he would have to supplement his income either as a bettor or, during the inevitable losing streaks, by temporary employment in a variety of other jobs. A close-up magician was the ideal solution, because, whatever his skills, he works in a profession that cannot earn him a great deal of money. I had written several articles about magic and magicians and had become friends with a few, most notably Michael Skinner, a master prestidigitator who works at the Golden Nugget in Las Vegas. I myself have no talent for magic, and I'm the sort of person who can't put tacks into a piece of cork without stabbing himself. But I do know what it takes to be a great sleight-of-hand artist, and I've used that knowledge to create Shifty, who has become almost as real to me as my own children.

In the writing workshops that I now teach at the University of California at San Diego, I urge my students not to think of fiction as a form entirely separate from other kinds of writing. Novelists need to acquire reportorial and research skills and should cultivate them in order to increase their knowledge of society and its workings. I also stress discipline and a regular pattern of work, the adoption of a rhythm into which the writer can lose himself every day. Ivory-tower writing and waiting for inspiration are anathema to me and result in an elitist, self-defeating attitude toward one's work. The computer will not do the work for you nor is it essential to the process. I myself work on lined yellow pads with No. 2 pencils and don't get around to typing the material up until I've rewritten and polished the text so that I feel it's ready to be read by someone else. Rewriting is the key to good writing. As for writer's block, my answer to that problem is a quick glance at my bank statement.

§ 60

CREATING CHARACTERS WHO "LIVE"

BY ANNE PERRY

BEING INVITED TO WRITE THIS has concentrated my mind on what has been until now rather a "seat of the pants" affair. I have written about characters either because I liked them, or because I thoroughly enjoyed disliking them. Those I liked I often identified with—such as Charlotte, Pitt, Great Aunt Vespasia; or had fun knowing vicariously—Emily, Micah Drummond or Somerset Carlisle, all of whom appear in most or all of my novels.

Through the characters I identify with, I can express my own feelings of anger, gentleness, shock, compassion, etc. But there are ways in which those I dislike are even more fun, and also project many of the qualities I feel deeply about. I relish their outrageous remarks, their total selfishness or bigotry and the hypocrisy of people like Charlotte's grandmama, who is a fearful old woman, and yet she does no real harm to anyone. I feel a kind of pity for her because she has outlived her friends, her usefulness, her social importance or hope of it, and the style of living to which she was educated and taught to expect.

Uncle Eustace (Cardington Crescent) was pompous, thoughtless, hypocritical, and he did an almost immeasurable damage through his arrogance and insensitivity. Yet in the end I pitied him when he caught one dreadful glimpse of understanding and began to see himself as he was. Perhaps that is a great deal of the key: Do not set people up merely to knock them down. Have as few characters as possible for whom you yourself feel no warmth or pity, and none at all for whom there is no comprehensible motive.

For a plot to be powerful, the reader has to believe that all the characters would really behave as they do. The moment something does not make sense, the spell is broken. And for readers to care—which is the essence of success—there must be characters in your novel whom readers like and feel involved with.

I find it helpful to make a one-page biographical sketch of characters who have more than walk-on parts, noting such things as age, anything important in their family background, such as parents' occupation, financial or social status, siblings, education, ambitions (especially if thwarted). And note their present hobbies or interests, love affairs (actual or desired), emotional events, wounds real and fancied, personal characteristics, temper, fears, obsessions.

Physical appearance must be consistent with personality. Strength of will, stubbornness, vacillation are often visible in a face. Passion and appetite usually show in a mouth, as do rigidity, indecision, insensitivity. Not only does facial construction say a lot about a person, but so also do movement, expression, pitch of voice and verbal tricks or habits. Body "language" can reveal a great deal, too; hands can indicate much, especially fingers, moving or at rest.

I find it useful when creating a character to start with a particular face I have seen in a newspaper photograph, a film, painting, or even in a waxwork. One of the best and most powerful I ever used was suggested by a waxwork of Cardinal Richelieu. As the character grows, you may move away from the model, but it helps with consistency of physical descriptions to have a firm starting point.

It is said that at twenty we have the face that nature gave us, at fifty the one we deserve! Your fifty-year-old characters should reveal their strengths and their weaknesses to anyone astute enough to read them.

It is a good idea to give at least some physical description of your character the first time the reader meets him. Readers will build some picture of their own if you don't, and then if their picture does not coincide with yours when it emerges later in the book, readers will be upset; you will have destroyed the character as they knew him.

It is usually far more effective to "show" your characters rather than describe them. Dialogue is obviously one of the best ways of doing this. The feelings characters express and the words they choose are very strong indications of personality, and much sharper to the reader than descriptions of vices, virtues, wit, gentleness, etc.

Try to key your descriptions to one or two features, an emotional sketch, an impression, not a photographic portrait from which characters could be identified on a police blotter. Shape and coloring can be less important than expression, or one outstanding feature. There are also less obvious features—eyebrows, hairline, curve of cheek or throat, ears, and, of course, teeth. A description—blue eyes, brown hair, straight nose, wide mouth—says far less about the person than something more personal, such as humorous eyes, uncertain mouth, quick to laugh but curiously sulky in repose. Above all, avoid sentimentality and clichés, such as "twinkling eyes" or "generous mouth." Try recalling someone you met a long time ago; which features can you still visualize? It will probably be only one or two, but they evoke the person for you.

The reactions of other characters to your hero/heroine can be very enlightening and reveal a great deal about the hero/heroine—and about the other characters as well. You can also show a great deal about a character by his reactions to a situation. You can demonstrate all sorts of emotions, weaknesses, strengths, bigotries, assumptions, compassion, wit—almost anything. And showing another character's reaction to the same situation can highlight the contrast between them powerfully, subtly, delicately.

Ask half a dozen people to describe an event to you, and you will probably find they all noticed different aspects of it, depending on their natures, likes and dislikes, preconceptions, or whatever. Remember this when your characters recount an event or react to one. Also, as time goes by, memory can become highly selective and much colored by our emotions. To some extent, we see what we expect to see; and believe what fits in with what we already think we know.

One of the most effective ways of illustrating character and heightening drama is the use of a small scene, a cameo—anything from a paragraph to a page long that is a heightened and vivid illustration of a particular characteristic. It will stay with the reader longer than a page of description and have a much sharper emotional effect.

You can use a scene or event from the past, but I believe one from the present is usually more effective. The "cameo" scene might be the failure to see a joke; a sudden appreciation of beauty and the ache to share it, to preserve it; a flash of temper that betrays fear; or something ridiculous that reveals the vulnerability of the character.

This scene from my novel *Bethlehem Road* is an example, not for what it says about suffragettes in 1888, but for the bigotry, the vulnerability, and the sadness of Lady Mary Carfax, and why she behaves as she does:

"What they are is very easy," Lady Mary replied. "They are women who have failed to make a suitable marriage, or who have an unnaturally masculine turn of mind and desire to dominate rather than be the domestic, gracious, and sensitive creatures they were intended to be, both by God and nature. . . . Why any woman should choose otherwise I cannot imagine—except, of course, as a revenge upon those of us who are normal, whom they cannot or will not emulate. . . ." Mary Carfax's pretense at pity was a sham; she had forgotten and forgiven nothing.

I hope these ideas on depicting character will help you to create your own characters with success—and pleasure.

61

CHARACTER: THE KEY ELEMENT IN MYSTERY NOVELS

BY JAMES COLBERT

BY DEFINITION, TO BE A MYSTERY a novel must have a murder at the beginning that is solved by the end. And by convention there must be a solution, whether or not there is an apprehension. This is the contract assumed by the reader when he or she picks up a book classified as a mystery. Yet despite this murder-solution requisite, mysteries offer the writer great freedom, a basic structure around which to work plot, setting, and most important, character.

Without doubt, character is the most important element of a mystery. A clever plot helps, certainly, as does a strong sense of place, but those elements are secondary, best used to show how the central character thinks and responds to events and environment. One writer may have a native Floridian solving murders while another may send a New York City detective to Florida. While Florida, of course, remains the same, the interesting thing for the reader is to see how the character responds, how he or she integrates the sense of the place into an overall experience. The same is true of the plot. No matter how interesting, unless uncovered by a central character readers find engaging, events take on a flat, two-dimensional quality. "Just the facts, ma'am. Just the facts" has its place, all right, but that place is in a newspaper, not a mystery.

So how does a writer go about portraying an engaging character? The answer to that is as multi-faceted and as complex as the character must be, and it is accomplished one small step at a time. Think of a police artist putting together a composite sketch of a suspect. Thin sheets of transparent plastic, each with slightly different lines are laid one over another, composing different parts of the face until a whole picture emerges. While the medium is different, the technique is not dissimilar to the one a writer uses. First sheet: How tall is the character, and how much does he weigh? How is he built? Second sheet: What color hair does he have? What are his distinguishing characteristics? Third sheet: What is the setting, and what is the character thinking? Small elements are put together, one over another, until a whole picture emerges.

Where the police artist leaves off with the physical portrait, however, the writer is just beginning because the reader wants to know, well, what's this guy really *like?* Is he threatening or non-threatening? Well-read or illiterate? Optimistic or pessimistic? What kind of car does he drive? What does he eat? The nuances, eccentricities, habits, way of thinking and quirks are what separate a description of a character from one who starts to *live*; and all those things are revealed as the character responds to his surroundings and reacts to events—in a very good mystery, dynamic events make the character *grow.*

Growth and change are intrinsic, inevitable elements of the human condition. The growing and the changing, however, usually occur very slowly, day by day, not very noticeably. Within the usually limited time frame of a novel, this change is often very difficult to portray, but the mystery has the advantage of a dynamic structure. A murder occurs at the beginning and is solved by the end. Events, feelings, new understandings are speeded up, compressed into a very short time. As a result, it is credible that the characters change fairly quickly in response. Really successful mysteries allow the reader not just to know a character but to grow with him, to learn his lessons as he did, without actually having to endure the violent crime. Observe Burke in Andrew Vachss's novel, *Blossom,* or listen to the first-person narrator in Scott Turow's *Presumed Innocent.* Notice how they change during the course of the book. Observe what they learn and how the new understandings affect them. And watch how, with the characters firmly in hand, the authors thrust them into the events that form the respective plots.

Plots are usually very simple ideas extended. Even the most complex plot can be described briefly. (Excellent examples of this can be found in your Sunday paper, in the film listings where even very involved movies are summarized in a line or two.) But unlike the step-by-step development of characters, plots appear complex at the outset and become more and more simple. Elements are stripped away rather than added. What appears confusing, even chaotic, at the start makes sense later on when other motives and actions are revealed: In retrospect, all the twists and turns make sense. The reader is left with a clear sense of order, a good sense of character, and, one hopes, a strong sense of place.

Evoking a place is stage setting in its most basic form. Remember, it is crucial to have the stage set for the central character—and not the other way round. Overlong descriptions of a place and a recitation of facts about it are best left to travel guides, which is not to say that setting is *un*important. But it *is* secondary. When successfully used, setting becomes the character and helps to reveal his or her foibles and way of life. In John D. MacDonald's Travis Magee novels, Travis Magee's houseboat, for example, is very much a part of Travis Magee, accommodating, even making possible, a way of life that is so much a part of him that when he travels, he seems to embody one *place* confronting another. Readers envy Travis the beachbum freedom of his life, and we understand how it feels to leave the beach and go, say, to New York City or to Mexico—or, for that matter, just to go to work. The setting is integral to Travis Magee and enriches the whole series; but while it may be difficult to imagine him anywhere else, the fact is, readers can. (MacDonald even tells us how to go about it whenever Travis considers his options.) For the writer, however, the single most important facet of technique, as important in its own way as making character primary, is to make use of what you know.

If presented well, there is no human experience that is uninteresting. Very good books have been written about what might, from all appearances, be very mundane lives. Yet mystery writers too often feel the need to write not what they know but what they perceive they *should* be writing about. As a result, the characters they create do not ring true, or in particular, they are tough when they should not be, or have no real sense of what violence is really like. But despite the hard-boiled school of detective fiction, it is *not* necessary for a central character in a mystery to be either tough or violent—the book can, in fact, be just as interesting when a character conveys some squeamishness or distaste for violence. Not all detectives have to be built like linebackers and display a penchant for brutal confrontation.

The simple fact is, what you know is what will ring true. Andrew Vachss writes about violence and violent people because he knows his subject; but Tony Hillerman eschews that and writes about Navajo Indians, which is what *he* knows. Scott Turow, the lawyer, writes about legal proceedings. All three have written very good books. But since Dashiell Hammett's *Continental Op*, far too many mystery writers have felt it mandatory to make their investigators tough, even when the writer has no notion of what real toughness is all about. The result is facade rather than substance—and the reader will sense it. In fiction, certainly, there is a need for imagination, but the imagination must spring from knowledge, not speculation. The most credible, most substantive books are those in which the author's grasp of his or her subject shows through. Allow your character to know what you know and do not attempt to impose on him what you feel he *should* know. Your character will appear shallow if you do, shallow, and most damning of all, contrived. With respect to that, it is important, too, that you consider your story first, *then* the genre it happens to fall into.

With my first novel, *Profit and Sheen*, I wasn't even aware that I had written a mystery until the first review came out. What makes me appear rather dense in one way worked to my advantage in another: I told my story as well as I knew how and was completely unencumbered by any feeling of restriction. The point is, tell your story as well as you know how and see how it comes out. *Then* worry about genre. If you start out with the expressed intent of writing a mystery, well and good; if you follow the rules. But if what you have in mind is a story with only some elements of a mystery, tell your story first and do not try to change it to conform to some vague idea of what a mystery should be. Your publisher will classify your book for you; genre classification is a subjective thing, nothing more than a handle, really, an easy and convenient way of breaking down different works into groups more for marketing purposes than for readers.

There are, of course, other aspects of writing a mystery to consider, but these are more difficult to pin down. Most notable among them, however, are point of view and voice. Selecting the right point of view is extremely important, because it determines what the reader will and will not learn. Voice is, really, the application of point of view to a consistent rhythm, a *voice* the reader hears. More often than not, point of view is intrinsic to the writing itself (the writer will begin "I . . ." or "He . . ."), but voice requires a certain conscious effort on the writer's part, an attempt to convey the story consistently through or around the central character—even when that central character's vision is rather limited or, to the writer, unattractive. The success of the voice is directly related to how true the writer remains to his character and how willing the writer is to remain "transparent."

If you work within the given structure, writing a mystery is not so different from writing any other kind of novel. Good mysteries do, in fact, have all the elements common to all good fiction: engaging characters, strong sense of place, compelling plot, believable voice. Allow the structure to work for you, write as honestly as you know how, and everything else will fall into place.

62

SETTING IS MORE THAN PLACE

By William G. Tapply

AN INTERVIEWER RECENTLY ASKED ME WHY I choose to set my mystery novels in New England instead of, say, Nebraska. I was tempted to answer with the old vaudeville punchline: "Everybody's got to be somewhere." Every story has to have a setting.

Instead I told the interviewer the simple truth: My choice of New England was easy—New England is where I've lived my entire life. It's what I know best. I couldn't write about Nebraska.

I define setting broadly. It's more than place. Setting comprises all the conditions under which things happen—region, geography, neighborhood, buildings, interiors, climate, weather, time of day, season of year.

I feel fortunate. My New England provides me with a rich variety of settings from which to select. I can send my narrator/lawyer/sleuth Brady Coyne from the inner city of Boston to the wilderness of the Maine woods, from the sand dunes of Cape Cod to the farmland of the Connecticut Valley, from exclusive addresses on Beacon Hill to working class neighborhoods in Medford. New England has whatever my stories might call for.

New England also gives me the full cycle of the seasons and all the weather and climate that accompany them. It gives me Locke-Ober and pizza joints, museums and theaters, factories and office buildings, mansions and apartments, skyscrapers and fishing lodges, condominiums and farmhouses.

I don't know about Nebraska. I suspect that if I lived there and knew it as intimately as I know New England I'd find a similar wealth of possibilities. I have, in fact, sent Brady to parts of North Carolina and Montana that I'm familiar with. What's important is knowing my settings well enough to invoke the details that will bring them to life and be useful in my stories.

Settings must strike our readers as realistic. A realistic setting persuades readers to suspend their disbelief and accept the premise that our stories really happened. The easiest and best way to do this is to write knowledgeably about real places, places where our readers live or have visited, or, at least, places they have read about or seen pictures of. Readers, I have learned, love to find in a novel a place they know. They enjoy comparing their impressions of Durgin Park or the New England Aquarium with Brady Coyne's. They like to hear what strikes Brady as noteworthy about Newbury Street, the Combat Zone, the Deerfield River, or the Boston Harbor.

You must get actual places precisely right or you risk losing your readers' trust. No matter how much you might dislike it, you cannot avoid research. You *must* hang out in the places you intend to write about. Observe the people, listen to the sounds, sniff the smells, note the colors and textures of the place. I have spent hours loitering in Boston's Chinatown and prowling the corridors in the East Cambridge courthouse. I've wandered around the Mt. Auburn Hospital and the Peabody Museum, looking for the telling detail that makes the place unique and that will allow me to make it ring true for every reader who has been there.

Research need not be unpleasant, in fact. I make it a point to eat in every restaurant I write about, no matter how familiar it already is to me, at least twice—once just before writing the scene to fix it in my mind, and once again afterward to make sure I've rendered it accurately.

A realistic setting doesn't really have to exist, however, and the fiction writer shouldn't feel limited to using actual places if doing so will alter the story he wants to tell. A fictional setting can still be true. My rule of thumb is this: If the setting you need exists, use it; if it doesn't exist, make it up but make it true. I built Gert's on the North Shore and Marie's in Kenmore Square—where no such restaurants stand—because my stories demand there be restaurants like them there. Readers are continually asking me how to find Gert's and Marie's, which I take to mean that I have rendered them realistically.

I made up a hardscrabble farm in Lanesboro and a horse farm in Harvard—fictitious but realistic places in actual Massachusetts communities. In my first Brady Coyne novel, I moved a rocky hunk of Rhode Island coastline to Massachusetts, committed a murder there, and named it Charity's Point because that storyline required it. I've had readers tell me they believe they have been there. In *The Vulgar Boatman*, I invented the town of Windsor Harbor. Had I tried to set that tale in a real community north of Boston, too many readers would have known that no events such as the ones I invented actually happened there. They would have been unable to suspend their disbelief.

Gert's and Marie's, the farms in Lanesboro and Harvard, Charity's Point, and Windsor Harbor were like the characters that populated the books. Although they were not *real*, they were all *true*—places like them exist, and they *could* be where I put them.

Setting can—and should—serve as more than a backdrop for the action of the story. The conditions under which the action occurs should do double or triple duty for you. Setting can create mood and tone for your fiction. The places where they live and work can reveal the personalities and motivations of your fictional characters. Places, weather, climate, season of year, and time of day can cause things to happen in a story as surely as characters can.

Shakespeare and Conan Doyle understood how setting can establish mood and foreshadow events. The "dark and stormy night" had its purpose, as did the spooky mansion on the remote moor or the thick fog of a London evening. Contemporary writers can use thunderstorms and abandoned warehouses and the barrooms and alleys of city slums in the same way. Robert Louis Stevenson once said, "Some places speak distinctly. Certain dank gardens cry aloud for murder; certain old houses demand to be haunted; certain coasts are set apart for shipwrecks." Find such places. Use them.

But be wary. Such obvious settings can too easily become literary clichés. Misuse them, or overuse them, and they lose their punch. Clever writers understand the power of going against stereotypes. Seek subtlety and irony. Murder can be committed on a sunny May morning in a suburban backyard, too, and when it does, the horror of it is intensified by the contrast.

Carefully selected details of setting can delineate the characters who populate the place. Match the pictures or calendars that hang on every office wall with some trait of the man who works there. Is the policeman's desk littered with half-empty styrofoam coffee cups? What kind of tablecloths does your restaurant use? What music is piped into the elevator of the office building? Does a week's worth of newspapers litter the front porch of that Brookline mansion? Does a specimen jar containing a smoker's lung sit on the desk of the forensic pathologist? Does the lawyer keep a bag of golf clubs in the corner of his office? Does a stack of old *Field & Stream* magazines sit on the table in the dentist's waiting room? Such well-chosen particulars can reveal as much about a character as his dress, manner of speech, or physical appearance.

Think of your settings as characters in your stories. Settings need not be passive. They can act and interact with your characters. Rainstorms cause automobile accidents. Snowstorms cover footprints and stall traffic. Laboratories contain chemicals that spill and release toxic fumes. The bitter cold of a Boston winter kills homeless people. Water released from a dam raises the water level in a river and drowns wading fishermen.

Your choice of setting may, at first, be arbitrary and general—the city where you work, the village where you live. But as you begin writing, you will need to search out particular places where the events of your story will unfold. Visit them often enough to absorb them. If you're lucky, you'll find that your real settings will begin to work for you. You'll see a person whose face you'll want to use. You'll overhear a snatch of conversation that fits a storytelling need. You'll note a detail you didn't expect that suggests a new direction for your plot. On one background-ing mission to a rural farmyard, I came upon a "honey wagon" pumping out a large septic tank. This suggested to me an unusually grisly way for a villain to dispose of a dead body; this murder method found its way into my story.

The secret of a successfully rendered setting lies *not* in piling ex-haustive detail upon repetitive particulars. There's no need to lug your typewriter around a room describing the designs of the furniture, the colors of the rugs and drapes, the brands of the whiskey on the sidebar. Extended descriptive passages, no matter how poetic and clever, only serve to stall the momentum of your story and bore your reader.

Setting is important. It serves many purposes. But don't get carried away. It *is* only a setting, the conditions in which your characters can play out their conflicts. The key to creating effective settings lies in finding the *exactly right* detail that will suggest all of the others. Be spare and suggestive. Look for a water stain on the ceiling or a cigarette burn on the sofa. You may need nothing else to create the picture you want in your reader's imagination. As Elmore Leonard says, "I try to leave out the parts that people skip."

NONFICTION: ARTICLES AND BOOKS

63

How to Get the Story Behind the Story

By Judith Broadhurst

THERE ARE TWO WAYS TO WRITE A FEATURE OR A PROFILE. Maybe more, but writing is a lot like what Duke Ellington said about music. There are only two kinds: good and bad.

With the first method, you base your whole article on the interview with the prime player. Unless you stumble upon one of those rare creatures who spouts one provocative quote after another, such features usually read like a puff piece written by a publicist rather than a journalist. Worse, you risk missing the real story altogether.

With the second way, you go backstage and find the supporting characters. That's what makes your article lively and gives it depth. It develops rather then merely reports, and becomes as much like a play or a short story as an article. The key to getting this story behind the story is filling in the background. And that takes hard work.

"There's no trick to interviewing someone who is easy to get to," Nora Ephron once said. "The trick is in interviewing the people around them so that, when you go into the interview, you know what the questions are."

Part of the trick, too, is asking yourself questions before you jump in. Use your library, the local newspaper morgue, and online computer research to gather information on the scope of your story, then narrow it to two or three potential angles.

Look at each possible angle as a wheel, with a hub, spokes, and a rim. Talk with the people on the rim first. They'll tell you which of the spokes are the mainstays for the hub. Think of the ones closer to the hub as the spokespeople; they're the ones who can lead you straight to the heart of the story. Listen closely when they go off on tangents. Keep your mind and ears open, because these people might surprise you and spin you off in a better direction than the one you planned to take.

Case in point: When *Pacific* magazine asked me to write a one-year-later piece about the California earthquake of 1989, the appropriate gist seemed obvious. What the quake hadn't destroyed in 15 seconds, the city demolished in the weeks and months that followed to prevent more disasters from the aftershocks. A year later, downtown Santa Cruz still looked like a war zone. The daily din was, "What's holding things up, and when does the rebuilding start?"

So, on the surface, the story was about political maneuvers and redevelopment financing and building plans. Wrong. That story was a continuing saga covered in daily newspaper reports week after week. It had to be repeated and updated, yet the reasons for the delays were complex. It took much legwork and many background interviews to grasp the situation well enough to explain it simply and clearly. But that part of the article ran as a sidebar.

That wasn't the plan. My focus shifted because I started by working my way around the perimeter of the nuts-and-bolts part of the story. I talked with people directly and indirectly affected by the fate of the central business district. This was the reconnaissance phase that Ephron advises. I wanted to be well-armed by the time I closed in on the key players to ask them questions.

"Statistics," I thought, "I've got to get the facts and figures straight." So I called the Red Cross, United Way, and staff members of special disaster relief projects. The spouse-abuse rate had tripled, they told me, and didn't level off for months afterward. Alcohol- and drug-related incidents increased. The housing shortage was still critical.

The Red Cross caseworker mentioned Peter, a 74-year-old man who was one of the many low-income, elderly people left homeless when a rent-subsidized hotel collapsed. Yes, they said, they would set up a phone interview with him. The anonymity of the telephone helped. Peter told me of the despair he felt when he lost what little he had left in the world. He was too old to start over, he said. It all looked hopeless to him, and he was on the brink of suicide when he called the Red Cross for help—and became a volunteer instead. His words were poignant, and gave the statistics life and meaning.

His tale made me curious about how the other most vulnerable among us, the children, were coping. After three inquiries, I found a counselor who connected me with the mother of Jenny, an eight-year-old. Jenny coped well for months after the quake. Then she suddenly regressed into the fearful behavior of a child half her age. More calls. Yes, other counselors and parents were seeing the same thing in children—and in themselves—as the anniversary of the quake loomed.

At the end of each new call I asked, "Are there any other people in the area I might talk to so I won't miss anything important? Or do you know of any professionals who deal with this kind of problem?" That led to interviews with numerous local people with diverse views and agendas, and to three phone interviews with international experts.

More than 70 interviews later, Jenny's trauma became the lead of the story. The real story had, indeed, become obvious. Every person I talked with, from co-workers, to store owners, to the mayor, expressed fear. The grown-ups also vented their anger against everyone from bureaucrats to God. But even the anger was just a camouflage for fear. So the story that started out as a soft news feature became a human interest piece, yet the saga of the rebuilding problems was there, too. Many people called to say they read the story. Every one of them said it made them cry, yet I couldn't help but feel glad. I had done my job.

Just the opposite happened years before with a feature story for *Houston City Magazine*. They titled it "Up in Flames," and I intended it to be one of those inspirational, human interest pieces. In the span of three days, the apartment building I lived in caught on fire twice. Half the building burnt to the ground. Strangers came from nowhere, without prompting, to help save our belongings. They hauled every item out of our apartments in nothing flat, stacked it all in the parking lot, unattended, and nary a thing was stolen. Touching, I thought, and a fine testament to humankind, with the operative word *kind*.

Halfway into doing interviews for the story, it turned into an investigative piece all because I asked myself, the apartment management, and the fire department at the outset, "What caused the fire?" They gave me contradictory answers, so I started poking around. It was a casual comment, filled with innuendo, and the frustration in the voice of one construction worker that changed the focus to an exposé of building code violations. The article itself was inflammatory, but filled with verifiable facts and personal anecdotes. It was picked up, pronto, by the daily newspapers and TV news crews. The controversy put such heat on city council that, within a year, they passed two new fire-prevention ordinances.

In both cases, had I stuck with my original premise or a rigid list of questions or people to interview, the stories would have been quite different and much weaker. The same applies to writing profiles. You've got to interview the people who know the subjects, who've worked with them, played with them, gone to school with them, who love them and hate them, before you sit down with the subjects themselves. Otherwise, your profiles will be superficial and little more than publicity releases.

The point is, to get the story behind the story, you have to go behind the scenes. You have to become thoroughly familiar with all perspectives, and talk with the people on the fringes. Sometimes, they won't talk on the record. But I've yet to find an instance when they wouldn't tell you someone who would, or give you enough information to dig into public records and come up with questions that the right people had to answer, on the record.

Through diverse sources and through tracing those spokes to the center, you get a well-rounded story rather than a flat one. You know when you're headed in the right direction when you begin hearing the same things over and over from different people. After you've heard it three to five times, stop. Follow their leads. Compile facts and figures by topic. Keep the individual interviews on separate pages or index cards, or in separate computer files. Be sure to record each person's name, title, and phone number on a source list which you can later pass on to the editor or fact-checkers.

Now here's the truly hard part. The problem with such extensive research and interviewing is sorting it out and writing an article that is clear, concise and lively enough to communicate with average readers and hold their interest. And here's how you do that.

Put everything aside for a day or two. Keep it in your mind, but don't concentrate on it purposely. Let it gestate. Then write down the single, most important message the story must get across. Choose the next two most critical points. Do this quickly, without analyzing much. Trust your intuition.

Next, find each quote or fact that supports those points. Log them. It makes no difference whether you fuss with a formal outline, scribble on cards or maneuver text between split screens on your computer. Just get all that information into some semblance of order.

Highlight the best quotes. "Best" means punchy, pithy, crucial and credible. It also means three-quarters or more of the quotes you have, you can't use, except as background. But they'll linger in your mind, and strengthen your story.

Remember, too, that you can paraphrase or summarize, and that readers expect you to interpret for them and to build bridges between quotes. As a guideline, don't quote more than two people for every thousand words. Three, tops. So, if you have a 3,000-word article, you can get by with quoting six to nine people. If you quote that many, however, you may confuse or distract the readers so much that they never make it to the end. What a waste of all your work.

By this time, the story itself will probably reveal to you whether it needs an anecdotal, a summary, or a teaser lead. Don't open with a quote unless you have a very compelling reason to do so. Now start writing.

Forget great prose. Do the first draft straight through. Put it aside again for a day or two, and don't peek! Then go back to it, and edit ruthlessly. As always, force yourself to kill your darlings. And bear in mind that it's just as important to know when to stop as to know where to start.

Tell the readers a story. Make sure it flows, logically and emotionally, and make sure it draws them in by making it relevant to their lives. Set the scene. Bring the perspective down to individual people whenever you can. Illustrate with quotes, as lively and as succinct as they come.

Pay attention to structure. Explain the problem, how it developed and who's doing what to solve it. Let them know how well that is or isn't working. Go from where we are, to where we were, to where we're going. That applies to profiles, too, but the focus remains on one person.

Have someone unfamiliar with the subject read your final draft. Feel free to ignore their advice. But, if there's a section where they really get stuck or misunderstand, fix it.

Let it gel one more time, overnight. Then attack it fresh, just to hone and polish. Turn it in to the editor, along with your source list. Be sure to keep your notes and tapes for at least a month after the story runs.

That's it. Pat yourself on the back for a job well done.

64

SELL YOUR HIDDEN GOLD WITH A QUERY

BY TOM JENKINS

A ONE-PAGE QUERY LETTER IS THE FIRST step in selling your article to a magazine or newspaper. No matter how well you write, you need to market your work; otherwise, it may remain hidden gold.

A written query shows you respect the editor's time—it can be answered at his or her convenience—and indicates your trust that the editor can judge your worth as a writer by reading your writing sample: the query letter.

A query letter should do the following: (1) grab interest; (2) summarize your idea; (3) show you can organize and write simply; (4) sketch your qualifications; and (5) make it easy for the editor to respond.

1. *Grab interest*

No one knows the magazine better than its editor, so in reading a query letter, how long does it take him to know if an article idea fits his publication? The first few words of your query, therefore, are crucial: You may not get another chance. It is obvious you need to grab his interest immediately and keep it throughout the letter. If you can do it in the query, the editor will know you can probably do it in the article you are proposing.

The opener should be brief, arouse a bit of curiosity, and at times suggest a point of view.

Bamboozlement. That was the cry of an English teacher recently as advertising copy writing, a favorite target of the ignorant, became the subject of attack.

This was the opener of my query for an article intending to show the effectiveness of written advertising copy. Acknowledging the flaws and gimmickry of "adblat," I went on to give examples of good advertising copy. The result was an article that appeared in a local newspaper.

Sometimes you can get attention with a single and accurate superlative: "The oldest living organism on earth is alive and well in California: the bristlecone pine." This query opener led to an article published in *Garden* magazine. That was ten years ago.

Since that time, horticulturists have learned that a drab and common shrub growing in the Southwest deserts is older: the creosote bush, one of which is believed to be 11,700 years old. I queried *Garden* again with an opener comparing the bristlecone with the creosote bush, and that led to an article that the magazine bought and published.

Sometimes you can arouse interest and give information at the same time, often in presenting a query about an unusual person. I came across a 52-year-old man whose past nervous condition had caused ulcerative colitis resulting in surgery to remove eight inches of his colon. My query to *Signs of the Times* opened with the following:

He rides a bicycle, bowls, flies an ultralight and skydives, but he also carries his own portable toilet with him everywhere. This is not a gag but the truth about a courageous man. Robert Kidwell is an ostomate.

The article was published under the title, "Faith Can Fly."

2. *Summarize your idea*

Your query letter should reflect your careful study of the readership, editorial needs, and style of the magazine to which you are writing. A query letter is specific; it is not a form letter sent to multiple publishers simultaneously, hoping for a lucky hit. You are not just proposing an article; you are proposing an article for a particular publication.

Your letter should give an overview of your topic and treatment with just enough details to show the editor you not only know your material but also how to present it.

In a query to *Desert* magazine, I wrote:

Misunderstood, maligned, and condemned throughout the West, the nation's cleverest wild animal is a needed predator: the coyote.

With hair-trigger reflexes and superbly sensitive senses, the coyote's ability to adjust and survive in the wilds is uncanny. It can sprint at 40 mph and cover 200 miles in a single day in search of food.

A social animal, attached to family and clan, the coyote has been undaunted by the growth of communities, suburban sprawl and compound 1080. Once concentrated almost entirely in the West, the coyote has turned up as far east as Maine, replacing the larger but less intelligent wolf as a wildlife predator.

The response was favorable, asking for the manuscript on speculation. The article appeared under the title, "The Controversial Predator."

Occasionally, a brief listing (but not a separate or complicated outline) in the body of the one-page query letter can give a structured overview some editors prefer. In a query to *Computer Decisions,* I suggested an article about how computerizing geographic data can save money for public utilities that depend upon large numbers of cumbersome, manually controlled maps.

The query included the following list:

With your approval, the article could be organized as follows:
1. Identify the basic problems of costly, nonintegrated and outdated maps that are manually controlled by a gas, electric, telephone or water utility company.
2. Explain how integrating and automating the maps can save money.
3. Give the details of a particular public utility, probably a telephone company, that saves money by using this kind of map management.

The associate editor responded with handwritten comments on the query letter itself, and I wrote the manuscript accordingly. "Big Saving in Computer Management of Maps" appeared in the magazine six months later.

Usually, your article idea is presented—in a kind of extended summary—in the opener and throughout the entire letter. When I read a newspaper item about a local college professor involved in an excavation project in downtown Mexico City, I perked up. I arranged an appointment with him and was impressed, both by him and the article possibilities. My query opened as follows:

Beneath the busy streets of downtown Mexico City, another city is buried. It is the sacred center of an entire empire, including the Great Temple of Tenochtitlan of the Aztec people (circa 1521), a 15-story architectural marvel incongruously devoted to human sacrifice.

I went on to summarize the quest of the University of Colorado's Dr. David Carrasco and his students to accumulate a priceless archive of ritual findings for the college. The managing editor of *Westways* liked the idea, but gave me the assignment only if I collected better photos than those I had submitted with the query. I did so, got an O.K., and the resulting article, "Digging Up a Dynasty," appeared in *Westways*.

3. *Show you can organize and write simply*

Organize your query letter in discrete but related parts, all contributing to the unity of your idea. Then say it simply. Don't try to impress an editor with multisyllabic words and elaborate phrases. Occasionally, you can use a quote to get attention and stress your point. In one query letter, I began with a two-word quote:

"Money walks."
This was the caption of a full-page photo in a national magazine. It was an Easter Seals advertisement showing a small boy, a polio victim, resting on his crutches and looking down at his dog at his side as the dog looked up at him.

The boy's desire to walk was depicted by the photo; the reader's opportunity to give money for research to help make his walking possible was conveyed by the two simple words. The photo by itself was incomplete; the copywriter's words made it complete. I added:

A picture isn't always worth a thousand words. No photo can do what the two words, "Money walks," can do. Those words grab more than the eyes. They grip the mind.
Such use of language is copywriting at its best.

This part of the query became part of the published article, entitled, "In Defense of Advertising Copywriting."
You can use plain words and write a query about a common subject:

It's a simple thing, really. It happens every year. In the fall, aspen leaves turn from green to gold. But the spectacle is stunning no matter how many times you've seen it.

This opener to my query to *Travel & Leisure* became part of the first paragraph of the article as published. The piece described a one-day aspen-viewing trip in the high country of Colorado. After one of the editors made some helpful suggestions, I included side roads, places to eat, and practical advice on what to bring and wear.

4. *Sketch your qualifications*

An editor wants to know if you can handle the article you are

306

proposing. Although you can demonstrate your control of language in the query letter, your past success in published articles, as well as your education and work experience, are reasonable indicators of your ability to deal with a chosen subject.

Indicate your qualifications in the query. You can list them or combine the information with your proposed topic in the same paragraph. In a query that proposed a piece about an unorthodox inventor, I wrote as follows:

Frederick Fisher has built a prototype for a solar-powered crematorium. Yes, a device to make after-the-fact use of the same sun that gave life.

This kind of irony fits in with other articles I have written about paradox and the oddities of human nature. They include an acre of coffins, an automobile with a 1937 license plate parked in a driveway, untouched for 32 years, and a freelance cartoonist who draws 60 cartoons a week for 60 different newspapers with no written contract for payment.

The article, entitled "Burn Me Up," was accepted and appeared in an alternative newsweekly, *Westword*.

If you have not published anything yet and therefore have no "official" publishing credentials, let your choice of an appropriate idea targeted to a particular magazine contribute to your credibility as a writer. Refer to whatever applicable background you have as a worker, researcher, traveler, collector, hobbyist or adventurer. Remember that your credentials also encompass your imagination, creativity, and intuitive powers. Be alert and observe carefully. You will find article ideas everywhere. An example: An item on a televised news broadcast about a missing railroad train engine caught my interest. I drove to the search site and became even more interested. This led me to the library and an eventual query:

On a proverbial dark and stormy night in 1878, Kiowa Creek flooded, washing out bridges and sending a Kansas-Pacific railroad train into the raging waters. Afterward, train cars were found, some smashed and almost entirely buried in the sandy creekbed.

But the locomotive was never recovered.

Today, 100 years later, a search is taking place.

I went on to tell about the excited people behind the search, including novelist Clive Cussler *(Raise the Titanic)*. The query to *True West* brought a go-ahead. I sent in the article and two weeks later a check came in the mail.

5. *Make it easy for the editor to respond*

It's an old but valid story. Always include an SASE or a self-addressed postcard for the editor who may not want to send a letter back to you. What could be simpler than a self-addressed postcard? You can even type on the reverse of it: Yes _____ No _____ Deadline _____ Photos preferred _____. Or variations of this. All the editor needs to do is make a check mark or two and perhaps indicate a word count. Nothing to dictate or write, no letter or envelope to type, and no stamping or metering. The editor will appreciate your thoughtfulness and assume you are organized and considerate.

I am not without my share of rejections; who isn't? It is unlikely that any of us can be 100 percent efficient in free-lance letter queries, but with practice you can come close. If you can query successfully, you will become a published writer.

There is no shortcut. It isn't an easy process, but it is a workable one. You need to know as much as you can about the publication you are querying. You need to know what articles it has published during the past year; you need to study them. Then you can write a query letter that will reveal your hidden gold.

65

LEADS THAT LEAD TO ARTICLE SALES

By Samm Sinclair Baker

A "HOOK" IN THE OPENING PARAGRAPH of your article can make the difference between luring the editor to read on, or boring him and killing your chances of making a sale. It is, in fact, the first essential for writing a salable article.

What makes a successful article lead? Here are my simple one-two-three guidelines for articles that sell—and actual openings from articles published in widely read and respected publications:

1) Open with an attention-getter.
2) Include an appealing promise.
3) Move on with a convincing follow-through.

I developed this sales-making procedure during over thirty years as a successful advertising writer because it worked for ads I wrote to (1) get attention, (2) make an inviting promise, (3) clinch the sale with a solid follow-through. In ads, this combination sold products again and again. Later, when I became a full-time free-lance writer, the approach worked to sell articles and books.

Examine how the following beginning of an article on home decorating and general interest uses the three guidelines:

Are you willing to try anything, anywhere, once?
Do you think that mirrors belong on your bathroom wall or on the ceiling above your bed? This numerology quiz will provide you with some answers to these questions and more . . .

If you were the editor of a woman's magazine, you would probably be prompted to read further because you know that many of your readers would be intrigued and interested. However, if the article started something like this, "A numerology quiz and your answers can reveal a

309

lot . . ." the editor would probably reject it fast, telling herself, "Our readers are fed up with ho-hum quizzes."

Consider how the editor's attention is captured here by the first line, "Are you willing to try anything, anywhere, once?"

Study other first-line examples of hooks that worked to make sales, all from popular magazines:

(Family problems) "Why can't my daughter understand me?" asks a Chicago woman. *(Modern Maturity)*

(Flowers, gardens) Special care in cutting flowers and keeping them indoors in water can extend their life a week or more . . . *(Woman's Day)*

(Health, beauty, diet) Would you like to take inches off the problem spots of your figure, starting tomorrow? *(Family Circle)*

(Interview with a photography model) "I stand stark naked in the middle of a photographic studio, surrounded by lights, not knowing what to do with my body . . ." *(New Woman)*

(Daily living, health) There's one sure thing about stress, you can't get away from it, but here's how you can get blessed relief starting now . . . (Gannett Newspapers *Sunday Magazine*)

(Activity, exercise) Most people who start a dull, boring exercise routine soon get exhausted just from counting, but here's how you can get enjoyment and full benefits from your exercising . . . *(Family Circle)*

Note how the first sentence hook and 1-2-3 guidelines apply to most nonfiction published in magazines to seize and hold your attention quickly. You may find exceptions when the author is well known or the opening is reprinted from a best-selling book, or some other exceptions. By and large, I've proved that these guides can work for you at any stage.

Making the "impossible" possible

I had been told by many that it was impossible for a newcomer to break into the pages of a Sunday newspaper magazine with a huge circulation, since the competition from big-name writers was so keen. I had just left my advertising agency work to become a full-time writer, my lifelong ambition. I said to myself, "The devil with the difficulties. I'll take a chance as a beginner." Ignoring common barriers has proved effective for me many times since, as it can for you. Here's how I, as a beginning free lancer, broke through with an article. It began:

Seven years ago, I taught and learned a lesson in happier living that has been a great help to me. It came from hearing nine dreary little words that you've probably heard dozens, even hundreds of times. Those nine ruinous words are, *"I'm not as young as I used to be."*

My idea for the personal experience, inspirational piece was sparked by a conversation I overheard on a railroad platform while I was awaiting a commuting train. I wrote it up, sent it to the editor cold. Bingo! It was accepted for their very popular first page "Words To Live By" feature. The sizable check was clipped to a note stating, "The opening lines appealed to me as a common experience."

Ignoring all discouraging cautions prompted me to move full speed ahead to write more articles and an inspirational how-to book, *Conscious Happiness*. Mindful always of the value of an opening hook, I started the book this way:

Conscious Happiness is free. It can enrich your life tremendously—yet it doesn't cost you a cent from now on. But nobody else can pay for it and give it to you as a gift. You must earn it yourself by wanting it enough so you work at it daily. Once you attain it, you can keep and enjoy its great benefits for the rest of your more rewarding life . . .

When a specific type of article sells for you, follow it up. I tried another idea based on personal experience but not inspirational. I wrote my piece and sent it to a leading pocket-size magazine.

An editor called to say that he wanted the article and to check whether the proposed fee was satisfactory (it took me three seconds to emit a breathless "yeah!"). He said, "There have been many articles offered to us on office sex, so your subject isn't new. But right from the opening lines it involved me and would also grab our readers." The piece began:

This is neither a sociological study nor a report in depth. It is not an exposé. It is a candid, clear-eyed discussion of sex in the office, based on what I've seen, heard, and know from working in various offices—from the mail room to the president's suite, in factories, advertising agencies, in small and large businesses . . .

To get the right sales-making lead-in, I had rewritten the opening more than a dozen times before submitting it. I finally found it by discarding the extraneous first paragraph and reshaping the second.

311

This tip has worked for me many times since: Consider cutting out the first try, then start with your second, third, or fourth paragraph.

Here's the compelling beginning of an article (not mine) from a recent issue of *Reader's Digest*. You could have written it without expert knowledge by enlisting an interviewee or coauthor, if you felt that you needed one:

Everywhere you look, childrearing experts are giving advice on how to communicate with children. Much of it is theoretical and not that useful. So we asked a different group of experts—good parents, trained by years of trial and error—to tell us their secrets . . .

Realize that basically all you would need to write this article yourself is the idea and the effort of interviewing some parents, including friends probably in your area.

Check, recheck, triple-check

With everything you write, remember to keep reviewing the lead-ins against the three checkpoints. Never let up. I'm in the middle of writing a proposal for a nonfiction book. Upon rereading it for the umpteenth time, I still had the nagging feeling that the opening paragraph was not provocative enough. I reexamined the lead to see if it covered the three checkpoints. The lines failed the test, so I rewrote the opening, which is greatly improved.

I'm sure now that the proposal has far more power to involve an editor and publisher. If I hadn't checked again, I'd have risked turn-down trouble.

It's worth heeding Goethe's warning: "If you miss the first buttonhole, you will not succeed in buttoning your coat."

66

THE REVIEWER'S CRAFT

BY SVEN BIRKERTS

I CALL THIS SHORT REFLECTION "The Reviewer's Craft" rather than "The Reviewer's Art" because I want to confine myself to making useful rather than more philosophic kinds of observations. But as I begin, I feel an almost irresistible pressure to set down a few high-toned generalizations. I suppose that it comes with the terrain. Just as one almost never begins a review without making at least one reflective, high-altitude circle around one's prey, so do I succumb here.

First: I don't imagine that anyone actually *sets out* to become a critic or reviewer. One usually ends up there. Maybe "ends up" sounds too darkly fatalistic—the critic generally *arrives* at his vocation after exploratory travels elsewhere. Often that "elsewhere" involves other, often "nobler" and more "creative" kinds of writing. It may, however, be a very happy arrival (it was for me).

I came to reviewing out of writing fiction and working in bookstores. The change from one genre to another was enormously liberating. Reviewing allowed me to spread the word about what I perceived to be neglected works of literature; no less important, it let me see my name in print after frustrating years of rejection. This latter incentive is not to be underestimated.

Though I began reviewing with the idea that it was a temporary expedient, a way of keeping my hand in while I waited for bigger things to happen, I soon came to face certain truths: that I loved what I was doing, that it came to me naturally (indeed, I saw that it was the critical side of my character that had blocked my attempts at fiction), and, best of all, that it was by no means a trivial or ephemeral endeavor. The intellect, the creative impulse, and the linguistic urge were all engaged fully—depending, of course, on the nature of the book—and there was ample room for self-expression.

Naturally, every person's experience is different. I can report only

313

how things fell out for me. For starters, I was lucky enough to connect straight off with a responsive and appreciative editor who liked a review I had written on speculation and asked for others. From that point on there was always a next step, a new assignment.

I have been reviewing for more than ten years now. A great deal has changed for me over this time. A peripheral concern has moved to the center of my life; I now pursue it as a vocation, with complete involvement. I look for the assignments I want; I try to publish in magazines that can pay me something for my work (I have written hundreds of pages gratis . . .); I juggle demands and schedules in such a way that I am often working on three or four pieces at once: reading for one, taking notes for another, putting final touches on yet a third. But for all this immersion—sometimes to the point of exhaustion—the pleasure is undiminished. And this I attribute to my choice of field: literature. While the work I read is serious, often difficult, it continually gives me the excitement and renewal that belong to art. I find that the thrill of starting to read a new novel or collection of poetry is as great as it was the first few times. What's more, the ambition of touching readers and influencing their responses to books only grows stronger.

This leads me to my last generality: the question of why one might want to be a reviewer. I see the evaluation and discussion of books as an indispensable part of what might be called the "conversation of culture." By taking up and sustaining the movement of ideas in print, one is siding with mind and sensibility against the forces of the blip and the byte. The more artistically, interestingly, and convincingly a reviewer can serve the cause of books, the greater his contribution.

Now, about the "craft" of reviewing. . . .

First, the bad news. It is all but impossible to make a living as a part-time reviewer. Unless you are lucky enough to get a berth as the regular reviewer at one of the more prestigious magazines or newspapers, you will be doing your work alongside your other work. You will fight hard to keep the different parts of your life separate. You will steal time from your other employer, jotting mysterious notes on memo pads, thinking about openings. You will feel a strong temptation to let the reviewing slide so that you can enjoy a bit more leisure time. Try to resist the temptation, but don't become joyless or humorless. *Never* work only out of a sense of duty; it will show in the prose. The world does not need one more scrap of dutiful, uninspired writing.

It is not for the money that one reviews—obviously. Passion is essential. Passion for reading—books, magazines, other reviews, trade journals. Passion, too, for thinking, meditating, digesting—for living through the afterlife of books. Passion, most certainly, for writing. But—no less important—for rewriting, and rewriting again. You cannot succeed as a reviewer if you cannot bear to see your sentences trimmed, your paragraphs pruned, your best metaphors scotched; if you cannot bear, in short, to hear that your finished copy is anything but finished. This is especially true when you begin reviewing. Later, with some luck, you will find your way to one or two congenial editors. They will admire your work and give you certain leeway. You will, in turn, internalize their standards and be better able to give them what they are looking for the first time around.

Most of the advice that follows is addressed to the would-be or beginning reviewer. Nothing I say has the status of being axiomatic. These are the things that my experience has taught me—period.

• Try as much as possible to follow the twists and warps of your own character; stay with the grain. This means using your experiences, interests, and particular kinds of expertise to best advantage. Make yourself conspicuous by doing a certain kind of review very well. If you have a special interest in psychology or women's issues or Latin American literature, begin there. Find the journals that address themselves to readers with those same interests and examine them as potential markets for your work. Don't worry that you will be typecast or straitjacketed. It is much easier to branch out later from a position of strength than to try to be everything to everyone.

When you have found one or more publications that you would like to write for, do some further research. Read several dozen reviews published in those journals and see if there is anything that could be called a "house style." Spend some time in bookstores to acquaint yourself with titles and authors of current books in the field to get a sense of the landscape. Then, go the library and read through some current issues of *Publishers Weekly* and *Kirkus Reviews*. Look for early reviews of books that you might be interested in proposing for review.

• The next step is to write an honest, non-pretentious (and not overlong) letter to the reviews editor of the journal in question. Identify yourself, cite your relevant interests and experiences, and ask if they would be interested in having a review of X, Y, or Z on speculation (always suggest several possibilities). Show some familiarity with the journal and the kind of material it publishes. If you have any writing samples—"clips" of other reviews—include one or two of the best ones. If you think you have an angle on the book(s) proposed, give some explanation. At this point you have done all you can. You can only hope that the editor is responsive and that the chance will be offered. (Give the editor about two weeks to respond—after that, follow up with a note or a phone call.)

• How to write a review. It should go without saying that you read the book. Not only must you read it, but you must read it better—more searchingly, more thoughtfully—than anyone else. This is your real job as a reviewer: You are the ideal intelligence sent out to greet the work; you have to introduce and explain it to others. Ideally, therefore, you will read it more than once. You will also—ideally—have read certain background material, enough to know the larger context of the book. The more you know, the better is your chance to make the kinds of interesting connections that lift a review out of the mold of unimaginative summary.

Under the best circumstances, you will have time between finishing the book and beginning your review. I find this brooding period absolutely essential. It not only helps to clarify the book's outlines, revealing more sharply what is important and what is not, but it also gives you time to locate your true response. Many books can seduce at close quarters and later prove to be second-rate. Give yourself a chance to cool from your first ardors, or your initial distaste.

I am a great believer in letting the unconscious intelligence do its share of the work. The longer I can walk around in a condition of attentive idleness, the more likely is the shape of my response to emerge on its own. There is also an art to knowing when it's time to stop mulling and start writing. For me, that time comes when I can make out the outlines of my opening paragraph, when I can feel the tone and momentum of my first pitch. Generally at this point the first sentence is ready—it sets a rhythm and indicates a direction.

• Do everything you can to keep your review within assigned word limits. Apart from writing clear, polished prose, this is the fastest way to win the love of an editor: write pieces that don't need to be cut or inflated to meet space requirements. This takes a certain amount of practice, but it does eventually become second nature. A good reviewer knows how to think 500-word thoughts, 1000-word thoughts, and so on. He knows, too, the formula for balance for any given word length—just how much description, how much quotation, and how much rendering of judgment.

- Be punctual—get the review in on time, or before deadline. Don't ever call an editor at the last possible moment to ask for an extension. If there is a problem coming, call in and give warning.

- Be ready to take the "phone edit" call. Have your piece where you can find it. Be attentive and flexible; don't waste time being defensive. A good editor is usually right about your prose—believe it or not. Editors will repeatedly ask for changes, cuts, and substitutions. Be ready to think fast—but make sure you understand the editor's suggestions. Do as much as you can to help. But never let an editor talk you into saying something you don't believe. Don't allow the piece to be printed if you are not happy with it—just because you want to see your name in print. There is nothing more dispiriting than seeing your by-line on a piece of writing that you are ashamed of; it will keep you awake nights.

- Learn to compartmentalize projects. If you are serious about becoming a reviewer, you will have to learn to keep three or four balls in the air at a time. There is no other way to produce as steadily as you need to for your name to stay alive in the public mind. Moreover, not only is it possible to have several projects going at once—at different stages—it's actually good for the work. Ideas and energies have a way of crossing project boundaries: Your thinking about structuralism will enrich your review of a biography of Charles Dickens. Also, having several projects going at once keeps you from the kind of one-track obsession that often leads to paralysis.

- The rewards? Money, no. But books . . . Jiffy bag after Jiffy bag. The mailman walks with a lighter step after he has stopped at your door. What else? A sense of daily independence. Of mental fitness: There is no better way to keep the brain in aerobic trim. And reading: What other profession allows you to read in bed in the middle of the afternoon (after you hit the big time, that is)? At some point or another every reviewer confides his secret to someone: "I can't believe I get paid to do this. . . ." Well, that feeling comes rarely. But when it comes, it makes a nice counterweight to the interminable chore of composition.

317

67

WRITING AND SELLING TRAVEL ARTICLES

BY JANET STEINBERG

TO THE OUTSIDE OBSERVER, that illusive magic carpet known as "Travel Writing" is glamour . . . excitement . . . adventure. It is sunrise in Bali . . . sunset in Spain; piranhas in the Amazon . . . pyramids along the Nile.

To the struggling free lancer, trying to make a living in this limited field can be instant frustration and starvation. However, if you are endowed with stamina, determination, and the financial means to get you through those first lean years, travel writing can be a most rewarding profession.

The following tips, garnered from more than a decade of travel writing experience, should be helpful to you along the way.

Write as if you are talking to your best friend: With pen in hand, pretend you've picked up the phone to tell your friend about the wonderful place you've just visited. Tell which sights are not to be missed and which are a waste of time and money. Tell where to eat—in a variety of price ranges—and what dish must absolutely be tried. Go beyond the overhyped shopping malls to the unusual boutiques that specialize in goods unique to that area.

Write to assault your readers' sense: The opening paragraph should immerse your readers in the destination and make them want to go there more than any other place in the world. Through your words they should be able to see the sun rise in Bali . . . hear the cacophony of sounds in the Casbah . . . smell the spice-laden, cow-dunged streets of India.

Anecdotes make good opening paragraphs: Quote the joke that the cab driver told you or begin with the tour guide's remark that put the entire busload of tourists into stitches.

Write to entertain: Travelers, both real and armchair, need to be entertained as well as informed. Otherwise, you will lose them after the first few paragraphs. Your facts must be current and informative but not boring. If it's in-depth research your readers want, they will turn to an encyclopedia or comprehensive guidebook.

Make your first sentence powerful: Let it paint a picture, arouse curiosity . . . or even anger. "I'm just wild about Harry," a successful travel article began. Playing upon the old song title, it compels readers to learn just who Harry is and what he is doing in the travel section.

"I love calories! I love cholesterol! I love Fauchon!" Who or what is Fauchon? Curious readers have to read beyond this award-winning opening. "Auschwitz is the flip side of Disneyworld." This first sentence of another prize-winning travel article instilled anger in some readers until they continued for the explanation. But they *did* continue.

Breathe new life into the old: Make antiquity come alive as you uncover the past. Your readers might have difficulty picturing Mark Antony and Cleopatra walking along the Arcadian Way in Ephesus, Turkey. However, a mention of Charlton Heston gliding down those ancient marble streets in his chariot will conjure up a myriad of images in the minds of millions of movie buffs.

Seek unexplored subjects and unique angles: When you visit a destination, think of all the articles you've read about that place. Then go one step farther. Skip the overdone Warsaw ghetto. Instead, write about the ghetto in Venice, Italy. Forget the tourist-trap restaurants in the old walled city of Dubrovnik. Instead, write about that secluded seafood spot, thirty minutes down the road on the Yugoslavian Riviera. A day in Rio may be hackneyed for most publications, but a day on nearby Paqueta Island is new and refreshing.

Visit the destination: If you want authenticity and credibility, let your readers know you've been to the spot about which you are writing. Describe something you ate or something you bought. Quote a local resident. Don't write from a brochure. Readers can peruse those without your help.

Timely events are a time bomb: Unless you have a regular market and are insured of immediate publication, don't write about events occurring currently or in the near future. By the time an editor gets around to reading—and using—your story, it may be dead.

Be aware of the shrinking newspaper market: Where once the free lancer was a major force in the travel sections of Sunday newspapers, today these sections are filled mostly with pieces by staff writers or articles obtained from outside news services.

Expand your markets: Forget the traditional newspaper markets and concentrate on secondary markets such as magazines targeting sports, business, art, and senior citizens.

Go behind the scenes: The kitchen at Air France . . . the flight attendants' training center at Singapore Airlines . . . the semi-annual sale at Harrods; the cockpit of the *Concorde* . . . the kennel of the *QE2* . . . the shop on the *Orient Express*. All topics not likely to be overdone.

Think ahead: Jump the gun. If your city is planning a bicentennial in two years, now is the time to query that travel magazine. If the local senior citizens club sponsors an annual motor coach tour for fall leafing, query seniors' magazines, a year ahead, to see if they'd like an on-the-coach reporter.

Work with a local travel agency: Convince them of the importance of a monthly newsletter or insert to go with their regular mailings. Payment can be much better than what you'd get for a newspaper article—and much steadier.

Work with a local public relations firm: Though your byline may never see the light of day, the pay for travel-related press releases is much better than for newspaper articles. The same holds true for writing for the tourist offices of various cities or countries.

Rely on round-ups: Grouping short items on one subject or theme into a single article is a favorite of editors. The world's best: golf courses . . . tennis camps . . . adventure travel . . . honeymoons. The world's worst: restaurants . . . cruises . . . shopping, etc.

Professional travel tips: Even though you might overpack when you travel, the reading public still wants you to tell them how to travel lightly. They also want to know what type of luggage you recommend, how to deal with jet lag and what to do about nasty customs officials.

Be a photographer: Even though you may not know a shutter from a lens, learn to take your own pictures. Presenting a complete package to an editor gives you the leading edge. Smart cameras make it easy for dumb photographers.

Don't try to be what you're not: Sophisticated readers want travel articles written by sophisticated writers. Adventurers want to read about trekking the Himalayas by someone who has trekked them.

Leave golf vacations to golfers, shopping sprees to shoppers. Don't try to write for a publication that features a lifestyle totally foreign to you.

Give editors what they want: When magazines request a query, send a query; when they request an SASE (self-addressed, stamped envelope), send an SASE. Familiarize yourself with the writing style of the publication you're aiming for, noting the number of words in the average article. Editors prefer not to edit.

Be accurate: Establishing a long-term relationship with an editor is directly dependent upon the reliability of your work. Many travel writers offer readability; not as many offer credibility.

Include consumer information: An informative sidebar is a necessity with most travel articles. The reader needs to know how to get there; what documentation is required; what the local currency is and the best place to get it; what the weather's like; appropriate clothing at different times of year, etc.

Submit clean copy: No matter how enjoyable and informative your article may be, an editor will pitch out a messy manuscript rather than suffer eye strain trying to decipher it.

68

How to Write a Profile

By Lou Ann Walker

ONE OF THE FIRST PROFILES I EVER READ was of Candice Bergen. I remember every detail vividly: what her room looked like, how she was dressed, the ideas she found frivolous, what mattered to her. As a teenager, I thought young Bergen was a wonderful role model. She believed in hard work and challenge, and ignoring her detractors. Not long ago, *New York Woman* magazine asked me to write a cover story on Bergen. I became very nervous. She was too glamorous to talk to, I thought. After the reams of copy that had been written about her, how could I make her come alive on paper? And then I reminded myself that I was curious about how she had developed over the years. I realized the challenge was to capture her essence, to rediscover what had enthralled me before, and to present Bergen in a new way.

To write a profile, you don't have the muss or fuss of figuring out what your topic is. You have a finite number of facts, and you can't get lost in too many subplots. Your job is to make the reader think that he or she has had a long, candlelit dinner full of shared intimacies and revelations. And, yes, usually laughs. Using your interview and research materials can be a far more creative and enriching process than writing most journalistic stories. After all, you're a detective, a psychologist, and a sage all rolled into one. The more talents you have, the better. Getting a *good* interview is 75% of the battle. Here are some tactics for making a profile come alive.

Getting the interview right

The interview, I've come to realize, is really a skillfully crafted performance, a *pas de deux*. Here are some tips for making the "dance" work.

1. Be creative in setting up an interview. Sometimes, particularly

with celebrities, I'll have an intermediary, a press agent, or a magazine editor tell me some of the activities the subject likes. Then, if I call the subject directly, I'm armed with a notion of the kind of article I'll do, and some of the topics I'll focus on. Usually home turf for the person is best. An office is all right, but often people are stiffer in that setting. Hollywood child star and comedienne Jane Withers taught me that if you're going to a restaurant, call ahead and ask the maitre d' for the quietest table.

One of the best tactics is to stay with a person all day, particularly on a movie set. Academy Award winning actress Marlee Matlin allowed me to tag along on a free day, and we had a most illuminating time. I let her drive me all over Los Angeles. (Frankly, it was a death-defying stunt. She's so excitable that when she uses her hands to sign, she often takes both of them off the steering wheel.) She took me to visit her elderly grandmother in a nursing home, and I could see the family affection. We went to a Beverly Hills restaurant where she used her TTY (telecommunications device for the deaf) on the phone at our table to have a conversation with her boyfriend, an actor on location in Canada. It was these small moments that made our interview memorable.

2. Become friendly with the people who work with the person you're interviewing. Charming a secretary who is snooty can lead to important revelations. One such secretary confided in me that the actress I was interviewing was just breaking up with a man and dating someone new. I never would have found that out if I hadn't done a little buttering up.

3. Research, research, research. *Before* you meet the person, you need to know everything you can. There is a warmth, a relaxation, that subjects undergo when writers have done their homework. Knowing background can help you read deeper meanings into answers.

4. Make a list of questions. For days before an interview, I ask myself what I want to know about the subject. Why does this politician care so much about drug task forces? Was someone in his family mugged? I think up questions while I'm driving around, or jogging. I rarely look at my list during the interview, but it's there just in case there's an awkward silence or the subject freezes up.

5. Don't be afraid to ask dumb questions. I've gotten many of my best answers that way. Keep a few stock questions in reserve for dry spells. "What are your best qualities? What are your worst?" might not

seem to have Pulitzer-winning potential, yet you'd be surprised where they may lead. Don't be afraid of silences, by the way. People often free associate in riveting ways. My favorite question is: "Why?"

6. Go with the conversational flow. If someone starts opening up about the worst day of his or her life, don't suddenly say, "What year were you born?"

7. The number one worst sin of interviewers: Talking too much. Many interviewers are really more interested in talking about themselves than they are in the subject. Your time with a person is precious. Use it to find out what you need for your profile. Being a bit forthcoming is useful, but Joe DiMaggio would probably not be terribly interested in your son's Little League score.

8. Play poker. In other words, don't pounce on perceived indiscretions on your subject's part. Stay cool, and later on bring up that name your subject dropped to find out what response you get. Don't get testy if there are interruptions. You might get revealing material from an overheard phone conversation.

9. Be compulsive. I use a tape recorder and write notes at the same time. I know of too many instances when batteries died, and I've also discovered that background noise drowns out a person's voice. It's better to have notes than nothing at all. But develop the technique of writing while looking your subject square in the eye as much as possible. Also, at some point, you must be compulsive about facts; you have to figure out if the explorer moved to New Zealand before or after he lived in Timbuktu.

10. Don't waste time. The best interviews aren't necessarily the longest. Use your judgment. Several shorter interviews are probably better for the subject than one marathon. Too much information can be hard to sift through. And you'll repeat yourself. But don't be shortchanged. Before leaving an interview, ask the person for a number where he or she can be reached if you have more questions or need to check some facts.

11. Ask about friends or acquaintances you can talk to. It's useful to interview other well-known people about a celebrity, but they'll probably give you pat answers. An old high school pal or college roommate will often provide more illuminating material. Ask to look at photo albums. Or places where certain events took place.

12. Never be intimidated. Remember, the subject, no matter how

important, had traumas and defeats as well as successes. And whether it was good or bad, most people like talking about their childhood. You don't have to be ingratiating. Sometimes winning a subject's trust means shaking the person up a bit or disagreeing with a point. As an interviewer, you're like a psychologist, figuring out what makes that person tick. Use your knowledge of human nature every way you can. There are times when you need to be confrontational, say with a senator who has been stripped of his congressional seat. But you don't need to be argumentative while interviewing a puppeteer for the local paper. Have a good understanding of what your editor wants.

13. Some time ago *The New Yorker* ran a two-part article by Janet Malcolm about the relationship between a writer and his subject. Malcolm's premise is that an interviewer is a seducer, then betrays the subject with what is written. Certainly there's an element of that in a story. But it's also true that many subjects are seducing writers, trying to manipulate the portrait. Be prepared for such seduction. If someone says: "You're going to write a nice article, aren't you?" don't dissemble. Be ready to say: "I'm going to write a fair piece."

14. Get people to be specific. Ask for examples. Most people talk in generalities to reporters. They think they sound more intelligent when, in actuality, it just makes for a dry story. You need anecdotes and details. If someone says, "I'm a very poor storyteller," your retort should be, "Give me an example." That, surprisingly enough, can turn out to be, "Well, when I met Winston Churchill . . ."

15. Observe and make notes about everything. Jot down the person's eye color, what photos are on the desk, the type of decor. After I walk out the door I usually stand in the hallway or sit in my car writing down impressions while they're still fresh.

Capturing the person on paper

1. Get reacquainted with the person. I generally type out all my notes, even if it takes a lot of time, as a way of imagining myself with the subject again. Usually when I'm typing, lines or images stand out, and I can tell immediately what the beginning and end of the piece will be.

2. Play around with structure. You're telling a story. Make it entertaining. Read other profiles for techniques for weaving together background with the present. It's just plain boring to write: "So-and-so was born in 1946. . . ." You want bounce and verve in your writing, even if

your subject was dry as dust. Make a dateline for the person. Or a chart to show the ups and downs of someone's career. Or maybe make a list of memorable quotations. I recently interviewed a 91-year-old woman doctor who still sees patients every day. She had so many crusty quotes, I couldn't possibly fit them all in. So I settled on a box with her "prescriptions" for modern man. It worked wonderfully well.

3. Make associations. Do some free-floating thinking about figures in history whose careers parallel your subject's. Or that your character looks like Meryl Streep but acts like Madonna. Push your creative buttons. Otherwise, you're a quotation box.

4. Examine the text closely. Throw out the canned responses immediately—unless you're making the point that someone is in a rut. Having read published articles about your subject, you know what is really fresh. Scan the answers for themes. For example, a television producer I recently interviewed used the word "control" over and over again. Having won a battle with cancer, she was re-establishing dominion over her own life. From the opening sentence, I built the piece around this producer's tug-of-war with life.

5. Give your analysis. The reader wants you to explain how or why the subject said what he or she said. You are the guide in this expedition. So lead.

6. Vary the tone. No life is all happy or sad. No profile should sound the same note again and again.

7. An infallible rule: You can never, ever tell how people are going to react to what you write. I did a tough portrait of a well-known actress. It was not a puff piece, but I was absolutely scrupulous in telling the truth about her failures and successes. She later wrote me it was the best article ever written about her. Her husband thought so, too. Intelligent subjects don't want to come off sounding like Milquetoasts. They want you to come up with original angles, not press release rehashes. It's balance you're after.

Finally, advice no one else will give you: Don't be afraid to turn down an assignment if you have negative feelings about the subject. I'm not saying you have to like the person you're interviewing. Tension can be good. But if you have no respect for the person's work or beliefs, then the interview will suffer.

The best way to be true to an interview subject is to be true to yourself. An editor I often write for recently told me that she realized my secret. I'm wide-eyed and non-judgmental, so people just open up to me. It can be a curse in a supermarket line or on a long plane trip, but I've come to realize it's one of my strong suits. If you're an enthusiastic person, there's no sense trying to mask that with a somber demeanor. If you're serious, don't try for the jollies. Just channel your interests and your behavior to get and write the best story you can.

Over the course of time, the people who write the best profiles are the ones who are, quite simply, captivated by others: That's what makes almost all wonderful writers. Simple fascination with humankind.

69

READ ALL ABOUT IT!

BY CERI EAGLING

LIKE ALL BEGINNING ARTICLE WRITERS, I suspect, I secretly scorned free-lancing for our community newspapers. A weekly newspaper serving a town of 10,000 was not at all what I had in mind for my prose when I first started. Many months later, however, when not only *Cosmopolitan* and *The Atlantic*, but also *Redbook, Yankee Magazine,* and *The Boston Globe* had returned my submissions without regret, I thought again about the field and decided it was worth trying.

It soon became apparent to me that sending my manuscripts to community newspapers increased my chances of acceptance a thousandfold. Editors of small-town newspapers are not remote figures unlikely to see your submissions, but they deal directly with all aspects of their weekly publications, including responding to potential contributors.

Community newspapers are chronically short of writers to cover routine town business; school committee and library trustee meetings; and other events that call for straightforward reporting skills. They also regularly publish articles that give a writer opportunities to develop a personal style: opinion columns, for example, in which contributors express views on varied subjects in styles that range from crusading to nostalgic, and feature articles dealing with human interest issues like the achievements and dilemmas particular individuals face and have to resolve.

If you have no clips of any of your previously published work to show an editor, write a sample article, typed double-spaced, on a topic of your choosing, with a cover letter stating your interest in free-lancing for the newspaper. Almost any local editor will treat this approach seriously. If you follow up your letter with a telephone call, in all probability you will be able to discuss future possibilities with the editor directly.

Mention any ideas you have for articles, but if your interest lies in feature writing, bear in mind that a community newspaper requires every article to have a *local* slant. World or national events are relevant only if they affect your community, or if someone in that town witnessed or participated in them in some way—insular, perhaps, but my experience indicates that by keeping your eyes and ears (and, incidentally, your mind) open, you will quickly come to appreciate the breadth and variety of your fellow citizens' experiences. The family in your town that took in its twenty-fifth foster child. Or the retired state trooper who opened a costume rental agency. Find out more about the high school student who has developed a potentially marketable gadget, or consider the teen-ager whose parents want to educate her at home.

Material abounds in the town you live in, and story ideas arise naturally from daily contact with the residents and institutions. You can, of course, broaden the scope of your articles beyond the borders of your town when your subject has some bearing on the outside world.

Ignore disparaging remarks about local newspapers. Submit only your best work; use the same criteria of excellence in writing that bears your byline, whether the article appears in your local paper or in a more prestigious publication.

Begin by thinking of yourself as a professional. When you have an editor's go-ahead to develop an idea you've queried him about, set yourself a precise deadline, even if the editor seems flexible. Significant events in town government, a local fire, or other "hard" news will always take priority over feature articles or opinion pieces, which stay timely longer. Even when your article is submitted on time and accepted, it may not appear immediately, but meeting deadlines will establish you as a reliable contributor and free you for new projects. Most important, a firm deadline provides the external pressure a writer needs to "concentrate the mind."

Be punctual for your appointments: If you set 2:00 P.M. for an interview, be sure to be there on time (or a few minutes early). If you promise to call your interviewee at 11:30 A.M. the next day, do so. It's all part of being a professional.

To make your article interesting to the newspaper's readers, you first have to make it interesting to yourself; if you don't, it will show in your writing. When you are planning your questions for an interview, therefore, ask yourself what you would like to learn from the subject. Which aspects pique your curiosity? If you wonder how the hobby your subject is so deeply involved with fits into the person's family life and schedule, make a note to inquire. Have these and other questions ready when you go to the interview, and ask them all, if time permits. But be open to any new insights or directions your interviewee suggests in his replies. Being responsive to his or her remarks and views will almost invariably produce richer results. Concrete facts and statistics do and should lend weight and authority to your work, but your genuine interest in knowing why people do what they do and how it affects their lives and other people will make your features more readable.

What you gain from an interview will not be an article, but rather, the raw material for an article. Every writer develops his own methods, but my first step after an interview is to arrange notes under various headings, each on a separate piece of paper (or several pieces). All comments that don't obviously fit in a category go on another sheet. I also make a note of facts and items that I need to check.

Invariably, details that you forgot to ask about or that occur to you later may require a follow-up telephone call. Check spellings of names, for instance; just because your interviewee has a common name, don't assume that you know how to spell it. Find out whether it's Debby, Debbie, or Debi, or if the person likes to have his middle name used as well as his first and last. Be sure to get it right. People dislike having their names appear incorrectly in print. If another person is mentioned in the course of your interview, go to that person and ask him exactly what he said or did. Writing for a small-town paper provides excellent training in accuracy, if only because you will meet your subject again.

After you have arranged your interview notes, read them over. A chronological list of facts alone rarely makes electrifying reading. Decide which aspect of the notes you took stands out—a single phrase made by your subject or some pivotal event in his experience which generated change or growth. It could equally well be something you perceived as significant or relevant: an ornament in the office; a small decorative feature or a repeated gesture or turn of phrase that will help characterize the person or his work. Depending on circumstances, the opening of your article may be intriguing, entertaining, or moving, but if it lacks liveliness, it will lose its impact.

Conciseness is also a good quality to cultivate, especially in writing for newspapers, where space is limited. Inexperience may make you include every detail you found in the course of your research, or every idea that occurs to you for an opinion piece, but you must limit yourself to what is relevant. Experience will teach you to recognize which facts will enhance your article and which will bog it down. You have to steel yourself to select only those details that shed light on your subject or add color to your style, and to reject those that may be fascinating, but are not pertinent.

If you leave the pruning to the editor, be prepared for the consequences. The editor certainly will prune, and you may not like the results. Ascertain in advance the approximate length the editor expects, and cut your manuscript accordingly before you submit it. I have found it useful to keep a copy of my original manuscript as submitted, in order to compare it with the published version. Sometimes I have learned a lesson in clarity.

Recognition as a writer by your fellow citizens is a potent morale builder. Though your newspaper's circulation may be small, the direct feedback from your readers provides an immediate reward, since local papers tend to publish accepted material in a fraction of the time usually taken by large-circulation publications. Also, publication in your local paper may bring requests for reprints that will reach a different and wider audience.

A feature writer for a local paper should refrain from exposing sensitive aspects of a local subject's life simply for the sake of revealing "the whole truth"—unless, of course, it is actually relevant to the article. As a reputable interviewer, you should establish which of the subject's remarks during the interview are off the record (if any), and which you are free to quote.

Occasionally, interviewees will ask to see your manuscript before you submit it. Refuse politely. Never confuse your role as professional writer with that of accommodating acquaintance. If the subject of your article has doubts about your reporting integrity, suggest the names of two or three previous interviewees who will vouch for your fairness and accuracy, but don't allow anyone except your editor to meddle with your text. Be wary too of the person who proposes himself for an interview. Decide whether his story holds genuine interest for your readers, or is merely free advertisement for his business.

One reason ambitious writers pass over the local or regional newspaper market is that their bank balances change little as a result of sales in this field. On the other hand, receiving a continuous stream of rejection slips from major publications brings even fewer financial rewards and is demoralizing besides. Of course, you should continue to try for the big time, too, but allow yourself a periodic taste of small-time success along the way. You may even find that the skills you develop in writing about local situations—clarity, conciseness, your ability to focus on a subject—may give your more ambitious writing projects the quality they require to be accepted for publication. Confidence and experience gained from interviewing fellow townspeople will improve your chances of conducting successful interviews with more famous people later on.

If your ultimate goal lies in writing fiction, consider how the insights you glean from researching community events may fuel future short stories; or how you may be able to graft a personality trait observed in someone you interview onto a character in your novel.

70

THE ART OF INTERVIEWING

BY WENDELL ANDERSON

INTERVIEWS ARE A HELPFUL RESEARCH TOOL for the nonfiction writer. Information obtained firsthand from experts adds credibility and authenticity to an article. I've sold articles on ways to enjoy a stress-free Christmas, how to grow popcorn, how to decorate the office with house plants, ways to raise money to start a business, and many other topics—all based on research conducted through interviews.

Interviews are the best way to gather anecdotes and quotes that enliven and add color to nonfiction writing. An engaging anecdote or quote can make an article memorable, but quoted material requires careful handling. Should every word uttered by the subject be taken down verbatim? What about grammatical errors, slang, or obscenities? When can you change the subject's words?

Magazines, newspapers, and individual writers differ on only one point regarding quoted material: whether to "clean up" a quotation. Some won't, for fear it could change the picture one gives of a subject. Other writers will make changes if direct quotes may embarrass a subject. The standard practice is to correct grammatical errors and to omit obscenities unless you are including them to benefit the reader. Otherwise, there is universal agreement that only the subject's exact words may be enclosed in quotation marks. So, if you quote indirectly, not using the exact words but giving only the gist of what your subject says, quotation marks are not used. In fairness to your subject and your readers, however, make sure the indirect quotations are accurate restatements of the subject's original words, and use language as similar to the subject's in tone and meaning as possible, taking care to keep the statements in proper context.

If you have questions about a quotation, verify its accuracy with the subject or don't use it. Misquoted material can never really be corrected and could close off future interviews with that subject—and further publication in the magazine that ran it.

While the only way to be sure of capturing quotes verbatim is to use a tape recorder, you can jot down a few ideas, impressions, observations, or additional questions as the interview progresses. Always ask the interviewee for permission to tape the conversation; taping without the interviewee's knowledge or permission is unethical and an invasion of privacy.

To record telephone interviews, you can use a special, inexpensive device available at stores like Radio Shack. Otherwise, you will have to take quick, but careful, notes. (You may want to learn a simple short-hand system, or devise one of your own.)

Before you go to an interview, do your homework. Knowing as many facts as you can about your subject is flattering and encourages him or her to respond better to you. At a minimum, learn your subject's title and background, and be sure to spell his or her name correctly—including middle initials.

Also, learn all you can about your topic in advance. Don't ask the interviewee for information you can easily get elsewhere beforehand, and don't rely on the interviewee as your sole reference. Experts can sometimes be out of touch or simply wrong. Statistics, in particular, can be troublesome. If you can, verify numbers you get from an interviewee with another source or from published material in the library.

When you've done your research, you're ready to prepare your questions. Thorough research will help you develop questions that appear spontaneous, conversational, and natural. Writing down your questions will help you keep the interview focused. Always ask open-ended questions that require an answer other than "yes" or "no." For example, instead of *Did you really fall into a vat of chocolate?* ask, *What was it like to fall into a vat of chocolate?*

Avoid leading questions. Instead of, *Was the UFO shaped like a saucer or like a cigar?*, ask, *What was the UFO shaped like?* Let subjects use their own words.

Save difficult or controversial questions for the end of the interview; you want to put the subject at ease before you ask tough questions, and when you do, be prepared to explain why.

Rely on your written questions, but remain flexible. Watch for ideas

334

that flow naturally from the conversation, and follow tangents that lead down productive paths.

When setting up the interview, let the subject know approximately how long the interview will take. People are usually willing to talk within a specified time. Be punctual and respect the subject's schedule. Choose an environment in which your subject will be most comfortable. I like to interview people where they are most natural and relaxed, in their homes or in their places of work. I once interviewed a florist in his truck as he drove around picking up supplies and making deliveries.

Good interviewers are courteous but assertive, professional and objective, but interested and determined. Show your professionalism by having your questions and equipment organized ahead of time. Have your tape recorder loaded and ready before you go to the interview, and have blank tapes and back-up batteries on hand. Fumbling with a tape recorder makes you look like an amateur.

Be honest with subjects about your work. Let them know if you're working on spec or on assignment. Tell them that what they say may or may not be quoted in print. Some people want to be quoted or referred to by name and may feel slighted if they're not.

Whether you agree or disagree with what your subject says, keep your opinions to yourself. Even though you are—as you should be— well informed about the topic under discussion, let your subjects feel that *they* are the experts, leading you through a complex topic or issue.

Follow the basic rules of listening. Wait until the subject finishes speaking before asking the next question. You can't talk and listen at the same time. Occasionally, you may interject a brief comment to show you are paying attention. But don't talk too much; the subject's comments are more important than yours. The idea is to control the conversation without dominating it. Looking at your watch or staring into space are sure signs of boredom.

Of course, not all interviews run smoothly. It's up to you to keep an interview on track and get the information you want.

When the subject goes off on an innocent tangent, try to get him or her back on track by asking your prepared questions. If the subject says he doesn't understand a question, repeat or rephrase it. When the subject answers in monosyllables, try to draw him or her out by saying something like, *I'm still not quite clear about. . .* , or, *I don't mean to repeat myself, but. . . ,* then repeat the question. Or ask questions that begin with "why" or "how." This forces the subject to define a position or to elaborate on it.

With wary subjects, you can use what some reporters call the "Columbo technique" (named for the TV detective): As you're headed for the door, turn around and say, *Oh, by the way. . . .* The subject is often disarmed at this point and may offer further information.

A technique that sometimes works well with reluctant subjects is the third-person technique: Instead of asking questions, say, *I suppose you've heard that your opponent said. . . ,* or, *I suppose your critics could say. . . .*

Sometimes you may have to go "off the record" to get an interviewee to open up. Doing so can provide leads or facts that you verify with other sources. While off the record, you can say, *I like what you just said; can I use that part?* If you've established a good rapport, the subject will often consent.

Professional ethics dictate that if you promise to go off the record, you keep your promise. If you publish facts or opinions that you agreed not to, you may be infringing on privacy rights, and, at the least, betraying a trust.

End your interview by asking, *Is there anything else you'd like to tell me?* Give the subject a chance to help you. And be sure you can get in touch with your subject if you have questions that arise while you're writing the article. When working on a piece for which the subject is the main resource, I usually refer to it as "our article," establishing a feeling of collaboration. Then if at some later time I have to return for further information or confirmation, the subject is usually more willing to continue working with someone viewed as a collaborator, rather than an interviewer.

Review your notes as soon as possible after the interview, while it's still fresh in your mind; many valuable quotes and facts have been lost because writers couldn't read their own scribbles.

Generally, it's a mistake to show subjects your article before it's published. Most people will want to edit it. They will say things like, "I didn't say that," or, "I didn't really mean to say that." Their perspective may be distorted by their own self-interest. Check with your subject if you have any doubts about facts, direct quotes, or paraphrases, but not for tone or style. But in the end, the finished piece is your responsibility.

Keep in mind that an interview is a conversation between two people. The better you relate to your subject, the better your interview, and ultimately, your article.

⚜ 71

WRITING THE PRO/CON ARTICLE

BY BARBARA MCGARRY PETERS

SKILLED WRITERS WHO TYPICALLY SAIL THROUGH FACTUAL NEWS reports or how-tos often shy away from controversial subjects. It's easy to understand why. Pro/con articles have inherent perils and pitfalls and so are tricky to do well.

Why then enter the fray? A well-written pro/con piece brings several rewards. One payoff is the insight you gain from successfully thrashing out a complex problem with no obvious answer. Another is the satisfaction of helping your readers make a difficult choice. A third is the challenge of writing an honest article that's fit to print—and getting paid for it.

Here are seven guidelines that might help you, as they've helped me, with the writing process.

1. *Choose a point of view.* This will be your story line. This doesn't mean you should come down hard on one side or the other. That would be courting rejection. Your point of view comes from an organizing principle—a point at which the two sides meet or at least brush by one another. From this unifying thread or central idea, you can move in either direction, and your article takes shape.

Without this strong theme, you may end up with a string of ideas not clearly linked to a developing story line. This happened to me when I was trying too hard to write a well-balanced piece. To the editor, my article appeared "disjointed and choppy—jumping back and forth abruptly without moving in a particular direction." Wanting to present both sides of the argument without taking sides and keep within the word limit, I had cut the connective tissue that held the article together. As a result the editor was as perplexed about the problem at the end of the article as he was at the beginning. But, thanks to his detailed rejection letter with suggestions for revision, I refashioned my article, and it appeared in print a month later.

2. *Get to the point quickly and stick to it.* Don't stumble or back your way into the article. Use punchy words and snappy, short sentences to capture your readers' interest. Your lead should announce your theme. Make it clear who your target audience is: for example, women or men of a special age group. Soon after you present the pro side, acknowledge the con position.

After you state your theme, tell readers your reason for writing the piece, and why you are writing it now. Has there been a fresh development that makes the article newsworthy? Your "angle" or "hook" could be a report from a recent conference, a political speech, a public announcement, or the publication of a scientific study.

Begin with general statements, then zoom in on details. But don't tell the readers anything they don't have to know. Irrelevant or tangential facts clutter the page and mask the story line. Scrutinize each sentence of your draft, and ask yourself: "Can my reader make a decision without knowing this?"

3. *Give evidence of thorough research.* Steep yourself in the subject, and interview experts from a wide range of disciplines. Controversies often affect people in a variety of ways: physical, emotional, social, political, and spiritual. It's important to include quotes on all aspects of a complex problem because one part of the problem might have a bearing on another. For instance, an article on the pros and cons of postmenopausal hormone treatment might include specialists in disease prevention and health promotion, gynecology, heart and bone disease, breast and uterine cancer, and genetic research. An article on the abortion controversy might include specialists in law, sociology, women's and children's health, psychology, medical research, religion, and ethics. Weave the experts' quotes into the article with smooth transitions, so that they reinforce your idea without slowing the pace.

Devote at least one paragraph to every argument. Imagine your reader asking you to clarify a point. What could you do to make the idea clearer, more understandable, persuasive?

4. *Keep your focus on general guidelines.* Don't overwhelm your reader with statistics related to the arguments, such as figures on

mortality, disease, or divorce rates or voter preferences. Statistics are virtually meaningless in a complex problem, especially one that involves more than one person. Even if risks were certain, making a choice between options would still be difficult, because there is always a trade-off between benefits and risks. And too many numbers confuse readers and slow the pace of the article.

5. *Keep your tone neutral.* A "let's reason together" tone is most likely to keep a reader's attention. Use concrete words for emotional effect. Avoid inflammatory words. If you're trying to remain objective and an angry tone slips into your writing, you'll lose most editors fast. It's tempting to use colorful, emotion-packed quotes, but your editor may become convinced you're promoting one side and will reject your article.

Avoid judgmental words or phrases; specious reasoning; unfair or weak arguments; uninformed, offensive remarks of unknown origin; questionable, simplistic, or vague accusatory comments.

6. *Save your strongest pro and con arguments for last.* It is the end of your article that will stick in your reader's mind. Don't discount the fact that many readers habitually take a peek at the end before they even finish the lead. A strong conclusion gives the reader something to think about—a clinching bit of evidence, a promising resource, a challenging question.

Wrap up your article by rephrasing your theme, and then leave readers with a new, provocative idea that invites them to weigh the implications of their decision.

7. *Ask a colleague or friend who is objective to read the manuscript for clarity,* to make sure it is not condescending, preachy, or insulting to your readers' intelligence. What questions have not been answered about the subject that should be? This step will help root out ambiguous sentences and unconvincing arguments.

Following these seven tips will greatly improve your chances of acceptance, but there still may be some frustrations along the way when you write about a controversial topic. The only writers who seem to have an easy time with it are those who refuse to consider both sides of the question.

340

What if you tackle a hot issue and find yourself with a pile of conflicting research, all supposedly valid arguments from leaders in the field? You must try to put things into perspective and consider the humorous aspects. As Bertrand Russell said, "The most savage controversies are those about matters . . . to which there is no good evidence either way."

72

THE MYSTERIOUS ART OF BIOGRAPHY

BY PATRICIA BOSWORTH

SINCE BIOGRAPHY IS THE MOST POPULAR FORM OF NONFICTION TODAY, there is an increasing interest in learning the craft. The rules, however, change with every project. The only rule you must follow is that you cannot make up the facts about a life, but you can imagine the form they take.

Thus, Nancy Mitford's classic *Zelda* is completely different in tone and style from W. A. Swanberg's *Citizen Hearst*. And the monumental *Power Broker* by Robert Caro cannot be compared to Richard Ellman's superb biography of James Joyce, except to say they are both master-pieces.

In my month-long workshop on biography writing (far too short a time), I kept repeating a series of questions and considerations for my students to mull over. For the purposes of this article, I'll list them and try to elaborate on them.

For starters: *What makes the life you want to write about "significant"?*

Usually some sort of outstanding accomplishment, a distinct quality of mind that sets a character apart.

How does a life express itself?

In an action or actions. In writing my biography about the 1960s photographer Diane Arbus, I discovered that Arbus invariably chose terrifying worlds to record with her camera. And not just because those worlds fascinated her, but because she wanted to overcome her fears about them. She felt it was essential to take risks; she lived every day believing that.

Along with an action, the power of documentation—evidence from interviews and letters and diaries—cannot be overlooked. Nancy Mitford, who has been working on a biography of Edna St. Vincent Millay for over a decade, finally met the poet's elderly sister. That meeting led her to a huge cache of personal papers—some 56,000 documents—the biggest collection on a major American literary figure remaining in private hands.

Archival sleuthing can often result in vivid, multilayered portraits, but it's not easy; ideally, one should possess the combined skills of an historian, a psychiatrist, and a novelist. Whenever I get depressed by that thought, I quote Mark Twain's definition of biography: "Biography is the clothes and buttons of a man; but the real biography of a man is lived in his head 24 hours a day, and *that* you can never know."

If one is lucky, one comes away with the essence of a character—a version of a life. But there is always more than one version. Although Mark Twain doesn't say so, *I* say, never write about someone who doesn't interest you. You must be obsessed by the character you're exploring, because to write a good biography takes five years or more. Leon Edel spent 25 years writing his splendid study of Henry James. It can be pretty deadly if you don't like—or worse, don't respect—the character you're investigating. (For instance, under no circumstances would I tackle a biography of mass murderer Charles Manson.) I want to be inspired and enlightened and challenged; I want to learn something.

Another task to set yourself: Look for the minor characters in a life, characters who may bring your major character to life, as, say, David McCullough did with Theodore Roosevelt in *Morning on Horseback*. McCullough paid close attention to every Roosevelt sibling.

Just as important, find a "voice" or "voices" you're comfortable with. In a book I'm writing now—a memoir/biography of my father, the late Bartley C. Crum, an activist lawyer who was blacklisted in the 1950s after defending "The Hollywood Ten"—I juxtapose excerpts from his and my mother's journals, reminiscences from colleagues and friends, as well as from my own memories. Then, I am dotting the narrative with letters from my father's contemporaries, men he worked with, such as Earl Warren, Henry Cabot Lodge, and Harry Truman. Letters from historical figures such as Warren are not only "voices"; they express a lot about America in the last fifty years.

As for settings, if at all possible, visit the places you'll be writing about. While I was researching my biography of Montgomery Clift, I had the opportunity to wander through his ghostly New York brownstone. The bar he'd built remained in the spacious double living room; the birch trees he'd planted "in honor of Chekhov" still rustled in his garden. And the bedroom that he'd slept in (and died in) was exactly as he'd left it, complete with cigarette burns on the floor.

Watching out for backgrounds and settings doesn't mean neglecting themes like power or the relationships between individuals and eras. There are many kinds of power, one of the most complicated being the power within relationships as dramatized, say, by Phyllis Rose's *Parallel Lives,* a study of Victorian marriages.

Speaking of themes, I seem to repeat the same theme in every biography I write. I choose as subjects essentially decent, good people who are driven, creatively obsessed about completing one or more tasks. Always at some peak point in their lives, they suffer a terrible tragedy (an accident or a death). How they work it out, or incorporate it into their lives in order to survive, is something I never tire of exploring.

At the same time, I try to remember the responsibility I have in *revealing* the life. How much "right" do I have to interpret, to speculate, to analyze, to give away secrets?

A biographer must be selective and discreet, particularly if friends and relatives of the subject are still alive. (I hasten to add that it is easier to write about a dead subject than a live one.) But it isn't necessary to use everything—certainly not all the "dirt." Selection of detail is crucial. It can make or break a biography.

Selection of detail can set the tone and suggest character and relationship. For example, my father often referred to my mother as his "child bride"; she never corrected him, but once confided in the depths of her journal, "Oh, how I wish someone would call me 'sweet woman' just once!"

Details, incidents, anecdotes—they piece the story of a life into a narrative. And everybody's life is composed of a first, second, and third act. And in the last act many things are finally resolved.

When all is said and done, what do the facts add up to? What does a life *mean*? These are central questions every biographer asks and must answer in the writing of a successful biography. And of course, there is no one answer; the answer is different for every book.

Then there is the revision. A biographer likes to spend a great deal of time revising endless chapters and scenes and paragraphs, so I now find a sharp pleasure in rewriting. I didn't at first.

I recall when I handed in the fourth draft of my Arbus biography to

Knopf (I'd been writing the book for five years), my editor read it and then very gently told me I would have to rewrite the entire book because so far I hadn't trusted myself or the material enough: I was still too "tentative"; I needed to "throw myself into the experience." He was absolutely correct.

For me, the ultimate fascination of biography is that, like all art forms, it works in mysteries. A good biographer never stops asking questions and never stops looking for clues.

§ 73

READ MY QUIPS!

BY SELMA GLASSER

THE KIND OF WRITING I DO OFFERS READERS playful relaxation for serious material. It's entertaining and recreational. What fun I have!

I pull out an arsenal of pizzazz to create powerful word play or witticisms. I give simple words or phrases new sparkle, variety, energy, and meaning. Timely subjects act as dynamic idea generators, recognizable because of their relevance to topics of the day. Just being alert and observant can pay off.

The best part is that it's almost "instant income" with a minimal number of words or time invested, from idea to submission. The rate of pay can range from $10–$1,000 or more, trips all over the world, to bylines in major publications.

For example, on a car stopped in front of me in heavy traffic, I noticed a bumper sticker that read, ANSWER MY PRAYERS. PLEASE STEAL THIS CAR. I sold it to *Reader's Digest*. Recently, I received $60 for a three-word cartoon idea for "Dennis, the Menace." In studying Hank Ketchum's work, I noted that each cartoon depicted a young boy's actions with adult phraseology. Mine showed Dennis using his crayons, asking his mother: "Need anything colorized?!"

It's a good idea to get the slant before submitting any cartoon, filler, or contest entry. Always avoid the obvious.

When the Netherlands offered a trip to Holland, instead of writing about windmills and tulips, my entry declared: IT'S TIME I GOT IN DUTCH!

This brought me a prize of ten days as guest of Queen Beatrix, and yes, I did get to meet her at a social event in honor of the prize winners.

An idea for light verse presented itself when I overheard a discussion about *problem drinkers*. I paraphrased those two words and sold this verse:

Problem Thinkers

Advice on marriage, love or sex, our columnists provide,
They're clever, sensible and wise and very qualified;
But surely, problems cross their path, at home, where they reside,
I wonder, where they turn for help, in whom do they confide?

Taking a traditional Christmas song and changing the season, I wrote a poem for *Good Housekeeping* entitled: "On the Twelfth Day of August." It was a take-off showing a mother's plight when youngsters are on vacation.

In a national grocery competition, I parodied another famous poem by starting off:

How do I love thee? Let me count the ways:
I love thee on big (double) coupon days . . .

and ended with:

I love thee for trying so hard to please,
And for making my shopping a breeze!

In keeping with the summer season (after a severe sunburn), I wrote and sold:

Burning to Return

Vacationing is pretty sound,
For those who want to get unwound,
But truthfully, here's what I found:
I'm happiest when homeward browned.

The popular phrase "remedial reading" was reworked on another summer theme in this way:

What Goes Down Must Come Up

Though I spend weeks of spading, top soiling and pleading,
My plot's a sad lot, which is surely not leading . . .
I'm thinking of taking remedial weeding!

Naturally, the seasonal verses were submitted six to eight months prior to the summertime. In mid-July when visitors flocked to my vacation home, I thought of this verse about Christmas:

LET'S ENACT THE SANTA "CLAUS"

The constant stream of people here,
To wish us Yuletide cheer,
Proves Santa has the right idea:
Visit people once a year!

Ordinary words or phrases in their literal meaning can help you invent a funny filler. For example, I put together a few that sold to *Saturday Evening Post*, with the title, "Fun Facts":

A GET-WELL CARD	What you would send someone prospecting for oil
VIRUS	What the electric company does for us
MINNEHAHA	Short laugh
CARTOON	Auto song
UNMANNED VEHICLE	Car driven by a female

I wrote a similar filler for *Good Housekeeping* called, "Two-Way Brain Teaser":

What do boys do when they see a fence?	CLIMATE
What's fear of relatives?	KINDRED
What's an oversized hairpiece?	BIGWIG
What do you do when you give up spinach?	SCRAP IRON
Where should folks take their automobiles swimming?	IN CAR POOLS

Following the same line of pun-fun, I took the word "Friday" and gave it the double entendre treatment in this epigram sold to *Good Housekeeping:*

The only person who got all his work done by Friday was Robinson Crusoe.

Clichés and proverbs reworked can be another easy way to get published. How about the expression "little things count"? Here's how I sold that one:

A kindergarten teacher is a woman who knows how to make little things count.

I reread some old proverbs and adapted a few for this feature:

Still water causes ecology problems.
Absence makes the heart grow fonder, but presents get better results.
All work and no play makes jack.
Cleanliness is next to impossible.
As you sow so shall you mow.
Every cloud has a silver airliner.

Occasionally, a filler published in one magazine can be reprinted in *Reader's Digest*. In that case, the writer gets paid twice. Using my word-storming formula (analogy), this epigram sold first to *Good Housekeeping* and later to *Reader's Digest:*

Remarks that are uncalled for are usually delivered. (Postal analogs: uncalled for . . . delivered)

Playboy has been known to use analogies. Here are a few sold to them:

A man with money to burn usually meets his match . . . (analogy here is burn-match)
Alimony: disinterest compounded annually (note financial analogs)

A TV booklet distributed free at supermarkets each month offers lots of cash and groceries with an annual Grand Slam Prize for the Best of the Year. I hit the jackpot using an analogy to write about the advertisers in musical terminology:

It takes genius to arrange a harmonious medley of merchants who offer scores of services . . . It's the easiest way to shop and get Bach in no time flat, and that beats the band!

(Note also the use of puns and alliteration.)

This analogy technique is the easiest device you can use to coax words onto the page. When asked to review a play called *Angry Housewives,* presented by a local theater group, I started this way:

The percolating plot starts on a low burner but boils over with bubbling talent. It's a well-done show cooking with gags.

(It never hurts to insert a pun for extra punch.)

Another fun game I play is "terse verse," which calls for a rhymed definition for a given word. I've written columns called "Rime Time" and "Phraze Craze." One picked up and reprinted by *Reader's Digest* read:

A fat cat is a flabby tabby.

A few others:

An animal doctor is a pet vet.
A royal court jester is a crown clown.
A matchmaker is a knotter plotter.
An unwed Santa is a single Kringle.
A hot house is a swelter shelter.

Reader's Digest reprinted my list of definitions of ordinary words. This time, the meanings were defined in colors. For example:

Nudist—come azure
Economist—cost of living rose
Psychologist—Freudian gilt
Politician—bipartisan slate
Gangster—come and get me copper

For *Catholic Digest,* I rhymed a shortie like this:

Outdoor theater sign: "Closed for the season. Reason? Freezin'."

Rhyme, parody, or pun wherever you can. Once you get your mind working along these lines, you'll see how much fun it is. Just today, I heard a western song called: "I'm a Legend in my Time." Immediately, I thought of the late Richard Armour (my mentor) as "a legend in his rhyme." Listening to Bob Hope sing his theme song, "Thanks for the Memories," made me think of "franks for the memories." As soon as some ad agency or contest needs a slogan for hot dogs, I'm ready! The TV game show called "The Phrase That Pays" brought to mind that "The Re-Phrase That Pays" is what this article is all about.

§ 74

THE LIBRARY: A RESEARCHER'S BEST FRIEND

BY MARGARET G. BIGGER

WOULDN'T IT BE GREAT TO HAVE A NETWORK of friends to help you with research and even contact other resource people for you? You do. In virtually every county in every state, the library stands ready to offer assistance not just from 9 to 5 weekdays, but often at night and on weekends, too. And, like true friends, libraries rarely charge for their services.

Reference department workers at most public libraries will reply to questions by phone about census statistics, national organizations, famous people, and an enormous variety of other topics easily found in their reference books. I ask only one question per call and only something that would likely be found in a book on the main floor in the reference area (not in the stacks or other remote sections). Recently, I called a reference librarian to find out the attendance at the 1989 Rose Bowl game; though she could tell me the number of seats in the stadium, she could not immediately locate the exact information I needed. She took down my name and phone number, and at noon the next day, she called to say she was still looking; by evening she called in triumph with the answer: "101,668!"

To do more involved research, you will have to go to a library, preferably the main library. A telephone call first, however, will determine whether a particular library or branch has material on your topic. Card catalogues, the *Readers' Guide to Periodical Literature,* and encyclopedias are handy tools, but the experienced librarian can help you find resources you may not think of. Be specific when you explain your needs.

World almanacs and atlases may be the best quick-fact books, but you should also consider these: *The Book of Answers* explores topics from the calendar to medicine, and from inventions to defense. *The Lincoln Library of Essential Information* has facts about major subjects, plus 3,600 brief biographies of noteworthy people who lived during 4,000 years of recorded history. To find out about well-known personalities, try biographical dictionaries, *Who's Who* and *Who Was Who* volumes, for which there are indexes.

If you want quotes from an important person, *Names & Numbers (A Journalist's Guide to the Most Needed Information Sources & Contacts)* has more than 20,000 listings arranged in such categories as the media, government, emergency agencies, business, sports, consumers, economics, education, religion, science and technology, politics, most newsworthy Americans, recreation-arts-entertainment, sports, and weather. Also, under "world," you will find international organizations, U.N. agencies, foreign embassies, U.S. embassies and the desks or country offices in the State Department. *Names and Numbers* will tell you whether your library is a regional depository for U.S. government documents.

Similar reference books include *The New Address Book: How to Reach Anyone Who's Anyone,* listing over 3,500 celebrities, corporate executives and other VIP's; *Information USA* (U.S. government experts); *Encyclopedia of Associations* (contact persons for national organizations, associations, and fraternities); and *Dial an Expert,* a consumer's sourcebook of free and low-cost information available by phone.

Of course, many of the people you wish to reach will be listed in current phone books. Many public libraries (or business branches) have not only phone books from towns and cities throughout that state, but microfiche of both white and yellow pages of the nation's largest cities. Catalogues from colleges across the country, manufacturers' directories, corporate annual reports, government documents, and recent magazines are also available on microfiche.

At the main library in my city, old city directories, census records, and back issues of local newspapers since the turn of the century and earlier are on microfilm. I found old newspapers invaluable in my research for a book about the 1920s and 1930s; they gave me a "feel" for the times. Later, they provided clues to finding living relatives of people I named in the book, to whom my publisher sent pre-publication brochures. Obituaries, social columns, news stories, and even ads for local businesses were great sources. I made extensive use of out-of-town telephone book microfiche to locate current home or business addresses.

While working on a biography, I found information in old city directories about the subject's relatives who were unknown by living descendants. Those directories listed all the adults living in the household at the time, as well as their occupations.

The New York Times, The Wall Street Journal, and *The Christian Science Monitor* are also available on microfilm at many regional libraries. Indexes for these are in book form, and many have on-line data bases for newspapers. Vu/Text indexes major Knight-Ridder newspapers and a few magazines. Dialogue provides the largest data base for periodicals and journals. If your library has one of these or a similar index service, you can do a "global" or a regional search for even a narrow topic. A bibliography will flash on the computer screen; you choose the article you need, and the entire article will be printed out.

For listings of markets for your work, you may want to consult *Ulrich's International Periodicals Directory, Gale Directory of Publications, The Writer's Handbook, The Literary Market Place, Standard Periodical Directory, Magazine Industry Market Place, International Writers' & Artists' Yearbook, Editor & Publisher International Yearbook,* and *Editor & Publisher Syndicate Directory.*

Make use of your library's photocopier. At small cost, you can reproduce pages to read later at your own desk. Some microfiche reading machines and microfilm machines will photocopy a specific page for as little as ten cents.

Through the Interlibrary Loan system, you can borrow material not available in your hometown library. Many major libraries have an on-line data base that can locate particular books, and for a minimal fee, you can get photocopies of magazine or newspaper articles from another library. A book or microfilm can be transferred to your library within about two weeks, usually at no charge or for a small insurance fee. You may borrow the book for a couple of weeks, but the microfilm must be viewed in the local library.

If you find that a certain town has source material you want, address a letter to the head librarian or reference librarian there, explaining what you are looking for and where you think that information might be found. Always provide a self-addressed, stamped envelope. If appropriate, leave space after each question, so the librarian can fill in the answers without having to write a separate letter. Allow several weeks for a response. You can try phoning for quick reference data, or you might say in your letter that you will call on a certain day for the answers.

While checking old tales about a specific area in Oklahoma, I asked small-town librarians there to help me locate people who might have been present at a particular event. As a result, I got first-person accounts—far more valuable than newspaper versions. In one instance, a librarian posted my letter on the Town Hall bulletin board, and an elderly woman validated information about a murder that had been deliberately expunged from public records!

Although I don't know the names of many of the librarians who have helped me over the years—they often prefer to remain anonymous—in one of my books, I acknowledged thirty-three "for their continued personal interest in seeking answers to a cascade of obscure questions."

§ 75

HOW TO INCREASE YOUR RATE OF ACCEPTANCE

BY RICHARD MATTHEWS

IN FREE LANCING, ENERGY AND PERSISTENCE ARE THE KEY to increasing your rate of acceptance. Having six proposals out is good; a dozen is better; and if you can get up to two dozen, that's best of all. The only way to keep writing articles that sell is to convince editors—on a regular basis—that you can produce what readers want. What counts in free lancing is acceptance, and there's *always* more you can do to make sure you get writing assignments with increasing frequency—and one thing is to regard a "thank you, but no" as no big deal.

Too many writers mistake a single rejection as reason for abandoning an idea, but if a proposal is rejected, revise, reslant, and resubmit it to another publication that might be receptive to the same general idea tailored to its editorial content. Restructuring an idea with a different set of readers in mind often meets with success the second time around.

A good article query is slanted toward the interests of a publication's readers, but a proposal is often based on an idea that may be made to lean in several different directions. For example, a proposed feature about a museum's display of 19th-century furnishings might have failed to catch one editor's eye; but a profile, say, of the museum's innovative curator, submitted to a magazine focused on people, or a query about the museum's collection of antique oil lamps sent to a collectibles publication may succeed where the first one didn't. The point is, you've probably done enough research to tilt the proposal toward several different audiences. Consider *all* the publications that might consider an article before giving up on the idea.

Whatever you do, don't let ideas sit around. One morale booster I often find helpful is to compile a list of all the publications that might be interested in some aspect of an idea (as distinct from a narrowly focused proposal written for a specific publication) and then use the list to keep recycling the idea till it sells. Don't send the same proposal to two magazines simultaneously; if both accept, you'll irritate both editors. But if a proposal is returned, mail it to another publication as quickly as possible. You may have to rewrite the query, but each idea (proposal/query/manuscript) that can be rescued is a potential return on your investment in the original research.

A possible exception to the rule against simultaneous submissions may be newspapers. If you have an idea for a newspaper article on, say, a news-based event, you might send the same proposal to several newspapers at the same time, always informing editors you've done so. And if one editor gives you a go-ahead, you should so inform the others. As a general rule, however, I avoid simultaneous submissions; I prefer to send my proposals one at a time, unless, of course, the same basic idea can be offered in sufficiently restructured form so that no conflict is possible.

Keep active idea files and fill them with clippings, information, contacts, and sources, and notes about the subjects they deal with. At some point, begin identifying all the publications that might be interested in what you know about a subject and start cross-referencing "idea files" with "publication files." I make it a point to be familiar with as many magazines as I can and to start a folder for each one. (A library well stocked with periodicals is worth at least a once-a-month browse.) I fill the folder with newspaper clippings, notes to myself about proposals I've sent to other publications, writer's guidelines, and most important, information and feature story ideas I think might be appropriate for the publication.

Let's say you want to write an article on boomerangs. If you approach the subject as a sport, there are a half dozen sports-oriented, recreation, or outdoor publications that might be interested. But what about the fellow who handcrafts fine wooden boomerangs, or the person who holds seven patents on boomerangs and sells them through mail order? Try a craft magazine for the first, a business publication for the second, a local newspaper for either one if you do the local angle. And if there's a boomerang tournament coming up, consider covering it locally, regionally, or even nationally, depending on its possibilities. Think about other approaches to the subject as well: What do you know or what can you find out about the history of boomerangs, their popularity in Australia, or their use in hunting? And if throwing and catching boomerangs is good exercise, don't neglect magazines devoted to health and fitness.

I've sold articles about people who make or throw boomerangs to four publications, and have written about maple sugaring in New England for no fewer than seven magazines and newspapers over a three-year period. Each article was unique, and though the amounts I was paid for them varied, money kept coming in.

Consider, too, starting a card file to remind yourself of upcoming dates for seasonal and anniversary material. A piece appropriate for a spring issue should be proposed as much as a year in advance. If an idea is tied to a date or holiday, a six- to eight-month lead time—especially if you have to recycle the proposal—is about the minimum. Some publications provide writers with editorial planning calendars that identify which of future issues will be devoted to specific subject areas. When sending for guidelines it's a good idea to ask for these. It's not unusual to sell articles that take more than a year to show up in print.

In marketing material, consider the entire range of publications available to free-lance writers. A historical piece that *American History Illustrated* refused might interest *American Heritage,* or an editor of a regional history magazine, or any of the many state magazines. If you have an idea for a feature on a unique collectible, by all means consider *Country Living,* or *Country Home,* but try regular collectible and general interest publications first. Hobby magazines, craft publications, journals devoted to nostalgia, to antiques, to flea markets and yard sales—any of these might buy a specific piece from you where a better known magazine might not. There are also hundreds of smaller publications devoted to specialty subjects like railroading, off-road travel, jogging, boating, home decorating, gardening, business management, education, health, etc., many of them willing to give on-speculation encouragement to writers with well-focused proposals addressed to the special interests of their readers.

An increasing number of national magazines, including such varied publications as *Omni, Esquire, Yankee, Popular Mechanics,* and *Modern Maturity* include what I call "short-take" sections: news, business, or human interest items that lend themselves to treatment in 50 to 300 words. I've sold such pieces to *The New York Times, Country Accents, The Hartford Courant, Country Journal, Farm & Ranch,* and *Vermont Life.* Short pieces offer a way of getting in over the transom so that

357

when you propose a 3,000-word feature to the editor, you can refer to your first appearance (or appearances) in the publication. Some longer articles may also lend themselves to short treatment spinoffs after the original article has appeared, but always inform editors of an idea's publication history.

Keep in mind, too, that if there's any reason at all for an editor to remember or recognize your name, remind him of it the next time you write.

And finally, the most personally satisfying of my strategies: my "Retrievable Rejections" file. Many rejections are little more than unsigned forms, about as personal as a shipping invoice. But occasionally a rejection slip arrives with a hand-written note. It may be nothing more than a brief reason for the rejection scribbled at the bottom of a form, but sometimes it's an invitation to submit again. I prize whatever is personal and encouraging. I file them away for future reference. When I have an idea and don't know where to send it, I sift through the file to find possibilities and send off proposals.

That file has been a gold mine. Seldom do I make it into a magazine on the first try; sometimes it has taken up to three years before an idea sells, but fully half the publications I've finally "cracked" came out of my Retrievable Rejections folder.

The difference between an amateur and a pro may well be that stack of rejections and how the writer handles it. Learning the craft; writing more and better proposals; targeting them to specialized markets; accumulating lists of ideas and publications that might accept your articles, and later breathing new life into them, based on newly acquired information—over the long haul, that's the surest way to success.

§76

WRITING THE PERSONAL EXPERIENCE ARTICLE

BY HOWARD SCOTT

IN THE SEARCH FOR SUBJECTS, many writers ignore an obvious possibility: their own personal experiences. Although these events do need some drama, tension, and a resolution (or solution), they don't have to be earth-shattering or catastrophic. Most of us have such experiences, and writers can make them come alive on paper.

Personal experience articles are in demand. They're a staple of women's magazines, which though hard to break into, pay excellent rates. Sunday newspaper magazine supplements and daily newspapers often use personal pieces, as do specific-focus magazines.

Think of a personal experience as a series of events that happened to you, and might be worth sharing with others. For example, when a roadblock was set up, clogging our usually quiet street with traffic for two weeks, our four-year-old hid each time a 16-wheeler rumbled by. To help her overcome her fear, we took her outside every day to watch the vehicles and wave to the drivers, made up stories about them, and read the truck signs to her. At the end of two weeks, she was sad to see the roadblock removed. The next day I sat down and wrote an account of the experience. The result was an article called "The Detour," which showed how a problem turned into a learning experience. It appeared in *Sesame Street Magazine*.

What else constitutes personal experience? Have you ever spent time with a famous person, lived through a medical crisis, lived in or visited an exotic place, taken up any strange hobbies? Have you had a close brush with death—an accident or a sickness, recovered from a disabling addiction, attempted and accomplished a difficult feat? Have you ever served on a jury, been audited? These are all good possibilities for personal experience articles.

Of course, the experience does not have to be your own. You can write a piece about a memorable event that a friend or relative or colleague went through. I once wrote an article about a friend whose jewelry store was robbed—"I've Been Robbed . . . Please Come Right Away." It was published in my local newspaper in Quincy, Massachusetts.

To proceed, think about the event, frame it in terms of the action, the characters, the outcome, and most important, the insight you gained. What helpful advice can be learned from the events reported? Is it revealing of human nature? Is it controversial?

Many publications look for controversial topics. For example, an article I wrote telling about a traumatic week I spent in a Boston hospital, during which 100 doctors tried to figure out what was wrong with me (it turned out to be a common controllable thyroid condition), showed how the medical establishment can miss obvious symptoms. To Bostonians, so proud of their medical facilities and expertise, this was heresy. However, *Boston Magazine* published my article describing this experience: "In the Midst of Life."

The writing is the easy part: Usually, there is no research required. It simply takes a straightforward recounting of the events as they occurred. Don't hold anything back, and when you have finished the first draft, put it aside and relax or work on something else. Then, with a clear, dispassionate eye, rewrite, cut, and prune to create a clear, readable piece. If some aspect of it doesn't add to the effect, omit it. Tighten the description, including only a few telling details. Limit the statements of how you felt to two or three key moments; change the emotional reactions into specific actions. For example, instead of "I was terrified," write, "My hands shook." In other words, show, don't tell.

In my medical story, one pivotal moment came at the hospital, when I finally had to face facts and tell my parents. The article reads:

I called my folks Sunday at their Florida home. My father answered. I said, "Dad, I have some bad news. I'm at _____ Hospital. The doctors think there's something seriously wrong with me, but they can't . . ." I couldn't finish. My wife reached for the phone. Crying, I tightened my grip. I tried to continue, but only sobs came out. My wife finally took the receiver and calmly explained what was happening.

I didn't have to state my emotions. They were clear through the action. That's showing, not telling.

Whenever possible, link emotional statements with objects in the story. In a personal experience article on a fire that destroyed half my house, one telling instant came the morning after the fire, when I saw the extent of the damage. I wrote: "Looking at the scorched maple tree in the front yard, with its blackened bark and leafless branches, I realized that was how I felt: scorched, barren, violated." ("Rising from the Ashes," *Providence Sunday Journal Magazine,* November 25, 1990) See how the burnt tree is used to reflect and amplify an emotional state.

The control of your emotions is important. Too much, and the horror is dissipated through overkill. Too little, and there's an irritating detachment. Let the story build up its own momentum, so that the reader will feel your emotions as you lived through the event. Save the actual statements of feelings for the pivotal climaxes in the narrative.

Of course all the basics of good writing apply: Keep the piece smooth, flowing, cohesive, and tight. Avoid overuse of adjectives. Use short sentences and a simple vocabulary. Stay in one point of view. Create vivid scenes. If possible, end with a surprise twist.

To place your manuscript, study market listings for publications that use personal experience pieces. Go to the library and locate examples from those magazines. Study several of the articles, noting their style and structure. How do they convey emotion? Are the articles instructive? Do they give specific solutions that readers will be able to apply to similar situations they experience? Do they use real names and facts, or are the identities of individuals and places obscured? Do the articles include sidebars giving do's and don'ts or background information or instruction? Based on which publications seem compatible with your approach, submit your article.

Contrary to the conventional advice in some writing guides, I suggest that you complete your personal experience article before you choose a market, because with this kind of piece, the drama of the event, its impact, and the quality of your writing will determine acceptance or rejection.

In all of my personal experience pieces, I have used actual names. In my first story, this was risky, because, in effect, I accused a private insurance adjuster of colluding with the builder. But these were the facts as they occurred, and, frankly, I wanted the chips to fall as they may. I asked the editor, and he said to go ahead and use real names. If an editor tells you not to use real names, change them, noting when they are first used that they are not the real names.

The key to getting published is to keep the manuscript in the mail. If you receive several rejections, ask yourself whether the people to whom you told your experience were visibly moved by it. If so, it is probably publishable, and you should keep trying. One caveat, however: Get the piece down on paper *before* you tell it to friends, to retain its emotional impact.

My fire story was rejected by eight publications, over an eighteen-month period, before it found a home. But that was of no consequence, since the fire could have occurred at any time. Interestingly enough, *The Providence Sunday Journal Magazine* ignored its usual market requirements—to feature only Rhode Island settings—when it published my Massachusetts personal experience piece. If you think you have an article that has strong, universal appeal, keep sending it out.

Photos are a big help, but not essential. When we had our fire, I knew the incident would someday see print, so I took many pictures, both color and black-and-white. The two photos the magazine chose were of the charred ruins and a shot of me bending down picking up debris. But this was the only time I included photos with the submission, and that's because they were terrific "grabber" shots.

Obviously, you don't know in advance if you're going to have an experience worth writing about. But when such an event does occur, take notes either during or after it happens. When we decided to travel to Florida by train rather than by plane for our annual winter getaway, I felt there was article potential in our doing so. Accordingly, I took notes—number of cars, number of passengers, costs, club car hours—and I jotted down some observations. This one page of comments helped me write "Taking the Train to Florida—a Chance to See the Country," for the *Boston Globe* Travel section (February 19, 1989).

What can you expect to be paid? Of course, that depends on where you place the piece. An article I wrote on building a room addition by starting with a room-raising weekend with 16 friends appeared in the *Boston Globe* Home section on July 7, 1986, and paid $60. But my *Sesame Street Magazine* piece on the roadblock paid $750. In general, publications pay better than average for a good personal experience piece. The national-circulation women's magazines pay $2,000 to $2,500. Regional publications and Sunday newspaper magazines range in the $400 to $800 category. The *Providence Sunday Journal* paid $450 for my fire story.

Writing personal experience articles can bring you the satisfaction of seeing your name in print and sharing an important event in your life with readers who may profit from it.

77

How to Write a How-to That Sells

By Gail Luttman

ANY ACTIVITY THAT INTERESTS YOU—from canoeing to cooking to collecting Civil War relics to cutting your own hair—is a potential how-to article. And whether you are an expert or a novice, you are qualified to write about it.

Where to start

The most successful introductions to how-to pieces state a problem and then propose one or more possible solutions, perferably those relating to the seven basic human motivators.

Ego—Does your solution to the problem improve the way you look, the way you feel about yourself, your ability to relate to others?

Economy—Does it save money, protect the environment, improve quality without increasing cost?

Health—Does it give you more energy, promote safety practices, increase your psychological well-being?

Romance—Does it enhance sex appeal, create a cozy atmosphere, improve personal relationships?

Family—Does it entertain children, foster loyalty, help research family history?

Leisure—Does it enliven holiday activities, provide an engrossing hobby, help plan exciting vacations?

Individuality—Does the activity appeal to the universal desire for uniqueness by offering something new, different or better?

These motivators often overlap. A hobby may bring in income. Dieting may improve both health and self-image. An inexpensive bungalow of unusual construction may serve as a romantic retreat. The more motivators you appeal to, the greater interest you will generate in your how-to.

Moving on

After piquing the reader's interest, offer a brief explanation of what the activity involves, couched in enthusiastic words that inspire confidence. Can the skill be learned in five easy steps? Fifteen minutes a day? Does it require a special setting, or will a corner of the garage do? What special tools or materials are needed?

Rather than barrage readers at the beginning with a large number of tools or materials required, you may want to list them in a sidebar, a separate boxed-off article that accompanies the main story. Sidebars are a great way to include data or lengthy explanations without interrupting the narrative flow. Some editors favor articles with one, two, or even three sidebars if the article is very long or complex.

Definitions of unfamiliar terms might go into a vocabulary sidebar, especially when they are numerous; on the other hand, if special words are few or are easy to define, it is better to explain their meanings as you go along.

Whenever possible, describe new concepts by drawing a comparison with something familiar. In a piece about building stone walls, for example, a description of the proper consistency of mortar as "buttery" sparks instant recognition.

Complicated procedures don't seem quite as confusing when written up in short, uncomplicated sentences of the sort found in cookbooks. Explicitness also ensures clarity. Vague directions such as "measure out six to eight cups of water" or "cut two to three yards of string" leave the reader wondering which of the two stated amounts to use.

Clarity is also improved by separating general principles from specific procedures. If you are writing about how to build a chicken coop, for example, after the introductory remarks, explain how the layout and dimensions are established, then include some specific plans. In a how-to about cooking a Christmas goose, first describe how to roast the goose, then offer some favorite recipes. In that way you'll satisfy both the creative reader who likes to improvise and the less adventuresome reader who feels more comfortable with step-by-step instructions.

The final and best way to ensure clarity is with illustrations. The less commonplace the subject, the more important photographs and sketches become, and they are essential when dimensions are involved. In addition, the market is more receptive to illustrated how-tos. But don't despair if you are not an accomplished photographer or artist; many how-to magazines have illustrators who will enhance your article with clear, easy-to-follow illustrations.

Organization

The subject of a how-to usually dictates whether to organize the steps chronologically or to start with simple procedures and work toward difficult ones. If two steps are to be taken at the same time, it is important to make that clear. In bread baking, for instance, point out that yeast should be softening in warm water while the other ingredients are being measured.

Repetition can help or hinder reader understanding. Too much repetition causes readers to lose interest. In a short article, a brief reference to the original explanation is usually all that's needed. But if the article is very long or complex and the explanation is relatively short, repetition is better than asking readers to flip pages back to find the required information.

Include a timetable for each step to help readers gauge their progress. How long does concrete take to set? Eggs to hatch? Wine to ferment? Do varying conditions influence timing? Can or should any deliberate measures be taken to speed things up or slow them down? What specific signs might the reader watch for as the project nears completion?

Finally, what can go wrong? Think twice before including a separate how-not-to section or a trouble-shooting sidebar. Faced with a long list of things that can go wrong, a reader might understandably wonder whether the whole thing is worth the bother. But, in general, as long as a how-to is clearly written and well organized, it doesn't hurt to point out danger spots along the way.

Research, including interviews with appropriate experts, supplies background that adds depth and authority to how-tos, thereby increasing reader interest and credibility. It also helps a writer discover whether his experiences are typical or not. If not, avoid making sweeping or questionable generalizations.

When consulting authoritative sources, watch out for regional variations in the terms and methods you plan to describe, especially when you're writing for a national magazine. Mention chicken wire and a southerner is likely to picture what the westerner calls lifestock fencing. Talk about reupholstering a divan or davenport, and there are readers who won't realize you are discussing a couch or a sofa. Before you write your article, look up alternative terminology from other areas.

Voice

Of course, the target audience determines how to approach your subject. If you are describing a new weaving technique to experienced weavers, you may use standard terms freely without defining them. But you should define any words that are specific to the new technique and you should definitely explain why the new technique is worth learning.

It is your job as a how-to writer to make certain that all readers achieve the same level of information by the time they reach the heart of your piece, and to do it without talking down. You can manage this by pretending you are writing a detailed letter to an interested friend.

You will find your most effective how-to voice by writing your article as if you were addressing a particular person who engages you in especially lively conversation. If you can't think of anyone suitable, invent someone. By writing expressly for that single reader, real or fictitious, you will delight all your readers with the personal tone of your how-to.

78

NINE STEPS FOR OUTLINING NONFICTION

BY SHIRLEY BARTLEY

BOOKS PILED HIGH ON THE FLOOR; manila folders, magazines, and mounds of paper yellowing with age on dusty shelves; desk drawers filled to overflowing with notecards, notebooks, and newspaper clippings. These are a few of the telltale signs of creative disorder. As long as the mess clutters just an office, the only one who complains is the writer. But if this state of disarray transfers itself to one's work then you have a real problem.

Trouble presenting ideas in an orderly manner can be your biggest obstacle to nonfiction sales. Your manuscripts are disorganized if your written ideas seem thrown together like pieces of a jigsaw puzzle. Outlining will help you find the pattern for those pieces. It can be a creative part of planning and writing nonfiction. The following nine-step process will help you organize both nonfiction articles and books; only length and scope differentiate the two.

1. *Narrow your topic statement*
Like an artist's sketch, an outline is a preliminary picture. However, using an outline is not like painting by number; rather, the process produces complex and original portraits.

As an example, let's say that I begin my work week by searching my files for an intriguing topic. I pull out a thick folder on gems as I fantasize about the ones I would buy with the money I make from writing.

After flipping through my research file, I limit the topic to the pros and cons of investing in genuine gem stones. Next, I remind myself that I should slant my piece toward the consumer. I list specific slants that have recently appeared in print. What's missing? I jot down several ideas. I conclude that what is needed is an article on the dangers of telephone sales of flawed gems.

2. *Invent new ideas about your topic*

Explore new patterns of thought. Within your chosen slant, try to get beyond empty generalities and banal observations. Write down as many variations on your focus as possible.

You should experience no dearth of creative ideas. If you do, you need to rethink your original slant and possibly start over with a new angle.

Suppose, as I brainstorm, I come up with several new ideas, including the history of the gem-scam operators, likely customers, types of gems telephone con artists typically sell, and so on.

3. *List ideas under general headings*

Use notecards to catalogue your ideas and data. Cards can be labeled with general headings such as history, present problems, extent and significance of problem, definition of key terms, solutions, and so on.

4. *Arrange ideas into a logical pattern.* What matters most is the organizing principle that lies behind the selection and arrangement of material.

There are numerous options from which to choose. Standard ways of organizing material include a *chronological* arrangement—*past, present,* and *future;* a *spatial* arrangement, in which the topics are connected by their relation to each other in space; *cause and effect; step-by-step;* an *inductive* pattern, in which you move from specifics to a conclusion; a *deductive* pattern, where you move from generalizations to conclusions, citing specific cases; a *hierarchical* pattern, which goes from least important to most important, or vice versa; *problem and solution;* and even a *random* pattern, which can be used if the main headings are of equal importance.

Returning to my gem-selling example, I organize my ideas chronologically. This is one of the easiest arrangements to master, while still preserving a readily identifiable logic. As the following sample outline illustrates, each main heading is a short, declarative sentence, which emphasizes one critical idea. Evidence is relegated to the sub-subheadings.

Title: Buying gems by phone is a risky business.

Introduction: Higher prices, a weakened dollar, and a nervous stock market are causing consumers to experiment with nontraditional investments such as gems. Con men are preying on investors.

Body:

I. **In the past, con men have pitched gems by phone.**
   A. Scams started in the late 1970s when the price of diamonds soared.
      1. Inflation was over ten percent and nervous investors looked for new money-making strategies.
      2. According to a New York appraiser, in 1977 a 1-carat diamond was worth $11,000. By 1980, same diamond sold for up to $60,000. By 1982, same diamond was worth less than $15,000.
   B. Hungry for fast profits, armchair investors got scalped by professional con men.
      1. Example of Texas huckster who targeted only oil-rich investors who had money to burn.
         a. Specialty of "Diamond Jim" was phoning only "serious" investors such as those with over $25,000 to invest in a single stone.
         b. By the time consumers caught on to the scam, "Diamond Jim" had vanished without a trace.
      2. Example of how *Fair Credit Billing Act of 1974* protected one consumer who bought flawed stones using a credit card. Law states that consumer is protected from having to pay for flawed merchandise when it is charged.
         a. This case was a rare one since most consumers paid with personal checks, cashier's checks or money orders.
         b. This law was not sufficient to stop con men.

II. **At present, gem-scam operators are bilking consumers out of hundreds of millions of dollars.**
   A. Hucksters are selling flawed colored gems.
      1. Florida state attorney general's office reports that sapphires, rubies, topazes, and emeralds are being sold over the phone.
         a. Stones are genuine but flawed.
         b. Colored stones are assessed on a purely subjective basis. No standards for clarity and color as there are for diamonds.
      2. Example of one investor who bought a Thai ruby over the phone for $24,000. Since it is imperfect and doesn't reflect the light, the stone is worth only $4,000.
   B. Anyone can be a victim.
      1. Florida state attorney general's office reports that hucksters get mailing lists of periodicals or the clientele of a brokerage house.
      2. Example of how a consumer gets hooked during a two-call process. First call offers gems for sale. Second call from a "different" firm offers to buy back same gems at a higher price. Therefore, the consumer gets hooked by the bait of fast and easy profits.
   C. Problem is significant on a national basis.
      1. Federal Trade Commission reports that individual scam operators are taking in millions of dollars.
      2. Jewelry-industry analysts report that thousands of people have been victimized and don't even know it.

3. According to the California state attorney general's office, problem is getting worse since scam operators set up their phone banks in one state and then flee to another.

III. **In the future, consumers would be safer if the following recommendations are followed.**

A. Protecting consumers against any type of telephone fraud should be a national priority.

1. Federal watchdog agency which would work with state authorities should be created. Purpose would be to stop all phone scams.

a. Consumers would be able to call and report suspicious phone offers.

b. Program would not be prohibitively costly.

2. State agencies would work in tandem with federal.

B. Protect consumers by establishing objective standards for colored stones.

1. Gemologist in Tulsa reports on advantages of verifiable and objective standards for colored stones.

2. Jewelry appraised in Houston recommends the type of standards that can be used.

3. Widely publicized standards would reduce marketability of huckster's stones.

Conclusion: Consumers should protect themselves from gem-scam operators by refusing to buy any gems over the phone. Purchases should be made only from reputable dealers. Consumers should invest in gems that have been appraised by experts, and remember the Latin motto: *Caveat emptor.*

5. *Accumulate data*

Check your outline for any holes. Is it heavy on factual data but short on authoritative testimony?

Fearing rejection, most writers err on the side of over-researching a topic. An outline can save you time and quell your anxieties, since it tells you exactly how much data you need and where it goes.

6. *Rethink the logic of your outline*

An outline establishes logical connections between ideas. Delete material that interferes with the logical sequence of your ideas. A good outline will help you catch errors of thought, language, or data.

I originally used a chronological pattern for my gem-selling example, but after rethinking my outline, I decided that the slant would be much stronger for consumers if I used a problem-and-solution pattern. Accordingly, I quickly reorganized my ideas and data.

371

7. *Ask your outline questions*

With a clean copy of your outline in hand, try to find out what you have left out or overlooked.

My favorite question is: "So what?" I use this question as a test for provocativeness. Asking a question such as this helps to delete fallacies of reasoning or boring bits of data.

8. *Do more research*

While it is easy to do too much research, it is also easy to do too little. An outline shows if you have made statements that you cannot prove. A short phone call or a brief trip to the library can do the trick.

9. *Transform your outline into a final manuscript*

An effective outline is the bare bones of the article. It must be fleshed out with lively style and, of course, convincing material. Outlining is one of the nuts and bolts of the writing trade that can make the difference between rejection and acceptance.

79

WRITING BIOGRAPHIES: THE PROBLEMS AND THE PROCESS

BY KATHERINE RAMSLAND

BIOGRAPHERS ARE FIXED ON THEIR heroes in a very peculiar manner," said Sigmund Freud. By that he meant that writing a biography is motivated by some psychological preoccupation. It is difficult for biographers to sustain such demanding work without intense emotional involvement with their subjects. Biographers must be prepared to make a major commitment, to immerse themselves totally in the point of view of another person so they can recreate that person's life with accuracy.

Choosing the subject

Most biographers write about their subjects because they know them, admire them, or believe a biography will make a contribution. Some biographers rework old material in new ways, and much of the "detective work" is already done. Those who introduce the subject for the first time must spend considerable effort collecting data. Writers of "authorized" biographies have access to private papers, while others have to struggle along without such cooperation. If the subject is living, the biographer faces problems not a factor when the subject is dead.

The choice of subject is also dictated by publishers' criteria. An academic publisher may want a scholarly book on an existing body of information, emphasizing literary criticism, while a commercial biography must demonstrate its market value, i.e., its readability and appeal to the general reader.

Dealing with research

Basically, there are two methods for dealing with facts. One is to collect them first, and organize them later. This prevents premature interpretations from highlighting some facts over others. The second method involves collecting just enough facts to set up a general guide for future directions. Your own personality will dictate which one you choose.

Both methods benefit from an active and passive phase. After a flurry of fact-gathering, allow your unconscious mind to go to work to reveal meaningful patterns as well as gaps in research. To be understood, facts must be absorbed and digested in the context of other information.

Inevitably you will be faced with an inordinate amount of data that needs careful organization and interpretation. Facts are malleable; they can be magnified out of proportion, interpreted out of context, minimized or suppressed. The first rule is to resist the impulse to appear omniscient. No person's life can be known completely. At best, a biography is a *perspective* based on the biographer's vision. Undocumented conjecture, while sometimes necessary, should be so acknowledged. The point is to create from raw data an organic portrait that reveals the significance of the subject's life or work. Not all of the facts will contribute to this goal. However, an abundance of facts must still be gathered to pinpoint those that give shape to how the subject's life was lived. There are many sources for locating that material.

1. Information may already be written in archives, letters, diaries, media profiles, unpublished manuscripts, and in earlier biographies.

2. Interviewing people who had personal acquaintance with the subject is essential. If the subject is living, he or she may give you a list. Otherwise, surviving family members can be helpful. Friends and relatives provide perspectives that can corroborate or broaden your understanding. Sometimes these contacts will be made over the phone or by mail, but often they will be face-to-face. Some people will be eager to cooperate; others may be reluctant. Friends will seek to protect, enemies to malign. You need tact, patience, persistence and discernment to obtain as many perspectives as possible. Prepare questions ahead of time. In the immediacy of an interview it is easy to forget points you wanted to raise.

All comments should be recorded, if possible. Do not count on being able to reconstruct a conversation later, especially as you begin to accumulate data. Biographies evolve. Your first impressions may not correspond to later insights. I am constantly surprised as I read over transcripts how items jump out at me that I had earlier overlooked. Had I just taken notes, those items would have been lost to me. Always ask permission to record, even over the phone. Be prepared to take notes if they say no.

3. Visit places that have meaning for the subject. Anne Rice lived in New Orleans. In writing her biography, I walked the streets she walked, and experiencing some of the same sensory impressions as she did— the smell of magnolias, the noise of rattling streetcars—gave me a perspective on her childhood.

4. You should have some grasp of the social and cultural influences that affected the subject.

5. General reference books on relevant subjects are helpful. I read books on psychology, sociology, alcoholism, and creativity to enhance understanding. Also, reading short profiles of other personalities can suggest new directions and help the writer create vivid impressions.

6. Reading books that influenced your subject can yield surprising insights.

7. Your own intuition is important. Note your emotional connections. You may have to make reasonable guesses about the subject's motivations, and using the facts you *do* have along with your intuition can help you make logical associations.

8. Photographs can reveal a great deal about a person's character and emotional development.

The idea of research is to find unifying themes among seemingly contradictory events or actions. Keep your eyes open for ideas or events that changed the person's *perspective* so you can monitor his or her emotional pulse. The points at which subjects' lives are most vivid to them are the points with which readers will identify most.

There is no end to the amount of factual data you can accumulate. One way you can organize and focus this research is to make an outline that provides logical progression and continuity. And you can structure your outline by choosing a biographical model.

Choosing a model

Biography involves both content and form. The form is like the plot of a novel: it makes the diverse elements work together to serve the purpose of the whole. Facts and quotes must be accurate, and critical interpretations interesting, but there is a consensus among contemporary biographers that there be enough flexibility of form to allow a

375

biographer to make a work unique. In other words, biographers are free to give their books an *aesthetic* unity and to interpret the stages of this subject. The choice of a model is important to this process.

1. Interpretive models guide readers, typically through psychological explanations, to reveal the motives that make sense of the subject's choices.

2. Objective models use all the known facts to document how the subject lived. This method is viewed more as historical than artistic.

3. Dramatic models *show* the subject through fictional devices, telling the life story through a series of vignettes and events. Virginia Woolf first coined the term "creative fact" to describe a fact that suggests or creates mood and character, even as it provides information. In such biographies, the "facts" are interpreted by the writer's imagination, thus replacing objectivity with intimacy. These biographies read more like novels than factual nonfiction.

The strength of a biography lies in creating the moments that reveal the most profound psychological truths—the motivations, transformations, and points of conflict—in the life of the subject. Biographers make choices in their writing as did the subjects in their lives. The writer's goal is to enable readers to *see* the subjects and to grasp how they acted and reacted, intentionally and unconsciously.

Many biographers make use of fictional devices, constructing their books with "plots," and paying special attention to creating tone and mood. Chapter endings may be "cliff-hangers," and using anecdotes with dialogue can provide details.

Ask yourself how closely you should stick to "just the facts." Dramatic styles take more license than objective styles. However, even the most fact-oriented biography can utilize fictional devices to create tension, advance the story, give information and reveal character.

For example, dialogue and physical impressions can be constructed from memory or from recordings to create scenes at important moments in the lives of the subjects. You can write dialogue by quoting from an exchange of letters, or if the subject is living, use what he or she recalls in dialogue.

Short chapters can give the feeling of tension, impatience, and urgency, as does Gerald Clarke's *Capote*. Metaphors and imagery deliver powerful impressions. The idea is to reveal the essence of the person, and to accomplish this, figurative language is sometimes superior to facts.

Uncomfortable discoveries

You may be confronted with information about your subject that gives you pause: sexual misconduct, cruelty, bigotry or marital discord. Perhaps the subject has even created a false picture of his or her life to manipulate public opinion. If the subject is still alive, and especially if he or she is cooperative, such information will raise important questions. How much must be revealed to facilitate an understanding of the person's life and how much is really just gratuitous gossip?

Arguments can be made for either side. Advocates of full revelation might consider one of the following points:

1. On the "objective" model, suppressing anything is an interpretation; to achieve objectivity, *all* facts must be revealed.

2. The dramatic model feeds on personal information—the more personal the better—to make the work truly vivid.

3. Some biographers idealize their subjects and justify avoiding the "dark" areas as unimportant in order to keep to their view of the person. For example, it was once thought that biographies of women should not disclose (for the "higher purposes" of society) information that detracted from their femininity. Carol Heilbrun, in *Writing a Woman's Life,* disagrees. She urges biographers of women to include "unfeminine" anger, dissatisfaction with roles, and quests for sensuality and power. Presenting the *whole* person takes priority.

Yet there are also arguments *against* full disclosure. For example:

1. People still alive may be harmed by the revelations.

2. Gossip detracts from scholarship. If the biographer reveals the information only to play up scandal, then he or she is not playing fair—(though including this type of information often adds to the readability of the book).

There are no easy answers to writing biography, and authors must decide for themselves what information will best serve their purpose. The purpose of biography is not to "spill the beans," but to deliver an interesting and comprehensive portrait guided by principles, imposed partly by the author and partly by the need for continuity, accuracy, depth, and focus.

POETRY

80

BEING TOUGH, BEING GENTLE

BY WILLIAM STAFFORD

CHEKHOV HAS A STORY ABOUT AN OLD CABBIE who drives his horse all day—through miserable weather and with many passengers—always wanting to tell someone about what is nearest his heart. No one has time to listen, and at the end of the day while unhitching his horse the cabbie finally finds a listener: He tells his unbearable trouble to his horse.

Sometimes we writers must feel like that cabbie. We have to provide what editors want to publish, what readers want to read. We drive hard all day, ignoring what is so near our hearts that we don't know how to handle it.

It's too private, too personal. Sometimes we can hardly face, even within our own selves, those significant feelings.

But surely what my whole life most wants to say can motivate my writing. Surely I need not abandon what I value, just in order to be fashionable, or to meet some editor's whim. What kind of life—what kind of vocation—is that?

So—how to be serious, emotional, have a real life—but not fall into sentimentality. How can we carry our most fervent feelings right into the living room of our readers and still be firm, solid, satisfying, convincing?

First, we can remember the usual warnings: "Show me, don't tell me." "Avoid clichés." "Get images and sense impressions into the lines." "Don't just say 'love,' 'beauty,' 'heart,' 'tears'." "When you find yourself terribly fond of what you are saying, watch out!" "You can't do it with adjectives. . . ."

We can observe these warnings. We can curry our writings by applying remedies. But somehow just observing such rules is not enough. They trim away, but they don't supply the fire we need. And they don't invite us to cut loose with our whole sentient being.

Once a writing class met at a game reserve—"Malheur"—in eastern Oregon. The place seethed with birds, and miles of cattails, willows, wandering waterways, buttes where coyotes howled. When as teacher I drove out there, the class gathered at a picnic table, and we looked around. One of the students said, "This place is beautiful."

Another chimed in, "This is the most beautiful place I have ever seen."

The next one got even more creative: "Hey, I've never even dreamed of so beautiful a part of the world!"

And I said, "We have to get out of here."

Our senses were overloaded, and we were not able to lean back enough to muster evidence rather than incoherent cries.

Maybe that's it. Maybe we have to practice writing about topics that allow us some degree of balance, of emotional stability from whence we can lever into the language some evidence for what we are feeling. That's the safe way. But we don't want to be safe at the cost of shying from our most enticing subjects.

Here is how in a workshop recently one writer—Lou Crabtree—achieved control by putting her ultimate topic, "Burial," into the form of an Indian ceremony:

> In the morning
> they will bury you
> standing on the north side
> the south the west
> not one will stand
> no shadow will fall
> on the east side
> no evil spirit between
> you and sunrise. . . .

Another writer in the workshop headed bravely into that most difficult of "sentimental" topics, a poem about her dog. She avoided some booby traps by *denying* her feelings (you can't mention something without its having an effect; it will be present, but it may be saved from being discounted by the reader). She called her poem "Sorrow":

> The black dog by the road
> two days in a row can't be yours.
> He died nine years ago. It's been
> that long since you saw him last.

379

> The plumed curl of his tail as he left
> through woods and you holding
> the leash limp in your hands. . . .

The elements of sentiment are present, but insulated by being denied. Ruth Moose, the author of "Sorrow," was able to spell out a touching experience but still be "tough."

These writers found ways to express honest feelings, and in each instance they brought *additional* material into the text. From their example, and from other such experiences, I want to suggest that one way out of sentimentality is to allow—to embrace, even—more feeling, not less. We can be as honest and fervent as our emotions suggest, and can explore those emotions, write them out fully and warmly, adding the particulars that identify exactly how the experiences come about.

We can tell the place, the people, the stray backgrounds that go together and create momentum—tell the reader exactly how it is, not our summary of how we feel, but an elaboration of encounters that bloom into something new.

Don't try to impose your feelings on the reader by asserting fervently *that* you have emotion, but instead, ask yourself *why*. Was there a scene that accompanied your feelings? What time of day was it? Does any sound relate to your feeling? There must have been something that made you react, that makes you react now. Make the reader encounter the human involvements that command our emotions. The reader must face the evidence, not just your soliciting of a feeling.

For—remember—literature and the writing of it do more than just express the self: Literature creates whole new continents of experience. David Copperfield, for instance, is not just oppressed by a cruel parent—his deadly, hard new father appears with a name: Murdstone. When that father oppresses him, David doesn't only feel bad; he gets shipped away into a whole succession of momentous encounters, where he doesn't just meet strange people—he meets exactly identified characters, like an old man named Mr. Dick who flies kites and frequently gets immobilized by thinking of King Charles's head.

These examples remind us that writers don't just assert summary feelings: Emily Dickinson doesn't just recollect a death in the family—she hears a fly buzz, and Death in the form of a kindly hack driver picks her up and starts down a long—a never-ending—road.

Writing—literature—springs new experiences into being; it is much more than just partially achieved recollections transferred from a fervent author to an accepting reader: A new life springs into focus, by being told. To create means to change, to change writer and reader.

I never came back to earth after reading Chekhov.

Now when I reach for my book—or my pen—Mr. Murdstone raises his heavy cane. I hear a fly buzz. Beyond the hedge in a gush of color and laughter Mr. Dick releases his gigantic staggering kite to the wind.

Isn't it strange, how we can link stray parts of our consciousness into one sequential line of thought? It doesn't have to be great, or important; it just has to get on a track and ramble along. At least, such was my feeling when I began one morning to jot down stray impulses about my own processes of writing. I wasn't out to amaze anyone, merely to explore a few relations with other writers. I got excited—what reverberations I felt from my recollections of reading. I wanted to bring in Martin Luther King, Mahatma Gandhi, many glorious characters with their richly syllabled names. . . .

The Way I Write*

In the mornings I lie partly propped up
the way Thomas Jefferson did when he slept
at Monticello. Then I stop and
Look away like Emily Dickinson when
she was thinking about the carriage and the fly.

When someone disturbs me I come back
like Pascal from those infinite spaces,
but I don't have his great reassurances
of math following along with me; so somehow
the world around me is even scarier.

Besides, the world on fire of Saint Teresa
surrounds me, and the wild faces Dante
awakened on his descent through those dark
forbidden caverns. But over my roof bends
my own kind sky and the mouse-nibble sound of now.

The sky has waited a long time
for this day. Trees have reached out,
the river has scrambled to get where it is.
And here I bring my little mind
to the edge of the ocean and let it think.

My head lolls to one side as thoughts
pour onto the page, important
additions but immediately obsolete, like waves.

The ocean and I have many pebbles
to find and wash off and roll into shape.

"What happens to all these rocks?" "They
become sand." "And then?" My hand stops.
Thomas Jefferson, Emily Dickinson,
Pascal, Dante—they all pause too.
The sky waits. I lean forward and write.

—William Stafford

*Reprinted by permission from *The Virginia Quarterly Review* (Summer 1990).

§ 81

RECEIVING A POEM

By Donald M. Murray

I AM WRITING THIS ARTICLE AS I AM IN THE PROCESS of making myself receptive to poetry: I can command myself to write non-fiction or fiction but I have to receive poetry.

This is not *the* way to write poetry. There is no correct way to write anything, certainly not poetry. This is merely an honest account of the writing of a poem that has not yet arrived with the promise to record precisely what happens.

Last night I knew I would attempt this experiment of writing an article *about* writing poetry *while* writing poetry. I often make my brain aware of the next day's writing. I don't think about the writing but create a climate of awareness.

The morning started badly. I woke too early, slept a bit late, had no time for my morning walk when lines of what may become poetry are often received. I felt this project hopeless, but as I drove back from the store—we were out of juice; I wanted muffins; I had to get the paper—I spotted a neighbor, a forestry expert walking his teenager somewhere. The boy carried a cooler, the father a stool and I made a strange speculation, "He was going out to watch a tree grow." That line might become a poem.

And it was that line that released another line: "August is the month of leaving." I sat in the garage for a moment, not yet speaking silently to myself of the full meaning of August in our family, instead forcing myself to think the line came because of a humorous column I was thinking of writing about what polite lies we speak as dreadful summer guests depart. But I knew that August was the month, fourteen years ago, when our middle daughter died at 20.

Now I will attempt some writing that *may* become a poem, following that fragment—"August is the month of leaving"—to see where it will lead, what connections it will make. The result is usually a clump of half-poetry, half prose in which I write fast, paying some, but not too much attention to line breaks.

I start to censor myself. I do not want to write about Lee's death; I do not want to think about her premature departure. But I may have no choice. I will write about August and see what happens.

~~The tide at Ocean Park~~
The morning tide at Ocean Park is out
and I run toward the sun to make my last
collection: razor clam shell, seaweed collar,
driftwood cane. Look back and draw,
with my big toe, this summer's cottage
and myself running toward me, knowing the tide
will return

In August my wool uniform itched as I saw
  Grandma
for the last time. She thought I was leaving
for Waterloo where her great-uncle for whom
I was named had taken a ball in the leg. But
I limped from football and would dance on air
swinging from the parachute kite and discover
all wars are the same.

In August I first learned to swim, took my first
wife blueberrying and in August, the month of
  buzzing
~~and~~ heat, we had the fight over vichyssoise my
  second
wife will not forget. In those last slow days
of August when summersun (paints?) pools of
  brightness
on the lawn and I watch the maple's shadows record
the breeze, we got that call that made us drive madly
home.

Lee told us how sweet her sisters had been in her
  fevered
hours, smiled and gently shut us out of her
                       [interrupted by phone call]
slow dying. [anger/rage] My woods are filled with
  leaves,
daisies, tall swaying trees but I walk to the rock
wall, [calm?] not touching the vulnerable blossom
  of the
daylily that opened this hour and will not last
the night.

I followed the poem wherever it took me, and, as it so often happens, my writing took me where I did not want to go. I felt physically ill toward the end of its writing, but I also felt I must write it. This not-yet-poem demanded to be heard.

I tried to stay in the poem, not to think but to record. I was on the beach, then—for no reason outside the poem—at Grandma's bedside, then in other Augusts before and after my war without understanding their meaning or connection, and then at Lee's bedside.

I put a parenthesis and question mark around "paints" that I thought a cliché, but I did not want to stop and interrupt the flow. When the phone rings or someone comes by, I stop in mid-line as many writers do, so I can pick it up and re-enter the writing. I was aware in the corner of my eye that the poem seemed to be in stanzas but did not know there were 7-7-8-7 lines until I now count them. I don't like many of the line breaks that seem to end on weak words and do not flow into the next line or stanza, but all that is a matter for the next draft.

I have never made bracketed notes to myself—"anger/rage" and "calm?"—within a draft before but went back and inserted them today to indicate a change of mood that *may* take place in the revision of the poem. I do think I have a text to work on and will let it sit for a while.

This was written on my computer. Usually the first drafts are written by hand in my daybook, but today I paste a printout of the poem in my daybook. I have to visit my laptop in computer hospital in Massachusetts, and the poem keeps on writing a new third stanza in my head. Finally, I stop by the road and scribble down:

It was my ninth August when I drowned, crystal bright spray, the sudden roof of water, blue warm then cold green. My 13th August I learned to swim underwater, daring the blackgreen death. The sudden rising. It was Vermont August, pools of brightness on lawn, the dance of maple leaf shadows when we heard the phone ring ring and suddenly drove home.

It was pretty bad but maybe there was something going on. I tossed the censor and my daybook on the back seat and drove on. In Massachusetts I stopped in a Friendly's, asked for a back booth, and while waiting for my soup and sandwich, played with what I had, trying not to be critical but to see what was working, to release the poem if one was on the page. I put what was inserted in bold type and show what I crossed out.

August is the Month of Leaving

The morning tide at Ocean Park is out
and I run toward the sun to make my last
collection: razor clam shell, seaweed collar,
driftwood cane. Look back and draw,
with my big toe, this summer's cottage
and myself running toward me, knowing the tide
will return.

~~In August m~~My wool uniform itched **in August** as
   I saw Grandma
for the last time. She thought I was leaving
for Waterloo where her great-uncle ~~for whom~~ **wore**
my name into battle. He took ~~I was named had~~
   ~~taken~~ a ball
     in the leg. But **saved the flag his brother**
     dropped.
I ~~limped from football and~~ would dance on air,
swinging from the parachute, ~~kite~~ and discover
   all wars
are the same.

~~In August I first learned to swim, took my first~~
~~wife blueberrying and in August, the month of~~
   ~~buzzing~~
~~and heat, we had the fight over vichyssoise my~~
   ~~second~~
~~wife will not forget. In those last slow days~~
~~of August when summersun (paints?) pools~~
   ~~of brightness~~
~~on the lawn and I watch the maple's shadows record~~
~~the breeze, we got that call that made us drive~~
   ~~madly~~
~~home~~.

~~It was~~ my ninth August ~~when~~ I drowned, crystal
   bright
spray, the ~~sudden~~ **rising** roof of water, blue warm
   then cold
     blackgreen sinking down.
My 13th August I learned to swim underwater
   (laughing?)
     holding my breath, ~~daring the blackgreen~~
   ~~death~~. The
     sudden rising. It was **a** Vermont
August, pools of brightness ~~on~~ **dappled** lawn, the
   dance of
     maple leaf

shadows when we heard the phone ring ring ring
  and ~~suddenly~~
    madly
drove home.

Lee told us ~~how sweet~~ her sisters had ~~been~~ **cooled**
  ~~in~~ her fevered **face**
~~hours,~~ smiled ~~and~~ **then** gently shut us out of her
slow dying. ~~[angry/rage]~~ My woods are ~~filled~~ **lush**
  with
    ~~leaves~~ **blooms, swollen the poison ivy vine**
~~daisies, tall swaying trees but I walk to the rock~~
~~wall, [calm?] not touching the vulnerable blossom~~
  ~~of the~~
I watch lush August in my woods then ~~But I Still~~
  But eye the
    yellow-orange ~~the~~ **flame of the**
daylily that opened this hour and will not last
the night.

   It is embarrassing to reveal such bad writing, but it is important that
inexperienced writers learn that writers have to write badly to write
well. I have learned to leave alone what I think works—the first
stanza—but I am most excited by those pages where syntax breaks
down, where language is struggling toward meaning.
   I need to write this poem on the eve of the anniversary of my
daughter's death, but I do not know what it means. I have no precon-
ceived theme, no idea; if I did, I would not need to write. The meaning
is in the writing of the poem. I don't know if I will end in anger or with
comfort, perhaps neither or both. I hope I will celebrate Lee's brief life,
but I am open to a complex of meanings or a meaning that will change
each time I read the poem. I know my readers will read according to
their own personal history of loss and their own needs at the moment of
reading. The poem—or any other piece of writing—does not belong to
me or to the reader; the magic is that each reading creates a text that
lies between us to which we both contribute.
   The next morning I come to my desk eager to type out the poem
anew, knowing it will change. If I am lucky, it will reveal itself to me if I
listen to the evolving lines.
   I type through it quickly, paying attention to the organic growth of the
poem, to the lines and how they break. I work on that first stanza that
had been untouched in yesterday's writing. I write easily, hearing the

poem, now looking back, now worrying a bit about its shape—the shorter lines in the first stanza—and copy it out again to work in close, word by word, space by space, line by line.

I print out the poem I have been given, read it once or twice again, then decide I have a poem I can show my wife and mail to Lee's sisters. I have learned to be careful to whom I show my writing and follow one rule: *Show drafts only to those who make me want to write when I leave.*

In the next days I share it with a few poet friends and a poetry group to which I belong. I listen to their response but do not accept all their counsel. I must respect the poem.

I continue, during the day and evening to read the poem lightly, almost casually, to hear what it is saying. I often read what is not yet on the page. In such a reading, I hear myself say, in the fifth line from the bottom, "fear" instead of "hate." "Fear" was a gift, and I am grateful to receive it. I had never felt right about "hate," but "fear" seems just right; it tells me just what I feel as I observe my August woods.

Stepping back from my writing desk after this sequence of drafts, I discover I have:

- Fleshed out the first stanza, making the innocent experience of August more complete. But, of course, it is not so innocent. There is an erasing tide.
- Tried to write with specific details, proper nouns and active verbs. I do not want to tell the reader what to think or how to feel, but to make the reader think and feel.
- Made the lines—usually—end on a solid piece of information but also provide the energy that will drive to the next line—and to the end of the poem.
- Enjoyed, in a mysterious, profound way, the writing of the poem. Although the subject is painful, it was helpful for me to write it. It is a sublime form of fun to play with language, listening to the lines that lead, the words that reveal, to live on the page, a life that may seem, at times, as intense as experience itself. As a writer, I lead the twice—or thrice—lived life.

I will submit the poem for publication and when it returns, put it in the mail again, but the pleasure of publication, if it comes, is nothing compared to those moments of concentration when I was lost in its receiving, when it revealed to me how I feel as August returns.

This is the poem as it is finished—for the moment:

August is the Month of Leaving

The morning tide at Ocean Park is out and I run
toward the sun to make my last collection: razor
clam shell, seaweed collar, green bottle from Spain
[no message, no Pirate map], my first driftwood
cane. I used its crooked point to draw this summer's
cottage, the next door wolfhound I feared. I know
the incoming

tide will create memory. In August I saw Grandma
for the last time. My wool uniform itched. She ordered
me to defeat Napoleon at Waterloo. Her great-uncle wore
my name into battle, held high the colors his brother
dropped. I would dance on air, swinging in my parachute
but landing would learn his Belgium lesson: we die
alone

as I drowned my ninth August, crystal bright spray,
the rising roof of water and the blackgreen cold before
my rescue. In my thirteenth summer I learned the projectile
dive, to swim under water, holding my breath, to rise.
And thirteen years ago this August we were in Vermont,
sunlight dappled on the long green lawn when the phone
rang

and we madly drove home. In the hospital Lee told us
her sisters had so gently cooled her fevered face, then
shut us out of her five day dying. I fear August
in my woods, so much green, sun, so many dancing shadows
but still I stand by the yellow-orange flame of the daylilly
that blooms that August morning yet will not survive
the night.

82

THE POET WITHIN YOU

BY DAVID KIRBY

I FIGURE POETRY is a way of beating the odds. The world is never going to give you everything you want, so why not look elsewhere? In a wonderful book called *The Crisis of Creativity* (now regrettably out of print) by George Seidel, it is stated that the artist will always have one thing no one else can have: a life within a life.

And that's only the start. If you have talent and luck and you work like a son of a gun, you might even end up, as the poet John Berryman says, adding to "the store of available reality."

But at least you can have a life within a life, no matter who you are. Not all of us can be great poets. If that were so, the Nobel Prize would be in every box of breakfast cereal—you'd get up, write your poem for the day, and collect your prize. But every literate person has it in him- or herself to be a good poet. Indeed, I have wonderful news for you— each of us is a poet already, or at least we used to be. It's just that most of us have gone into early retirement.

Seriously, when interviewers ask the marvelously gifted William Stafford when he started to write poetry, Stafford often replies, "When did you stop?" All children put words together imaginatively; just talk to one and you'll see what I mean. But then they grow up and enter the world of bills and backaches. They start chasing that dollar, and suddenly their time is limited. Poetry is usually the first thing to go. People get so busy with their lives that they forget to have a life within a life. But you have a life anyway, right? So forget about it for a minute—it'll still be there when you come back—and let's talk about the poet within you.

The first thing you need to do is forget that all poets are supposed to be erratic or unstable. Flaubert was quite clear on this point. He said, "Be regular and orderly in your life, like a bourgeois, so that you may be violent and original in your work." In other words, there's no point

390

in sapping your resources by pursuing some phony "artistic" lifestyle. First, the outer person has to be calm and self-disciplined; only then can the inner one be truly spontaneous.

And that means getting organized. Here are a few rules I use to make my life as orderly and bourgeois as possible, so that the poet within me can be as wild as he wants to be.

1) *Start small.* Most beginning writers tackle the big themes: love, death, the meaning of life. But don't we already know everything there is to know about these subjects? Love is wonderful, death is terrible, life is mysterious. So start small and work your way up. Take a phrase you overheard, a snippet of memory, a dream fragment, and make a poem of that. Once the details are in place, the big theme (whatever it is) will follow, but the details have to come first.

2) *Write about what you remember.* It is a commonplace that you should write about what you know, but usually the present is too close for us to see it clearly. We have to move away from the events in our lives before we can see them in such a way that we can write about them engagingly. Don't waste time on the guy you saw talking to his dog this morning; take a few notes, if you like, but if he's memorable, he'll pop into your mind later, when you really need him. Instead, why not write a poem about the girl in your third-grade class who could throw a baseball better than any of the boys and all the problems that caused? By putting these memories down on paper and shaping them, you're enriching not only your own life but also the lives of others.

3) *Be a sponge.* Shakespeare was. His plays are based on historical accounts and on lesser plays by earlier playwrights. So what are you, better than Shakespeare? I once wrote a poem called "The Last Song on the Jukebox" that was published in a magazine and then in a collection of my poetry and now in an anthology that is widely used on college campuses; people seem to like it pretty well. Looking back at the poem, I can hear in it echoes of two country songs that I used to be able to sing in their entireties but have since forgotten. Somebody says something in my poem that is a variation on something a character says in a novel called *Ray,* by the talented Barry Hannah. And the overall tone of "The Last Song on the Jukebox" owes much to a poet I heard reading his own work one night. His voice was perfect—it had just the right twang to it—so I used it for the speaker in my poem. Now that I

think about it, I realize that I didn't like the guy's poetry that much. That didn't stop me from adapting his twang to my purpose.

4) *Play dumb.* Just about anything can be turned into a poem if you play dumb about it, because when you're smart, everything makes sense to you and you go about your business, whereas when you're dumb, you have to slow down, stop, figure things out. Recently, in Chicago, I saw a man being arrested. The police had cuffed him and were hauling him away while an elderly woman shook with rage and screamed after them as they all climbed into the paddywagon. "Liar!" she shouted, "liar!" You mean you can get arrested just for lying, I said to myself? Is that only in Chicago, or does the law apply everywhere? Now if I were a smart person, I might have figured out what really happened: Probably the guy grabbed her purse, and she called the cops, and he said he didn't do it, and she said he *did* do it, and so on. But by being dumb, I got a flying start on a poem. I haven't finished the poem yet, but as you can see, I have already given myself a lot to work with, thanks to my astonishingly low IQ.

5) *Reverse your field.* When you catch yourself on the verge of saying something obvious, don't just stop; instead, say the opposite of what you were going to say in the first place. Listen to the poet within you. If you want to eat a chocolate bar, that's not poetry; everybody likes chocolate. But suppose the chocolate bar wanted to eat you? Now that's a poem. Here's another example: I'm thinking of ending my liar-in-Chicago poem with something about husbands and wives and how they have to be truthful to each other, and I can see myself heading toward a stanza in which the speaker wonders what his wife really means when she says (and this would be the last line of the poem), "I love you." The problem is that that's too pat for a last line, too cloying, too sentimental, an easy out. Instead, since people who are really crazy about each other sometimes kid around in a mock-hostile way, why not have the speaker wonder whether the wife is telling the truth or not when she laughs and hits him on the arm and says, "I hate you, you big lug!" Such an unexpected statement would come as a surprise to the reader, although first it will have come as a surprise to me, who was heading in the opposite direction before I realized that I needed to reverse my field.

6) *Work on several poems at once.* For one thing, you won't end up giving too much attention to a poem that doesn't need it—like children, some poems do better if you don't breathe down their necks all the time. For another, if you're working on just one poem and it isn't going anywhere, you're likely to feel terribly frustrated, whereas if one poem is dying on the vine and three others are doing pretty well, you'll feel as though you are ahead of the game (because you will be). Also, sometimes our poems are smarter than we are, and a word or a line or a stanza that isn't right for one poem will often migrate to another and find a home for itself there. Poems are happiest in the company of other poems, so don't try to create them in a vacuum. You probably wouldn't try to write four novels at once, but there's no reason why you shouldn't take advantage of poetry's brevity and get several poems going simultaneously.

7) *Give yourself time.* This is actually related to the preceding rule, since you wouldn't tend to rush a poem if you were working on several of them at once. I have a friend whose daughter is learning how to cook. But she's a little impatient, so when she has a recipe that says you should bake the cake at 350 degrees for thirty minutes, she doesn't see why you can't cook it at 700 degrees for fifteen minutes. If you take this approach to poetry, your poems are going to end up like my friend's daughter's cakes, charred on the outside and raw in the middle. If you saw a stunningly handsome stranger walking down the street, would you run up to him and shout, "Marry me"? Of course not—he might say yes! Poems are the same way, and if you try to make them yours too soon, you won't be happy with the results, I promise you. Be coy, be flirtatious; draw the poem out a little and see what it's really about. There's no hurry, because you've got all those other poems you're working on, remember?

8) *Find a perfect reader.* A perfect reader is like a perfect tennis partner, someone who is a little better than you are (so you feel challenged), but not that much better (so you don't get demoralized). And like an ideal tennis partner, a good reader is going to be hard to find. You don't play tennis with your mother, so don't expect her to critique your writing.

Anyway, what kind of mother would tell her own child that his poetry is terrible? That's what friends are for. So no parents. And no room-mates, either: people are always saying to me, "You're going to love this poem; my roommate says it's the best thing I've ever written." What else would a roommate say? You can hardly go on living with someone, after you've told him to throw his notebook away and take up basket-weaving. Just as you would play tennis with a couple of dozen people before you pick the one you want to play with every Saturday, so too should you pass your poems around until you find the one person who can show you their strengths and weaknesses without inflating or deflating your ego too much. If you're lucky, you'll then do what I did when I found my perfect reader—you'll marry her (or him).

If you have a knack for language and you follow these rules and you get a break from time to time and you look both ways whenever you cross the street, after a while you will find you have created for yourself a life within a life. You will have awakened—reawakened, actually—the poet within you. And even if this isn't your year to win the Nobel Prize, I have to say that I never met anybody who didn't break out into a big happy smile when I introduced myself as a poet. I don't know what it is; maybe people associate me with Homer or Milton. At any rate, every-one seems happy to know there is a poet in the neighborhood.

Well, not everybody. Once I was negotiating with a man to buy his house, and I was getting the better of him. So the man lost his temper and said I didn't know what I was doing, I *couldn't* know, because I was a poet and I ought to go back to my poems and leave business affairs to men like him, practical, level-headed men. For a couple of days, I felt pretty rotten, although the whole thing turned out spledidly for me, since I later found another house I liked even better than his. Mean-while, the practical level-headed fellow had lost a great buyer; like Flaubert, I believe in paying my bills on time.

And I got my revenge: I wrote a poem about him.

83

How to Write a Funny Poem

By Jack Prelutsky

WRITING HUMOROUS VERSE is hard work. For the humor to succeed, every part of the poem must be just right: It requires delicacy. If the poet uses too heavy a hand, the poem goes beyond being funny and turns into something disquieting or even grotesque. Conversely, if the poet doesn't push the idea far enough, the incongruities that are supposed to make the poem funny bypass the reader.

Humorous poetry is often highly underrated. The reader responds easily to humor with laughter, often unaware of the mental and technical gymnastics that the poet has performed to elicit this response. Physiological studies have shown that the body has a much easier time laughing than getting angry. Since humor is such a facile emotion, the reader assumes that the funny poem is also a simple poem—about as complicated as slipping on a banana peel.

How do I make a poem funny? Exactly what are these gymnastics? I'll start with one that is a favorite, and then continue with several others that should be standard in any humorist's repertoire.

I love the technique of asking serious questions about a silly idea. You can make almost anything funny by starting with an absolutely nonsensical premise, and asking common sense questions about it. I once was in a supermarket selecting some boneless chicken breasts for dinner, and it suddenly occurred to me to ask the question, "What about the rest of the chicken—was that boneless, too?" And if so, where did it live, what did it do, and what did the other chickens think of it? When I'd finished answering my "serious" questions, I had the groundwork for a poem, "Ballad of a Boneless Chicken," which appears in *The New Kid on the Block.*

While I was writing the poem, one last question occurred to me: Exactly what sort of egg does a boneless chicken lay? The answer provided me with a surprising, yet somehow logical conclusion.

Ballad of a Boneless Chicken

I'm a basic boneless chicken,
yes, I have no bones inside,
I'm without a trace of rib cage,
yet I hold myself with pride,
other hens appear offended
by my total lack of bones,
they discuss me impolitely
in derogatory tones.

I am absolutely boneless,
I am boneless through and through,
I have neither neck nor thighbones,
and my back is boneless too,
and I haven't got a wishbone,
not a bone within my breast,
so I rarely care to travel
from the comfort of my nest.

I have feathers fine and fluffy,
I have lovely little wings,
but I lack the superstructure
to support these splendid things.
Since a chicken finds it tricky
to parade on boneless legs,
I stick closely to the hen house,
laying little scrambled eggs.

Another of my tricks is to find that one small special something in the ordinary, or to add something unexpected to the apparently mundane. For example, in *The New Kid on the Block,* I have a poem called, "Euphonica Jarre." Euphonica would be unexceptional, were it not for one preposterous talent—she's the world's worst singer. In this poem, I applied another device, one familiar to all humorists—*exaggeration!* To make Euphonica outlandishly funny, I decided that her vocalizing should cause unlikely events, such as ships running aground, trees defoliating themselves, and the onset of avalanches.

Euphonica Jarre

Euphonica Jarre has a voice that's bizarre,
but Euphonica warbles all day,
as windowpanes shatter and chefs spoil the batter
and mannequins moan with dismay.

Mighty ships run aground at her horrible sound,
pretty pictures fall out of their frames,
trees drop off their branches,
rocks start avalanches,
and flower beds burst into flames.

When she opens her mouth, even eagles head south,
little fish truly wish they could drown,
the buzzards all hover, as tigers take cover,
and rats pack their bags and leave town.

Milk turns into butter and butterflies mutter
and bees look for something to sting,
pigs peel off their skins, a tornado begins
when Euphonica Jarre starts to sing.

In *The New Kid on the Block,* there's another poem called, "Forty Performing Bananas," which illustrates the tactic of making something extraordinary out of the ordinary. On the surface, there's nothing unusual about bananas. They're found in every food market, and we take them for granted when we slice them over our breakfast cereal. However, they become uniquely foolish when imbued with the skill to sing and dance. Some inanimate objects are just naturally amusing when they're anthropomorphized. Performing bananas are among them; airborne hot dogs, which appear in my newest book, *Something Big Has Been Here,* are another.

By the way, I use a lot of wordplay in the banana poem: their features are "appealing" and their fans "drive here in bunches." It's probably already occurred to you, but I'd like to mention that I routinely combine several techniques in a poem and can wind up with some complex results. Another way to find humor in the ordinary is to take this item or idea and keep amplifying it until it reaches a totally absurd conclusion. When I was writing *Something Big Has Been Here,* I was struck with the notion of an uncuttable meat loaf. It's an old joke, and there are dozens of examples on TV and film. I searched for an approach that would allow the reader to experience that old joke in a new way. In this case, the meat loaf in question resists all attempts to slice, hammer, drill or chisel it. The implements become more and more exotic, the speaker resorts to bows and arrows, a blowtorch, a power saw, and finally a hippopotamus to trample it. Nevertheless, the meat loaf remains intact. Though I could have ended the whole business here, I decided to employ an additional tactic, that of combining two different ideas that normally don't belong together, further stretching credulity. I conclude the poem by accepting the meat loaf for what it is (indestructible) and reveal that additional meat loaves are now being manufactured as building materials. Of course, no builder would use meat loaves to erect a house, but by making such an absurd leap, I made the poem even funnier.

I'd like to touch on a rather obvious resource for any poet who writes humor: letting the humor grow out of the words themselves. There are numerous kinds of wordplay: puns, anagrams, spoonerisms, and malapropisms. I love puns, and in *Something Big Has Been Here,* I expanded on the sayings that children write to each other in their autograph books when I composed the poem, "I Wave Good-bye When Butter Flies." In this list of puns, you can watch a pillow fight, sew on a cabbage patch, dance at a basket ball, etc.

I Wave Good-bye When Butter Flies

> I wave good-bye when butter flies
> and cheer a boxing match,
> I've often watched my pillow fight,
> I've sewn a cabbage patch,
> I like to dance at basket balls
> or lead a rubber band,
> I've marveled at a spelling bee,
> I've helped a peanut stand.
>
> It's possible a pencil points,
> but does a lemon drop?
> Does coffee break or chocolate kiss,
> and will a soda pop?
> I share my milk with drinking straws,
> my meals with chewing gum,
> and should I see my pocket change,
> I'll hear my kettle drum.
>
> It makes me sad when lettuce leaves,
> I laugh when dinner rolls,
> I wonder if the kitchen sinks
> and if a salad bowls,
> I've listened to a diamond ring,
> I've waved a football fan,
> and if a chimney sweeps the floor,
> I'm sure the garbage can.

Another common technique to achieve humor is the surprise ending. My use of this device is the result of being so astounded and delighted by the O. Henry stories I read as a child. One of my most successful uses of a surprise ending is in the title poem of my book, *The New Kid on the Block*. I recite a complaint about a neighborhood bully, the new kid who punches, tweaks my arm, pulls my hair, likes to fight, is twice my size, and just at the point when everyone has conjured up an image of some big, loutish boy, I end the poem with the following lines:

". . . that new kid's really bad, I don't care for her at all."

I admit that the punch line's humor depends heavily on the shameless use of one of contemporary society's most common stereotypes, but it has never failed to draw laughter whenever I've recited the poem to an audience. This is a good place to remind everyone that much of our humor is culture bound. Very often, what may be hilarious to an American audience may draw blank looks from residents of the Himalayas. Actually, I don't have to go as far as Tibet to make an apt comparison; there are many moments on the British "Benny Hill" television show that draw blank looks from me.

One last device I'll mention is irony. It can be as simple as in my poem, "My Dog, He is an Ugly Dog" (from *The New Kid on the Block*), where I list all the things wrong with my dog: He's oddly built, sometimes has an offensive aroma, has fleas, is noisy, stupid, and greedy. Nevertheless, despite this litany of his drawbacks, I declare that he's the only dog for me.

In my poem, "I Met a Rat of Culture" (from *Something Big Has Been Here*), the irony becomes a bit more sophisticated when I describe a learned and highly skilled rodent; he's handsomely attired, recites poetry (a bit of irony within irony), speaks many languages, is knowledgeable about all the arts and sciences, and so on, but at the end of the poem, he reveals his true nature: ". . .but he squealed and promptly vanished at the entrance of my cat, for despite his erudition, he was nothing but a rat."

There are several other methods I incorporate, but I'll leave them to some desperate graduate student to uncover. A few involve simple observation and focusing on incongruities. That's what happened when I was squirrel-watching, and noticed that their tails looked like question marks. I wrote a poem in which I concluded that it's pointless for them to wear question marks, inasmuch as "there's little squirrels care to know." ("Squirrels," from *Something Big Has Been Here*.) And there's always the riddle trick, when you start with the punch line and work backward, as I did in "A Wolf is at the Laundromat" from *The New Kid on the Block*. You learn in the last line that the unusually polite wolf doing its laundry is not to be feared, since it is nothing more than a "wash-and-wear-wolf."

So much for the mechanics of making a poem humorous. What do you do when you're stuck for a really funny idea? Watch an "I Love Lucy" rerun—it hasn't failed me yet.

§ 84

INSIDE A POEM

BY EVE MERRIAM

INSIDE A POEM are the feelings that we all have but usually don't put into words. The feeling of being happy for some special reason or perhaps for no reason at all. The feeling of sadness at the end of summer or just feeling lonely even with family or friends around. For like nature, human nature changes from one mood to another: from sunshiny to stormy, from raging wind to calm and serene, and then blowing up a storm once again. It is the purpose—and the pleasure—of poetry to express these emotions out in the open.

When something is too beautiful or too terrible or even too funny for words: then it is time for poetry.

Although written on the printed page, poetry is always meant to be heard aloud as a conversation between the writer and reader. And yet, it takes many forms, some that may even seem to be like prose. It may tell a story, as fiction does, or it may present facts, as nonfiction does. It may have no rhyming scheme, because a poem doesn't always have to rhyme; nor does it always have to have a regular beat or meter to the line; nor are there always capital letters at the beginning of each line. And some free verse seems to have no formal rhythmic pattern at all. Yet there is a difference between prose and poetry, and it can always be clearly seen.

The difference is this: that poetry speaks directly to and for our emotions. There is no middle ground; nothing standing in between to run interference for us, to soften the blow or reduce the impact. In a novel, we generally takes sides: We may sympathize with one group against another, and we may come to identify with one particular character. But in a poem, there is only one central character and it is always the same person. It is the "I" of the poet who is really you the reader.

It is possible to be a spectator at many things, to sit back as an

401

observer and watch what is going on. Not in poetry. Here you are always on center stage, directly involved in the action every moment. And so whether a poem is written about some emotion that was felt long ago, or whether it springs from a more immediate source, the time inside a poem always seems to be in the present tense. Another reason a poem seems so immediate is that the language is highly concentrated: All non-essential words have been left out so that the essence of the emotion can come through.

When a poem succeeds in untangling our feelings and putting them into words, two interesting things happen—and they happen at the same moment. It is a little like the intermingling of hot and cold currents in a lake when you are swimming. First, it is a relief to be taken out of ourselves and to have our mood expressed—whether it is a joyful or sad one, serious or comic. We find that we are not alone in our emotions; the poet feels as we do. At the same time, our feelings are made more sharply individual for us as our vivid emotions are relived again in the life of the poem. A paradox takes place as we read: A double feeling that we are the same as others and yet we are unique— that is the inner message of a poem. "Yes," we may think as we read a verse describing a parent, "that is how I sometimes feel about my father, too, and yet—" and our mind goes leaping from the poet's images to images of our own.

Reading prose once is usually enough. We follow the story through to the end, for we want to find out what happens; then we are satisfied to be finished with the experience. But reading a poem once is only the beginning. For a poem is written like a surprise package: There are always more layers to unwrap. Prose *is* what it is; a poem suggests. The music and the meaning will shine through more clearly the second time around—or perhaps the third, or even the thirteenth. Do not expect it to be crystal-clear at once; remember that a crystal has many facets. As a crystal can be turned in the sunlight to reveal all the colors of the rainbow, so a poem can be turned over and over in your mind and new meanings and new music will radiate. For a good poem contains both meaning and music. Even nonsense verse contains a certain sense of logic, ridiculous as it may sound. And without song in its syllables, the most lofty verse will fall flat on its prosy face. Why so? Again because a poem, unlike prose, appeals directly to the emotions; and in order to do so effectively the words have to be chosen not only for what they express, but also for how they sound. Music is an emotional experience, and when music is added to the meaning of words there is a double force. And so the poet learns to use language as an orchestra. Word-music can be a velvet lullaby or a rough-booted march, depending on what effect one wishes to create.

Poets use many tools and tricks. It is their job to play with words, to juggle and toss the words until they are arranged in the most satisfactory pattern. Awareness of the tools and tricks available may increase our pleasure in reading as well as writing poetry. Poets may use established verse forms like the couplet, the quatrain, the limerick, the sonnet, among others, and surely will use such figures of speech as metaphor and simile. They may also use alliteration, assonance, and onomatopoeia as subtle kinds of music, less obvious and sometimes more haunting than rhyme.

As we learn how the poet makes the wheels go round, we may come to enjoy poetry all the more. And along the way, we may learn such useful things as how to avoid clichés in our own poetry writing and speech, and how to increase our vocabulary. But most useful of all is learning how to enjoy reading a poem for its own sake—that is to say, for our own.

85

WRITING POETRY: THE MAGIC AND THE POWER

BY T. ALAN BROUGHTON

SPRING—WHICH IN VERMONT is a form of late winter. My four-year-old son and I are taking advantage of a pocket of sunshine to blow bubbles on the front lawn. He likes to wave the wand, then see if he can recapture one of the larger bubbles, perching it on the tip where he can watch it make oily, transparent shifts through the colors of the rainbow. Sometimes, with a wave of generosity, he will free the bubble again to rise into its ultimate journey. Today an uncertain breeze is blowing whatever he makes straight up, or sideways, or into our faces.

He holds out his wand, stares at me through the soapy hole that will become a bubble, and says, "I am magic even though the bubbles have the power."

"What?"

But like any professional oracle he does not repeat or explain. The hand waves, the bubbles coalesce out of air, he dips again and runs across the lawn, trailing a cloud behind him.

I have begun to write down such statements when I can, although I swear I will try not to embarrass him with them when he is older, if he finds them so. An only child has enough self-consciousness to deal with. But this statement won't let go. It snags me the way an image, a word, an incident—glimpsed through my own eyes or vicariously—will when they demand to become a poem. But this time I'm going to blow it off in prose, here, in a brief essay about the making of bubbles that are poems.

Write a poem. That is the first, terrifying instruction I often give my students in a writing class. Ninety percent, if not more, of the instruction in such a course is concerned with revision. Skill, technique, examples of fine poems and some of their drafts, assignments based on specific objectives—these are matters that can be taught consciously with the hope that they will become so well learned that they are innate. But that first assignment, its terror and, if it works, its joy, is directed toward that other part of the process—the unknown, the constantly new, the unlearned that can be learned only in the moment of doing. I give the assignment not to discourage or crush a shaky talent, but to let each of those writers know what every writer feels like, no matter how experienced, when sitting down to make a new poem.

I read poetry not only to find out more of its secrets, even if I cannot use them, but also to remind myself that poems can be written. In the silence of one's mind, no matter how many stacks of books have been filed there, no matter how much knowledge about line-lengths or figures of speech has been stored away, the image of the blank page or screen is fitting metaphor for the fearful ignorance of beginning. By now I have written thousands of poems, only a handful of which I would want anyone to read, although, sometimes to my embarrassment, more than a handful have been published. But no one *wants* to write the same poem again and again, even if some of us are doomed by the limits of talent to do so. The resistance writers so often describe as being present each morning (or evening if they are night-writers) is inevitable. "Momentum" is perhaps an appropriate term to use in sports where a team is melding into a tribe rather than being a mere gathering of disparate individuals, but for the single writer in the solitude of study or park bench, each poem is discovering again that poems can be written.

Which is where the joy resides, and probably also where the need to do it again and again, even for a whole lifetime, originates. Words begin to happen. Perhaps the first few are brutally and impatiently crossed out, the pen for a moment thrown down in impatience. Try again. The next few stick like burrs—at least through this first version. Later one may delete them without regret. But it is happening, whether line by line, image by image, sound by sound, or all together. Each writer will do it in her or his own way—out loud, standing up, lying down, in notebooks, on scraps of paper, on the greenish glow of a screen.

It is a moment that no one can take away from the writer, no matter how fiercely some critic will respond later to the object made. At least my premise is that this is what makes the difference between the writer who persists and the one who gives it a try and goes on to prefer real estate or engineering or the teaching of literature. It is not just the hope that the next poem will be the best poem that keeps the poet going, but also the simple surprise that more poems are there and that the magic is available.

Which is not to say that the process is without its practical side. The distortion in my description so far is that even if "momentum" is not the right term, there is some accumulation of experience. Those students who find the first assignment so daunting that they return with deep circles under their eyes and one of those poems about "how I am trying to write a poem and not succeeding and this is it" can be helped along. Such help can be only tentative and personal, but like any talisman, once used to enter the next level in the cave, it can be thrown away and that person can find his or her own better means.

1. For the moment, forget what any other poet has written about. Write out of your own experience. Despite the anxiety that we are just like everyone else, the fear that we are lost in the *pluribus* rather than standing out as *unum,* the miracle of existence is that each one of us is uncloned, comes piled with genes never before accumulated in quite the same pattern. Enjoy. Now. Because the price for that, of course, is that you must die. What you have done, seen, reacted to, absorbed, dreamed, imagined is not exactly like anyone else's experience. Because you are a member of the human species, the larger patterns are similar—which does enable you to hope that what you write sufficiently incarnates those patterns to be accessible to others. But the intensity will come from those fine, small differences that make you and your poem an-other.

2. So the corollary is be concrete, be specific, sing out of the sensuous facts of your own body. Large abstract terms are the voice of the herd lowing to itself—Love, Hope, Joy, Defeat. We need them—the smoothed objects of ritual naming that help us believe we know what we have done and seen. But to journey into them, we need a map of their huge domains as detailed as the description of their hedges and weeds, the sound a specific woman's voice makes when it calls from the window of a particular house. Perhaps the sound will add up to Loneliness or Loss, but your reader will believe that only when he is tricked into hearing the voice, and he will believe what he has heard is much richer and more complex than the single term.

3. And that complexity is what the words poems use can give us—

especially in Metaphor, that yoking of the disparate or opposite, the comparison that is known but often unacknowledged until the poet shows it to us.

Translated loosely, and for a New England readership, Moritake's haiku could be "A fallen leaf returning to the branch." It is meaningless without its title: "Butterfly." Two utterly known, utterly common objects. A leaf, a butterfly. They are superimposed. The delight may be small—a leaf seen as a butterfly, a butterfly seen as a leaf. The basis of comparison is motion—that faltering, fluttering, seemingly indeterminate flight of both. The poet's ability to defy gravity is the surprise. Small effect. But is it so small if, after having read the poem, one always sees the two objects in their flights differently from before?

The yoking of disparate elements is a larger pattern of poems, that incorporation of the Yin and Yang of the world. In writing through the first drafts, part of the struggle is in keeping the mind open to illogic, to prevent all the training we have had since childhood in being "reasonable" from taking over. At the moment of writing, the mind is not so much concentrating on belief as admitting that whatever the poem has started to say, is saying at this very moment I am putting down words, it may be about something else, a something else I could never have imagined without doing what I am doing now—writing it into existence. Perhaps in the first draft that "otherness" will show only in glints, and then revision will be in sleuthing, trying to find those unexpected moments.

Bear in mind that metaphor does not reside in images alone, but in situations also. I remember once trying to write a poem that I thought was a story about a boy falling from a flagpole. He had come to a place with his father to fix the pole. The narrator was a man watching, describing the event that happened to virtual strangers even if he had hired them. What I discovered was a poem that was really about the man and his marriage, the terrible descent he and his wife and his own small son were going through. The foreground remained the death of the boy climber, but the foreground was the way to present the other descents. In another instance, a poem I thought was to be about stopping by the side of the road and hearing Mozart coming through the air from the open window of someone's truck becomes yoked with a death in the nearby woods, a suicide and its investigation that might seem to be as far removed from a Mozart Serenade as possible.

Serenade for Winds

We know life so little that it is very little in our power to distinguish right from wrong, just from unjust, and to say that one is unfortunate because one suffers, which has not been proved. (Van Gogh, to his brother Theo and sister-in-law Jo.)

Clustered beside the road are a van,
pick-up, two sedans. In another season
we might imagine hunters tracking deer
or lugging sixpacks away from their wives.
But the Seal of State on one door warns
a new fact has burned its brand on the landscape.

From the vacant truck a radio plays
Mozart into the summer breeze.
Now an oboe floats above
the bass of bassoon, a clarinet
lures the horn to join
this conversation on the waves.

We have stopped to check the map
but might believe that only this
was why we drove for hours—
leaves lifted in a freshet,
all else forgotten and offstage
when air and music are one.

In the forest a trooper stops
a witness from cutting the rope
with his knife. Procedures require
cameras and tape, a careful report.
A man's body, halted by noose
and gravity, slowly swings
from the maple's limb.
In an hour or two a wife
and elder son will try
through taut jaw to say
they're not surprised, blame him,
the State, or bank, or all.

Only a few bars remain.
Cut him down. Let him drop
on the layered leaves.
The notes rise into the silence of air
through which the body must descend.

That's enough for starters, at least for me when I sit down to try to find a new poem. Everyone who knows poets intimately has to learn to forgive them for their metaphor-hounding. Any little act or word can be snatched up and transformed by poems. I hope my son, if he sees this years from now, will forgive my plagiarizing. But I couldn't have found a better way to say it—that moment of sharing between poet and poem when the day's last word announces itself, when that bubble called a poem begins to take its translucent form. "I am magic, even though the bubbles have the power."

86

FINDING THE SUBJECT FOR YOUR POEM

BY JOYCE PESEROFF

POEMS EVOLVE IN MANY WAYS. Sometimes they spring from a striking image preserved in a notebook, sometimes from a bit of overheard conversation that teases and intrigues, or a story that demands to be told. A poem may arise, full of energy, driven by the propulsive rhythm of a sentence or a phrase. I have written from all of these possibilities, but most often I begin with the desire to write about a subject—spring, a Maine landscape, or a birthday party; or my aging uncle, or my aerobic exercise class. All of these subjects—whether ancient as a classic text or commonplace and contemporary—offer prospects for a poet writing today. Yet in half of these poems, the topic was not immediately obvious to me; in fact, I began by writing about some other subject entirely.

Because poetry involves unconscious as well as conscious processes—like an iceberg, nine-tenths of a poet's work may lie below the surface of the mind—a poem's true subject may not reveal itself at once. I begin a poem with real interest and excitement, only to bog down around the third stanza. Energy that first generated line after enjambed line packed with vivid language evaporates; the urgency with which I began the poem later eludes me. I file the drafts in a "wait" folder and, grumbling, turn to other work.

When this happens, I know that I need to give my psyche time, as well as space, to discover what the poem is really about. Rather than abandon such promising starts, I go back, willing to cut and rewrite. With patience and openness to new directions, I find the poem's true subject—perhaps a difficult or uncomfortable one, perhaps merely more complex than first imagined—revealed. Let me give three examples of how such rewriting—and rethinking—works.

The first problem is common to novice poets, but more experienced ones also need to recognize what I call the "runway" problem. These

410

poems start with a long, often expository, foreground before they really take off. Example: A baby, at six months, has her final DPT shot; she's furious with the nurse who administers the needle. I begin a poem about her infant rage and go on to write about the mass immunizations begun in the 1950s with Salk's discovery of the polio vaccine. As I continue, trying to link this bit of history to the baby, I realize that it is *my* childhood I want to write about: the mysteriousness of grownups invading that world of children; the second-grader who cried invisibly behind a screen set up by the public health nurse. Soon I realize that although the baby's response was the key to my memories, it doesn't belong in the poem. It was the "runway" for my own experiences to emerge, brought forward by images of shots and nurses common to both scenarios.

Perhaps I will use the discarded material somewhere else. Often enough, in order to preserve the integrity of a poem, a writer must cut the line or stanza that pleases her most, even—and sometimes especially—if it was the sentence that started her writing in the first place.

My second example involves a poem I had been thinking about for a long time. I wanted to describe an incident my mother had mentioned when we were both looking through a box of family photographs: When I was four years old, my friends' parents had threatened to boycott a birthday party because my mother had invited the son of our apartment building's only black family. After hearing a poet I esteem read new work about her upbringing in the old *de jure* segregated South, I was moved to write about this incident in New York City's *de facto* segregated housing projects.

I got stuck while describing the room full of children—the hats, the cake, the furniture too large for them. I decided to look more closely at the *characters* I had introduced, possibly adding some, while exploring their family relationships. Although I did use material about the black boy's sisters, this did not lead to a satisfying resolution to the poem.

After character, I examined the poem's *setting*. Was there more to say about the place where I grew up? I had written about that subject before and didn't want to repeat myself; images and the emotion arising from them must be freshly discovered, not ready-made. Otherwise, a poet finds what Yeats called "rhetoric" doing the work of the imagination.

Finally, I returned to the source of the poem—the box of photographs. When I *dramatized* this scene between me and my mother, I found I could use it to frame the poem. The party became a flashback, which I rewrote in the past tense.

What else was in that box of photographs? I developed a new series of *images:*

Julian

Halloween—a sulky gypsy pines
for her sister's store-bought costume,
disdaining yards of Mother's precious scarves
and clinking necklaces . . .
          two women

rigged in a tight suit and lacy tablecloth
(bridegroom and pregnant bride)
who knocked door to door for drinks,
   demanded bread,
upset our cupboard for two cans of soup . . .

The images forced me to recall my mother's fury at these begging women, the same vulgar parents who nearly ruined a child's party because they felt superior to blacks. More and more of the poem's emotion seemed to center not on the boy, Julian, but on my mother.

I added her presence to the poem's first lines and concluded with images of my mother alone, drinking coffee and working a crossword puzzle. The birthday party—original impulse for the poem—shrank from two stanzas to four lines. The theme of "Julian," I discovered through rewriting, was not segregation but isolation, and its subject not, after all, the title character.

This last example began as two separate poems, one about fall and the onset of winter, the other about my grandmother's death. A careful reader might immediately notice the affinity between these subjects, since the first is often used as a metaphor for the second:

October

September cooling to October
stops the throat with a doughy phlegm—
a hundred years ago "lung fever"
killed thousands, left the rest
to cabin fever—then, for whoever emerged
from that white chrysalis: spring.
Dying, my grandmother became a student
of migration, tallying species

412

at the hospital feeder. I almost believed
the evening grosbeak put on earth
to soothe her, and the V of geese a sign
of direction in adversity.

It was the image of "fever" in the first half of "October" that alerted
me to its connection with the untitled poem about my grandmother. I
cut all description from my "fall into winter" poem that didn't share
references to disease. From the second poem, I eliminated all details of
hospital routine except the ones that involved the natural world: the
feeder and the flying birds. I linked these two poems through their
shared imagery and in the process noticed that my subject had shifted
subtly: Instead of an elegy, I had written a testament to a living woman's
courage in the face of death.

These are three examples I was able to salvage from the "wait" file
and place, when completed, in a manuscript. I have many more poems
that still need work as I approach their true subject. It may take months
for a poem's subject to become clear to me. Often, I have to distract my
conscious mind so that the unconscious might do the work of association and identification. Here are some suggestions that may help both
with their proper tasks:

1) Save all drafts; throw nothing out. The image you discarded ten
pages ago may give you the one necessary clue to your subject. The way
you broke a line may suggest new connections as it shifts the emphasis
of your poem from one word to another. This is the reason word
processors are not useful to poets, at least during composition: You'd
have to stop and print each version as you write it, in order not to lose
anything.

2) Don't hurry. A poem may take months, or years, to complete. And
even then, you may have to put it aside for another month or year before
you're sure it's finished.

3) Look carefully at any two poems you begin at the same time. They
may hold themes in common and point to concerns below the surface of
your words. Look for images that recur, or a turn of phrase you repeat.
As in "October," sometimes what begins as two poems may end as one.

4) Be ruthless with cuts. The loveliest, vowel-filled line does a poem
no good if it distracts from what playwrights call the "through-line"—
the inevitable chain of action leading to a satisfying conclusion. Be sure

413

your poems begin at the beginning, and not several sentences before. Sacrifice your most cherished stanza if it is irrelevant to what your poem is about. Save it for the next poem—for, just as two poems may turn out to be halves of one long lyric, one draft may contain the impulse for two or more successful poems.

87

BUILDING CONFIDENCE IN YOURSELF
AS A POET

BY JAMES APPLEWHITE

THE WRITING OF A POEM from first draft to publishable version tends to fall into several phases. Getting a first draft down on paper is, or ought to be, a pleasurable process. Poetry incorporates an element of play. Word-sounds that echo against each other (in internal and end-line rhyme, consonance, assonance, and alliteration) are a kind of technical signature of this play, which extends through image, metaphor and whole narrative contour. That is, the poet's mind in the process of composing allows itself the child-freedom of lip-and-tongue eroticism, of language indulged *as if* in nonsense syllables. The idea of a poem is itself a playful invention, a bending or troping away from the literal into the figurative. "God a mighty," I still hear the field hand saying, "this here morning is cold as blue blazes." I *saw* the cold—materialized, active—in those "blazes," in those flames.

I like to alter Coleridge's image of the poet as a charioteer driving onward with loosely held reins. Instead of a horse as representative of that bodily, kinetic, spontaneous source of sound, association, and undisclosed motive, I propose the more contemporary machine of the bingo parlor. It is a kind of glass-sided till, within which numbered ping pong balls are steadily blown upward, like bubbles in the muses' fountain. You, the conscious half of the writer, are standing above, receiving into your hands these syllables of an evolving riddle breathed from beneath. It is like a popcorn machine, sounds a bit like one, and maybe the smell of popcorn blows through the tent. You don't accept every proposal for a word in your poem, or every rhythmic impulse, that so "pops up." You select, take some but push some back, asking for better imagination, a fresher number. Language, after all, is generic, a possession in common, and every sound and sense has been used to death. Some of "what comes" is inevitably cliché.

This is my image for stage one of the writing, and a point for appreciating a delicate balance. Coleridge had his driver—my caller of numbers—hold the reins loosely. The horse must, to some extent, have its head. A kind of momentum, expressed most obviously in the rhythm and sound, needs to develop, If the caller waits for too long to pick out one of the balls, they may pile up in frustration and cause a blockage. What wants and needs to be said has to get itself in motion. Altering the image, the words that begin to come are like the knotted scarves pulled by the magician from his hat. One is linked to another, and pulling them into motion the first time is necessary for the whole strip to unfurl.

For this stage of composition, then, I advise a willing suspension of disbelief in the validity of what you are saying. I don't mean that you should be wholly uncritical, but I do mean that you should allow yourself the freedom and self-approval to write without inhibition. You can't hit a golf or tennis ball or skate or dive if you are so self-conscious that your movements are deliberate and forced. You learn how to do it by practice, then *do* it, in a movement that is whole, feels spontaneous, and causes a certain delight.

The times to put the harder pressure on yourself are *before* this first writing, and after. What is available to you as you write is in part dependent upon your preparation. Wide reading, study, and analysis of poetry, reading aloud, developing access to your deeper sources of subject matter, all help enrich the mix of what is bubbling up from "below." Discriminating insight into language—sound as well as sense—should have become habitual in you *before* this moment. Put pressure on yourself to read and to understand, to know yourself, to begin the extraction of insights that lead to the richer interior. But don't freeze up when you should be intuitive. Admit to yourself that you love this verbalization of the irrational, this bingo game in which you fill in for yourself the missing columns of self-knowledge.

Getting down the first draft is phase one. You may, for a lyric-length poem, write it in one sitting, or begin it in one session, in the morning, and then continue for a bit more that evening before going to bed. *Phase one* goes on for as long as conception is still glowing inside your head. At this point, the text is illuminated by what you intended.

Here is the first draft of my poem, "Clear Winter." The reader will note that the published version (see page 373) is a few lines shorter, and that changes have been made in word order, word choice, and above all, in the rhythmic momentum or "flow." The finished poem runs on more

416

swiftly, as I had from the beginning intended. But in the first attempt, I was unable quite to capture in writing the seamless movement I had felt. Still all the elements of the final poem are present in this first draft. This is a remarkably complete first version, for me. Even so, the poem had to go through a series of versions, before I was able to bring back those spontaneous phrases and movements from the manuscript and give them a more finely tuned setting.

Clear Winter
(First draft, January 8, 1985)

Confusion of seasons is over.
Today was clear winter.
Light that on trunks was warm
Looked bare and bleak
On chill limbs against chill air.
I saw everywhere corpses of trees
Piled mercilessly by past
High water, crotch-chunk
Of one upon trunk of another.
I worry about my brother.
Angular cedars with crowns
Thinned of needles in death
Seem some desert tribe
Overtaken by an angel of death.
Finally I climbed clear
Of the river valley where memory
Surrounded with its proxy history
Tree-corpses. I saw air clear
In its isolation and pure
As a star. We are unable
to endure this light
The cold whets like a knife.
I stand above this used,
Abused river land and
Hypothesize the being
We cannot undertand, who
Begins springs with fire of a star,
Who is the clarity of air
And the far zero dark.
I sniff for the scent of some fire,
For coffee or leaf smoke or
cigarette scent. All are purely
Absent. I turn toward home,
Alone as a pane of ice
This keen sun shines through.
I will kiss my warm wife,

> And under the first star,
> Gather cedar for a fire.

Phase two begins when the first glow has faded, or has begun to. *Then* there is the shock of recognition, as you encounter the text you have produced. It is not necessarily disappointing. You may be happily surprised by the electricity in some phrases. You may also note lapses, stretches of dead language, redundancy. Now, with the text in hand, you apply maximum pressure. The poem won't be inhibited. It already exists. *Always* keep the first draft. You aren't a painter who loses the early version in revision. Be as self-critical as you can be. Call everything into question. Go from self-love to self-hate. But avoid extremes. A *balanced* appreciation, an objective appraisal of weaknesses and failings in your own writing is needed. It is essential for you to recognize excellence as well as to admit fault.

You want to see the poem clearly, as it is, and for many poets (including myself), this requires part of phase two to be a revision that questions everything, that entertains the possibility that the whole poem may be a failure. I tend to over-revise at this point, possibly to over-rationalize, and perhaps to make the poetic statement artificially complete, too explicit. Since I seem to need to do this, I allow it to happen, knowing that it is part of phase two: critically confronting the poem.

Phase three emphasizes the fact that the "real poem" knows more than "I" do, that ideally it combines the phase-one spontaneity and the phase-two appraisal. Thinking too much about it, trying all possible combinations of key words in troublesome phrases, is only another effort on your part to see the essence of the poem clearly. Thus, phase three involves a kind of "forgetting" of this highly conscious, trial-and-error revision. I let the text rest, like dough between kneadings. This may be for weeks or months. Then something will reawaken interest. I will recall the true poem, the real poem, from the confusion of various versions. Sometimes I literally recall the poem by writing it out afresh as I remember it at this point, perhaps with help from earlier drafts, especially the first. Often I find that the revision has helped pare away the nonessential, and to prepare a place for what in the first draft was really final. I cherish the sense that for each real poem there is some absolute, inevitable form toward which I have been fumbling through successive drafts. This is in part an illusion, for even "final" texts get

418

revised. You should never turn down what you consider better insight. The real poem seems to gather up into itself the many competing glimpses scattered through various versions. I think of prose as linear, a link through time, but a poem is more a circle, which, when completed, does not end. It looks forward and backward, resisting the erosion of more revisions.

I am myself a runner, and *River Writing: An Eno Journal* was largely composed while I was running along the Eno River in all seasons, all weathers. It started accidentally, but once begun, my premise came to be that the poem would be founded on whatever I saw or thought during the run. The river is over the ridge behind my house, so I could go out and return without interruption. (By the way, *shield* yourself from interruption during the time you set aside to write. If writing is as important to you as you think it is, treat it as such. Give it that central importance in your life.)

The finished version of "Clear Winter" is four lines shorter than the first draft, and words have been cut or substituted in a number of lines that remain. These changes help allow the rhythm of lines to fuse one into the other, so that the whole seems a single movement. For example, "chill limbs against chill air" becomes "chill limbs high in chill air." The first draft let the word *death* appear twice at the ends of lines, and the word *star* appears twice. It also allows the word *corpses* to come in too soon. It was as if my first impulse had known generally what it wanted, but had had to move toward that goal by trial and error. But notice that except for a change in tense, the ending stands as first imagined and drafted.

Here is the published version of "Clear Winter":

Clear Winter
(Published in *River Writing: An Eno Journal,*
Princeton University Press, 1988)

Confusion of seasons is over.
Today was clear winter.
Light that on trunks seemed warm
Looked bleak and bare
On chill limbs high in chill air.
I saw bodies of trees
Piled mercilessly by past
High water, crotch-chunk

Of one upon trunk of another.
Angular cedars, their crowns
Thinned of needles by drought,
Seemed a desert tribe
Overtaken by an angel of death.
Finally I climbed clear
Of the valley which memory
Stocked with its proxy
Corpses. I saw air
In its isolation now pure.
We are unable to endure
This light the cold whets to steel.
I stood above river land
And hypothesized the being
We cannot understand, who
Begins things with flame of a star,
Who is the zero far dark.
I sniffed for scent of some smoke,
For coffee, leaf-smolder or
Cigarette odor. All unendurably
Absent. I turned toward home,
Alone as a pane of ice
The keen sun shines through.
I kissed my warm wife
And under the first star
Gathered cedar for a fire.

Here is the lesson I learned from the poems in *River Writing*. It is good sometimes to let the cadences and larger structures of your poetry and its emotional momentum build. Learn to write with ease, with relaxation. You can't really run faster or farther over the long haul simply by bearing down harder. You have to raise the level of your effort, then relax, and trust that preparation. Then perfect the draft later. With joy. As Fred Astaire said to a new partner, "Don't be nervous, but don't make a mistake." Learning not to be nervous, not to make yourself nervous, because of your relaxation and confidence in revision, will help you prevent making a mistake. And remember that the only real mistake in poetry is not ever to get the poem written.

But the key element for most poets who are learning the process is knowing when and how to apply the pressure. Writing poetry is like training for athletic competition. Performance in the event—the writing of the poem—is largely a product of conditioning, associated with analysis of form and technique. But you don't perform that analysis in the act of writing. You somewhat analyze the problem before you, but finally you have to get in there and perform. You don't sit there anxiously wondering whether the last word was really the right one. You don't sit there worrying whether the poem will finally be any good. Time will tell.

JUVENILE AND YOUNG ADULT

88

Is It Good Enough for Children?

By Madeleine L'Engle

A WHILE AGO WHEN I WAS TEACHING A COURSE on techniques of fiction, a young woman came up to me and said, "I do hope you're going to teach us something about writing for children, because that's why I'm taking this course."

"What have I been teaching you?" I asked her.

"Well—writing."

"Don't you write when you write for children?"

"Yes, but—isn't it different?"

No, I assured her, it isn't different. The techniques of fiction are the techniques of fiction, and they hold as true for Beatrix Potter as they do for Dostoevsky.

But the idea that writing for children isn't the same as writing for adults is prevalent indeed, and usually goes along with the conviction that it isn't quite as good. If you're a good enough writer for adults, the implication is, of course, you don't write for children. You write for children only when you can't make it in the real world, because writing for children is easier.

Wrong, wrong, wrong!

I had written several regular trade novels before a publisher asked me to write about my Swiss boarding school experiences. Nobody had told me that you write differently when you write for children, so I didn't. I just wrote the best book I possibly could; it was called *And Both Were Young.* After that I wrote *Camilla,* which has been reissued as a young adult novel, and then *Meet the Austins.* It's hard today for me to understand that this simple little book had a very hard time finding a publisher because it's about a death and how an ordinary family reacts to that death. Death at that time was taboo. Children weren't supposed to know about it. I had a couple of offers of publication if I'd take the death out. But the reaction of the family—children as well as the parents—to the death was the core of the book.

Nowadays what we offer children makes *Meet the Austins* seem pale, and on the whole, I think that's just as well, because children know a lot more than most grown-ups give them credit for. *Meet the Austins* came out of my own family's experience with several deaths. To have tried to hide those deaths from our children would have been blind stupidity. All hiding does is confuse children and add to their fears. It is not subject matter that should be taboo, but the way it is handled.

A number of years ago—the first year I was actually making reasonable money from my writing—my sister-in-law was visiting us, and when my husband told her how much I had earned that year, she was impressed and commented, "And to think most people would have had to word so hard for that!"

Well, it is work, it's most certainly work; wonderful work, but work. Revision, revision, revision. Long hours spent not only in the actual writing, but in research. I think the best thing I learned in college was how to do research, so that I could go right on studying after I had graduated.

Of course, it is not *only* work; it is work that makes the incomprehensible comprehensible. Leonard Bernstein says that for him music is cosmos in chaos. That is true for writing a story, too. Aristotle says that what is plausible and impossible is better than what is possible and implausible.

That means that story must be *true*, not necessarily *factual*, but true. This is not easy for a lot of people to understand. When I was a school child, one of my teachers accused me of telling a story. She was not complimenting me on my fertile imagination; she was accusing me of telling a lie.

Facts are fine; we need facts. But story takes us to a world that is beyond facts, out on the other side of facts. And there is considerable fear of this world.

The writer Keith Miller told me of a young woman who was determined that her three preschool children were going to grow up in the real world. She was not, she vowed, going to sully their minds with myth, fantasy, fairy tales. They were going to know the truth—and for truth, read fact—and the truth would make them free.

One Saturday, after a week of rain and sniffles, the sun came out, so she piled the children into her little red VW bug and took them to the Animal Farm. The parking lot was crowded, but a VW bug is small, and she managed to find a place for it. She and the children had a wonderful day, petting the animals, going on rides, enjoying the sunshine. Suddenly, she looked at her watch and found it was far later than she realized. She and the children ran to where the VW bug was parked, and to their horror, found the whole front end was bashed in.

Outraged, she took herself off to the ranger's office. As he saw her approach, he laughed and said, "I'll bet you're the lady with the red VW bug."

"It isn't funny," she snapped.

"Now, calm down, lady, and let me tell you what happened. You know the elephant your children had such fun riding? She's a circus-trained elephant, and she was trained to sit on a red bucket. When she saw your car, she just did what she was trained to do and sat on it. Your engine's in the back, so you can drive it home without any trouble. And don't worry. Our insurance will take care of it. Just go on home, and we'll get back to you on Monday."

Slightly mollified, she and the kids got into the car and took off. But she was later than ever, so when she saw what looked like a very minor accident on the road, she didn't stop, but drove on.

Shortly, the flashing light and the siren came along, and she was pulled over. "Lady, don't you know that in this state it's a crime to leave the scene of an accident?" the trooper asked.

"But I wasn't in an accident," she protested.

"I suppose your car came that way," she said, pointing to the bashed-in front.

"No. An elephant sat on it."

"Lady, would you mind blowing into this little balloon?"

That taught her that facts alone are not enough; that facts, indeed, do not make up the whole truth. After that she read fairy tales to her children and encouraged them in their games of Make Believe and Let's Pretend.

I learned very early that if I wanted to find out the truth, to find out why people did terrible things to each other, or sometimes wonderful things—why there was war, why children are abused—I was more likely to find the truth in story than in the encyclopedia. Again and again I read *Emily of the New Moon,* by Lucy Maud Montgomery, because

Emily's father was dying of diseased lungs, and so was mine. Emily had a difficult time at school, and so did I. Emily wanted to be a writer, and so did I. Emily knew that there was more to the world than provable fact, and so did I. I read fairy tales, the myths of all nations, science fiction, the fantasies and family stories of E. Nesbit. I read Jules Verne and H. G. Wells. And I read my parents' books, particularly those with lots of conversation in them. What was not in my frame of reference went right over my head.

We tend to find what we look for. If we look for dirt, we'll find dirt, whether it's there or not. A very nice letter I received from a reader said that she found *A Ring of Endless Light* very helpful to her in coming to terms with the death of a friend, but that another friend had asked her how it was that I used dirty words. I wrote back saying that I was not going to reread my book looking for dirty words, but that as far as I could remember, the only word in the book that could possibly be construed as dirty was *zuggy*, which I'd made up to avoid using dirty words. And wasn't looking for dirty words an ugly way to read a book?

One of my favorite books is Frances Hodgson Burnett's *The Secret Garden*. I read it one rainy weekend to a group of little girls, and a generation later to my granddaughters up in an old brass bed in the attic. Mary Lennox is a self-centered, spoiled-rotten little heroine, and I think we all recognize at least a little of ourselves in her. The secret garden is as much the garden of Mary's heart as it is the physical walled garden. By the end of the book, warmth and love and concern for others have come to Mary's heart, when Colin, the sick boy, is able to walk and run again. And Dickon, the gardener's boy, looks at the beauty of the restored garden and says, "It's magic!" But "magic" is one of the key words that has become taboo to today's self-appointed censors, so, with complete disregard of content, they would add *The Secret Garden* to the pyre. I shudder. This attitude is extreme. It is also dangerous.

It comes down to the old question of separate standards, separate for adults and children. The only standard to be used in judging a children's book is: *Is it a good book?* Is it good enough for me? Because if a children's book is not good enough for all of us, it is not good enough for children.

§ 89

WRITING THE WESTERN NOVEL FOR YOUNG ADULTS

BY JOAN LOWERY NIXON

THE WEST TO ME IS A STATE OF MIND. Those who settled the West were easterners and southerners and immigrants from all over the world, hard-working people who had courage and hope and the imagination to visualize the promise in our vast expanse of unsettled, untamed land. Their lives were difficult and filled with challenges, and it's the uniqueness of these challenges that fascinates young adult readers today. While immersed in stories set west of the Mississippi in the last half of the eighteen-hundreds, modern readers are discovering concepts like *sacrifice* and *self-denial* and *unwavering commitment to an ideal*— concepts that are not too common in today's very different world.

Many authors who write about the West are history buffs with a deep knowledge of the period and place; but for those who are not so knowledgeable, there are three books that can spark ideas and lead to further productive research: *The World Almanac of the American West,* John S. Bowman, General Editor (Ballantine Books); *The Reader's Encyclopedia of the American West,* Edited by Howard R. Lamar (Crowell Publishers); and *Historical Atlas of the Outlaw West,* by Richard Patterson (Johnson Books, Boulder, Colorado).

Plotting the historical western novel usually begins with an event or an important moment in history. For example, in browsing through my copy of *Historical Atlas of the Outlaw West* I read about the town of Leadville, Colorado, during 1879, its worst year. The decent people of Leadville were robbed at gunpoint in broad daylight and beset by "lot jumpers" who'd kill them and take over their property. There were countless unsolved or unpunished murders and an ineffectual law enforcement system. Finally, in desperation, as a warning to *all* outlaws in the area, a group of seven-hundred men who called themselves "The Merchants' Protective Patrol" dragged two prisoners out of the jail and

426

hanged them from the framework of a building under construction across the road from the elegant Tabor Opera House, which was to hold its grand opening that evening. This vigilante action shook up the town. Some thought it was right, because a number of criminals left Leadville; but others felt that killing for any reason was wrong.

With the present-day increase in the crime rate throughout the country and the passionately argued issue of gun control, I thought this event would be an issue that would touch the lives of contemporary young readers, so I decided to set my story in Leadville.

My first step in writing the story was to research Leadville thoroughly. I read everything I could find about the local politics, the civic problems, and the economics of Leadville. It was primarily a mining town, and in 1879 it was the home of the wealthy Horace Tabor. I even found a newspaper account of Jesse and Frank James quietly working a claim at nearby Soda Springs. But reading about a place is never enough for me. I have to discover for myself how it looks and feels. When I discovered that walking in Leadville's thin air made me wheeze, I knew my characters would do the same until they became used to the high altitude.

I bought some books and pamphlets written by residents about Leadville's history. Because of its wonderful local detail, material of this sort is a treasure. Whenever I visit an area to do research, I try to take in all the regional historical museums. Some collections are housed in huge buildings; some fill only a room or two in a tiny restored pioneer house; but I've never failed to learn something of significance at each stop.

A logical question often raised by writers interested in trying their hand at the western historical young adult novel is how to include all the material gathered in the course of your research so the readers will find it interesting. The answer is, you don't. But the research gives you the factual background you need to write a good book.

Even though most western novels are probably sparked by a memorable historical event, you must keep this important point in mind: The main character is always the most important part of any novel—not the period, not the place, not the history—and how she or he reacts to what is taking place. What is she thinking? If she's frightened or curious or angry or unhappy or excited, this is what readers want to know.

An author's goal is to have young readers relate wholeheartedly to the main character of the story, and it's no harder to do in historical novels than in contemporary ones—but the *emotions* of the main characters must be felt and understood by your readers. For example: You could write a contemporary story about a teenage girl named Elizabeth who is furious with her father. He's suddenly become fed up with New York crime, noise, and traffic and has decided to move his family to a small town in Montana, where he is going to open a franchised branch of a popular fast-food restaurant. This means that Liz—note the contemporary nickname—will have to leave her friends, her school; give up her frequent visits to museums, concerts, and theatre, and adapt to a lifestyle she's sure she'll hate.

Or you could move Elizabeth into the mid-eighteen-hundreds, where she'd probably be called Beth. Her father is excited about the fortunes being made in some of the mining towns in California. He decides to share in the boom by packing up his family, moving to Sacramento, and opening a general store to sell supplies to the miners and the families settling the area. Beth is furious that her father has made this choice regardless of the wishes of his family. She doesn't want to leave her friends, her friendly neighborhood, and her grandparents—whom she realizes she may never see again.

The stories would be told through Liz's and Beth's emotional reactions: their emotions are exactly the same, emotions today's readers could understand with no difficulty. Music, clothing, food, manners, family relationships, transportation—everything that would make up life, whether it was lived in 1992 or 1850—are essential to the story, but they provide only background material for Liz or Beth and their emotions.

For the protagonist in my Leadville story, I chose a seventeen-year-old girl. Her father left the family to make his fortune when she was only seven. He has never returned, and the last of his infrequent letters to her mother came from Leadville. The girl remembers her father affectionately as a warm, fun-loving person. He had shared his love of poetry with her, and she treasures that memory.

I gave her a soft name—Sarah—and she's very much like her father—a dreamer and a poet—a fact about which her mother often reminds her. I gave Sarah a fourteen-year-old sister named Susannah, a name with more bounce and spunk. Susannah is a solid, practical person, very much like their mother who has supported her daughters and herself by turning their home in Chicago into a well-run boarding house.

Naming your characters correctly is important. While some period names are found in material being researched, it's also helpful to have at hand *First Names First* by Leslie Alan Dunkling (Universe Books, New York, NY), in which both popular and unusual first names from the past and the present are included.

Before my Leadville story opens, Sarah's and Susannah's mother has died, and a greedy aunt and uncle have moved in, taking over the boarding house. In 1879 the girls would have had no legal rights to their inheritance, so someone needs to find their father and bring him home to straighten things out.

It would have been easy to have Sarah just pack her bag and head West after her father, but that action wouldn't have fit her temperament. *Susannah* is the one who would easily have traveled alone, but Susannah is too young, so she bullies Sarah into making the trip. Through the problems and dangers Sarah encounters on the journey and in Leadville, she discovers some surprising facts about her own capabilities. I told their story through two books: *High Trail to Danger* and *A Deadly Promise* (Bantam).

In the western historical novel, you'll want to make your characters' dialogue true to the period by using colloquialisms, slang, and occasional phrases from that time; but be sure to use contractions so speech patterns won't sound formal and stilted—a turn-off for young readers.

Writing western historical novels for young adults is immensely satisfying. It gives me the opportunity to show that history isn't simply a collection of dates and wars and kings and presidents, but that *children* have always helped make history, that *children* are not only important to the past but are helping to shape history being made today.

And I hope that the characters in my western history-based stories will not only carry today's young readers through stories filled with adventure and excitement, but will also show them that the western state of mind was responsible for handling problems with determination and courage, because in the 1990s, determination and courage may be the qualities our children will need to count on the most.

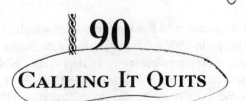

90
CALLING IT QUITS

BY LOIS LOWRY

"You put <u>what</u> in it?" my son asked, his fork halfway to his mouth.
"Ginger snaps," I repeated. "Crushed ginger snaps."
"I thought that's what you said." I watched while he put his fork back down on his plate and then pushed the plate away from him. It was clear to me that my son, normally a good sport, was not going to eat my innovative beef stew.
It was clear to me, after I tasted it myself, that he had made the right decision.

SOMETIMES IN THE PROCESS OF CREATING, it is very difficult to know when to quit adding things.

Some years back, I received in the mail the first foreign edition of my first young adult book, *A Summer to Die*. Fortunately it was French. Later I would receive, with a gulp of astonishment, the Finnish, the Afrikaans, the Catalan; but this first one was French. French I can read.

And so I leafed through the pages, savoring the odd, startling sense of recognition that I had, seeing my own words translated into another language.

On the last page, I read the line of dialogue with which I had concluded the book. " 'Meg,' he laughed, putting one arm over my shoulders, 'you were beautiful all along.' " There it was, in French.

But there was something else, as well. I blinked in surprise, seeing it. In French, the book concluded: "They walked on."

They walked on? Of course they *had* walked on, those two characters, Meg and Will. I knew they had, and I had trusted the reader to know that they had. But I hadn't written that line. The translator had.

I don't know why. I can only guess that the translator simply couldn't resist that urge that makes all of us throw a crushed ginger snap into the stew now and then.

Knowing when to stop is one of the toughest tasks a writer faces.

Is there a rule that one can follow? Probably not. But there is, I think, a test against which the writer can measure his ending, his stopping place.

When something more is going to take place, but the characters have been so fully drawn, and the preceding events so carefully shaped that the reader, on reflection, knows what more will happen, and is satisfied by it—then the book ends.

In essence, you, as writer, will have successfully taught the reader to continue writing the book in his mind.

What about the concept of resolution, then? Isn't the writer supposed to tie up the loose ends of the story neatly at the conclusion? And if everything is neatly packaged and tied, then how on earth can something more take place?

Your story—your plot—your theme— is only a portion of the lives of the characters you have created. Their lives, if you have made them real to the reader, are going to continue in the reader's mind.

Your role is only a part of that process. And you need to know when and how to get out when your role is finished. As author, you tie up and resolve the piece of a life you have chosen to examine. Then you leave, gracefully. The life continues, but you are no longer looking at it.

You have engaged and directed the imagination of the reader; and then you have turned the reader loose.

Writing this, I looked at the endings of some of my own books, to see if they followed any kind of pattern.

In one, *Anastasia on Her Own,* a mother and daughter are laughing and tap-dancing together up a flight of stairs.

In *Find a Stranger, Say Goodbye,* a young girl is packing to go away; she is deciding what to take and what to leave behind.

The narrator and her mother in *Rabble Starkey* are together in a car, heading into a somewhat uncertain future. (Not coincidentally, that book is published in Great Britain under the title *The Road Ahead.*)

The forms of these endings are different. Some are descriptive, some consist of dialogue. Some are lighthearted, others more introspective.

But they do seem to have a few elements in common:

431

They all include the main character—sometimes more than one—in the final scene.

Each of them, in various forms, reflects a sense of motion, of flow, of moving forward.

And each in its own way contains a kind of conclusive statement.

Anastasia fell in behind her mother and tried to follow the complicated hops, turns, and shuffles her mother was doing. Together they tap-danced down the hall and up the stairs. It was silly, she thought; but it was fun. And it sure felt good, having her mother back in charge.

—*Anastasia on Her Own*

It was the throwing away that was the hardest. But she did it, until the trunk was packed, the trash can was filled, and the room was bare of everything except the memories; those would always be there, Natalie knew.

—*Find a Stranger, Say Goodbye*

She sped up a little, driving real careful, and when we went around the curve I looked, and it was all a blur. But there was nothing there. There was only Sweet Hosanna and me, and outside the whole world, quiet in the early morning, green and strewn with brand new blossoms, like the ones on my very best dress.

—*Rabble Starkey*

The common elements that you can see and hear in those ending paragraphs are a little like the basics in a good stew; maybe you could equate them to a garlic clove, a bay leaf, and a dollop of wine.

As for the crushed ginger snap? The ingredient that qualifies as overkill and makes the whole thing just a little nauseating?

Well, I confess that those three passages have one more thing in common. Each one was tough to end. Like the translator who added another sentence to my book, I wanted to go on, too. I wanted to add crushed ginger snaps: more sentences, more images, embellishments, explanations, embroidery.

And if I had? Take a look:

She sped up a little, driving real careful, and when we went around the curve I looked, and it was all a blur. But there was nothing there. There was only Sweet Hosanna and me, and outside the whole world, quiet in the early morning, green and strewn with brand new blossoms, like the ones on my very best dress.

What would the future hold for us? I had no way of knowing. But I remembered how, in the past years, my mother had worked and saved to bring us this far. I looked at her now, her eyes intent on the road, and I could see the determination . . .

Et cetera. You can't read it—I couldn't *write* it—without a feeling of wanting to push your plate away. It's too much. It's unnecessary. It is, in a word, sickening.

The letters I get so often from kids provide me, unintentionally, with a reminder of the impact of a good ending. Boy, if anyone in the world knows how to *end*, it's a kid writing a letter.

"Well," they say, "I have to quit now."

⸿91

Dialogue: Let Your Characters Do the Talking

By Eve Bunting

Frankly, my dear, I don't give a damn!" So spoke Rhett to Scarlett in one of the best known lines of dialogue ever written. With that statement he signified the end of his patience, his tolerance, and maybe even his love.

Dialogue, real and believable, can say so much. Consider what we learn about the grandmother, come to visit for the first time in Pam Conrad's novel, *My Daniel.*

> "Do you know how to milk a cow, Grandma?"
> "I know how to milk it, feed it, slaughter it, skin it, drain it, quarter it, roast it, and eat it," she answered, getting up from her seat.

The author could have told us that the grandmother was feisty, competent and had a sense of humor. She didn't. She let Grandma speak for herself.

In *Scorpions,* by Walter Dean Myers, the mother of Jamal, Sassy, and Randy reminisces. Randy is in jail, and somehow she has to find the money to bail him out:

> "One day"—Mama's eyes looked far away—"I was walking downtown with Randy in my arms. I was waiting for a light to change when this white lady stopped and looked at him. I looked at her and she was smiling and I smiled back at her, and that was the best feeling in the whole world. You got a baby, and you hope so much for it. . . ."

We don't have to be told of the mother's heartbreak and disappointment and continuing love for her son. Her own words do that more effectively.

But good dialogue can do more than strengthen characterization. It can move your plot along.

In my young adult novel *The Ghost Children,* Matt and his little sister, Abby, have come to live with Aunt Gerda. Aunt Gerda has wooden dolls that she calls her "children." Matt suspects Clay Greeley and his friends, the twins, of vandalizing the house and the dolls. He goes to confront them:

"This bozo's real brave," one twin told the other.
"Well, he'd have to be, wouldn't he, living up there with the witch and the talking dolls."

This is the first time Matt has outside verification of his suspicion that the dolls talk.

"Go ahead and tell them what you heard," Clay Greeley ordered.
"Well, it was real dark. It was just about one in the morning . . ."
"The doll way in back was saying something about the moon and lightning . . ."

Red alert for Matt and for the reader, too. Here the dialogue furthered the plot and heightened the suspense at the same time.

Dialogue can play an important role, even in picture books. In my book *The Mother's Day Mice,* there is a discussion between Biggest Mouse, Middle and Little Mouse. It is right at the beginning, the early morning of Mother's Day:

Biggest studied his watch. "We have two hours before Mother wakes up. Middle and I know what we're getting for her and where to find it." He looked at Little Mouse and waited.
"I know what I'm getting, too," Little Mouse said. "Honeysuckle."
Biggest shook his head. "Little Mouse! Honeysuckle grows only on Honeysuckle Cottage. And we know who lives in Honeysuckle Cottage. You have to find something else for Mother."

In this short exchange, the problem is set up without resorting to exposition. We discover that there is a time limit involved and that a problem lies ahead for Little Mouse. Will he be able to overcome it?

Dialogue can also reveal the theme, or basic truth of your book in a subtle way so that it doesn't seem too much like a Sunday sermon!

There were a lot of important things I wanted to say in my novel *A Sudden Silence.* Jesse's brother, Bry, has been killed by a hit-and-run drunk driver. Jesse believes that if he can find that driver, his own guilt will end. For hadn't he been there when the car struck, and hadn't he

435

saved himself but failed to save his brother? If he finds the driver, won't that exonerate Jesse? I wanted to say to the reader: "Guilt does not go away that easily. Blaming someone else does not mean you ever stop blaming yourself, too."

In this scene, close to the end, Jesse is talking to his dad:

> "Dad?" I began. "I keep thinking that maybe I could have saved Bry somehow. I can't get away from that. If I'd jumped forward. . . . I saved myself, Dad."
>
> "I don't know what to tell you, Jesse. No use saying you'll get over it. You probably never will. . . . Everybody's left with something to regret, Jesse. We just have to go on the best we can."

There! I let my characters say it for me.

So how does one write vital, meaningful dialogue that deepens characterization, furthers the plot, expands the theme, and sounds real?

First, the author must come out of self and become the characters. Know everything about them before you begin, their likes and dislikes, their strengths and weaknesses, their fears and triumphs. Live with them. Know them so well that a false word coming out of one of their mouths sounds contrived. Not easy, you say? No, not easy. As a "past-young woman" myself who writes books for teenagers and middle graders I have to be constantly alert. I have to remember that "those days" are gone and "these days" are here. I have to adapt. You have to, too.

One way to do this is to eavesdrop. Or, to put it less sneakily, listen, if possible, unobserved.

When I wrote *Sixth Grade Sleepover*, I eavesdropped openly, asking permission to visit a sixth-grade classroom. For the first few days, the children were certainly aware of my presence at the back of the room and on the playground at recess and lunch. But as time passed and I stayed quiet, I became simply a part of the classroom, like their pet rabbit in his cage. That is when I got my truest material. What ten-year-old can you listen to? Which grade school can you go to? Is there a McDonald's where you can sit at a table with a cup of coffee, next to a bunch of teenagers, and make notes in your notebook? Do you have a young child or a grandchild? If you write picture books, then you are lucky. One of my own picture books came straight out of the mouths of my son and my three-year-old granddaughter. He was lying on her bed, trying to get her to take a nap.

436

"Teddy's napping.
The big, yellow dump truck is napping.
Come lie next to Daddy."
"Susie wants a drink of water."
"Susie needs her balloon and her . . ."

Eavesdropping can pay off for those of us lurking outside a granddaughter's door. My picture book *No Nap* is there to prove it!

Listen! Listen when you are in the mall, or in the market, or waiting in line at the theatre.

One girl, probably junior high, is talking to her friend. "I swear, he's a major babe."

I quickly make a note. So "major babe" is what they say now? However, there is a trap here. Slang dates quickly. But slang used sparingly and judiciously can give a feeling of today to your book. I will probably change the phrase somewhat, keeping the feel but making it more mine. How about "top babe"? Then I'll be safe if "major babe" flares and disappears. There is nothing more out of date than out-of-date slang. An exclamation such as "Out of sight!" is, I believe, out of sight already, and "Far out!" is so far out it is lost in space.

Along with slang, dialect, if used at all, has to be handled cautiously in children's books. It is difficult for many young people—and almost impossible for one who has a reading problem—to understand. In my books with an Irish background, I try for an Irish turn of speech, an Irish cadence, and stay away from the brogue.

Try to avoid pointless chatter that goes nowhere. If your characters use meaningless dialogue in your first draft, take it out of your second draft. It simply slows the action and is a major cause of story sag. And remember, one character never tells a second character something he already knows simply to give information to the reader. For example, two sisters are talking. "We lived in Brigham City for four months. You were three years older than I was. Papa sold insurance." Her sister knows all that. The author must find a better way to tell the reader.

When you are handling several characters in a story, particularly several of the same age and sex, it is important to make each one sound a little different. One way to do this is to give one character a gesture to go with her speech. For instance:

"I did not! How could you think such a thing?" Cassandra pushed back her long, blonde hair.

437

Let that be her habit. But don't have her overdo it to the point of absurdity. Let one character have a favorite word, or a manner of speaking. Have one always overdramatize, or constantly make rather goofy puns. In my book, *Someone is Hiding on Alcatraz Island,* Jelly Bean talked through his nose, as if he always had a cold. Maxie could never stand still, and his speech was as jerky as his body movements. You can find something that will make your character an individual and keep him distinctive in the reader's mind.

Above all, dialogue must sound natural. Ordinary people and especially ordinary children don't use flowery images in everyday conversation.

"Oh, how beautiful the pool looks. It's almost as if the sun is trapped in the sparkling water."

No. A kid would be more likely to say: "The pool looks great. Last one in's a rotten egg!" Or perhaps now it's "Last one in's a rotten banana." I'll have to eavesdrop and find out.

The repeated use of "he said" and "she said" to identify the speaker is difficult for some authors to accept. Rather than be repetitious they try variations. Some, such as asked, answered, whispered, murmured, are fine. Others are not.

"What a wonderful evening," Tony breathed, moving closer to Kay.
"Isn't it?" she sighed. "Look at the stars."

Try breathing or sighing real words sometime. Much better to stay with "he said," "she said." Better yet, use a tag line.

Tony moved closer to Kay. "What a wonderful evening."
She turned to face him. "Isn't it? Look at the stars."

The tag line identifies who is speaking and also sets the scene more visually.

So many memorable books contain memorable spoken lines.

"I'll huff and I'll puff and I'll blow your house down."
"Who's been sleeping in *my* bed?"
"Don't go into Mr. McGregor's garden; your father had an accident there."

Understand what good dialogue can do for the tale you tell. Train your ear to listen, then step back, and let your characters speak for themselves.

92

PUTTING YOUR CHARACTERS TO WORK IN MYSTERY FICTION

BY MARY BLOUNT CHRISTIAN

IF WE HAVE DONE OUR JOBS WELL, our characters are real to our young readers. In fact, they are not "characters" at all, but people—living, breathing people who are bumbling through their troubles like the rest of us and who occasionally triumph, making all of us feel better about ourselves.

I gave as much thought to creating that clever Old English Sheepdog, Sebastian (Super Sleuth), as I have to any of my human characters. Detective John Quincy Jones, his human caretaker, is like a single parent. And while Sebastian is a much better detective than John, he, like my young readers, must depend on the kindness of others for his very existence. Sebastian can't open doors or dog food cans. He has no money of his own, and although he thinks in English, he speaks only Canine, which means he has a difficult time putting his ideas across to people.

He is much smarter than others realize. And he is sharply reprimanded when he does something naughty but is rarely, if ever, applauded for accomplishments. My young readers identify with these experiences and readily accept Sebastian as a peer, ignoring the fact that he's hairy and four-footed.

Reader identification is your best tool in making a story believable. It allows the readers to suspend disbelief in some pretty unbelievable adventures.

It's highly improbable that eight- and ten-year-olds, or even teens (and certainly not dogs), will be faced with the sorts of mysteries I confront them with in my stories. I must create people who are so believable, so real that they make the story work, as improbable as it may seem on the surface.

Introducing these people and their peculiarities to readers should never be rushed. Writers are like anthropologists, slowly brushing away

439

the surface clutter to reveal the wondrous secrets, one layer at a time. That is my favorite part of the writing process, because I find surprises at every layer.

Most of my stories begin with a vague situation and only a general idea about whom I need to carry my story: the gender, the age, the surface flaws and strengths.

I carry a small notebook with me all the time, and I jot down brief reminders of people I've observed with potential for characterization. As a "people collector," I may immediately remember someone I've observed—that toothless waitress with the smear of ketchup across the front of her apron, that shifty-eyed guy with hands the size of hams hanging out from his horse blanket coat—from whom I might get the idea for the fictional character I need.

That image remains blurry, however, until I find the right name for him or her, and I am every bit as attentive to my characters' names as I was to naming my offspring.

For contemporary given names I pore through *Name Your Baby* (Bantam). For popular names, there are the school directories and the birth announcements in the newspapers. If I want a name that is rural and rugged or from a past century, I use *Bible Names* (Ark Products) or *Who's Who in the Bible* (Spire). For more unusual names or ethnic names I consult *The New Age Baby Name Book* (Warner). Last names are as important as first names. Just be sure to select names that fit the origins and backgrounds of your characters. This, too, helps in developing your character.

I go through these books until one of the names finally "connects" with that blurry figure, and the features begin to sharpen. I knew I couldn't name my fictional dog hero after our own dog, though he was the inspiration for the character. Who would have believed a hero named Popsicle? The minute I found my name Sebastian, the image of a not-so-perfect Old English sheepdog, an undercover canine, became clear, and the story began to gel for me.

When I wanted to write a near-slapstick mystery with a hero who took himself a little too seriously, I chose Fenton P. Smith for his name, a mix of the usual and unusual and a bit of mystery thrown in, too, just like my character.

Once I'm sure the name and physical image are properly merged, I do the "Baskin-Robbins" test, probably because I'm a perpetual dieter, and this lets me visit vicariously the forbidden ice cream store. I can learn a lot just by observing my character in that setting.

Does he order vanilla, chocolate, or strawberry when confronted with all those luscious choices? He's probably a traditionalist, slow to take risks. As a mystery hero, he'll need to get pushed to the limit before he'll fight back.

Does he go for the raspberry truffles orange blossom flavor-of-the-month—without asking for a sample first? He's easily influenced and ready to follow the suspect down a dark alley. Does he get a dish or a cone, a double or single dip? Draw your own conclusions; there are no calories.

I go home with him and march right into his room, opening drawers and closet doors, peering under the bed. Are things jammed into drawers or divided and neatly stacked? Is that a stack of automotive magazines shoved under the bed? And is that a pair of hockey skates next to the baseball cleats?

The choice of furniture and curtains may be his mom's, but that poster from the movie *Top Gun* is his own.

I've learned a lot about my character, and I haven't even been through his billfold yet. Of course, I will! We carry our identities with us—in our billfolds, in our purses. There are pictures of our loved ones, our special friends, maybe even our pets. We can tell if he has a driver's license, a student I.D., a private pilot's license, membership in specific organizations, whether or not he has one or several credit cards or any cash.

With these tidbits of information, which I'll jot on a sheet of paper, I will list his position in the family (only, middle, oldest child, etc.), his religious background, his attitudes toward children, the elderly, and animals, his ethnic background, his personal ambitions and needs. When I know enough about him, I may write one or more scenes of conflict, just to hear his voice, listen to his inner thoughts, and watch his physical reactions. Does he slouch when he believes himself alone but stand straight in the presence of others? How does he enter a room? Does he repeat a phrase often? How does he sound when he's talking to his best friend, his teacher, his parent, his girlfriend?

And I won't neglect the other members of my little band of characters, either. The anti-hero has a past that has shaped his attitudes and personality, too. And he won't see himself as the villain. He'll have what

441

are to him valid reasons for behaving as he does. Also, he is a villain because of what he does, not because of what he looks like. So I make a sketch for him, too, and for anyone else who will play a major part in the story.

Imagine all the events in our characters' lives, from birth to death, strung together in a chain; our story is about one tiny link of that chain. We see only that section directly in front of us. Yet, everything our characters do that we can see is influenced by their past experiences. Their futures depend on what they do while we observe them, so if we want them to have reasonably happy futures, it's up to us to send our characters on life's journey with the personalities that will make it so.

You wouldn't send a mountain climber up Pike's Peak without a safety rope and pick. Neither should you send a character into a mystery without curiosity, stamina, and a strong feeling of self-preservation. Whether or not he recognizes these qualities in himself in the beginning, they must already be in place when the story starts, or the glue and Band-Aids will show, and your story will lack believability.

The sheet of information will grow as I write the first draft, peeling away the layers of protective covering that my character, like all of us, has built around himself. When a scene isn't working for me, I go back to my information sheet where I had noted, for example, that at the age of five my character was trapped in a burning house until he was rescued by a firefighter. That's how I knew how he would react now to a house fire. And, because my sketch also indicated that his father had died in a hit-and-run accident, I knew he'd feel strongly about catching a hit-and-run driver.

There is more than just knowing how your character would react to a given situation, though. I had sold several stories with only so-so reviews from the critics until I was lucky enough to attend a workshop given by Tony Hillerman. What he said changed my writing technique and my reviews for the better.

He reminded us that it is sensory detail that bonds the reader to the main character and makes the unbelievable seem true. He told us to write our first drafts, then go back and see that every typed page had at least two sensory details observed through the viewpoint character. Now I experience the story with all my senses: taste, smell, touch, sight, sound. I am thus bonded with my character, and so is my reader.

93

WRITING NONFICTION BOOKS FOR YOUNG READERS

BY JAMES CROSS GIBLIN

WHERE do you get the ideas for your nonfiction books?" is often the first thing I'm asked when I speak to writers. My usual reply is, "From anywhere and everywhere."

I've found a good place to start in the search for ideas is with your own interests and enthusiasms. It also helps if you can make use of personal experience. For example, the idea for my *The Skyscraper Book* (Crowell) really had its beginnings when I was a child, and loved to be taken up to the observation deck of the Terminal Tower, the tallest building in my home city of Cleveland.

Years later, after I moved to New York, I rented an apartment that was just a few blocks away from the Flatiron Building, one of the city's earliest and most striking skyscrapers. No matter how many times I passed the building, I always saw something new when I looked up at the carved decorations on its surface.

Although I had edited many books for children, I'd never thought of writing for a young audience until I was invited to contribute a 500-word essay to *The New York Kid's Book*. I chose the Flatiron Building as my topic because I wanted to find out more about it myself.

That piece led to an expanded magazine article (for *Cricket*) called "Buildings That Scrape the Sky," and then to *The Skyscraper Book*. In the latter I was finally able to tell the story behind Cleveland's Terminal Tower, the skyscraper that had fascinated me forty years earlier.

Besides looking first to your own interests and knowledge, you should also be open to ideas that may come your way by luck or chance. The idea of *Chimney Sweeps* (Crowell) literally came to me out of the blue when I was flying to Oklahoma City on business.

The plane stopped in Chicago and a tall, rangy young man carrying what I thought was a musical instrument case took the seat next to me. We started to talk, and I discovered that the man—whose name was Christopher Curtis—was a chimney sweep, and his case contained samples of the brushes he manufactured at his own small factory in Vermont. He was on his way to Oklahoma City to conduct a seminar for local sweeps on how to clean chimneys more efficiently.

Chris went on to tell me a little about the history of chimney sweeping and its revival as a profession in the last decade, because of the energy crisis. In turn, I told him I was a writer of children's books, and that he'd fired my interest in chimney sweeps as a possible subject.

We exchanged business cards, and a month or so later I wrote to tell him that I'd followed up on the idea and had started researching the book on chimney sweeps. I asked him if he'd be willing to read the manuscript for accuracy. He agreed to do so and volunteered to supply photographs of present-day sweeps that could be used (and were) as illustrations in the book.

According to an old English superstition, it's lucky to meet a chimney sweep. Well, meeting Christopher Curtis was certainly lucky for me!

Evaluating an idea

Once you have an idea for a book, the next step is to decide whether or not it's worth pursuing. The first thing I do is check R. R. Bowker's annual *Subject Guide to Children's Books in Print,* available in the reference department of most libraries, to see what else has been written on the subject. With *Chimney Sweeps,* there was nothing at all. In the case of *The Skyscraper Book,* I discovered that there were several books about *how* skyscrapers are constructed, but none with a focus on *why* and *by whom* they're constructed, which was the angle of the book I wanted to write. There may be many books on a given subject, but if you find a fresh or different slant, there'll probably be room in the market for yours, too.

Another thing to weigh when evaluating an idea is the matter of levels: A subject worth treating in a book usually has more than one. For instance, when I began researching *Chimney Sweeps,* I soon realized that besides the obvious human and social history, the subject also touched on economic and technological history. Weaving those different levels together made the book more interesting to write—and I believe it makes it more interesting for readers also.

A third important factor to consider is what age group to write the book for. That decision has to be based on two things: the nature of the subject and a knowledge of the market for children's books. I aimed *Chimney Sweeps* at an older audience, because I felt that the subject required more of a sense of history than younger readers would have. At the same time, I kept the text as simple and compact as possible, because I knew that there's a much greater demand today for children's nonfiction geared to the upper elementary grades than there is for Young Adult nonfiction.

After you've checked out your idea and decided what slant to take with it, and what age group to write for, it's time to begin the research. An entire article could be devoted to research methods alone. The one thing I feel it's safe to say after writing seven books is that each project requires its own approach, and you have to discover it as you go along.

When I was researching *The Scarecrow Book* (Crown, 1980), I came up against one stone wall after another. It seemed no one had ever bothered to write anything about scarecrows. Research became a matter of following up on the skimpiest of clues. For example, a brief mention in a magazine article that the Japanese had a scarecrow god led me to the Orientalia Division of the Library of Congress, where a staff member kindly translated a passage from a Japanese encyclopedia describing the god and its relation to Japanese scarecrows.

The Skyscraper Book presented the opposite problem. There was so much background material available on skyscrapers that I could easily have spent ten years researching the subject and never come to the end. Choices had to be made early on. I settled on the eight or ten New York skyscrapers I wanted to discuss and sought detailed information only on those. I did the same thing with skyscrapers in Chicago and other cities around the country.

Chimney Sweeps opened up the exciting area of primary source material. On a visit to the Economics Division of the New York Public Library, I discovered the yellowing transcripts of early 19th-century British investigations into the deplorable living and working conditions of child sweeps.

Fireworks, Picnics, and Flags: The Story of The Fourth of July Symbols (Clarion) introduced me to the pleasures of on-site research. I had spent two days at beautiful Independence National Historical Park in Philadelphia. I toured Independence Hall, visited the rented rooms nearby where Thomas Jefferson drafted the Declaration of Independence, and watched a group of third-grade youngsters touch the Liberty Bell in its pavilion. I won't soon forget the looks of awe on their faces.

Whenever I go out on a research expedition, I always take along a supply of 4 × 6-inch cards. At the top of each one, I write the subject for handy reference when I file the cards alphabetically in a metal box. I also write the title, author, publisher, and date of the book I'm reading so that I'll have all that information on hand when I compile the bibliography for my book. Then I go on to jot down the facts I think I might be able to use.

I try to check each fact against at least two other sources before including it in the text. Such double-checking can turn up myths that have long passed as truths. For instance, while researching *Fireworks, Picnics, and Flags,* I read two books that said an old bell-ringer sat in the tower of Independence Hall almost all day on July 4, 1776. He was waiting for word that independence had been declared so that he could ring the Liberty Bell.

At last, in late afternoon, a small boy ran up the steps of the tower and shouted, "Ring, Grandfather! Ring for Liberty!" The old man did so at once, letting all of Philadelphia know that America was no longer a British colony. It makes a fine story—but according to the third source I checked, it simply isn't true.

By no means will all of the facts I find appear in the finished book. Only a small part of any author's research shows up in the final manuscript. But I think a reader can feel the presence of the rest beneath the surface, lending substance and authority to the writing.

Picture research

With most of my books, I've gathered the illustrations as well as written the text, and this has led me into the fascinating area of picture research. On *The Scarecrow Book,* for example, I discovered the resources of the Prints and Photographs Division of the Library of Congress, where I located several stunning photographs of Southern scarecrows taken during the 1930s. Later, in a back issue of *Time* magazine, I came across a story about Senji Kataoka, a public relations officer with the Ministry of Agriculture in Tokyo, whose hobby was taking pictures of scarecrows. Over the years, the article said, Mr.

446

Kataoka had photographed more than 2000 examples in the countryside around Tokyo.

I decided to follow up on this lead, remote as it might prove to be. From the Japanese consulate in New York I obtained the address of the Ministry of Agriculture in Tokyo, and wrote Mr. Kataoka there. Six weeks later his answer arrived in neatly printed English, along with eight beautiful color snapshots of scarecrows. I wrote back saying I needed black-and-white photos for the book and Mr. Kataoka immediately mailed me a dozen, four of which were used in the chapter on Japanese scarecrows. Another appeared on the jacket. When I asked Mr. Kataoka how much he wanted for his photos, he said just a copy of the book.

Experiences such as these have taught me several important things about doing picture research. The first is: Never start with commercial photographic agencies. They charge high reproduction fees which are likely to put you in the red if your contract states that you are responsible for paying such costs.

Instead, try non-profit sources like U.S. government agencies, which provide photographs for just the cost of the prints; art and natural history museums, which charge modest fees; and national tourist offices, which will usually give you photographs free of charge, asking only that you credit them as the source.

Other good sources of free photos are the manufacturers of various products. Their public relations departments will be happy to send you high quality photographs of everything from tractors to inflatable vinyl scarecrows in return for an acknowledgment in your book.

Selling

Writers often ask me if they should complete all the research for a nonfiction book before trying to sell the idea to a publisher. That's usually not necessary. However, if you're a beginner you should do enough research to make sure there's sufficient material for a book. Then you'll need to write a full outline and draft one or two sample chapters. After that, you can send query letters to publishers and ask if they'd like to look at your material.

If a publisher is interested, you should be prepared to rewrite your sample chapters several times before being offered a contract. That happened to me with my first book, *The Scarecrow Book,* and looking back now I'm glad it did. For it helped me and my collaborator, Dale Ferguson, to sharpen the focus of that book.

Of course it's different after you become an established author. Then both you and your editors know what you can do, and generally a two- or three-page proposal describing your new book idea will be enough for the publisher to make a decision.

Once you have your contract for the book in hand, you can proceed with the writing of the manuscript. Some authors use electric type-writers, others have turned to word processors. I write longhand in a spiral notebook and mark in the margins the date each passage was drafted. That encourages me as I inch through the notebook, working mainly on Saturdays and Sundays and during vacations from my full-time editorial job.

Achieving a consistent personal voice in a nonfiction book takes me at least three drafts. In the first, I get down the basic material of the paragraph or section. In the second, I make certain the organization is logical and interesting, and I then begin to smooth out those spots where the style of the original research source may be too clearly in evidence. In the third draft, I polish the section until the tone and voice are entirely mine.

After I deliver to the editor the completed manuscript and the il-lustrations I've gathered, I may heave a sigh of relief. But chances are my work won't be over. The editor may feel that extensive revisions are necessary; sections of the manuscript may have to be reorganized, others rewritten. Perhaps the editor will want mc to compile a bibliogra-phy, or a glossary of unfamiliar words used in the text.

At last everything is in place, and a year or so later—during which time the manuscript has been copyedited, designed, and set in type—the finished book arrives in the mail. That's an exciting moment, fol-lowed by a few anxious weeks as you wait for the first reviews to appear. The verdict of the critics isn't the final one, though. There's yet another stage in the life of any children's book: the reaction of young readers.

Perhaps a boy will come up to me after a library talk and tell me that he was inspired to find out more about the skyscrapers in his city after reading *The Skyscraper Book.* Or a girl will write to say that the chapter on a day in the life of a climbing boy in *Chimney Sweeps* made her cry. It's only then that I know I'm on the way toward achieving my goal—to write lively, accurate, and entertaining books for young people.

❧ 94

TEN COMMON ERRORS IN WRITING FOR CHILDREN

BY LINDA LEE MAIFAIR

A STORY FOR CHILDREN must do all the things an adult story does, and do it just as well, but in fewer words and simpler language. Where do would-be authors of juvenile fiction go wrong? The following are among the most common errors in writing for children:

(1) *Adult point of view.* Children want to read about children—children like themselves or as they'd like to be, facing the sort of problems they might face or doing things they've only dreamed about.

They like to identify with the central child characters, living the story's events and facing the characters' problems right along with them. They want to see the situation through the eyes and heart of someone who sees it the way they might see it themselves.

(2) *Multiple point of view.* Although adult fiction sometimes has a multiple point of view, children's stories should not. With less sophisticated reading abilities and very strong identification with the central characters, children are not as willing or able to change viewpoints in the course of a story.

Even shifting back and forth between two equally important characters with relatively the same perspective—like best friends or twin brothers—can be confusing and disconcerting for young readers, requiring them to divide their attention and change personalities vicariously as often as the viewpoint changes.

(3) *Stilted dialogue.* Young readers must be able to accept the youngsters in their stories as "real" children. Part of this reality comes from giving the characters the mannerisms, expressions, and actions of real kids. A great deal of it, however, comes from having young characters *sound* like real children.

Many juvenile characters talk the way authors who have little experience with real children the same age *think* young people talk. This is

449

about as successful as a writer who has never been to England trying to write dialogue for a Scotland Yard detective based on the way he or she *thinks* an Englishman would talk. Awkward, dated, and misused slang and phonetically unreadable dialect are no substitute for plain, spontaneous childlike (as opposed to *childish*) chatter.

Other young characters with flaws are all too often presented merely as miniature adults, stuffy and insufferable. They say things real youngsters would never say in words they would never use. Spouting polysyllabic vocabulary in compound-complex sentences, they never use contractions or utter gross, childish insults or expressions of disgust. Their speech is too mature, too difficult, too wordy and too wise.

(4) *Summaries posing as stories.* Many beginning writers of juvenile fiction leave out the dialogue completely. Because it is extremely difficult to develop both plot and character within the constraints of the juvenile story, they summarize rather than *show* what happened. There is no dialogue, no play-by-play action, no scenes, long or short. The result may, in fact, be a workable, interesting plotline, a place to start, but it isn't a story.

(5) *Lack of conflict.* Stories for young readers should do more than recount an isolated experience, no matter how interesting, pleasant, or "educational." They must have a plot that moves forward, logically and inevitably toward a climax and resolution. A fun day at the zoo or a carefree vacation on Grandpa's farm is seldom enough.

The story must revolve around some sort of problem. The conflict, though not necessarily earth-shattering, must be appropriate and relevant for both the child character and reader. It must also be a conflict that matters, the outcome of which will affect the main character's life and spirit in some way, hopefully for the better.

The plot will evolve from his or her thwarted but persistent efforts to solve the problem. The theme or "lesson" of the story should emerge from the ways the character has changed and what he or she has learned about life in the process.

(6) *Missing climax.* The problem in a juvenile story must be followed through to resolution, building first to a climax, a "darkest moment" and high point of tension, for the character and reader to work and worry through together.

Often the writer uses up the juvenile story's short, strict word limits before he or she reaches this climax, the part the readers would find most exciting. Rather than cutting down the beginning and balancing the development, climax and resolution, the unwary writer tends to rush through the climax or skip it entirely, trying to tie everything together in the few words that remain.

Problems solved too suddenly, too neatly, too miraculously; telling readers what happened after the fact instead of letting them see and hear what goes on as it evolves, leaves readers frustrated, unsatisfied, and cheated, as if someone had fast-forwarded to the end of a really exciting adventure movie without letting the viewers witness the big showdown or how the hero got everything to work out in the end. The climax should be the biggest, strongest scene in the story, the young readers' reward for staying with the character and caring about what happens to him or her.

(7) *Characters uninvolved in the solution of the problem.* In many stories for children, a parent, teacher, coach or other adult intercedes to solve the problems, impart the lesson, and make sure everything ends happily ever after. This is very unsatisfying and unfair to both the young reader and the young character. Young readers expect characters to *do* something about their problems, something the readers themselves may not be able to do, empowerment they may experience only through their stories. It's also one way children learn, safely and vicariously, that actions have consequences, and people must take responsibility for them.

The characters will make mistakes, and there will be obstacles, many of their own creation, all of which makes for a more interesting plot, but the characters have to take action and make decisions that lead logically to the resolution of the story, if not of the conflict itself.

The young protagonists may not, realistically, be able to handle the situation on their own. Ten-year-old sleuths cannot follow, trap and apprehend dangerous criminals singlehandedly. The main child character may need adult assistance, but he must remain an active participant, not merely an observer, throughout the big scene and at the end.

(8) *Starting too soon.* When you have to tell a story in under a thousand words, you don't have the space to go into the history of the character, trace his family back three generations or introduce each cast member in minute, physical and psychological detail, particularly in the critical first paragraph or two of the story.

The story should begin as close to the main action and problem as

451

possible, getting the readers into the thick of things and making them wonder how it's all going to turn out. Necessary background information and details should be woven into the fabric of the story as it moves forward, using bits of dialogue and narration.

A story about a catastrophe on a camping trip shouldn't start when the child is packing his backpack *unless* what he takes or forgets has an impact on the outcome of the story. A story about a Saturday morning basketball game shouldn't start at school on Friday afternoon, *unless* something happens that is crucial to the plot. A story about a new girl who is ostracized by the "in" crowd shouldn't start with Mom's pancake breakfast, but with the opening buzzer of the game, or with the girl's face smarting in angry, embarrassed response to a snubbing remark or action.

(9) *Going on too long.* When the problem is resolved, stop. Don't let the characters stand around analyzing or recapping what happened. Don't follow everyone back home for cookies and milk. Don't lessen the impact of the climax or shift the reader's attention to minor characters or entirely new, unrelated situations. And don't summarize what will happen for the next ten years of the character's life; young readers can't conceptualize that far in the future.

(10) *Sermonizing.* Some editors, especially those of religious and denominational magazines for young people, like their readers to be left with what one calls "moral residue," a "lesson" beyond the simple entertainment value of the story. But such lessons must be handled subtly.

Having an adult character lecture a child who has misbehaved in some way, serious or minor, is not acceptable or appealing to young readers. Equally unacceptable, as well as totally unrealistic, is having the "reformed" young character go on at length about what he or she has learned and how repentant he feels, vowing never to err again.

The writer must let the events of the story—the way a character handles a situation, the consequences of his actions, and the resultant changes in his attitude and behavior—demonstrate the "moral" of the story instead of hitting the reader over the head with it at the end.

Though weaknesses in juvenile fiction take many forms, they are symptomatic of a single underlying, unforgivable sin committed by too many would-be writers: the failure to understand and respect both this unique and special audience and the challenges involved in creating worthwhile stories for children.

452

95

THINK PICTURE BOOK

BY EVE BUNTING

THE BAD NEWS IS THAT NO, picture books are not easy to write. The good news is that there are some useful guidelines in picture book writing, and although they will never guarantee a sale, they will at least put you on course if writing a beautiful picture book is your heart's desire. So let's think picture book.

Most obviously, *think pictures*. Perceive your story as a moving slide show, vivid, arresting, and dramatic. Give the illustrator something to work with. If you are both author and illustrator you will be doing yourself the same favor. Incidentally, it is not necessary for you to provide the pictures. The publisher will take care of that for you.

Remember, static scenes without variety do not make a good slide presentation.

I once had a friend show me a picture book manuscript she'd written.

"It's so cute," she said. "But I've sent it out and sent it out, and no one wants to buy it. Why?"

In the book, a cat stands before a mirror, trying on hats—a cowboy hat, a fireman's helmet, a baseball cap, etc. One character, one scene, one action, repeated over and over.

"He could be a very cute cat," I said. "But nothing happens."

My friend looked puzzled and a little irritated by my lack of perception.

"Something does happen," she said. "He changes hats."

I amended my words. "Not enough happens."

That cat in the mirror would make a dull slide show and a dull picture book.

An art director in a major publishing house once told me: "The words in a picture book should be a gift to the illustrator."

I had always believed that the illustrator's paintings were gifts to the writers, adding dimensions often undreamed of. And that is true. But it has to work the other way around, too. What the art director meant was that if the scenes in the text are varied, imaginative, plentiful, the illustrator doesn't have to struggle and the book is what it should be, a happy collaboration. To achieve this, keep in mind that the scenes should roll forward in an ever-moving diversity of character and action. This does not always happen naturally for me. I have to work at it. You can, too.

When you've finished your manuscript, divide it by drawing lines across the text to mark what you see as the natural ending of a page. Or set up a dummy by taking eight sheets of blank paper and folding them horizontally to make a 32-page book (32 pages is the usual picture book length, less three or four for front matter: title page, copyright, and dedication). Write your text on each dummy page. Do you have enough pictures? Do you have too many words? Look for balance. Visualize your little reader, or listener, impatient to get on with it, to turn the page to find out what happens next.

If I see an ungainly chunk of text in my own work, I deliberately set out to "break" it up with picture possibilities.

For instance, in *The Mother's Day Mice,* there is a scene in which the three little mice are watching Honeysuckle Cottage, waiting and hoping that the cat on the porch will go away. It is important here that I give the impression of time passing, since Little Mouse needs to hear many repeats of the song being played on the piano inside the cottage. When I read what I'd written, I realized I had a static scene. So I added:

(Middle Mouse) set his strawberry on the ground and a beetle came on the run. Middle picked it up again and shooed the beetle away.
Little Mouse began creeping toward the cottage on his belly.
Biggest yanked him back by his tail.

These few lines add action and a little humor. They use all three mouse characters and a new peripheral character, the beetle, is placed on the scene. But better, better, better, they add two picture possibilities. And Jan Brett, the illustrator, used both charmingly.

Adding scenes is not that difficult. But it is harder because of the second unbreakable law of the picture book—*think short*. Think 1,000 words, or less. Think concise. Say what you need to say in the most economical way possible that makes sense and that sounds poetic, because a poetic telling is the essence of the picture book.

A few weeks ago I visited a school where examples of "pretty sentences from picture books" were pinned on the wall of the library.

"We talk about them," the librarian told me. "We ask: 'Why did the author say it this way instead of another way?' We listen to the sounds of the words and the cadence of the sentence and look for images."

So "pretty" sentences are a must, if we want to make it on the wall. Not overblown, though. Not gushy or sentimentally sweet.

Isn't it more breathtaking to read, "The air hissed to the beat of wings" *(The Man Who Could Call Down Owls)* than, "There was the sound of wings in the air"? Try to use the actual "sound" word. The air *hissed;* the bus *wheezed;* the leaves *flurried* in the wind.

Long passages of undiluted description are out in the picture book. But I believe short descriptions add immeasurably to the texture of the story and enhance the word awareness of even the youngest reader. A line or two can set the scene:

Milk bottles stood on front steps, waiting to be let in. The sky was the color of his mother's pearl brooch. The one she wore on Sundays. *(St. Patrick's Day in the Morning)*

Crows cawed in the white air. The arms of the trees scratched at the sky. *(The Valentine Bears)*

Our table seemed monstrously big. Chairs, hump-backed, clawed and crouched around it. *(Ghost's Hour, Spook's Hour)*

Enough description, but not too much.

A picture book, then, must be short, not abrupt. It must be pure, not sterile. There is room for a story and for a few beautiful word pictures, too.

There is also room to say something valuable. A picture book that does not has no value of itself. Heavy or deeply moralistic, no. Worthwhile, yes. The treasure is well hidden, but it's there for the child to feel and understand. In *Ghost's Hour, Spook's Hour,* I am saying: "No need to be afraid of the dark. The scary things can be explained away. See? No need to be afraid." Those actual words never appear in the text. They are self-evident as Jake and his trusty dog, Biff, search the dark house for Mom and Dad while in the hallway the big clock strikes midnight—ghost's hour, spook's hour.

On a trip to mainland China a few years ago, I spent some time browsing in a bookstore and brought back with me a picture book entitled *A Boy and His Kitten* (for children from 4 to 8). The story is about Maomao who will not go to bed. He and his kitten play through the night hours, disturbing his good little sister.

"How troublesome are those children who do not go to bed," the text says.

In the morning, little sister, who presumably got some sleep, is up at dawn doing her morning exercises. Alas for Maomao and his kitten who are now sleeping the day away:

> For them, it is too late
> To breathe the fresh morning air,
> Or hear their teacher's interesting stories.
> Oh, what a great pity it is
> for Maomao and his kitten!
>
> Our little friends,
> Be not like these two.
> Early to bed,
> And early to rise,
> Keeps you fit and wise.

One has to hope that the story lost a little something in the translation!

You must try not to do this in the picture books you write. In fact, I venture to say, do this and you'll never have a picture book. So *think subtle*. The worthwhile thing you have to say will come across just as clearly and much more palatably.

The picture book writer, perhaps more than writers in any other genre, must *think original*. The field is overflowing with books about cats and dogs, horses and ponies, dinosaurs, rabbits, ducks, mice; boys who are having terrible, awful days, girls who can be anything they want to be; moms, dads, pesky little sisters—all subjects that interest little kids. But writers need to find the *new* angle. As in Carol and Donald Carrick's book: *What Happened to Patrick's Dinosaurs?* The dinosaurs, Patrick says, liked helping people to build houses and lay roads. But after a while the people were willing to sit back and let the dinosaurs do it. They didn't help themselves. So the dinosaurs, for the sake of the people and still helping them, took off in space ships. And *that's* what happened! A nice, original touch and a theme that is there without being belabored.

When I wrote *Scary, Scary Halloween,* I knew of the numerous picture books about this popular holiday. What was there to say that hadn't already been said? So I did trick or treating from a cat's point of view, a mama cat, hiding under the house with her baby kittens, waiting fearfully for the monsters, who are the children in costume, to leave. When they do—

> It's quiet now, the monsters gone
> The streets are ours until the dawn.
> We're out, we prowlers of the night
> Who snap and snarl and claw and bite.
> We stalk the shadows, dark, unseen . . .
> Goodbye 'til next year, Halloween.

A different angle? I think so, and the editor agreed.

When you think picture book, think lasting and forever, because that is what the best picture books are. How many children have been frightened and reassured by *Where the Wild Things Are* (Maurice Sendak)? How many have learned to read for pleasure through the good graces of Dr. Seuss and *The Cat in the Hat* or *Green Eggs and Ham*? How many have gone to sleep to the lullaby lull of *Goodnight Moon*? How many will? A picture book is not temporary, it is not ephemeral. It is as lasting as truth itself and should, said Arnold Lobel, "Rise out of the lives and passions of its creators." It should be unique and ageless and seemingly effortless in its smooth, easy flow.

For all the effort involved, the pruning and shaping and sculpting of words, you will be rewarded with joy as you hold in your hand this small polished jewel that is *your* picture book.

PLAYWRITING

96

New Writing for the Theatre

By Shelley Berc and Robert Hedley

HAVE YOU EVER FOUND YOURSELF SITTING DOWN to write a play and discovered that the ideas and feelings you wished to convey were not served by the traditional route of exposition, development, and denouement; that the world you were perceiving was plotless, fragmented, and collage-like? Perhaps you even felt defeated before you started because you didn't know the "rules"?

One of the most fascinating things we've discovered working with new playwrights, as we do at the Iowa Playwrights Workshop, is that many of their plays or plays-in-progress do not conform to the usual notion of dramatic writing. In fact, when these students attempt to "fix" their plays in conventional ways—a little character development here, a bit more plot there—the plays fall apart. Many of today's playwrights are mapping out a new dramatic territory and are writing the rules of its domain, rather than trying to superimpose a traditional style or structure upon it.

Not since the end of the nineteenth century has there been less consensus over what playwriting is or should be. The realistic play with its concentration on true-to-life, psychologically motivated action is losing its hold on dramatic writing. Playwrights, in increasing greater numbers, are finding themselves attracted to a variety of theatrical styles and approaches that confound our sense of the linear, character-focused play. Many playwrights find that the subject matter and dramatic structure associated with realism do not reflect the fragmented, multisensory, technologically swift nature of life today.

This new writing for the stage is likely to replace psychologically motivated characters with mercurial ones; linear plot with a series of non-linear events that resemble jam sessions on a theme; realistic, informational dialogue with language arias that exist to create momentary metaphysical landscapes. Actually, such elements in one form or another have been a staple of avant-garde theatre for nearly a century. Now, however, they are becoming part of mainstream dramatic writing and can even be called the new classic style. As the world becomes a place where many things are done simultaneously, in which total communication across hemispheres is just a fax away, playwrights are losing patience with single-minded theatre pieces that systematically follow through a central idea or problem for two or three acts, with characters who consistently respond out of psychological motivation.

Internationally acclaimed playwrights such as Heiner Mueller, Irene Fornes, and Manfred Karge are all in their own unique ways creating scripts that speak to today's concerns in a dramatic language and structure that may wholly disregard plot, conflict, dialogue, even character. What then are the elements of postmodern playwriting, and what do they say about the future place of the playwright in the world and on the stage?

Let's take, for example, Manfred Karge's *Man to Man*. The play has only one character, a woman who impersonates her husband after his death so she can take his job and survive in Nazi Germany. As performed at the Royal Court Theatre in London, it opened with a woman lying on the floor amidst the domestic debris of her life. There is no pretense about making the set look like a real room; we see only fragments of the character's life—a few bottles, a record player, a chair, a TV—as if we were sifting through an archaeological site.

For the next fifty minutes (the length of plays is changing, too) this woman tells us the story of her life in terms of its personal, political, economic, and mythological aspects. No single notion of how to perceive her existence is given weight over another. To this end, the text is mercurial in its transitions rather than causal, fragmented in its plot rather than linear, evocative in its development rather than factual.

The text of *Man to Man* hardly looks like a play at all in the usual sense. It is divided into a series of numbered passages that combine prose, verse, slogans, captions, quotes, puns, political references, and a fairy tale. It is a language picked up and spit out like a grab bag of political and cultural history. Several genres of language, from the literary quotation to the billboard advertisement, create the pastiche of this woman's life. More important, the language here does not exist primarily for the purposes of conveying information, developing character, or tracing a tragic flaw. In *Man to Man*, language is both main character and prime action; its forms comment on each other; its vying genres combust and collide, turning the world as we comfortably know it upside down and freeing us to perceive anew.

In many of the new plays that attract critical attention, conventional playwriting wisdom is inadequate. The idea that to write plays that speak eloquently and powerfully, one must start with Aristotle and spend time with Ibsen has not been true for some time and is now particularly untrue. Linearity and character modesty—that is, the assumption that somebody else must reveal the character's story—are less important than ever. Consistency of tone and authorial absence, bulwarks of realism, are directly refused as today's new plays celebrate verbal fluency and imagination. The audience is not asked to suspend its disbelief or allowed to hide voyeuristically behind a "fourth wall."

This is not to suggest that plays of consequence, beauty, power, or outrageousness are not being written in traditional forms, but that impatience or restlessness with those forms is now a part of the young playwright's make-up. It seems no longer possible, for example, to pretend that stage events are taking place without being observed, that a few hundred eyes are not peering out from the darkness. Likewise, it appears to be impossible for characters to restrain the urge to speak directly to their audience. Verbal literacy—that is, a knowledge of what language can be asked to do and a recognition of what it has done in all its uses, misuses, and variations—is on the rise, leading, yet again, to an impatience with plays whose characters are unaware that they inhabit a stage and hence speak only to the fictional point. In the new plays, the boundaries between what is funny and what is sad, what is tragic or trivial, beautiful or trite have been stretched and blurred to an unprecedented extent in direct reflection of our social and historical times.

While the terms in which many of the new plays address the audience are often abstract and complex, their relationship with the audience is astonishingly direct. Characters often tell the audience flat out what it needs to know, rather than going through a long, slow list of clues that become the plot structure. By getting the facts over with quickly (as the Greeks did ages ago in their plays), the playwright can concentrate on the political, historical, and metaphysical concerns he or she wants to relate. Scenes no longer develop one to another in a storylike trance in which all things lead inevitably to the climax. Rather, they often exist like medieval triptychs in which certain selected images springing from a well-known theme play against each other, illuminating and interpreting the story by its very fracture and incompleteness. Audience response is built through a series of impressions, aural and visceral, carefully arranged to create an idea or image through juxtaposition, irony, parallelism, or repetition.

One of the most interesting trends in new plays is the monodrama, or one-person play. Unlike realism, in which the audience watches the story evolve through key physical and emotional actions, the new monodramas in particular rely heavily on action through language. As storyteller, the playwright uses forms of language in rhythmic variation to provide dynamic action without the trappings of verisimilitude. The monodramas are often a mix of autobiography and cultural mythology. Through a series of impressions, the multiplicity of life is examined, honed down to the microcosm of the lone character. Monodramas examine the self as social creature and the self as mythological hero. Dramatic tension is found in the battle between the disparate identities of the self. Dialogue in the monodrama, when not between these warring selves, is between the character and the audience. Hence, each member of the audience actually becomes a character, and a true dialogue between performer and observer occurs.

The trends and developments are not meant to serve as a prescription nor a set of new rules to replace the old. A play by Irene Fornes, for example, is profoundly different from the Karge play cited here but just as relevant. What is important for the aspiring playwright to recognize is a sense of the freedom and imagination in the newer forms, as well as the reemergence of language as a primary player in the drama.

But let's be more specific. How can beginning playwrights help themselves? First of all it is important to read widely in order to understand what is going on in theater writing today. While publications such as *The Fireside Theatre* are excellent for mainstream writing, the newest pieces can be found in the *Wordplay* collections; the various *PAJ* volumes; *TCG, Plays International, American Theatre,* and other magazines; and in anthologies like *7 Different Plays.* For the inexperienced writer, it is liberating to see the methods and structures used by writers tackling contemporary issues.

In working with their ideas, aspiring playwrights must learn to trust their instincts. While it's not easy for a new playwright to know whether he or she is on the road to creating plays in a nonlinear, lyric, evocative style or merely being sloppy in character delineation and plot development, little good will result from listening to the critical inner voice that compares everything to *Death of a Salesman*. The experience of a new play is a total experience, including its form. Not being a "slice of life," such an experience does not demand consistency of language, place, character, or other normal conditions. Indeed, an impulse or instinct to use multiple forms may indicate the only means of expressing your idea.

But let's conclude with a few basics for you to keep in mind as you write or revise your plays:

1) The one thing traditional playwriting and some of the newer forms have in common is specificity of detail and clarity of expressed ideas.

2) When you are writing a play, make sure you are listening to what *it* is telling *you*, rather than what you think you want to say. Follow your impulses. Listen to your characters. Forget rules, forget doors, forget politeness. Never ask yourself whether it's logical or not.

3) If the play is telling you primarily about the sound and rhythm of a certain day, you must consider that the play may be more of a dramatization of the essence of that day than of the characters or stories you've tried to put in it. The characters and the stories have been there and will be there, at least in your notebook. That day, that flavor, may not. Just because it doesn't resemble plays you know doesn't mean that it won't become a new, important play.

4) Remember that playwrights can and do dramatize anything—from a day to a poem to a piece of architecture. Dramatic action, the mainspring of the theatrical experience, does not necessarily mean physical or psychological action. Action can also mean a movement of ideas or images or words or intentions.

5) Try to put the world you see in your mind on the stage. Explore the thoughts, the words, the visions that own you, and reach for ways to translate them in terms of actors, sets, and audience. Don't settle for what you know or have seen.

6) Be courageous. You are individual when you write like yourself. When you try to put your ideas in someone else's form you often betray those ideas.

Many of the new techniques are as old as the Greeks, but the varied and joyous way in which styles and genres of the theatre are being put together is wholly new and magical; an invitation to the mind to explore the farthest reaches of its imaginative strength.

97

TEN GOLDEN RULES FOR PLAYWRIGHTS

BY MARSHA NORMAN

Budding playwrights often write to ask me advice on getting started—and succeeding—in writing plays. The following are a few basics that I hope aspiring playwrights will find helpful.—M.N.

1. Read at least four hours every day, and don't let anybody ask you what you're doing just sitting there reading.

2. Don't write about your present life. You don't have a clue what it's about yet. Write about your past. Write about something that terrified you, something you *still* think is unfair, something that you have not been able to forget in all the time that's passed since it happened.

3. Don't write in order to tell the audience how smart you are. The audience is not the least bit interested in the playwright. The audience only wants to know about the characters. If the audience begins to suspect that the thing onstage was actually written by some other person, they're going to quit listening. So keep yourself out of it!

4. If you have characters you cannot write fairly, cut them out. Grudges have no place in the theatre. Nobody cares about your grudges but you, and you are not enough to fill a house.

5. There must be one central character. One. Everybody write that down. Just one. And he or she must want something. And by the end of the play, he or she must either get it or not. Period. No exceptions.

6. You must tell the audience right away what is at stake in the evening, i.e. how they know when they can go home. They are, in a sense, the jury. You present the evidence, and then they say whether it seems true to them. If it does, it will run, because they will tell all their friends to come see this true thing, God bless them. If it does not seem true to them, try to find out why and don't do it any more.

7. If, while you are writing, thoughts of critics, audience members or family members occur to you, stop writing and go read until you have successfully forgotten them.

464

8. Don't talk about your play while you are writing it. Good plays are always the product of a single vision, a single point of view. Your friends will be helpful later, after the play's direction is established. A play is one thing you can get too much help with. If you must break this rule, try not to say what you have learned by talking. Or just let other people talk and you listen. Don't talk the play away.

9. Keep pads of paper near all your chairs. You will be in your chairs a good bit (see Rule 1), and you will have thoughts for your play. Write them down. But don't get up from reading to do it. Go right back to the reading once the thoughts are on the paper.

10. Never go to your typewriter until you know what the first sentence is that day. It is definitely unhealthy to sit in front of a silent typewriter for any length of time. If, after you have typed the first sentence, you can't think of a second one, go read. There is only one good reason to write a play, and that is that there is no other way to take care of it, whatever it is. There are too many made-up plays being written these days. So if it doesn't spill out faster than you can write it, don't write it at all. Or write about something that does spill out. Spilling out is what the theatre is about. Writing is for novels.

98

IF THE PLAY'S *YOUR* THING . . .

BY EDITH TARBESCU

IF YOU HAVE NEVER WRITTEN A PLAY or if you are just starting one, you will probably feel like a sailor contemplating charts. Then suddenly it will dawn on you—you don't always get where you're going by moving in a straight line. Sometimes you have to tack back and forth in order to reach your destination. The same goes for playwriting.

Starting out

Just the way a novice sailor doesn't cross the Atlantic Ocean his first time out (or even his second or third), you should probably not attempt a three-act play, or even a two-act play, until you've had some experience. A one-act play is enough of a challenge, and best of all, it can be as long or as short as you want. Even ten minutes. But to get your sealegs even before attempting a one-act play, you could start with a scene. As a result of that single scene, one of the characters may begin to take on a life of his own. If that happens, you can write additional scenes. After you've written several scenes, you can think about adding or subtracting until you have a one-act play. But don't pad; length isn't a determining factor in the quality of the play.

For this first scene, you will need to decide on a place and time, in addition to the characters. Keep it simple. Remember: This is not the movies or television. A simple set or even a bare stage with props and lighting can be extremely effective. The time can be the present, the past, or the future, but be consistent, and if you set it in the past, check historical facts.

Next, ask yourself some basic questions, particularly about your characters, since people are at the heart of your play. You might even want to write a character sketch of each one, or if you're basing your play on a real person, ask yourself what characteristics this person has that make him or her interesting. If a certain character is taken from

466

real life, you would do well to change specific details so you don't get hung up on facts that may inhibit the dramatic impact. Reality is only the springboard for a play. Whether you write a character sketch or not, ask yourself two things: What are these characters like, deep down? And what do they want from each other? Motivations should also emanate from the characters, not the writer.

It's also important to keep in mind that you *must* have conflict; without it, a play is stagnant. If characters don't *want,* nothing happens; all you'll have is conversation. You don't bring people together on a stage just to converse about the weather. And even if that were so, there would probably still be *hidden* needs. For example, somebody owes somebody else money, and the person decides to collect. If the other one refuses to pay, they have a conflict. In real life, they may simply argue or discuss their situation. On stage, somebody must take action. Maybe the person who's owed the money informs the debtor's husband or wife. Or maybe he decides to hire a third party to rough up his so-called friend. There must always be action and reaction. Don't resort to the obvious; try to be imaginative. A character may get stymied in his attempt to resolve a situation and then has to try something else. In this way, scenes continue to build, and each character maintains a certain momentum, going after what he wants until he's satisfied.

Don't let a character achieve his goal too easily. By making it diffi-cult—by putting your characters up against a wall—you will also gain insight into their individual characteristics. How would they respond in a certain situation? Would they resort to violence? Revenge? Bribery? Dirty dealing? Most of all, well-drawn characters are never passive. They must *want* something—and pursue it.

Stage directions

As far as stage directions are concerned, keep them as short as possible except, of course, for entrances and exits, and try not to give instructions to directors. Descriptions of characters should be included on the first page under "Cast of Characters." These descriptions should be brief, too, e.g., MARY JONES, *mid-thirties.* Stage descriptions should not be elaborate, and the way a line is spoken need not be defined; that's the director's job. The emotion and tone should be inherent in the dialogue itself. Therefore, leave out words such as *humorously, gently, furiously,* etc. Also, actors don't like to be told when to bang their fist on a table or when to pick up a prop or put it down. The rule about descriptions is, the sparer the better.

Dialogue or conversation?

Dialogue is not conversation. Small talk on stage is boring and doesn't lead anywhere. We hear a lot of small talk on television, but a stage play is not a half-hour situation-comedy, and there is no canned laughter in the theater. If you're writing a comedy, let the humor flow naturally and come from the characters. Try not to be glib. A play filled with superficial one-liners often lacks depth and will soon be forgotten.

Characters speak in a short, sometimes clipped manner. Watch out for those long monologues that cover half a page. Check to see if you have too many and if they're necessary or could be shortened. One way to break up a long speech is to have another character interrupt. In real life, people interrupt all the time.

Dialogue is a means of revealing what a specific character wants. Sometimes, however, characters try to get what they want in a devious or circuitous manner. There are instances where a character isn't in conflict with another person (or persons); he is in conflict with himself. This will prompt him to behave in a certain manner, resulting in specific actions and reactions.

Try out your dialogue by saying the lines out loud. Or get a group of people together and have each person take a part. Your "actors" will tell you if your lines are believable. They'll also tell you if your characters' motivations are credible.

Your characters should have different "voices." If they all sound alike, you need to go back and find each character's unique personality and way of speaking.

Movement is action

A play is *behavior*. As we watch a play, we are seeing characters behave toward each other in a certain manner. That behavior can be good, bad, immoral, loving, hateful, ad infinitum. A quick sketch can give the audience all the background they need. In Tennessee Williams's *The Glass Menagerie,* the protagonist, Tom, says, "My father fell in love with long distance." Then Williams *shows* us what happened to those left behind, and how they reacted. We see the characters in conflict with themselves and with each other. What makes a play compelling to an audience is the interaction between characters, not a long spiel of narrative information.

Where to begin . . .

This is easier said than done, but remember, scenes are your building blocks. You can add or take away or reverse scenes.

As far as the beginning is concerned, don't be afraid of false starts. Your first few attempts might be your way of getting to know your characters, their individual needs (or wants), and their secrets. You don't know someone intimately until you've lived with him a while. Keep in mind, too, that writing a scene or monologue can help you understand a character better. After you've achieved that goal, you can throw that scene away, but the insight gained from writing it will inform the rest of the work.

As a novice playwright, don't worry—at least in the beginning—about plotting or writing an outline. Concentrate on your characters; allow them to surprise you. Be a voyeur. Your characters may lead you places you never expected to go. Once you've learned to create characters that are interesting, not just stereotypes that will bore you and your audience, you can begin to shape those scenes you've written. By molding your material, scene by scene, you will begin to see your plot more fully. You will also be amazed at the twists and turns your story has taken. If you *listen* to your characters, they will take you with them.

. . . and when to stop

Once you've mastered characterization, writing dialogue, and shaping scenes into one-act plays, you can begin to work with the other elements that drive a play: plotting, tension, suspense, etc. But in the beginning, you should concentrate on your characters' wants; keep your dialogue from meandering; and deal honestly with your characters' emotions.

Remember, too, that people in plays don't always speak the King's English. Don't allow the dialogue to sound stiff, and don't attempt to make it poetic. Keep it straightforward, at least in the beginning. And make sure they don't all sound alike!

It's all a matter of combining the basic techniques and skills you've learned with imagination and determination.

❧ 99

AN OBJECT LESSON FOR PLAYWRIGHTS

By Jeffrey Sweet

THE EXPERIMENT GOES SOMETHING LIKE THIS: You place a sheet of paper over a magnet. Then you pour iron filings onto the paper. Almost instantly, the filings arrange themselves into a pattern. The pattern indicates the outline of the magnetic field.

You don't *see* the field. You see the *pattern* the filings make because of the *presence* of the field.

And yes, this does have something to do with writing plays.

By way of demonstration, here's a short scene that takes place in a suburban living room between a man and a teenage boy. As it begins, the boy is heading out the door when the man stops him by saying—

MAN: What's that in your hand?
BOY: Nothing.
MAN: Open it, please.
BOY: Dad—
MAN (*Firmly*): Open your hand. (*The boy opens it to reveal a key.*) Well?
BOY: I'm only going out for an hour.
MAN: Give it to me.
BOY: There's someplace I have to be.
MAN: You give that key to me now or I'll ground you another week. (*The man opens his hand. The boy hesitates, then puts the key into the man's hand.*)

Not a lot of dialogue. But look at how much we learn in this short passage: The man and boy are father and son. The father wields his authority with a firm hand. The son is not above trying to pull a fast one to get around his father's orders. The son wants to go out for an hour and he needs the key to do so, leading to a reasonable guess that the key is for the family car, which he is not supposed to be using. Additionally, from the father's threat to extend the son's grounding, we gather the son is currently being punished.

470

Just as the pattern the iron filings form indicates the magnetic field acting upon them, so the contest over the car key indicates the dramatic field in existence between the father and son.

To rephrase this into a general principle: You can often dramatize what is going on between your characters through the way they negotiate over an object.

This technique is particularly useful because it allows the audience to figure a good deal out for themselves, obviating the writer from having to go through tedious explanations. Notice, for instance, that in the scene above, the father doesn't say anything like, "I'm very disappointed in your behavior." Nor does the son say, "I'm upset about the way you restrict my movements." Both of these statements indeed would be accurate expressions of their feelings, but how much more effective it is to allow the viewer, by analyzing the negotiation over the key, to arrive at his or her own conclusions as to the nature of the relationship between the characters.

The great plays are filled with brilliant negotiations over objects. Whenever Shakespeare introduces an object onstage, you can be sure it will be used to strong dramatic effect. In fact, according to chroniclers of the time, it was with a scene containing the resourceful use of objects that Shakespeare first established his reputation as a hot young playwright.

Act I, Scene 4 of *Henry VI, Part 3*. The Duke of York, who with his sons has led a revolt against Henry VI, has been captured by Margaret, Henry VI's bloodthirsty queen. Margaret steps forward to taunt York. She shows him a handkerchief with a red stain on it, and informs him in a casual way that it was dipped in the blood of his youngest and much-beloved son Rutland, whom one of her followers has just killed. "And if thine eyes can water for his death," she says, "I give thee this to dry thy cheeks withal," and does indeed offer it to him. (In one particularly effective production I saw, York refused to take the handkerchief, so she draped it over his shoulder.) Continuing with her cruel sport, Margaret goes on to say, in essence, "So you want to be a king, hunh? Well, let's see how you'd look in a crown." And she makes a paper crown and puts it onto his head and remarks sarcastically, "Ay, marry, sir, now looks he like a king!"

Powerful stuff, the power of which derives largely from the *physicalization* of York's downfall and Margaret's sadism by the introduc-

471

tion of two imaginatively chosen objects. The paper crown is a particularly strong choice. Being paper, of course it doesn't have the value of the real crown, an adroit way of conveying the contempt with which Margaret views York's aspirations for the throne.

This use of objects is a technique Shakespeare employed to great advantage in his other plays. Think of Hamlet holding Yorick's skull. Think of the way Iago uses Desdemona's handkerchief (another handkerchief!) to goad Othello. Think of the counterfeit letter used to beguile Malvolio in *Twelfth Night*.

It is a technique that modern playwrights have also employed to great effect. Much of the action in Lillian Hellman's *The Little Foxes* revolves around a safe deposit box and bonds stolen from it. In Frederick Knott's *Wait Until Dark,* the villains' actions are motivated by the desire to get their hands on a doll stuffed with drugs. In William Gibson's *The Miracle Worker,* Annie Sullivan and Helen Keller go head to head over a variety of objects—a key, a plate of food, a pile of silverware and so on.

What's more, the *transformation* or *destruction* of an object introduced onstage can give a scene even greater impact.

At the beginning of the third act of Neil Simon's *The Odd Couple,* Oscar and Felix are feuding. Oscar sees that Felix is eating a plate of pasta and decides to spoil it by spraying it with an aerosol. Oscar makes a derisive remark about Felix's spaghetti. Felix laughs at Oscar's ignorance. "It's not spaghetti. It's linguini!" Whereupon, Oscar picks up the plate, goes to the kitchen door, hurls the food at an unseen wall and announces, "Now it's garbage!" The transformation of the food to garbage graphically dramatizes the disintegration of Felix and Oscar's relationship.

In Tennessee Williams's *The Glass Menagerie,* the shy Laura shows Jim, the gentleman caller, her favorite piece of a collection of glass figures, a unicorn. In an effort to raise her spirits, Jim begins to waltz with Laura, but, during the dance, they bump into the table on which the unicorn is sitting. It falls to the floor and its horn breaks off. Later, when she realizes that Jim's visit will not be the beginning of the relationship between them for which she had hoped (during the scene, he reveals he has recently become engaged), Laura gives him the damaged unicorn as a souvenir. The shattering of the unicorn gives particular emphasis to a scene concerned with the shattering of Laura's illusions.

This technique—the negotiation over objects—may be extended to the negotiation over things that are not physical objects. In *A Streetcar Named Desire,* Tennessee Williams has his principals clash memorably over a variety of props (Blanche's trunk, clothes and letters, the deed to Belle Reve, etc.), but they also contest other elements.

At one point, for instance, Blanche turns on the radio. Stanley, in the middle of a poker game with friends, finds the music distracting and orders Blanche to turn it off. A little later, when she turns it on again, Stanley grabs the radio and tosses it out the window. Clearly, then, one can negotiate over sound. (Certainly, as anyone who has had to endure the sound of a boom box on the street, one can negotiate over volume.)

Shortly after she arrives, Blanche covers the naked lightbulbs in Stanley and Stella's apartment with Chinese lanterns. Late in the play, when Mitch confronts her with the truth about her past, he yanks off the lanterns so as to be able to see her clearly. A negotiation over light. (See also the battles between the father and sons over the use of light in Eugene O'Neill's *Long Day's Journey Into Night.*)

In the climactic confrontation, Blanche, feeling threatened by Stanley, wants to walk past him and asks him to move out of her way. He insists she has plenty of room to get by and then backs her into the bedroom. A negotiation over space. (Much of *The Odd Couple,* too, is about the negotiation over space, as two men of different habits and natures try to share one apartment.)

So, characters may negotiate over objects, over sound, over light and over space. Also over time, over temperature, over elevation—over anything, in fact, to which a character might attach value.

Including *people.* Returning to *Streetcar,* notice that Blanche and Stanley carry on a play-long struggle over Stella, and Stanley wins. For that matter, *any* play concerning a triangle, romantic or otherwise, inevitably involves two parties negotiating over the third.

On a more abstract level, the negotiation may be over ideas. Much of David Mamet's *American Buffalo* concerns Teach and Donny arguing over how to steal a set of rare coins from an apartment. Their differing approaches to the plan go a long way toward establishing the differences in their characters and highlighting the ethical issues which are the heart of this remarkable work. And so, too, virtually anything George Bernard Shaw wrote. He almost always defines his characters on the basis of their conflicting opinions on intellectual matters.

Yes, what I'm describing is a technical device. But it's no artificial

473

trick. One of the reasons this technique works so well onstage is that it reflects the way people behave in real life.

For we are constantly negotiating with each other. When two people on a date debate whether to see a kung fu movie or a revival of *Singing in the Rain,* they're revealing their differing tastes through the arguments they advance in support of their respective choices. When children fight over who's going to sleep in the upper bunk, the resolution of their controversy tells a great deal about which child has what powers and prerogatives. When a wife upbraids her husband for constantly leaving the cap off the tube of toothpaste, one may quickly glean something of the health of their marriage.

To bring such negotiations to the stage is to reveal to the audience the ways people use whatever tools are at hand to pursue their objectives with each other. It is to show how, in contests over such seemingly mundane objects as a key, a credit card, a handkerchief, or an alarm clock, human beings often inadvertently reveal the deeper issues between them.

❧ 100

CONFLICT: THE HEARTBEAT OF A PLAY

BY D. R. ANDERSEN

EVERY PLAYWRIGHT is a Dr. Frankenstein trying to breathe life into a page for the stage. In a good play, the heartbeat must be thundering. And the heartbeat of a play is conflict.

Simply put, conflict exists when a character wants something and can't get it. Conflict may sometimes be internal—as when a character struggles to choose between or among opposing desires. For example, Alma in Tennessee Williams's *Summer and Smoke* longs to yield to her sexual yearnings but is prevented by the repressed and conventional side of her nature.

Conflict in drama may also be external—as when a character struggles against another *character* (Oscar and Felix in Neil Simon's *The Odd Couple*); against *society* (Nora in Ibsen's *A Doll's House*); against *nature* (the mountain climbers in Patrick Meyers' *K2*); or against *fate* (Sophocles' *Oedipus*).

In most plays, the conflict is a combination of internal and external struggles. In fact, internal conflict is often externalized for dramatic impact. In Philip Barry's *Holiday,* for instance, the hero's inner dilemma is outwardly expressed in his attraction to two sisters—one who represents the safe but boring world of convention, and the other who is a symbol of the uncertain but exciting life of adventure.

Granted that a conflict may be internal or external; that a character may be in conflict with another character, society, nature or fate; and that most plays are a combination of internal and external conflict, many plays that have these basic elements of conflict do not have a thundering heartbeat. Why? These plays lack one, some, or all of the five magic ingredients of rousing, attention-grabbing-and-holding conflict.

The five magic ingredients

I. *Never let your audience forget what your protagonist wants.*

You can achieve this in a number of ways. Often the protagonist or another character states and periodically restates in dialogue what is at stake. Or in some plays, he explains what he wants directly to the audience in the form of a monologue. As you read or watch plays you admire, take note of the obvious and ingenious techniques playwrights use to tell the reader or audience what the characters' goals are.

Sometimes the method used to keep your audience alerted to your protagonist's goal/concern/need is a direct reflection of the protagonist's personality. In the following three short passages from my play *Graduation Day,*[1] a mother and father with very traditional values have a conversation while waiting to meet their rebellious daughter, who has told them she has a big surprise. Notice how the protagonist—Mrs. Whittaker—nervously and comically manipulates the conversation, reminding her husband and the audience of her concern for her daughter Jane:

MRS. WHITTAKER
(Knocking on the door)
Jane. Jane. It's Mom and Dad.
(Pause)
No answer. What should we do, Tom?
MR. WHITTAKER
Let's go in.
MRS. WHITTAKER
Suppose we find Jane in a compromising situation?
MR. WHITTAKER
Nobody at Smith College has ever been found in a compromising situation.

* * *

MRS. WHITTAKER
Tom, you know, this was my freshman room.
MR. WHITTAKER
Of course, I know.
MRS. WHITTAKER
And Jane's. It was Jane's freshman room too, Tom. Remember?

* * *

MR. WHITTAKER
Mary, you get in the craziest moods at these reunions. I may never bring you back again.

---

1. First produced by Playwrights Horizons in New York, starring Polly Holliday.

MRS. WHITTAKER

Do you know why you fell in love with me, Tom?

MR. WHITTAKER

I fell in love with you the minute I saw you eat pancakes.

MRS. WHITTAKER

That's a sound basis for a relationship. Tom, where do you suppose Jane is? And more frightening, what do you suppose she wants to tell us? She said just enough on the phone to suggest that she's going to be bringing a boy here for us to meet.

MR. WHITTAKER

A man, Mary, a man.

MRS. WHITTAKER

Oh, God. I never even considered that possibility. Suppose Jane brings a fiancé—our age—like Pia Zadora did.

MR. WHITTAKER

Don't you want Jane to live her own life?

MRS. WHITTAKER

No. Especially not her own life. Practically anyone else's. But not her own.

MR. WHITTAKER

What *do* you want for Jane?

MRS. WHITTAKER

I don't see why Jane can't fall in love with a plain Harvard Business School student, let's say. Someone who'll be steady and dependable.

And so it goes. The protagonist discusses a number of topics, but she inevitably leads the conversation back to her overriding concern. Mrs. Whittaker's desire to see her daughter do the right thing and marry wisely is always uppermost in the mind and conversation of the character.

In this one act, a comic effect is achieved by having Mrs. Whittaker insistently remind the audience what she wants. Once you have clearly established what a character wants, you can then write powerful and often hilarious scenes in which the audience, already knowing the character's point of view, is able to anticipate his reaction.

II. *Show your protagonist struggling to achieve what he wants.*

This principle is, of course, the basic writing advice to *show*, not tell, and it was a major concern for me when I was writing *The House Where I Was Born*.[2]

The plot: A young man, Leo, has returned from the Vietnam War, a psychosomatic mute because of the atrocities he witnessed. He comes back to a crumbling old house in a decaying suburb, a home populated

---

2. First produced by Playwrights Horizons in New York.

477

by a callous stepfather; a mother who survives on aphorisms and by bending reality to diminish her despair; a half-crazy aunt; and a grandfather who refuses to buckle under to the pressures from his family to sell the home.

I set out to dramatize Leo's painful battle to free himself of memories of the war and to begin a new life. However, each time I worked on the scene in the play when Leo first comes home, his dialogue seemed to trivialize his emotions.

Then it occurred to me that Leo should not speak at all during the first act; that his inability to speak would *show* an audience his suffering and pain far better than his words could.

At the end of the third act, when Leo regains some hope, some strength to go on, every speech I wrote for him also rang false. The problem, I eventually realized, was that as playwright, I was *telling* the audience that a change had taken place, instead of *showing* the change as it took place.

In the final draft, I solved this dramatic problem by having Leo, who had loved music all his life, sit down at the piano and begin playing and singing Christmas carols while his surprised and relieved family joined in.

First silence, then singing, served my play better than mere telling.

III. *Create honest, understandable, and striking obstacles against which your protagonist must struggle.*

Many plays fail because their characters' problems seem too easily solved. I wrestled with this issue when I was writing *Oh Promise Me!*[3] a play that takes place in a private boarding house for the elderly. The play's original title was *Mr. Farner Wants a Double Bed*. The plot involved the attempt of an elderly man and woman—an unmarried couple—to share a double bed in a rooming house run by a repressed and oppressive owner. I wanted to explore contemporary attitudes toward the elderly, particularly as they concerned sexuality.

The more I played with the idea, the more I repeatedly heard an inner voice saying, "Chances are the couple could find some place to live where nobody cared if they were married or not." This voice—like the

---

3. Winner of the Jane Chambers Memorial Playwriting Award.

audience watching a play without an honest, understandable, convincing obstacle for the protagonist—kept saying, "So what?"

The writer's response: "Suppose, instead of a man and a woman, the couple is two men." Here was a real obstacle: Two elderly, gay men, growing feeble, want to sleep together in a double bed under the roof of an unsympathetic and unyielding landlord.

Suddenly, the play was off and running.

IV. *In the final scene or scenes, make sure your protagonist achieves what he wants; comes to understand that there is something else he wants; or accepts (defiantly, humbly, etc.) that he cannot have what he wants.*

If we spend time in the theater watching a character battle for something, we want to know the outcome—whatever it may be.

In my psychological thriller *Trick or Treat*,[4] Kate, a writer in her forties, has been badly burned in a love affair and is unable to decide whether to accept or reject a new relationship. She is involved at present with Toby, a younger man, but—as the following dialogue reveals—she insists on keeping him at a cool distance.

KATE
That does it, Toby. We're getting out of this place.
TOBY
Okay. Tomorrow we'll check into the local Howard Johnson's.
KATE
I want to go home—to New York—to my own apartment.
TOBY
Okay. Okay. If you insist. Besides, Howard Johnson's is not to be entered into lightly.
KATE
Huh?
TOBY
It's an old college rule. You'd never shell out for a room at Howard Johnson's—unless you were *very* serious about the girl.
KATE
I'll remember that. The day I agree to check into a Howard Johnson's—you'll know I've made a serious commitment to our relationship.

In the course of the play, Kate faces a number of trials—including a threat to her life—as she tries to expose the fraudulent leader of a

---

4. First produced by the Main Street Theater, New York, New York.

religious cult. Through these trials—with Toby by her side—Kate comes to realize that she's ready to forget the past and give herself over to a new relationship. This critical decision is humorously expressed in the last seconds of the play:

KATE

Do you love me, Toby?

TOBY

Yes, I do. I found that out tonight . . . when I thought I might be losing you forever. Do you love me?

KATE

Yes. And I can prove it.

TOBY

How?

KATE

Take me to Howard Johnson's—please! Take me to Howard Johnson's!

The curtain falls and the audience knows that the heroine has made an unequivocal decision.

V. *Make sure that the audience ultimately sympathizes with the protagonist's yearning to achieve his goal, however outlandish his behavior.*

This may be the most important of the five magic ingredients of conflict. It may also be the most elusive. To oversimplify, in a good play, the protagonist must be very likable and/or have a goal that is universal.

In the plays I've had produced, one character seems to win the sympathy of the audience hands down. In my romantic comedy *Funny Valentines,*[5] Andy Robbins, a writer of children's books, is that character. Andy is sloppy, disorganized, and easily distracted, and—this is his likable trait—he's painfully aware of his shortcomings and admits them openly. Here's Andy speaking for himself:

ANDY

Judging by my appearance, you might take me to be a complete physical and emotional wreck. Well, I can't deny it. And it's gotten worse—much worse—since Ellen left. You know that's true.

---

5. Published by Samuel French; winner of the Cummings/Taylor Playwriting Award; produced in Canada under the title *Drôles de Valentins*.

480

Andy is willing to admit his failings to old friends and strangers alike. Here he's talking to an attractive young woman he's just met.

ANDY
You don't have to be consoling just because I haven't finished a book lately. I won't burst into tears or create a scene. No. I lied. I might burst into tears—I'm warning you.

ZAN
I didn't mean to imply . . . (*She laughs.*)

ANDY
Why are you laughing?

ZAN
You stapled your shirt.

ANDY
What's so odd about that? Millions of derelicts do it every day.

ZAN
And your glasses are wired together with a pipe cleaner.

ANDY
I didn't think twine would be as attractive.

In addition to liking Andy, audiences seem to sympathize with his goal of wanting to grow up and get back together with his collaborator and ex-wife, Ellen.

Whether you're wondering where to find an idea for a one-act play or beginning to refine the rough draft of a new full-length work or starting rehearsals of one of your plays, take your cue from the five magic ingredients of conflict. Whatever your experience as a playwright and whatever your current project, understanding the nature of dramatic conflict and how to achieve it will prove invaluable at every point in the writing and staging process.

* * *

Five exercises for creating dramatic conflict

Try these exercises to develop your skill in handling conflict.

1. Choose five plays you like. Summarize each in one sentence, stating what the protagonist wants. For example, Hamlet wants to avenge his father's murder.
2. Write one page of dialogue in which character A asks character B to do something that character B doesn't want to do. Have character A

make a request in three different ways, each showing a different emotion—guilt, enthusiasm, humility, anger.

3. Write a speech in which a character talks to another character and conveys what he wants without explicitly stating his goal.

4. Choose a famous play you enjoy. Rewrite the last page or two so that the outcome of the conflict for the protagonist is entirely different from the original.

5. Flip through today's newspaper until you find a story about a person—famous or unknown—who interests you. Then summarize the story in one sentence, stating what the person wants. For example: X wants to save an endangered species of bird. Next list the obstacles the person is facing in trying to get what he wants:

   • A developer wants to build a shopping mall where the remaining members of the endangered species live.

   • Pollution from a nearby factory is threatening the birds' food supply.

Finally, write several short scenes in which X (the protagonist) confronts the people (the antagonists) who represent the cause of each obstacle. (In this example, the antagonist would be the developer or the owner of the factory.) Decide which of the scenes you've written is the most dramatically satisfying. Identify the reasons you think it is the best scene.

WHERE TO SELL

Where to Sell

This year's edition of *The Writer's Handbook* includes a completely revised and updated list of free-lance markets, and writers at all levels of experience should be encouraged by the number and wide variety of opportunities available to them. Editors, publishers, and producers rely on free lancers for a wide range of material, from articles and fiction to play scripts, op-ed pieces, how-tos, and children's books, and they are very receptive to the work of newcomers.

The field of specialized publications, including travel, city and regional magazines, and those covering such areas as health, science, consumer issues, sports, and hobbies and crafts, remains one of the best markets for beginning free lancers. Editors of these magazines are in constant need of authoritative articles (for which the payment is usually quite high), and writers with experience in and enthusiasm for a particular field, whether it's gardening, woodworking, bicycling, stamp collecting, bridge, or car repair, will find their knowledge particularly helpful, as there is usually at least one publication devoted to every one of these areas. Such interests and activities can generate more than one article if a different angle is used for each magazine and the writer keeps the audience and editorial content firmly in mind.

The market for technical, computer, health, and personal finance writing is also very strong, with articles on these topics appearing in almost every publication on the newsstands today. For these subjects, editors are looking for writers who can translate technical material into lively, readable prose, often the most important factor in determining a sale.

While some of the more established markets may seem difficult to break into, especially for the beginner, there are thousands of lesser-known publications where editors will consider submissions from first-time free lancers. City and regional publications offer some of the best opportunities, since these editors generally like to work with local writers and often use a wide variety of material, from features to fillers. Many newspapers accept op-ed pieces, and are most receptive to pieces on topics not covered by syndicated columnists (politics, economics, and foreign affairs); pieces with a regional slant are particularly welcome here.

It is important for writers to keep in mind the number of opportunities that exist for nonfiction, because the paying markets for fiction are somewhat limited. Many general-interest and women's magazines do publish short stories; however, beginners will find these markets extremely competitive, with their work being judged against that of experienced professionals. We highly recommend that new writers look into the small, literary, and college publications, which always welcome the work of talented beginners. Payment usually is made only in copies, but publication in literary journals can lead to recognition by editors of larger circulation magazines, who often look to the smaller publications for new talent. A growing number of regional, specialized, and Sunday magazines use short stories and are particularly interested in local writers.

The market for poetry in general-interest magazines continues to be tight, and the advice for poets, as for fiction writers, is to try to get established and build up a list of publishing credits by submitting material to literary journals. Poets should look also to local newspapers, which often use verse, especially if it is related to holidays or other special occasions.

Community, regional, and civic theaters and college dramatic groups offer new playwrights the best opportunities for staged production in this competitive market. Indeed, many of today's well-known playwrights received their first recognition in regional theaters, and aspiring writers who can get their work produced by one of these have taken a significant step toward breaking into this field. In addition to producing plays and giving dramatic readings, many theaters also sponsor competitions or new play festivals.

As for the television market, unfortunately it is inaccessible without an agent, and most writers break into it only after a careful study of the medium and a long apprenticeship.

While the book publishing field remains competitive, beginners should be especially encouraged by the many first novels published over the past few years, with more editors than ever before seeking out new works of fiction. An increasing number of publishers are broadening their nonfiction lines as well, and editors at many hardcover and paperback houses are on the lookout for new authors, especially those with a knowledge of or training in a particular field. Writers of juvenile and young adult books will be pleased to hear that in response to a growing audience of young readers and increased sales, many publishers are greatly expanding their lists of children's books.

Small presses across the country continue to flourish—in fact, they are currently publishing more books by name authors and more books on mainstream subjects, than at any other time in recent years—offering writers an attractive alternative for their manuscripts.

All information in these lists concerning the needs and requirements of magazines, book publishing companies, and theaters comes directly from the editors, publishers, and directors, but editors move and addresses change, as do requirements. No published listing can give as clear a picture of editorial needs and tastes as a careful study of several issues of a magazine, and writers should never submit material without first thoroughly researching the prospective market. If a magazine is not available in the local library, write directly to the editor for a sample copy (often sent free or at a small cost). Contact the publicity department of a book publisher for an up-to-date catalogue or a theater for a current schedule. Many companies also offer a formal set of writers guidelines, available for an SASE upon request.

ARTICLE MARKETS

The magazines in the following list are in the market for free-lance articles of many types. Unless otherwise stated in these listings, a writer should submit a query first, including a brief description of the proposed article and any relevant qualifications or credits. A few editors want to see samples of published work, if available. Manuscripts must be typed double-space on good white bond paper (8 ½ × 11), with name, address, and telephone number at the top left- or right-hand corner of the paper. Do not use erasable or onion skin paper, since it is difficult to work with, and always keep a copy of the manuscript, in case it is lost in the mail. Submit photos or slides *only* if the editor has specifically requested them. A self-addressed envelope with sufficient postage to cover the return of the manuscript or the answer to a query should accompany all submissions. Response time may vary from two to eight weeks, depending on the size of the magazine and the volume of mail it receives. If an editor doesn't respond within what seems to be a reasonable amount of time, it's perfectly acceptable to send a polite inquiry. Many publications have writers guidelines, outlining their editorial requirements and submission procedures; these can be obtained by sending a self-addressed, stamped envelope (SASE) to the editor. Also, be sure to ask for a sample copy: Editors indicate the most consistent mistake free lancers make is failing to study several issues of the magazine to which they are submitting material.

GENERAL-INTEREST PUBLICATIONS

ACCENT/TRAVELOG—P.O. Box 10010, Ogden, UT 84409. Caroll Shreeve, V.P. of Pub. Articles, 1,200 words, about travel, having fun, fitness, sightseeing, the ordinary and the usual in foreign and domestic destinations. "Avoid budget approaches and emphasize the use of travel professionals." Must include excellent transparencies. Queries required. Guidelines with SASE. Pays 15¢ a word, $35 for photos, $50 for cover photo, on acceptance.

ALLIED PUBLICATIONS—1776 Lake Worth Rd., Lake Worth, FL 33460. Articles, to 1,500 words: business, management, fashion, careers, travel (foreign and domestic), beauty, hairstyling, general interest, home, and family. Photos, cartoons, humor. Write for terms of payment. Guidelines. Publishes *Trip & Tour, Modern Office, Woman Beautiful, Home, Exhibit*.

AMERICAN HERITAGE—60 Fifth Ave., New York, NY 10011. Richard F. Snow, Ed. Articles, 750 to 5,000 words, on U.S. history and background of American life and culture from the beginning to recent times. No fiction. Pays $300 to $1,500, on acceptance. Query. SASE.

AMERICAN HISTORY ILLUSTRATED—6405 Flank Dr., P.O. Box 8200, Harrisburg, PA 17105. Well-researched articles, 3,000 to 5,000 words. Style should be popular, not scholarly. No travelogues, fiction, or puzzles. Pays $200 to $1,000, on acceptance. Query.

THE AMERICAN LEGION MAGAZINE—Box 1055, Indianapolis, IN

46206. Daniel S. Wheeler, Ed.-in-Chief. Articles, 750 to 1,800 words, on current world affairs, public policy, and subjects of contemporary interest. Pays $100 to $1,000, on acceptance. Query.

AMERICAN VISIONS, THE MAGAZINE OF AFRO-AMERICAN CULTURE—The Carter G. Woodson House, 1538 9th St. N.W., Washington, DC 20001. Joanne Harris, Ed. Articles, 1,500 to 3,000 words, and columns, 750 to 2,000 words, on African-American history and culture with a focus on the arts. Pays from $100 to $1,000, on publication. Query first.

AMERICAS—OAS, 19th and Constitution Ave. N.W., Washington, DC 20006. Rebecca Read Medrano, Ed. Features, 2,500 to 5,000 words, on Latin America and the Caribbean. Wide focus: anthropology, the arts, travel, science, and development. "We prefer stories that can be well illustrated." No political material. Query. Pays from $250, on publication.

AMTRAK EXPRESS—1301 Carolina St., Greensboro, NC 27401. Melinda L. Stovall, Ed. Published for Amtrak passengers. Articles, 1,500 to 1,800 words, on sports and leisure, business, travel within Amtrak coverage area, health, American innovation, and rail experiences. "The magazine highlights life in the United States and features aspects of train travel across the country and throughout history. Articles should be well-researched, current, lively, informative, and balanced." No fiction or reprints. Pays $350 to $500, on acceptance. Query with SASE.

THE ATLANTIC—745 Boylston St., Boston, MA 02116. William Whitworth, Ed. Non-polemic, meticulously researched articles on public issues, politics, social sciences, education, business, literature, and the arts. Ideal length: 3,000 to 6,000 words, though short pieces (1,000 to 2,000 words) are also welcome and longer text pieces will be considered. Pays excellent rates.

BETTER HOMES AND GARDENS—1716 Locust St., Des Moines, IA 50336. David Jordan, Ed. Articles, to 2,000 words, on home and family entertainment, building, decorating, food, money management, health, travel, pets, environment, and cars. Pays top rates, on acceptance. Query.

BON APPETIT—5900 Wilshire Blvd., Los Angeles, CA 90036. Barbara Fairchild, Exec. Ed. Articles on fine cooking (menu format or single focus), cooking classes, and gastronomically focused travel. Query with samples of published work. Pays varying rates, on acceptance.

BOSTONIA—10 Lenox St., Brookline, MA 02146. Keith Botsford, Ed. Articles, to 3,000 words, on politics, literature, music, art, travel, food, and wine. Pays $150 to $1,000, on acceptance. Queries required.

CAPPER'S—616 Jefferson St., Topeka, KS 66607–1188. Nancy Peavler, Ed. Articles, 300 to 500 words: human-interest, personal experience for women's section, historical. Pays varying rates, on publication.

CAR AUDIO AND ELECTRONICS—21700 Oxnard St., Woodland Hills, CA 91367. Bill Neill, Ed. Features, 1,000 to 2,000 words, on electronic products for the car: audio systems, security systems, CBs, radar detectors, cellular telephones, etc. Pays $300 to $1,000, on acceptance.

CHATELAINE—MacLean Hunter Bldg., 777 Bay St., Toronto, Ont., Canada M5W 1A7. Elizabeth Parr, Sr. Ed. Articles, 1,500 to 3,500 words, for Canadian women, on current issues, personalities, medicine, psychology, etc., covering all aspects of Canadian life. "Upfront" columns, 500 words, on relationships, health, nutrition, fitness, parenting. Pays from $350 for columns, from $1,250 for features, on acceptance.

THE CHRISTIAN SCIENCE MONITOR—One Norway St., Boston, MA 02115. David Holmstrom, Feature Ed. Articles, 800 words, on arts, education, food, sports, science, and lifestyle; interviews, literary essays for "Home Forum" page; guest columns for "Opinion Page." Pay varies, on acceptance. Original material only.

COLUMBIA—1 Columbus Plaza, New Haven, CT 06507–0901. Richard McMunn, Ed. Journal of the Knights of Columbus. Articles, 500 to 1,500 words, on a wide variety of topics of interest to K. of C. members, their families, and the Catholic layman: current events, religion, education, art, etc. Must include substantial quotes from a variety of sources and be illustrated with color photos. Pays $250 to $500, including art, on acceptance.

THE COMPASS—Grand Central Towers, 230 E. 44th St., Suite 14B, New York, NY 10017. J.A. Randall, Ed. True stories, to 2,500 words, on the sea, sea trades, and aviation. Pays to $600, on acceptance. Query with SASE.

CONNOISSEUR—Hearst Corp., 1790 Broadway, 18th Fl., New York, NY 10019. Robert Sabat, Man Ed. Articles for readers "interested in learning about excellence in all areas of art." Topics include fine, decorative, and performing arts, architecture and design, food, fashion, and travel; include pertinent service data. Length varies; query required.

CONSUMERS DIGEST—5705 N. Lincoln Ave., Chicago, IL 60659. John Manos, Ed. Articles, 500 to 3,000 words, on subjects of interest to consumers: products and services, automobiles, health, fitness, consumer legal affairs, and personal money management. Photos. Pays from 35¢ to 50¢ a word, extra for photos, on publication. Buys all rights. Query with resumé and published clips.

COSMOPOLITAN—224 W. 57th St., New York, NY 10019. Helen Gurley Brown, Ed. Guy Flatley, Man. Ed. Articles, to 3,000 words, and features, 500 to 2,000 words, on issues affecting young career women. Query.

COUNTRY—5400 S. 60th, Greendale, WI 53129. Dan Matel, Asst. Ed. People-centered articles, 500 to 1,000 words, for a rural audience. (No articles on farm production techniques.) Fillers, 50 to 200 words. Taboos: tobacco, liquor, and sex. Pays $75 to $150, on acceptance. Query.

COUNTRY JOURNAL—P.O. Box 8200, Harrisburg, PA 17105. Peter V. Fossel, Ed. Articles, 2,500 to 3,000 words, for country and small-town residents; practical, informative pieces, essays, humor, and reports on contemporary rural life. Pays $500 to $1,500, on acceptance. Send SASE for guidelines. Query with SASE.

DALLAS LIFE MAGAZINE—*The Dallas Morning News*, Communications Center, P.O. Box 655237, Dallas, TX 75265. Mike Maza, Man. Ed. Well-researched articles and profiles, 1,000 to 3,000 words, on contemporary issues, personalities, on subjects of strictly Dallas-related interest. Pays from 20¢ a word, on acceptance. Query.

DAWN—628 N. Eutaw, Baltimore, MD 21201. Charles Brown, Ed. Illustrated feature articles, 750 to 1,000 words, on subjects of interest to black families. Pays $100, on publication. Query.

THE ELKS MAGAZINE—425 W. Diversey Parkway, Chicago, IL 60614. Fred D. Oakes, Ed. Articles, 3,000 words, on business, sports, and topics of current interest, for non-urban audience with above-average income. Informative or humorous pieces, to 2,500 words. Pays $150 to $500 for articles, on acceptance. Query.

EMERGE—599 Broadway, 12th Floor, New York, NY 10012. Wilmer Ames, Pub./Ed.-in-Chief. Feature articles, 1,500 to 2,000 words, of interest to middle-class black Americans. Also, Q-and-A interviews, 2,000 words, with 750 word introductions; international pieces, 500 to 1,000 words, from an Afrocentric perspective; short pieces, 750 words, on health, local hero; and "Dateline U.S.A." pieces, 150 to 300 words, on news stories and events around the country. Query. Pays from 50¢ a word, after acceptance.

ESQUIRE—1790 Broadway, New York, NY 10019. Terry McDonell, Ed.-in-Chief. David Hirshey, Articles Ed. Articles, 2,500 to 4,000 words, for intelligent adult audience. Pay varies, on acceptance. Query with published clips; complete manuscripts from unpublished writers. SASE required.

ESSENCE—1500 Broadway, New York, NY 10036. Susan L. Taylor, Ed.-in-Chief. Provocative articles, 1,500 to 2,500 words, about black women in America today: self-help, how-to pieces, business and finance, health, celebrity profiles, and political issues. Short items, 300 to 750 words, on work, parenting, and health. Query required; send complete manuscript only for "Brothers," and "Interiors" columns. Pays varying rates, on acceptance.

EXHIBIT—See *Allied Publications*.

FAMILY CIRCLE—110 Fifth Ave., New York, NY 10011. Susan Ungaro, Exec. Ed. Ellen Stoianoff, Sr. Ed., Nancy Josephson, Health Ed. Articles, to 2,500 words, on "women who have made a difference," marriage, family, and child-rearing issues; consumer affairs, health and fitness, humor and personal opinion essays. Query required. Pays $1 a word, on acceptance.

FORUM, THE INTERNATIONAL JOURNAL ON HUMAN RELATIONS—1965 Broadway, New York, NY 10023–5965. True, first-person erotic adventures. Pays $800 to $1,000, on acceptance. Send manuscript or proposal.

GLAMOUR—350 Madison Ave., New York, NY 10017. Ruth Whitney, Ed.-in-Chief. Susan Pelzer, Art. Ed. Editorial approach is "how-to" for women, 18 to 35. Articles on careers, health, psychology, interpersonal relationships, etc. Fashion, health, and beauty material staff-written. Pays from $1,000 for 1,500- to 2,000-word articles, from $1,500 for longer pieces, on acceptance.

GLOBE—5401 N.W. Broken Sound Blvd., Boca Raton, FL 33487. Robert Taylor, Man. Ed. Factual articles, 500 to 1,000 words, with photos: exposés, celebrity interviews, consumer and human-interest pieces. Pays $50 to $1,500.

GOLDEN YEARS—P.O. Box 537, Melbourne, FL 32902–0537. Carol Brenner Hittner, Ed. Bimonthly for people over the age of 50. Pieces on unique hobbies, beauty and fashion, sports, and travel, 600 words. Pays 10¢ a word, on publication.

GOOD HOUSEKEEPING—959 Eighth Ave., New York, NY 10019. Joan Thursh, Articles Ed. Personal-experience articles, 2,500 words, on a unique or trend-setting event; family relationships; personal medical pieces dealing with an unusual illness, treatment, and result; personal problems and how they were solved. Short essays, 750 to 1,000 words, on family life or relationships. Pays top rates, on acceptance. Queries preferred. Guidelines.

GOOD READING MAGAZINE—Litchfield, IL 62056. Peggy Kuethe, Assoc. Ed. Articles, 500 to 1,000 words, with B&W photos, on current subjects of general interest: travel, business, personal experiences, relationships. Pays $10 to $100.

GRIT—208 W. Third St., Williamsport, PA 17701. Alvin Elmer, Assoc. Ed. Articles, to 800 words, with photos, on interesting people, communities, jobs, recreation, families, and coping. Pays 15¢ a word, extra for photos, on acceptance.

HARPER'S MAGAZINE—666 Broadway, New York, NY 10012. Address Editor. Articles, 2,000 to 5,000 words. Query with SASE.

HG: HOUSE & GARDEN—350 Madison Ave., New York, NY 10017. Priscilla Flood, Man. Ed. Michael Boodro, Articles Ed. Articles on decorating, architecture, gardens, the arts. Rarely buys unsolicited manuscripts. Query.

HISTORIC PRESERVATION—1785 Massachusetts Ave. N.W., Washington, DC 20036. Anne Elizabeth Powell, Ed. Lively feature articles from published writers, 1,500 to 4,000 words, on residential restoration, preservation issues, and people involved in preserving America's heritage. High-quality photos. Pays $300 to $1,000, extra for photos, on acceptance. Query.

HOME—See *Allied Publications*.

HOUSE BEAUTIFUL—1700 Broadway, New York, NY 10019. Elaine Greene, Ed. Articles related to the home. Pieces on architecture, design, travel, and gardening; mostly staff-written. Pays varying rates, on acceptance. Query with detailed outline. Guidelines.

INQUIRER MAGAZINE—*Philadelphia Inquirer*, P.O. Box 8263, 400 N. Broad St., Philadelphia, PA 19101. Fred Mann, Ed. Local-interest features, 500 to 7,000 words. Profiles of national figures in politics, entertainment, etc. Pays varying rates, on publication. Query.

INSIDE MAGAZINE—226 S. 16th St., Philadelphia, PA 19102-3392. Jane Biberman, Ed. Articles, 1,500 to 3,000 words, on Jewish issues, health, finance, and the arts. Queries required; send clips if available. Pays $75 to $600, within four weeks of acceptance.

KEY HORIZONS—Gateway Plaza, 950 N. Meridian, Suite 1200, Indianapolis, IN 46204. Joan Todd, Man. Ed. Quarterly. General-interest articles and department pieces, 300 to 3,000 words, for readers ages 55 and older living in Indiana and western Pennsylvania. Topics include personal finance, wellness, cooking, nostalgia, family trends, and travel. Pays $75 to $500, $25 to $50 for photos, on publication.

KIWANIS—3636 Woodview Trace, Indianapolis, IN 46268. Chuck Jonak, Exec. Ed. Articles, 2,500 to 3,000 words, on home; family; international issues; the social, health, and emotional needs of youth (especially under age six); career and community concerns of business and professional people. No travel pieces, interviews, profiles. Pays $400 to $1,000, on acceptance. Query. Guidelines.

LADIES' HOME JOURNAL—100 Park Ave., New York, NY 10017. Lynn Langway, Exec. Ed. Jane Farrell, Articles Ed. Articles on contemporary subjects of interest to women. Query required. Not responsible for unsolicited manuscripts.

LISTEN MAGAZINE—Pacific Press Pub. Assn., P.O. Box 7000, Boise, ID 83707. Lincoln Steed, Ed. Articles, 1,200 to 1,500 words, on problems of alcohol and drug abuse, for teenagers; personality profiles. Photos. Pays 5¢ to 7¢ a word, extra for photos, on acceptance. Query. Guidelines.

MCCALL'S—110 Fifth Ave., New York, NY 10011. Kate White, Ed.-in-Chief. Andrea Thompson, Articles Ed. Interesting, unusual, and topical narratives, reports on social trends relating to women of all ages, 1,000 to 3,000 words. Human-interest stories. Pays top rates, on acceptance.

MADEMOISELLE—350 Madison Ave., New York, NY 10017. Liz Logan, Articles Ed. Articles, 1,500 to 2,000 words, on subjects of interest to single, working women in ther 20s. Pays from $1,750 for full-length articles, on acceptance. Query.

MD MAGAZINE—10 Astor Pl., New York, NY 10003. Helen Smith, Ed.

Articles, 750 to 2,500 words, for doctors, on the arts, history, other aspects of culture; fresh angle required. Pays 50¢ to $1 per word, on publication. Query by mail only.

METROPOLITAN HOME—750 Third Ave., New York, NY 10017. Service and informational articles for residents of houses, co-ops, lofts, and condominiums, on real estate, equity, wine and spirits, collecting, trends, travel, etc. Interior design and home furnishing articles with emphasis on lifestyle. Pay varies. Query.

MODERN MATURITY—3200 E. Carson St., Lakewood, CA 90712. J. Henry Fenwick, Ed. Articles, to 2,000 words, on careers, workplace, human interest, living, finance, relationships, and consumerism, for persons over 50. Photos. Pays $500 to $2,500, extra for photos, on acceptance. Query first.

MODERN OFFICE—See *Allied Publications.*

THE MOTHER EARTH NEWS—24 E. 23rd St., 5th Fl., New York, NY 10010. Owen Lipstein, Ed. Articles for rural and urban readers: home improvements, how-tos, indoor and outdoor gardening, family pastimes, self-help, health, food, ecology, energy, and consumerism. Pays varying rates, on acceptance. Guidelines.

MOTHER JONES—1663 Mission St., San Francisco, CA 94103. Douglas Foster, Ed. Investigative articles, political essays, cultural analyses. "OutFront" pieces, 250 words, about change, "either good, bad, or strange." Pays $750 to $2,000, after acceptance. Query in writing only.

MS.: THE WORLD OF WOMEN—230 Park Ave., 7th Fl., New York, NY 10169. Address Manuscript Ed. Articles relating to feminism, women's roles, and social change; reporting, profiles, essays, theory, and analysis. Pays market rates. Query with SASE required.

NATIONAL ENQUIRER—Lantana, FL 33464. Articles, of any length, for mass audience: topical news, the occult, how-to, scientific discoveries, human drama, adventure, personalities. Photos. Pays from $325. Query or send complete manuscript.

NEW WOMAN—215 Lexington Ave., New York, NY 10016. Karen Walden, Ed.-in-Chief. Articles on personal and professional relationships, health, fitness, lifestyle, money and career issues. Editorial focus is on self-discovery, self-development, and self-esteem. "Read the magazine to become familiar with our needs, and request writers' guidelines with SASE. We look for originality, solid research, and a friendly, accessible style." Pays varying rates, on acceptance.

NEW YORK—755 Second Ave., New York, NY 10017. Edward Kosner, Ed. Laurie Jones, Man. Ed. Feature articles of interest to New Yorkers, on current events in the metropolitan New York area. Pays $850 to $3,500, on acceptance. Query required; not responsible for unsolicited material.

THE NEW YORK ANTIQUE ALMANAC—Box 335, Lawrence, NY 11559. Carol Nadel, Ed. Articles on antiques, shows, shops, art, investments, collectibles, collecting suggestions, nostalgia, related humor. Photos. Pays $5 to $75, extra for photos, on publication.

THE NEW YORK TIMES MAGAZINE—229 W. 43rd St., New York, NY 10036. Address Articles Ed. Timely articles, approximately 3,000 words, on news items, forthcoming events, trends, culture, entertainment, etc. Pays to $2,500 for major articles, on acceptance. Query with clips.

THE NEW YORKER—20 W. 43rd St., New York, NY 10036. Address the

Editors. Factual and biographical articles for "Profiles," "Reporter at Large," etc. Pays good rates, on acceptance. Query.

NEWSWEEK—444 Madison Ave., New York, NY 10022. Original opinion essays, 1,000 to 1,100 words, for "My Turn" column: must contain verifiable facts. Submit manuscript with SASE. Pays $1,000, on publication.

OMNI—1965 Broadway, New York, NY 10023–5965. Keith Ferrell, Ed. Articles, 2,500 to 3,000 words, on scientific aspects of the future: space, machine intelligence, ESP, origin of life, future arts, lifestyles, etc. Pays $750 to $2,500, less for short features, on acceptance. Query.

PARADE—750 Third Ave., New York, NY 10017. Fran Carpentier, Sr. Articles Ed. National Sunday newspaper supplement. Factual and authoritative articles, 1,000 to 1,500 words, on subjects of national interest: health, consumer and environmental issues, science, the family, sports, etc. Profiles of well-known personalities and service pieces. No fiction, poetry, games, or puzzles. Pays from $1,000. Query.

PENTHOUSE—1965 Broadway, New York, NY 10023–5965. Peter Bloch, Ed. Barbara Rice, Man. Ed. General-interest or controversial articles, to 5,000 words. Pays from 20¢ a word, on acceptance.

PEOPLE IN ACTION/SPORTS PARADE—Box 10010, Ogden, UT 84409. Caroll Shreeve, Pub. (Formerly separate publications; they have been combined.) Personality profiles, 1,200 words, of celebrities in sports, entertainment, fine arts, science, etc. Celebrities must be nationally or internationally known for their participation in their field, have positive values, and be making a contribution to society. "High quality color transparencies are a must; query for details." Pays 15¢ a word, $35 for photos, $50 for cover photos, on acceptance.

PEOPLE WEEKLY—Time-Life Bldg., Rockefeller Ctr., New York, NY 10020. John Saar, Asst. Man. Ed. Considers article proposals only, three to four paragraphs, on timely, entertaining, and topical personalities. Pays good rates, on acceptance. "Vast majority of material is staff written."

PHILIP MORRIS MAGAZINE—153 Waverly Pl., 3rd Floor, New York, NY 10014. Frank Gannon, Ed. Profiles of American innovators, entertainers, sports figures, animal conservationists. Also U.S. travel destinations, food. Pays on publication.

PLAYBOY—680 N. Lakeshore Dr., Chicago, IL 60611. John Rezek, Articles Ed. Sophisticated articles, 4,000 to 6,000 words, of interest to urban men. Humor: satire. Pays to $3,000, on acceptance. Query.

PLAYGIRL—801 Second Ave., New York, NY 10017. Barbara Haigh, Ed.-in-Chief. Articles, 2,000 to 2,500 words, for women ages 18 to 34. Pays negotiable rates. Query with clips to Nonfiction Editor.

PRIME TIMES—2802 International Ln., Suite 120, Madison, WI 53704. Rod Clark, Exec. Ed. Articles, 500 to 1,800 words, for dynamic, creative mid-lifers. Departments, 850 to 1,000 words. Pays $125 to $750, on publication. Query. Guidelines with SASE.

REAL PEOPLE—950 Third Ave., New York, NY 10022–2705. Alex Polner, Ed. True stories, to 500 words, on the bizarre: occult, UFOs, strange occurrences, everyday weirdness, etc. Pays $50, on publication; send submissions to "Real Bizarre" column. Queries for interviews, 1,000 to 1,800 words, with national celebrities also considered; pays $100 to $350, on publication.

REDBOOK—224 W. 57th St., New York, NY 10019. Diane Salvatore, Sr. Ed. Sally Lee, Sr. Ed. Toni Gerber Hope, Articles Ed. Articles, 1,000 to 3,500 words, on subjects related to relationships, sex, current social issues, psychology, marriage, the family, and parenting. Payment varies, on acceptance. Query.

ROLLING STONE—1290 Ave. of the Americas, 2nd Fl., New York, NY 10104. Magazine of American music, culture, and politics. No fiction. Query. "We rarely accept free-lance material."

THE ROTARIAN—1560 Sherman Ave., Evanston, IL 60201. Willmon L. White, Ed. Articles, 1,200 to 2,000 words, on international social and economic issues, business and management, human relationships, travel, sports, environment, science and technology; humor. Pays good rates, on acceptance. Query.

SATELLITE ORBIT—8330 Boone Blvd., Suite 600, Vienna, VA 22182. Mike Doan, Ed. Television-related articles, 750 to 2,500 words, personality profiles, general sports pieces, items on hardware, and articles of interest to the satellite and cable TV viewer. Query with clips. Pay varies, on acceptance.

THE SATURDAY EVENING POST—1100 Waterway Blvd., Indianapolis, IN 46202. Ted Kreiter, Exec. Ed. Family-oriented articles, 1,500 to 3,000 words: humor, preventive medicine, destination-oriented travel pieces (not personal experience), celebrity profiles, the arts, and sciences. Pieces on sports and home repair (with photos). Pays varying rates, on publication. Queries preferred.

SELF—350 Madison Ave., New York, NY 10017. Alexandra Penney, Ed.-in-Chief. Articles for young women with a particular interest in health, nutrition, fitness, relationships, fashion and beauty, and related lifestyle subjects. Pays from $1 a word. Query.

SMITHSONIAN MAGAZINE—900 Jefferson Dr., Washington, DC 20560. Marlane A. Liddell, Articles Ed. Articles on history, art, natural history, physical science, profiles, etc. Query.

SOAP OPERA DIGEST—45 W. 25th St., New York, NY 10010. Jason Bonderoff, Man. Ed. Investigative reports and profiles, to 1,500 words, about New York- or Los Angeles-based soaps. Pays from $250, on acceptance. Query with clips.

SPORTS ILLUSTRATED—1271 Ave. of the Americas, New York, NY 10020. No unsolicited material.

SPORTS PARADE—See *People in Action.*

SUNDAY JOURNAL MAGAZINE—*Providence Sunday Journal*, 75 Fountain St., Providence, RI 02902. Elliot Krieger, Ed. Features on some aspect of life in New England, especially Rhode Island and S.E. Massachusetts. Pays $100 to $500, on publication.

TDC: THE DISCOVERY CHANNEL—7700 Wisconsin Ave., Bethesda, MD 20814. Rebecca Farwell, Ed. Monthly magazine that amplifies and develops (but does not review or retell) the topics and genres covered by the Discovery cable TV channel, including science and technology, nature and ecology, human adventure, history, people and places. "Our objective is to approach nonfiction subjects in a literary style. We are always looking for writing with strong 'you are there' feeling. Articles are commissioned by staff, though queries are sometimes considered." Send letter of introduction, resumé, areas of expertise, and published clips.

THE TOASTMASTER—P.O. Box 9052, Mission Viejo, CA 92690. Suzanne Frey, Ed. Member-supported monthly. Articles, 1,500 to 2,500 words, on decision making, speech outlining, introducing speakers, leadership development, speaking techniques, etc. Pays $100 to $250, on acceptance.

TOWN & COUNTRY—1700 Broadway, New York, NY 10019. Address Features Dept. Considers one-page proposals for articles. Rarely buys unsolicited manuscripts.

TRAVEL & LEISURE—1120 Ave. of the Americas, New York, NY 10036. Ila Stanger, Ed.-in-Chief. Articles, 800 to 3,000 words, on destinations and leisure-time activities. Short pieces for "Travel & Health," "Travel & Money," and "Taking Off." Regional pieces for regional editions. Pays on acceptance: $2,000 to $3,000 for features; $500 to $1,200 for regionals; $50 to $300 for short pieces. Query.

TRIP & TOUR—See *Allied Publications.*

TROPIC—*The Miami Herald*, One Herald Plaza, Miami, FL 33132. Tom Shroder, Exec. Ed. Essays and articles, 1,000 to 4,000 words, on current trends and issues, light or heavy for sophisticated audience. No fiction or poetry. Limited humor. Pays $200 to $1,000, on publication. SASE. Allow four to six weeks for response.

TV GUIDE—Radnor, PA 19088. Jack Curry, Man. Ed. Short, light, brightly written pieces about humorous or offbeat angles of television and industry trends. (Majority of personality pieces are staff written.) Pays on acceptance. Query.

VANITY FAIR—350 Madison Ave., New York, NY 10017. Wayne Lawson, Ed. Articles. Pays on acceptance. Query.

VILLAGE VOICE—842 Broadway, New York, NY 10003. Sarah Jewler, Man. Ed. Articles, 500 to 2,000 words, on current or controversial topics. Pays $75 to $450, on acceptance. Query or send manuscript with SASE.

VISTA—999 Ponce, Suite 600, Coral Gables, FL 33134. Renato Perez, Sr. Ed. Articles, to 1,500 words, for English-speaking Hispanic Americans, on job advancement, bilingualism, immigration, the media, fashion, education, medicine, sports, and food. Profiles, 100 words, of Hispanic Americans in unusual jobs; photos welcome. Pays 20¢ a word, on acceptance. Query required.

VOGUE—350 Madison Ave., New York, NY 10017. Address Features Ed. Articles, to 1,500 words, on women, entertainment and the arts, travel, medicine, and health. General features. Query.

VOLKSWAGEN WORLD—Volkswagen of America, 3800 Hamlin Rd., Auburn, MI 48057. Marlene Goldsmith, Ed. Articles, 600 to 1,200 words, for Volkswagen owners: profiles of well-known personalities who drive VWs; inspirational or human-interest pieces; travel; humor; high-tech German product pieces; German travel. Photos. Pays $200 per printed page, on acceptance. Query. Guidelines.

WASHINGTON JOURNALISM REVIEW—4716 Pontiac St., #301, College Park, MD 20740–2493. Bill Monroe, Ed. Articles, 500 to 3,000 words, on print or electronic journalism. Pays 20¢ a word, on publication. Query.

WASHINGTON POST MAGAZINE—*The Washington Post*, 1150 15th St. N.W., Washington, DC 20071. Linton Weeks, Man. Ed. Essays, profiles, and Washington-oriented general-interest pieces, to 5,000 words, on business, arts and culture, politics, science, sports, education, children, relationships, behavior, etc. Pays from $1,000, after acceptance.

WEEKLY WORLD NEWS—600 S. East Coast Ave., Lantana, FL 33462. Edward Clontz, Ed. Bizarre news pieces, about 500 to 1,000 words. Query first. Pays $125 to $500, on publication.

WISCONSIN—*The Milwaukee Journal Magazine*, P.O. Box 661, Milwaukee, WI 53201. Alan Borsuk, Ed. Trend stories, essays, humor, personal-experience pieces, profiles, 500 to 2,000 words, with strong Wisconsin emphasis. Pays $75 to $650, on publication.

WOMAN BEAUTIFUL—See *Allied Publications*.

WOMAN'S DAY—1633 Broadway, New York, NY 10019. Rebecca Greer, Articles Ed. Articles, 500 to 2,500 words, on subjects of interest to women: marriage, education, family health, child rearing, money management, interpersonal relationships, changing lifestyles, etc. Dramatic first-person narratives about women who have experienced medical miracles or other triumphs, or have overcome common problems, such as alcoholism. Query first. Pays top rates, on acceptance.

WOMAN'S WORLD—270 Sylvan Ave., Englewood Cliffs, NJ 07632. Articles, 600 to 1,800 words, of interest to middle-income women between the ages of 18 and 60, on love, romance, careers, medicine, health, psychology, family life, travel; dramatic stories of adventure or crisis, investigative reports. Send SASE for guidelines. Pays $300 to $900, on acceptance. Query.

WORKING WOMAN—230 Park Ave., New York, NY 10169. Lynn Povich, Ed. Articles, 1,000 to 2,500 words, on business and personal aspects of working women's lives. Pays from $400, on acceptance.

YANKEE—Dublin, NH 03444. Judson D. Hale, Ed. Articles, to 3,000 words, with New England angle. Photos. Pays $150 to $1,000 (average $750), on acceptance.

YOUR HOME/INDOORS & OUT—Box 10010, Ogden, UT 84409. Caroll Shreeve, V.P. of Pub. Articles, 1,200 words, on fresh ideas in home decor, ranging from floor and wall coverings to home furnishings. Latest in home construction (exteriors, interiors, building materials, design, entertaining, and lifestyle), the outdoors at home (landscaping, pools, patios, gardens, etc.), home management, and home buying and selling. Avoid do-it-yourself approaches. Emphasis on the use of home improvement professionals. Must include excellent transparencies. Queries required. Guidelines. Pays 15¢ a word and $35 for photos, $50 for cover photo, on acceptance.

CURRENT EVENTS, POLITICS

AFRICA REPORT—833 U.N. Pl., New York, NY 10017. Margaret A. Novicki, Ed. Well-researched articles by specialists, 1,000 to 2,500 words, with photos, on current African affairs. Pays $150 to $250, on publication.

THE AMERICAN LEGION MAGAZINE—Box 1055, Indianapolis, IN 46206. Daniel S. Wheeler, Ed.-in-Chief. Articles, 750 to 1,800 words, on current world affairs, public policy, and subjects of contemporary interest. Pays $500 to $1,000, on acceptance. Query.

THE AMERICAN SCHOLAR—1811 Q St. N.W., Washington, DC 20009. Joseph Epstein, Ed. Non-technical articles and essays, 3,500 to 4,000 words, on current affairs, the American cultural scene, politics, arts, religion, and science. Pays to $500, on acceptance.

THE AMICUS JOURNAL—Natural Resources Defense Council, 40 W. 20th St., New York, NY 10011. Peter Borrelli, Ed. Investigative articles, book reviews, and poetry related to national and international environmental policy. Pays varying rates, on acceptance. Queries required.

THE ATLANTIC—745 Boylston St., Boston, MA 02116. William Whitworth, Ed. In-depth articles on public issues, politics, social sciences, education, business, literature, and the arts, with emphasis on information rather than opinion. Ideal length: 3,000 to 6,000 words, though short pieces, 1,000 to 2,000 words, are also welcome. Pays excellent rates, on acceptance.

CHURCH & STATE—8120 Fenton St., Silver Spring, MD 20910. Joseph L. Conn, Man. Ed. Articles, 600 to 2,600 words, on religious liberty and church-state relations issues. Pays varying rates, on acceptance. Query.

COMMENTARY—165 E. 56th St., New York, NY 10022. Norman Podhoretz, Ed. Articles, 5,000 to 7,000 words, on contemporary issues, Jewish affairs, social sciences, community life, religious thought, culture. Serious fiction; book reviews. Pays on publication.

COMMONWEAL—15 Dutch St., New York, NY 10038. Margaret O'Brien Steinfels, Ed. Catholic. Articles, to 3,000 words, on political, social, religious, and literary subjects. Pays 3¢ a word, on acceptance.

THE CRISIS—4017 24th St., #8, San Francisco, CA 94114. Fred Beauford, Ed. Articles, to 1,500 words, on the arts, civil rights, and problems and achievements of blacks and other minorities. Pays $75 to $500, on acceptance.

ENVIRONMENT—4000 Albemarle St. N.W., Washington, DC 20016. Barbara T. Richman, Man. Ed. Articles, 2,500 to 5,000 words, on environmental, scientific, and technological policy and decision-making issues. Pays $100 to $300, on publication. Query.

FOREIGN SERVICE JOURNAL—2101 E St. N.W., Washington, D.C. 20037. Articles on American diplomacy, foreign affairs, and subjects of interest to Americans representing U.S. abroad. Query.

THE FREEMAN—Foundation for Economic Education, Irvington-on-Hudson, NY 10533. Brian Summers, Sr. Ed. Articles, to 3,500 words, on economic, political, and moral implications of private property, voluntary exchange, and individual choice. Pays 10¢ a word, on publication.

INQUIRER MAGAZINE—*Philadelphia Inquirer*, P.O. Box 8263, 400 N. Broad St., Philadelphia, PA 19101. Fred Mann, Ed. Local-interest features, 500 to 7,000 words. Profiles of national figures in politics, entertainment, etc. Pays varying rates, on publication. Query.

LABOR'S HERITAGE—10000 New Hampshire Ave., Silver Spring, MD 20903. Stuart Kaufman, Ed. Quarterly journal of The George Meany Memorial Archives. Publishes 15- to 30-page articles to be read by labor scholars, labor union members, and the general public. Pays in copies.

MIDSTREAM—110 E. 59th St., New York, NY 10022. Joel Carmichael, Ed. Articles of international and Jewish concern. Pays 5¢ a word, after publication.

MOMENT—3000 Connecticut Ave. N.W., Suite 300, Washington, DC 20008. Suzanne Singer, Man. Ed. Sophisticated articles and some fiction, 2,500 to 5,000 words, on Jewish topics. Columns, to 1,500 words, on current issues in MidEast, American Jewry, Israel, pluralism. Pays $50 to $400, on publication.

MOTHER JONES—1663 Mission St., San Francisco, CA 94103. Doug Foster, Ed. Investigative articles, political essays, cultural analyses. Pays $1,000 to $3,000 for feature articles, after acceptance. Query.

THE NATION—72 Fifth Ave., New York, NY 10011. Victor Navasky, Ed.

Articles, 1,500 to 2,500 words, on politics and culture from a liberal/left perspective. Pays $75 per published page, to $300, on publication. Query.

THE NEW YORK TIMES MAGAZINE—229 W. 43rd St., New York, NY 10036. Address Articles Ed. Timely articles, approximately 4,000 words, on news items, trends, culture, etc. Pays $1,000 for short pieces, $2,500 for major articles, on acceptance. Query with clips.

THE NEW YORKER—20 W. 43rd St., New York, NY 10036. Address the Editors. Factual and biographical articles, for "Profiles," "Reporter at Large," "Annals of Crime," "Onward and Upward with the Arts," etc. Pays good rates, on acceptance. Query.

NUCLEAR TIMES: ISSUES & ACTIVISM FOR GLOBAL SURVIVAL— P.O. Box 351, Kenmore Station, Boston, MA 02215. Sonia Shah, Man. Ed. News and feature articles, 500 to 4,000 words, on peace, justice, the environment, nuclear disarmament, military policy, and militarization of American culture. Pays from 25¢ a word, two to four weeks after acceptance.

ON THE ISSUES—CHOICES Women's Medical Center, Inc., 97–77 Queens Blvd., Forest Hills, NY 11374–3317. Beverly Lowy, Man. Ed. "The Magazine of Substance for Progressive Women." Articles, up to 2,500 words, on political or social issues. Movie, music, and book reviews, 500 to 750 words. Query. Payment varies, on publication.

THE PROGRESSIVE—409 E. Main St., Madison, WI 53703. Erwin Knoll, Ed. Articles, 1,000 to 3,500 words, on political and social problems. Light features. Pays $75 to $300, on publication.

PUBLIC CITIZEN MAGAZINE—2000 P St. N.W., Suite 610, Washington, DC 20036. Ana Radelat, Ed. Investigative reports and articles of timely political interest, for members of Public Citizen: consumer rights, health and safety, environmental protection, safe energy, tax reform, and government and corporate accountability. Photos, illustrations. Pays to $500.

REGARDIE'S—1010 Wisconsin Ave. N.W., Suite 600, Washington, DC 20007. Brian Kelly, Ed. Profiles and investigations of the "high and mighty" in the DC area: "We require aggressive reporting and imaginative, entertaining writing." Pays 50¢ a word, on publication. Queries required.

ROLL CALL: THE NEWSPAPER OF CAPITOL HILL—900 2nd St. N.E., Washington, DC 20002. James K. Glassman, Ed. Factual, breezy articles with political or Congressional angle: Congressional historical and human-interest subjects, political lore, etc. Political satire and humor. Pays on publication.

THE ROTARIAN—1560 Sherman Ave., Evanston, IL 60201. Willmon L. White, Ed. Articles, 1,200 to 2,000 words, on international social and economic issues, business and management, environment, science and technology. "No direct political or religious slants." Pays good rates, on acceptance. Query.

SATURDAY NIGHT—36 Toronto St., Suite 1160, Toronto, Ont., Canada M5C 2C5. John Fraser, Ed. Canada's oldest magazine of politics, social issues, culture, and business. Features, 1,000 to 3,000 words, and columns, 800 to 1,000 words; fiction, to 3,000 words. Must have Canadian tie-in. Payment varies, on acceptance.

TROPIC—*The Miami Herald*, One Herald Plaza, Miami, FL 33132. Tom Shroder, Ed. Essays and articles on current trends and issues, light or heavy, 1,000 to 4,000 words, for sophisticated audience. Pays $200 to $1,000, on publication. Query with SASE; 4 to 6 weeks for response.

VFW MAGAZINE—406 West 34th St., Kansas City, MO 64111. Richard K. Kolb, Ed. Magazine for Veterans of Foreign Wars and their families. Articles, 1,500 words, on current issues and history, with veteran angle. Photos. Pays from $500, extra for photos, on acceptance. Guidelines.

VILLAGE VOICE—842 Broadway, New York, NY 10003. Sarah Jewler, Man. Ed. Articles, 500 to 2,000 words, on current or controversial topics. Pays $75 to $450, on publication. Query or send manuscript with SASE.

THE WASHINGTON MONTHLY—1611 Connecticut Ave. N.W., Washington, DC 20009. Charles Peters, Ed. Investigative articles, 1,500 to 5,000 words, on politics, government and the political culture. Pays 10¢ a word, on publication. Query.

WASHINGTON POST MAGAZINE—*The Washington Post*, 1150 15th St. N.W., Washington, DC 20071. Linton Weeks, Man. Ed. Essays, profiles, and general-interest pieces, to 5,000 words, on Washington-oriented politics and related issues. Pays from $1,000, after acceptance. SASE required.

REGIONAL AND CITY PUBLICATIONS

ADIRONDACK LIFE—P.O. Box 97, Jay, NY 12941. Tom Hughes, Ed. Features, to 3,000 words, on outdoor and environmental activities and issues, arts, wilderness, profiles, history, and fiction; focus is on the Adirondack region and north country of New York State. Pays to 25¢ a word, on acceptance. Query.

ALOHA, THE MAGAZINE OF HAWAII—49 South Hotel St., #309, Honolulu, HI 96813. Cheryl Chee Tsutsumi, Ed. Articles, 1,500 to 4,000 words, on the life, customs, and people of Hawaii and the Pacific. Poetry. Fiction. Pays $150 to $400 for full-length features, on publication. Query first.

ARIZONA HIGHWAYS—2039 W. Lewis Ave., Phoenix, AZ 85009. Robert J. Early, Ed. Articles, 1,500 to 2,000 words, on travel in Arizona; pieces on adventure, humor, lifestyles, nostalgia, history, archaeology, nature, etc. Pays 30¢ to 45¢ a word, on acceptance. Query first.

ARKANSAS TIMES—Box 34010, Little Rock, AR 72203. Richard Martin, Ed. Articles, to 6,000 words, on Arkansas history, people, travel, politics. All articles must have strong AR orientation. Pays to $500, on acceptance.

ATLANTA—1360 Peachtree St., Suite 1800, Atlanta, GA 30309. Lee Walburn, Ed. Articles, 1,500 to 5,000 words, on Atlanta subjects or personalities. Pays $600 to $1,200, on publication. Query.

THE ATLANTIC ADVOCATE—P.O. Box 3370, Gleaner Bldg., Prospect St., Fredericton, N.B., Canada E3B 5A2. Marilee Little, Ed. Well-researched articles on Atlantic Canada and general-interest subjects; fiction, to 1,500 words. Pays to 8¢ a word, on publication.

ATLANTIC CITY MAGAZINE—1270 W. Washington Ave., Suite 100, Cardiff, NJ 08232. Ken Weatherford, Ed. Lively articles, 500 to 4,000 words, on Atlantic City and southern New Jersey, for locals and tourists: entertainment, casinos, business, recreation, personalities, environment, local color. Pays $100 to $700, on publication. Query.

BACK HOME IN KENTUCKY—P.O. Box 1627, Franklin, TN 37064. Nanci P. Gregg, Man. Ed. Articles on Kentucky history, travel, craftsmen and artisans, Kentucky cooks, "colorful" characters, and limited personal nostalgia specifically related to Kentucky. Pays $25 to $100 for articles with B&W or color photos. Queries preferred.

BALTIMORE MAGAZINE—16 S. Calvert St., Suite 1000, Baltimore, MD 21202. Stan Heuisler, Ed. Articles, 500 to 3,000 words, on people, places, and things in the Baltimore metropolitan area. Consumer advice, investigative pieces, profiles, humor, and personal experience pieces. Payment varies, on publication. Query required.

THE BIG APPLE PARENTS' PAPER—928 Broadway, Suite 709, New York, NY 10010. Helen Rosengren Freedman, Ed. Articles, 600 to 750 words, for New York City parents. Pays $50 to $75, within 60 days of acceptance, plus $25 cover bonus. Buys first NY-area rights.

BIRMINGHAM—2027 First Ave. N., Birmingham, AL 35203. Joe O'Donnell, Ed. Personality profiles, features, business, and nostalgia pieces, to 2,500 words, with Birmingham tie-in. Pays $50 to $175, on publication.

BLUE RIDGE COUNTRY—P.O. Box 21535, Roanoke, VA 24018. Kurt Rheinheimer, Ed. Bimonthly. Regional articles, 1,200 to 2,000 words, that "explore and extol the beauty, history, and travel opportunities in the mountain regions of Virginia, North Carolina, West Virginia, Tennessee, Kentucky, Maryland, South Carolina, and Georgia." Color slides or B&W prints considered. Pays $200 for features, extra for photos, on publication. Queries preferred.

BOCA RATON—JES Publishing, Amtec Center, Suite 100, 6413 Congress Ave., Boca Raton, FL 33487. Darrell Hofheinz, Ed. Articles, 800 to 3,000 words, on Florida topics, personalities, and travel. Pays $50 to $500, on publication. Query with clips required.

THE BOSTON GLOBE MAGAZINE—*The Boston Globe*, Boston, MA 02107. Ande Zellman, Ed. General-interest articles on local, national, and international topics and profiles, 2,500 to 5,000 words. Query and SASE required.

BOSTON MAGAZINE—300 Massachusetts Ave., Boston, MA 02115. Betsy Buffington, Man. Ed. Informative, entertaining features, 1,000 to 3,000 words, on Boston area personalities, institutions, and phenomena. Query. Pays to $2,000, on publication.

BOUNDARY WATERS JOURNAL—9396 Rocky Ledge Rd., Ely, MN 55731. Stuart Osthoff, Ed. Articles, 2,000 to 3,000 words, on recreation and natural resources in Minnesota's Boundary Waters region, including canoe routes, fishing, wildlife, history, and lifestyles of residents. Pays $200 to $400, on publication.

BUFFALO SPREE MAGAZINE—Box 38, Buffalo, NY 14226. Johanna Shotell, Ed. Articles, to 1,800 words. Pays $75 to $100, $25 for poetry, on publication.

BUSINESS IN BROWARD—2455 E. Sunrise Blvd., Suite 300, Ft. Lauderdale, FL 33304. T. Constance Coyne, Ed. Small business regional bimonthly; 2,500-word articles for eastern Florida county. Pay varies, on acceptance. Same address and requirements for *Business in Palm Beach County.*

CALIFORNIA BUSINESS—4221 Wilshire Blvd., Suite 400, Los Angeles, CA 90010. Samuel Lipsman, Ed. Articles, 500 to 3,500 words, on California-based businesses. Payment varies, on acceptance. Query.

CAPE COD LIFE—P.O. Box 222, Osterville, MA 02655. Brian F. Shortsleeve, Pub. Articles on Cape Cod current events, business, art, history, gardening, and lifestyle, 2,000 words. Pays 10¢ a word, 30 days after publication. Queries preferred.

CARIBBEAN TRAVEL AND LIFE—8403 Colesville Rd., Silver Spring, MD 20910. Veronica Gould Stoddart, Ed. Articles, 500 to 3,000 words, on all aspects of travel, recreation, leisure, and culture in the Caribbean, Bahamas, and Bermuda. Pays $75 to $550, on publication. Query with published clips.

CHESAPEAKE BAY MAGAZINE—1819 Bay Ridge Ave., Annapolis, MD 21403. Jean Waller, Ed. Articles, 8 to 10 typed pages, related to the Chesapeake Bay area. Profiles. Photos. Pays on publication. Query first.

CHICAGO—414 N. Orleans, Chicago, IL 60610. Joanne Trestrail, Man. Ed. Articles, 1,000 to 5,000 words, related to Chicago. Pays varying rates, on acceptance. Query.

CHICAGO HISTORY—Clark St. at North Ave., Chicago, IL 60614. Russell Lewis, Ed. Articles, to 4,500 words, on Chicago's urban, political, social, and cultural history. Pays to $250, on publication. Query.

CHICAGO TRIBUNE MAGAZINE—*Chicago Tribune*, 435 N. Michigan Ave., Rm. 532, Chicago, IL 60611. Profiles and articles, to 6,000 words, on public and social issues on the personal, local, or national level. Prefer regional slant. Query. Pays $250 to $1,500, on publication.

CINCINNATI MAGAZINE—409 Broadway, Cincinnati, OH 45202. Laura Pulfer, Ed./Pub. Articles, 1,000 to 3,000 words, on Cincinnati people and issues. Pays $75 to $100 for 1,000 words, on acceptance. Query with writing sample.

CITY NEWS—2 Park Ave., Suite 2012, New York, NY 10016. Leslie Elgort, Ed. Bimonthly. Articles, 750 to 1,500 words, poetry, fillers, and humor of interest to New York City teenagers; B&W photos. Payment varies, on publication.

CITY SPORTS MAGAZINE—P.O. Box 193693, San Francisco, CA 94119. Chris Newbound, Ed. Articles, 500 to 2,000 words, on participant sports, family recreation, travel, and the active lifestyle. Pays $100 to $650, on publication. Query. Limited market.

CLINTON STREET—Box 3588, Portland, OR 97208. David Milholland, Ed. Articles, to 15 pages, and creative fiction, 2 to 20 pages. "Eclectic blend of politics, culture, humor, and art." Compelling first-person accounts welcome. Pays $50 to $200, on publication.

COLORADO BUSINESS—7009 S. Potomac, Englewood, CO 80112. Jeff Rundles, Ed. Articles, varying length, on business and economic trends in Colorado. Pays on publication. Query.

COLORADO HOMES & LIFESTYLES—7009 S. Potomac, Englewood, CO 80112. Darla J. Worden, Pub. Articles on topics related to Colorado: travel, fashion, design and decorating, architecture, gardening, luxury real estate, art, celebrity lifestyles, people, food, antiques, collecting, and entertaining. Pays to 20¢ a word, on acceptance.

CONNECTICUT—789 Reservoir Ave., Bridgeport, CT 06606. Charles Monagan, Ed. Articles, 1,500 to 3,500 words, on Connecticut topics, issues, people, and lifestyles. Pays $500 to $1,500, within 30 days of acceptance.

CRAIN'S DETROIT BUSINESS—1400 Woodbridge, Detroit, MI 48207. Mary Kramer, Ed. Business articles, 500 to 1,000 words, about Detroit, for Detroit business readers. Pays $100 to $200, on publication. Query required.

CREATING EXCELLENCE—New World Publishing, P.O. Box 2048, S.

Burlington, VT 05407. David Robinson, Ed. Inspirational and practical business-oriented articles, profiles, and essays related to Vermont. Pays $50 to $250, on publication.

D—3988 N. Central Expressway, Suite 1200, Dallas, TX 75204. Ruth Fitzgibbons, Ed. In-depth investigative pieces on current trends and problems, personality profiles, and general-interest articles on the arts, travel, and business, for upper-class residents of Dallas. Pays $350 to $500 for departments, $800 to $1,200 for features. Written queries only.

DALLAS LIFE MAGAZINE—*The Dallas Morning News*, P.O. Box 655237, Communications Center, Dallas, TX 75265. Mike Maza, Man. Ed. Well-researched articles and profiles, 1,000 to 3,000 words, on contemporary issues, personalities, or subjects of strictly Dallas-related interest. Pays from 25¢ a word, on acceptance. Query required.

DELAWARE TODAY—P.O. Box 4440, Wilmington, DE 19807. Lise Monty, Ed. Service articles, profiles, news, etc., on topics of local interest. Pays $75 to $125 for department pieces, $125 to $300 for features, on publication. Queries with clips required.

DETROIT FREE PRESS MAGAZINE—*Detroit Free Press*, 321 W. Lafayette Blvd., Detroit, MI 48231. Articles, to 5,000 words, on issues, lifestyles. Personality profiles; essays; humor. Pays from $150. Query appreciated.

DETROIT MONTHLY—1400 Woodbridge, Detroit, MI 48207. Brux Austin, Ed. Articles on Detroit-area people, issues, lifestyles, and business. Payment varies. Query required.

DOWN EAST—Camden, ME 04843. Davis Thomas, Ed. Articles, 1,500 to 2,500 words, on all aspects of life in Maine. Photos. Pays to 20¢ a word, extra for photos, on acceptance. Query.

ERIE & CHAUTAUQUA MAGAZINE—Charles H. Strong Bldg., 1250 Tower Ln., Erie, PA 16505. Kim Kalvelage, Man. Ed. Feature articles, to 2,500 words, on issues of interest to upscale readers in the Erie, Warren, and Crawford counties (PA), and Chautauqua (NY) county. Pieces with regional relevance. Pays after publication. Query preferred, with writing samples. Buys all rights. Guidelines available.

FLORIDA HOME & GARDEN—800 Douglas Rd., Suite 500, Coral Gables, FL 33134. Kathryn Howard, Ed. Features,1,000 to 2,000 words, and department pieces, 1,000 words, about Florida interior design, architecture, landscape architecture, gardening, cuisine, trendy new products, travel (Florida and Caribbean), and home entertaining. Pays $200 to $400, photos extra.

FLORIDA KEYS MAGAZINE—P.O. Box 2921, Key Largo, FL 33037. Gibbons Cline, Ed. Articles, 1,000 to 2,000 words, on the Florida Keys: history, environment, natural history, profiles, etc. Fillers, humor. Photos. Pays varying rates, on publication.

FLORIDA WILDLIFE—620 S. Meridian St., Tallahassee, FL 32399–1600. Andrea H. Blount, Ed. Bimonthly of the Florida Game and Fresh Water Fish Commission. Articles, 800 to 1,200 words, that promote native flora and fauna, hunting, fishing in Florida's fresh waters, outdoor ethics, and conservation of Florida's natural resources. Pays $50 to $200, on publication.

GEORGIA JOURNAL—Grimes Publications, P.O. Box 27, Athens, GA 30603–0027. Millard B. Grimes, Ed. and Pub. Articles, 1,000 to 2,000 words, on people, history, events, travel, etc., in and around GA. Poetry, to 20 lines. Pays $50 to $250, on publication.

GOLDEN STATE—555 19th St., San Francisco, CA 94107. Anne Evers, Ed. Family- and activity-oriented articles on California attractions. Query with clips. Payment varies, on publication.

GRAND RAPIDS—40 Pearl St. N.W., #1040, Grand Rapids, MI 49503. Carole Valade Smith, Ed. Service articles (dining guide, travel, personal finance, humor) and issue-oriented pieces related to Grand Rapids, Michigan. Pays $35 to $200, on publication. Query.

GULF COAST GOLFER—See *North Texas Golfer.*

GULFSHORE LIFE—2975 S. Horseshoe Dr., Naples, FL 33942. Janis Lyn Johnson, Ed. Articles, 800 to 3,000 words, on southwest Florida personalities, travel, sports, business, interior design, arts, history, and nature. Pays $150 to $300. Query.

HAWAII—Box 6050, Mission Viejo, CA 92690. Dennis Shattuck, Ed. Bimonthly. Articles, 1,000 to 5,000 words, related to Hawaii. Pays 10¢ a word, on publication. Query.

HIGH COUNTRY NEWS—Box 1090, Paonia, CO 81428. Betsy Marston, Ed. Articles on environmental issues, public lands management, energy, and natural resource issues; profiles of western innovators; pieces on western politics. Poetry. B&W photos. Pays $2 to $4 per column inch, on publication, for 750-word roundups and 2,000-word features. Query first.

HONOLULU—36 Merchant St., Honolulu, HI 96813. Ed Cassidy, Ed. Features highlighting contemporary life in the Hawaiian islands: politics, sports, history, people, arts, events. Pays $500, on publication. Columns and department pieces are mostly staff-written. Queries required.

HOUSTON METROPOLITAN MAGAZINE—P.O. Box 25386, Houston, TX 77265. Mike Peters, Man. Ed. Gabrielle Cosgriff, Ed. Dir. Articles with strong Houston-area angles. Issue-oriented features, profiles, lifestyle pieces. Also gardening and design pieces; department columns ("City Insight," "Art Beat," "Metropolitan Marketplace"). Pays $50 to $500 for columns; $600 to $1,000 for features.

ILLINOIS ENTERTAINER—2250 E. Devon, Suite 150, Des Plaines, IL 60018. Michael C. Harris, Ed. Articles, 500 to 1,500 words, on local and national entertainment (emphasis on alternative music) in the greater Chicago area. Personality profiles; interviews; reviews. Photos. Pays varying rates, on publication. Query preferred.

ILLINOIS MAGAZINE—P.O. Box 40, Litchfield, IL 62056. Peggy Kuethe, Ed. Bimonthly. Regional articles, 100 to 2,000 words, on travel, history, current events, points of interest, and biography. No exposés or personal experience pieces. Pays $15 to $250, on publication.

INDIANAPOLIS MONTHLY—950 N. Meridin St., Suite 1200, Indianapolis, IN 46204. Deborah Paul, Ed./Pub. Sam Stall, Man. Ed. Articles, 1,000 words, on health, sports, politics, business, interior design, travel, and Indiana personalities. All material must have a regional focus. Pays varying rates, on publication.

INDUSTRY MAGAZINE—441 Stuart St., Boston, MA 02116. Alan R. Earls, Ed./Pub. Articles, 500 to 1,500 words, related to business and industry in Massachusetts. Pays negotiable rates, on acceptance. Queries required.

INQUIRER MAGAZINE—*Philadelphia Inquirer*, 400 N. Broad St., Philadelphia, PA 19101. Fred Mann, Ed. Articles, 1,500 to 2,000 words, and 3,000 to 7,000 words, on politics, science, arts and culture, business, lifestyles and entertain-

502

ment, sports, health, psychology, education, religion, and humor. Short pieces, 850 words, for "Up Front." Pays varying rates. Query.

INSIDE CHICAGO—2501 W. Peterson Ave., Chicago, IL 60659. Barbara Young, Ed. Features, to 3,000 words, and articles, to 1,500 words, on Chicago-related trends, profiles of Chicagoans, entrepreneuring, arts, and lifestyle. Short reports, 200 to 400 words. Department pieces, 900 to 1,000 words. Pays varying rates. Query.

THE IOWAN MAGAZINE—108 Third St., Suite 350, Des Moines, IA 50309. Charles W. Roberts, Ed. Articles, 1,000 to 3,000 words, on business, arts, people, and history of Iowa. Photos a plus. Pays $200 to $600, on publication. Query required.

ISLAND LIFE—P.O. Box 929, Sanibel Island, FL 33957. Joan Hooper, Ed. Articles, 500 to 1,200 words, with photos, on unique or historical places in Florida, southwest Gulf Coast (Sanibel, Captiva, Marco). Pays on publication. SASE.

JACKSONVILLE TODAY—White Publishing Co., 1325 San Marco Blvd., Suite 900, Jacksonville, FL 32207. Ed Grimm, Ed. Features, 2,000 to 3,000 words, relating to Jacksonville and North Florida personalities. Pays $200 to $350, on publication. Query required.

KANSAS!—Kansas Dept. of Commerce, 400 W. Eighth Ave., 5th Fl., Topeka, KS 66603–3957. Andrea Glenn, Ed. Quarterly. Articles, five to seven typed pages, on the people, places, history, and events of Kansas. Color slides. Pays to $250, on acceptance. Query.

KENTUCKY LIVING—P.O. Box 32170, Louisville, KY 40232. Gary Luhr, Ed. Articles, 800 to 2,000 words, with strong Kentucky angle: profiles (of people, places, events), history, biography, recreation, travel, leisure or lifestyle, and book excerpts. Pays $125 to $300, on acceptance. Guidelines available.

KEY HORIZONS—Gateway Plaza, 950 N. Meridian, Suite 1200, Indianapolis, IN 46204. Joan Todd, Man. Ed. Quarterly. General-interest articles and department pieces, 300 to 3,000 words, for readers 55 and older living in Indiana and western Pennsylvania. Topics include personal finance, wellness, cooking, nostalgia, family trends, and travel. Pays $75 to $500, $25 to $50 for photos, on publication.

L.A. WEST—919 Santa Monica Blvd., Santa Monica, CA 90401. Mary Daily, Ed. Features, 850 to 1,200 words, relating to western Los Angeles; humorous essays on current lifestyles; profiles, 350 to 500 words, on westside professionals; travel pieces, 800 words, on foreign and domestic destinations. Pays $75 to $600, on publication. Queries preferred. Guidelines.

LAKE SUPERIOR MAGAZINE—P.O. Box 16417, Duluth, MN 55816–0417. Paul Hayden, Ed. Articles with unusual twists on Lake Superior regional subjects: historical pieces that highlight the people, places, and events that affect the Lake Superior region. Pictorial essays; humor and occasional poetry. Quality photos enhance submission. "Writers must have a thorough knowledge of the subject and how it relates to our region." Pays to $400, extra for photos, after publication. Query first.

LOS ANGELES MAGAZINE—1888 Century Park E., Suite 920, Los Angeles, CA 90067. Lew Harris, Ed. Articles, to 3,000 words, of interest to sophisticated, affluent southern Californians, preferably with local focus on a lifestyle topic. Pays from 10¢ a word, on acceptance. Query.

LOS ANGELES READER—5550 Wilshire Blvd., Suite 301, Los Angeles, CA 90036. James Vowell, Ed. Articles, 750 to 5,000 words, on subjects relating to the Los Angeles area; special emphasis on feature journalism, entertainment, and the arts. Pays $25 to $300, on publication. Query preferred.

LOUISVILLE—One Riverfront Plaza, Louisville, KY 40202. James Oppel, Jr., Ed. Articles, 1,000 to 2,000 words, on community issues, personalities, and entertainment in the Louisville area. Photos. Pays from $50, on acceptance. Query; articles on assignment only. Limited free-lance market.

MARYLAND—c/o Dept. of Economic and Employment Development, 30 Hudson St., Annapolis, MD 21401. D. Patrick Hornberger, Ed. Dir. Articles, 800 to 2,200 words, on Maryland subjects. Pay varies, on acceptance. Query preferred. Guidelines.

MEMPHIS—MM Corp., Box 256, Memphis, TN 38101. Leanne Kleinmann, Ed. Articles, 1,500 to 4,000 words, on a wide variety of topics related to Memphis and the Mid-South region: politics, education, sports, business, etc. Profiles; investigative pieces. Pays $75 to $1,000, on publication. Query. Guidelines available.

MICHIGAN LIVING—1 Auto Club Dr., Dearborn, MI 48126. Len Barnes, Ed. Travel articles, 500 to 1,500 words, on tourist attractions and recreational opportunities in the U.S. and Canada, with emphasis on Michigan: places to go, things to do, costs, etc. Color photos. Pays $150 to $380, extra for photos, on acceptance.

MID-WEST OUTDOORS—111 Shore Dr., Hinsdale, IL 60521. Gene Laulunen, Ed. Articles, 1,500 words, with photos, on where, when, and how to fish and hunt, within 500 miles of Chicago. Pays $25, on publication.

MILWAUKEE MAGAZINE—312 E. Buffalo, Milwaukee, WI 53202. David Fryxell, Ed. Profiles, investigative articles, and historical pieces, 3,000 to 6,000 words; local tie-in a must. Some regional fiction. Pays from $800, on publication. Query preferred.

MPLS. ST. PAUL—12 S. 6th St., Suite 400, Minneapolis, MN 55402. Claude Peck, Man. Ed. In-depth articles, features, profiles, and service pieces, 400 to 3,000 words, with Minneapolis-St. Paul focus. Pays to $1,000.

MINNESOTA MONTHLY—15 S. Ninth St., Suite 320, Minneapolis, MN 55402. Jodie Ahern, Man. Ed. Articles, to 4,000 words, on the people, places, events, and issues in Minnesota; fiction, to 3,000 words; poetry, to 50 lines. Pays $50 to $800, on acceptance. Query for nonfiction only.

MONTANA MAGAZINE—P.O. Box 5630, Helena, MT 59604. Carolyn Cunningham, Ed. Where-to-go items, regional profiles, photo essays. Montana-oriented only. B&W prints, color slides. Pays $75 to $350, on publication.

NEVADA—1800 East Hwy. 50, Suite 200, Carson City, NV 89710. David Moore, Ed. Articles, 500 to 700 or 1,500 to 1,800 words, on topics related to Nevada: travel, history, profiles, humor, and place. Photos. Pay varies, on publication.

NEW ALASKAN—Rt. 1, Box 677, Ketchikan, AK 99901. R.W. Pickrell, Ed. Articles, 1,000 to 5,000 words, and fiction; must be related to southeast Alaska. Pays 1 ½¢ a word, on publication.

NEW DOMINION—2000 N. 14th St., Suite 750, Arlington, VA 22201. Philip Hayward, Ed. "The Magazine for and about Northern Virginia." Articles, 600 to 2,000 words, on regional business and lifestyles. Query with writing samples. Pays $5.50 per column inch, on publication.

NEW HAMPSHIRE PROFILES MAGAZINE—P.O. Box 370, Stratham,

NH 03885. Suki Casanave, Ed. Articles, 500 to 3,000 words, on New Hampshire people, places, events, and issues. Pays $100 to $450, on publication. Queries welcome.

NEW JERSEY MONTHLY—P.O. Box 920, Morristown, NJ 07963–0920. Jan Bresnick, Ed. Articles, profiles, and service pieces, 2,000 to 3,000 words; department pieces on health, business, education, travel, sports, local politics, and arts, 1,000 to 1,500 words, with New Jersey tie-in. Pays $35 to $100 for shorts, $400 to $600 for departments, $600 to $1,750 for features, on acceptance. Query with SASE and magazine clips. Guidelines.

NEW MEXICO MAGAZINE—Joseph M. Montoya Bldg., 1100 St. Francis Dr., Santa Fe, NM 87503. Address Ed. Articles, 250 to 2,000 words, on New Mexico subjects. Pays about 25¢ a word, on acceptance.

NEW ORLEANS MAGAZINE—111 Veterans Blvd., Metairie, LA 70005. Errol Laborde, Ed. Articles, 3 to 15 triple-spaced pages, on New Orleans area people and issues. Photos. Pays $15 to $500, extra for photos, on publication. Query.

NEW YORK—755 Second Ave., New York, NY 10017. Edward Kosner, Ed. Laurie Jones, Man. Ed. Feature articles on subjects of interest to New Yorkers. Payment negotiated, made on acceptance. Query required.

NEW YORK ALIVE—Box 9001, Mt. Vernon, NY 10552. Michelle Eldredge, Ed. Articles aimed at developing knowledge of and appreciation for New York State. Features, 3,000 words maximum, on lifestyle, sports, travel and leisure, history, and the arts. Department pieces for regular columns, including "Great Escapes" (travel ideas) and "Expressly New York" (unusual places, products, or events in New York). Pays $200 to $350 for features, $50 to $150 for departments. Query preferred.

NORTH DAKOTA HORIZONS—P.O. Box 2467, Fargo, ND 58108. Sheldon Green, Ed. Quarterly. Articles, about 3,000 words, on the people, places, and events that affect life in North Dakota. Photos. Pays $75 to $300, on publication.

NORTH GEORGIA JOURNAL—65 Roswell St., Bldg. 100, Alpharetta, GA 30201. Olin Jackson, Pub./Ed. History, travel, and lifestyle features, 2,000 to 3,000 words, on North Georgia. History features need human-interest approach and must be written in first person; include interviews. Photos a plus. Pays $75 to $350, on acceptance. Query.

NORTH TEXAS GOLFER—9182 Old Katy Rd., Suite 212, Irving, TX 77055. Bob Gray, Ed. Articles, 800 to 1,500 words, involving local golfers or related directly to north Texas. Pays from $50 to $250, on publication. Query. Same requirements for *Gulf Coast Golfer* (related to south Texas).

NORTHEAST MAGAZINE—*The Hartford Courant*, 285 Broad St., Hartford, CT 06115. Lary Bloom, Ed. Articles and short essays, 750 to 3,000 words, that reflect the concerns of Connecticut residents. Pays $250 to $1,000, on acceptance.

NORTHERN LIGHTS—Box 8084, Missoula, MT 59807–8084. Address Editor. Thoughtful articles, 500 to 3,000 words, about the contemporary West. Occasional fiction. "We're open to virtually any subject as long as it deals with our region (the Rocky Mountains) in some way." Pays to 10¢ a word, on publication.

NORTHWEST—1320 S.W. Broadway, Portland, OR 97201. Ellen E. Heltzel, Ed. Sunday magazine of *The Sunday Oregonian*. Articles, to 3,000 words, on Pacific Northwest issues and personalities: regional travel, science and business, outdoor recreation, and lifestyle trends. Personal essays. Local angle essential. Pays $75 to $1,000. Query first.

NORTHWEST LIVING!—130 Second Ave. S., Edmonds, WA 98020–3512. Terry W. Sheely, Ed. Lively, informative articles, 400 to 1,000 words, on the natural resources of the Northwest: homes, gardens, people, travel, history, etc. Color photos essential. Shorts, 100 to 400 words. Pays to $300, on publication. Query with SASE for guidelines.

NORTHWEST PRIME TIMES—10829 N.E. 68th St., Kirkland, WA 98033. Neil Strother, Pub./Ed. News and features aimed at 50 and up audience. Pays $25 to $50 on publication. Limited market.

NORTHWEST REGIONAL MAGAZINES—P.O. Box 18000, Florence, OR 97439. Address Dave Peden or Judy Fleagle. All submissions considered for use in *Oregon Coast, Northwest Travel,* and *Oregon Coast Getaway Guide*. Articles, 1,200 to 1,500 words, pertaining to the Pacific Northwest, on travel, history, town/ city profiles, and nature. News releases, 200 to 500 words. Articles with photos or slides preferred. Pays $75 to $200, on publication. Guidelines.

NORTHWEST TRAVEL—See *Northwest Regional Magazines.*

OH! IDAHO—Peak Media, Box 925, Hailey, ID 83333. Laurie Sammis, Ed. "Articulate, image-oriented" features, 1,500 to 2,000 words, on Idaho's residents, recreation, and other Idaho topics. Department pieces, 1,200 words, on a wide variety of subjects, including food and travel in Idaho. Pays from 10¢ a word, on publication. Query. Guidelines.

OHIO MAGAZINE—62 E. Broad St., Columbus, OH 43215. Ellen Stein Burbach, Ed. Profiles of people, cities, and towns of Ohio; pieces on historic sites, tourist attractions, little-known spots. Lengths and payment vary. Query.

OKLAHOMA TODAY—Box 53384, Oklahoma City, OK 73152. Sue Carter, Ed. Travel articles; profiles, history, nature and outdoor recreation, and arts articles. All material must have regional tie-in. Queries for 1,000- to 2,000-word articles preferred. Pays $100 to $300, on acceptance. SASE for guidelines.

ORANGE COAST—245-D Fischer, Suite 8, Costa Mesa, CA 92626. Palmer Jones, Ed. Articles of interest to educated Southern Californians. Pieces, 1,000 to 1,500 words, for regular departments: "Escape" (local travel), "Access," "Spotlight," "Selects," "Guide," and "Focus." Feature articles, 1,500 to 2,500 words: investigative, lifestyle, business trends in the area, and issue-oriented topics. Query. Pays $250 for features, $100 for columns, on acceptance. Guidelines.

OREGON COAST—See *Northwest Regional Magazines.*

ORLANDO MAGAZINE—P.O. Box 2207, Orlando, FL 32802. Michael Candelaria, Ed. Articles and profiles, 1,000 to 1,500 words, on business, lifestyle, home and garden. Photos a plus. Pays $150 to $250, on publication. Query required.

OTTAWA MAGAZINE—192 Bank St., Ottawa, Ont., Canada K2P 1W8. Marion Soubliere, Assoc. Ed. Articles, investigative journalism, and profiles, 2,000 to 2,500 words, relating to the social issues and cultural and consumer interests of Ottawa City. Query with five or six article ideas, resumé, and published clips. Payment varies, on acceptance.

PALM SPRINGS LIFE—Desert Publications, 303 North Indian Canyon Dr., P.O. Box 2724, Palm Springs, CA 92263. Jamie Lee Pricer, Ed. Articles, 1,000 to 2,000 words, of interest to "wealthy, upscale people who live and/or play in the desert": food, interior design, luxury cars, shopping, sports, homes, personalities, desert issues, arts, and culture. Pays $150 to $400 for features, $30 to $60 for short profiles, on publication. Query required.

PARENTGUIDE NEWS—2 Park Ave., Suite 2012, New York, NY 10016. Leslie Elgort, Ed. Monthly. Articles, 1,000 to 1,500 words, related to New York families and parenting: trends, profiles, special programs, special products. Payment varies, on publication.

PENNSYLVANIA HERITAGE—P.O. Box 1026, Harrisburg, PA 17108–1026. Michael J. O'Malley III, Ed. Quarterly of the Pennsylvania Historical Museum Commission. Articles, 3,000 to 4,000 words, on fine and decorative arts, architecture, archaeology, oral history, exhibits, industry and technology, travel, and folklore, written with an eye toward illustration. Photographic essays. Pieces should "introduce readers to the state's rich culture and historic legacy." Pays $300 to $500; extra for photos and drawings, on acceptance.

PENNSYLVANIA MAGAZINE—Box 576, Camp Hill, PA 17011. Albert E. Holliday, Ed. General-interest features with a Pennsylvania flavor. All articles must be accompanied by photos or illustrations. Send photocopies of illustration. SASE required. Guidelines.

PERSIMMON HILL—1700 N.E. 63rd St., Oklahoma City, OK 73111. M.J. Van Deventer, Ed. Published by the National Cowboy Hall of Fame. Articles, 1,500 to 3,000 words, on Western history and art, cowboys, ranching, and nature. Top-quality illustrations a must. Pays from $100 to $250, on acceptance.

PHILADELPHIA—1500 Walnut St., Philadelphia, PA 19102. Laurence Stains, Articles Ed. Articles, 1,000 to 5,000 words, for sophisticated audience, relating to Philadelphia area. No fiction or poetry. Pays on acceptance. Query.

PHOENIX MAGAZINE—4707 N. 12th St., Phoenix, AZ 85014. Richard Vonier, Ed. Articles, 1,000 to 3,000 words, on topics of interest to Phoenix-area residents. Pays $300 to $1,500, on publication. Queries preferred.

PITTSBURGH—4802 Fifth Ave., Pittsburgh, PA 15213. Bruce VanWyngarden, Ed. Articles, 850 to 3,000 words, with western Pennsylvania slant, two- to four-month lead time. Pays on publication.

PORTLAND MONTHLY MAGAZINE—578 Congress St., Portland, ME 04101. Colin Sargent, Ed. Articles on local people, fashion, culture, and trends. Fiction, to 750 words. Pays on publication. Query preferred.

RECREATION NEWS—P.O. Box 32335, Washington, DC 20007. Sam E. Polson, Ed. Articles, 1,500 to 2,000 words, on recreation for government workers in the Washington, D.C. area. Light, first-person accounts, 800 words, for "Sporting Life" column. "Articles should have a conversational tone that's lean and brisk." Queries preferred. Pays $50 for reprints to $350 for cover articles, on publication. Guidelines.

REGARDIE'S—1010 Wisconsin Ave. N.W., Suite 600, Washington, DC 20007. Brian Kelly, Ed. Profiles and investigations of the "high and mighty" in the DC area: "We require aggressive reporting and imaginative, entertaining writing." Pays 50¢ a word, on publication. Queries required.

RHODE ISLAND MONTHLY—18 Imperial Pl., Providence, RI 02903. Vicki Sanders, Man. Ed. Features, 1,000 to 4,000 words, ranging from investigative reporting and in-depth profiles to service pieces and visual stories, on Rhode Island and southeastern Massachusetts. Seasonal material, 1,000 to 2,000 words. Fillers, 150 to 250 words, on places, customs, people, events, products and services, restaurants and food. Pays $250 to $900 for features; $25 to $50 for shorts, on publication. Query.

ROCKFORD MAGAZINE—331 E. State St., Box 678, Rockford, IL 61105.

Elaine Johnson, Ed. General-interest magazine covering Rockford and northern Illinois. Feature articles, 3,000 to 4,000 words, and departments, 1,500 to 2,500 words, on city and area personalities, politics, events, business, family, travel destinations, etc. "Nothing predictable or routine." Query with samples and clips. Pays from 5¢ a word, on acceptance.

RURAL LIVING—4201 Dominion Blvd., Suite 101, Glen Allen, VA 23060. Richard G. Johnstone, Jr., Ed. Features, 1,000 to 1,500 words, on people, places, historic sites in Virginia and Maryland's Eastern Shore. Queries preferred. Pays $100 to $150 for articles, on publication.

RURALITE—P.O. Box 558, Forest Grove, OR 97116. Address Ed. or Feature Ed. Articles, 800 to 2,000 words, of interest to a primarily rural and small-town audience in Oregon, Washington, Idaho, Nevada, northern California, and Alaska. "Think pieces" affecting rural/urban interests, biographies, local history and celebrations, self-help, etc. Humorous articles and animal pieces. No fiction or poetry. No sentimental nostalgia. Pays $30 to $400, on acceptance. Queries required. Guidelines.

SAN DIEGO MAGAZINE—4206 W. Point Loma Blvd., P.O. Box 85409, San Diego, CA 92138. Virginia Butterfield, Assoc. Ed. Articles, 1,500 to 3,000 words, on local personalities, politics, lifestyles, business, history, etc., relating to San Diego area. Photos. Pays $250 to $600, on publication. Query with clips.

SAN DIEGO READER—P.O. Box 85803, San Diego, CA 92186. Jim Holman, Ed. Articles, 2,500 to 10,000 words, on the San Diego region. Literate nonfiction. Pays $500 to $2,000, on publication.

SAN FRANCISCO BUSINESS TIMES—325 Fifth St., San Francisco, CA 94107. Tim Clark, Ed. Business-oriented articles, about 20 column inches. Limited free-lance market. Pays $75 to $100, on publication. Query.

SAN FRANCISCO FOCUS—680 Eighth St., San Francisco, CA 94103. Mark Powelson, Ed. Service features, profiles of local newsmakers, and investigative pieces of local issues, 2,500 to 3,000 words. Pays $250 to $750, on acceptance. Query required.

SEATTLE HOME AND GARDEN—201 Dexter Ave. N., Suite 101, Seattle, WA 98109. Jo Brown, Man. Ed. Home and garden articles, 500 to 2,000 words, relating directly to the Northwest. Pays $100 to $800, on publication. Guidelines.

SEATTLE'S CHILD—P.O. Box 22578, Seattle, WA 98122. Ann Bergman, Ed. Articles, 400 to 2,500 words, of interest to parents, educators, and childcare providers of children under 12, and investigative reports and consumer tips on issues affecting families in the Puget Sound region. Pays $75 to $400, on publication. Query required.

SENIOR MAGAZINE—3565 S. Higuera St., San Luis Obispo, CA 93401. Personality profiles and health articles, 600 to 900 words, and book reviews (of new books or outstanding older titles) of interest to senior citizens of California. Pays $1.50 per inch, $10 to $25 for B&W photos, on publication.

SILENT SPORTS—717 10th St., P.O. Box 152, Waupaca, WI 54981. Upper Midwest monthly on bicycling, cross-country skiing, running, canoeing, hiking, backpacking, and other "silent" sports; articles, 1,000 to 2,000 words. Pays $40 to $100 for features; $20 to $50 for fillers, on publication. Query.

SOUTH CAROLINA WILDLIFE—P.O. Box 167, Columbia, SC 29202–0167. Address Man. Ed. Articles, 1,000 to 3,000 words, with regional outdoors focus: conservation, natural history and wildlife, recreation. Profiles, natural history. Pays from 10¢ a word. Query.

SOUTH FLORIDA MAGAZINE—800 Douglas Rd., Suite 500, Coral Gables, FL 33134. Marilyn Moore, Ed. Features, 2,000 to 3,500 words, and department pieces, 900 to 1,300 words, on a variety of subjects related to south Florida. Short, bright items, 200 to 400 words, for "Undercurrents." Pays $75 to $900, within 30 days of acceptance.

SOUTHERN OUTDOORS—5845 Carmichael Pkwy., Montgomery, AL 36117. Larry Teague, Ed. How-to articles, 200 to 600 words or 1,500 to 2,000 words, on hunting and fishing, for fishermen and hunters in the Southern states. Pays 15¢ a word, on acceptance. Query.

SOUTHWEST ART—Franklin Tower, 5444 Westheimer, Suite 1440, Houston, TX 77056. Susan McGarry, Ed. Articles, 1,800 to 2,200 words, on the artists, art collectors, museum exhibitions, gallery events and dealers, art history, and art trends west of the Mississippi River. Particularly interested in representational or figurative arts. Pays from $300, on acceptance. Query with slides of artwork to be featured.

THE STATE: DOWN HOME IN NORTH CAROLINA—128 S. Tryon St., Suite 2200, Charlotte, NC 28202. Angela Terez, Man. Ed. Articles, 750 to 2,000 words, on people, history, and places in North Carolina. Photos. Pays on publication.

SUNDAY JOURNAL MAGAZINE—*Providence Sunday Journal*, 75 Fountain St., Providence, RI 02902. Elliot Krieger, Ed. Nonfiction, 1,000 to 3,000 words, with a New England focus. Pays $100 to $500, on publication.

SUNSET MAGAZINE—80 Willow Rd., Menlo Park, CA 94025. William Marken, Ed. Western regional. Very limited free-lance market.

SUNSHINE: THE MAGAZINE OF SOUTH FLORIDA—*The Sun-Sentinel*, 200 E. Las Olas Blvd., Ft. Lauderdale, FL 33301–2293. John Parkyn, Ed. Articles, 1,000 to 3,000 words, on topics of interest to south Floridians. Pays $250 to $1,000, on acceptance. Query first. Guidelines.

TALLAHASSEE MAGAZINE—2365 Centerville Rd., Tallahassee, FL 32308. Dave Fiore, Ed. Articles, 800 to 1,100 words, with a positive outlook on the life, people, and history of the north Florida area. Pays on publication. Query.

TAMPA BAY LIFE: THE BAY AREA'S MAGAZINE—6200 Courtney Campbell Causeway, Suite 580, Tampa, FL 33607–1458. Larry Marscheck, Ed. Dir. Articles, 850 to 3,000 words, on the people, events, and issues shaping the Tampa Bay region's future. Pays $125 to $300 for department pieces; $400 to $600 for features, on publication.

TEXAS HIGHWAYS MAGAZINE—State Dept. of Highways and Public Transportation, P.O. Box 141009, Austin, TX 78714–1009. Tommie Pinkard, Ed. Texas travel, history, and scenic features, 200 to 1,800 words. Pays 40¢ to 60¢ a word, $80 to $500 per photo, on acceptance. Guidelines for writers and photographers.

TEXAS MONTHLY—P.O. Box 1569, Austin, TX 78767. Gregory Curtis, Ed. Features, 2,500 to 5,000 words, and departments, to 2,500 words, on art, architecture, food, education, business, politics, etc. "We like solidly researched pieces that uncover issues of public concern, reveal offbeat and previously unreported topics, or use a novel approach to familiar topics." Pays varying rates, on acceptance. Queries required.

TIMELINE—1982 Velma Ave., Columbus, OH 43211–2497. Christopher S. Duckworth, Ed. Articles, 1,000 to 6,000 words, on history of Ohio (politics, economics, social, and natural history) for lay readers in the Midwest. Pays $100 to $900, on acceptance. Queries preferred.

TOLEDO MAGAZINE—*The Blade*, Toledo, OH 43660. Sue Stankey, Ed. Articles, to 5,000 words, on Toledo-area personalities, events, etc. Pays $50 to $500, on publication. Query with SASE.

TORONTO LIFE—59 Front St. E., Toronto, Ont., Canada M5E 1B3. Marq De Villiers, Ed. Articles, 1,500 to 4,500 words, on Toronto. Pays $1,500 to $3,500, on acceptance. Query.

TROPIC—*The Miami Herald*, One Herald Plaza, Miami, FL 33132. Tom Shroder, Exec. Ed. General-interest articles, 750 to 3,000 words, for south Florida readers. Pays $200 to $1,000, on acceptance. Send SASE.

TUCSON LIFESTYLE—Old Pueblo Press, 7000 E. Tanque Verde, Tucson, AZ 85715. Sue Giles, Ed.-in-Chief. Features on local businesses, lifestyles, the arts, homes, and fashion. Payment varies, on acceptance. Query preferred.

TWIN CITIES READER—5500 Wayzata Blvd., Minneapolis, MN 55416. Glen Warchol, Ed.-in-Chief. Articles, 2 to 4 printed pages, on cultural phenomena, city politics, and general-interest subjects, for local readers ages 25 to 44. Pays to $5 to $8 per inch, on publication.

VALLEY MAGAZINE—16800 Devonshire, Suite 275, Granada Hills, CA 91344. Barbara Wernik, Ed. Articles, 1,000 to 1,500 words, on celebrities, issues, education, health, business, dining, and entertaining, etc., in the San Fernando Valley. Pays $100 to $350, within eight weeks of acceptance.

VENTURA COUNTY & COAST REPORTER—1583 Spinnaker Dr., Suite 213, Ventura, CA 93001. Nancy Cloutier, Ed. Articles, 3 to 5 pages, on any locally slanted topic. Pays $10, on publication.

VERMONT LIFE—61 Elm St., Montpelier, VT 05602. Tom Slayton, Ed.-in-Chief. Articles, 500 to 3,000 words, on Vermont subjects only. Pays 20¢ a word, extra for photos. Query perferred.

VIRGINIA BUSINESS—411 E. Franklin St., Suite 105, Richmond, VA 23219. James Bacon, Ed. Articles, 1,000 to 2,500 words, related to the business scene in Virginia. Pays varying rates, on acceptance. Query required.

VIRGINIA WILDLIFE—P.O. Box 11104, Richmond, VA 23230–1104. Monthly of the Commission of Game and Inland Fisheries. Articles, 1,500 to 2,500 words, with Virginia tie-in, on conservation and related topics, including fishing, hunting, wildlife management, outdoor safety, and ethics, etc. Articles must be accompanied by color photos. Query with SASE. Pays 10¢ a word, extra for photos, on publication.

WASHINGTON POST MAGAZINE—*The Washington Post*, 1150 15th St. N.W., Washington, DC 20071. Linton Weeks, Man. Ed. Personal-experience essays, profiles, and general-interest pieces, to 6,000 words, on business, arts and culture, politics, science, sports, education, children, relationships, behavior, etc. Articles should be of interest to people living in Washington, D.C. area. Pays from $100, on acceptance. Limited market.

THE WASHINGTONIAN—1828 L St. N.W., Suite 200, Washington, DC 20036. John Limpert, Ed. Helpful, informative articles, 1,000 to 4,000 words, on DC-related topics. Pays 50¢ a word.

WE ALASKANS MAGAZINE—*Anchorage Daily News*, Box 149001, Anchorage, AK 99514–9001. George Bryson, Ed. Articles, 500 to 1,000 words, and features, 3,000 to 4,000 words, on Alaska topics only. Profiles, narratives, fiction, and humor. Pays $50 to $150 for short articles, $300 to $500 for features, on publication.

THE WEEKLY, SEATTLE'S NEWS MAGAZINE—1931 Second Ave., Seattle, WA 98101. David Brewster, Ed. Articles, 700 to 4,000 words, with a Northwest perspective. Pays $75 to $800, on publication. Query. Guidelines.

WESTERN SPORTSMAN—P.O. Box 737, Regina, Sask., Canada S4P 3A8. Roger Francis, Ed. Informative articles, to 2,500 words, on hunting, fishing, and outdoor experiences in Alberta, Saskatchewan, and Manitoba. How-tos, humor, cartoons. Photos. Pays $75 to $400, on publication.

WESTWAYS—2601 S. Figueroa St., Los Angeles, CA 90007. Eric Seyfarth, Man. Ed. Articles, 1,000 to 1,500 words, and photo essays, on western U.S., Canada, and Mexico: history, contemporary living, travel, personalities, etc. Photos. Pays from 20¢ a word, extra for photos, 30 days before publication. Query.

WINDY CITY SPORTS—1450 W. Randolph, Chicago, IL 60607. Maryclaire Collins, Ed. Articles, to 1,500 words, on amateur sports in the Chicago area. Queries required. Pays $100, on publication.

WISCONSIN—*The Milwaukee Journal Magazine*, Journal/Sentinel, Inc., Box 661, Milwaukee, WI 53201. Alan Borsuk, Ed. Articles, 500 to 2,000 words, on business, politics, arts, science with strong Wisconsin emphasis. Personal-experience essays, profiles and investigative articles. Pays $75 to $500, on publication. Query.

WISCONSIN TRAILS—P.O. Box 5650, Madison, WI 53705. Geri Nixon, Man. Ed. Articles, 1,500 to 3,000 words, on regional topics: outdoors, lifestyle, events, adventure, travel; profiles of artists, craftspeople, and regional personalities. Fiction, with regional slant. Fillers. Pays $100 to $450, on acceptance and on publication. Query.

WISCONSIN WEST MAGAZINE—2000 Oxford Ave., Box 8, Eau Claire, WI 54703. Articles on current issues for residents of western Wisconsin; profiles of restaurants, B&B inns, weekend leisure activities and getaways, and famous people of western Wisconsin; and historical pieces. Short humor. Payment varies, on publication.

YANKEE—Yankee Publishing Co., Dublin, NH 03444. Judson D. Hale, Ed. Articles and fiction, about 2,500 words, on New England and residents. Pays about $800 for features, on acceptance.

YANKEE MAGAZINE'S TRAVEL GUIDE TO NEW ENGLAND AND ITS NEIGHBORS—Main St., Dublin, NH 03444. Janice Brand, Ed. Articles, 500 to 2,000 words, on activities, attractions, places to visit in New England. Photos. Pays on acceptance. Query with outline and writing samples required.

TRAVEL ARTICLES

AAA WORLD—1000 AAA Dr., Heathrow, FL 32746–5063. Douglas Damerst, Ed. Articles, 600 to 1,500 words, on consumer automotive and travel concerns. Pays $200 to $800, on acceptance. Query with writing samples required. Articles by assignment only.

ACCENT/TRAVELOG—Box 10010, Ogden, UT 84409. June Krambule, Ed.

Articles, 1,200 words, on travel destinations, ways to travel, and travel tips. Pays 15¢ a word, $35 for color photos, on acceptance. Query first.

ADVENTURE ROAD—The Condé Nast Publications, 360 Madison Ave., New York, NY 10017. Marilyn Holstein, Ed. Official publication of the Amoco Motor Club. Articles, 1,500 words, on destinations in North America, Mexico, and the Caribbean. Photos. Pays $300 to $800, on acceptance. Query required.

AIRFARE: THE MAGAZINE FOR AIRLINE EMPLOYEES—6401 Congress #100, Boca Raton, FL 33487. Ratu Kamlani, Ed. Travel articles, 1,000 to 2,500 words, with photos, on shopping, sightseeing, dining, and night life for airline employees. Prices, discount information, and addresses must be included. Pays $150, after publication.

ARIZONA HIGHWAYS—2039 W. Lewis Ave., Phoenix, AZ 85009. Richard G. Stahl, Man. Ed. Informal, well-researched travel articles, 2,000 to 2,500 words, focusing on a specific city or region in Arizona and environs. Also articles dealing with nature, environment, flora and fauna, history, anthropology, archaeology, hiking, boating, industry. Pays 30¢ to 45¢ a word, on acceptance. Query with published clips. Guidelines.

BLUE RIDGE COUNTRY—P.O. Box 21535, Roanoke, VA 24018. Kurt Rheinheimer, Ed. Regional travel articles, 1,200 to 2,000 words, on destinations in the mountain regions of Virginia, North Carolina, West Virginia, Tennessee, Kentucky, Maryland, South Carolina, and Georgia. Color slides and B&W prints considered. Pays $200 for features, extra for photos, on publication. Queries preferred.

BRITISH HERITAGE—P.O. Box 8200, Harrisburg, PA 17105–8200. Gail Huganir, Ed. Travel articles on places to visit in the British Isles, 800 to 1,000 words. Include detailed historical information with a "For the Visitor" sidebar. Pays $100 to $200, on acceptance.

CALIFORNIA HIGHWAY PATROLMAN—2030 V St., Sacramento, CA 95818–1730. Carol Perri, Ed. Travel articles, to 2,000 words, focusing on places in California and the West Coast. "We prefer out-of-the-way stops instead of regular tourist destinations." Query or send completed manuscript with photos. SASE required. Pays 2 ½¢ a word, $5 for B&W photos, on publication.

CANADIAN—1305 11th Ave. S.W., Suite 306, Calgary, Alberta, Canada T3C 3P6. Alister Thomas, Ed. Monthly inflight magazine of Canadian Airlines International. Travel pieces, 1,000 to 1,500 words. Payment varies, on acceptance. Query.

CARIBBEAN TRAVEL AND LIFE—8403 Colesville Rd., Suite 830, Silver Spring, MD 20910. Veronica Gould Stoddart, Ed. Lively, informative articles, 500 to 2,500 words, on all aspects of travel, leisure, recreation, and culture in the Caribbean, Bahamas, and Bermuda, for up-scale, sophisticated readers. Photos. Pays $75 to $550, on publication. Query.

COLORADO HOMES & LIFESTYLES—7009 S. Potomac, Englewood, CO 80112. Darla Worden, Pub. Travel articles on cities, regions, establishments in Colorado; roundups and travel pieces with unusual angles; 1,000 to 1,500 words. Pays $140, on acceptance. Query.

CRUISE TRAVEL—990 Grove St., Evanston, IL 60201. Charles Doherty, Man. Ed. Ship-, port-, and cruise-of-the-month features, 800 to 2,000 words; cruise guides; cruise roundups; cruise company profiles; travel suggestions for one-day port stops. Payment varies, on acceptance. Query with sample color photos.

DISCOVERY—One Illinois Center, 111 E. Wacker Dr., Suite 1700, Chicago, IL 60601. Scott Powers, Ed. Articles, 1,000 to 2,500 words, on travel topics that explore the world and its people; pieces should be geared to the automotive traveler. Photos on assignment only. Pays from $800, on acceptance. Query with published clips required.

EARLY AMERICAN LIFE—Box 8200, Harrisburg, PA 17105–8200. Frances Carnahan, Ed. Travel features about historic sites and country inns, 1,000 to 3,000 words. Pays $100 to $600, on acceptance. Query.

EMERGE—599 Broadway, 12th Floor, New York, NY 10012. Wilmer Ames, Pub./Ed.-in-Chief. Travel articles of interest to middle-class black Americans for "Intrepid Traveler." Sophisticated adventure in out-of-the-way places or unusual views of familiar places. "We don't want typical travelogues or how-to service pieces." Pays from 50¢ a word, after acceptance.

ENDLESS VACATION—Box 80260, Indianapolis, IN 46280. Helen W. O'Guinn, Ed. Travel features, to 1,500 words; international scope. Pays on acceptance. Query preferred. Guidelines. Limited market.

FAMILY CIRCLE—110 Fifth Ave., New York, NY 10011. Sylvia Barsotti, Special Features Ed. Travel articles, to 2,000 words. Concept travel pieces should appeal to a national audience and focus on both luxury and affordable activities for families; prefer service-filled, theme-oriented travel pieces or first-person family vacation stories. Pay rates vary, on acceptance. Query first.

FRIENDLY EXCHANGE—Locust at 17th, Des Moines, IA 50336. Adele Malott, Ed. Articles, 1,000 to 1,800 words, of interest to active midwestern and western families, on travel and leisure. Photos. Pays $300 to $800, extra for photos. Query preferred. Send SASE for guidelines.

GOLDEN STATE—555 19th St., San Francisco, CA 94107. Anne Evers, Ed. Family- and activity-oriented articles on California attractions. Query with clips. Payment varies, on publication.

GREAT EXPEDITIONS—Box 8000–411, Sumas, WA 98295–8000. Craig Henderson, Ed. Articles, 700 to 2,500 words, on independent, adventurous, budget-conscious travel and unusual destinations. Pays $30 to $65, on publication. Guidelines.

GUIDE TO LIVING OVERSEAS—See *Transitions Abroad*.

GULFSHORE LIFE—Collier Park of Commerce, 2975 S. Horseshoe Dr., Naples, FL 33942. Janis Lyn Johnson, Ed. Florida travel articles focusing on the unusual and unique, 1,800 to 2,400 words. Don't want "typical" Sunshine-State destinations. Pay negotiable, on publication. Queries required.

INNSIDER—821 Wanda, Ferndale, MI 48220. Cynthia La Ferle, Ed. Bimonthly "for travelers actively seeking quality accommodations in country inns, bed-and-breakfast inns, and other historic lodgings." Inn profiles (1,500 words; 1,800 to 3,000 words for profiles of two or more inns); book reviews (300 words); and sidebars (to 400 words). Color photos welcome; mention availability when querying. Pays within 60 days of acceptance: $375 to $650 for inn profiles; $65 for book reviews; $70 to $90 for sidebars; $75 to $100 per photo. Guidelines.

INTERNATIONAL LIVING—824 E. Baltimore St., Baltimore, MD 21202. Kathleen Peddicord, Ed. Newsletter. Short pieces and features, 200 to 2,000 words, with useful information on investing, shopping, travel, employment, education, real estate, and lifestyles overseas. Pays $100 to $400, after publication.

ISLANDS—3886 State St., Santa Barbara, CA 93105. Destination features, 1,000 to 3,000 words, on islands around the world as well as department pieces and front-of-the-book items on island-related topics. Pays about 50¢ a word, on publication. Query required. Guidelines.

LIFE IN THE TIMES—The Times Journal Co., Springfield, VA 22159–0200. Margaret Roth, Ed. Travel articles, 750 to 900 words, narrowly focused. "Rather than an article on New York City, we'd prefer one on some particular aspect of the trip." Also features on food, 500 to 1,000 words; and short, personal-experience pieces, 750 words, of interest to military people and their families around the world. Pays $125 for travel articles, from $25 to $150 for short pieces, to $350 for general-interest features up to 2,000 words, on acceptance.

MICHIGAN LIVING—Automobile Club of Michigan, 1 Auto Club Dr., Dearborn, MI 48126. Len Barnes, Ed. Informative travel articles, 500 to 1,500 words, on U.S. & Canadian tourist attractions and recreational opportunities; special interest in Michigan.

THE MIDWEST MOTORIST—12901 N. Forty Dr., St. Louis, MO 63141. Michael Right, Ed. Articles 1,000 to 1,500 words, with color slides, on domestic and foreign travel. Pays from $150, on acceptance.

NATIONAL GEOGRAPHIC—17th and M Sts. N.W., Washington, DC 20036. William P.E. Graves, Ed. First-person articles on geography, exploration, natural history, archaeology, and science. Half staff written; half written by recognized authorities and published authors. Does not consider unsolicited manuscripts.

NATIONAL MOTORIST—Bayside Plaza, 188 The Embarcadero, San Francisco, CA 94105. Jane Offers, Ed. Illustrated articles, 500 to 1,100 words, for California motorists, on motoring in the West, car care, roads, personalities, places, etc. Color slides. Pays from 10¢ a word, on acceptance. Pays for photos on publication. SASE required.

NEW WOMAN—215 Lexington Ave., New York, NY 10016. Karen Walden, Ed.-in-Chief. Armchair travel pieces; women's personal experience and "what I learned from this experience" pieces, 1,000 to 2,000 words. Pays $500 to $2,000, on acceptance. Query required.

THE NEW YORK TIMES—229 W. 43rd St., New York, NY 10036. Nancy Newhouse, Travel Ed. Considers queries only; include writer's background, description of proposed article. No unsolicited manuscripts or photos. Pays on acceptance.

NORTHWEST LIVING!—130 Second Ave. S., Edmonds, WA 98020–3512. Terry W. Sheely, Ed. Articles, 400 to 1,500 words, on regional travel and natural resources. Color slides or B&W prints. Query with SASE required.

NORTHWEST REGIONAL MAGAZINES—P.O. Box 18000, Florence, OR 97439. Address Dave Peden or Judy Fleagle. All submissions considered for use in *Oregon Coast, Northwest Travel,* and *Oregon Coast Getaway Guide.* Articles, 1,200 to 1,500 words, on travel, history, town/city profiles, and nature. News releases, 200 to 500 words. Articles with photos or slides preferred. Pays $75 to $200, on publication. Guidelines.

NORTHWEST TRAVEL—See *Northwest Regional Magazines.*

OFF DUTY MAGAZINE—3303 Harbor Blvd., Suite C-2, Costa Mesa, CA 92626. Gary Burch, U.S. Ed. Travel articles, 1,800 to 2,000 words, for active-duty military Americans (age 20 to 40) and their families, on U.S. regions or cities. Must have wide scope; no out-of-the-way places. Military angle essential. Photos. Pays from 20¢ a word, extra for photos, on acceptance. Query required. Guidelines. Limited market.

OREGON COAST—See *Northwest Regional Magazines*.

OREGON COAST GETAWAY GUIDE—See *Northwest Regional Magazines*.

PACIFIC TRAVEL—1540 Gilbreth Rd., Burlingame, CA 94010. Kumar Pati, Pub. Articles, 4 to 6 pages, about travel, tourism, entertainment, fashion, culture, and business in Asia and the Pacific Rim countries. Departments include: news in brief, business opportunities, vacation information, etc. Profiles of hotels and restaurants, tourist information, and transportation. "Articles should be written in first person about personal experience. Submit eight photos, of which we'll publish about four." Payment varies, on publication. Guidelines.

RV TIMES MAGAZINE—Royal Productions, Inc., Box 6294, Richmond, VA 23230. Alice P. Supple, Ed. Articles and fiction, 500 to 2,000 words, related to outdoor or leisure activities, travel attractions in the Maryland, Virginia, New Jersey, New York, Delaware, and Pennsylvania areas. Pays 7¢ a word (to $90), on publication.

SACRAMENTO MAGAZINE—P.O. Box 2424, Sacramento, CA 95812–2424. Jan Haag, Ed. Articles, 1,000 to 1,500 words, on destinations within a six-hour drive of Sacramento. Pay varies, on acceptance. Query.

SPECIALTY TRAVEL INDEX—305 San Anselmo Ave., #217, San Anselmo, CA 94960. C. Steen Hansen, Co-Publisher/Ed. Semiannual directory of adventure vacation tour companies, destinations, and vacation packages. Articles, 1,000 to 2,000 words, with how-to travel information, humor, and opinion. Pays 20¢ per word, on publication. Slides and photos considered. Queries preferred.

TEXAS HIGHWAYS MAGAZINE—State Dept. of Highways and Public Transportation, P.O. Box 141009, Austin, TX 78714–1009. Tommie Pinkard, Ed. Travel, historical, cultural, scenic features on Texas, 200 to 1,800 words. Pays 40¢ to 50¢, on acceptance; photos $80 to $500. Guidelines.

TOURS & RESORTS—World Publishing Co., 990 Grove St., Evanston, IL 60201–4370. Ray Gudas, Man. Ed. Features on U.S. and international vacation destinations and resorts, 1,000 to 1,500 words; also essays, nostalgia, humor, tour company profiles, travel tips, and service articles, 800 to 1,500 words. Pays up to $350, on acceptance. Top-quality color slides a must. Query.

TRANSITIONS ABROAD—18 Hulst Rd., Box 344, Amherst, MA 01004. Dr. Clayton A. Hubbs, Ed. Articles for overseas travelers who seek an in-depth experience of the culture: work, study, travel, budget tips. Include practical, first-hand information. Emphasis on establishing meaningful contact with people and socially responsible, ecology-minded travel. "Eager to work with inexperienced writers who travel to learn and want to share information." B&W photos a plus. Pays $1.50 per column inch, after publication. Same requirements for *Guide to Living Overseas*, for nontourist (educational, cultural, vocational) travel abroad. Query preferred. Guidelines.

TRAVEL AGE WEST—100 Grant Ave., San Francisco, CA 94108. Robert Carlsen, Man. Ed. Articles, 800 to 1,000 words, with photos, on any aspect of travel useful to travel agents, including names, addresses, prices, etc.; news or trend angle preferred. Pays $2 per column inch, after publication.

TRAVEL & LEISURE—1120 Ave. of the Americas, New York, NY 10036. Ila Stanger, Ed.-in-Chief. Articles, 800 to 3,000 words, on destinations and travel-related activities. Regional pieces for regional editions. Short pieces for "Travel & Health," "Travel & Money," and "Taking Off." Pays on acceptance: $2,000 to $3,000 for features; $500 to $1,200 for regionals; $50 to $300 for short pieces. Query; articles on assignment.

TRAVEL HOLIDAY—Travel Publication, Inc., 28 W. 23rd St., 10th Floor, NewYork, NY 10010. Elizabeth Hettich, Man. Ed. Informative, lively features, 1,400 to 3,000 words, on foreign and domestic travel. Query with published clips.

TRAVEL SMART—Dobbs Ferry, NY 10522. Short pieces, 250 to 1,000 words, about interesting, unusual and/or economical places. Give specific details on hotels, restaurants, transportation, and costs. Pays on publication.

VISTA/USA—Box 161, Convent Station, NJ 07961. Kathleen M. Caccavale, Ed. Travel articles, 1,200 to 2,000 words, on U.S., Canada, Mexico, and the Caribbean. Also, pieces on general-interest topics, hobby/collecting, culture, and Americana. "Flavor of the area, not service oriented." Shorts, 500 to 1,000 words, on "Minitrips," "CloseFocus," "American Vignettes." Pays from $500 for features, from $150 for shorts, on acceptance. Query with writing sample and outline. Limited market.

VOLKSWAGEN WORLD—Volkswagen of America, Inc., 3800 Hamlin Rd., Auburn Hills, MI 48057. Marlene Goldsmith, Ed. Travel articles on unique places or with a unique angle, to 750 words. Pays $150 per printed page, on acceptance. Query.

WESTWAYS—2601 S. Figueroa St., Los Angeles, CA 90007. Eric Seyfarth, Man. Ed. Travel articles on where to go, what to see, and how to get there, 1,300 to 1,500 words. Domestic travel articles are limited to western U.S., Canada, and Hawaii; foreign travel articles are also of interest. Quality color transparencies should be available. Pays 25¢ a word, 30 days before publication.

YANKEE MAGAZINE'S TRAVEL GUIDE TO NEW ENGLAND—Main St., Dublin, NH 03444. Janice Brand, Ed. Articles, 500 to 2,000 words, on destinations in New England. Photos. Pays on acceptance. Query with outline and writing samples.

INFLIGHT MAGAZINES

ABOARD—North-South Net, Inc., 100 Almeria Ave., Suite 220, Coral Gables, FL 33134. Georgina Fernandez, Ed. Inflight magazine of eight Latin American international airlines in Chile, Dominican Republic, Ecuador, Guatemala, El Salvador, Bolivia, Nicaragua, and Honduras. Articles, 1,200 to 1,500 words, with photos. Pieces on science, sports, home, fashion, and gastronomy. No political stories. Pays $150, with photos, on acceptance and on publication. Query required.

ALASKA AIRLINES MAGAZINE—2701 First Ave., Suite 250, Seattle, WA 98121. Giselle Smith, Man. Ed. Articles, 800 to 2,500 words, on lifestyle topics, business, travel, and profiles of regional personalities for West Coast business travelers. Query. Payment varies, on publication.

AMERICA WEST AIRLINES MAGAZINE—Skyword Marketing, Inc., 7500 N. Dreamy Draw Dr., Suite 240, Phoenix, AZ 85020. Michael Derr, Ed. Articles celebrating creativity, 750 to 2,000 words; regional angle helpful. Pays from $250 to $750, on acceptance. Query with clips required. Guidelines.

AMERICAN WAY—P.O. Box 619640, DFW Airport, TX 75261–9640. Doug Crichton, Ed. American Airlines' inflight magazine. Features of interest to the business traveler, emphasizing travel, adventure, business, and the arts/culture. Pays from $900, on acceptance. Query.

CANADIAN—1305 11th Ave. S.W., Suite 306, Calgary, Alberta, Canada T3C 3P6. Alister Thomas, Ed. Monthly. Articles, 1,000 to 1,500 words, on travel and business for Canadian Airlines International travelers. Payment varies, on acceptance. Query.

SKY—12955 Biscayne Blvd., North Miami, FL 33181. Lidia de Leon, Ed. Delta Air Lines' inflight magazine. Articles on business, lifestyle, high tech, sports, the arts, etc. Color slides. Pays varying rates, on acceptance. Query.

WOMEN'S PUBLICATIONS

BBW: BIG BEAUTIFUL WOMAN—9171 Wilshire Blvd., Suite 300, Beverly Hills, CA 90210. Carole Shaw, Ed.-in-Chief. Articles, 1,500 words, of interest to women ages 25 to 50, especially large-size women, including interviews with successful large-size women and personal accounts of how to cope with difficult situations. Tips on restaurants, airlines, stores, etc., that treat large women with respect. Payment varies, on publication. Query.

BLACK ELEGANCE—475 Park Ave. S., New York, NY 10016. Sharyn J. Skeeter, Ed. Articles, 1,000 to 2,000 words, on fashion, beauty, relationships, home design, careers, personal finance, and personalities, for black women ages 25 to 45. Short interviews. Include photos if available. Pays $150 to $225, on publication. Query. Guidelines.

BRIDAL GUIDE—Globe Communications Corp., 441 Lexington Ave., New York, NY 10017. Deborah Harding, Ed. Mary McHugh, Articles Ed. Bimonthly covering wedding planning, fashion, beauty, contemporary relationships, honeymoon travel, and plans for the first home. Regular departments include: finance, sex, remarriage, and advice for the groom. Prefers queries for articles 800 to 1,600 words. Pays $200 to $600, on acceptance.

BRIDE'S & YOUR HOME—(formerly *Bride's Magazine*) 350 Madison Ave., New York, NY 10017. Andrea Feld, Man. Ed. Articles, 800 to 3,000 words, for engaged couples or newlyweds, on communication, sex, housing, finances, careers, remarriage, step-parenting, health, birth control, pregnancy, babies, religion, in-laws, relationships, and wedding planning. Three major editorial subjects: home, wedding, and honeymoon travel. Pays $300 to $1,000, on acceptance.

CAPPER'S—616 Jefferson St., Topeka, KS 66607-1188. Nancy Peavler, Ed. Human-interest, personal-experience, historical articles, 300 to 700 words. Poetry, to 15 lines, on nature, home, family. Novel-length fiction for serialization. Letters on women's interests, recipes, hints, for "Heart of the Home." Jokes. Children's writing and art section. Pays varying rates, on publication.

CHATELAINE—Maclean Hunter Bldg., 777 Bay St., Toronto, Ont., Canada M5W 1A7. Elizabeth Parr, Sr. Ed. Articles, 2,500 words, on current issues and personalities of interest to Canadian women. Pays from $1,200 for 1,500 to 3,000 words; from $350 for 500-word "Up-front" columns (relationships, health, parents/kids), on acceptance. Send query with outline or manuscript with international reply coupon.

COMPLETE WOMAN—1165 N. Clark, Chicago, IL 60610. Susan Handy, Man. Ed. Articles, 1,500 to 2,000 words, with how-to sidebars, giving practical advice to women on careers, health, personal relationships, etc. Also interested in reprints. Pays varying rates, on publication. Send manuscript or query with SASE.

COSMOPOLITAN—224 W. 57th St., New York, NY 10019. Helen Gurley Brown, Ed. Betty Nichols Kelly, Fiction and Books Ed. Articles, to 3,500 words, and features, 500 to 2,500 words, on issues affecting young career women, with emphasis on jobs and personal life. Fiction on male-female relationships: short shorts, 1,500 to 3,000 words; short stories, 3,000 to 4,000 words; condensed published novels, 25,000 words. SASE required.

COUNTRY WOMAN—P.O. Box 643, Milwaukee, WI 53201. Kathy Pohl, Man. Ed. Profiles of country women (photo/feature packages), inspirational, reflective pieces. Personal-experience, nostalgia, humor, service-oriented articles, original crafts, and how-to features, to 1,000 words, of interest to country women. Pays $40 to $150, on acceptance.

ELLE—1633 Broadway, New York, NY 10019. Rona Berg, Editorial Board. Articles, varying lengths, for fashion-conscious women, ages 20 to 50. Subjects include beauty, health, careers, fitness, travel, and lifestyles. Pays top rates, on publication. Query required.

ESSENCE—1500 Broadway, New York, NY 10036. Harriette Cole, Contemporary Living Ed. Provocative articles, 800 to 2,500 words, about black women in America today: self-help, how-to pieces, business and finance, health, celebrity profiles, art, travel, and political issues. Short items, 500 to 750 words, on work, parenting, and health. Features and fiction, 800 to 2,500 words. Pays varying rates, on acceptance. Query for articles.

EXECUTIVE FEMALE—127 W. 24th St., New York, NY 10011. Diane Burley, Ed. Features, 6 to 12 pages, on managing people, time, and careers, for women in business. Articles, 4 to 6 pages, for "More Money," "Profiles," and "Viewpoint." Pays varying rates, on publication. Limited market.

FAMILY CIRCLE—110 Fifth Ave., New York, NY 10011. Susan Ungaro, Exec. Ed. Articles, 2,000 words, on "women who have made a difference," marriage, family, and child-care and elder-care issues; consumer affairs, travel, humor, health, nutrition and fitness, personal opinion essays. Query required. Pays top rates, on acceptance.

FIRST FOR WOMEN—P.O. Box 1649, Englewood Cliffs, NJ 07632. Jackie Highe, Ed. Bibi Wein, Fiction Ed. Query first for articles. Send manuscript for fiction. Mainstream stories, 3,500 to 4,500 words, reflecting the concerns of contemporary women; no formula or experimental fiction. Tightly structured short-shorts, 850 to 1,000 words. "A humorous twist is welcome in fiction." Pay varies, on acceptance. Allow 8 to 12 weeks for response. SASE required.

GLAMOUR—350 Madison Ave., New York, NY 10017. Ruth Whitney, Ed.-in-Chief. Barbara Coffey, Man. Ed. How-to articles, from 1,500 words, on careers, health, psychology, interpersonal relationships, etc., for women ages 18 to 35. Fashion and beauty pieces staff written. Submit queries to Lisa Bain, Articles Ed. Pays from $500, on acceptance.

GOOD HOUSEKEEPING—959 Eighth Ave., New York, NY 10019. Joan Thursh, Articles Ed. Lee Quarfoot, Fiction Ed. In-depth articles and features on controversial problems, topical social issues; dramatic personal narratives with unusual experiences of average families; new or unusual medical information, personal medical stories. No submissions on food, beauty, needlework, or crafts. Short stories, 2,000 to 5,000 words, with strong identification for women, by published writers and "beginners with demonstrable talent." Unsolicited fiction not returned; if no response in six weeks, assume work was unsuitable. Include SASE with nonfiction submissions. Pays top rates, on acceptance.

IDEALS—P.O. Box 140300, Nashville, TN 37214–0300. Nancy Skarmeas, Assoc. Ed. Articles, 600 to 800 words; poetry, 12 to 50 lines, no free verse. Light, reminiscent pieces of interest to women. Pays $10 for poems. Guidelines.

518

LADIES' HOME JOURNAL—100 Park Ave., New York, NY 10017. Myrna Blyth, Pub. Dir./Ed.-in-Chief. Articles of interest to women. Send queries with outlines to: Lynn Langway, Exec. Ed. (news/general interest); Jane Farrell, Articles Ed. (news/human interest); Nelly Edmondson Gupta (health/medical); Jill Rachlin (celebrity/entertainment); Pamela Guthrie O'Brien (psychology); Lois Johnson (beauty/fashion/fitness); Jan Hazard (food); Shana Aborn (personal experience); Mary Mohler, Man. Ed. (children and families). Fiction accepted through literary agents only; humorous poetry accepted for "Last Laughs" column. Guidelines.

LADY'S CIRCLE—111 E. 35th St., New York, NY 10016. Mary F. Bemis, Ed. How-to, food, and crafts articles for homemakers. Short fiction. "Upbeat" pieces for over-50 audience. Pays $125 for articles, $10 for pet peeves, $5 for recipes or helpful hints, on publication.

LEAR'S—655 Madison Ave., New York, NY 10021. Audreen Ballard, Exec. Ed. "Literate, lively, and compelling" articles, 800 to 1,200 words, for women, on health, finance, contemporary issues, personalities, and leisure. Query with clips and SASE. Pays $1 a word, on acceptance.

MCCALL'S—110 Fifth Ave., New York, NY 10011. Andrea Thompson, Articles Ed. Articles, 1,000 to 3,000 words, on current issues, human interest, family relationships. Pays top rates ($750 for "The Mothers' Page"), on acceptance

MADEMOISELLE—350 Madison Ave., New York, NY 10017. Liz Logan, Articles Ed. Eileen Schnurr, Fiction Ed. Articles, 1,500 to 2,500 words, on work, relationships, health, and trends of interest to single, working women in their mid-twenties. Reporting pieces, essays, first-person accounts, and humor. No how-to. Submit query with clips and SASE. Pays excellent rates, on acceptance.

MODERN BRIDE—475 Park Ave. South, New York, NY 10016. Mary Ann Cavlin, Man. Ed. Articles, 1,800 to 2,000 words, for bride and groom, on wedding planning, financial planning, juggling career and home, etc. Query Travel Editor Geri Bain with articles on honeymoon travel. Pays $600 to $1,200, on acceptance.

MS.: THE WORLD OF WOMEN—230 Park Ave., 7th Fl., New York, NY 10169. Address Manuscript Editor with SASE. Articles relating to feminism, women's roles, and social change; national and international news reporting, profiles, essays, theory, and analysis. Query with SASE required. No fiction or poetry accepted, acknowledged, or returned.

NA'AMAT WOMAN—200 Madison Ave., Suite 2120, New York, NY 10016. Judith Sokoloff, Ed. Articles on Jewish culture, women's issues, social and political topics, and Israel, 1,500 to 2,500 words. Short stories with a Jewish theme. Pays 8¢ a word, on publication. Query or send manuscript.

NEW WOMAN—215 Lexington Ave., New York, NY 10016. Karen Walden, Ed.-in-Chief. Articles, for women ages 25 to 49, on self-improvement, self-esteem, self-discovery. Features: relationships, careers, health and fitness, money, fashion, beauty, food and nutrition, travel features with self-discovery angle, and essays by and about women pacesetters. Pays about $1 a word, on acceptance. Query with SASE.

NEW YORK WOMAN—1120 Sixth Ave., 9th Fl., New York, NY 10036. Betsy Carter, Ed. Articles, 500 to 3,000 words, for women ages 25 to 45, living in the New York metropolitan area. Pays $1 a word, on publication. Queries with SASE required.

ON THE ISSUES—Choices Women's Medical Center, Inc., 97–77 Queens Blvd., Forest Hills, NY 11374–3317. Beverly Lowy, Man. Ed. "The Magazine of

Substance for Progressive Women." Articles, to 2,500 words, on political or social issues. Movie, music, and book reviews, 500 to 750 words. Query. Payment varies, on publication.

PLAYGIRL—801 Second Ave., New York, NY 10017. Barbara Haigh, Ed.-in-Chief. In-depth articles for contemporary women. Humor, celebrity interviews. No free-lance fiction. Pays varying rates. Query first with clips. Guidelines.

RADIANCE: THE MAGAZINE FOR LARGE WOMEN—P.O. Box 31703, Oakland, CA 94604. Alice Ansfield, Ed./Pub. Quarterly. Articles, 1,500 to 2,500 words, that provide information, inspiration, and resources for women of all large sizes. Features include information on health, media, fashion, and politics that relate to issues of body size. Fiction and poetry also welcome. Pays to $100, on publication.

REDBOOK—224 W. 57th St., New York, NY 10019. Dawn Raffel, Fiction Ed. Toni Hope, Articles Ed. Fiction and articles for women ages 25 to 40. Pays from $1,000 for short stories to 25 typed pages; to $850 for short shorts, to 9 typed pages; $750 for personal-experience pieces, 1,000 to 2,000 words, on solving problems in marriage, family life, or community, for "Young Mother's Story." Query for articles only. SASE required.

SELF—350 Madison Ave., New York, NY 10017. Alexandra Penney, Ed.-in-Chief. Query for articles on current women's issues. No poetry. Payment varies. Include SASE.

VOGUE—350 Madison Ave., New York, NY 10017. Address Features Ed. Articles, to 1,500 words, on women, entertainment and the arts, travel, medicine, and health. General features. No unsolicited manuscripts. Query first. Pays good rates, on acceptance.

WOMAN'S DAY—1633 Broadway, New York, NY 10019. Rebecca Greer, Articles Ed. Human-interest or helpful articles, to 2,500 words, on marriage, child-rearing, health, careers, relationships, money management. Dramatic first-person narratives of medical miracles, rescues, women's experiences, etc. Pays top rates, on acceptance. Query.

WOMAN'S WORLD—270 Sylvan Ave., Englewood Cliffs, NJ 07632. Marilyn Webb, Feature Ed. Articles, 600 to 1,800 words, of interest to middle-income women between the ages of 18 and 60, on love, romance, careers, psychology, family life, investigative stories, dramatic adventures or crises. Send SASE for guidelines. Pays $300 to $750, on acceptance. Query.

WOMEN IN BUSINESS—American Business Women's Assn., 9100 Ward Pkwy., Box 8728, Kansas City, MO 64114–0728. Wendy S. Myers, Ed. Features, 1,000 to 1,500 words, for working women ages 35 to 55. No profiles. Pays on acceptance. Written query required.

WOMEN'S CIRCLE—P.O. Box 299, Lynnfield, MA 01940. Marjorie Pearl, Ed. Success stories on home-based female entrepreneurs. How-to articles on contemporary craft and needlework projects. Unique money-saving ideas and recipes. Pays varying rates, on acceptance.

WORKING MOTHER—Lang Communication, 230 Park Ave., New York, NY 10169. Address Editorial Dept. Articles, to 1,000 words, that help women in their task of juggling job, home, and family. "We like humorous pieces that solve or illuminate a problem unique to our readers." Payment varies, on acceptance.

WORKING WOMAN—230 Park Ave., New York, NY 10169. Lynn Povich, Ed.-in-Chief. Articles, 1,000 to 2,500 words, on business and personal aspects of the lives of working women. Pays from $400, on acceptance.

HOME AND LIFESTYLE PUBLICATIONS

THE AMERICAN ROSE MAGAZINE—P.O. Box 30,000, Shreveport, LA 71130. Kris McKnight, Exec. Dir. Articles on home rose gardens: varieties, products, helpful advice, rose care, etc.

BETTER HOMES AND GARDENS—1716 Locust St., Des Moines, IA 50336. David Jordan, Ed. Articles, to 2,000 words, on home and family entertainment, money management, health, travel, pets, and cars. Pays top rates, on acceptance. Query.

THE CHRISTIAN SCIENCE MONITOR—One Norway St., Boston, MA 02115. David Holmstrom, Features Ed. Newspaper. Articles on lifestyle trends, women's rights, family, parenting, and consumerism. Pays varying rates, on acceptance.

CONNECTICUT FAMILY—See *New York Family.*

CONNOISSEUR—Hearst Corp., 1790 Broadway, 18th Fl., New York, NY 10019. Robert Sabat, Man. Ed. Articles for readers "interested in learning about excellence in all areas of art." Topics include fine, decorative, and performing arts, architecture and design, food, fashion, and travel; include pertinent service data. Length varies; query required. Pays about $1 a word, on acceptance.

CONSUMERS DIGEST—5705 N. Lincoln Ave., Chicago, IL 60659. John Manos, Ed. Articles, 500 to 3,000 words, on subjects of interest to consumers: products and services, automobiles, health, fitness, consumer legal affairs, and personal money management. Photos. Pays from 40¢ a word, extra for photos, on publication. Buys all rights. Query with resumé and published clips.

COUNTRY—5400 S. 60th St., Greendale, WI 53129. Dan Matel, Asst. Ed. Pieces on interesting rural and country people who have unusual hobbies or businesses, 500 to 1,500 words; liberal use of direct quotes. Good, candid, color photos required. Pays on acceptance. Queries preferred.

DECORATING REMODELING—110 Fifth Ave., New York, NY 10011. Olivia Bell Buehl, Ed. Columns on finance and collecting. Articles on home decorating, remodeling, architecture, and gardening. Query first. Payment varies, on acceptance.

EAST WEST: THE JOURNAL OF NATURAL HEALTH & LIVING—17 Station St., Box 1200, Brookline, MA 02147. Features, 1,500 to 2,500 words, on holistic health, natural foods, herbal remedies, etc. Interviews. Photos. Pays 20¢ a word, extra for photos, on acceptance.

ELLE DECOR—1633 Broadway, New York, NY 10019. Mitchell Owens, Articles Ed. "Personality profiles, 500 to 2,000 words, of new artists, designers, and craftspeople are a good way to catch our attention." Query. Pays $1 a word, on acceptance.

FARM AND RANCH LIVING—5400 S. 60th St., Greendale, WI 53129. Bob Ottum, Ed. Articles, 2,000 words, on rural people and situations; nostalgia pieces, profiles of interesting farms and farmers, ranches and ranchers. Pays $15 to $400, on acceptance and on publication.

FATE—P.O. Box 64383, St. Paul, MN 55164–0383. Donald Michael Kraig, Ed. Factual fillers and true stories, to 300 words, on strange or psychic happenings and mystic personal experiences. Pays $2 to $15.

FLORIDA HOME & GARDEN—800 Douglas Rd., Suite 500, Coral Gables, FL 33134. Kathryn Howard, Ed. Features, 800 to 1,000 words, and department pieces, 500 to 750 words, about Florida interior design, architecture, landscape architecture, gardening, trendy new products, art, travel (Florida, Caribbean, and Mexico's gulf coast), and home entertaining. Pays $200 to $400, extra for photos.

FLOWER & GARDEN MAGAZINE—4251 Pennsylvania, Kansas City, MO 64111. Practical how-to articles, 1,000 words, on lawn and garden advice. Query first. Good photos enhance submission. Pays varying rates, on acceptance. (Photos paid on publication.)

FOOD & WINE—1120 Ave. of the Americas, New York, NY 10036. Carole Lalli, Ed.-in-Chief. Warren Picower, Man. Ed. Current culinary or beverage ideas for dining and entertaining at home and out. Submit detailed proposal.

GARDEN DESIGN—Society of American Landscape Architects, 4401 Connecticut Ave. N.W., Fifth Fl., Washington, DC 20008. Karen D. Fishler, Ed. Garden-related features. Need articles, 800 to 1,500 words, on "private and public gardens, interviews with landscape designers and other personalities, and stories on art, architecture, furniture and fashion as they relate to the garden." Pays from 50¢ a word, on publication. Guidelines.

GROWING CHILD/GROWING PARENT—22 N. Second St., Lafayette, IN 47902–0620. Nancy Kleckner, Ed. Articles, to 1,500 words, on subjects of interest to parents of children under 6. No personal experience pieces or poetry. Guidelines.

HARROWSMITH COUNTRY LIFE—Ferry Rd., Charlotte, VT 05445. Address Editorial Dept. Investigative pieces, 4,000 to 5,000 words, on issues of ecology and the environment, rural life, gardening, energy-efficient housing, and healthful food. Short pieces for "Screed" (opinions) and "Gazette" (news briefs). Pays $500 to $1,500 for features, from $50 to $600 for department pieces, on acceptance. Query required. Send SASE for guidelines.

HEALTHY KIDS—Cahners Publishing, 475 Park Ave. S., New York, NY 10016. Phyllis Steinberg, Ed. Published in two editions: "Birth-3" (quarterly) and "4–10" Years (three times a year). Articles, 1,500 to 2,000 words, addressing the elements of raising a healthy, happy child (basic care, nutrition, analysis of the growing mind, behavior patterns, emergencies, etc.). "All articles should be written by experts or include interviews with appropriate pediatricians and other health-care professionals." Query. Pays $500 to $1,000, on acceptance.

THE HERB QUARTERLY—P. O. Box 548, Boiling Springs, PA 17007. Linda Sparrowe, Ed. Articles, 2,000 to 4,000 words, on herbs: practical uses, cultivation, gourmet cooking, landscaping, herb tradition, medicinal herbs, crafts ideas, unique garden designs, profiles of herb garden experts, practical how-tos for the herb businessperson. Include garden design when possible. Pays on publication. Guidelines.

HG: HOUSE & GARDEN—350 Madison Ave., New York, NY 10017. Nancy Novogrod, Ed.-in-Chief. Dana Cowin, Man. Ed. Articles on decorating, style, design, architecture, and the arts. No unsolicited articles.

HOME LIFE—127 Ninth Ave. N., Nashville, TN 37234. Charlie Warren, Ed. Southern Baptist. Articles, to 1,500 words, on Christian marriage, parenting, and family relationships. Pays to 5 ½¢ a word, on acceptance.

HORTICULTURE—Statler Bldg., 20 Park Plaza, Suite 1220, Boston, MA 02116. Deborah Starr, Articles Ed. Authoritative, well-written articles, 500 to 2,500 words, on all aspects of gardening. Pays competitive rates. Query first.

HOUSE BEAUTIFUL—1700 Broadway, New York, NY 10019. Elaine

Greene, Ed. Service articles related to the home. Pieces on design, travel, and gardening; mostly staff-written. Send for writer's guidelines. Query with detailed outline. SASE required.

INDEPENDENT LIVING—44 Broadway, Greenlawn, NY 11740. Anne Kelly, Ed. Articles, 1,000 to 2,000 words, addressing lifestyles of persons who have disabilities. Possible topics: home health care, travel, sports, family life, and sexuality. Pays 10¢ a word, on publication. Query.

LOG HOME GUIDE FOR BUILDERS & BUYERS—164 Middle Creek Rd., Cosby, TN 37722. Articles, 500 to 1,500 words, on building new, or restoring old, log homes, especially with solar or alternative heating systems, as well as pieces on decorating or profiles of interesting builders of log homes. Pays 20¢ a word, extra for photos, on publication. Limited market. Query first.

LOG HOME LIVING—P.O. Box 220039, Chantilly, VA 22022. Roland Sweet, Ed. Articles, 1,000 to 1,500 words, on modern manufactured and handcrafted kit log homes: homeowner profiles, design and decor features, home producer profiles, and technical articles. Pays $200 to $600, on acceptance.

MAGICAL BLEND—Box 11303, San Francisco, CA 94101. Julie Marchasin, Literary Ed. Positive, uplifting articles on spiritual exploration, lifestyles, occult, white magic, new age thought, and fantasy. Fiction and features to 5,000 words. Pays in copies.

MATURE OUTLOOK—Meredith Corp., 1716 Locust, Des Moines, IA 50336. Marjorie P. Groves, Ed. Articles, 500 to 2,000 words, for "energetic" readers over the age of 50, on travel and leisure topics, health, food, gardening, and personalities. Pays $200 to $1,500, on acceptance.

MILITARY LIFESTYLE MAGAZINE—4800 Montgomery Ln., Suite 710, Bethesda, MD 20814. Hope Daniels, Ed. Articles, 1,000 to 2,000 words, for military families in the U.S. and overseas; pieces on child raising, marriage, health, fitness, food, and issues concerning young military families; home decor and "portable" or "instant" gardening articles; fiction. Pays $300 to $700, on publication. Query first.

THE MOTHER EARTH NEWS—24 E. 23rd St., 5th Fl., New York, NY 10010. Owen Lipstein, Ed. Articles on country living: home improvement and construction, how-tos, indoor and outdoor gardening, crafts and projects, etc. Also self-help, health, food-related, ecology, energy, and consumerism pieces; profiles. Pays from $100 per published page, on acceptance. Address Submissions Ed.

NATIONAL GARDENING MAGAZINE—180 Flynn Ave., Burlington, VT 05401. Warren Schultz, Ed. Articles, 300 to 3,000 words: seed-to-table profiles of major crops; firsthand reports from experienced gardeners in this country's many growing regions; easy-to-follow gardening techniques; garden food recipes; coverage of fruits, vegetables, and ornamentals. Pays $75 to $450, extra for photos, on acceptance. Query preferred.

NEW AGE JOURNAL—342 Western Ave., Brighton, MA 02135. Peggy Taylor, Ed. Features, 2,000 to 4,000 words; columns, 750 to 1,500 words; short news items, 500 words; and first-person narratives, 750 to 1,500 words, for readers who take an active interest in holistic health, personal and spiritual growth, environmentalism, social responsibility, and contemporary social issues. Pays varying rates. Query or send completed manuscript.

NEW CHOICES FOR THE BEST YEARS—28 W. 23rd St., New York, NY 10010. Kate Greer, Ed.-in-Chief. Lifestyle/service magazine for people ages 45 to 65. Articles on careers, health/fitness, travel, gardening, relationships, entertaining, and finance. Columns on "Generations," "Collecting," nostalgia, the new voluntarism, pets, cars. Send complete manuscript with SASE. Payment varies, on acceptance.

NEW HOME—P.O. Box 2008, Laconia, NH 03247. Steven Maviglio, Man. Ed. Articles, 250 to 2,500 words, "that give upscale new homeowners whatever they need to make their home more comfortable, practical, and personal." Department pieces on landscaping, security, and interviews with professionals in their homes. Pays $200 to $1,000, on acceptance. Query required.

NEW YORK FAMILY—420 E. 79th St., New York, NY 10021. Felice Shapiro, Susan Ross, Eds. Articles related to family life in New York City and general parenting topics. Pays $50 to $100. Same requirements for *Westchester Family* and *Connecticut Family*.

PALM SPRINGS LIFE—Desert Publications, 303 North Indian Canyon Dr., P.O. Box 2724, Palm Springs, CA 92263. Jamie Pricer, Ed. Articles, 1,000 to 3,000 words, of interest to "wealthy, upscale people who live and/or play in the desert." Pays $150 to $400 for features, $30 to $75 for short profiles, on publication. Query required.

PARENTING—501 Second St., San Francisco, CA 94107. Rachael Grossman, Ed. Articles, 500 to 3,500 words, on education, health, fitness, nutrition, child development, psychology, and social issues, for parents of young children. Query.

PARENTS—685 Third Ave., New York, NY 10017. Ann Pleshette Murphy, Ed. Articles, 1,500 to 3,000 words, on parenting, family, women's and community issues, etc. Informal style with quotes from experts. Pays from $1,000, on acceptance. Query.

SELECT HOMES—50 Holly St., Toronto, Canada M4S 3B3. Lynette Jennings, Ed. How-to articles, profiles of Canadian homes, renovation features, 800 to 1,500 words. Pays from $400 to $800 (Canadian), on acceptance. Query with international reply coupons. Send SAE with international reply coupons for guidelines.

SWIMSUIT INTERNATIONAL—Swimsuit Publishers, 801 Second Ave., New York, NY 10017. Nicole Dorsey, Ed.-in-Chief. Articles, 1,000 to 1,500 words, on health, lifestyle, and swimwear-related topics. Payment varies. Query.

VIRTUE—P. O. Box 850, Sisters, OR 97759. Marlee Alex, Ed. Articles, 1,000 to 1,500 words, on the family, marriage, self-esteem, working mothers, opinions, food, crafts. Fiction and poetry. Pays 15¢ to 25¢ a word, on acceptance. Query required.

WESTCHESTER FAMILY—See *New York Family*.

WILDFIRE—Bear Tribe Publishing, P.O. Box 9167, Spokane, WA 99209–9167. Matthew Ryan, Ed. Articles, 1,000 to 2,500 words, with a strong nature-based focus on spirituality, personal development, alternative lifestyles, natural healings, and ecology. Fiction, 900 to 4,500 words, and poetry, 20 lines. Pays to $250, on publication.

WINE TIDINGS—5165 Sherbrooke St. W., Suite 414, Montreal, Quebec, Canada H4A 1T6. Barbara Leslie, Ed. Published eight times a year. Articles, 1,000 to 1,500 words, and 400- to 1,000-word shorts, with accurate wine information and written for a Canadian audience. Pays $100 to $300 for features, $30 to $150 for shorts, on publication. Photos, $20 to $50 for B&W or color; $200 to $400 for covers.

WORKBENCH—4251 Pennsylvania, Kansas City, MO 64111. Robert N. Hoffman, Exec. Ed. Illustrated how-to articles on home improvement and woodworking, with detailed instructions. Pays from $150 per printed page, on acceptance. Send SASE for writers' guidelines.

YOGA JOURNAL—2054 University Ave., Berkeley, CA 94704. Stephan Bodian, Ed. Articles, 1,200 to 4,000 words, on holistic health, spirituality, yoga, and transpersonal psychology; new age profiles; interviews. Pays $50 to $400, on publication.

SPORTS, OUTDOORS, RECREATION

THE AMERICAN FIELD—542 S. Dearborn, Chicago, IL 60605. B.J. Matthys, Man. Ed. Yarns about hunting trips, bird-shooting; articles to 1,500 words, on dogs and field trials, emphasizing conservation of game resources. Pays varying rates, on acceptance.

AMERICAN HANDGUNNER—591 Camino de la Reina, Suite 200, San Diego, CA 92108. Cameron Hopkins, Ed. Semi-technical articles on shooting sports, gun repair and alteration, handgun matches and tournaments, for lay readers. Pays $100 to $500, on publication. Query.

AMERICAN HUNTER—470 Spring Park Place, Suite 1000, Herndon, VA 22070–5227. Tom Fulgham, Ed. Articles, 1,400 to 2,000 words, on hunting. Photos. Pays on acceptance. Guidelines.

AMERICAN MOTORCYCLIST—American Motorcyclist Assn., Box 6114, Westerville, OH 43081–6114. Greg Harrison, Ed. Articles and fiction, to 3,000 words, on motorcycling: news coverage, personalities, tours. Photos. Pays varying rates, on publication. Query with SASE.

THE AMERICAN RIFLEMAN—470 Spring Park Place, Suite 1000, Herndon, VA 22070. Bill Parkerson, Ed. Factual articles on use and enjoyment of sporting firearms. Pays on acceptance.

AMERICAN SQUAREDANCE MAGAZINE—216 Williams St., P.O. Box 488, Huron, OH 44839. Cathie Burdick, Co-Ed. Articles and fiction, 1,000 to 1,500 words, related to square dancing. Poetry. Fillers to 100 words. Pays $2 per column inch.

ATLANTIC SALMON JOURNAL—P.O. Box 289, Guysborough, N.S., Canada B0H 1N0. Harry Bruce, Ed. Material related to Atlantic salmon: fishing, conservation, ecology, travel, politics, biology, how-tos, anecdotes, cuisine. Articles, 1,500 to 3,000 words. Pays $100 to $350, on publication.

AUTO RACING DIGEST—See *Inside Sports.*

BACKPACKER MAGAZINE—Rodale Press, 33 Minor St., Emmaus, PA 18049. John Viehman, Exec. Ed. Articles, 250 to 3,000 words, on self-propelled backcountry travel: backpacking, technique, kayaking/canoeing, mountaineering, nordic skiing, health, natural science. Photos. Pays varying rates. Query.

THE BACKSTRETCH—19899 W. 9 Mile Rd., Southfield, MI 48075–3960. Harriet Randall, Ed. United Thoroughbred Trainers of America. Feature articles, with photos, on subjects related to thoroughbred horse racing. Pays after publication. Sample issue and guidelines on request.

BASEBALL ILLUSTRATED—See *Hockey Illustrated.*

BASKETBALL DIGEST—See *Inside Sports*.

BASSIN'—15115 S. 76th E. Ave., Bixby, OK 74008. Gordon Sprouse, Man. Ed. Articles, 1,500 to 1,800 words, on how and where to bass fish, for the amateur fisherman. Pays $275 to $400, on acceptance.

BASSMASTER MAGAZINE—B.A.S.S. Publications, P.O. Box 17900, Montgomery, AL 36141. Dave Precht, Ed. Articles, 1,500 to 2,000 words, with photos, on freshwater black bass and striped bass. "Short Casts" pieces, 400 to 800 words, on news, views, and items of interest. Pays $200 to $400, on acceptance. Query.

BAY & DELTA YACHTSMAN—2019 Clement Ave., Alameda, CA 94501. Bill Parks, Ed. Cruising stories and features. Must have northern California tie-in. Photos and illustrations. Pays varying rates.

BC OUTDOORS—1132 Hamilton St., #202, Vancouver, B.C., Canada V6B 2S2. George Will, Ed. Articles, to 2,000 words, on fishing, hunting, conservation, and all forms of non-competitive outdoor recreation in British Columbia and Yukon. Photos. Pays from 15¢ to 25¢ a word, on acceptance.

BICYCLE GUIDE—545 Boylston St., Boston, MA 02116. Christopher Koch, Ed. "Our magazine covers all aspects of cycling from an enthusiast's perspective: racing, touring, sport riding, product reviews, and technical information. We depend on free lancers for touring articles, personality profiles, and race coverage." Queries are preferred. Pays varying rates, on publication.

BICYCLING—33 E. Minor St., Emmaus, PA 18098. James C. McCullagh, Ed. Articles, 500 to 2,500 words, on recreational riding, fitness training, nutrition, bike maintenance, equipment, racing and touring, for serious cyclists. Photos, illustrations. Pays $25 to $1,000, on acceptance. Guidelines.

BIKEREPORT—Bikecentennial, P.O. Box 8308, Missoula, MT 59807. Daniel D'Ambrosio, Ed. Accounts of bicycle tours in the U.S. and overseas, interviews, personal-experience pieces, humor, and news shorts, 1,200 to 2,500 words. Pays $25 to $65 per published page.

BIRD WATCHER'S DIGEST—P.O. Box 110, Marietta, OH 45750. Mary B. Bowers, Ed. Articles, 600 to 2,500 words, for bird watchers: first-person accounts; how-tos; pieces on endangered species; profiles. Cartoons. Pays from $50, on publication.

BLACK BELT—P.O. Box 918, Santa Clarita, CA 91380–9018. Articles related to self-defense: how-tos on fitness and technique; historical, travel, philosophical subjects. Pays $100 to $250, on publication. Guidelines.

BOAT PENNSYLVANIA—Pennsylvania Fish Commission, P.O. Box 1673, Harrisburg, PA 17105–1673. Art Michaels, Ed. Articles, 200 to 2,500 words, with photos, on boating in Pennsylvania: motorboating, sailing, waterskiing, canoeing, kayaking, and personal motorcraft. No pieces on fishing. Pays $50 to $250, on acceptance. Query. Guidelines.

BOUNDARY WATERS JOURNAL—9396 Rocky Ledge Rd., Ely, MN 55031. Stuart Osthoff, Ed. Articles, 2,000 to 3,000 words, on recreation and natural resources in Minnesota's Boundary Waters Canoe Area Wilderness and Ontario's Quetico Provincial Park. Regular features include canoe-route journals, fishing, camping, hiking, cross-country skiing, wildlife and nature, regional lifestyles, history, and events. Pays $200 to $400, on publication; $50 to $150 for photos.

BOW & ARROW HUNTING—Box HH, 34249 Camino Capistrano, Capistrano Beach, CA 92624. Roger Combs, Ed. Dir. Articles, 1,200 to 2,500 words, with

B&W photos, on bowhunting; profiles and technical pieces. Pays $50 to $300, on acceptance. Same address and mechanical requirements for *Gun World.*

BOWHUNTER MAGAZINE—Box 8200, Harrisburg, PA 17105–8200. M.R. James, Ed. Informative, entertaining features, 500 to 2,000 words, on bow-and-arrow hunting. Fillers. Photos. Pays $25 to $300, on acceptance. Study magazine first.

BOWHUNTING WORLD—319 Barry Ave. S., Suite 101, Wayzata, MN 55391. Tim Dehn, Ed. Articles, 1,800 to 3,000 words, on all aspects of bowhunting and competitive archery, with photos. Pays from $200, on acceptance, with premium for features available on double-density 5 ¼-inch disks, ASCII format preferred.

BOWLERS JOURNAL—200 S. Michigan Ave., Chicago, IL 60604. Mort Luby, Ed. Trade and consumer articles, 1,200 to 2,200 words, with photos, on bowling. Pays $75 to $200, on acceptance.

BOWLING—5301 S. 76th St., Greendale, WI 53129. Bill Vint, Ed. Articles, to 1,500 words, on amateur league and tournament bowling. Profiles. "Looking for unique, unusual stories about bowling people and places." Pays varying rates, on publication.

BOWLING DIGEST—See *Inside Sports.*

CALIFORNIA ANGLER—1921 E. Carnegie St., Suite N, Santa Ana, CA 92705. How-to and where-to articles, 2,000 words, for freshwater and saltwater anglers in California: travel, new products, fishing techniques, profiles. Photos. Pays $75 to $300, on acceptance. Query first.

CANOE—P.O. Box 3146, Kirkland, WA 98083. Les Johnson, Man. Ed. Features, 1,100 to 2,000 words; department pieces, 500 to 1,000 words. Topics include canoeing or kayaking adventures, destinations, boat and equipment reviews, technique and how-tos, short essays, camping, environment, humor, health, history, etc. Pays $5 per column inch, on publication. Query preferred. Guidelines.

CAR AND DRIVER—2002 Hogback Rd., Ann Arbor, MI 48105. William Jeanes, Ed. Articles, to 2,500 words, for enthusiasts, on new cars, classic cars, industry topics. "Ninety percent staff written. Query with clips. No unsolicited manuscripts." Pays to $2,500, on acceptance.

CAR CRAFT—8490 Sunset Blvd., Los Angeles, CA 90069. John Baechtel, Ed. Articles and photo features on unusual street machines, drag cars, racing events; technical pieces; action photos. Pays from $150 per page, on acceptance.

CASCADES EAST—716 N.E. Fourth St., P.O. Box 5784, Bend, OR 97708. Geoff Hill, Ed./Pub. Articles, 1,000 to 2,000 words, on outdoor activities (fishing, hunting, golfing, backpacking, rafting, skiing, snowmobiling, etc.), history, special events, and scenic tours in Central Oregon Cascades. Photos. Pays 5¢ to 10¢ a word, extra for photos, on publication.

CITY SPORTS MAGAZINE—P.O Box 193693, San Francisco, CA 94119. Chris Newbound, Ed. Articles, 200 to 2,000 words, on the active lifestyle, including service pieces, trend pieces, profiles, and nutrition. Pays $50 to $650, on publication. Query editor.

CROSS COUNTRY SKIER—319 Barry Ave. S., Wayzata, MN 55391. Jim Chase, Ed. Articles, to 3,000 words, on all aspects of cross-country skiing. Departments, 1,000 to 1,500 words, on ski maintenance, skiing techniques, health and fitness. Published October through February. Pays $300 to $700 for features, $100 to $350 for departments, on publication. Query.

CURRENTS—P.O. Box 6847, 314 N. 20th St., Suite 200, Colorado Springs, CO 80904. Address Greg Moore. Quarterly. "Voice of the National Organization for River Sports." Articles, 500 to 2,000 words, for kayakers, rafters, and river canoeists, pertaining to whitewater rivers and/or river running. Fillers. B&W action photos. Pays $35 and up for articles, $30 to $50 for photos, on publication. Queries preferred.

CYCLE WORLD—853 W. 17th St., Costa Mesa, CA 92627. David Edwards, Ed. Technical and feature articles, 1,500 to 2,500 words, for motorcycle enthusiasts. Photos. Pays $100 to $200 per page, on publication. Query.

CYCLING U.S.A.—U.S. Cycling Federation, 1750 E. Boulder St., Colorado Springs, CO 80909. Steve Penny, Ed. Articles, 500 to 1,500 words, on bicycle racing. Pays 15¢ a word, on publication. Query first.

THE DIVER—P.O. Box 313, Portland, CT 06480. Bob Taylor, Ed. Articles on divers, coaches, officials, springboard and platform techniques, training tips, etc. Pays $15 to $50, extra for photos ($5 to $25 for cartoons), on publication.

EQUUS—Fleet Street Corp., 656 Quince Orchard Rd., Gaithersburg, MD 20878. Laurie Prinz, Ed. Articles, 1,000 to 3,000 words, on all breeds of horses, covering their health, care, the latest advances in equine medicine and research, and horse-world events. "Attempt to speak as one horse-person to another." Pays $100 to $400, on acceptance.

FAMILY MOTOR COACHING—8291 Clough Pike, Cincinnati, OH 45244–2796. Pamela Wisby Kay, Ed. Monthly. Articles, 1,500 to 2,000 words, on technical topics and travel routes and destinations accessible by motorhome. Query preferred. Payment varies, on acceptance.

FIELD & STREAM—2 Park Ave., New York, NY 10016. Duncan Barnes, Ed. Articles, 1,500 to 2,000 words, with photos, on hunting, fishing. Fillers, 75 to 1,000 words. Cartoons. Pays from $800 for feature articles with photos, $75 to $500 for fillers, $100 for cartoons, on acceptance. Query for articles.

FISHING WORLD—51 Atlantic Ave., Floral Park, NY 11001. Keith Gardner, Ed. Features, to 2,500 words, with color transparencies, on fishing sites, technique, equipment. Pays to $500 for major features, $250 for shorter destination articles. Query preferred.

THE FLORIDA HORSE—P.O. Box 2106, Ocala, FL 32678. Bernie Dickman, Ed. Articles, 1,500 words, on Florida thoroughbred breeding and racing. Pays $100 to $200, on publication.

FLY FISHERMAN—6405 Flank Dr., Box 8200, Harrisburg, PA 17105. Philip Hanyok, Man. Ed. Query.

FLY ROD & REEL—P.O. Box 370, Camden, ME 04843. James E. Butler, Man. Ed. Flyfishing pieces, 2,000 to 2,500 words, and occasional fiction; articles on the culture and history of the areas being fished. Pays on publication. Query.

THE FLYFISHER—1387 Cambridge, Idaho Falls, ID 83401. Dennis G. Bitton, Ed. Articles, 500 to 3,000 words, on techniques, lore, history, and flyfishing personalities; how-to pieces. Serious or humorous short stories related to flyfishing. Pays from $50 to $200, after publication. Queries are preferred. Guidelines.

FOOTBALL DIGEST—Century Publishing Co., 990 Grove St., Evanston, IL

60201. Michael K. Herbert, Ed.-in-Chief. Profiles of pro stars, "think" pieces, 1,500 words, aimed at the pro football fan. Pays on publication. Guidelines.

FOOTBALL FORECAST—See *Hockey Illustrated.*

FUR-FISH-GAME—2878 E. Main St., Columbus, OH 43209. Mitch Cox, Ed. Illustrated articles, 800 to 2,500 words, preferably with how-to angle, on hunting, fishing, trapping, dogs, camping, or other outdoor topics. Some humorous or where-to articles. Pays $40 to $150, on acceptance.

GAME AND FISH PUBLICATIONS—P.O. Box 741, Marietta, GA 30061. Publishes 30 monthly outdoors magazines for 48 states. Articles, 1,500 to 2,500 words, on hunting and fishing. How-tos, where-tos, and adventure pieces. Profiles of successful hunters and fishermen. No hiking, canoeing, camping, or backpacking pieces. Pays $125 to $175 for state-specific articles, $200 to $250 for multi-state articles, before publication. Pays, $25 to $75 for photos.

GOAL—650 Fifth Ave., 33rd Fl., New York, NY 10019. Michael A. Berger, Ed. Official magazine of the National Hockey League. Player profiles and trend stories, 1,000 to 1,800 words, for hockey fans with knowledge of the game, by writers with understanding of the sport. Pays $150 to $300, on acceptance. Query.

GOLF DIGEST—5520 Park Ave., Trumbull, CT 06611. Jerry Tarde, Ed. Instructional articles, tournament reports, and features on players, to 2,500 words. Fiction, 1,000 to 2,000 words. Poetry, fillers, humor, photos. Pays varying rates, on acceptance. Query preferred.

GOLF FOR WOMEN—2130 Jackson Ave. W., Oxford, MS 38655. George Kehoe, Ed.-in-Chief. Golf-related articles of interest to women; fillers and humor. Instructional pieces staff written. Pays from 40¢ a word, on publication. Query first.

GOLF JOURNAL—Golf House, P.O. Box 708, Far Hills, NJ 07931–0708. Robert Sommers, Ed. U.S. Golf Assn. Articles on golf personalities, history, travel. Humor. Photos. Pays varying rates, on publication.

GOLF MAGAZINE—2 Park Ave., New York, NY 10016. Jim Frank, Ed. Articles, 1,000 words with photos, on golf history and travel (places to play around the world); profiles of professional tour players. Shorts, to 500 words. Pays 75¢ a word, on acceptance. Queries preferred.

THE GREYHOUND REVIEW—National Greyhound Association, Box 543, Abilene, KS 67410. Tim Horan, Man. Ed. Articles, 1,000 to 10,000 words, pertaining to the greyhound racing industry: how-to, historical nostalgia, interviews. Pays $85 to $150, on publication.

GULF COAST GOLFER—See *North Texas Golfer.*

GUN DIGEST—4092 Commercial Ave., Northbrook, IL 60062. Ken Warner, Ed. Well-researched articles, to 5,000 words, on guns and shooting, equipment, etc. Photos. Pays from 10¢ a word, on acceptance. Query.

GUN DOG—P.O. Box 35098, Des Moines, IA 50315. Bob Wilbanks, Man. Ed. Features, 1,000 to 2,500 words, with photos, on bird hunting: how-tos, where-tos, dog training, canine medicine, breeding strategy. Fiction. Humor. Pays $50 to $150 for fillers and short articles, $150 to $350 for features, on acceptance.

GUN WORLD—See *Bow & Arrow Hunting.*

GUNS & AMMO—8490 Sunset Blvd., Los Angeles, CA 90069. E. G. Bell, Jr., Ed. Technical and general articles, 1,500 to 3,000 words, on guns, ammunition, and target shooting. Photos, fillers. Pays from $150, on acceptance.

HANG GLIDING—U.S. Hang Gliding Assn., P.O. Box 8300, Colorado Springs, CO 80933–8300. Gilbert Dodgen, Ed. Articles, two to three pages, on hang gliding. Pays to $50, on publication. Query.

HOCKEY DIGEST—See *Inside Sports.*

HOCKEY ILLUSTRATED—Lexington Library, Inc., 355 Lexington Ave., New York, NY 10017. Stephen Ciacciarelli, Ed. Articles, 2,500 words, on hockey players, teams. Pays $125, on publication. Query. Same address and requirements for *Baseball Illustrated, Wrestling World, Pro Basketball Illustrated, Pro Football Illustrated, Basketball Annual* (college), *Baseball Preview, Baseball Forecast, Pro Football Preview, Football Forecast*, and *Basketball Forecast.*

HORSE & RIDER—P.O. Box 72001, San Clemente, CA 92672. Juli S. Thorson, Ed. Articles, 500 to 1,700 words, with photos, on Western riding and general horse care geared to the performance horse: training, feeding, grooming, health etc. Pays varying rates, on publication. Buys all rights. Guidelines.

HORSEMEN'S YANKEE PEDLAR—785 Southbridge St., Auburn, MA 01501. Nancy L. Khoury, Pub. News and feature-length articles, about horses and horsemen in the Northeast. Photos. Pays $2 per published inch, on publication. Query.

HORSEPLAY—P.O. Box 130, Gaithersburg, MD 20884. Cordelia Doucet, Ed. Articles, 700 to 3,000 words, on eventing, show jumping, horse shows, dressage, driving, and fox hunting, for horse enthusiasts. Pays 10¢ a word for all rights, 9¢ a word for first American rights, after publication. Query. SASE required.

HOT BIKE—2145 W. La Palma, Anaheim, CA 92801. Buck Lovell, Ed. Articles, 250 to 2,500 words, with photos, on Harley-Davidson motorcycles (contemporary and antique). Event coverage on high performance street and track and sport touring motorcycles, with emphasis on Harley Davidsons. Geographical motorcycle features. Pays $50 to $100 per printed page, on publication.

HOT ROD—8490 Sunset Blvd., Los Angeles, CA 90069. Jeff Smith, Ed. How-to pieces and articles, 500 to 5,000 words, on auto mechanics, hot rods, track and drag racing. Photo-features on custom or performance-modified cars. Pays to $250 per page, on publication.

HUNTING—8490 Sunset Blvd., Los Angeles, CA 90069. Craig Boddington, Ed. How-to articles on practical aspects of hunting. At least 15 photos required with articles. Pays $250 to $500 for articles with B&W photos, extra for color photos, on publication.

THE IN-FISHERMAN—Box 999, Brainerd, MN 56401–0999. Doug Stange, Ed. Published seven times yearly. How-to articles, 1,500 to 4,500 words, on all aspects of freshwater fishing. Humor, 1,000 to 1,500 words, for "Reflections" column. Pays $250 to $650, on acceptance.

INSIDE SPORTS—Century Publishing Co., 990 Grove St., Evanston, IL 60201. Michael K. Herbert, Ed. In-depth, insightful sports articles, player profiles, fillers, and humor. Same requirements for *Hockey Digest, Bowling Digest, Auto Racing Digest,* and *Basketball Digest.* Payment varies, on publication. Query. Guidelines.

INSIDE TEXAS RUNNING—9514 Bristlebrook Dr., Houston, TX 77083–6193. Joanne Schmidt, Ed. Articles and fillers on running, cycling, and triathlons in Texas. Pays $35 to $100, $10 for photos, on acceptance.

KEEPIN' TRACK OF VETTES—P.O. Box 48, Spring Valley, NY 10977.

Shelli Finkel, Ed. Articles of any length, with photos, relating to Corvettes. Pays $25 to $200, on publication.

KITPLANES—P.O. Box 6050, Mission Viejo, CA 92690. Dave Martin, Ed. Articles geared to the growing market of aircraft built from kits and plans by home craftsmen, on all aspects of design, construction, and performance, 1,000 to 4,000 words. Pays $150 to $350, on publication.

LAKELAND BOATING—1600 Orrington Ave., Suite 500, Evanston, IL 60201–5047. Sarah Wortham, Ed. Articles for boat owners on the Great Lakes and other area waterways, on long-distance cruising, short trips, maintenance, equipment, history, regional personalities and events, and environment. Photos. Pays on publication. Query first. Guidelines.

MEN'S FITNESS—21100 Erwin St., Woodland Hills, CA 91367. Jim Rosenthal, Fitness Ed. Ted Mason, Health Ed. Features, 1,500 to 2,500 words, and department pieces, 1,000 to 1,500 words: authoritative and practical articles dealing with fitness, health, and men's lifestyles. Pays $350 to $1,000, on acceptance.

MEN'S HEALTH—Rodale Press, 33 E. Minor Dr., Emmaus, PA 18098. Michael Lafavore, Exec. Ed. Articles, 1,000 to 2,500 words, on fitness, diet, health, relationships, sports, and travel, for men ages 25 to 55. Pays from 50¢ a word, on acceptance. Query first.

MICHIGAN OUT-OF-DOORS—P.O. Box 30235, Lansing, MI 48909. Kenneth S. Lowe, Ed. Features, 1,500 to 2,500 words, on hunting, fishing, camping, and conservation in Michigan. Pays $75 to $150, on acceptance.

MID-WEST OUTDOORS—111 Shore Dr., Hinsdale, IL 60521. Gene Laulunen, Ed. Articles, 1,000 to 1,500 words, with photos, on where, when, and how to fish and hunt in the Midwest. Pays $15 to $35, on publication.

MOTOR TREND—8490 Sunset Blvd., Los Angeles, CA 90069. Jeff Karr, Ed. Articles, 250 to 2,000 words, on autos, racing, events, and profiles. Photos. Pay varies, on acceptance. Query.

MOTORCYCLIST—8490 Sunset Blvd., Los Angeles, CA 90069. Art Friedman, Ed. Articles, 1,000 to 3,000 words. Action photos. Pays $100 to $200 per published page, on publication.

MOTORHOME MAGAZINE—29901 Agoura Rd., Agoura, CA 91301. Bob Livingston, Ed. Articles, to 2,000 words, with color slides, on motorhomes; travel and how-to pieces. Pays to $600, on acceptance.

MOUNTAIN BIKE—Rodale Press, 33 E. Minor St., Emmaus, PA 18098. Tim Blumenthal, Man. Ed. Articles, 1,200 to 2,000 words, on mountain bike touring; major off-road cycling events; political, sport, or land-access issues; riding techniques; fitness and training tips. Pays $200 to $650, on publication. Query first.

MUSCULAR DEVELOPMENT—351 W. 54th St., New York, NY 10019. Alan Paul, Ed. Articles, 1,000 to 2,500 words, personality profiles, training features, and diet and nutrition pieces. Photos. Pays $100 to $300 for articles; $35 for color photos, $20 for B&W, and $300 to $500 for cover photos.

MUSHING—P.O. Box 149, Ester, AK 99725–0149. Todd Hoener, Ed. How-tos, profiles, and features (1,500 to 2,000 words) and department pieces (500 to 1,000 words) for competitive and recreational dog drivers and skijorers. International audience. Photos. Pays $30 to $250, after acceptance. Queries preferred. Guidelines.

NATIONAL PARKS MAGAZINE—1776 Massachusetts Ave., Washington, DC 20002. Sue E. Dodge, Ed. Articles, 1,000 to 2,000 words, on natural history, wildlife, outdoors activities, and conservation as they relate to national parks; illustrated features on the natural, historic, and cultural resources of the National Park System. Pieces about legislation and other issues and events related to the parks. Pays $100 to $800, on acceptance. Query. Send for guidelines.

THE NEW ENGLAND SKIERS GUIDE—Box 1125, Waitsfield, VT 05673. Andrew Bigford, Ed. Annual (June closing). Articles on alpine and nordic skiing, equipment, and winter vacations at New England resorts. Rates vary.

NORTH TEXAS GOLFER—9182 Old Katy Rd., Suite 212, Houston, TX 77055. Bob Gray, Ed. Articles, 800 to 1,500 words, of interest to golfers in north Texas. Pays $50 to $250, on publication. Queries required. Same requirements for *Gulf Coast Golfer.*

NORTHEAST OUTDOORS—P.O. Box 2180, Waterbury, CT 06722–2180. Jean Wertz, Ed. Articles, 500 to 1,800 words, preferably with B&W photos, on camping in Northeast U.S.: recommended private campgrounds, camp cookery, recreational vehicle hints. Stress how-to, where-to. Cartoons. Pays $20 to $80, on publication. Guidelines.

OFFSHORE—220 Reservoir St., Needham Heights, MA 02194. Herbert Gliick, Ed. Articles, 1,200 to 2,500 words, on boats, people, and places along the New England, New York, and New Jersey coasts. Writers should be knowledgeable boaters. Photos a plus. Pays 15¢ to 20¢ a word.

OPEN WHEEL—P.O. Box 715, Ipswich, MA 01938. Dick Berggren, Ed. Articles, to 6,000 words, on open wheel drivers, races, and vehicles. Photos. Pays to $400 on publication.

OUTDOOR AMERICA—1401 Wilson Blvd., Level B, Arlington, VA 22209. Quarterly publication of the Izaak Walton League of America. Articles, 1,500 to 2,000 words, on natural resource conservation issues and outdoor recreation; especially fishing, hunting, and camping. Pays 20¢ a word for features. Query Articles Ed. with published clips.

OUTDOOR CANADA—703 Evans Ave., Suite 202, Toronto, Ont., Canada M9C 5E9. Ms. Teddi Brown, Ed. Published nine times yearly. Articles, 1,500 to 2,000 words, on outdoor sports, with an emphasis on fishing, for sportsmen and their families. Pays $200 to $600, on publication.

OUTDOOR LIFE—2 Park Ave., New York, NY 10016. Vin T. Sparano, Ed.-in-Chief. Short, instructive items on hunting, fishing, boats, outdoor equipment, and related subjects. Pays top rates, on acceptance.

OUTSIDE—1165 N. Clark, Chicago, IL 60610. High-quality articles, with photos, on sports, environmental issues, wilderness travel, adventure, etc. Pays varying rates. Query with clips.

PENNSYLVANIA ANGLER—Pennsylvania Fish Commission, P.O. Box 1673, Harrisburg, PA 17105–1673. Address Art Michaels, Ed. Articles, 250 to 2,500 words, with photos, on freshwater fishing in Pennsylvania. Pays $50 to $250, on acceptance. Must send SASE with all material. Query. Guidelines.

PENNSYLVANIA GAME NEWS—Game Commission, 2001 Elmerton Ave., Harrisburg, PA 17110–9797. Bob Mitchell, Ed. Articles, to 2,500 words, with photos, on outdoor subjects, except fishing and boating. Photos. Pays from 6¢ a word, extra for photos, on acceptance.

PETERSEN'S FISHING—8490 Sunset Blvd., Los Angeles, CA 90069. Robert Robb, Ed. "We're interested primarily in how-to articles (2,000 to 2,500 words), though pieces on where to fish, unusual techniques and equipment, and profiles of successful fisherman will also be considered. Photos must accompany all manuscripts, and we prefer to be queried first." Pays $300 to $400, on acceptance.

PETERSEN'S HUNTING—8490 Sunset Blvd., Los Angeles, CA 90069. Craig Boddington, Ed. How-to articles, 2,500 words, on all aspects of sport hunting. B&W photos; color slides. Pays $300 to $500, on acceptance. Query.

PGA MAGAZINE—The Quartron Group, 2155 Butterfield, Suite 200, Troy, MI 48084. Articles, 1,500 to 2,500 words, on golf-related subjects. Pays $300 to $500, on acceptance. Query.

PLEASURE BOATING—1995 N.E. 150th St., North Miami, FL 33181. Don Zern, Exec. Ed. Articles, 1,000 to 2,500 words, on fishing, cruising, recreational boating, travel, offshore racing, covering Florida, Bahamas, and Caribbean. Special sections on Florida Keys, Bahamas, Jamaica, Cayman Islands, and Puerto Rico. Pays varying rates, on publication. Query first. Study sample copies. Guidelines.

POWERBOAT—15917 Strathern St., Van Nuys, CA 91406. Lisa Nordskog, Ed. Articles, to 1,500 words, with photos, for high performance powerboat owners, on outstanding achievements, water-skiing, competitions; technical articles on hull and engine developments; how-to pieces. Pays $300 to $1,000, on acceptance. Query.

PRACTICAL HORSEMAN—Gum Tree Corner, Unionville, PA 19375. Joanne Tobey, Exec. Ed. How-to articles on English riding, training, and horse care. Pays on acceptance. Query.

PRIVATE PILOT—P.O. Box 6050, Mission Viejo, CA 92690–6050. Mary F. Silitch, Ed. Technically based aviation articles for general aviation pilots and aircraft owners, 1,000 to 4,000 words, for aviation enthusiasts. Photos. Pays $75 to $250, on publication. Query.

PRO BASKETBALL ILLUSTRATED—*See Hockey Illustrated.*

PRO FOOTBALL ILLUSTRATED—See *Hockey Illustrated.*

PURE BRED DOGS/AMERICAN KENNEL GAZETTE—51 Madison Ave., New York, NY 10010. Elizabeth Bodner, DVM, Exec. Ed. Audrey Pavia, Sr. Ed. Articles, 1,000 to 2,500 words, relating to pure-bred dogs. Pays from $100 to $300, on acceptance. Queries preferred.

RESTORATION—3153 E. Lincoln, Tucson, AZ 85714–2017. W.R. Haessner, Ed. Articles, 1,200 to 1,800 words, on restoration of autos, trucks, planes, trains, etc., and related building (bridges and structures). Photos. Pays varying rates (from $25 per page) on publication. Queries required.

RIDER—29901 Agoura Rd., Agoura Hills, CA 91301. Mark Tuttle Jr., Ed. Articles, with slides, to 3,000 words, with emphasis on travel, touring, commuting, and camping motorcyclists. Pays $100 to $500, on publication. Query.

RUNNER'S WORLD—Rodale Press, 33 E. Minor St., Emmaus, PA 18098. Bob Wischnia, Sr. Ed. Articles for "Human Race" (submit to Eileen Shovlin), "Finish Line" (to Cristina Negron), and "Health Watch" (to Megan Othersen) columns. Send feature articles or queries to Bob Wischnia. Payment varies, on acceptance. Query.

SAFARI—4800 West Gates Pass Rd., Tucson, AZ 85745. William Quimby, Publications Dir. Articles, 2,000 words, on big game hunting. Pays $200, on publication. Pays extra for photos.

SAIL—275 Washington St., Newton, MA 02158–1630. Patience Wales, Ed.

Articles, 1,500 to 3,500 words, features, 1,000 to 2,500 words, with photos, on sailboats, equipment, racing, and cruising. How-tos on navigation, sail trim, etc. Pays $75 to $1,000 on publication. Guidelines sent on request.

SAILING—125 E. Main St., Port Washington, WI 53074. M. L. Hutchins, Ed. Features, 700 to 1,500 words, with photos, on cruising and racing; first-person accounts; profiles of boats and regattas. Query for technical or how-to pieces. Pays varying rates, 30 days after publication. Guidelines.

SALT WATER SPORTSMAN—280 Summer St., Boston, MA 02210. Barry Gibson, Ed. Articles, 1,200 to 1,500 words, on how anglers can improve their skills, and on new places to fish off the coast of U.S. and Canada, Central America, the Caribbean, and Bermuda. Photos a plus. Pays $350 to $700, on acceptance. Query.

SCORE, CANADA'S GOLF MAGAZINE—287 MacPherson Ave., Toronto, Ont., Canada M4V 1A7. Bob Weeks, Man. Ed. Articles, 800 to 2,000 words, on travel, golf equipment, golf history, personality profiles, or prominent professionals. (Canadian content only.) Pays $125 to $600 for features, on assignment and publication. Query with published clips.

SEA KAYAKER—6327 Seaview Ave. N.W., Seattle, WA 98107–2664. Christopher Cunningham, Ed. Articles, 400 to 4,500 words, on ocean kayaking. Related fiction. Pays 5¢ to 10¢ a word, on publication. Query with clips and international reply coupons.

SEA, BEST BOATING IN THE WEST—17782 Cowan, Suite C, Irvine, CA 92714. Linda Yuskaitis, Exec. Ed. Features, 800 to 2,000 words, and news articles, 200 to 400 words, of interest to West Coast boating enthusiasts: profiles of boating personalities, cruise destinations, analyses of marine environmental issues, technical pieces on navigation and seamanship, news from western harbors. No fiction, first-person, poetry, or cartoons. Pays varing rates, on publication.

SHOTGUN SPORTS—P.O. Box 6810, Auburn, CA 95604. Frank Kodl, Ed. Official publication of The United States Sporting Clays Assoc. Articles with photos, on trap and skeet shooting, sporting clays, hunting with shotguns, reloading, gun tests, and instructional shooting. Pays $25 to $200, on publication.

THE SHOW—100 W. Harrison, North Tower, 5th Fl., Seattle, WA 98119. Kenneth Leiker, Ed. Bimonthly. Articles, 1,000 to 3,500 words, on the past, present, and future of baseball. Payment negotiable, on publication. Queries required.

SILENT SPORTS—717 10th St., P.O. Box 152, Waupaca, WI 54981. Upper Midwest monthly on bicycling, cross country skiing, running, canoeing, hiking, backpacking, and other "silent" sports; articles, 1,000 to 2,000 words. Pays $50 to $100 for features; $20 to $50 for fillers, on publication. Query.

SKI MAGAZINE—2 Park Ave., New York, NY 10016. Dick Needham, Ed. Articles, 1,300 to 2,000 words, for experienced skiers: profiles, humor, it-happened-to-me stories, and destination articles. Short, 100- to 300-word, news items for "Ski Life" column. Equipment and racing articles are staff written. Query first (with clips) for articles. Pays from $200, on acceptance.

SKI RACING—Box 1125, Rt. 100, Waitsfield, VT 05673. Articles on alpine and nordic racing, training, personalities. Photos. Rates vary.

SKIN DIVER MAGAZINE—8490 Sunset Blvd., Los Angeles, CA 90069. Bill Gleason, Pub./Ed. Illustrated articles, 500 to 2,000 words, on scuba diving activities, equipment, and dive sites. Pays $50 per published page, on publication.

SKYDIVING MAGAZINE—P. O. Box 1520, DeLand, FL 32721–1520. Michael Truffer, Ed. Timely news articles, 300 to 800 words, relating to sport and military parachuting. Fillers. Photos. Pays $25 to $200, extra for photos, on publication.

SNOWMOBILE—319 Barry Ave., S., Suite. 101, Wayzata, MN 55391. Dick Hendricks, Ed. Articles, 700 to 2,000 words, with color or B&W photos, related to snowmobiling: races and rallies, trail rides, personalities, travel. How-tos, humor; cartoons. Pays to $450, on publication. Query.

SOCCER AMERICA MAGAZINE—P. O. Box 23704, Oakland, CA 94623. Paul Kennedy, Ed. Articles, to 500 words, on soccer: news, profiles. Pays $50, for features, within 60 days of publication.

SOUTH CAROLINA WILDLIFE—P. O. Box 167, Columbia , SC 29202–0167. John E. Davis, Ed. Articles, 1,000 to 3,000 words, with regional outdoor focus: conservation, natural history, wildlife, and recreation. Profiles, how-tos. Pays on acceptance.

SOUTHERN OUTDOORS—5845 Carmichael Pkwy., Montgomery, AL 36117. Larry Teague, Ed. Essays, 1,200 to 1,500 words, related to the outdoors. Pays 15¢ to 20¢ a word, on acceptance.

SPORT MAGAZINE—8490 Sunset Blvd., Los Angeles, CA 90069. Don Evans, Ed. Dir. Query with clips. No fiction, poetry, or first person.

THE SPORTING NEWS—1212 N. Lindbergh Blvd., St. Louis, MO 63132. John D. Rawlings, Ed. Articles, 1,000 to 1,500 words, on baseball, football, basketball, hockey, and other sports. Pays $150 to $500, on publication.

SPORTS ILLUSTRATED—1271 Avenue of the Americas, New York, NY 10020. Chris Hunt, Articles Ed. No unsolicited material.

SPUR MAGAZINE—P. O. Box 85, Middleburg, VA 22117. Address Editorial Dept. Articles, 300 to 5,000 words, on thoroughbred racing, breeding, polo, show jumping, eventing, and steeplechasing. Profiles of people and farms. Historical and nostalgia pieces. Pays $50 to $400, on publication. Query.

STOCK CAR RACING—P. O. Box 715, Ipswich, MA 01938. Dick Berggren, Feature Ed. Articles, to 6,000 words, on stock car drivers, races, and vehicles. Photos. Pays to $400, on publication.

SURFER MAGAZINE—P. O. Box 1028, Dana Point, CA 92629. Court Overin, Pub. Steve Hawk, Ed. Articles, 500 to 5,000 words, on surfing, surfers, etc. Photos. Pays 10¢ to 15¢ a word, $10 to $600 for photos, on publication.

SURFING—P. O. Box 3010, San Clemente, CA 92674. Nick Carroll, Ed. Eric Fairbanks, Man. Ed. Short newsy and humorous articles, 200 to 500 words. No first-person travel articles; knowledge of sport essential. Pays varying rates, on publication.

TENNIS—5520 Park Ave., P. O. Box 0395, Trumbull, CT 06611–0395. Donna Doherty, Ed. Instructional articles, features, profiles of tennis stars, humor, 800 to 2,000 words. Photos. Pays from $300, on publication. Query.

TENNIS WEEK—124 E. 40th St., Suite 1101, New York, NY 10016. Eugene L. Scott, Pub. Steven Sheer, Ed. In-depth, researched articles, from 1,000 words, on current issues and personalities in the game. Pays $125, on publication.

TRAILER BOATS—20700 Belshaw Ave., P. O. Box 5427, Carson, CA 90249–5427. Wiley Poole, Ed. Technical and how-to articles, 500 to 2,000 words, on boat, trailer, or tow vehicle maintenance and operation; skiing, fishing, and cruising. Fillers, humor. Pays 10¢ to 15¢ a word, on publication.

TRAILER LIFE—29901 Agoura Rd., Agoura, CA 91301. Bill Estes, Ed. Articles, to 2,500 words, with photos, on trailering, truck campers, motorhomes, hobbies, and RV lifestyles. How-to pieces. Pays to $600, on acceptance. Send for guidelines.

TRAILS-A-WAY—Compass Publishing Group, 6489 Parkland Dr., Sarasota, FL 34243. Martha Higbie, Ed. RV-related travel articles, 1,000 to 1,200 words, for "the monthly magazine dedicated to Midwest camping families." Pay varies, on publication.

TREASURE DIVER—P.O. Drawer 7419, Van Nuys, CA 91409. Stanford Nielsen, Ed. Bimonthly. Articles (1,000 to 2,500 words) on or related to underwater adventure. Color slides or B&W photos must accompany submissions. Pays $1.50 per column inch, including photos; $75 per cover photo; made on publication.

TRIATHLETE—1415 Third St., Suite 303, Santa Monica, CA 90401. Richard Graham, Ed. Published 11 times yearly. Articles, varying lengths, pertaining to the sport of triathlon. "We can't use articles about marathons, long-distance cycling events, or rough-water swimming." Color slides. Pays 10¢ to 30¢ a word, on publication.

VELONEWS—1830 North 55th St., Boulder, CO 80301. John Wilcockson, Ed. Articles, 500 to 1,500 words, on competitive cycling, training, nutrition; profiles, interviews. No how-to or touring articles. "We focus on the elite of the sport." Pay varies, on publication.

VOLKSWAGEN WORLD—Volkswagen of America, 3800 Hamlin Rd., Auburn Hills, MI 48057. Marlene Goldsmith, Ed. Articles, 750 to 1,000 words, with or without color slides. Pays $150 to $325 per printed page, on acceptance. Query required. Guidelines.

WASHINGTON FISHING HOLES—P.O. Box 32, Sedro Wolley, WA 98284. Detailed articles, with specific maps, 800 to 1,500 words, on fishing in Washington. Local fishing how-tos. Photos. Pays on publication. Query. Send SASE for guidelines.

THE WATER SKIER—799 Overlook Dr., Winter Haven, FL 33884. Greg Nixon, Ed. Feature articles on waterskiing. Pays varying rates, on acceptance.

THE WESTERN HORSEMAN—P.O. Box 7980, Colorado Springs, CO 80933–7980. Pat Close, Ed. Articles, about 1,500 words, with photos, on care and training of horses; farm, ranch, and stable management; health care and veterinary medicine. Pays to $250, on acceptance.

WESTERN OUTDOORS—3197-E Airport Loop, Costa Mesa, CA 92626. Timely, factual articles on fishing and hunting, 1,200 to 1,500 words, of interest to western sportsmen. Pays $400 to $500, on acceptance. Query. Send first-class stamp for guidelines.

WESTERN SPORTSMAN—P.O. Box 737, Regina, Sask., Canada S4P 3A8. Roger Francis, Ed. Articles, to 2,500 words, on outdoor experiences in Alberta, Saskatchewan, and Manitoba; how-to pieces. Photos. Pays $75 to $325, on publication.

WINDRIDER—P.O. Box 2456, Winter Park, FL 32790. Debbie Snow, Ed. Features, instructional pieces, and tips, by experienced boardsailors. Fast action photos. Pays $50 to $75 for tips, $250 to $300 for features, extra for photos. Send for guidelines first.

WINDY CITY SPORTS—1450 W. Randolph, Chicago, IL 60607. Mary-claire Collins, Ed. Articles, 1,500 words, on amateur sports in Chicago. Query required. Pays $100, on publication.

WOMAN BOWLER—5301 S. 76th St., Greendale, WI 53129–1191. Karen Sytsma, Ed. Profiles, interviews, and news articles, to 1,000 words, for women bowlers. Pays varying rates, on acceptance. Query with outline.

WOMEN'S SPORTS & FITNESS—1919 14th St., Suite 421, Boulder, CO 80302. Margie McCloy, Ed. How-tos, profiles, active travel, and controversial issues in women's sports, 500 to 3,000 words. Fitness, nutrition, and health pieces also considered. Pays on publication.

WRESTLING WORLD—See *Hockey Illustrated.*

YACHTING—2 Park Ave., New York, NY 10016. Charles Barthold, Exec. Ed. Articles, 1,500 words, on upscale recreational power and sail boating. How-to and personal-experience pieces. Photos. Pays $350 to $1,000, on acceptance. Queries preferred.

AUTOMOTIVE MAGAZINES

AAA WORLD—AAA Headquarters, 1000 AAA Dr., Heathrow, FL 32746–5063. Douglas Damerst, Ed. Automobile and travel concerns, including automotive travel, purchasing, and upkeep, 750 to 1,500 words. Pays $300 to $600, on acceptance. Query with clips; articles are by assignment only.

AMERICAN MOTORCYCLIST—American Motorcyclist Assn., Box 6114, Westerville, OH 43081–6114. Greg Harrison, Ed. Articles and fiction, to 3,000 words, on motorcycling: news coverage, personalities, tours. Photos. Pays varying rates, on publication. Query with SASE.

CAR AND DRIVER—2002 Hogback Rd., Ann Arbor, MI 48105. William Jeanes, Ed. Articles, to 2,500 words, for enthusiasts, on new cars, classic cars, industry topics. "Ninety percent staff-written. Query with clips. No unsolicited manuscripts." Pays to $2,500, on acceptance.

CAR AUDIO AND ELECTRONICS—21700 Oxnard St., Woodland Hills, CA 91367. Bill Neill, Ed. Features, 1,000 to 2,000 words, on electronic products for the car: audio systems, cellular telephones, security systems, CBs, radar detectors, etc.; how to buy them; how they work; how to use them. "To write for us, you must know this subject thoroughly." Pays $200 to $1,000, on acceptance. Send manuscript or query.

CAR CRAFT—8490 Sunset Blvd., Los Angeles, CA 90069. John Baechtel, Ed. Articles and photo features on unusual street machines, drag cars, racing events; technical pieces; action photos. Pays from $150 per page, on acceptance.

CYCLE WORLD—853 W. 17th St., Costa Mesa, CA 92627. David Edwards, Ed. Technical and feature articles, 1,500 to 2,500 words, for motorcycle enthusiasts. Photos. Pays $100 to $200 per page, on publication. Query.

HOT BIKE—2145 W. La Palma, Anaheim, CA 92801. Buck Lovell, Ed. Articles, 250 to 2,500 words, with photos, on Harley-Davidson motorcycles (contemporary and antique). Event coverage on high performance street, track and sport touring Harley-Davidsons. Pays $50 to $100 per printed page, on publication.

HOT ROD—8490 Sunset Blvd., Los Angeles, CA 90069. Jeff Smith, Ed. How-to pieces and articles, 500 to 5,000 words, on auto mechanics, hot rods, track and drag racing. Photo features on custom or performance-modified cars. Pays $250 per page, on publication.

KEEPIN' TRACK OF VETTES—P.O. Box 48, Spring Valley, NY 10977. Shelli Finkel, Ed. Articles of any length, with photos, relating to Corvettes. Pays $25 to $200, on publication.

MOTOR TREND—8490 Sunset Blvd., Los Angeles, CA 90069. Jeff Karr, Ed. Articles, 250 to 2,000 words, on autos, racing, events, and profiles. Photos. Pay varies, on acceptance. Query.

MOTORCYCLIST—8490 Sunset Blvd., Los Angeles, CA 90069. Art Friedman, Ed. Articles, 1,000 to 3,000 words. Action photos. Pays $100 to $200 per published page, on publication.

OPEN WHEEL—See *Stock Car Racing*.

RESTORATION—3153 E. Lincoln, Tucson, AZ 85714–2017. W.R. Haessner, Ed. Articles, 1,200 to 1,800 words, on restoration of autos, trucks, planes, trains, etc., and related building (bridges, structures, etc.). Photos. Pays varying rates, from $25 a page, on publication. Queries required.

RIDER—29901 Agoura Rd., Agoura Hills, CA 91301. Mark Tuttle, Jr., Ed. Articles, with color slides, to 3,000 words, with emphasis on travel, touring, commuting, and camping motorcyclists. Pays $100 to $500, on publication. Query.

ROAD & TRACK—1499 Monrovia Ave., Newport Beach, CA 92663. Ellida Maki, Man. Ed. Monthly for knowledgeable car enthusiasts. Short automotive articles, to 450 words, of "timeless nature." Pays on publication. Query.

STOCK CAR RACING—P.O. Box 715, Ipswich, MA 01938. Dick Berggren, Ed. Features, technical automotive pieces, up to ten typed pages, for oval track racing enthusiasts. Fillers. Pays $75 to $350, on publication. Same requirements for *Open Wheel*.

TRUCKERS/USA—P.O. Box 323, Windber, PA 15963. David Adams, Ed. Monthly. Articles, 500 to 1,000 words, on the trucking business and marketing. Poetry and trucking-related fiction. Pays $50 for articles, $40 for color cover photos, on acceptance.

VOLKSWAGEN WORLD—Volkswagen of America, 3800 Hamlin Rd., Auburn Hills, MI 48057. Marlene Goldsmith, Ed. Articles, 750 to 1,000 words. Color slides a plus. Pays $150 to $325 per printed page, on acceptance. Query required. Guidelines.

FITNESS MAGAZINES

AMERICAN FITNESS—15250 Ventura Blvd., Suite 310, Sherman Oaks, CA 91403. Peg Jordan, Ed. Rhonda Wilson, Man. Ed. Articles, 500 to 1,500 words, on exercise, health, sports, nutrition, etc. Illustrations, photos, cartoons.

EAST WEST: THE JOURNAL OF NATURAL HEALTH & LIVING—17 Station St., Box 1200, Brookline, MA 02147. Features, 1,500 to 2,500 words, on holistic health, natural foods, herbal remedies, etc. Interviews. Photos. Pays 20¢ a word, extra for photos, on acceptance.

IDEA TODAY—6190 Cornerstone Ct. East, Suite 204, San Diego, CA 92121–3773. Patricia Ryan, Ed. Practical articles, 1,000 to 3,000 words, on new exercise programs, business management, nutrition, sports medicine, dance-exercise and one-to-one training techniques. Articles must be geared toward the aerobics instructor, exercise studio owner or manager, or personal trainer. Don't query for consumer or general health articles. Payment is negotiable, on acceptance. Query preferred.

INSIDE TEXAS RUNNING—9514 Bristlebrook Dr., Houston, TX 77083–6193. Joanne Schmidt, Ed. Articles and fillers on running, cycling, and triathlons in Texas. Pays $35 to $100, $10 to $25 for photos, on acceptance.

MEN'S FITNESS—21100 Erwin St., Woodland Hills, CA 91367. Jim Rosenthal, Fitness Ed. Features, 1,500 to 2,500 words, and department pieces, 1,000 to 1,500 words: "authoritative and practical articles dealing with fitness, health, and men's lifestyles." Pays $350 to $1,000, on acceptance.

MEN'S HEALTH—Rodale Press, 33 E. Minor Dr., Emmaus, PA 18098. Steve Slon, Man. Ed. Articles, 1,000 to 2,500 words, on fitness, diet, health, relationships, sports, and travel, for men ages 25 to 55. Pays from 50¢ a word, on acceptance. Query first.

MUSCULAR DEVELOPMENT—351 W. 54th St., New York, NY 10019. Alan Paul, Ed. Articles, 1,000 to 2,500 words, on competitive bodybuilding, power lifting, sports, and nutrition for serious weight training athletes: personality profiles, training features, and diet and nutrition pieces. Photos. Pays $100 to $300 for articles; $35 for color photos; $20 for B&W; and $300 to $500 for cover photos.

NEW BODY—1700 Broadway, New York, NY 10019. Nayda Rondon, Ed. Lively, readable service-oriented articles, 800 to 1,500 words, on exercise, nutrition, lifestyle, diet, and health for women aged 18 to 35. Writers should have some background in or knowledge of the health field. Also considers 500- to 600-word essays for "How I Lost It" column by writers who have lost weight and kept it off. Pays $100 to $300, on publication. Query.

THE PHYSICIAN AND SPORTSMEDICINE—4530 W. 77th St., Minneapolis, MN 55435. Terry Monahan, Man. Ed. News and feature articles. Clinical articles must be co-authored by physicians. Sports medicine angle necessary. Pays $150 to $1,000, on acceptance. Query first. Guidelines.

SHAPE—21100 Erwin St., Woodland Hills, CA 91367–3772. Elizabeth Turner, Asst. Ed. Articles, 1,200 to 1,500 words, with new and interesting ideas on the physical and mental side of getting and staying in shape; reports, 300 to 400 words, on journal research. Mostly expert bylines. Payment varies, on publication. Guidelines. Limited market.

VEGETARIAN TIMES—P.O. Box 570, Oak Park, IL 60303. Paul Obis, Pub. Articles, 750 to 2,500 words, on health, nutrition, exercise and fitness, meatless meals, etc. Personal-experience and historical pieces, profiles. Pays $25 to $500, on publication.

VIM & VIGOR—8805 N. 23rd Ave., Suite 11, Phoenix, AZ 85021. Fred Petrovsky, Ed. Positive articles, with accurate medical facts, on health and fitness, 1,200 to 2,000 words, by assignment only. Pays $350 to $450, on publication. Query.

WEIGHT WATCHERS MAGAZINE—360 Lexington Ave., New York, NY 10017. Susan Rees, Health and Fitness Editor. Articles on nutrition and health. Pays from $350, on acceptance. Query with clips required. Guidelines.

WOMEN'S SPORTS & FITNESS—1919 14th St., Suite 421, Boulder, CO 80302. Jane McConnell, Ed. How-tos, profiles, active travel, and controversial issues in women's sports, 500 to 3,000 words. Fitness, nutrition, and health pieces also considered. Pays on publication.

YOGA JOURNAL—2054 University Ave., Berkeley, CA 94704. Stephan Bodian, Ed. Articles, 1,200 to 4,000 words, on holistic health, meditation, consciousness, spirituality, and yoga. Pays $50 to $500, on publication.

CONSUMER/PERSONAL FINANCE

BETTER HOMES AND GARDENS—1716 Locust St., Des Moines, IA 50336. Articles, 750 to 1,000 words, on "any and all topics that would be of interest to family-oriented, middle-income people." Address Margaret V. Daly, Executive Features Editor, *Better Homes and Gardens*, 750 Third Ave., New York, NY 10017.

BLACK ENTERPRISE—130 Fifth Ave., New York, NY 10011. Earl G. Graves, Ed. Articles on money management, careers, political issues, entrepreneurship, high technology, and lifestyles for black professionals. Profiles. Pays on acceptance. Query.

CHANGING TIMES—See *Kiplinger's Personal Finance.*

CONSUMERS DIGEST—5705 N. Lincoln Ave., Chicago, IL 60659. John Manos, Ed. Articles, 500 to 3,000 words, on subjects of interest to consumers: products and services, automobiles, travel, health, fitness, consumer legal affairs, and personal money management. Photos. Pays from 35¢ to 50¢ a word, extra for photos, on acceptance. Query with resumé and clips.

FAMILY CIRCLE—110 Fifth Ave., New York, NY 10011. Susan Ungaro, Exec. Ed. Susan Sherry, Sr. Ed. Enterprising, creative, and practical articles, 1,000 to 1,500 words, on investing, starting a business, secrets of successful entrepreneurs, and consumer news on smart shopping. Query first with clips. Pays $1 a word, on acceptance.

GOLDEN YEARS—P.O. Box 537, Melbourne, FL 32902–0537. Carol Brenner Hittner, Ed. "We consider articles, to 600 words, on preretirement, retirement planning, real estate, travel, celebrity profiles, humor, and contemporary issues of particular interest to affluent people over 50." Pays on publication.

KIPLINGER'S PERSONAL FINANCE MAGAZINE—(formerly *Changing Times*) 1729 H St. N.W., Washington, DC 20006. Articles on personal finance (i.e., buying a stereo, mutual funds). Length and payment vary. Query required. Pays on acceptance.

KIWANIS—3636 Woodview Trace, Indianapolis, IN 46468. Chuck Jonak, Exec. Ed. Articles, 2,500 to 3,000 words, on financial planning for younger families in a variety of areas; pieces on financial planning for retirees and small business owners. Pays $400 to $1,000, on acceptance. Query required.

MODERN MATURITY—3200 E. Carson St., Lakewood, CA 90712. J. Henry Fenwick, Ed. Articles, 1,000 to 2,000 words, on a wide range of financial topics of interest to people over 50. Pays to $2,500. Queries required.

MONEY MAKER—5705 N. Lincoln Ave., Chicago, IL 60659. Dennis Fertig, Ed. Informative, jargon-free personal finance articles, to 2,500 words, for the general reader, on investment opportunities and personal finance. Pays 25¢ a word, on acceptance. Query with clips for assignment. (Do not send manuscripts on disks.)

THE MONEYPAPER—1010 Mamaroneck Ave., Mamaroneck, NY 10543. Vita Nelson, Ed. Financial news and money-saving ideas. Brief, well-researched articles on personal finance, money management: saving, earning, investing, taxes, insurance, and related subjects. Pays $75 for articles, on publication. Query with resumé and writing sample.

SELF—350 Madison Ave., New York, NY 10017. Ann Landi, Money/Careers Ed. Articles, 1,200 to 1,500 words, on money matters for career women in their 20s and 30s. Pays from $1,000, on acceptance. Query first.

WOMAN'S DAY—1633 Broadway, New York, NY 10019. Rebecca Greer, Articles Ed. Articles, to 2,500 words, on financial matters of interest to a broad range of women. Pays top rates, on acceptance. Query first.

PROFESSIONAL/TRADE PUBLICATIONS

ABA JOURNAL—American Bar Association, 750 N. Lake Shore Dr., Chicago, IL 60611. Gary A. Hengstler, Ed./Pub. Articles, to 3,000 words, on law-related topics: current events in the law and ideas that will help lawyers practice better and more efficiently. Writing should be in an informal, journalistic style. Pays from $1,000, on acceptance; buys all rights.

ACCESS CONTROL—6255 Barfield Rd., Atlanta, GA 30328. Steven Lasky, Ed./Assoc. Pub. Comprehensive case studies, from 3,000 words, on large-scale access control installations in industrial, commercial, governmental, retail, and transportational environments: door and card entry, gates and operators, turnstiles and portals, perimeter security fencing and its accessories, perimeter and interior sensors, CCTV technology, system design strategies, integration of hardware, and guard services. Photos. Pays from 20¢ a word, extra for photos, on publication. Query.

ACROSS THE BOARD—845 Third Ave., New York, NY 10022. Justin Martin, Asst. Ed. Articles, to 5,000 words, on a variety of topics of interest to business executives; straight business angle not required. Pays $100 to $1,000, on publication.

ALTERNATIVE ENERGY RETAILER—P.O. Box 2180, Waterbury, CT 06722. John Florian, Ed. Dir. Feature articles, 1,000 words, for retailers of alternative energy products: wood, coal, and fireplace products and services. Interviews with successful retailers, stressing the how-to. B&W photos. Pays $200, extra for photos, on publication. Query first.

AMERICAN BANKER—One State Street Plaza, New York, NY 10004. Ed Finn, Ed., Patricia Kitchen Stundza, Features Ed. Articles, 1,000 to 3,000 words, on banking and financial services, technology in banking, consumer financial services, human resources, management techniques. Pays varying rates, on publication. Query preferred.

AMERICAN COIN-OP—500 N. Dearborn St., Chicago, IL 60610–9988. Ben Russell, Ed. Articles, to 2,500 words, with photos, on successful coin-operated laundries: management, promotion, decor, maintenance, etc. Pays from 8¢ a word, $8 per B&W photo, two weeks prior to publication. Query. Send SASE for guidelines.

AMERICAN DEMOGRAPHICS—P.O. Box 68, Ithaca, NY 14851–9989. Brad Edmondson, Ed.-in-Chief. Articles, 500 to 2,000 words, on the four key elements of a consumer market (its size, its needs and wants, its ability to pay, and how it can be reached), with specific examples on how companies market to consumers. Readers include marketers, advertisers, and strategic planners. Pays $100 to $500, on acceptance. Query.

AMERICAN FARRIERS JOURNAL—63 Great Rd., Maynard, MA 01754. Susan G. Philbrick, Ed. Articles, 800 to 5,000 words, on general farriery issues, hoof care, tool selection, equine lameness, and horse handling. Pays 30¢ per published line, $10 per published illustration or photo, on publication. Query.

AMERICAN MEDICAL NEWS—515 N. State St., Chicago, IL 60610. Ronni Scheier, Asst. Exec. Ed. Features, 1,000 to 3,000 words, on socioeconomic developments of interest to physicians across the country. No pieces on health, clinical treatments, or research. Query required. Pays $500 to $1,500, on acceptance. Guidelines.

THE AMERICAN SALESMAN—424 N. Third St., P.O. Box 1, Burlington, IA 52601–0001. Barbara Boeding, Ed. Articles, 900 to 1,200 words, on techniques for increasing sales. Author photos requested on article acceptance. Buys all rights. (No advertising.) Pays 3¢ a word, on publication. Guidelines.

AMERICAN SALON—7500 Old Oak Blvd., Cleveland, OH 44130. Angela Watkins, Ed. Official publication of the National Cosmetology Assoc. Business and fashion articles of varying lengths for salon professionals. Payment varies, on publication. Query.

AMERICAN SCHOOL & UNIVERSITY—401 N. Broad St., Philadelphia, PA 19108. Joe Agron, Ed. Articles and case studies, 1,200 to 1,500 words, on design, construction, operation, and management of school and college facilities.

ARCHITECTURE—1130 Connecticut Ave. N.W., Suite 625, Washington, DC 20036. Address Man. Ed. Articles, to 3,000 words, on architecture, building technology, professional practice. Pays 50¢ a word.

AREA DEVELOPMENT MAGAZINE—400 Post Ave., Westbury, NY 11590. Tom Bergeron, Ed. Articles for top executives of industrial companies, on sites and facility planning. Pays $50 per manuscript page. Query.

ART BUSINESS NEWS—777 Summer St., P.O. Box 3837, Stamford, CT 06905. Jo Yanow-Schwartz, Ed. Articles, 1,000 words, for art dealers and framers, on trends and events of national importance to the art industry, and relevant business subjects. Pays from $75, on publication. Query preferred.

ART MATERIAL TRADE NEWS—6255 Barfield Rd., Atlanta, GA 30328–4369. Tom Cooper, Ed. Articles, from 800 words, for dealers, wholesalers, and manufacturers of artist materials; must be specific to trade. Pays to 15¢ a word, on publication. Query.

AUTOMATED BUILDER—P.O. Box 120, Carpinteria, CA 93014. Don Carlson, Ed. Articles, 500 to 750 words, on various types of home manufacturers and dealers. Query required. Pays $300, on acceptance, for articles with slides.

BARRISTER—American Bar Assn., 750 N. Lake Shore Dr., Chicago, IL 60611–4403. Vicki Quade, Ed. Articles, 250 to 3,000 words, on legal and social issues, for young lawyers. Pays $250 to $1,000, on acceptance. Query.

BARRON'S—200 Liberty St., New York, NY 10281. Alan Abelson, Ed. National-interest articles, 1,200 to 2,500 words, on business and finance. Query.

BEAUTY EDUCATION—(formerly *National Beauty School Journal*) 220 White Plains Rd., Tarrytown, NY 10591. Sheila Furjanic, Ed. Articles, 1,500 to 2,000 words, that provide beauty educators, trainers, and professionals in the cosmetology industry with information, skills, and techniques on such topics as hairstyling, makeup, aromatherapy, retailing, massage, and beauty careers. Send SASE for editorial calendar with monthly themes. Pays $150, on publication. Query.

542

BETTER BUSINESS—235 East 42nd St., New York, NY 10017. John F. Robinson, Pub. Articles, 10 to 12 double-spaced pages, for small businesses, minority businesses, and businesses owned by women. Query. SASE required.

BOATING INDUSTRY—390 Fifth Ave., New York, NY 10018. Richard W. Porter, Ed. Articles, 1,000 to 1,500 words, on marine management, merchandising and selling, for boat dealers. Photos. Pays varying rates, on publication. Query.

BUILDER—Hanley-Wood, Inc., 655 15th St. N.W., Suite 475, Washington, DC 20005. Mitchell B. Rouda, Ed. Articles, to 1,500 words, on trends and news in home building: design, marketing, new products, etc. Pays negotiable rates, on acceptance. Query.

BUSINESS MARKETING—740 N. Rush St., Chicago, IL 60611. Steve Yahn, Ed. Articles on selling, advertising, and promoting products and services to business buyers. Pays competitive rates, on acceptance. Queries are required.

BUSINESS TIMES—P.O. Box 580, 315 Peck St., New Haven, CT 06513. Joel MacClaren, Ed. Articles on Connecticut-based businesses and corporations. Query.

BUSINESS TODAY—P.O. Box 10010, 1720 Washington Blvd., Ogden, UT 84409. Caroll Shreeve, Pub./Ed.-in-Chief. Informative articles, 1,200 words, on business concerns of the businessperson/entrepreneur in U.S. and Canada. Pays 15¢ a word, $35 for color photos, on acceptance. Query. Send SASE for guidelines.

BUSINESS VIEW—See *Florida Business/Southwest.*

CALIFORNIA BUSINESS—4221 Wilshire Blvd., Suite 400, Los Angeles, CA 90010. G.B. Engel, Ed. Articles, 1,200 to 3,000 words, on business and econometric issues in California. Pays varying rates, on acceptance. Query.

CALIFORNIA LAWYER—1390 Market St., Suite 1210, San Francisco, CA 94102. Thomas Brom, Man. Ed. Articles, 2,500 to 3,000 words, for attorneys in California, on legal subjects (or the legal aspects of a given political or social issue); how-tos on improving legal skills and law office technology. Pays $300 to $1,200, on acceptance. Query.

CAMPGROUND MANAGEMENT—P.O. Box 5000, Lake Forest, IL 60045–5000. Mike Byrnes, Ed. Detailed articles, 500 to 2,000 words, on managing recreational vehicle campgrounds. Photos. Pays $50 to $200, after publication.

CHEESE MARKET NEWS—See *Dairy Foods Magazine.*

CHIEF EXECUTIVE—233 Park Ave. S., New York, NY 10003. J.P. Donlon, Ed. CEO bylines. Articles, 2,500 to 3,000 words, on management, financial, or business strategy. Departments on investments, amenities, and travel, 1,200 to 1,500 words. Features on CEOs at leisure, Q&A's with CEOs, other topics. Pays varying rates, on acceptance. Query required.

CHINA, GLASS & TABLEWARE—P.O. Box 2147, Clifton, NJ 07015. Amy Stavis, Ed. Case histories and interviews, 1,500 to 2,500 words, with photos, on merchandising of china and glassware. Pays $50 per page, on publication. Query.

CHRISTIAN RETAILING—600 Rinehart Rd., Lake Mary, FL 32746. Brian Peterson, Ed. Articles, 1,000 to 1,600 words, on new products, industry news, or topics related to running a profitable Christian retail store. Pays $50 to $200, on publication.

CLEANING MANAGEMENT MAGAZINE—13 Century Hill Dr., Latham, NY 12110–2197. Tom Williams, Ed. Articles, 800 to 1,200 words, on managing efficient cleaning and custodial/maintenance operations, profiles, photo features, or general interest articles directly related to the industry; also technical/mechanical how-tos. Photos encouraged. Query first. Pays to $200 for features, on publication. Guidelines.

COMMERCIAL CARRIER JOURNAL—Chilton Way, Radnor, PA 19089. Jerry Standley, Ed. Thoroughly researched, focused articles on private fleets and for-hire trucking operations. Pays from $50, on acceptance. Queries required.

COMPUTER GRAPHICS WORLD—One Technology Park Dr., Westford, MA 01886. Stephen Porter, Man. Ed. Articles, 1,000 to 3,000 words, on computer graphics technology and its use in science, engineering, architecture, film and broadcast, and graphic arts areas. Photos. Pays $600 to $1,200 per article, on acceptance. Query.

CONCRETE INTERNATIONAL—Box 19150, 22400 W. Seven Mile Rd., Detroit, MI 48219. William J. Semioli, Assoc. Pub. & Ed. Articles, 6 to 12 double-spaced pages, on concrete construction and design, with drawings and/or photos. Pays $100 per printed page, on publication. Query.

THE CONSTRUCTION SPECIFIER—Construction Specifications Institute, 601 Madison St., Alexandria, VA 22314. Kristina A. Kessler, Ed. Technical articles, 1,000 to 3,000 words, on the "nuts and bolts" of commercial construction, for architects, engineers, specifiers, contractors, and manufacturers. Pays 15¢ per word, on publication.

CONTRACTORS MARKET CENTER—See *Equipment World.*

CONVENIENCE STORE NEWS—7 Penn Plaza, New York, NY 10001. Barbara Grondin, Ed. Features and news items, 500 to 750 words, for convenience store owners, and operators. Photos, with captions. Pays $3 per column inch or negotiated price for features; extra for photos, on publication. Query.

COOKING FOR PROFIT—P.O. Box 267, Fond du Lac, WI 54936–0267. Colleen Phalen, Ed. Practical how-to articles, 1,000 words, on commercial food preparation, gas energy management; case studies, etc. Pays $75 to $250, on publication.

CORPORATE CASHFLOW—6255 Barfield Rd., Atlanta, GA 30328. Richard Gamble, Ed. Articles, 1,250 to 2,500 words, for treasury managers in public and private institutions: cash management; investments; domestic and international financing; credit and collection management; developments in law, economics, and tax. Pays $125 per published page, on publication. Query.

CRAIN'S CHICAGO BUSINESS—740 Rush St., Chicago, IL 60611. David Snyder, Man. Ed. Business articles about the Chicago metropolitan area exclusively. Pays $12 per column inch, on acceptance.

CREATING EXCELLENCE—New World Publishing, P.O. Box 2048, S. Burlington, VT 05407. David Robinson, Ed. Self-help and inspirational articles: profiles and essays related to business success. "Purpose is to inform and inspire people to be their best, personally and professionally." Vermont distribution only. Pays $75 to $250, on acceptance. Queries preferred.

CREDIT AND COLLECTION MANAGEMENT BULLETIN—Bureau of Business Practice, 24 Rope Ferry Rd., Waterford, CT 06386. Russell Case, Ed. Interviews, 500 to 1,250 words, for commercial and consumer credit managers, on innovations, successes, and problem solving. Query.

DAIRY FOODS MAGAZINE—Gorman Publishing Co., 8750 W. Bryn Mawr, Chicago, IL 60631. Mike Pehanich, Ed. Articles, to 2,500 words, on innovative dairies, dairy processing operations, marketing successes, new products, for milk handlers and makers of dairy products. Fillers, 25 to 150 words. Pays $25 to $300, $5 to $25 for fillers, on publication. Same requirements for *Cheese Market News*.

DEALERSCOPE MERCHANDISING—North American Publishing Co., 401 N. Broad St., Philadelphia, PA 19108. Murray Slovick, Ed. Articles, 750 to 3,000 words, for dealers and distributors of audio, video, personal computers for the home, office; satellite TV systems for the home; major appliances on sales, marketing, and finance. How-tos for retailers. Pays varying rates, on publication. Query with clips.

DENTAL ECONOMICS—P.O. Box 3408, Tulsa, OK 74101. Dick Hale, Ed. Articles, 1,200 to 3,500 words, on business side of dental practice, patient and staff communication, personal investments, etc. Pays $100 to $400, on acceptance.

DRUG TOPICS—Five Paragon Dr., Montvale, NJ 07645-1742. Valentine A. Cardinale, Ed. News items, 500 words, with photos, on drug retailers and associations. Merchandising features, 1,000 to 1,500 words. Pays $100 to $150 for news, $200 to $400 for features, on acceptance. Query for features.

EARNSHAW'S INFANTS & CHILDREN'S REVIEW—225 W. 34th St., Suite 1212, New York, NY 10001. Christina Gruber, Ed. Articles on retailers, retail promotions, and statistics for children's wear industry. Pays $50 to $200, on publication. Query. Limited market.

ELECTRICAL CONTRACTOR—7315 Wisconsin Ave., Suite 1300-West, Bethesda, MD 20814. Walt Albro, Ed. Articles, 1,000 to 1,500 words, with photos, on construction or management techniques for electrical contractors. Pays 24¢ to 75¢ a word, before publication. Query.

EMERGENCY—6300 Yarrow Dr., Carlsbad, CA 92009. Rhonda Foster, Ed. Features, to 3,000 words, and department pieces, to 2,000 words, of interest to paramedics, emergency medical technicians, flight nurses, and other pre-hospital personnel: disaster management, advanced and basic life support, assessment, treatment. Pays $100 to $400 for features, $50 to $250 for departments. Photos are a plus. Guidelines and editorial calendar available.

EMPLOYEE SERVICES MANAGEMENT—NESRA, 2400 S. Downing, Westchester, IL 60154. Elizabeth Martinet, Ed. Articles, 1,200 to 2,500 words, for human resource, fitness, and employee service professionals.

THE ENGRAVERS JOURNAL—26 Summit St., P.O. Box 318, Brighton, MI 48116. Rosemary Farrell, Man. Ed. Articles, of varying lengths, on topics related to the engraving industry or small business. Pays $60 to $175, on acceptance. Query.

ENTREPRENEUR—2392 Morse Ave., Irvine, CA 92714. Rieva Lesonsky, Ed.-in-Chief. Articles for established and aspiring independent business owners, on all aspects of running a business. Pay varies, on acceptance. Query.

ENTREPRENEURIAL WOMAN—2392 Morse Ave., Irvine, CA 92714. Rieva Lesonsky, Ed.-in-Chief. Profiles, 1,800 words, of female entrepreneurs; how-tos on running a business, and pieces on coping as a woman owning a business. Payment varies, on acceptance.

EQUIPMENT WORLD—(formerly *Contractors Market Center*) P.O. Box 2029, Tuscaloosa, AL 35403. Marcia Gruver, Ed. Features, 500 to 1,500 words, for contractors who buy, sell, and use heavy equipment; articles on equipment selection, application, maintenance, and replacement. Pay varies, on acceptance.

EXPORT MAGAZINE—386 Park Ave. South, New York, NY 10016. Jack Dobson, Ed. Articles, 1,000 to 1,200 words. From U.S.-based free lancers: articles on developments in hardware and appliances, air conditioning and refrigeration, sporting goods and leisure products. From overseas-based free lancers: articles on merchandising techniques of foreign retailers who import above-described items from the U.S. Pays $300 to $400 with photos, on acceptance. Query required.

FARM JOURNAL—230 W. Washington Sq., Philadelphia, PA 19105. Earl Ainsworth, Ed. Practical business articles, 500 to 1,500 words, with photos, on growing crops and raising livestock. Pays 20¢ to 50¢ a word, on acceptance. Query required.

FARM STORE—P.O. Box 2400, 12400 Whitewater Dr., Suite 160, Minnetonka, MN 55343. Julie Emnett, Ed. Articles, 500 to 1,500 words, of interest to farm store owners and managers. Payment varies, on publication. Query.

FINANCIAL WORLD—1328 Broadway, New York, NY 10001. Douglas A. McIntyre, Pub. Features and profiles of large companies and financial institutions and the people who run them. Pays varying rates, on publication. Queries are required.

FISHING TACKLE RETAILER MAGAZINE—P.O. Box 17151, Montgomery, AL 36141–0151. Dave Ellison, Ed. Articles, 300 to 1,250 words, for merchants who carry angling equipment: business focus is required, and writers should provide practical information for improving management and merchandising. Pays varying rates, on acceptance.

FITNESS MANAGEMENT—P.O. Box 1198, Solana Beach, CA 92075. Edward H. Pitts, Ed. Authoritative features, 750 to 2,500 words, and news shorts, 100 to 750 words, for owners, managers, and program directors of fitness centers. Content must be in keeping with current medical practice; no fads. Pays 8¢ a word, on publication. Query.

FLORIDA BUSINESS/SOUTHWEST—(formerly *Business View*) P.O. Box 9859, Naples, FL 33941. Eleanor K. Somer, Pub. Ken Gooderham, Ed. Innovative articles and columns, 750 to 2,000 words, on business, economics, finance; profiles of business leaders. Real estate and banking trends. Southwest Florida regional angle required. Pays $50 to $300, on publication. Query.

FLORIST—29200 Northwestern Hwy., P.O. Box 2227, Southfield, MI 48037–1099. Susan Nicholas, Man. Ed. Articles, to 2,000 words, with photos, on retail florist business improvement. Photos.

FLOWERS &—Teleflora Plaza, Suite 260, 12233 W. Olympic Blvd., Los Angeles, CA 90064. Marie Moneysmith, Ed.-in-Chief. Articles, 1,000 to 3,500 words, with how-to information for retail florists. Pays from $500, on acceptance. Query with clips.

FOOD MANAGEMENT—270 Madison Ave., 5th Fl., New York, NY 10016. Donna Boss, Ed. Articles on food service in hospitals, nursing homes, schools, colleges, prisons, businesses, and industrial sites. Trends and how-to pieces, with management tie-in. Query.

FREQUENT FLYER—1775 Broadway, New York, NY 10019. Joe Brancatelli, Exec. Ed. Articles, 1,000 to 3,000 words, on all aspects of frequent business travel, international trade, aviation, etc. Few pleasure travel articles; no personal experience pieces. Pays to $500, on acceptance. Query.

GARDEN DESIGN—Society of American Landscape Architects, 4401 Connecticut Ave. N.W., Fifth Fl., Washington, DC 20008. Deborah Papier, Exec. Ed. Garden-related features. Need articles, 800 to 1,500 words, on "private and public gardens, interviews with landscape designers and other personalities; also articles on art, architecture, furniture and fashion as they relate to the garden." Pays from 50¢ a word, on publication. Guidelines.

GENETIC ENGINEERING NEWS—1651 Third Ave., New York, NY 10128. John Sterling, Man. Ed. Features and news articles on all aspects of biotechnology. Pays varying rates, on acceptance. Query.

GLASS DIGEST—310 Madison Ave., New York, NY 10017. Charles Cumpston, Ed. Articles, 1,200 to 1,500 words, on building projects and glass/metal dealers, distributors, storefront and glazing contractors. Pays varying rates, on publication.

GOLF COURSE NEWS—38 Lafayette St., P.O. Box 997, Yarmouth, ME 04096. Mark Leslie, Man. Ed. Features, 500 to 1,500 words, on all aspects of golf course maintenance, design, building, and management. Pays $300 to $500 for features, on acceptance.

GOLF SHOP OPERATIONS—5520 Park Ave., Box 395, Trumbull, CT 06611–0395. Michael Schwanz, Ed. Articles, 200 to 800 words, with photos, on successful golf shop operations; new ideas for merchandising, display, bookkeeping. Short pieces on golf professionals and retailers. Pays $250 to $350, on publication. Query with outline.

GOVERNMENT EXECUTIVE—1730 M St. N.W., Suite 1100, Washington, DC 20036. Timothy Clark, Ed. Articles, 1,500 to 3,000 words, for civilian and military government workers at the management level.

GREENHOUSE MANAGER—P.O. Box 1868, Fort Worth, TX 76101. David Kuack, Ed. How-to articles, success stories, 500 to 1,800 words, accompanied by color slides, of interest to professional greenhouse growers. Profiles. Pays $50 to $300, on acceptance. Query required.

HARDWARE TRADE—2965 Broadmoor Valley Rd., Suite B, Colorado Springs, CO 80906. Marsha Jo Legler, Ed. Dir. Articles, 800 to 1,000 words, on unusual hardware and home center stores and promotions in the Northwest and Midwest. Photos. Query.

HARVARD BUSINESS REVIEW—Harvard Graduate School of Business Administration, Boston, MA 02163. Query editors, in writing, on new ideas about management of interest to senior executives.

HEALTH FOODS BUSINESS—567 Morris Ave., Elizabeth, NJ 07208. Gina Geslewitz, Ed. Articles, 1,200 words, with photos, profiling health food stores. Shorter pieces on trends, research findings, preventive medicine, alternative therapies. Interviews with doctors and nutritionists. Pays on publication. Query. Send for guidelines.

HEARTH & HOME—P.O. Box 2008, Laconia, NH 03247. Kenneth E. Daggett, Pub./Ed. Profiles and interviews, 1,000 to 1,800 words, with specialty retailers selling both casual furniture and hearth products (fireplaces, woodstoves, accessories, etc.). Pays $150 to $250, on acceptance.

HEATING/PIPING/AIR CONDITIONING—2 Illinois Center, Chicago, IL 60601. Robert T. Korte, Ed. Articles, to 5,000 words, on heating, piping, and air conditioning systems in industrial plants and large buildings; engineering information. Pays $60 per printed page, on publication. Query.

HOSPITAL SUPERVISOR'S BULLETIN—24 Rope Ferry Rd., Waterford, CT 06386. Michele Dunaj, Ed. Interviews, articles with non-medical hospital supervisors on departmental problem solving. Pays 12¢ to 15¢ a word. Query.

HOSPITALS—737 N. Michigan Ave., Chicago, IL 60611. Mary Grayson, Ed. Articles, 800 to 3,200 words, for hospital administrators. Pays varying rates, on acceptance. Query.

HUMAN RESOURCE EXECUTIVE—Axon Group, 747 Dresher Rd., Horsham, PA 19044–0980. David Shadovitz, Ed. Profiles and case stories, 1,800 to 2,200 words, of interest to people in the personnel profession. Pays varying rates, on acceptance. Queries required.

INCENTIVE MAGAZINE—633 Third Ave., New York, NY 10017. Regina Eisman, Sr. Ed. Articles on marketing, managing, incentive travel, and merchandise; motivation and incentive sales and merchandising strategies. Pays $125 to $800, on acceptance.

INCOME OPPORTUNITIES—380 Lexington Ave., New York, NY 10168–0035. Stephen Wagner, Ed. Helpful articles, 1,000 to 2,500 words, on how to make money full- or part-time; how to start a successful small business, improve sales, etc. Pays varying rates, on acceptance.

INCOME PLUS—73 Spring St., Suite 303, New York, NY 10012. Roxane Farmanfarmaian, Ed. How-to articles on starting a small business, franchise, or mail-order operation. Payment varies, on publication. Query.

INDEPENDENT BUSINESS—875 S. Westlake Blvd., Suite 211, Westlake Village, CA 91361. Daniel Kehrer, Ed. Articles, 500 to 2,000 words, of practical interest and value to small business owners. Pays $200 to $1,500, on acceptance. Query.

INSTITUTIONAL RESEARCH—See *Research Magazine*.

INTERNATIONAL DESIGN—330 W. 42nd St., New York, NY 10036. Annetta Hanna, Ed. Articles to 2,000 words, on product development, design management, graphic design, design history, fashion, art, and environments for designers and marketing executives. Profiles of designers and corporations that use design effectively. Pays $250 to $600, on publication.

JEMS, JOURNAL OF EMERGENCY MEDICAL SERVICES—P.O. Box 2789, Carlsbad, CA 92018. Diane Lofshult, Man. Ed. Articles, 1,500 to 3,000 words, of interest to emergency medical providers (from EMTs to paramedics to nurses and physicians) who work in the EMS industry worldwide.

LLAMAS—P.O. Box 1038, Dublin, OH 43017. Susan Ley, Asst. Ed. "The International Camelid Journal," published eight times yearly. Articles, 300 to 3,000 words, of interest to llama and alpaca owners. Pays $25 to $300, extra for photos, on acceptance. Query.

LOTUS—P.O. Box 9123, Cambridge, MA 02139. Rich Friedman, Ed.-in-Chief. Articles, 1,500 to 2,000 words, for business and professional people using electronic spreadsheets. Query with outline required. Pay varies, on final approval.

LP-GAS MAGAZINE—131 W. First St., Duluth, MN 55802. Zane Chastain, Ed. Articles, 1,500 to 2,500 words, with photos, on LP-gas dealer operations:

marketing, management, etc. Photos. Pays to 15¢ a word, extra for photos, on acceptance. Query.

MACHINE DESIGN—Penton Publications, 1100 Superior Ave., Cleveland, OH 44114. Leland E. Teschler, Exec. Ed. Articles, to 10 typed pages, on design-related topics for engineers. Pays varying rates, on publication. Submit outline or brief description.

MAGAZINE DESIGN & PRODUCTION—8340 Mission Rd., Suite 106, Prairie Village, KS 66206. Maureen Waters, Man. Ed. Articles, six to ten typed pages, on magazine design and production: printing, typesetting, design, computers, layout, etc. Pays $100 to $200, on acceptance. Query required.

MAINTENANCE TECHNOLOGY—1300 S. Grove Ave., Barrington, IL 60010. Robert C. Baldwin, Ed. Articles with how-to information on maintenance of electrical and electronic systems, mechanical systems and equipment, and plant facilities. Readers are maintenance managers, supervisors, and engineers in industrial plants and hospitals. Payment varies, on acceptance. Query.

MANAGE—2210 Arbor Blvd., Dayton, OH 45439. Doug Shaw, Ed. Articles, 1,500 to 2,200 words, on management and supervision for first-line and middle managers. "Please indicate word count on manuscript and enclose SASE." Pays 5¢ a word.

MANUFACTURING SYSTEMS—191 S. Gary, Carol Stream, IL 60188. Tom Inglesby, Ed. Articles, 500 to 2,000 words, on computer and information systems for industry executives seeking to increase productivity in manufacturing firms. Pays 10¢ to 20¢ a word, on acceptance. Query required.

MEMPHIS BUSINESS JOURNAL—88 Union, Suite 102, Memphis, TN 38103. Barney DuBois, Ed. Articles, to 2,000 words, on business, industry trade, agri-business, and finance in the mid-South trade area. Pays $80 to $200, on acceptance.

MINIATURES DEALER—21027 Crossroads Cir., P.O. Box 1612, Waukesha, WI 53187. Geraldine Willems, Ed. Articles, 1,000 to 1,500 words, on advertising, promotion, merchandising of miniatures and other small business concerns. Interviews with miniatures dealers. Pays to $175, on publication.

MIX MAGAZINE—6400 Hollis St., Suite 12, Emeryville, CA 94608. David Schwartz, Ed. Articles, varying lengths, for professionals, on audio, video, and music entertainment technology. Pays varies, on publication. Query.

MODERN HEALTHCARE—740 N. Rush St., Chicago, IL 60611. Clark Bell, Ed. Features on management, finance, building design and construction, and new technology for hospitals, health maintenance organizations, nursing homes, and other health care institutions. Pays $200 to $400, on publication. Very limited free-lance market.

MODERN OFFICE TECHNOLOGY—1100 Superior Ave., Cleveland, OH 44114. Lura Romei, Ed. Articles, three to four double-spaced, typed pages, on new concepts, management techniques, technologies, and applications for management executives. Payment varies, on acceptance. Query preferred.

MODERN TIRE DEALER—P.O. Box 8391, 341 White Pond Dr., Akron, OH 44320. Lloyd Stoyor, Ed. Tire retailing and automotive service articles, 1,000 to 1,500 words, with photos, on independent tire dealers and retreaders. Query; articles by assignment only. Pays $300 to $350, on publication.

NATIONAL BEAUTY SCHOOL JOURNAL—See *Beauty Education.*

NATIONAL FISHERMAN—120 Tillson Ave., Rockland, ME 04841. James W. Fullilove, Ed. Articles, 200 to 2,000 words, aimed at commercial fishermen and boat builders. Pays $4 to $6 per inch, extra for photos, on publication. Query preferred.

NATION'S BUSINESS—1615 H St. N.W., Washington, DC 20062. Articles on business-related topics, including management advice and success stories aimed at small- to medium-size businesses. Pays negotiable rates, on acceptance. Guidelines available.

NEPHROLOGY NEWS & ISSUES—13901 N. 73rd St., Suite 214, Scottsdale, AZ 85260. Mark E. Neumann, Ed. "We publish news articles, human-interest features, and opinion essays on dialysis, kidney transplants, and kidney disease." Pays varying rates, on publication. Photos a plus. Queries required.

NEVADA BUSINESS JOURNAL—3800 Howard Hughes Pkwy., Suite 120, Las Vegas, NV 89109. Lyle Brennan, Ed. Business articles, 1,500 to 2,500 words, of interest to Nevada readers; profiles, how-to articles. Pays $75 to $150 on publication. Query. Guidelines.

NEW CAREER WAYS NEWSLETTER—67 Melrose Ave., Haverhill, MA 01830. William J. Bond, Ed. How-to articles, 1,500 to 2,000 words, on new ways to succeed at work in the 1990s. Pays varying rates, on publication. Query with outline and SASE.

NORTH AMERICAN INTERNATIONAL BUSINESS—(formerly *Northeast International Business*) 401 Theodore Fremd Ave., Rye, NY 10580. David E. Moore, Exec. Ed. Articles, 1,000 to 1,500 words, on global marketing strategies, and short pieces (500 words), with tips on operating abroad. Profiles, 750 to 3,000 words, on individuals or companies. Pays 50¢ a word, on acceptance and on publication. Query.

NORTHEAST INTERNATIONAL BUSINESS—See *North American International Business.*

NSGA RETAIL FOCUS—National Sporting Goods Assoc., 1699 Wall St., Suite 700, Mt. Prospect, IL 60056. Cindy Savio, Man. Ed. Members magazine. Articles, 700 to 1,000 words, on sporting goods industry news and trends, the latest in new product information, and management and store operations. Payment varies, on publication. Query.

NURSINGWORLD JOURNAL—470 Boston Post Rd., Weston, MA 02193. Paul Kay, Ed. Articles, 800 to 1,500 words, for nurses, nurse educators, and students of nursing, etc., on all aspects of nursing. B&W photos. Pays from 25¢ per column inch, on publication.

OPPORTUNITY MAGAZINE—73 Spring St., Suite 303, New York, NY 10012. Donna Ruffini, Ed. Articles, 900 to 1,500 words, on sales psychology, sales techniques, successful small business careers, self-improvement. Pays $25 to $50, on publication.

OPTOMETRIC ECONOMICS—American Optometric Assn., 243 N. Lindbergh Blvd., St. Louis, MO 63141–7881. Dr. Jack Runninger, Ed. Monthly. Articles, 1,000 to 2,000 words, on private practice management for optometrists; direct, conversational style with how-to advice on how optometrists can build, improve, better manage, and enjoy their practices. Short humor and photos. Query. Payment varies, on acceptance.

PARTY & PAPER RETAILER—500 Summer St., Stamford, CT 06901. Trisha McMahon Drain, Ed. Monthly. Articles, 800 to 1,000 words, that offer employee management and retail marketing advice to the party store owner. "Articles grounded in facts and anecdotes are appreciated." Pay varies, on publication. Query with published clips.

PET BUSINESS—P.O. Box 2300, Miami, FL 33243. Karen Payne, Ed. Brief documented articles on animals and products found in pet stores; research findings; legislative/regulatory actions. Pays $4 per column inch, on publication. Photos, $10 to $20.

PETS/SUPPLIES/MARKETING—One E. First St., Duluth, MN 55802. Hugh Bishop, Ed. Articles, 1,000 to 1,200 words, with photos, on pet shops, and pet and product merchandising. Pays 10¢ a word, extra for photos. No fiction or news clippings. Query.

PHOTO MARKETING—3000 Picture Pl., Jackson, MI 49201. Margaret Hooks, Man. Ed. Business articles, 1,000 to 3,500 words, for owners and managers of camera/video stores or photo processing labs. Pays $150 to $500, extra for photos, on publication.

PHYSICAL THERAPY/OCCUPATIONAL THERAPY JOB NEWS— 470 Boston Post Rd., Weston, MA 02193. John C. Hinds, Jr. Articles, case studies, and profiles, 1,500 to 2,500 words, of interest to professional and student physical therapists. Guidelines available. Pays on publication.

PHYSICIANS FINANCIAL NEWS—PFN Publishing, 342 Madison Ave., Suite 1104, New York, NY 10173. Noreen Perrotta, Ed. Articles, 1,000 words, on investment and personal finance and non-clinical medical economic subjects. Pays $400, after acceptance. Queries required.

PHYSICIAN'S MANAGEMENT—7500 Old Oak Blvd., Cleveland, OH 44130. Bob Feigenbaum, Ed. Articles, about 2,500 words, on finance, investments, malpractice, and office management for primary care physicians. No clinical pieces. Pays $125 per printed page, on acceptance. Query with SASE.

PIZZA TODAY—P.O. Box 114, Santa Claus, IN 47579. Paula Werne, Ed. Pizza business management articles, to 2,500 words, of use to pizza entrepreneurs. Pizza business profiles. Pays $75 to $150 per published page, on publication.

P.O.B.—5820 Lilley Rd., Suite 5, Canton, MI 48187–3623. Victoria L. Dickinson, Ed. Technical and business articles, 1,000 to 4,000 words, for professionals and technicians in the surverying and mapping fields. Technical tips for field and office procedures and equipment maintenance. Pays $150 to $400, on acceptance.

POLICE MAGAZINE—6300 Yarrow Dr., Carlsbad, CA 92009–1597. Sean T. Hilferty, Ed. Articles and profiles, 1,000 to 3,000 words, on specialized groups, equipment, issues and trends of interest to people in the law enforcement profession. Pays $100 to $300, on acceptance.

POOL & SPA NEWS—3923 W. Sixth St., Los Angeles, CA 90020. News articles for the swimming pool, spa, and hot tub industry. Pays from 10¢ to 15¢ a word, extra for photos, on publication. Query first.

PRIVATE PRACTICE—Box 12489, Oklahoma City, OK 73157. Brian Sherman, Ed. Articles, 1,500 to 2,000 words, on state or local legislation affecting medical field. Pays $150 to $300, on publication.

PROGRESSIVE GROCER—Four Stamford Forum, Stamford, CT 06901. Priscilla Donegan, Man. Ed. Articles related to retail food operations; ideas for successful merchandising, promotions, and displays. Short pieces preferred. Cartoons and photos. Pay varies, on acceptance.

QUICK PRINTING—1680 S. W. Bayshore Blvd., Port St. Lucie, FL 34984. Bob Hall, Ed. Articles, 1,500 to 3,000 words, of interest to owners and operators of quick print shops, copy shops, and small commercial printers, on how to make their businesses more profitable; include figures. Pays from $75, on acceptance.

REAL ESTATE TODAY—National Association of Realtors, 430 N. Michigan Ave., Chicago, IL 60611–4087. Educational, how-to articles on all aspects of residential, finance, commercial-investment, and brokerage-management real estate, to 1,500 words. Query required.

REMODELING—Hanley-Wood, Inc., 655 15th St., Suite 475, Washington, DC 20005. Wendy A. Jordan, Ed. Articles, 250 to 1,700 words, on remodeling and industry news for residential and light commercial remodelers. Pays 20¢ a word, on acceptance. Query.

RESEARCH MAGAZINE—2201 Third St., P.O. Box 77905, San Francisco, CA 94107. Anne Evers, Ed. Articles of interest to stockbrokers, 1,000 to 3,000 words, on financial products, selling, how-tos, and financial trends. Pays from $300 to $900, on publication. Same requirements for *Institutional Research*, for institutional investors. Query.

RESTAURANTS USA—1200 17th St. N.W., Washington, DC 20036–3097. Sylvia Rivchun-Somerville, Ed. Publication of the National Restaurant Association. Articles, 1,500 to 3,500 words, on the food service and restaurant business. Pays $350 to $750, on acceptance. Query.

ROOFER MAGAZINE—12120 Amedicus Ln., Ft. Myers, FL 33907. Kaerrie Simons, Ed. Technical and non-technical articles, human-interest pieces, 500 to 1,500 words, on roofing-related topics: new roofing concepts, energy savings, pertinent issues, roofing contract profiles, industry concern. Humorous items welcome. No general business or computer articles. Photos a plus. Pays negotiable rates, on publication. Guidelines.

RV BUSINESS—29901 Agoura Rd., Agoura, CA 91301. Katherine Sharma, Exec. Ed. Articles, 1,500 to 2,500 words, on manufacturing, financing, selling, and servicing recreational vehicles. Articles on legislative matters affecting the industry. Pays varying rates.

THE SAFETY COMPLIANCE LETTER—24 Rope Ferry Rd., Waterford, CT 06386. Margot Loomis, Ed. Interview-based articles, 800 to 1,250 words, for safety professionals, on solving OSHA-related safety and health problems. Pays to 15¢ a word, on acceptance. Query.

SAFETY MANAGEMENT—24 Rope Ferry Rd., Waterford, CT 06386. Margot Loomis, Ed. Interview-based articles, 1,100 to 1,500 words, for safety professionals, on improving workplace safety and health. Pays to 15¢ a word, on acceptance. Query.

SALES & MARKETING MANAGEMENT—Bill Communications, Inc., 633 Third Ave., New York, NY 10017. Richard Kern, Ed. Short and feature articles of interest to sales and marketing executives. Looking for practical "news you can use." Pays varying rates, on acceptance. Queries preferred.

SIGN BUSINESS—P.O. Box 1416, Broomfield, CO 80038. Emerson Schwartzkopf, Ed. Articles specifically targeted to the sign business. Pays $50 to $200, on publication.

SNACK FOOD MAGAZINE—131 W. First St., Duluth, MN 55802. Jerry Hess, Ed. Articles, 600 to 1,500 words, on trade news, personalities, promotions, production in snack food manufacturing industry. Short pieces; photos. Pays 12¢ to 15¢ a word, $15 for photos, on acceptance. Query.

SOUTHERN LUMBERMAN—P.O. Box 681629, Franklin, TN 37068–1629. Nanci P. Gregg, Man. Ed. Articles on sawmill operations, interviews with industry leaders, how-to technical pieces with an emphasis on increasing sawmill production and efficiency. "Always looking for 'sweetheart' mill stories; we publish one per month." Pays $100 to $250 for articles with B&W photos. Queries preferred.

SOUVENIRS AND NOVELTIES—7000 Terminal Square, Suite 210, Upper Darby, PA 19082. Articles, 1,500 words, quoting souvenir shop managers on items that sell, display ideas, problems in selling, industry trends. Photos. Pays from $1 per column inch, extra for photos, on publication.

SPECIALTY STORE SERVICE BULLETIN—6604 W. Saginaw Hwy., Lansing, MI 48917. Ralph D. Ward, Ed. Articles on how to run a business: promotions, fashion trends, sales training, etc., for women's clothing store owners and managers. Payment varies, on acceptance. Query.

SUCCESSFUL FARMING—1716 Locust St., Des Moines, IA 50336. Gene Johnston, Man. Ed. Articles, to 2,000 words, for farming families, on all areas of business farming: money management, marketing, machinery, soils and crops, livestock, and buildings; profiles. Pays from $300, on acceptance. Query required.

TAVERN SPORTS INTERNATIONAL—200 S. Michigan Ave., Suite 1430, Chicago, IL 60604. Jocelyn Hathaway, Man. Ed. Features and profiles, 1,000 to 2,000 words, of interest to people in the coin-amusement and hospitality industries. Topics cover the promotion and marketing of recreational entertainment and legislative issues affecting the two industries. Color photos a plus. Payment varies, on publication.

TEA & COFFEE TRADE JOURNAL—130 W. 42nd St., New York, NY 10036. Jane P. McCabe, Ed. Articles, 3 to 5 pages, on trade issues reflecting the tea and coffee industry. Query first. Pays $5 per published inch, on publication.

TEXTILE WORLD—4170 Ashford-Dunwoody Rd. N.E., Suite 420, Atlanta, GA 30319. L.A. Christiansen, Ed. Articles, 500 to 2,000 words, with photos, on manufacturing and finishing textiles. Pays varying rates, on acceptance.

TILE WORLD/STONE WORLD—320 Kinderkamack Rd., Oradell, NJ 07649–2102. John Sailer, Ed. Articles, 750 to 1,500 words, on new trends in installing and designing with tile and stone. For architects, interior designers, and design professionals. Pays $115 per printed page, on publication. Query.

TODAY'S OR NURSE—6900 Grove Rd., Thorofare, NJ 08086. Mary Jo Krey, Ed. Clinical or general articles, from 2,000 words, of direct interest to operating room nurses.

TOURIST ATTRACTIONS AND PARKS—7000 Terminal Square, Suite 210, Upper Darby, PA 19082. Articles, 1,500 words, on successful management of parks and leisure attractions. News items, 250 and 500 words. Pays 7¢ a word, on publication. Query.

TRAILER/BODY BUILDERS—P.O. Box 66010, Houston, TX 77266. Paul Schenck, Ed. Articles on engineering, sales, and management ideas for truck body and truck trailer manufacturers. Pays from $100 per printed page, on acceptance.

TRAINING MAGAZINE—50 S. Ninth St., Minneapolis, MN 55402. Jack Gordon, Ed. Articles, 1,000 to 2,500 words, for managers of training and development activities in corporations, government, etc. Pays to 20¢ a word, on acceptance. Query.

TRAVEL COUNSELOR—(formerly *Travel People*) CMP Publications, 600 Community Dr., Manhassett, NY 11030. Linda Ball, Ed. Business and management how-to articles, 1,000 to 1,500 words, of successful travel industry workers. Pay varies, on acceptance.

TRAVEL PEOPLE—See *Travel Counselor.*

TRUCKERS/USA—P.O. Box 323, Windber, PA 15963. David Adams, Ed. Monthly. Articles, 500 to 1,00 words, on the trucking business and marketing. Trucking-related poetry and fiction. Payment varies, on publication.

VENDING TIMES—545 Eighth Ave., New York, NY 10018. Arthur E. Yohalem, Ed. Features and news articles, with photos, on vending machines. Pays varying rates, on acceptance. Query.

WESTERN FLYER—P.O. Box 98786, Tacoma, WA 98498–0786. Dave Sclair, Pub. Articles, 500 to 2,500 words, of interest to "general aviation" pilots. "Best shot for non-pilot writers is 'destination' series: attractions and activities near airports not necessarily aviation oriented." Pays $3 per column inch (approximately 40 words); $10 for B&W photos; $50 for color photos; within the first month following publication.

WINES & VINES—1800 Lincoln Ave., San Rafael, CA 94901. Philip E. Hiaring, Ed. Articles, 1,000 words, on grape and wine industry, emphasizing marketing and production. Pays 5¢ a word, on acceptance.

WOMEN IN BUSINESS—9100 Ward Parkway, Box 8728, Kansas City, MO 64114–0728. Wendy Myers, Ed. Publication of the American Business Women's Association. Features, 1,000 to 2,000 words, for career women from 25 to 55 years old; no profiles. Pays 15¢ a published word, on acceptance. Query.

WOODSHOP NEWS—Pratt St., Essex, CT 06426–1185. Ian C. Bowen, Ed. Features (one to three typed pages) for and about people who work with wood: business stories, profiles, news. Pays from $3 per column inch, on publication. Queries preferred.

WORKBOAT—P.O. Box 1348, Mandeville, LA 70470. Marilyn Barrett, Assoc. Ed. Features, to 2,000 words, and shorts, 500 to 1,000 words, providing current, lively information for work boat owners, operators, crew, suppliers, and regulators. Topics include construction and conversion; diesel engines and electronics; politics and industry; unusual vessels; new products; and profiles. Payment varies, on acceptance and on publication. Queries preferred.

WORLD OIL—Gulf Publishing Co., P.O. Box 2608, Houston, TX 77252. T.R. Wright, Jr., Ed. Engineering and operations articles, 3,000 to 4,000 words, on petroleum industry exploration, drilling, or production. Photos. Pays from $50 per printed page, on acceptance. Query.

WORLD SCREEN NEWS—49 E. 21st St., 6th Fl., New York, NY 10010. Gregory P. Fagan, Ed. Features and short pieces on trends in the business of international television programming (network, syndication, cable, and pay). Pays to $750, after publication.

WORLD WASTES—6255 Barfield Rd., Atlanta, GA 30328. Bill Wolpin, Ed./Pub. Katya Andresen, Asst. Ed. Case studies, 1,000 to 2,000 words, with photos, of refuse haulers, landfill operators, resource recovery operations, and transfer stations, with solutions to problems in field. Pays from $125 per printed page, on publication. Query preferred.

YOUNG FASHIONS—119 Fifth Ave., New York, NY 10003. Articles, 1,500 to 3,000 words, that help store owners and department store buyers of children's clothes with merchandising, fashion issues, or operations; how-to pieces. Pays $300 per article, on publication. Query required.

IN-HOUSE MAGAZINES

Publications circulated to company employees (sometimes called house magazines or house organs) and to members of associations and organizations are excellent, well-paying markets for writers at all levels of experience. Large corporations publish these magazines to promote good will, familiarize readers with the company's services and products, and interest customers in these products. And, many organizations publish house magazines designed to keep their members abreast of the issues and events concerning a particular cause or industry. Always read an in-house magazine before submitting an article; write to the editor for a sample copy (offering to pay for it) and the editorial guidelines. Stamped, self-addressed envelopes should be enclosed with any query or manuscript. The following list includes only a sampling of publications in this large market.

CALIFORNIA HIGHWAY PATROLMAN—2030 V St., Sacramento, CA 95818–1730. Carol Perri, Ed. Articles, on transportation safety, California history, travel, consumerism, past and present vehicles, humor, general items, etc. Photos a plus. Pays 2 ½ ¢ a word, $5 for B&W photos, on publication. Guidelines and/or sample copy with 9″ × 11″ SASE.

CATHOLIC FORESTER—P.O. Box 3012, 425 W. Shuman Blvd., Naperville, IL 60566–7012. Barbara Cunningham, Ed. Official publication of the Catholic Order of Foresters, a fraternal life insurance company for Catholics. General-interest articles, to 2,000 words. Fiction, to 3,000 words (prefer shorter), that deals with contemporary issues; no moralizing, explicit sex or violence. Pays from 10¢ a word, on acceptance.

COLUMBIA—1 Columbus Plaza, New Haven, CT 06507–0901. Richard McMunn, Ed. Journal of the Knights of Columbus. Articles, 1,500 words, for Catholic families. Must be accompanied by color photos or transparencies. No fiction. Pays to $500 for articles and photos, on acceptance.

THE COMPASS—Grand Central Towers, 230 E. 44th St., Suite 14B, New York, NY 10017. J.A. Randall, Ed. Articles, to 2,500 words, on the sea and deep sea trade; also articles on aviation. Pays to $600, on acceptance. Query with SASE.

THE ELKS MAGAZINE—425 W. Diversey Pkwy., Chicago, IL 60614. Judith L. Keogh, Man. Ed. Articles, to 2,500 words, on business, sports, and topics of current interest; for non-urban audience with above-average income. Informative or humorous pieces, to 2,500 words. Pays $150 to $400 for articles, on acceptance. Query.

FIREHOUSE—PTN Publishing Company, 445 Broad Hollow Rd., Melville, NY 11747. Thomas J. Rahilly, Exec. Ed. Articles, 500 to 2,000 words: on-the-scene accounts of fires, trends in firefighting equipment, controversial fire service issues, and lifestyles of firefighters. Pays $100 per typeset page; extra for photos. Query.

FOCUS—Turnkey Publications, 3420 Executive Center Dr., #250, Austin, TX 78731. Robin Perry, Ed. Magazine of the North American Data General Users Group. Articles, 700 to 4,000 words, on Data General computers. Photos a plus. Pays to $100, on publication. Query required.

FORD NEW HOLLAND NEWS—Ford New Holland, Inc., P.O. Box 1895, New Holland, PA 17557. Rosanne Macrina, Ed. Articles, to 1,500 words, with strong color photo support, on production, agriculture, research, and rural living. Pays on acceptance. Query.

FRIENDS, THE CHEVY OWNERS' MAGAZINE—30400 Van Dyke, Warren, MI 48093. Claire Hinsberg, Ed. Feature articles, 800 to 1,200 words, auto-travel related with specific focus; outdoor/adventure oriented; lifestyle; celebrity profiles; entertainment. Pays varying rates, extra for photos, on acceptance. Query.

THE FURROW—Deere & Company, John Deere Rd., Moline, IL 61265. George R. Sollenberger, Exec. Ed. Specialized, illustrated articles on farming. Pays to $1,000, on acceptance.

KIWANIS—3636 Woodview Trace, Indianapolis, IN 46268. Chuck Jonak, Exec. Ed. Articles, 2,500 words (sidebars, 250 to 350 words) on lifestyle, relationships, world view, education, trends, small business, religion, health, etc. No travel pieces, interviews, profiles. Pays $400 to $1,000, on acceptance. Query.

THE LION—300 22nd St., Oak Brook, IL 60521. Robert Kleinfelder, Sr. Ed. Official publication of Lions Clubs International. Articles, 800 to 2,000 words, and photo essays, on club activities. Pays from $50 to $600, including photos, on acceptance. Query.

THE MODERN WOODMEN—Modern Woodmen of America, 1701 1st Ave., Rock Island, IL 61201. Gloria Bergh, Mgr., Public Relations. Member publication for fraternal life insurance society. Family- and community-oriented, general-interest articles; some quality fiction. Color photos. Pays from $50, on acceptance. Publication not copyrighted.

MOTOR CLUB NEWS—484 Central Ave., Newark, NJ 07107. Marlene Timm, Man. Ed. Magazine of the Motor Club of America. Articles, 2,500 words, on automotive travel inside and outside the U.S., auto safety, and trends in the auto industry. "Issues are seasonal; articles often reflect travel destinations appropriate to the season." Queries are preferred; address Christy Colato, Ed. Asst. Pays $150, on acceptance.

OPTIMIST MAGAZINE—4494 Lindell Blvd., St. Louis, MO 63108. Gary S. Bradley, Ed. Articles, to 1,500 words, on activities of local optimist club, and techniques for personal and club success; also articles of general interest to the membership. Pays from $100, on acceptance. Query.

RESTAURANTS USA—1200 17th St. N.W., Washington, DC 20036-3097. Sylvia Rivchun-Somerville, Ed. Publication of the National Restaurant Association. Articles, 1,500 to 3,500 words, on the food service and restaurant business. Pays $350 to $750, on acceptance. Query.

THE RETIRED OFFICER MAGAZINE—201 N. Washington St., Alexandria, VA 22314. Articles, 800 to 2,000 words, of interest to military retirees and their families. Current military/national affairs: recent military history, health/medicine, and second-career opportunities. No fillers. Photos a plus. Pays to $500, on acceptance. Query Manuscripts Ed. Guidelines.

THE ROTARIAN—1560 Sherman Ave., Evanston, IL 60201. Willmon L.

White, Ed. Publication of Rotary International, world service organization of business and professional men and women. Articles, 1,200 to 2,000 words, on international social and economic issues, business and management, human relationships, travel, sports, environment, science and technology; humor. Pays good rates, on acceptance. Query.

SILVER CIRCLE—4900 Rivergrade Rd., Irwindale, CA 91706. Jay Binkly, Ed. National consumer-interest quarterly. Consumer service articles, 800 to 2,000 words, on money, health, home, gardening, food, travel, hobbies, etc. Query. Pays $250 to $1,500 (20% kill fee), on acceptance.

THE TOASTMASTER—P.O. Box 9052, Mission Viejo, CA 92690. Suzanne Frey, Ed. Member-supported monthly. Articles, 1,500 to 2,500 words, on decision making, speech outlining, introducing speakers, leadership development, speaking techniques, etc. Pays $100 to $250, on acceptance.

VFW MAGAZINE—406 W. 34th St., Kansas City, MO 64111. Richard K. Kolb, Ed. Magazine for Veterans of Foreign Wars and their families. Articles, to 1,500 words, on current issues and military history, with veteran angle. Photos. Pays to $500 for unsolicited articles, extra for photos, on acceptance. Guidelines.

WOODMEN OF THE WORLD MAGAZINE—1700 Farnam St., Omaha, NE 68102. George M. Herriott, Ed. Articles on history, insurance, family, health, science, etc. Photos. Pays 10¢ a word, extra for photos, on acceptance.

RELIGIOUS AND DENOMINATIONAL

ADVANCE—1445 Boonville Ave., Springfield, MO 65802. Harris Jansen, Ed. Articles, 1,200 words, slanted to ministers, on preaching, doctrine, practice; how-to features. Pays to 6¢ a word, on acceptance.

AMERICA—106 W. 56th St., New York, NY 10019–3893. George W. Hunt, S.J., Ed. Articles, 1,000 to 2,500 words, on current affairs, family life, literary trends. Pays $75 to $150, on acceptance.

AMERICAN BIBLE SOCIETY RECORD—1865 Broadway, New York, NY 10023. Clifford P. Macdonald, Man. Ed. Material related to work of American Bible Society: translating, publishing, distributing. Pays on acceptance. Query.

AMIT WOMAN—817 Broadway, New York, NY 10003–4761. Micheline Ratzersdorfer, Ed. Articles, 1,000 to 2,000 words, of interest to Jewish women: Middle East, Israel, history, holidays, travel. Pays to $75, on publication.

ANNALS OF ST. ANNE DE BEAUPRÉ—P.O. Box 1000, St. Anne de Beaupré, Quebec, Canada G0A 3C0. Roch Achard, C.Ss.R., Ed. Articles, 1,100 to 1,200 words, on Catholic subjects and on St. Anne. Pays 3¢ to 4¢ a word, on acceptance.

BAPTIST LEADER—American Baptist Churches-USA, P.O. Box 851, Valley Forge, PA 19482–0851. L. Isham, Ed. Practical how-to or thought-provoking articles, 1,200 to 1,600 words, for local church lay leaders and teachers.

BRIGADE LEADER—Box 150, Wheaton, IL 60189. Steve Neideck, Man. Ed. Inspirational articles, 1,000 to 1,800 words, for Christian men who lead boys, with an emphasis on fathering. Pays $60 to $150. Query only.

CATECHIST—2451 E. River Rd., Dayton, OH 45439. Patricia Fischer, Ed. Informational and how-to articles, 1,200 to 1,500 words, for Catholic teachers, coordinators, and administrators in religious education programs. Pays $25 to $75, on publication.

CATHOLIC DIGEST—P.O. Box 64090, St. Paul, MN 55164–0090. Address Articles Ed. Articles, 2,000 to 2,500 words, on Catholic and general subjects. Fillers, to 300 words, on instances of kindness rewarded, for "Hearts Are Trumps"; accounts of good deeds, for "People Are Like That." Pays from $200 for original articles, $100 for reprints, on acceptance; $4 to $50 for fillers, on publication.

CATHOLIC LIFE—See *PIME World.*

CATHOLIC NEAR EAST MAGAZINE—1011 First Ave., New York, NY 10022–4195. Thomas McHugh, Ed. Michael La Civita, Asst. Ed. A quarterly publication of Catholic Near East Welfare Assoc., a papal agency for humanitarian and pastoral support. Articles 1,500 to 2,000 words, on people of the Balkans, Eastern Europe, Egypt, Ethiopia, Middle East, and India; their religious affairs, heritage, culture, and current state of affairs. Special interest in Eastern Christian churches. Color photos for all articles. Query with SASE. Pays 15¢ a word, on publication.

CATHOLIC TWIN CIRCLE—12700 Ventura Blvd., Suite 200, Studio City, CA 91604. Loretta G. Seyer, Ed. Articles and interviews of interest to Catholics, 1,000 to 2,000 words, with photos. Strict attention to Catholic doctrine required. Enclose SASE. Pays 10¢ a word, on publication.

CHARISMA & CHRISTIAN LIFE—600 Rinehart Rd., Lake Mary, FL 32746. Jeff Dunn, Assignment Ed. Charismatic/evangelical Christian articles, 1,500 to 2,500 words, for developing the spiritual life. Photos. Pays varying rates, on publication.

THE CHRISTIAN CENTURY—407 S. Dearborn St., Chicago, IL 60605. James M. Wall, Ed. Ecumenical. Articles, 1,500 to 2,500 words, with a religious angle, on political and social issues, international affairs, culture, the arts. Poetry, to 20 lines. Photos. Pays about $25 per printed page, extra for photos, on publication.

CHRISTIAN HERALD—40 Overlook Dr., Chappaqua, NY 10514. Bob Chuvala, Ed. Evangelical. Articles, personal-experience pieces, to 1,200 words, on biblically oriented topics. Pays from 10¢ a word for full-length features, from $25 for short pieces, after acceptance. Query or send complete manuscript. No poetry.

CHRISTIAN SINGLE—MSN 140, 127 Ninth Ave. N., Nashville, TN 37234. Articles, 600 to 1,200 words, for single adults about leisure activities, issues related to single parents, inspiring personal experiences, humor, life from a Christian perspective. Pays 5 ½¢ a word, on acceptance, plus three complimentary copies. Query or send complete manuscript. Guidelines.

CHRISTIAN SOCIAL ACTION—100 Maryland Ave. N.E., Washington, DC 20002. Lee Ranck, Ed. Articles, 1,500 to 2,000 words, on social issues for concerned persons of faith. Pays $75 to $100, on publication.

CHRISTIANITY TODAY—465 Gundersen Dr., Carol Stream, IL 60188. Lyn Cryderan, Ed. David Neff, Man. Ed. Doctrinal social issues and interpretive essays, 1,500 to 3,000 words, from evangelical Protestant perspective. No fiction or poetry. Pays $300 to $500, on acceptance. Query required.

CHURCH ADMINISTRATION—127 Ninth Ave. N., Nashville, TN 37234. Gary Hardin, Ed. Southern Baptist. How-to articles, 1,500 to 1,800 words, on administrative planning, staffing, pastoral ministry, organization, and financing. Pays 5 ½¢ a word, on acceptance. Query.

CHURCH & STATE—8120 Fenton St., Silver Spring, MD 20910. Joseph L. Conn, Man. Ed. Articles, 600 to 2,600 words, on religious liberty and church-state relations issues. Pays varying rates, on acceptance. Query.

CHURCH EDUCATOR—Educational Ministries, Inc., 2861-C Saturn St., Brea, CA 92621. Robert G. Davidson, Ed. How-to articles, to 1,750 words, on Christian education: activity projects, crafts, learning centers, games, bulletin boards, etc., for all church school, junior and high school programs, and adult study group ideas. Allow 3 months for response. Pays 3¢ a word, on publication.

THE CHURCH HERALD—6157 28th St. S.E., Grand Rapids, MI 49546–6999. Jeffrey Japinga, Ed. Reformed Church in America. Articles, 500 to 1,500 words, on Christianity and culture, politics, marriage, and home. Pays $50 to $125, on acceptance. Query required.

CIRCUIT RIDER—P.O. Box 801, Nashville, TN 37202–0801. Keith Pohl, Ed. Articles for United Methodist pastors, 800 to 1,600 words. Pays $50 to $200, on acceptance. Query, with SASE, preferred.

COLUMBIA—1 Columbus Plaza, New Haven, CT 06507–0901. Richard McMunn, Ed. Knights of Columbus. Articles, 1,500 words, for Catholic families. Must be accompanied by color photos or transparencies. No fiction. Pays to $500 for articles with photos, on acceptance.

COMMENTARY—165 E. 56th St., New York, NY 10022. Norman Podhoretz, Ed. Articles, 5,000 to 7,000 words, on contemporary issues, Jewish affairs, social sciences, religious thought, culture. Serious fiction; book reviews. Pays on publication.

COMMONWEAL—15 Dutch St., New York, NY 10038. Margaret O'Brien Steinfels, Ed. Catholic. Articles, to 3,000 words, on political, religious, social, and literary subjects. Pays 3¢ a word, on acceptance.

CONFIDENT LIVING—Box 82808, Lincoln, NE 68501. Jan Reeser, Man. Ed. Articles, to 1,200 words, on relating biblical truths to daily living. Photos. Pays 7¢ to 15¢ a word, on acceptance. No simultaneous submissions. SASE required. Photos paid on publication.

DECISION—Billy Graham Evangelistic Association, 1300 Harmon Pl., Minneapolis, MN 55403–0779. Roger C. Palms, Ed. Christian testimonials and teaching articles on evangelism and Christian nurturing, 1,500 to 2,000 words. Vignettes, 400 to 1,000 words. Pays varying rates, on publication.

DISCOVERIES—6401 The Paseo, Kansas City, MO 64131. Latta Jo Knapp, Ed. Fiction for children (grades 3 to 6) 400 to 800 words, defining Christian experiences and demonstrating Christian values and beliefs. Pays 3 ½¢ a word for first rights; 5¢ a word for multi-use rights; on acceptance or publication.

DREAMS & VISIONS—Skysong Press, RR1, Washago, Ontario, Canada L0K 2B0. Wendy Stanton, Manuscript Ed. New frontiers in Christian fiction. Eclectic fiction, 2,000 to 7,500 words, that "has literary value and is unique and relevant to Christian readers today." Pays in copies and $100 reward to best of the year.

EVANGEL—Light and Life Press, Box 535002, Indianapolis, IN 46253–5002. Vera Bethel, Ed. Free Methodist. Personal experience articles, 1,000 words; short devotional items, 300 to 500 words; fiction, 1,200 words, showing personal faith in Christ to be instrumental in solving problems. Pays $10 to $25 for articles, $45 for fiction, $10 for poetry, on publication.

EVANGELICAL BEACON—901 E. 78th St., Minneapolis, MN 55420. Carol Madison, Ed. Evangelical Free Church. Articles, 500 to 2,000 words, that fit with the editorial theme. Send SASE for guidelines and editorial calendar. Pays 7¢ a word (3¢ a word for reprints), on publication.

FAITH TODAY—Box 8800, Sta. B, Willowdale, Ontario, Canada M2K 2R6. Brian C. Stiller, Ed. Audrey Dorsch, Man. Ed. Articles, 1,500 words, on current issues relating to the church in Canada. Pays negotiable rates, on publication. Queries are preferred.

THE GEM—Box 926, Findlay, OH 45839–0926. Marilyn Rayle Kern, Ed. Articles, 300 to 1,600 words, and fiction, 1,000 to 1,600 words: true-to-life experiences of God's help, of healed relationships, and of growing maturity in faith. For adolescents through senior citizens. Pays $15 for articles and fiction, $5 to $10 for fillers, after publication.

GROUP, THE YOUTH MINISTRY MAGAZINE—Box 481, Loveland, CO 80539. Rick Lawrence, Ed. Interdenominational magazine for leaders of junior and senior high school Christian youth groups. Articles, 500 to 1,700 words, about practical youth ministry principles, techniques, or activities. Short how-to pieces, to 300 words, for "Try This One." Pays to $150 for articles, $15 to $25 for department pieces, on acceptance. Guidelines available.

GUIDE—Review and Herald Publishing Co., 55 W. Oak Ridge Dr., Hagerstown, MD 21740. Stories and articles, to 1,200 words, for Christian youth, ages 10 to 14. Pays 3¢ to 4¢ a word, on acceptance.

HOME LIFE—127 Ninth Ave. N., Nashville, TN 37234. Charlie Warren, Ed. Mary P. Darby, Asst. Ed. Southern Baptist. Articles, preferably personal-experience, and fiction, to 1,500 words, on Christian marriage, parenthood, and family relationships. Human-interest pieces, 200 to 500 words; cartoons and short verse. Pays to 5 ½¢ a word, on acceptance.

INSIDE MAGAZINE—226 S. 16th St., Philadelphia, PA 19102–3392. Jane Biberman, Ed. Articles, 1,500 to 3,000 words, and fiction, 2,000 to 3,000 words, of interest to Jewish adults. Pays $100 to $500, on acceptance. Query.

THE JEWISH MONTHLY—B'nai B'rith International, 1640 Rhode Island Ave. N.W., Washington, DC 20036. Jeff Rubin, Ed. Articles, 500 to 3,000 words, on politics, religion, history, culture, and social issues of Jewish concern with an emphasis on people. Pays 10¢ to 25¢, on publication. Query with clips.

JOURNEY—Christian Board of Publication, Box 179, St. Louis, MO 63166. Michael E. Dixon, Ed. Fiction, 100 to 1,200 words; articles, 600 to 1,000 words; and poetry, to 20 lines. Accepts material for 12- to 16-year-olds. Pays 3¢ a word for prose, from $3 for poetry, on acceptance. Guidelines available.

KEY TO CHRISTIAN EDUCATION—8121 Hamilton Ave., Cincinnati, OH 45231–2396. Barbara Bolton and Lowellete Lauderdale, Eds. Articles, to 1,200 words, on teaching methods, and success stories for workers in Christian education. Pays varying rates, on acceptance.

LIGHT AND LIFE—P.O. Box 535002, Indianapolis, IN 46253–5002. Robert Haslam, Ed. Fresh, lively articles about practical Christian living, and sound treatments of vital issues facing the Evangelical in contemporary society. Pays 4¢ a word, on publication.

LIGUORIAN—Liguori, MO 63057–9999. Rev. Allan Weinert, Ed. Francine O'Connor, Man. Ed. Catholic. Articles and short stories, 1,500 to 2,000 words, on Christian values in modern life. Pays 10¢ to 12¢ a word, on acceptance.

THE LIVING LIGHT—U.S. Catholic Conference, Dept. of Education, 3211 4th St. N.W., Washington, DC 20017–1194. Berard L. Marthaler, Exec. Ed. Theoretical and practical articles, 1,500 to 4,000 words, on religious education, catechesis, and pastoral ministry.

LIVING WITH CHILDREN—MSN 140, 127 Ninth Ave. N., Nashville, TN 37234. Articles, 800 to 1,200 words, on parent-child relationships, told from a Christian perspective. Pays 5 ½¢ a word, after acceptance.

LIVING WITH PRESCHOOLERS—MSN 140, 127 Ninth Ave. N., Nashville, TN 37234. Articles, 800 to 1,200 words, and anecdotes, for Christian families. Pays 5 ½¢ a word, on acceptance.

LIVING WITH TEENAGERS—127 Ninth Ave. N., Nashville, TN 37234. Articles told from a Christian perspective for parents of teenagers; first-person approach preferred. Poetry, 4 to 16 lines. Pays 5 ½¢ a word, on acceptance, for articles.

THE LOOKOUT—8121 Hamilton Ave., Cincinnati, OH 45231. Simon J. Dahlman, Ed. Articles, 500 to 2,000 words, on family issues, Christian education, applying Christian faith to current issues, and people overcoming problems with Christian principles. Inspirational or humorous shorts, 500 to 800 words; fiction, to 2,000 words. Pays 4¢ to 7¢ a word, on acceptance.

THE LUTHERAN—8765 W. Higgins Rd., Chicago, IL 60631. Edgar R. Trexler, Ed. Articles, to 2,000 words, on Christian ideology, personal religious experiences, social and ethical issues, family life, church, and community. Pays $100 to $600, on acceptance. Query.

MATURE LIVING—127 Ninth Ave. N., Nashville, TN 37234. General-interest and travel articles, nostalgia and fiction, 900 words, for Christians, 60 years and older. Profiles, 25 lines; must include a B&W action photo. Brief, humorous items for "Cracker Barrel." Pays 5¢ a word, $25 for profile and photo, $5 for humor on acceptance. Buys all rights.

MATURE YEARS—201 Eighth Ave. S., P.O. Box 801, Nashville, TN 37202. Marvin W. Cropsey, Ed. United Methodist. Articles on retirement or related subjects, 1,500 to 2,000 words. Humorous and serious fiction, 1,500 to 1,800 words, for adults. Travel pieces with religious slant. Poetry, to 14 lines. Include Social Security no. with manuscript. Buys all rights.

MESSENGER OF THE SACRED HEART—661 Greenwood Ave., Toronto, Ont., Canada M4J 4B3. Articles and short stories, about 1,500 words, for American and Canadian Catholics. Pays from 4¢ a word, on acceptance.

MIDSTREAM—110 E. 59th St., New York, NY 10022. Joel Carmichael, Ed. Jewish-interest articles and book reviews. Fiction, to 3,000 words, and poetry. Pays 5¢ a word, after publication.

THE MIRACULOUS MEDAL—475 E. Chelten Ave., Philadelphia, PA 19144–5785. John W. Gouldrick, C.M., Ed. Dir. Catholic. Fiction, to 2,400 words. Religious verse, to 20 lines. Pays from 2¢ a word for fiction, from 50¢ a line for poetry, on acceptance.

MODERN LITURGY—160 E. Virginia St., #290, San Jose, CA 95112. John Gullen, S.J., Ed. Plays. Material must be related to Roman Catholic liturgy. Query only. Pays in copies and subscription.

MOMENT—3000 Connecticut Ave. N.W. , Suite 300, Washington, DC

20008. Suzanne Singer, Man. Ed. Sophisticated, issue-oriented articles, 2,500 to 5,000 words, on Jewish topics. Pays $150 to $400, on publication.

MOMENTUM—National Catholic Educational Assn., 1077 30th St. N.W., Suite 100, Washington, DC 20007–3852. Patricia Feistritzer, Ed. Articles, 500 to 1,500 words, on outstanding programs, issues, and research in education. Book reviews. Pays 2¢ a word, on publication. Query.

MOODY MAGAZINE—(formerly *Moody Monthly*) 820 N. La Salle Dr., Chicago, IL 60610. Andrew Scheer, Man. Ed. Anecdotal articles, 1,200 to 1,800 words, on the evangelical Christian experience in school, the home, and the workplace. Pays 10¢ to 15¢ a word, on acceptance. Query.

THE NATIONAL CHRISTIAN REPORTER—See *The United Methodist Reporter*.

NEW ERA—50 E. North Temple, Salt Lake City, UT 84150. Richard M. Romney, Man. Ed. Articles, 150 to 2,000 words, and fiction, to 2,000 words, for young Mormons. Poetry; photos. Pays 5¢ to 10¢ a word, 25¢ a line for poetry, on acceptance. Query.

NEW WORLD OUTLOOK—475 Riverside Dr., Rm. 1351, New York, NY 10115–0122. Alma Graham, Ed. Articles, 500 to 1,500 words, on United Methodist missions and Methodist-related programs and ministries. Focus on national, global, and women's and children's issues. Pays on publication.

OBLATES—15 S. 59th St., Belleville, IL 62223–4694. Priscilla Kurz, Manuscripts Ed. Jacqueline Lowery Corn, Man. Ed. Articles, 500 to 600 words, that inspire, uplift, and motivate through positive Christian values in everyday life. Inspirational poetry, to 16 lines. Pays $75 for articles, $25 for poems, on acceptance. Send complete manuscript only. Send 52¢ SASE for guidelines and sample copy.

OUR FAMILY—Box 249, Battleford, Sask., Canada S0M 0E0. Nestor Gregoire, Ed. Articles, 1,000 to 3,000 words, for Catholic families, on modern society, family, marriage, current affairs, and spiritual topics. Humor; verse. Pays 7¢ to 10¢ a word for articles, 75¢ to $1 a line for poetry, on acceptance. SAE with international reply coupons required with all submissions. Guidelines.

OUR SUNDAY VISITOR—Huntington, IN 46750. Greg Erlandson, Ed. In-depth features, 1,000 to 1,200 words, on the Catholic church in America today. Pays $150 to $250, on acceptance

PARISH FAMILY DIGEST—200 Noll Plaza, Huntington, IN 46750. Corine B. Erlandson, Ed. Articles, 750 to 1,000 words, on family life, Catholic profiles, inspiration, etc., for the Catholic reader. Also publishes short humorous anecdotes and light-hearted cartoons. Pays 5¢ a word, on acceptance.

PENTECOSTAL EVANGEL—1445 Boonville Ave., Springfield, MO 65802. Richard Champion, Ed. Assemblies of God. Religious, personal experience, and devotional articles, 400 to 1,000 words. Verse, 12 to 30 lines. Pays 6¢ a word, on acceptance.

PIME WORLD—(formerly *Catholic Life*) 35750 Moravian Dr., Fraser, MI 48026. Paul W. Witte, Man. Ed. Articles, 600 to 1,200 words, on Catholic missionary work in Hong Kong, India, Latin America, Africa. Photos. No fiction or poetry. Pays 6¢ a word, extra for photos, on publication.

PRESBYTERIAN SURVEY—100 Witherspoon, Louisville, KY 40202–1396. Kenneth E. Little, Ed./Pub. Articles, 1,200 words, of interest to members of the Presbyterian Church or ecumenical individuals. Pays to $150, on acceptance.

THE PRIEST—200 Noll Plaza, Huntington, IN 46750–4304. Robert A. Willems, Assoc. Ed. Articles, to 2,500 words, on life and ministry of priests, current theological developments, etc., for priests, permanent deacons, and seminarians. Pays $35 to $150, on acceptance.

PURPOSE—616 Walnut Ave., Scottdale, PA 15683–1999. James E. Horsch, Ed. Stories, articles, and fillers, to 900 words, on Christian discipleship themes, with good photos; pieces of history, biography, science, hobbies, from a Christian perspective. Fiction, to 900 words, on Christian problem solving. Poetry, to 12 lines. "Send complete manuscripts. No queries, please!" Pays to 5¢ a word, to $1 a line for poetry, on acceptance.

QUAKER LIFE—Friends United Meeting, 101 Quaker Hill Dr., Richmond, IN 47374–1980. James R. Newby, Ed. Carol Beals, Man. Ed. Articles and news for members of the Society of Friends. Brief poetry considered. "Almost all material solicited to match theme format." Pays in copies.

QUEEN—26 S. Saxon Ave., Bay Shore, NY 11706–8993. J. Patrick Gaffney, S.M.M., Ed. Publication of Montfort Missionaries. Articles and fiction, 1,000 to 2,000 words, related to the Virgin Mary. Poetry. Pay varies, on acceptance.

THE QUIET HOUR—850 N. Grove Ave., Elgin, IL 60120. Richard Lint, Ed. Short devotionals. Pays $15, on acceptance. By assignment only; query required.

THE RECONSTRUCTIONIST—Box 1336, Roslyn Heights, NY 11577. Rabbi Joy Levitt, Ed. Articles and fiction, 2,000 to 3,000 words, relating to Judaism. Poetry. Pays $18 to $36, on publication.

ST. ANTHONY MESSENGER—1615 Republic St., Cincinnati, OH 45210–1298. Norman Perry, O.F.M., Ed. Articles, 2,000 to 3,000 words, on personalities, major movements, family, religious and church issues, spiritual life, and social issues. Human interest pieces. Humor; fiction, 2,000 to 3,000 words. Pays 14¢ a word, on acceptance. Articles and stories should have religious implications. Query for nonfiction.

ST. JOSEPH'S MESSENGER—P.O. Box 288, Jersey City, NJ 07303–0288. Sister Ursula Maphet, Ed. Inspirational articles, 500 to 1,000 words, and fiction, 1,000 to 1,500 words. Verse, 4 to 40 lines.

SEEK—8121 Hamilton Ave., Cincinnati, OH 45231. Eileen H. Wilmoth, Ed. Articles and fiction, to 1,200 words, on inspirational and controversial topics and timely religious issues. Christian testimonials. Pays 5¢ to 7¢ a word, on acceptance. SASE for guidelines.

SHARING THE VICTORY—Fellowship of Christian Athletes, 8701 Leeds Rd., Kansas City, MO 64129. John Dodderidge, Ed. Articles, interviews, and profiles, to 1,000 words, for co-ed Christian athletes and coaches in high school, college, and pros. Pays from $50, on publication. Query required.

SIGNS OF THE TIMES—P. O. Box 7000, Boise, ID 83707. Greg Brothers, Ed. Seventh-Day Adventists. Feature articles on Christians who have performed community services; current issues from a biblical perspective; health, home, marriage, human-interest pieces; inspirational articles, 500 to 2,000 words. Pays 20¢ a word, on acceptance.

SISTERS TODAY—The Liturgical Press, St. John's Abbey, Collegeville, MN 56321–7500. Articles, 500 to 3,500 words, on theology, social justice issues, and religious issues for women and the Church. Poetry, to 34 lines. Pays $5 per printed page, $10 per poem, on publication; $50 for color cover photos and $25 for B&W inside photos. Send articles to: Sister Mary Anthony Wagner, O.S.B., Ed., St.

Benedict's Convent, St. Joseph, MN 56374–2099. Send poetry to: Sister Virginia Micka, C.S.J., College of Saint Catherine, Box 4162, St. Paul, MN 55105.

SOCIAL JUSTICE REVIEW—3835 Westminster Pl., St. Louis, MO 63108–3409. Rev. John H. Miller, C.S.C., Ed. Articles, 2,000 to 3,000 words, on social problems in light of Catholic teaching and current scientific studies. Pays 2¢ a word, on publication.

SPIRITUAL LIFE—2131 Lincoln Rd. N.E., Washington, DC 20002–1199. Steven Payne, O.C.D., Ed. Professional religious journal. Religious essays, 3,000 to 5,000 words, on spirituality in contemporary life. Pays from $50, on acceptance. Send 7x10 SASE with four first-class stamps for guidelines and sample issue.

SPIRITUALITY TODAY—3642 Lindell Blvd., St. Louis, MO 63108–3396. Regina Siegfried, A.S.C., Ed. Quarterly. Biblical, liturgical, theological, ecumenical, historical, and biographical articles, 3,500 words, about the challenges of contemporary Christian life. Pays from 1 ½¢ a word, on publication. Query required, with SASE. Guidelines.

SUNDAY DIGEST—850 N. Grove Ave., Elgin, IL 60120. Articles, 1,000 to 1,500 words, on Christian faith in contemporary life; inspirational and how-to articles; free-verse poetry. Anecdotes, 500 words. Pays $60 to $200 (less for reprints), on acceptance.

SUNDAY SCHOOL COUNSELOR—1445 Boonville Ave., Springfield, MO 65802–1894. Sylvia Lee, Ed. Articles, 1,000 to 1,500 words, on teaching and Sunday school people, for local Sunday school teachers. Pays 3¢ to 5¢ a word, on acceptance.

SUNSHINE MAGAZINE—Sunshine Press, Litchfield, IL 62056. Peggy Kuethe, Ed. Inspirational articles, to 600 words. Short stories, 1,000 words, and juveniles, 400 words. No heavily religious material or "born again" pieces. Pays varying rates, on acceptance.

TEACHERS INTERACTION—1333 S. Kirkwood Rd., St. Louis, MO 63122–7295. Martha S. Jander, Ed. Articles, 800 to 1,200 words; how-to pieces, to 100 words, for Lutheran volunteer church school teachers. Pays $10 to $35, on publication. Limited free-lance market.

THEOLOGY TODAY—Box 29, Princeton, NJ 08542. Hugh T. Kerr, Ed. Articles, 1,500 to 3,500 words, on theology, religion, and related social issues. Literary criticism. Pays $75 to $200, on publication.

THE UNITED CHURCH OBSERVER—84 Pleasant Blvd., Toronto, Ont., Canada M4T 2Z8. Factual articles, 1,500 to 2,500 words, on religious trends, human problems, social issues. No poetry. Pays after publication. Query.

THE UNITED METHODIST REPORTER—P.O. Box 660275, Dallas, TX 75266–0275. Spurgeon M. Dunnam, III, Ed. John Lovelace, Man. Ed. United Methodist newspaper. Religious features, to 500 words. Religious verse, 4 to 12 lines. Photos. "Tight-deadline, time-sensitive, nationally circulated weekly newspaper." Pays 4¢ a word, on publication. Send for guidelines. Same address and requirements for *The National Christian Reporter* (interdenominational).

UNITED SYNAGOGUE REVIEW—155 Fifth Ave., New York, NY 10010. Lois Goldrich, Ed. Articles, 1,000 to 1,200 words, on issues of interest to Conservative Jewish community. Query.

UNITY MAGAZINE—Unity School of Christianity, Unity Village, MO

64065. Philip White, Ed. Articles and poems: inspirational, religious, metaphysical, 500 to 1,500 words. Pays 5¢ to 9¢ a word, on acceptance.

VIRTUE—P. O. Box 850, Sisters, OR 97759. Marlee Alex, Ed. Articles and fiction for Christian women. Query only, except for "One Woman's Journal" and "In My Opinion."

VISTA MAGAZINE—P. O. Box 50434, Indianapolis, IN 46250–0434. Articles and adult fiction, on current Christian concerns and issues. First-person pieces, 750 to 1,200 words. Opinion pieces from an evangelical perspective, 500 to 750 words. Pays from 2¢ to 4¢ a word.

WITH—722 Main St., Box 347, Newton, KS 67114. Eddy Hall and Carol Duerksen, Eds. Fiction, 500 to 1,800 words; nonfiction, 500 to 1,500 words; and poetry, to 50 lines for Anabaptist-Mennonite teenagers. "We want to help teens understand the issues that affect them directly and indirectly, and help them make choices that reflect an Anabaptist-Mennonite understanding of living by the Spirit of Christ. Wholesome humor always gets a close read." B&W 8x10 photos accepted. Payment is 4¢ a word, on acceptance (2¢ a word for reprints).

YOUNG SALVATIONIST—The Salvation Army, 615 Slaters Ln., Alexandria, VA 22314. M. Lesa Salyer, Ed. Articles, 600 to 1,200 words, teach the Christian view to everyday living, for teenagers. Short shorts, first-person testimonies, 600 to 800 words. Pays 6¢ to 10¢ a word, on acceptance. SASE required. Guidelines.

HEALTH

ACCENT ON LIVING—P. O. Box 700, Bloomington, IL 61702. Raymond C. Cheever, Pub. Betty Garee, Ed. Articles, 250 to 1,000 words, about physically disabled people, including their careers, recreation, sports, self-help devices, and ideas that can make daily routines easier. Good photos a plus. Pays 10¢ a word, on publication. Query.

ADDICTION & RECOVERY—4959 Commerce Parkway, Cleveland, OH 44128. Brenda L. Lewison, Ed. Articles on all aspects of alcoholism and other drug addiction: treatment, legislation, education, prevention, and recovery. Send SASE for guidelines.

AMERICAN BABY—475 Park Ave. S., New York, NY 10016. Judith Nolte, Ed. Articles, 1,000 to 2,000 words, for new or expectant parents on prenatal or infant care. Pays varying rates, on acceptance.

AMERICAN FITNESS—15250 Ventura Blvd., Suite 310, Sherman Oaks, CA 91403. Peg Jordan, Ed. Rhonda Wilson, Man. Ed. Articles, 500 to 1,500 words, on exercise, health, sports, nutrition, etc. Illustrations, photos, cartoons.

AMERICAN JOURNAL OF NURSING—555 W. 57th St., New York, NY 10019. Mary B. Mallison, R.N., Ed. Articles, 1,500 to 2,000 words, with photos, on nursing. Query.

ARTHRITIS TODAY—The Arthritis Foundation, 1314 Spring St. N.W., Atlanta, GA 30309. Cindy McDaniel, Ed. Self-help, how-to, general interest, and inspirational articles (1,000 to 2,500 words) and short fillers (100 to 250 words) to help people with arthritis live more productive, independent, and pain-free lives. Pays from $350, on acceptance.

BABY TALK—636 Ave. of the Americas, New York, NY 10011. Susan Strecker, Ed. Articles, 1,500 to 3,000 words, by parents or professionals, on babies and baby care, etc. Pay varies, on acceptance. SASE required.

BETTER HEALTH—1384 Chapel St., New Haven, CT 06511. James F. Malerba, Pub. Dir. Wellness and prevention magazine affiliated with The Hospital of Saint Raphael of New Haven. Upbeat articles, 2,000 words, that encourage a healthier lifestyle. Pays $150 to $350, on acceptance. Query with SASE.

EAST WEST: THE JOURNAL OF NATURAL HEALTH & LIVING—17 Station St., Box 1200, Brookline, MA 02147. Features, 1,500 to 2,500 words, on holistic health, natural foods, herbal remedies, etc. Interviews. Photos. Pays 20¢ a word, extra for photos, on acceptance.

EXPECTING—685 Third Ave., New York, NY 10017. Evelyn A. Podsiadlo, Ed. Articles, 700 to 1,800 words, for expectant mothers. Pays $300 to $500, on acceptance.

HEALTH PROGRESS—4455 Woodson Rd., St. Louis, MO 63134–3797. Judy Cassidy, Ed. Journal of the Catholic Health Association. Features, 2,000 to 4,000 words, on hospital and nursing home management and administration, medical-moral questions, health care, public policy, technological developments in health care and their effects, nursing, financial and human resource management for healthcare administrators, and innovative programs in hospitals and long-term care facilities. Payment negotiable. Query.

HEALTH WATCH—455 S. 4th Ave., Suite 908, Louisville, KY 40202. Mollie Vento, Ed. Bimonthly. Articles on consumer health issues. "Strong reporting and research required." Mention availability of color slides in query. Payment varies, on acceptance.

HOSPITALS—737 N. Michigan Ave., Chicago, IL 60611. Mary Grayson, Ed. Articles, 800 to 1,500 words, for hospital administrators, on financing, staffing, coordinating, and providing facilities for health care services. Pays varying rates, on acceptance. Query.

IDEA TODAY—6190 Cornerstone Ct. East, Suite 204, San Diego, CA 92121–3773. Patricia Ryan, Ed. Practical articles, 1,000 to 3,000 words, on new exercise programs, business management, nutrition, sports medicine, and dance-exercise and one-to-one training techniques. Articles must be geared toward the aerobics instructor, exercise studio owner or manager, or personal trainer. No queries on topics for the consumer. No general health ideas wanted. Payment negotiable, on acceptance. Query preferred.

IN HEALTH—475 Gate Five Rd., Suite 225, Sausalito, CA 94965. Leslie Talmadge, Ed. Articles, 1,000 to 5,000 words, on health and medicine; pieces for "Food," "Fitness," "Vanities," "Drugs," "Mind," and "Family" departments. Pays 80¢ to $1 a word, on acceptance. Query with clips required.

LET'S LIVE—P.O. Box 74908, Los Angeles, CA 90004. Debra Jenkins Robinson, Ed. Articles, 1,000 to 1,500 words, on preventive medicine and nutrition, alternative medicine, diet, exercise, recipes, and natural beauty. Pays $150, on publication. Query.

MUSCULAR DEVELOPMENT—351 W. 54th St., New York, NY 10019. Alan Paul, Ed. Articles, five to ten typed pages, geared to serious weight training athletes, on any aspect of competitive body building, powerlifting, sports, and nutrition. Photos. Pays $50 to $300, on publication. Query.

NEW BODY—1700 Broadway, New York, NY 10019. Nayda Rondon, Ed. Well-researched, service-oriented articles, 800 to 1,500 words, on exercise, nutrition, lifestyle, diet, and health for women ages 18 to 35. Also considers submissions, 500 to 600 words, for "How I Lost It" column in which writers tell how they lost weight and have kept it off. Writers should have some background in or knowledge of the health field. Pays $100 to $300, on publication. Query.

NURSING 92—1111 Bethlehem Pike, Springhouse, PA 19477. Maryanne Wagner, Ed. Most articles are clinically oriented, and are written by nurses for nurses. Covers legal, ethical, management, and career aspects of nursing. Also includes narratives about personal nursing experiences. No poetry. Pays $25 to $250, on publication. Query.

NURSINGWORLD JOURNAL—470 Boston Post Rd., Weston, MA 02193. Eileen Devito, Man. Ed. Articles, 500 to 1,500 words, for and by nurses and nurse-educators, on aspects of current nursing issues. Pays from 25¢ per column inch, on publication.

THE PHYSICIAN AND SPORTSMEDICINE—4530 W. 77th St., Minneapolis, MN 55435. Terry Monahan, Man. Ed. News and feature articles; clinical articles coauthored with physician. Sports medicine angle necessary. Pays $150 to $1,000, on acceptance. Guidelines. Query required.

A POSITIVE APPROACH—1600 Malone, Municipal Airport, Millville, NJ 08332. Ann Miller, Ed. Articles, 500 words, on all aspects of the positive-thinking disabled/handicapped person's private and business life. Well-researched articles of interest to the visually and hearing impaired, veterans, the arthritic, and all categories of the disabled and handicapped, on interior design, barrier-free architecture, gardening, wardrobe, computers, and careers. No fiction or poetry. Pays in copies.

TODAY'S OR NURSE—6900 Grove Rd., Thorofare, NJ 08086. Mary Jo Krey, Ed. Clinical or general articles, from 2,000 words, of direct interest to operating room nurses.

VEGETARIAN TIMES—P.O. Box 570, Oak Park, IL 60303. Paul Obis, Pub. Articles, 750 to 2,500 words, on health, nutrition, exercise and fitness, meatless meals, etc. Personal-experience and historical pieces, profiles. Pays $25 to $500, on publication.

VIBRANT LIFE—55 W. Oak Ridge Dr., Hagerstown, MD 21740. Features, 750 to 1,500 words, on total health: physical, mental, and spiritual. Seeks upbeat articles on the family and how to live happier, healthier lives; Christian slant. Pays $80 to $250, on acceptance.

VIM & VIGOR—8805 N. 23rd Ave., Suite 11, Phoenix, AZ 85021. Fred Petrovsky, Ed. Positive health and fitness articles, 1,200 to 2,000 words, with accurate medical facts. By assignment only. Pays $350 to $450, on publication. Query.

YOGA JOURNAL—2054 University Ave., Berkeley, CA 94704. Stephan Bodian, Ed. Articles, 1,200 to 4,000 words, on holistic health, meditation, consciousness, spirituality, and yoga. Pays $50 to $500, on publication.

YOUR HEALTH—1720 Washington Blvd., Box 10010, Ogden, UT 84409. Caroll Shreeve, Pub. Articles, 1,200 words, on individual health care needs: prevention, treatment, low-impact aerobics, fitness, nutrition, etc. Color photos required. Pays 15¢ a word, on acceptance. Guidelines.

EDUCATION

BEAUTY EDUCATION—(formerly *National Beauty School Journal*), 220 White Plains Rd., Tarrytown, NY 10591. Sheila Furjanic, Ed. Articles, 1,500 to 2,000 words, that provide beauty educators, trainers, and professionals in the cosmetology industry with information, skills, and techniques on such topics as hairstyling, makeup, aromatherapy, retailing, massage, and beauty careers. Send SASE for editorial calendar with monthly themes. Pays $150, on publication. Query.

CAREER WOMAN—See *Minority Engineer.*

CAREERS AND THE DISABLED—See *Minority Engineer.*

CLASSROOM COMPUTER LEARNING—See *Technology & Learning.*

EQUAL OPPORTUNITY—See *Minority Engineer.*

FOUNDATION NEWS—1828 L St. N.W., Washington, DC 20036. Arlie W. Schardt, Ed. Articles, to 2,000 words, on national or regional activities supported by, or of interest to, grant makers and the nonprofit sector. Pays to $1,500, on acceptance. Query.

GIFTED EDUCATION PRESS NEWSLETTER—P.O. Box 1586, 10201 Yuma Ct., Manassas, VA 22110. Maurice Fisher, Pub. Articles, to 3,000 words, written by educators, laypersons, and parents of gifted children, on the problems of identifying and teaching gifted children and adolescents. "Interested in incisive analyses of current programs for the gifted and recommendations for improving the education of gifted students. Particularly interested in the problems of teaching humanities, science, ethics, literature, and history to the gifted. Looking for highly imaginative and knowledgeable writers." Query required. Pays with subscription.

HOME EDUCATION MAGAZINE—P.O. Box 1083, Tonasket, WA 98855–1083. Helen E. Hegener, Man. Ed. Informative articles, 750 to 2,000 words, on all aspects of the growing homeschool movement. Send complete manuscript or detailed query with SASE. Pays about 2¢ a word, on publication.

THE HORN BOOK MAGAZINE—14 Beacon St., Boston, MA 02108. Anita Silvey, Ed. Articles, 600 to 2,800 words, on books for young readers and related subjects for librarians, teachers, parents, etc. Pays $25 per printed page, on publication. Query.

INDEPENDENT LIVING MAGAZINE—See *Minority Engineer.*

INSTRUCTOR MAGAZINE—Scholastic, Inc., 730 Broadway, New York, NY 10003. Debra Martorelli, Ed. Articles, 300 to 1,500 words, for teachers in grades K through 8. Payment varies, on acceptance.

ITC COMMUNICATOR—International Training in Communication, 4249 Elzevir Rd., Woodland Hills, CA 91364. JoAnn Levy, Ed. Educational articles, 200 to 800 words, on leadership, language, speech presentation, meetings procedures, personal and professional development, written and spoken communication techniques. SASE required. Pays in copies.

JOURNAL OF CAREER PLANNING & EMPLOYMENT—62 Highland Ave., Bethlehem, PA 18017. Mimi Collins, Ed. Bill Beebe, Assoc. Ed. Quarterly. Articles, 3,000 to 4,000 words, on topics related to career planning, placement, recruitment, and employment of new college graduates. Pays $200 to $400, on acceptance. Query first with clips. Guidelines available.

KEY TO CHRISTIAN EDUCATION—8121 Hamilton Ave., Cincinnati, OH 45231–2396. Barbara Bolton and Lowellette Lauderdale, Eds. Fillers and articles, to 1,200 words, on Christian education; tips for teachers in the local church. Pays varying rates, on acceptance.

LEARNING 92/93—1111 Bethlehem Pike, Springhouse, PA 19477. Charlene Gaynor, Ed. How-to, why-to, and personal-experience articles, to 3,000 words, for teachers of grades K through 8. Tested classroom ideas for curriculum roundups, to 600 words. Pays to $300 for features, on acceptance.

MEDIA & METHODS—1429 Walnut St., Philadelphia, PA 19102. Michele Sokoloff, Ed. Articles, 800 to 1,000 words, on media, technologies, and methods used to enhance instruction and learning in high school and university classrooms. Pays $50 to $200, on publication. Query required.

MINORITY ENGINEER—44 Broadway, Greenlawn, NY 11740. James Schneider, Exec. Ed. Articles, 1,000 to 1,500 words, for college students, on career opportunities in engineering, techniques of job hunting, and role-model profiles of professional minority engineers. Interviews. Pays 10¢ a word, on publication. Query. Same address and requirements for *Equal Opportunity, Career Woman* (query Eileen Nester), and *Careers and the Disabled*. For *Independent Living Magazine* and *Woman Engineer*, a career-guidance quarterly, query Editor Anne Kelly.

MOMENTUM—National Catholic Educational Assn., 1077 30th St. N.W., Suite 100, Washington, DC 20007–3852. Patricia Feistritzer, Ed. Articles, 500 to 1,500 words, on outstanding programs, issues, and research in education. Book reviews. Query or send complete manuscript. No simultaneous submissions. Pays 2¢ a word, on publication.

NATIONAL BEAUTY SCHOOL JOURNAL—See *Beauty Education*.

PHI DELTA KAPPAN—8th and Union Sts., Box 789, Bloomington, IN 47402–0789. Pauline Gough, Ed. Articles, 1,000 to 4,000 words, on educational research, service, and leadership; issues, trends, and policy. Pays from $250, on publication.

SCHOOL ARTS MAGAZINE—50 Portland St., Worcester, MA 01608. Kent Anderson, Ed. Articles, 800 to 1,000 words, on art education with special application to the classroom. Photos. Pays varying rates, on publication.

SCHOOL SAFETY—National School Safety Center, 16830 Ventura Blvd., Encino, CA 91436. Ronald D. Stephens, Exec. Ed. Published three times during the school year. Articles, 2,000 to 3,000 words, of use to educators, law enforcers, judges, and legislators on the prevention of drugs, gangs, weapons, bullying, discipline problems, and vandalism; also on-site security and character development as they relate to students and schools. Articles are pro-bono; no payment made.

SCHOOL SHOP/TECH DIRECTIONS—Box 8623, Ann Arbor, MI 48107. Susanne Peckham, Man. Ed. Articles, 1 to 10 double-spaced typed pages, for teachers and administrators in industrial, technological, and vocational educational fields, with particular interest in classroom projects and computer uses. Pays $25 to $150, on publication. Guidelines.

TEACHING K-8—40 Richards Ave., Norwalk, CT 06854. Patricia Boderick, Ed. Dir. Articles, 1,200 words, on the profession of teaching for those who work with children. Queries are not necessary. Pays to $35, on publication.

TECHNOLOGY & LEARNING—(formerly *Classroom Computer Learning*) Peter Li, Inc., 2169 E. Francisco Blvd. E., Suite A-4, San Rafael, CA 94901. Holly Brady, Ed. Articles, to 3,000 words, for teachers of grades K through 12, about uses of computers and related technology in the classroom: human-interest and philosophical articles, how-to pieces, software reviews, and hands-on ideas. Pay varies, on acceptance.

TODAY'S CATHOLIC TEACHER—2451 E. River Rd., Dayton, OH 45439–1597. Stephen Brittan, Ed. Articles, 600 to 800 words, 1,000 to 1,200 words, and 1,200 to 1,500 words, on education, parent-teacher relationships, innovative teaching, teaching techniques, etc., of interest to educators. Pays $15 to $175, on publication. SASE required. Query first. Guidelines.

WILSON LIBRARY BULLETIN—950 University Ave., Bronx, NY 10452. Mary Jo Godwin, Ed. Articles, 2,500 to 3,000 words, on libraries, communications, and information systems. News, reports, features. Pays from $250, extra for photos, on publication.

WOMAN ENGINEER—See *Minority Engineer*.

FARMING AND AGRICULTURE

ACRES USA—10008 E. 60 Terrace, Kansas City, MO 64133. Charles Walters, Jr., Ed. Articles on biological agriculture: technology, economics, public policy, and current events. "Our emphasis is on production of quality food without the use of toxic chemicals." Pays 6¢ a word, on acceptance. Query.

AMERICAN BEE JOURNAL—51 N. Second St., Hamilton, IL 62341. Joe M. Graham, Ed. Articles on beekeeping, for professionals. Photos. Pays 75¢ a column inch, extra for photos, on publication.

BEEF—7900 International Dr., Minneapolis, MN 55425. Paul D. Andre, Ed. Articles on beef cattle feeding, cowherds, stocker operations, and related phases of the cattle industry. Pays to $300, on acceptance.

BUCKEYE FARM NEWS—Ohio Farm Bureau Federation, Two Nationwide Plaza, Box 479, Columbus, OH 43216–0479. Susie Taylor, Copy Ed. Occasional articles, to 600 words, related to agriculture. Pays on publication. Query.

DAIRY GOAT JOURNAL—W. 2997 Markert Rd., Helenville, WI 53137. Dave Thompson, Ed. Articles, to 1,500 words, on successful dairy goat owners, youths and interesting people associated with dairy goats. "Especially interested in practical husbandry ideas." Photos. Pays $50 to $250, on publication. Query.

FARM AND RANCH LIVING—5400 S. 60th St., Greendale, WI 53129. Bob Ottum, Ed. Articles, 2,000 words, on rural people and situations; nostalgia pieces; profiles of interesting farms and farmers, ranches and ranchers. Pays $15 to $400, on acceptance and on publication.

FARM INDUSTRY NEWS—7900 International Dr., Minneapolis, MN 55425. Joe Degnan, Ed. Articles for farmers, on new products, machinery, equipment, chemicals, and seeds. Pays $175 to $400, on acceptance. Query required.

FARM JOURNAL—230 W. Washington Sq., Philadelphia, PA 19105. Earl Ainsworth, Ed. Articles, 500 to 1,500 words, with photos, on the business of farming, for farmers. Pays 20¢ to 50¢ a word, on acceptance. Query.

FARM STORE—P.O. Box 2400, 12400 Whitewater Dr., Suite 160, Minnetonka, MN 55343. Julie Emnett, Ed. Articles, 500 to 1,500 words, that offer "business know-how for today's agribusiness professional." Payment varies, on publication. Query.

FLORIDA GROWER & RANCHER—1331 N. Mills Ave., Orlando, FL 32803. Frank Garner, Ed. Articles and case histories on Florida farmers, growers, and ranchers. Pays on publication. Query; buys little freelance material.

THE FURROW—Deere & Company, John Deere Rd., Moline, IL 61265. George Sollenberger, Exec. Ed. Specialized, illustrated articles on farming. Pays to $1,000, on acceptance.

HARROWSMITH—Telemedia Publishing, Inc., Camden East, Ont., Canada

570

KOK 1J0. Michael Webster, Ed. Articles, 700 to 4,000 words, on country life, homesteading, husbandry, organic gardening, and alternative energy with a Canadian slant. Pays $150 to $1,500, on acceptance. Query with SAE/international reply coupon.

HARROWSMITH COUNTRY LIFE—Ferry Rd., Charlotte, VT 05445. Address Ed. Dept. Investigative pieces, 4,000 to 5,000 words, on ecology, energy, health, gardening, do-it-yourself projects, and the food chain. Short pieces for "Screed" (opinions) and "Gazette" (news briefs). Pays $500 to $1,500 for features, $50 to $600 for department pieces, on acceptance. Query required. Send SASE for guidelines.

PEANUT FARMER—P.O. Box 95075, Raleigh, NC 27625. Mary Evans, Man. Ed. Articles, 500 to 2,000 words, on production and management practices in peanut farming. Pays $50 to $350, on publication.

PENNSYLVANIA FARMER—704 Lisburn Rd., Camp Hill, PA 17011. John R. Vogel, Ed. Articles on farmers in Pennsylvania, New Jersey, Delaware, Maryland, and West Virginia; timely business-of-farming concepts and successful farm management operations.

RURAL HERITAGE—P.O. Box 516, Albia, IA 52531. Allan Young, Pub. How-to and feature articles, 300 to 2,500 words, related to draft horses and rural living. Pays 3¢ to 10¢ a word, $5 to $25 for photos, on publication.

SHEEP! MAGAZINE—W. 2997 Markert Rd., Helenville, WI 53137. Dave Thompson, Ed. Articles, to 1,500 words, on successful shepherds, woolcrafts, sheep raising, and sheep dogs. "Especially interested in people who raise sheep successfully as a sideline enterprise." Photos. Pays $80 to $300, extra for photos, on publication. Query first.

SMALL ACREAGE MANAGEMENT—Rt. 1, Box 146, Silex, MO 63377. Kelly Klober, Ed. Articles, 500 to 800 words, on land uses for small farm owners. Pays 1¢ to 3¢ a word, on publication. Query.

SMALL FARMER'S JOURNAL—P.O. Box 2805, Eugene, OR 97402–0318. Address the Editors. How-tos, humor, practical work horse information, livestock and produce marketing, gardening information, and articles appropriate to the independent family farm. Pays negotiable rates, on publication. Query first.

TOPICS IN VETERINARY MEDICINE—812 Springdale Dr., Exton, PA 19341–2803. Kathleen Etchison, Ed. Technical articles, 1,200 to 1,500 words, and clinical features, 500 words, on veterinary medicine. Photos. Pays $300, $150 for shorter pieces, extra for photos, on publication.

WALLACES FARMER—1501 42nd St., #501, W. Des Moines, IA 50265. Monte Sesker, Ed. Features, 600 to 700 words, on farming in IA, MN, ND, and SD; methods and equipment; interviews with farmers. Query.

THE WESTERN PRODUCER—Box 2500, Saskatoon, Saskatchewan, Canada S7K 2C4. Address Man. Ed. Articles, to 1,000 words, on agricultural and rural subjects, preferably with a Canadian slant. Photos. Pays from 15¢ a word, $15 for B&W photos and cartoons, on acceptance.

ENVIRONMENT, CONSERVATION, WILDLIFE, NATURAL HISTORY

THE AMERICAN FIELD—542 S. Dearborn, Chicago, IL 60605. B.J. Matthys, Man. Ed. Yarns about hunting trips, bird-shooting; articles, to 1,500 words, on dogs and field trials, emphasizing conservation of game resources. Pays varying rates, on acceptance.

AMERICAN FORESTS—1516 P St. N.W., Washington, DC 20005. Bill Rooney, Ed. Well-documented articles, to 2,000 words, with photos, on recreational and commercial uses and management of forests. Photos. Pays on acceptance.

THE AMICUS JOURNAL—Natural Resources Defense Council, 40 W. 20th St., New York, NY 10011. Francesca Lyman, Ed. Investigative articles, book reviews, and poetry related to national and international environmental policy. Pays varying rates, on acceptance. Queries required.

ANIMALS—Massachusetts Society for the Prevention of Cruelty to Animals, 350 S. Huntington Ave., Boston, MA 02130. Marjorie Kinder, Ed. Asst. Informative, well-researched articles, to 3,000 words, on animal welfare and pet care, conservation, international wildlife, and environmental issues affecting animals; no personal accounts or favorite pet stories. Pays to $300, on publication. Query.

ATLANTIC SALMON JOURNAL—P.O. Box 289, Guysborough, N.S., Canada B0H 1N0. Harry Bruce, Ed. Articles, 1,500 to 3,000 words. Material related to Atlantic salmon: fishing, conservation, ecology, travel, politics, biology, how-tos, anecdotes, cuisine. Pays $100 to $350, on publication.

AUDUBON—950 Third Ave., New York, NY 10022. Michael W. Robbins, Ed. Bimonthly. Articles (1,800 to 4,500 words) on conservation and environmental issues, natural history, ecology, and related subjects. Payment varies, on acceptance. Query.

BIRD WATCHER'S DIGEST—P.O. Box 110, Marietta, OH 45750. Mary B. Bowers, Ed. Articles, 600 to 2,500 words, for bird watchers: first-person accounts; how-tos; pieces on endangered species; profiles. Cartoons. Pays from $50, on publication.

BUZZWORM—2305 Canyon Blvd., Boulder, CO 80302. Elizabeth Darby Junkin, Man. Ed. Bimonthly. Articles on environmental and natural resources issues worldwide: endangered species, new ideas in conservation, and personalities. Query with clips and resumé. Pays $200 to $1,500, after publication.

ENVIRONMENTAL ACTION—6930 Carroll Ave., 6th Fl., Takoma Park, MD 20912. Barbara Ruben and Hawley Truax, Eds. News and features, varying lengths, on a broad range of political and/or environmental topics: energy, toxic materials, recycling, solid waste, etc. Book reviews; environmentally related consumer goods. Pays $250 to $400 for features, $50 for book reviews, $75 for short news articles, $25 to $100 for photos, on publication. Query with clips and resumé required.

EQUINOX—7 Queen Victoria Rd., Camden East, Ont., Canada K0K 1J0. Jody Morgan, Asst. Ed. Articles, 3,000 to 6,000 words, on popular geography, wildlife, astronomy, science, the arts, travel, and adventure. Department pieces, 300 to 800 words, for "Nexus" (science and medicine) and "Habitat" (synthetic and natural environment). Pays $1,500 to $3,000, for features, $100 to $500 for short pieces, on acceptance.

FLORIDA WILDLIFE—620 S. Meridian St., Tallahassee, FL 32399–1600. Andrea H. Blount, Ed. Bimonthly of the Florida Game and Fresh Water Fish Commission. Articles, 800 to 1,200 words, that promote native flora and fauna, hunting, fishing in Florida's fresh waters, outdoor ethics, and conservation of Florida's natural resources. Pays $50 to $200, on publication.

GARBAGE—435 Ninth St., Brooklyn, NY 11215. Patricia Poore, Ed. Articles, 2,500 to 4,000 words, that tailor scientific and technical information to the environmental interests of a lay audience. Topics include food/health; gardening; how-to (ideas for improving efficiency and cutting down on waste); environmental science and technology; lifestyles. Occasionally publish short news items. Query with published clips. Payment varies, on acceptance.

HARROWSMITH COUNTRY LIFE—Ferry Rd., Charlotte, VT 05445. Address Editorial Dept. Investigative articles, 4,000 to 5,000 words, on ecology, energy, health, gardening, and the food chain. Short pieces for "Screed" (opinions) and "Gazette" (news briefs). Do-it-yourself projects. Pays $500 to $1,500 for features, from $50 to $600 for department pieces, on acceptance. Query with SASE required. Guidelines.

INTERNATIONAL WILDLIFE—8925 Leesburg Pike, Vienna, VA 22184. Jan Boysen, Assoc. Ed. Short features, 700 words, and 1,500- to 2,500-word articles that make nature (and human use and stewardship of it) understandable and interesting. Pays $500 for one-page features, $1,800 for full-length articles, on acceptance. Query. Limited free-lance needs. Guidelines.

THE LOOKOUT—Seamen's Church Institute, 241 Water St., New York, NY 10038. Andrea Laine, Ed. Factual articles on the sea and merchant seafarers. Features, 200 to 1,500 words, on the merchant marines, maritime art and artifacts, the marine environment, maritime history, book reviews, etc. Photos. Pays $25 to $100, on publication.

NATIONAL GEOGRAPHIC—17th and M Sts. N.W., Washington, DC 20036. William P.E. Graves, Ed. First-person, general-interest, heavily illustrated articles on science, natural history, exploration, and geographical regions. Query required.

NATIONAL PARKS MAGAZINE—1776 Massachusetts Ave., Washington, DC 20002. Sue E. Dodge, Ed. Articles, 1,000 to 2,000 words, on natural history, wildlife, outdoor activities, and conservation as they relate to national parks: illustrated features on the natural, historic, and cultural resources of the national park system. Pieces about legislation and other issues and events related to the parks. Pays $100 to $800, on acceptance. Query. Send for guidelines.

NATIONAL WILDLIFE—8925 Leesburg Pike, Vienna, VA 22184. Mark Wexler, Ed. Articles, 1,000 to 2,500 words, on wildlife, conservation, environment; outdoor how-to pieces. Photos. Pays on acceptance. Query.

NATURAL HISTORY—American Museum of Natural History, Central Park West at 79th St., New York, NY 10024. Alan Ternes, Ed.-in-Chief. Informative articles, to 3,000 words, by experts, on anthropology and natural sciences. Pays $1,000 for features, on acceptance. Query.

OUTDOOR AMERICA—1401 Wilson Blvd., Level B, Arlington, VA 22209. Quarterly publication of the Izaak Walton League of America. Articles, 1,500 to 2,000 words, on natural resource conservation issues and outdoor recreation; especially fishing, hunting, and camping. Pays 20¢ a word. Query Articles Ed. with published clippings.

SEA FRONTIERS—4600 Rickenbacker Causeway, Virginia Key, Miami, FL 33149. Bonnie Bilyeu Gordon, Ed. Illustrated articles, 500 to 3,000 words, on scientific advances related to the sea, biological, physical, chemical, or geological phenomena, ecology, conservation, etc., written in a popular style for lay readers. Send SASE for guidelines. Pays 25¢ a word, on acceptance. Query.

SIERRA—730 Polk St., San Francisco, CA 94109. Jonathan F. King, Ed.-in-

Chief. Articles, 750 to 2,500 words, on environmental and conservation topics, politics, travel, hiking, backpacking, skiing, rafting, cycling. Photos. Pays from $500 to $2,000, extra for photos, on acceptance. Query with SASE and clips.

SMITHSONIAN MAGAZINE—900 Jefferson Dr., Washington, DC 20560. Marlane A. Liddell, Articles Ed. Articles on history, art, natural history, physical science, profiles, etc. Query.

SPORTS AFIELD—250 W. 55th St., New York, NY 10019. Tom Paugh, Ed. Articles, 2,000 words, with quality photos, on hunting, fishing, natural history, conservation, personal experiences. How-to pieces; humor, fiction. Pays top rates, on acceptance.

VIRGINIA WILDLIFE—P.O. Box 11104, Richmond, VA 23230–1104. Monthly of the Commission of Game and Inland Fisheries. Articles, 1,500 to 2,500 words, on conservation and related topics, including fishing, hunting, wildlife management, outdoor safety, ethics, etc. All material must have Virginia tie-in and be accompanied by color photos. Query with SASE. Pays 10¢ a word, extra for photos, on acceptance.

WILDLIFE CONSERVATION—New York Zoological Society, Bronx, NY 10460. Nancy Simmons, Sr. Ed. First-person articles, 1,500 to 2,000 words, on "popular" natural history, "based on author's research and experience as opposed to textbook approach." Payment varies, on acceptance. Guidelines.

ZOO LIFE—11661 San Vicente Blvd., Suite 402, Los Angeles, CA 90049. Audrey Tawa, Ed. Quarterly. Articles, 1,500 to 2,000 words, on the work zoos and aquariums are doing in the fields of animal conservation and education. Mention possibility of photos when querying. Pays 30¢ a word, on publication. Payment for photos negotiable. Guidelines.

MEDIA AND THE ARTS

AHA! HISPANIC ARTS NEWS—Assoc. of Hispanic Arts, 173 E. 116th St., New York, NY 10029–1302. Dolores Prida, Ed. Editorials, reviews, monthly calendars, feature articles, and listings by artistic discipline. Query required.

AIRBRUSH ACTION—400 Madison Ave., Lakewood, NJ 08701. Address the Editors. Articles, 500 to 3,000 words, on airbrush, graphics, and art-related topics. Pays $75 to $300, on publication. Query.

THE AMERICAN ART JOURNAL—40 W. 57th St., 5th Fl., New York, NY 10019–4044. Jane Van N. Turano, Ed. Quarterly. Scholarly articles, 2,000 to 10,000 words, on American art of the 17th through the early 20th centuries. Photos. Pays $200 to $500, on acceptance.

AMERICAN INDIAN ART MAGAZINE—7314 E. Osborn Dr., Scottsdale, AZ 85251. Roanne P. Goldfein, Man. Ed. Detailed articles, 10 typed pages, on American Indian arts: painting, carving, beadwork, basketry, textiles, ceramics, jewelry, etc. Pays varying rates, on publication. Query.

AMERICAN THEATRE—355 Lexington Ave., New York, NY 10017. Jim O'Quinn, Ed. Features, 500 to 4,000 words, on the theater and theater-related subjects. Payment negotiable, on publication. Query.

ART & ANTIQUES—633 3rd Ave., New York, NY 10017. Jeffrey Schaire, Ed. Investigative pieces or personal narratives, 1,500 words, and news items, 300 to 500 words, on art or antiques. Pays $1 a word, on publication. Query first.

THE ARTIST'S MAGAZINE—1507 Dana Ave., Cincinnati, OH 45207. Michael Ward, Ed. Features, 1,200 to 2,500 words, and department pieces for the working artist. Poems, to 20 lines, on art and the creative process. Single-panel cartoons. Pays $150 to $350 for articles; $50 for cartoons, on acceptance. Guidelines. Query.

ARTS ATLANTIC—P.O. Box 848, Charlottetown, P.E.I., Canada C1A 7L9. Joseph Sherman, Ed. Articles and reviews, 600 to 3,000 words, on visual, performing, and literary arts, crafts in Atlantic Canada. Also, "idea and concept" articles of universal appeal. Pays from 15¢ a word, on publication; flat rates for interviews. Query.

BLUEGRASS UNLIMITED—Box 111, Broad Run, VA 22014–0111. Peter V. Kuykendall, Ed. Articles, to 3,500 words, on bluegrass and traditional country music. Photos. Pays 6¢ to 8¢ a word, extra for photos.

CLAVIER MAGAZINE—200 Northfield Rd., Northfield, IL 60093. Kingsley Day, Ed. Practical articles, interviews, master classes, and humor pieces, 2,000 words, for keyboard performers and teachers. Pays $40 to $80 a published page, on publication.

DANCE MAGAZINE—33 W. 60th St., New York, NY 10023. Richard Philp, Ed.-in-Chief. Features on dance, personalities, techniques, health issues, and trends. Photos. Query; limited free-lance market.

DANCE TEACHER NOW—3020 Beacon Blvd., West Sacramento, CA 95691–3436. K.C. Patrick, Ed. Articles, 1,000 to 2,500 words, for professional dance educators, dancers, and other dance professionals on practical information for the teacher and/or business owner, economic and historical issues related to the profession. Profiles of schools, methods, and people who are leaving their mark on dance. Must be thoroughly researched. Pays $200 to $350, on acceptance. Query preferred.

DARKROOM PHOTOGRAPHY—9171 Wilshire Blvd., Suite 300, Beverly Hills, CA 90210. Thom Harrop, Ed. Articles on photographic techniques and photographic portfolios, 1,000 to 2,500 words, with photos, for all levels of photographers. Pays $100 to $700. Query.

DRAMATICS—Educational Theatre Assoc., 3368 Central Pkwy., Cincinnati, OH 45225–2392. Don Corathers, Ed. Articles, interviews, how-tos, 750 to 4,000 words, for high school students on the performing arts with an emphasis on theater practice: acting, directing, playwriting, technical subjects. Prefer articles that "could be used by a better-than-average high school teacher to teach students something about the performing arts." Pays $15 to $200 honorarium. Manuscripts preferred; graphics and photos accepted.

THE ENGRAVERS JOURNAL—26 Summit St., Box 318, Brighton, MI 48116. Rosemary Farrell, Man. Ed. Articles, varying lengths, on topics related to the engraving industry and small business operations. Pays $60 to $175, on acceptance. Query first.

FILM QUARTERLY—Univ. of California Press, 2120 Berkeley Way, Berkeley, CA 94720. Ann Martin, Ed. Film reviews, historical and critical articles, book reviews, to 6,000 words. Pays on publication. Query.

FLUTE TALK—Instrumentalist Publishing Co., 200 Northfield Rd., Northfield, IL 60093. Kathleen Goll-Wilson, Ed. Articles, 6 to 12 typed pages, on flute performance and pedagogy; fillers; photos and line drawings. Thorough knowledge of music or the instrument a must. Pays honorarium, on publication. Queries preferred.

INDUSTRIAL PHOTOGRAPHY—445 Broadhollow Rd., Melville, NY 11747. Steve Shaw, Ed. Articles on techniques and trends in current professional photography; audiovisuals, etc., for industrial photographers and executives. Query.

INTERNATIONAL MUSICIAN—Paramount Bldg., 1501 Broadway, Suite 600, New York, NY 10036. Articles, 1,500 to 2,000 words, for professional musicians. Pays varying rates, on acceptance. Query.

JAZZIZ—P. O. Box 8309, Gainesville, FL 32605. Michael Fagien, Ed.-in-Chief. Feature articles on all aspects of adult contemporary music: interviews, profiles, concept pieces. "Departments include reviews of a variety of music genres, radio and video." Emphasis on new releases. Send resumé with manuscript. Pays varying rates, on acceptance. Query.

KEYBOARD MAGAZINE—20085 Stevens Creek, Cupertino, CA 95014. Dominic Milano, Ed. Articles, 1,000 to 5,000 words, on keyboard instruments, MIDI and computer technology, and players. Photos. Pays $175 to $500, on acceptance. Query.

MEDIA HISTORY DIGEST—c/o Editor & Publisher, 11 W. 19th St., New York, NY 10011. Hiley H. Ward, Ed. Articles, 1,500 to 2,000 words, on the history of print media, for wide consumer interest. Puzzles and humor related to media history. Pays varying rates, on publication. Query.

MODERN DRUMMER—870 Pompton Ave., Cedar Grove, NJ 07009. Ronald L. Spagnardi, Ed. Articles, 500 to 2,000 words, on drumming: how-tos, interviews. Pays $50 to $500, on publication.

MUSIC MAGAZINE—P. O. Box 313, Port Credit P.S., Mississauga, Ontario, Canada L5G 4L8. Articles, with photos, on musicians, conductors, and composers, for all classical music buffs. Pays $100 to $300, on publication. Query required. Guidelines.

NEW ENGLAND ENTERTAINMENT DIGEST—45 Willard St., W. Quincy, MA 02169. Michael R. McCaffrey, Pub. News features and reviews on arts and entertainment in New England. Light verse. Pays $10 to $25, $1 to $2 for verse, on publication.

OPERA NEWS—The Metropolitan Opera Guild, 70 Lincoln Center Plaza, New York, NY 10023–6593. Patrick J. Smith, Ed. Articles, 600 to 2,500 words, on all aspects of opera. Pays 20¢ a word, on publication. Query.

PERFORMANCE—1203 Lake St., Suite 200, Fort Worth, TX 76102–4504. Don Waitt, Pub./Ed.-in-Chief. Reports on the touring industry: concert promoters, booking agents, concert venues and clubs, as well as support services, such as lighting, sound and staging companies. Pays 35¢ per column line, on publication.

PETERSEN'S PHOTOGRAPHIC—8490 Sunset Blvd., Los Angeles, CA 90069. Bill Hurter, Ed. Articles and how-to pieces, with photos, on travel, video, and darkroom photography, for beginners, advanced amateurs, and professionals. Pays $60 per printed page, on publication.

PHOTOMETHODS—Box 490, Hicksville, NY 11802–0490. David Silverman, Ed.-in-Chief. Articles, 1,500 to 3,000 words, on innovative techniques in imaging for industry (still, film, video), working situations, and management. Pays from $150, on publication. Query.

POPULAR PHOTOGRAPHY—1633 Broadway, New York, NY 10019. Jason Schneider, Ed. Dir. How-to articles, 500 to 2,000 words, for amateur photographers. Query first with outline and photos.

PREVUE—P.O. Box 974, Reading, PA 19603. J. Steranko, Ed. Lively articles on films and film-makers, entertainment features and celebrity interviews, 4 to 25 pages. Pays varying rates, on acceptance. Query with clips.

PROFESSIONAL STAINED GLASS—Rte. 6 at Dingle Ridge Rd., Brewster, NY 10509. Julie Sloan, Man. Ed. Practical articles of interest to stained glass professionals. Abundant opportunity for energetic and enterprising free lancers. Pays $100 to $250, on publication. Query required.

ROLLING STONE—1290 Ave. of the Americas, 2nd Fl., New York, NY 10104. Magazine of American music, culture, and politics. No fiction. Query. Rarely accepts free-lance material.

SHEET MUSIC MAGAZINE—223 Katonah Ave., Katonah, NY 10536. Josephine Sblendorio, Man. Ed. Pieces, 1,000 to 2,000 words, for pianists and organists, on musicians and composers, how-tos, and book reviews (to 500 words); no hard rock or heavy metal subjects. Pays $75 to $200, on publication.

SUN TRACKS—Box 2510, Phoenix, AZ 85002. Robert Baird, Music Ed. Music section of *New Times*. Long and short features, record reviews, and interviews. Pays $25 to $500, on publication. Query.

THEATRE CRAFTS MAGAZINE—135 Fifth Ave., New York, NY 10010. Patricia MacKay, Pub. David Barbour, Man. Ed. Articles, 500 to 2,500 words, on design, technical, and management aspects of theater, opera, dance, television, and film, for those in performing arts and entertainment trade. Pays on acceptance. Query.

VIDEO MAGAZINE—460 W. 34th St., New York, NY 10001. Stan Pinkwas, Man. Ed. How-to and service articles on home video equipment, technology, and programming. Interviews and human-interest features related to above subjects, from 800 to 2,500 words. Pays varying rates, on acceptance. Query.

VIDEOMAKER—P.O. Box 4591, Chico, CA 95927. Bradley Kent, Ed. "The Video Camera User's Magazine." Authoritative, how-to articles geared at hobbyist and professional video camera/camcorder users: instructionals, innovative applications, tools and tips, industry developments, new products, etc. Pays varying rates, on publication. Queries preferred.

WASHINGTON JOURNALISM REVIEW—4716 Pontiac St., #301, College Park, MD 20740–2493. Bill Monroe, Ed. Articles, 500 to 3,000 words, on print or electronic journalism. Pays 20¢ a word, on publication. Query.

HOBBIES, CRAFTS, COLLECTING

AMERICAN WOODWORKER—Rodale Press, 33 E. Minor St., Emmaus, PA 18098. David Sloan, Ed. "A how-to bimonthly for the woodworking enthusiast." Technical or anecdotal articles (to 2,000 words) relating to woodworking or furniture design. Fillers, drawings, slides and photos considered. Pays from $150 per published page, on publication; regular contributors paid on acceptance. Queries preferred. Guidelines.

ANTIQUE MONTHLY—2100 Powers Ferry Road, Atlanta, GA 30339. Kenna Simmons, Man. Ed. Articles, 750 to 1,200 words, on trends and the exhibition and sales (auctions, antique shops, etc.) of decorative arts and antiques, with B&W photos or color slides. Heavy emphasis on news and timely material. Pays varying rates, on publication.

THE ANTIQUE TRADER WEEKLY—Box 1050, Dubuque, IA 52001. Kyle

D. Husfloen, Ed. Articles, 1,000 to 2,000 words, on all types of antiques and collectors' items. Photos. Pays from $25 to $200, on publication. Query preferred. Buys all rights.

ANTIQUES & AUCTION NEWS—P.O. Box 500, Mount Joy, PA 17552. Weekly newspaper. Factual articles, 600 to 1,500 words, on antiques, collectors, and collections. Query required. Photos. Pays $5 to $20, after publication.

ANTIQUEWEEK—P.O. Box 90, Knightstown, IN 46148. Tom Hoepf, Ed., Central Edition; Connie Swaim, Ed., Eastern Edition. Weekly antique, auction, and collectors newspaper. Articles, 500 to 1,500 words, on antiques, collectibles, restorations, genealogy, auction and antique show reports. Photos. Pays from $40 to $150 for in-depth articles, on publication. Query. Guidelines.

AOPA PILOT—421 Aviation Way, Frederick, MD 21701. Mark R. Twombly, Ed. Magazine of the Aircraft Owners and Pilots Assn. Articles, to 2,500 words, with photos, on general aviation for beginning and experienced pilots. Pays to $750.

AQUARIUM FISH—P.O. Box 6050, Mission Viejo, CA 92690. Edward Bauman, Ed. Articles, 2,000 to 4,000 words, on freshwater, saltwater, and pond fish, with or without color transparencies. (No "pet fish" stories, please.) Payment varies, on publication.

THE AUTOGRAPH COLLECTOR'S MAGAZINE—P.O. Box 55328, Stockton, CA 95205. Joe Kraus, Ed. Articles, 100 to 1,500 words, on all areas of autograph collecting: preservation, framing, and storage, specialty collections, documents and letters, collectors and dealers. Queries preferred. Pays 5¢ a word, $3 for illustrations, $10 for photos, and $25 for cartoons, on publication.

BIRD TALK—Box 6050, Mission Viejo, CA 92690. Karyn New, Ed. Articles for pet bird owners: care and feeding, training, safety, outstanding personal adventures, exotic birds in their native countries, profiles of celebrities' pet birds, travel to bird parks or shows. Pays 10¢ a word, after publication. Query or send manuscript; good transparencies a plus.

BIRD WATCHER'S DIGEST—P.O. Box 110, Marietta, OH 45750. Mary B. Bowers, Ed. Articles, 600 to 3,000 words, on bird-watching experiences and expeditions: information about rare sightings; updates on endangered species. Pays from $50, on publication. Allow eight weeks for response.

THE BLADE MAGAZINE—P.O. Box 22007, Chattanooga, TN 37422. J. Bruce Voyles, Ed. Articles, 500 to 3,000 words: historical pieces on knives and old knife factories, etc.; interviews with knifemakers; celebrities who use/collect knives; knife trends, handmade and factory; values on collectible knives and knife accessories; how to use knives, sharpen; etc. Study magazine first. Pays from 5¢ a word, on publication.

BYLINE—Box 130596, Edmond, OK 73013. Marcia Preston, Ed.-in-Chief. Kathryn Fanning, Man. Ed. General fiction, 2,000 to 4,000 words. Nonfiction, 1,500- to 1,800-word features and 300- to 800-word special departments. Poetry, 10 to 30 lines preferred. Nonfiction and poetry must be about writing. Humor, 400 to 800 words, about writing. "We seek practical and motivational material that tells writers how they can succeed, not why they can't. Overdone topics: writers' block, the muse, rejection slips." Pays $5 to $10 for poetry; $15 to $35 for departments; $50 for features and short fiction, on acceptance.

CARD PLAYER—1455 E. Tropicana Ave., Suite 450, Las Vegas, NV 89119. June Field, Ed./Pub. "The Magazine for Those Who Play to Win." Articles on events, personalities, legal issues, new casinos, tournaments, and prizes. Also articles on strategies, theory and game psychology to improve play. Occasionally use humor, cartoons, puzzles, or anecdotal material. Pays $50, on publication; $25 to $35 for fillers. (For longer stories, features, or special coverage, pays $75 to $100.) Guidelines.

CHESS LIFE—186 Route 9W, New Windsor, NY 12553–7698. Glenn Petersen, Ed. Articles, 500 to 3,000 words, for members of the U.S. Chess Federation, on news, profiles, technical aspects of chess. Features on all aspects of chess: history, humor, puzzles, etc. Fiction, 500 to 2,000 words, related to chess. Photos. Pays varying rates, on acceptance. Query; limited free-lance market.

CLASSIC TOY TRAINS—21027 Crossroads Cir., Waukesha, WI 53187. Articles, with photos, on toy train layouts and collections. Also train manufacturing history and repair/maintenance. Pays $75 per printed page, on acceptance. Query.

COLLECTOR EDITIONS—170 Fifth Ave., New York, NY 10010. Joan Muyskens Pursley, Ed. Articles, 750 to 1,500 words, on collectibles, mainly glass, porcelain, and prints. Pays $150 to $350, within 30 days of acceptance. Query with photos.

COLLECTORS NEWS—P.O. Box 156, Grundy Center, IA 50638. Linda Kruger, Ed. Articles, to 1,500 words, on private collections, antiques, and collectibles, especially 20th-century nostalgia, Americana, glass and china, music, furniture, transportation, timepieces, jewelry, and lamps; include B&W photos. Pays 75¢ per column inch; $1 per inch for front-page articles, on publication.

COUNTED CROSS-STITCH PLUS—306 E. Parr Rd., Berne, IN 46711. Lana Schurb, Ed. How-to and instructional counted cross-stitch. Book and product reviews. Pays varying rates, on publication.

COUNTRY FOLK ART MAGAZINE—8393 E. Holly Rd., Holly, MI 48442–8819. Julie L. Semrau, Man. Ed. Historical, gardening, collectibles, and how-to pieces, 750 to 2,000 words, with a creative slant on American country folk art. Pays $150 to $300, on acceptance. Submit pieces on seasonal topics one year in advance.

COUNTRY HANDCRAFTS—5400 S. 60th St., Greendale, WI 53129. Kathy Pohl, Exec. Ed. All types of craft designs (needlepoint, quilting, woodworking, etc.) with complete instructions and full-size patterns. Pays from $50 to $300, on acceptance, for all rights.

CRAFTS 'N THINGS—Dept. W, 701 Lee St., Suite 1000, Des Plaines, IL 60016–4570. Julie Stephani, Ed. How-to articles on all kinds of crafts projects, with instructions. Pays $50 to $250, on publication. Send manuscript with instructions and photograph of the finished item.

CROSS STITCH SAMPLER—(formerly *Needlewords*) 7 Olde Ridge Village, Chadds Ford, PA 19317. Deborah N. DeSimone, Ed. Articles, 500 to 1,500 words, about counted cross-stitch, drawn thread, or themes revolving around stitching (samplers, needlework tools, etc.). Queries required. Payment varies, on publication.

DOG FANCY—P.O. Box 6050, Mission Viejo, CA 92690. Kim Thornton, Ed. Articles, 1,500 to 3,000 words, on dog care, health, grooming, breeds, activities, events, etc. Photos. Pays 5¢ a word, on publication.

DOLLS, THE COLLECTOR'S MAGAZINE—170 Fifth Ave., New York, NY 10010. Joan Muyskens Pursley, Ed. Articles, 500 to 2,500 words, for knowledgeable doll collectors: sharply focused with a strong collecting angle, and concrete information (value, identification, restoration, etc.). Pays $100 to $350, after acceptance. Query.

FIBERARTS—50 College St., Asheville, NC 28801. Ann Batchelder, Ed. Published five times yearly. Articles, 400 to 1,200 words, on contemporary trends in fiber sculpture, weaving, surface design, quilting, stitchery, papermaking, felting, basketry, and wearable art. Query with photos of subject, outline, and synopsis. Pays varying rates, on publication.

FINESCALE MODELER—P.O. Box 1612, Waukesha, WI 53187. Bob Hayden, Ed. How-to articles for people who make nonoperating scale models of aircraft, automobiles, boats, figures. Photos and drawings should accompany articles. One-page model-building hints and tips. Pays from $30 per published page, on acceptance. Query preferred.

THE HOME SHOP MACHINIST—2779 Aero Park Dr., Box 1810, Traverse City, MI 49685. Joe D. Rice, Ed. How-to articles on precision metalworking and foundry work. Accuracy and attention to detail a must. Pays $40 per published page, extra for photos and illustrations, on publication. Send SASE for writer's guidelines.

KITPLANES—P.O. Box 6050, Mission Viejo, CA 92690. Dave Martin, Ed. Articles geared to the growing market of aircraft built from kits and plans by home craftsmen, on all aspects of design, construction, and performance, 1,000 to 4,000 words. Pays $60 per page, on publication.

LOST TREASURE—P.O. Box 1589, Grove, OK 74344. Debi Williams, Man. Ed. Factual articles, 1,000 to 1,800 words, on treasure hunting, metal detecting, prospecting techniques, and legendary lost treasure. Profiles. Pays 4¢ a word; preference given to stories with photos. Photos: Pays $5 each for B&W; $100 for color slides for cover. Send SASE with 52¢ postage for guidelines.

MILITARY HISTORY—602 S. King St., Suite 300, Leesburg, VA 22075. C. Brian Kelly, Ed. Bimonthly on the strategy, tactics, and personalities of military history. Department pieces, 2,000 words, on espionage, weaponry, personality, and travel. Features, 4,000 words, with 500-word sidebars. Pays $200 to $400, on publication. Query. Guidelines.

MINIATURE COLLECTOR—P.O. Box 631, Boiling Springs, PA 17007. James Keough, Ed./Pub. Articles, 800 to 1,200 words, with photos, on outstanding 1/12-scale (dollhouse) miniatures and the people who make and collect them. Original, illustrated how-to projects for making miniatures. Pays varying rates, within 30 days of acceptance. Query with photos.

MODEL RAILROADER—21027 Crossroads Cir., Waukesha, WI 53187. Russ Larson, Ed. Articles, with photos of layout and equipment, on model railroads. Pays $75 per printed page, on acceptance. Query.

NEEDLEWORDS—See *Cross Stitch Sampler.*

NEW ENGLAND ANTIQUES JOURNAL—4 Church St., Ware, MA 01082. Jody Young, Gen. Mgr. Well-researched articles, to 2,500 words, on antiques of interest to collectors and/or dealers, auction and antiques show reviews, to 1,000 words, antiques market news, to 500 words; photos desired. Pays to $150, on publication. Query or send manuscript. Reports in two to four weeks.

THE NEW YORK ANTIQUE ALMANAC—Box 335, Lawrence, NY 11559. Carol Nadel, Ed. Articles on antiques, shows, shops, art, investments, collectibles, collecting suggestions; related humor. Photos. Pays $5 to $75, extra for photos, on publication.

NOSTALGIA WORLD—Box 231, North Haven, CT 06473. Richard Mason, Jr., Ed. Articles, 1,500 to 3,000 words, on all kinds of collectibles: records, TV memorabilia (Munsters, Star Trek, Dark Shadows, Elvira, etc.), comics, gum cards, toys, sheet music, monsters, magazines, dolls, movie posters, etc. Pays $10 to $50, on publication.

NUTSHELL NEWS—21027 Crossroads Cir., P.O. Box 1612, Waukesha, WI 53187. Sybil Harp, Ed. Articles, 1,200 to 1,500 words, for architectural scale miniatures enthusiasts, collectors, craftspeople, and hobbyists. Interested in artisan profiles, tours of collections, and how-to projects. "Writers must be knowledgeable miniaturists." Color slides or B&W prints required. Pays $50 per published page, on acceptance. Query first.

PETERSEN'S PHOTOGRAPHIC—8490 Sunset Blvd., Los Angeles, CA 90069. Bill Hurter, Ed. How-to articles on all phases of still photography of interest to the amateur and advanced photographer. Pays $60 per printed page for article accompanied by photos, on publication.

PLATE WORLD—9200 N. Maryland Ave., Niles, IL 60648. Alyson Sulaski Wyckoff, Ed. Articles on artists, collectors, manufacturers, retailers of limited-edition (only) collector's plates. No antiques. Internationally oriented. Pays varying rates, on acceptance. Query first with writing samples.

POPULAR MECHANICS—224 W. 57th St., New York, NY 10019. Deborah Frank, Man. Ed. Articles, 300 to 2,000 words, on latest developments in mechanics, industry, science; features on hobbies with a mechanical slant; how-tos on home, shop, and crafts projects; features on outdoor adventures, boating, and electronics. Photos and sketches a plus. Pays to $1,000, $25 to $100 for short pieces, on acceptance. Buys all rights.

POPULAR PHOTOGRAPHY—1633 Broadway, New York, NY 10019. Jason Schneider, Ed. Dir. Illustrated articles of interest to serious amateur photographers, especially how-to picture-taking pieces, 500 to 2,000 words. Payment varies. Query with outline.

THE PROFESSIONAL QUILTER—Oliver Press, Box 75277, St. Paul, MN 55175. Jeannie M. Spears, Ed. Articles, 500 to 1,500 words, for small businesses related to the quilting field: business and marketing skills, personality profiles. Graphics, if applicable; no how-to-quilt articles. Pays $25 to $75, on publication. Guidelines.

QUICK & EASY CRAFTS—306 E. Parr Rd., Berne, IN 46711. Beth Schwartz, Ed. How-to and instructional needlecrafts and other arts and crafts, book reviews, and tips. Photos. Pays varying rates, on publication.

RAILROAD MODEL CRAFTSMAN—P.O. Box 700, Newton, NJ 07860–0700. William C. Schaumburg, Ed. How-to articles on scale model railroading; cars, operation, scenery, etc. Pays on publication.

R/C MODELER MAGAZINE—P.O. Box 487, Sierra Madre, CA 91025. Patricia E. Crews, Ed. Technical and semi-technical how-to articles on radio-controlled model aircraft, boats, helicopters, and cars. Query.

RESTORATION—3153 E. Lincoln, Tucson, AZ 85714–2017. W.R. Haessner, Ed. Articles, 1,200 to 1,800 words, on restoring autos, trucks, planes, trains, etc. Photos and art required. Pays $50 per page, on publication. Query.

THE ROBB REPORT—1 Acton Pl., Acton, MA 01720. Attn: Toby Perelmuter. Feature articles on investment opportunities, classic and collectible autos, entrepreneurship, technology, lifestyles, home interiors, boats, travel, etc. Pays on publication. Query with SASE and published clips.

SCHOOL MATES—U.S. Chess Federation, 186 Route 9W, New Windsor, NY 12553–7698. Jennie L. Simon, Ed. Articles and fiction, to 1,000 words, and short fillers, related to chess for beginning chess players (not necessarily children). "Instructive, but room for fun puzzles, anecdotes, etc. All chess related." Pays about $40 per 1,000 words, on publication. Query; limited free-lance market.

SEW NEWS—P.O. Box 1790, News Plaza, Peoria, IL 61656. Linda Turner Griepentrog, Ed. Articles, to 3,000 words, "that teach a specific technique, inspire a reader to try new sewing projects, or inform a reader about an interesting person, company, or project related to sewing, textiles, or fashion." Emphasis is on fashion (not craft) sewing. Pays $25 to $400, on acceptance. Queries required; no unsolicited manuscripts accepted.

SPORTS CARD TRADER—3 Fairchild Ct., Plainview, NY 11803. Address Editorial Office. Articles, from 1,000 words, related to baseball, football, basketball, and hockey cards; collecting and investing and fillers. Queries preferred. Pays 7¢ per word, on publication.

SPORTS COLLECTORS DIGEST—Krause Publications, 700 E. State St., Iola, WI 54990. Tom Mortenson, Ed. Articles, 750 to 2,000, on old baseball card sets and other collectibles. Pays $50 to $100, on publication.

TEDDY BEAR REVIEW—P.O. Box 1239, Hanover, PA 17331. Chris Revi, Ed. Articles on antique and contemporary teddy bears for makers, collectors, and enthusiasts. Pays $50 to $200, within 30 days of acceptance. Query with photos.

THREADS MAGAZINE—Taunton Press, 63 S. Main St., Box 355, Newtown, CT 06470. Address the Editors. A bimonthly devoted to design, materials, and techniques in sewing and textile arts. Articles and department pieces about materials, tools, techniques, people, and design, especially in garment making, knitting, quilting, and stitchery. Pays $150 per published page, on publication.

TREASURE—6688 Split Rock Ave., Twenty-Nine Palms, CA 92277. Jim Williams, Ed. Articles, to 2,500 words, and fillers, 300 words, of interest to treasure hunters: How-to (building projects and hunting techniques); Search (where to look for treasure); and Found (stories of discovered treasure). Photos and illustrations welcome. Pays from $30 for fillers, to $125 for features, on publication. Same address and requirements for *Treasure Search* and *Treasure Found.*

TROPICAL FISH HOBBYIST—1 T.F.H. Plaza, Neptune City, NJ 07753. Ray Hunziker, Ed. Articles, 500 to 3,000 words, for beginning and experienced tropical and marine fish enthusiasts. Photos. Pays $35 to $250, on acceptance. Query.

VINTAGE FASHIONS—900 Frederick St., Cumberland, MD 21502. Carolyn Cook, Ed. Articles, to 1,200 words, on vintage clothing (except furs), jewelry, and accessories. Pieces on the care and preservation of vintage items. Photos. Queries preferred. Payment varies, on publication.

WEST ART—Box 6868, Auburn, CA 95604–6868. Martha Garcia, Ed. Features, 350 to 700 words, on fine arts and crafts. No hobbies. Photos. Pays 50¢ per column inch, on publication. SASE required.

WESTERN & EASTERN TREASURES—P.O. Box 1095, Arcata, CA 95521. Rosemary Anderson, Man. Ed. Illustrated articles, to 1,500 words, on treasure hunting and how-to metal detecting tips. Pays 2¢ a word, extra for photos, on publication.

WIN MAGAZINE—16760 Stagg St., #213, Van Nuys, CA 91406–1642.

Cecil Suzuki, Ed. Gambling-related articles, 1,000 to 3,000 words, and fiction. Pays on publication.

THE WINE SPECTATOR—Opera Plaza, Suite 2014, 601 Van Ness Ave., San Francisco, CA 94102. Jim Gordon, Man. Ed. Features, 600 to 2,000 words, preferably with photos, on news and people in the wine world. Pays from $100, extra for photos, on publication. Query required.

WOODENBOAT MAGAZINE—P.O. Box 78, Brooklin, ME 04616. Jonathan Wilson, Ed. How-to and technical articles, 4,000 words, on construction, repair, and maintenance of wooden boats; design, history, and use of wooden boats; and profiles of outstanding wooden boat builders and designers. Pays $6 per column inch. Query preferred.

WOODWORK—42 Digital Dr., Suite 5, Novato, CA 94949. Graham Blackburn, Ed. Published six times yearly. Articles on all aspects of woodworking (simple, complex, technical, or aesthetic) with illustrations and cut lists. Topics include personalities, joinery, shows, carving, how-to, finishing, etc. Pays $150 per published page; $20 to $150 for "Techniques" department pieces, on publication. Queries or outlines preferred.

THE WORKBASKET—4251 Pennsylvania, Kansas City, MO 64111. Roma Jean Rice, Ed. Instructions and models for original knit, crochet, and tat items. (Designs must fit theme of issue.) How-tos on crafts and gardening, 400 to 1,200 words, with photos. Pays 7¢ a word for articles, extra for photos, on acceptance; negotiable rates for instructional items.

WORKBENCH—4251 Pennsylvania Ave., Kansas City, MO 64111. Robert N. Hoffman, Exec. Ed. Articles on do-it-yourself home improvement and maintenance projects and general woodworking articles for beginning and expert craftsmen. Complete working drawings with accurate dimensions, step-by-step instructions, lists of materials, in-progress photos, and photos of the finished product must accompany submission. Queries welcome. Pays from $150 per published page, on acceptance.

YELLOWBACK LIBRARY—P.O. Box 36172, Des Moines, IA 50315. Gil O'Gara, Ed. Articles, 300 to 2,000 words, on boys/girls series literature (Hardy Boys, Nancy Drew, Tom Swift, etc.) for collectors, researchers, and dealers. "Especially welcome are interviews with, or articles by past and present writers of juvenile series fiction." Pays in copies.

YESTERYEAR—P.O. Box 2, Princeton, WI 54968. Michael Jacobi, Ed. Articles on antiques and collectibles, for readers in Wisconsin, Illinois, Iowa, Minnesota, and surrounding states. Photos. Will consider regular columns on collecting or antiques. Pays from $10, on publication.

ZYMURGY—Box 1679, Boulder, CO 80306–1679. Charles N. Papazian, Ed. Articles appealing to beer lovers and homebrewers. Pays in merchandise and books. Query.

POPULAR & TECHNICAL SCIENCE; COMPUTERS

A+/INCIDER—(formerly *Incider*) IDG Communications/Peterborough, 80 Elm St., Peterborough, NH 03458. Paul Statt, Sr. Ed. Features, 2,000 to 2,500 words, and product reviews, 1,000 to 1,500 words, of interest to Apple II and Macintosh computer users. Short hints and news, to 100 words. Pays from $25 to $500, on acceptance. Query.

AD ASTRA—National Space Society, 922 Pennsylvania Ave. S.E., Washington, DC 20003–2140. A. Royce Dalby, Ed.-in-Chief. Lively, non-technical features, to 3,000 words, on all aspects of international space program. Particularly interested in "Living in Space" articles; space settlements; lunar and Mars bases. Pays $150 to $250, on publication. Query; guidelines available.

AIR & SPACE—370 L'Enfant Promenade, 10th Fl., Washington, DC 20024–2518. George Larson, Ed. General-interest articles, 1,000 to 3,500 words, on aerospace experience, past, present, and future; travel, space, history, biographies, essays, commentary. Pays varying rates, on acceptance. Query first.

AMERICAN HERITAGE OF INVENTION & TECHNOLOGY—60 Fifth Ave., New York, NY 10011. Frederick Allen, Ed. Articles, 2,000 to 5,000 words, on history of technology in America, for the sophisticated general reader. Query. Pays on acceptance.

AMIGA WORLD—IDG Communications, 80 Elm St., Peterborough, NH 03458. Barbara Gefvert, Sr. Ed. Janine Jackson, Reviews Ed. Articles, 1,500 to 3,000 words: product roundups and comparisons of major products, explanations of new technologies, applications and programming tutorials relating to Amiga systems. Single and comparative reviews, 800 to 1,500 words, on just-released Amiga hardware and software products. Pays $450 to $800 for articles, $200 and up for reviews, on publication. Query preferred; for reviews, list credentials for covering specific types of products.

ARCHAEOLOGY—15 Park Row, New York, NY 10038. Peter A. Young, Ed.-in-Chief. Articles on archaeology by professionals or lay people with a solid knowledge of the field. Pays $500 to $1,000, on acceptance. Query required.

ASTRONOMY—P.O. Box 1612, Waukesha, WI 53187. Richard Berry, Ed.-in-Chief. Articles on astronomy, astrophysics, space programs, research. Hobby pieces on equipment; short news items. Pays varying rates, on acceptance.

BIOSCIENCE—American Institute of Biological Science, 730 11th St. N.W., Washington, DC 20001. Anna Maria Gillis, Features Ed. Articles, two to four journal pages, on new developments in biology or on science policy, for professional biologists. Pays $300 per journal page, on publication. Query required.

BYTE MAGAZINE—One Phoenix Mill Ln., Peterborough, NH 03458. Frederic Langa, Ed. Features on new technology, how-to articles, and reviews of computers and software, varying lengths, for sophisticated users of personal computers. Payment is competitive. Query. Guidelines.

CBT DIRECTIONS—Weingarten Publications, 38 Chauncy St., Boston, MA 02111. Floyd Kemske, Ed. Articles (2,500 words) and news items (from 500 words) on computer-based training, interactive video, and multimedia for industry and government professionals in program development. Pays $100 to $600, on acceptance. Query.

CLASSROOM COMPUTER LEARNING—See *Technology & Learning*.

COMPUTE!—324 W. Wendover Ave., Suite 200, Greensboro, NC 27408–8439. Peter Scisco, Ed. In-depth feature articles on using the personal computer at home, work, and school. Industry news, interviews with leaders in the pc field, product information, hardware and software reviews. For users of Amiga, Commodore 64/128, IBM, Tandy, and compatibles.

COMPUTE GAZETTE—324 W. Wendover Ave., Suite 200, Greensboro, NC 27408. David Hensley, Man. Ed. Tom Netsel, Ed. Articles, to 2,000 words, on

Commodore 64/128, including home, education, and business applications, games, and programming. Original programs and artwork also accepted.

COMPUTER CRAFT—(formerly *Modern Electronics*) 76 N. Broadway, Hicksville, NY 11801. Art Salsberg, Ed.-in-Chief. How-to features, technical tutorials, and construction projects related to personal computer and microcontroller equipment. Emphasizes enhancements, modifications, and applications. Lengths vary. Query with outline required. Pays $90 to $150 per published page, on acceptance.

DATACENTER MANAGER—International Computer Programs, Inc., 8900 Keystone Crossing, Suite 1100, Indianapolis, IN 46240–2183. Mark Taber, Ed. Articles, 2,000 to 3,000 words, on the software and utilities that drive computer systems, communications, and data center operations. Pays $600 to $800, on acceptance.

DESIGN MANAGEMENT—Communications Channels, 6255 Barfield Rd., Atlanta, GA 30328. Eric Torrey, Ed. Articles, 1,500 to 2,000 words, on news, trends concerning CAD, engineering and architecture, computer graphics, reprographics, and related design fields. Pays on publication. Query required.

DIGITAL NEWS—33 West St., Boston, MA 02111. Charles Babcock, Ed. Newspaper articles of varying lengths, covering products, applications, and events related to Digital's VAX line of computers. Pay varies, on acceptance. Query required.

EARTH—Kalmbach Publications, P.O. Box 1612, Waukesha, WI 53187. Steve Zaburunov, Ed. Bimonthly. Articles, 3,000 to 5,000 words, on the latest discoveries in geology and the earth sciences. Earth-related poetry, to 5 lines. Landscape drawings and color photos. Payment varies, on acceptance; photos paid on publication. Guidelines.

ENVIRONMENT—4000 Albemarle St. N.W., Washington, DC 20016. Barbara T. Richman, Man. Ed. Factual articles, 2,500 to 5,000 words, on scientific, technological, and environmental policy and decision-making issues. Pays $100 to $300. Query.

FINAL FRONTIER—1516 West Lake St., Suite 102, Minneapolis, MN 55408. Jeremiah Creedon, Ed. Articles, 1,500 to 3,000 words; columns, 800 words; and shorts, 250 words, about people, events, and "exciting possibilities" of the world's space programs. Pays about 25¢ a word, on acceptance. Query.

FOCUS—Turnkey Publications, 3420 Executive Center Dr., #250, Austin, TX 78731. Robin Perry, Ed. Articles, 700 to 4,000 words, on Data General computers. Photos a plus. Pays to $100, on publication. Query required.

THE FUTURIST—World Future Society, 4916 Elmo Ave., Bethesda, MD 20814. Timothy Willard, Man. Ed. Features, 1,000 to 5,000 words, on subjects pertaining to the future: environment, education, science, technology, etc. Pays in copies.

GENETIC ENGINEERING NEWS—1651 Third Ave., New York, NY 10128. John Sterling, Man. Ed. Articles on all aspects of biotechnology; feature articles and news articles. Pays varying rates, on acceptance. Query.

GEOBYTE—American Association of Petroleum Geologists, P.O. Box 979, Tulsa, OK 74101–0979. Ken Milam, Man. Ed. Articles, 20 typed pages, on computer applications in exploration and production of oil, gas, and energy minerals for geophysicists, geologists, and petroleum engineers. Pay varies, on acceptance. Queries preferred.

HOME OFFICE COMPUTING—Scholastic, Inc., 730 Broadway, New York, NY 10003. Mike Espindle, Man. Ed. Articles of interest to people operating businesses out of their homes: product roundups, profiles of successful businesses, marketing and financial tips and advice. Payment varies, on acceptance.

INCIDER—See *A + /Incider.*

INFOMART MAGAZINE—Infomart Corporate Communications, 1950 Stemmons Fwy., Suite 6038, Dallas, TX 75207. Address Jeff Anderson or Roy Miller. Articles, 100 to 800 words, on high-tech and business topics for chief information officers and management information system directors. Query. Payment is negotiable.

LINK-UP—143 Old Marlton Pike, Medford, NJ 08055. Joseph A. Webb, Ed. Dir. How-to pieces, hardware and software reviews, and current trends, 600 to 2,500 words, for business and education professionals who use computers and modems at work and at home. Pays $90 to $220, on publication. Book reviews, 500 to 800 words, $55. Photos a plus.

LOTUS—P. O. Box 9123, Cambridge, MA 02139. Rich Friedman, Ed.-in-Chief. Articles, 1,500 to 2,000 words, on business and professional applications of Lotus software. Query with outline required. Pay varies, on final approval.

MACWORLD—Editorial Proposals, 501 Second St., Suite 600, San Francisco, CA 94107. Reviews, news, consumer, and how-to articles relating to Macintosh personal computers; varying lengths. Query or send outline with screenshots, if applicable. Pays from $300 to $3,500, on acceptance. Send SASE for writers guidelines.

MOBILE OFFICE—21600 Oxnard St., Suite 480, Woodland Hills, CA 91367. Michael Meresman, Ed. Monthly. Articles, 1,500 to 2,000 words, and fillers on applications for mobile electronics. Query. Payment varies, on publication.

MODERN ELECTRONICS—See *Computer Craft.*

NETWORK WORLD—161 Worcester Rd., Framingham, MA 01701-9171. John Gallant, Ed. Articles, to 2,500 words, about applications of communications technology for management level users of data, voice, and video communications systems. Pays varying rates, on acceptance.

NIBBLE—P.O. Box 256, Lincoln, MA 01773-0256. Andrew Maddox, Man. Ed. Programs and programming methods, as well as short articles, reviews, and general-interest pieces for Apple II Computer users. Include program and article on disk. Send cover letter and sample program runs with manuscript. Pays $200 to $500 for major articles, $50 to $200 for shorter pieces. Guidelines.

OMNI—1965 Broadway, New York, NY 10023-5965. Keith Ferrell, Ed. Articles, 1,000 to 3,500 words, on scientific aspects of the future: space colonies, cloning, machine intelligence, ESP, origin of life, future arts, lifestyles, etc. Pays $800 to $3,500, $150 for short items, on acceptance. Query.

PCM MAGAZINE—Falsoft, Inc., 9509 US Highway 42, P.O. Box 385, Prospect, KY 40059. Judi Hutchinson, Ed. Articles and computer programs for Tandy portables and MS-DOS computers. Pays varying rates, on publication.

POPULAR ELECTRONICS—500-B Bi-County Blvd., Farmingdale, NY 11735. Carl Laron, Ed. Features, 1,500 to 2,500 words, for electronics hobbyists and experimenters. "Our readers are science oriented, understand computer theory and operation, and like to build electronics projects." Fillers and cartoons. Pays $25 to $350, on acceptance.

586

PUBLISH—Integrated Media, Inc., 501 Second St., San Francisco, CA 94107. Sandra Rosenzweig, Ed.-in-Chief. Features (1,200 to 2,000 words) and reviews (300 to 800 words) on all aspects of computerized publishing. Pays $400 for short articles and reviews, $900 and up for full-length features and reviews, on acceptance. Query James Martin, Exec. Ed.

RADIO-ELECTRONICS—500-B Bi-County Blvd., Farmingdale, NY 11735. Brian C. Fenton, Ed. Technical articles, 1,500 to 3,000 words, on all areas related to electronics. Pays $50 to $500, on acceptance.

THE RAINBOW—Falsoft, Inc., 9509 U. S. Highway 42, P. O. Box 385, Prospect, KY 40059. Tony Olive, Submissions Ed. Articles and computer programs for Tandy color computers. Pays varying rates, on publication.

SCIENCE PROBE!—500-B Bi-County Blvd., Farmingdale, NY 11735. Forrest M. Mims, III, Ed. Quarterly. Articles, 2,500 to 3,000 words, geared toward amateur scientists of all ages; color slides should be available with all articles. Pays $350 to $1,000, on acceptance.

THE SCIENCES—2 E. 63rd St., New York, NY 10021. Peter G. Brown, Ed. Essays and features, 2,000 to 4,000 words, and book reviews, on all scientific disciplines. Pays honorarium, on publication. Query.

SEA FRONTIERS—4600 Rickenbacker Causeway, Virginia Key, Miami, FL 33149. Bonnie Bilyeu Gordon, Ed. Illustrated articles, 500 to 3,000 words, on scientific advances related to the sea, biological, physical, chemical, or geological phenomena, ecology, conservation, etc., written in a popular style for lay readers. Send SASE for guidelines. Pays 25¢ a word, on acceptance. Query.

SHAREWARE MAGAZINE—1030D E. Duane Ave., Sunnyvale, CA 94086. Claudia Graziano, Man. Ed. Reviews of shareware programs and articles on related topics, 1,000 to 4,000 words. Payment varies, on publication. Query.

TECHNOLOGY & LEARNING—(formerly *Classroom Computer Learning*) Peter Li, Inc., 2169 E. Francisco Blvd., Suite A-4, San Rafael, CA 94901. Holly Brady, Ed. Articles, to 3,000 words, on computer use in the classroom: human-interest, philosophical articles, how-to pieces, software reviews, and hands-on ideas, for teachers of grades K through 12. Pay varies, on acceptance.

TECHNOLOGY REVIEW—MIT, W59–200, Cambridge, MA 02139. Steve Marcus, Ed. General-interest articles and more technical features, 1,500 to 5,000 words, on technology, the environment, and society. Pay varies, on publication. Query.

VOICE PROCESSING MAGAZINE—P.O. Box 42382, Houston, TX 77242. Kim Wilson Padgett, Ed. Technical articles, 2,000 to 2,400 words, and applications of voice mail and messaging, voice response, call processing, and voice/data networking. Pays flat fee. Query.

ANIMALS

AMERICAN FARRIERS JOURNAL—63 Great Rd., Maynard, MA 01754. Susan Philbrick, Ed. Articles, 800 to 5,000 words, on general farrier issues, hoof care, tool selection, equine lameness, and horse handling. Pays 30¢ per published line, $10 per published illustration or photo, on publication. Query.

AQUARIUM FISH—P.O. Box 6050, Mission Viejo, CA 92690. Edward Bauman, Ed. Articles, 2,000 to 4,000 words, on freshwater, saltwater, and pond fish, with or without color transparencies. (No "pet fish" stories, please.) Payment varies, on publication.

BIRD TALK—Box 6050, Mission Viejo, CA 92690. Karyn New, Ed. Articles for pet bird owners: care and feeding, training, safety, outstanding personal adventures, exotic birds in their native countries, profiles of celebrities' birds, travel to bird parks or bird shows. Pays 7¢ to 10¢ a word, after publication. Query or send manuscript; good transparencies a plus.

CAT FANCY—P.O. Box 6050, Mission Viejo, CA 92690. Kate Segnar, Ed. Fiction and nonfiction, to 3,000 words, on cat care, health, grooming, etc. Pays 5¢ a word, on publication.

DAIRY GOAT JOURNAL—W. 2997 Markert Rd., Helenville, WI 53137. Dave Thompson, Ed. Articles, to 1,500 words, on successful dairy goat owners, youths and interesting people associated with dairy goats. "Especially interested in practical husbandry ideas." Photos. Pays $50 to $250, on publication. Query.

DOG FANCY—P. O. Box 6050, Mission Viejo, CA 92690. Kim Thornton, Ed. Articles, 1,500 to 3,000 words, on dog care, health, grooming, breeds, activities, events, etc. Photos. Pays from 5¢ a word, on publication.

EQUUS—Fleet Street Corp., 656 Quince Orchard Rd., Gaithersburg, MD 20878. Laurie Prinz, Ed. Articles, 1,000 to 3,000 words, on all breeds of horses, covering their health, care, the latest advances in equine medicine and research. "Attempt to speak as one horse-person to another." Pays $100 to $400, on acceptance.

HORSE & RIDER—P.O. Box 72001, San Clemente, CA 92672. Juli Thorson, Ed. Sue M. Copeland, Man. Ed. Articles, 500 to 3,000 words, with photos, on western riding and general horse care: training, feeding, health, grooming, etc. Pays varying rates, on publication. Buys all rights. Guidelines.

HORSE ILLUSTRATED—P.O. Box 6050, Mission Viejo, CA 92690. Sharon Ralls Lemon, Ed. Articles, 1,500 to 2,500 words, on all aspects of owning and caring for horses. Photos. Pays 7¢ to 10¢ a word, on publication.

HORSEMEN'S YANKEE PEDLAR—785 Southbridge St., Auburn, MA 01501. Nancy L. Khoury, Pub. News and feature-length articles, about horses and horsemen in the Northeast. Photos. Pays $2 per published inch, on publication. Query.

HORSEPLAY—P.O. Box 130, Gaithersburg, MD 20884. Cordelia Doucet, Ed. Articles, 700 to 3,000 words, on eventing, show jumping, horse shows, dressage, driving, and fox hunting, for horse enthusiasts. Pays 10¢ a word, buys all rights, after publication.

LLAMAS—P.O. Box 1038, Dublin, OH 43017. Susan Ley, Asst. Ed. "The International Camelid Jounal," published 8 times yearly. Articles, 300 to 3,000 words, of interest to llama and alpaca owners. Pays $25 to $300, extra for photos, on acceptance. Query.

MUSHING—P.O. Box 149, Ester, AK 99725–0149. Todd Hoener, Pub. How-tos, profiles, interviews, and features, 1,500 to 2,000 words, and department pieces, 500 to 1,000 words, for competitive and recreational dog drivers and skijorers. International audience. Photos. Pays $30 to $250, after acceptance. Queries preferred. Guidelines.

PRACTICAL HORSEMAN—Gum Tree Corner, Unionville, PA 19375.

Joanne Tobey, Exec. Ed. How-to articles on horse care, English riding, and training. Pays on acceptance. Query.

PURE BRED DOGS/AMERICAN KENNEL GAZETTE—51 Madison Ave., New York, NY 10010. Elizabeth Bodner, DVM, Exec. Ed. Audrey Pavia, Sr. Ed. Articles, 1,000 to 2,500 words, relating to pure-bred dogs. Pays from $100 to $300, on acceptance. Query preferred.

SHEEP! MAGAZINE—W. 2997 Markert Rd., Helenville, WI 53137. Dave Thompson, Ed. Articles, to 1,500 words, on successful shepherds, woolcrafts, sheep raising, and sheep dogs. "Especially interested in people who raise sheep successfully as a sideline enterprise." Photos. Pays $80 to $300, extra for photos, on publication. Query first.

TROPICAL FISH HOBBYIST—1 T.F.H. Plaza, Neptune City, NJ 07753. Ray Hunziker, Ed. Articles, 500 to 3,000 words, for beginning and experienced tropical and marine fish enthusiasts. Photos. Pays $35 to $250, on acceptance. Query.

WILDLIFE CONSERVATION—New York Zoological Society, Bronx, NY 10460. Nancy Simmons, Sr. Ed. Articles, 1,500 to 2,000 words, that "probe conservation controversies to search for answers and help save threatened species." Payment varies, on acceptance. Guidelines.

PARENTING, CHILD CARE, AND DEVELOPMENT

AMERICAN BABY—475 Park Ave. S., New York, NY 10016. Judith Nolte, Ed. Articles, 1,000 to 2,000 words, for new or expectant parents on prenatal and infant care. Pays varying rates, on acceptance.

BABY TALK—636 Ave. of the Americas, New York, NY 10011. Susan Strecker, Ed. Articles, 1,500 to 3,000 words, by parents or professionals, on babies, baby care, etc. Pays varying rates, on acceptance. SASE required.

THE BIG APPLE PARENTS' PAPER—928 Broadway, Suite 709, New York, NY 10010. Helen Rosengren Freedman, Ed. Articles, 600 to 750 words, for NYC parents. Pays $50 to $75, (plus $25 cover bonus), on publication. Buys first NY-area rights.

GROWING CHILD/GROWING PARENT—22 N. Second St., Lafayette, IN 47902–0620. Nancy Kleckner, Ed. Articles, to 1,500 words, on subjects of interest to parents of children under 6, with emphasis on the issues, problems, and choices of being a parent. No personal-experience pieces or poetry. Pays 8¢ to 15¢ a word, on acceptance. Query.

HEALTHY KIDS—Cahners Publishing, 475 Park Ave. S., New York, NY 10016. Phyllis Steinberg, Ed. Published in two editions: "Birth-3" (quarterly) and "4–10 Years" (three times a year). Articles, 1,500 to 2,000 words, on the elements of raising a healthy, happy child (basic care, analysis of the growing mind, behavior patterns, nutrition, emergencies, etc.). "All articles should be written by experts or include interviews with appropriate pediatricians and other health-care professionals." Query. Pays $500 to $1,000, on acceptance.

LIVING WITH CHILDREN—MSN 140, 127 Ninth Ave. N., Nashville, TN 37234. Articles, 800 to 1,200 words, on parent-child relationships, told from a Christian perspective. Pays 5 ½¢ a word, after acceptance.

LIVING WITH PRESCHOOLERS—MSN 140, 127 Ninth Ave. N., Nashville, TN 37234. Articles, 800 to 1,200 words, and anecdotes, for Christian families. Pays 5 ½¢ a word, on acceptance.

LIVING WITH TEENAGERS—127 Ninth Ave. N., Nashville, TN 37234. Articles told from a Christian perspective for parents of teenagers; first-person approach preferred. Poetry, 4 to 16 lines. Pays 5 ½¢ a word, on acceptance, for articles.

NEW YORK FAMILY—420 E. 79th St., New York, NY 10021. Felice Shapiro, Susan Ross, Eds. Stephen Morison, Assoc. Ed. Articles related to family life in New York City. Pays $50 to $100, on publication. Same requirements for *Westchester Family*, for parents in Westchester County, NY, and *Connecticut Family*.

PARENTGUIDE NEWS—2 Park Ave., Suite 2012, New York, NY 10016. Leslie Elgort, Ed. Monthly. Articles, 1,000 to 1,500 words, related to New York families and parenting: trends, profiles, special programs and products, etc. Humor, jokes, puzzles, and photos also considered. Payment varies, on publication.

PARENTING—501 Second St., San Francisco, CA 94107. David Markus, Ed. Articles, 500 to 3,500 words, for parents of children up to 10, but especially under 6. Topics include education, health, fitness, nutrition, child development, psychology, and social issues. Query.

PARENTS—685 Third Ave., New York, NY 10017. Ann Pleshette Murphy, Ed.-in-Chief. Articles, 1,500 to 3,000 words, on parenting, family, women's and community issues, etc. Informal style with quotes from experts. Pays from $1,000, on acceptance. Query.

SEATTLE'S CHILD—P.O. Box 22578, Seattle, WA 98122. Ann Bergman, Ed. Articles, 400 to 2,500 words, of interest to parents, educators, and childcare providers of children under 12, plus investigative reports and consumer tips on issues affecting families in the Puget Sound region. Pays $75 to $400, on publication. Query required.

WORKING MOTHER—230 Park Ave., New York, NY 10169. Address Editorial Dept. Articles, to 1,000 words, that help women in their task of juggling job, home, and family. Payment varies, on acceptance.

MILITARY

THE AMERICAN LEGION MAGAZINE—Box 1055, Indianapolis, IN 46206. Daniel S. Wheeler, Ed.-in-Chief. Articles, 750 to 1,800 words, on current world affairs, public policy, and subjects of contemporary interest. Pays $100 to $1,000, on acceptance. Query.

ARMY MAGAZINE—2425 Wilson Blvd., Arlington, VA 22201–3385. L. James Binder, Ed.-in-Chief. Features, to 5,000 words, on military subjects. Essays, humor, history, news reports, first-person anecdotes. Pays 12¢ to 18¢ a word, $10 to $25 for anecdotes, on publication.

LEATHERNECK—Box 1775, Quantico, VA 22134–0776. William V.H. White, Ed. Articles, to 3,000 words, with photos, on U.S. Marines. Pays $50 per printed page, on acceptance. Query.

LIFE IN THE TIMES—The Times Journal Co., Springfield, VA 22159–0200. Margaret Roth, Ed. Travel articles, 900 words; and general-interest features, up to 3,000 words, of interest to military people and their families around the world. Pays from $125 to $350, on acceptance. Query first.

MILITARY HISTORY—602 S. King St., Suite 300, Leesburg, VA 22075. C. Brian Kelly, Ed. Bimonthly on the strategy, tactics, and personalities of military history. Department pieces, 2,000 words, on espionage, weaponry, personality, and travel. Features, 4,000 words, with 500-word sidebars. Pays $200 to $400, on publication. Query. Guidelines.

MILITARY LIFESTYLE MAGAZINE—4800 Montgomery Ln., Suite 710, Bethesda, MD 20814–5341. Hope Daniels, Ed. Articles, 1,000 to 1,800 words, for active-duty military families in the U.S. and overseas, on lifestyles, child-raising, health, food, fashion, travel, sports and leisure; short fiction. Pays $300 to $800, on publication. Query first. No poetry, no historical reminiscences.

OFF DUTY MAGAZINE—3303 Harbor Blvd., Suite C-2, Costa Mesa, CA 92626. Gary Burch, U.S. Ed. Travel articles, 1,800 to 2,000 words, for active-duty military Americans (age 20 to 40) and their families, on U.S. regions or cities. Must have wide scope; no out-of-the-way places. Military angle essential. Photos. Pays from 20¢ a word, extra for photos, on acceptance. Query required. Guidelines. Limited market.

THE RETIRED OFFICER MAGAZINE—201 N. Washington St., Alexandria, VA 22314. Articles, 800 to 2,000 words, of interest to military retirees and their families. Current military/political affairs: recent military history (especially Vietnam and Korea), humor, travel, hobbies, military family lifestyles, wellness, and second-career job opportunities. Photos a plus. Pays to $500, on acceptance. Queries required, no unsolicited manuscripts; address Manuscript Ed. Guidelines.

VFW MAGAZINE—406 West 34th St., Kansas City, MO 64111. Richard K. Kolb, Ed. Magazine for Veterans of Foreign Wars and their families. Articles, 1,500 words, on current events, veteran affairs, and military history, with veteran angle. Photos. Pays from $500, extra for photos, on acceptance. Guidelines. Query first.

HISTORICAL

AMERICAN HERITAGE—60 Fifth Ave., New York, NY 10011. Richard F. Snow, Ed. Articles, 750 to 5,000 words, on U.S. history and background of American life and culture from the beginning to recent times. No fiction. Pays from $300 to $1,500, on acceptance. Query. SASE.

AMERICAN HERITAGE OF INVENTION & TECHNOLOGY—60 Fifth Ave., New York, NY 10011. Frederick Allen, Ed. Articles, 2,000 to 5,000 words, on history of technology in America, for the sophisticated general reader. Query. Pays on acceptance.

AMERICAN HISTORY ILLUSTRATED—6405 Flank Dr., P.O. Box 8200, Harrisburg, PA 17105. Articles, 3,000 to 5,000 words, soundly researched. Style should be popular, not scholarly. No travelogues, fiction, or puzzles. Pays $300 to $650, on acceptance. Query with SASE required.

CHICAGO HISTORY—Clark St. at North Ave., Chicago, IL 60614. Russell Lewis, Ed. Articles, to 4,500 words, on political, social, and cultural history. Pays to $250, on publication. Query.

EARLY AMERICAN LIFE—Box 8200, Harrisburg, PA 17105–8200. Frances Carnahan, Ed. Illustrated articles, 1,000 to 3,000 words, on early American life: arts, crafts, furnishings, architecture; travel features about historic sites and country inns. Pays $50 to $500, on acceptance. Query.

THE HIGHLANDER—P.O. Box 397, Barrington, IL 60011. Angus Ray, Ed.

Bimonthly. Articles, 1,300 to 1,900 words, related to Scottish history. "We are not concerned with modern Scotland or current problems in Scotland." Pays $100 to $150, on acceptance.

HISTORIC PRESERVATION—1785 Massachusetts Ave. N.W., Washington, DC 20036. Anne Elizabeth Powell, Ed. Lively feature articles from published writers, 1,500 to 4,000 words, on residential restoration, preservation issues, and people involved in preserving America's heritage. High-quality photos. Pays $300 to $1,000, extra for photos, on acceptance. Query required.

LABOR'S HERITAGE—10000 New Hampshire Ave., Silver Spring, MD 20903. Stuart Kaufman, Ed. Quarterly journal of The George Meany Memorial Archives. Articles, 20 to 30 pages, for labor scholars, labor union members, and the general public. Pays in copies.

MILITARY HISTORY—602 S. King St., Suite 300, Leesburg, VA 22075. C. Brian Kelly, Ed. Bimonthly on the strategy, tactics, and personalities of military history. Department pieces, 2,000 words, on espionage, weaponry, personality, and travel. Features, 4,000 words, with 500-word sidebars. Pays $200 to $400, on publication. Query. Guidelines.

OLD WEST—See *True West*.

PENNSYLVANIA HERITAGE—P.O. Box 1026, Harrisburg, PA 17108–1026. Michael J. O'Malley III, Ed. Quarterly of the Pennsylvania Historical and Museum Commission. Articles, 3,000 to 4,000 words, that "introduce readers to the state's rich culture and historic legacy and involve them in such a way as to ensure that Pennsylvania past has a future." Pays $300 to $500, up to $100 for photos or drawings, on acceptance.

PERSIMMON HILL—1700 N.E. 63rd St., Oklahoma City, OK 73111. M.J. Van Deventer, Ed. Published by the National Cowboy Hall of Fame. Articles, 1,500 to 3,000 words, on Western history and art, cowboys, ranching, and nature. Top-quality illustrations a must. Pays from $100 to $250, on acceptance.

TRUE WEST—P.O. Box 2107, Stillwater, OK 74076–2107. John Joerschke, Ed. True stories, 500 to 4,500 words, with photos, about the Old West to 1930. Some contemporary stories with historical slant. Source list required. Pays 3¢ to 6¢ a word, extra for B&W photos, on acceptance. Same address and requirements for *Old West*.

COLLEGE, CAREERS

THE BLACK COLLEGIAN—1240 S. Broad St., New Orleans, LA 70125. K. Kazi-Ferrouillet, Man. Ed. Articles, to 2,000 words, on experiences of African-American students, careers, and how-to subjects. Pays on publication. Query.

CAMPUS LIFE—465 Gundersen Dr., Carol Stream, IL 60188. Jim Long, Ed. Articles reflecting Christian values and world view, for high school and college students. Humor, general fiction, and true, first-person experiences. "If we have a choice of fiction, how-to, and a strong first-person story, we'll go with the true story every time." Photo essays, cartoons. Pays from $125, on acceptance. Query.

CAMPUS USA—1801 Rockville Pike, Suite 216, Rockville, MD 20852. Gerald S. Snyder, Ed. Articles (500 to 1,200 words) on the tastes, feelings, and moods of today's college students: careers, computing, travel, movies, music, fashion, and sports. Pays $200 for "Campus USA WallBoards" on computers, business, music, lifestyles, sports, and health. Query required.

CAREER WOMAN—See *Minority Engineer.*

CAREERS AND THE DISABLED—See *Minority Engineer.*

CIRCLE K—3636 Woodview Trace, Indianapolis, IN 46268. Nicholas K. Drake, Exec. Ed. Serious and light articles, 2,000 to 2,500 words, on careers, college issues, leadership development, self-help, community service and involvement. Pays $225 to $400, on acceptance. Queries preferred.

COLLEGE BROADCASTER—National Assoc. of College Broadcasters, Box 1955, Brown University, Providence, RI 02912. Articles, 500 to 2,000 words, on college radio and TV station operations and media careers. Published eight times yearly. Query. Pays in copies.

EQUAL OPPORTUNITY—See *Minority Engineer.*

JOURNAL OF CAREER PLANNING & EMPLOYMENT—62 Highland Ave., Bethlehem, PA 18017. Mimi Collins, Ed. Bill Beebe, Assoc. Ed. Quarterly. Articles, 3,000 to 4,000 words, on topics related to career planning, placement, recruitment, and employment of new college graduates. Pays $200 to $400, on acceptance. Query first with clips. Guidelines.

KEY.DC—5323 41st St. N.W., Washington, DC 20015. Soraya Chemaly, Ed. Tabloid. Profiles and informational features, 900 to 2,000 words, of interest to college students in Washington, DC. "Distributed to 22 area colleges and universities. Primarily arts and entertainment with regular profiles and issue/news/information features and supplements." Query for articles and fillers. Pays 5¢ a word for profiles and features; 3¢ word for supplements, on publication.

MINORITY ENGINEER—44 Broadway, Greenlawn, NY 11740. James Schneider, Exec. Ed. Articles, 1,000 to 1,500 words, for college students, on career opportunities in engineering fields; techniques of job hunting; developments in and applications of new technologies. Interviews. Profiles. Pays 10¢ a word, on publication. Query. Same address and requirements for *Woman Engineer, Equal Opportunity, Career Woman,* and *Careers and the Disabled.*

STUDENT LEADERSHIP—P.O. Box 7895, Madison, WI 53707–7895. Jeff Yourison, Ed. Articles, to 2,000 words, and poetry for college students. All material should reflect a Christian world view. Queries required.

UCLA MAGAZINE—405 Hilgard Ave., Los Angeles, CA 90024–1391. Mark Wheeler, Ed. Quarterly. Articles, 2,000 words, related to UCLA through research, alumni, students, etc. Queries required. Pays to $900, on acceptance.

WHAT'S NEW MAGAZINE—8305 Paces Oaks Blvd., Suite 438, Charlotte, NC 28213. Bob Leja, Ed. General-interest articles, 150 to 300 words, on music, movies, books, cars, travel, sports, food, wine, consumer electronics, computers, arts, and entertainment. Pays varying rates, on publication. Query required.

WOMAN ENGINEER—See *Minority Engineer.*

OP-ED MARKETS

Op-ed pages in newspapers (those that run opposite the editorials) offer writers an excellent opportunity to air their opinions, views, ideas, and insights on a wide spectrum of subjects and in styles, from the highly personal and informal essay to the more serious commentary on politics, foreign affairs, and news events. Humor and nostalgia often find a place here. Often newspapers will buy exclusive rights to a piece in a specific geographic area, and the writer is free to resell the piece outside that area.

THE ARGUS LEADER—P.O. Box 5034, Sioux Falls, SD 57117–5034. Rob Swenson, Editorial Page Ed. Articles, to 850 words, on a wide variety of subjects for "Different Voices" column. Prefer local writers with an expertise on their subject. No payment made.

ARIZONA REPUBLIC—120 East Van Buren, Phoenix, AZ 85004. James Hill, Ed. Articles, 800 to 1,000 words, on domestic and foreign affairs, environment, religion, politics, law, etc. Pays $150, on publication. Query. Exclusive rights: AZ.

THE BALTIMORE SUN—P.O. Box 1377, Baltimore, MD 21278–0001. Hal Piper, Opinion-Commentary Page Ed. Articles, 600 to 1,500 words, on a wide range of topics: politics, education, foreign affairs, lifestyles, etc. Humor. Payment varies, on publication. Exclusive rights: MD and DC.

THE BOSTON GLOBE—P.O. Box 2378, Boston, MA 02107–2378. Marjorie Pritchard, Ed. Articles, to 700 words, on economics, education, environment, foreign affairs, and regional interest. Send complete manuscript. Pays $100, on publication. Exclusive rights: New England.

BOSTON HERALD—One Herald Sq., Boston, MA 02106. Editorial Page Ed. Pieces, 600 to 800 words, on economics, foreign affairs, politics, regional interest, and seasonal topics. Payment varies, on publication. Prefer submissions from regional writers. Exclusive rights: MA, RI, and NH.

THE CAPITAL TIMES—P.O. Box 8060, Madison, WI 53708. Phil Haslanger, Ed. Articles, 600 to 700 words, on education, environment, regional interest, and religion. Pays $25, on publication.

THE CHARLOTTE OBSERVER—P.O. Box 32188, Charlotte, NC 28232. Jane McAlister Pope, Ed. Well-written, thought-provoking articles, to 700 words. Prefer local writers. Pays $50, on publication. "No simultaneous submissions in NC or SC."

THE CHICAGO TRIBUNE—435 N. Michigan Ave., Chicago, IL 60611. Richard Liefer, Op-Ed Page Ed. Pieces, to 800 words, on domestic affairs, environment, regional interest, and science. "Writers must be experts in their fields." Pays about $150, on publication. SASE required.

THE CHRISTIAN SCIENCE MONITOR—One Norway St., Boston, MA 02115. Scott Baldauf, Ed. Pieces, 700 to 800 words, on domestic affairs, economics, education, environment, foreign affairs, law, and politics. Pays $100 to $150, on acceptance. "We retain all rights for 90 days after publication. Submissions must be exclusive."

THE CHRONICLE—901 Mission St., San Francisco, CA 94103. Stephen Schwartz, Ed. Articles, 800 to 1,000 words, on a wide range of subjects. Pays $50 to $150, on publication. Query with SASE. "No anti-gay or racist pieces." Exclusive rights: Bay area.

THE CLEVELAND PLAIN DEALER—1801 Superior Ave., Cleveland, OH 44114. Jim Strang, Op-Ed Ed. Pieces, 700 to 900 words, on a wide variety of subjects. Pays $50, on publication.

DALLAS MORNING NEWS—Communications Center, P.O. Box 655237, Dallas, TX 75265. Carolyn Barta, "Viewpoints" Ed. Pieces, 750 words, on politics, education, foreign and domestic affairs, seasonal and regional issues. No humor. Pay averages $75, on publication. SASE required. Exclusive rights: Dallas/Ft. Worth area.

DALLAS TIMES HERALD—1101 Pacific, Dallas, TX 75202. Articles, 700 words, on politics, education, economics, foreign and domestic affairs. Send complete manuscript. No payment.

DENVER POST—P.O. Box 1709, Denver, CO 80201. Bob Ewegen, Ed. Articles, 400 to 700 words, with local or regional angle. Pays $35 to $50, on publication. Query.

DES MOINES REGISTER—P.O. Box 957, Des Moines, IA 50304. "Opinion" Page Ed. Articles, 500 to 850 words, on all topics. Pays $35 to $75, on publication. Exclusive rights: IA.

THE DETROIT FREE PRESS—321 W. Lafayette St., Detroit, MI 48231. Address Op-Ed Editor. Opinion pieces, to 1,000 words, on domestic and foreign affairs, economics, education, environment, law, politics, and regional interest. Pays $50 to $100, on publication. Query. Exclusive rights: MI and northern OH.

THE DETROIT NEWS—615 Lafayette Blvd., Detroit, MI 48226. Richard Burr, Ed. Pieces, 600 to 900 words, on a wide variety of subjects. Pays $75, on publication.

THE FLINT JOURNAL—200 E. First St., Flint, MI 48502. Articles, 650 words, of regional interest by local writers. No payment. Limited market.

FORT WORTH STAR-TELEGRAM—P.O. Box 1870, Fort Worth, TX 76101. Ann Thompson, Op-Ed Ed. Articles, to 900 words, on a variety of subjects. No human interest, lifestyle, nostalgia, religious, or seasonal material. "Most of our limited space goes to local writers on local topics." Pays $75, on publication. Exclusive rights: Dallas area.

FRESNO BEE—1626 E St., Fresno, CA 93786–0001. Tom Kirwan, Ed. Articles, 800 words: human interest, nostalgia, regional interest, and seasonal material. "Our main interest is in material that hasn't been done to death in editorials and syndicated columns; material in which the writer has personal knowledge or experience." Send complete manuscript. Pays $100, on acceptance.

THE HOUSTON POST—P.O. Box 4747, Houston, TX 77210–4747. Lynne Millar, Ed. Opinions and current affairs pieces, 900 words, on wide variety of topics. Send complete manuscript. Pays $40, on publication. Exclusive rights: Houston area.

INDIANAPOLIS STAR—P.O. Box 145, Indianapolis, IN 46206–0145. John H. Lyst, Ed. Articles, 700 to 800 words, of regional interest. Pays $40, on publication. Exclusive rights: IN.

JOURNAL AMERICAN—P.O. Box 90130, Bellevue, WA 98009–9230. Karl Thunemann, Editorial Page Ed. Articles, to 600 words, by local authors on local and regional issues. "Very limited market." No payment.

LONG BEACH PRESS-TELEGRAM—604 Pine Ave., Long Beach, CA 90844. John J. Fried, Ed. Articles, 750 to 900 words, on lifestyles and regional topics. Writers must be local. "Articles on baby boomer issues are of interest to us." Pays $75, on publication. Exclusive rights: Los Angeles area.

LOS ANGELES TIMES—Times Mirror Sq., Los Angeles, CA 90053. Op-Ed Ed. Commentary pieces, to 800 words, on many subjects. "Not interested in nostalgia or first-person reaction to faraway events." Payment varies, on publication. Limited market. SASE required.

LOUISVILLE COURIER-JOURNAL—525 W. Broadway, Louisville, KY 40202. Op-Ed Ed. Pieces, 750 words, on regional topics. Author must live in the area. Pays $25 to $50, on publication. Very limited market.

THE NEW YORK TIMES—229 W. 43rd St., New York, NY 10036. Address Op-Ed, 10th Floor. Pieces, 850 words, on topics including public policy, science, lifestyles, and ideas. "Send copy of the article and clips. No queries!" Pays $150, on publication. Buys first North American rights.

NEWSDAY—"Viewpoints," 235 Pinelawn Rd., Melville, NY 11747. Noel Rubinton, "Viewpoints" Ed. Pieces, 700 to 800 words, on a variety of topics. Pays $150, on publication.

THE OREGONIAN—1320 S.W. Broadway, Portland, OR 97201. Address Forum Ed. Articles, 900 to 1,000 words, on a wide variety of subjects. Send complete manuscript. Pays $100, on publication.

PITTSBURGH POST GAZETTE—50 Blvd. of the Allies, Pittsburgh, PA 15222. Editorial Page Ed. Articles, to 800 words, on a variety of subjects. No humor. Pays $75 to $150, on publication. SASE required.

PORTLAND PRESS HERALD—P.O. Box 1460, Portland, ME 04104. Op-Ed Page Ed. Articles, 750 words, on any topic with regional tie-in. Writers must live in Maine or New Hampshire. Pays $50, on publication. Query. Exclusive rights: ME and NH.

THE SACRAMENTO BEE—2100 Q St., Sacramento, CA 95852. Rhea Wilson, Opinion Ed. Op-ed pieces, to 1,000 words; topics of state and regional interest only. Pays $150, on publication. Query.

ST. LOUIS POST-DISPATCH—900 N. Tucker Blvd., St. Louis, MO 63101. Donna Korando, Ed. Articles, 700 words, on economics, education, science, politics, foreign and domestic affairs, and the environment. Pays $70, on publication. "Goal is to have half of the articles by local writers."

ST. PAUL PIONEER PRESS DISPATCH—345 Cedar St., St. Paul, MN 55101. Robert J.R. Johnson, Ed. Uses pieces, to 750 words, on a variety of topics. Prefer authors with a connection to the area. Pays $50, on publication.

THE SAN FRANCISCO CHRONICLE—901 Mission St., San Francisco, CA 94103. Marsha Vande Berg, Open Forum Ed. Articles, 500 and 700 words, "that are relevant to public policy debates and push the debates one or two steps forward." Also, well-crafted humor pieces. Pays to $150 ($75 for unsolicited pieces), on publication.

SAN FRANCISCO EXAMINER—110 5th St., San Francisco, CA 94103. Op-Ed Ed. Well-written articles, 500 to 650 words, on any subject. "No foreign policy analysis by amateurs." Payment varies, on publication.

SAN JOSE MERCURY NEWS—750 Ridder Park Dr., San Jose, CA 95190. Articles, 750 words, on any subject. Prefer local writers. Pays $75, on publication. Exclusive rights: Bay area.

SEATTLE POST-INTELLIGENCER—P.O. Box 1109, Seattle, WA 98111. Charles J. Dunsire, Editorial Page Ed. Articles, 750 to 800 words, on foreign and domestic affairs, environment, education, politics, regional interest, religion, science, and seasonal material. Prefer writers who live in the area. Pays $75 to $150, on publication. SASE required. Very limited market.

TULSA WORLD—P.O. Box 1770, Tulsa, OK 74102. Articles, about 1,500 words, on subjects of local or regional interest. Payment varies, on publication. Query. Exclusive rights: Tulsa area.

USA TODAY—P.O. Box 500, Washington, DC 20044. Sid Hurlburt, Ed./ Columns. Articles, 380 to 430 words. Very limited market. Query. "Because topics are presented in debate format, most of our guest columnists are commissioned to specifically react to the contrary view." Pays $125, on publication.

THE WALL STREET JOURNAL—Editorial Page, 200 Liberty St., New York, NY 10281. Melanie Kirkpatrick, Editorials Ed. Articles, to 1,500 words, on politics, economics, law, education, environment, humor (occasionally), and foreign and domestic affairs. Articles must be of national interest by writers with expertise in their field. Pays $150 to $300, on publication.

WASHINGTON TIMES—3600 New York Ave. N.E., Washington, DC 20002. Charles Wheeler, Ed. Articles, 800 to 1,000 words, on a variety of subjects. No pieces written in the first-person. "Syndicated columnists cover the 'big' issues; find an area that is off the beaten path." Pays $150, on publication. Exclusive rights: DC and Baltimore area.

ADULT MAGAZINES

CAVALIER—2600 Douglas Rd., Suite 600, Coral Gables, FL 33134. Nye Willden, Man. Ed. Articles with photos, and fiction, 1,500 to 3,000 words, for sophisticated young men. Pays to $400 for articles, to $250 for fiction, on publication. Query for articles.

CHIC—9171 Wilshire Blvd., Suite 300, Beverly Hills, CA 90210. Doug Oliver, Exec. Ed. Sex-related articles, interviews, erotic fiction, 2,500 to 3,500 words. Query for articles. Pays $750 for articles, $500 for fiction, on acceptance.

FORUM, THE INTERNATIONAL JOURNAL OF HUMAN RELA-TIONS—1965 Broadway, New York, NY 10023–5965. Don Myrus, Ed. Articles, 2,500 words; interested in well-written, erotic fiction and essays on matters of a sexual nature. Payment varies, on acceptance. Query.

GALLERY—401 Park Ave. S., New York, NY 10016–8802. Marc Lichter, Ed.-in-Chief. Barry Janoff, Man. Ed. Articles, investigative pieces, interviews, profiles, to 3,500 words, for sophisticated men. Short humor, satire, service pieces, and fiction. Photos. Pays varying rates, half on acceptance, half on publication. Query.

GENESIS—1776 Broadway, 20th Fl., New York, NY 10019. Henry Krinkle, Ed. Articles, 2,500 words; celebrity interviews, 2,500 words. Sexually explicit non-fiction features, 3,000 words. Photo essays. Pays 60 days after acceptance. Query.

HARVEY FOR LOVING PEOPLE—Suite 2305, 450 Seventh Ave., New York, NY 10001. Harvey Shapiro, Ed./Pub. Sexually oriented articles and fiction, to 2,500 words. Pays on publication. Query for articles.

PENTHOUSE—1965 Broadway, New York, NY 10023. Peter Bloch, Ed. General-interest profiles, interviews, or investigative articles, to 5,000 words. Interviews, 5,000 words, with introductions. Pays to $1 a word, on acceptance.

PLAYBOY—680 N. Lakeshore Dr., Chicago, IL 60611. John Rezek, Articles Ed. Alice K. Turner, Fiction Ed. Articles, 3,500 to 6,000 words, and sophisticated fiction, 1,000 to 10,000 words (5,000 preferred), for urban men. Humor; satire. Science fiction. Pays to $5,000 for articles, to $5,000 for fiction, $1,000 for short-shorts, on acceptance.

PLAYERS—8060 Melrose Ave., Los Angeles, CA 90046. Joe Nazel, Ed. Articles, 1,000 to 3,000 words, for black men: politics, economics, travel, fashion, grooming, entertainment, sports, interviews, fiction, humor, satire, health, and sex. Photos a plus. Pays on publication.

PLAYGIRL—801 Second Ave., New York, NY 10017. Susan Bax, Man. Ed. Articles, 1,500 words, for women 18 to 34. Celebrity interviews, 1,500 to 2,000 words. Humor. Pays varying rates, on acceptance.

FICTION MARKETS

This list gives the fiction requirements of general- and special-interest magazines, including those that publish detective and mystery, science fiction and fantasy, romance and confession stories. Other good markets for short fiction are the *College, Literary and Little Magazines* where, though payment is modest (usually in copies only), publication can help a beginning writer achieve recognition by editors at the larger magazines. Juvenile fiction markets are listed under *Juvenile, Teenage, and Young Adult Magazines*. Publishers of book-length fiction manuscripts are listed under *Book Publishers*.

All manuscripts must be typed double-space and submitted with self-addressed envelopes bearing postage sufficient for the return of the material. Use good white paper; onion skin and erasable bond are not acceptable. *Always* keep a copy of the manuscript, since occasionally a manuscript is lost in the mail. Magazines may take several weeks—often longer—to read and report on submissions. If an editor has not reported on a manuscript after a reasonable amount of time, write a brief, courteous letter of inquiry.

ABORIGINAL SF—P.O. Box 2449, Woburn, MA 01888–0849. Charles C. Ryan, Ed. Stories, 2,500 to 6,000 words, with a unique scientific idea, human or alien character, plot, and theme of lasting value; "must be science fiction; no fantasy, horror, or sword and sorcery." Pays $250. Send SASE for guidelines.

AFTER HOURS—P.O. Box 538, Sunset Beach, CA 90742–0538. William G. Raley, Ed. Quarterly. Fantasy and horror, to 6,000 words, set after sundown. "If it's too weird or off-the-wall for other magazines, send it here." Pays 1¢ per word, on acceptance, plus one copy.

AIM MAGAZINE—P.O. Box 20554, Chicago, IL 60620. Ruth Apilado, Ed. Short stories, 800 to 3,000 words, geared to promoting racial harmony and peace. Pays from $15 to $25, on publication. Annual contest.

ALFRED HITCHCOCK'S MYSTERY MAGAZINE—380 Lexington Ave., New York, NY 10168–0035. Cathleen Jordan, Ed. Well-plotted, plausible mystery, suspense, detection and crime stories, to 14,000 words; "ghost stories, humor, futuristic or atmospheric tales are all possible, as long as they include a crime or the suggestion of one." Pays 5¢ a word, on acceptance. Guidelines with SASE.

ALOHA, THE MAGAZINE OF HAWAII AND THE PACIFIC—49 S. Hotel St., Suite 309, Honolulu, HI 96813. Cheryl Tsutsumi, Ed. Fiction to 4,000 words, with a Hawaii focus. Pays $150 to $300, on publication. Query.

AMAZING STORIES—Box 111, Lake Geneva, WI 53147. Mr. Kim Mohan, Ed. Janis Wells, Asst. Ed. Monthly. Original, previously unpublished science fiction, fantasy, and horror, 1,000 to 25,000 words. Pays 6¢ to 10¢ a word, on acceptance.

ANALOG: SCIENCE FICTION/SCIENCE FACT—380 Lexington Ave., New York, NY 10168–0035. Stanley Schmidt, Ed. Science fiction, with strong characters in believable future or alien setting: short stories, 2,000 to 7,500 words; novelettes, 10,000 to 20,000 words; serials, to 70,000 words. Pays 5¢ to 8¢ a word, on acceptance. Query for novels.

THE ATLANTIC—745 Boylston St., Boston, MA 02116. William Whitworth, Ed. Short stories, 2,000 to 6,000 words, of highest literary quality, with "fully developed narratives, distinctive characterization, freshness in language, and a resolution of some kind." Pays excellent rates, on acceptance.

THE ATLANTIC ADVOCATE—P.O. Box 3370, Fredericton, N.B., Canada E3B 5A2. Marilee Little, Ed. Fiction, 1,000 to 1,500 words, with regional angle. Pays to 10¢ a word, on publication.

ATLANTIC SALMON JOURNAL—P.O. Box 289, Guysborough, Canada B0H 1N0. Harry Bruce, Ed. Address submissions to Beth Jackson. Fiction, 1,500 to 2,500 words, related to angling or conservation of Atlantic salmon. Pays $100 to $325, on publication.

THE BOSTON GLOBE MAGAZINE—*The Boston Globe*, Boston, MA 02107. Ande Zellman, Ed. Short stories, to 3,000 words. Include SASE. Pays on acceptance.

BOYS' LIFE—1325 Walnut Hill Ln., P.O. Box 152079, Irving, TX 75015–2079. Kathy Vilim DaGroomes, Fiction Ed. Publication of the Boy Scouts of America. Humor, mystery, SF, adventure, 500 to 1,200 words, for 8- to 18-year-old boys; study back issues. Pays from $750, on acceptance. Send SASE for guidelines.

BUFFALO SPREE MAGAZINE—Box 38, Buffalo, NY 14226. Johanna V. Shotell, Ed. Fiction and humor, to 1,800 words, for readers in the western New York region. Pays $75 to $100, on publication.

CAMPUS LIFE—465 Gundersen Dr., Carol Stream, IL 60188. James Long, Ed. Fiction and humor, reflecting Christian values (no overtly religious material), 1,000 to 4,000 words, for high school and college students. Pays from $150 to $400, on acceptance. Limited free-lance market. Queries only; SASE.

CAPPER'S—616 Jefferson Ave., Topeka, KS 66607–1188. Nancy Peavler, Ed. Short novel-length family-oriented or romance stories. Also very limited market for short stories, 5,000 to 7,500 words, that can be divided into two or three installments. Pays $75 to $250. Submit complete manuscript.

CAT FANCY—P.O. Box 6050, Mission Viejo, CA 92690. K.E. Segnar, Ed. Fiction and nonfiction, to 3,000 words, about cats. Pays 5¢ a word, on publication.

CATHOLIC FORESTER—P.O. Box 3012, 425 W. Shuman Blvd., Naperville, IL 60566–7012. Barbara A. Cunningham, Ed. Official publication of the Catholic Order of Foresters. Fiction, to 3,000 words (prefer shorter); "looking for more contemporary, meaningful stories dealing with life today." No sex or violence or "preachy" stories; religious angle not required. Pays from 5¢ a word, on acceptance.

599

CAVALIER—2600 Douglas Rd., Suite 600, Coral Gables, FL 33134. Maurice DeWalt, Fiction Ed. Sexually oriented fiction, to 3,000 words, for sophisticated young men. Pays to $250, on publication.

COBBLESTONE—30 Grove St., Peterborough, NH 03458–1454. Carolyn P. Yoder, Ed.-in-Chief. Fiction must relate to monthly theme, 500 to 1,200 words, for children aged 8 to 14 years. Pays 10¢ to 15¢ a word, on publication. Send SASE for editorial guidelines.

COMMENTARY—165 E. 56th St., New York, NY 10022. Marion Magid, Ed. Fiction, of high literary quality, on contemporary social or Jewish issues. Pays on publication.

COSMOPOLITAN—224 W. 57th St., New York, NY 10019. Betty Kelly, Fiction and Books Ed. Short shorts, 1,500 to 3,000 words, and short stories, 4,000 to 6,000 words, focusing on contemporary man-woman relationships. Solid, upbeat plots, sharp characterization; female protagonists preferred. "Submission cannot be returned without SASE." Pays $800 for short shorts; from $1,000 for short stories.

COUNTRY WOMAN—P.O. Box 643, Milwaukee, WI 53201. Kathy Pohl, Man. Ed. Fiction, 750 to 1,000 words, of interest to rural women; protagonist must be a country woman. "Stories should focus on life in the country, its problems and joys, as experienced by country women; must be upbeat and positive." Pays $90 to $125, on acceptance.

CRICKET—Box 300, Peru, IL 61354–0300. Marianne Carus, Pub./Ed.-in-Chief. Fiction, 200 to 1,500 words, for 6- to 14-year-olds. Pays to 25¢ a word, on publication. Return envelope and postage required.

DISCOVERIES—6401 The Paseo, Kansas City, MO 64131. Latta Jo Knapp, Middler Ed. Fiction, 600 to 1,000 words, for children grades 3 to 6, defining Christian experiences and values. Pays 3 ½¢ a word, on acceptance.

DIVER MAGAZINE—295–10991 Shellbridge Way, Richmond, B.C., Canada V6X 3C6. Peter Vassilopoulos, Pub./Ed. Fiction related to diving. Humor. Pays $2.50 per column inch, on publication. Query.

EASYRIDERS MAGAZINE—P. O. Box 3000, Agoura Hills, CA 91301–0800. Keith R. Ball, Ed. Fiction, 3,000 to 5,000 words. Pays from 15¢ a word, on acceptance.

ELLERY QUEEN'S MYSTERY MAGAZINE—380 Lexington Ave., New York, NY 10017. Janet Hutchings, Ed. High-quality detective, crime, and mystery stories, 4,000 to 6,000 words; "we like a mix of classic detection and suspenseful crime." "First Stories" by unpublished writers. Pays 3¢ to 8¢ a word, on acceptance.

EMERGE—599 Broadway, 12th Floor, New York, NY 10012. Wilmer Ames, Pub./Ed.-in-Chief. High-quality fiction of interest to middle-class black Americans. Pays from 50¢ a word, after acceptance.

ESQUIRE—1790 Broadway, New York, NY 10019. Terry McDonell, Ed.-in-Chief. Send finished manuscript of short story. (Only one at a time.) No full-length novels. No pornography, science fiction, or "true romance" stories.

EVANGEL—Light and Life Press, Box 535002, Indianapolis, IN 46253–5002. Vera Bethel, Ed. Free Methodist. Fiction, 1,200 words, with personal faith in Christ shown as instrumental in solving problems. Pays $45, on publication.

FAITH 'N STUFF—c/o *Guideposts*, 747 Third Ave., New York, NY 10017. Mary Lou Carney, Ed. Bible-based bimonthly for 7- to 12-year-olds. Problem fiction, 1,500 words, with "realistic dialogue and sharp imagery. No preachy stories about Bible-toting children." Pays $75 to $250 for all rights, on acceptance. No reprints.

FAMILY CIRCLE—110 Fifth Ave., New York, NY 10011. Kathy Sagan, Fiction Ed. Very limited market: seeks quality short stories and short shorts that reflect real-life situations and seasonal material. No unsolicited manuscripts.

FICTION INTERNATIONAL—English Dept., San Diego State Univ., San Diego, CA 92182. Harold Jaffe and Larry McCaffery, Eds. Post-modernist and politically committed fiction and theory. Submit between Sept. 1st and Dec. 15th.

FIRST FOR WOMEN—P.O. Box 1649, Englewood Cliffs, NJ 07632. Bibi Wein, Fiction Ed. Well-written, mainstream stories, 3,000 to 4,000 words, reflecting the concerns of contemporary women; no formula or experimental fiction. Also: short-shorts, 850 to 1,000 words. A humorous twist is welcome. Pay varies, on acceptance. SASE. Do not query for fiction. Allow 8 to 10 weeks for response, less for short-shorts.

FLY ROD & REEL—P.O. Box 370, Camden, ME 04843. James E. Butler, Man. Ed. Occasional fiction, 2,000 to 2,500 words, related to fly fishing. Special annual fiction issue published in summer. Payment varies, on publication.

GALLERY—401 Park Ave. S., New York, NY 10016–8802. Barry Janoff, Ed. Dir. Peter Emshwiller, Fiction Ed. Fiction, to 3,000 words, for sophisticated men. "We are not looking for SF, mystery, 40s-style detective, or stories involving aliens from other planets. We do look for interesting stories that enable readers to view life in an off-beat, unusual, or insightful manner: fiction with believable characters and actions." Pays varying rates, half on acceptance, half on publication.

GOLF DIGEST—5520 Park Ave., Trumbull, CT 06611. Jerry Tarde, Ed. Unusual or humorous stories, to 2,000 words, about golf; golf "fables," to 1,000 words. Pays 50¢ a word, on acceptance.

GOOD HOUSEKEEPING—959 Eighth Ave., New York, NY 10019. Lee Quarfoot, Fiction Ed. Short stories, 1,000 to 3,000 words, with strong identification figures for women, by published writers and "beginners with demonstrable talent." Novel condensations or excerpts. "Writers whose work interests us will hear from us within 4 to 5 weeks of receipt of manuscript. Please send inexpensive copies of your work; and do not enclose SASEs or postage. We can no longer return or critique manuscripts. We do accept multiple submissions." Pays top rates, on acceptance.

GUN DOG—1901 Bell Ave., Des Moines, IA 50315. Bob Wilbanks, Man. Ed. Occasional fiction, humor related to gun dogs and bird hunting. Pays $100 to $350, on acceptance.

HICALL—1445 Boonville Ave., Springfield, MO 65802–1894. Deanna Harris, Ed. Fiction, to 1,500 words, for 15- to 19-year-olds. Strong evangelical emphasis a must: believable characters working out their problems according to biblical principles. Pays 3¢ a word for first rights, on acceptance. Reprints considered.

HIGHLIGHTS FOR CHILDREN—803 Church St., Honesdale, PA 18431–1824. Kent L. Brown Jr., Ed. Fiction on sports, humor, adventure, mystery, etc., 900 words, for 9- to 12-year-olds. Easy rebus form, 100 to 150 words, and easy-to-read stories, to 500 words, for beginning readers. "We are partial to stories in which the protagonist solves a dilemma through his own resources, rather than through luck or magic." Pays from 14¢ a word, on acceptance. Buys all rights.

HOMETOWN PRESS—2007 Gallatin St., Huntsville, AL 35801. Jeffrey C.

Hindman, M.D., Ed.-in-Chief. Fiction, 800 to 2,500 words, well-crafted and tightly written, suitable for family reading. New and unpublished writers welcome. SASE for guidelines.

ISAAC ASIMOV'S SCIENCE FICTION MAGAZINE—380 Lexington Ave., New York, NY 10168–0035. Gardner Dozois, Ed. Short science fiction and fantasies, to 15,000 words. Pays 6¢ to 8¢ a word, on acceptance.

LADIES' HOME JOURNAL—100 Park Ave., New York, NY 10017. Fiction with strong identification for women. Short stories and full-length manuscripts accepted through agents only, and from writers with mainstream publishing credits.

LOLLIPOPS—Good Apple, Inc., P. O. Box 299, Carthage, IL 62321–0299. Jerry Aten, Ed. Teaching ideas and activities covering all areas of the curriculum for preschool to second-grade children. Rates vary.

THE LOOKOUT—8121 Hamilton Ave., Cincinnati, OH 45231. Simon J. Dahlman, Ed. Inspirational short-shorts, 500 to 2,000 words. Pays to 7¢ a word, on acceptance. No historical fiction, science fiction, or fantasy.

MADEMOISELLE—350 Madison Ave., New York, NY 10017. Eileen Schnurr, Fiction Ed. Short stories, 1,500 to 5,000 words, of interest to young single women. Looking for strong voices, fresh insights, generally classic form; no genre fiction. Male point-of-view about personal relationships welcome. Pays $1,000 to $1,500 for short shorts, up to $2,000 for stories, on acceptance. No fiction manuscripts will be returned: "If after a period of two months you have not heard from us, feel free to submit to other publications."

THE MAGAZINE OF FANTASY AND SCIENCE FICTION—Box 11526, Eugene, OR 97440. Kristine K. Rusch, Ed. Fantasy and science fiction stories, to 10,000 words. Pays 5¢ to 7¢ a word, on acceptance.

MATURE LIVING—127 Ninth Ave. N., Nashville, TN 37234. Judy Pregel, Asst. Ed. Fiction, 900 to 1,200 words, for senior adults. Must be consistent with Christian principles. Pays 5¢ a word, on acceptance.

MIDSTREAM—110 E. 59th St., New York, NY 10022. M. S. Solow, Asst. Ed. Fiction on Jewish themes, to 3,000 words. Pays 5¢ a word, after publication.

MILITARY LIFESTYLE MAGAZINE—4800 Montgomery Ln., Suite 710, Bethesda, MD 20814–5341. Hope Daniels, Ed. Fiction, to 2,000 words, for military families in the U.S. and overseas. Pays from $500, on publication. Annual fiction contest.

NA'AMAT WOMAN—200 Madison Ave., 21st Fl., New York, NY 10016. Judith A. Sokoloff, Ed. Short stories, approximately 2,500 words, with Jewish theme. Pays 8¢ a word, on publication.

THE NEW YORKER—20 W. 43rd St., New York, NY 10036. Fiction Dept. Short stories, humor, and satire. Pays according to length, on acceptance. Include SASE.

OMNI—1965 Broadway, New York, NY 10023–5965. Ellen Datlow, Fiction Ed. Strong, realistic science fiction, to 12,000 words. Some contemporary hard-edged fantasy. Pays to $2,250, on acceptance.

PENTHOUSE—1965 Broadway, New York, NY 10023. No unsolicited manuscripts.

PLAYBOY—680 N. Lakeshore Dr., Chicago, IL 60611. Alice K. Turner, Fiction Ed. Quality fiction, 1,000 to 8,000 words (average 6,000): suspense, mystery, adventure, and sports short stories; stories about contemporary relationships; science fiction. Active plots, masterful pacing, and strong characterization. Pays from $2,000 to $5,000, on acceptance. Query first; often overstocked.

PLOUGHSHARES—Emerson College, 100 Beacon St., Boston, MA 02116. Address Editors. Serious fiction, to 6,000 words. Poetry. Pays $10 to $50, on publication. Reading periods and themes vary; check most recent issue.

PURPOSE.—616 Walnut Ave., Scottdale, PA 15683–1999. James E. Horsch, Ed. Fiction, 900 words, on problem solving from a Christian point of view. Poetry, 3 to 12 lines. Pays up to 5¢ a word, to $1 per line for poetry, on acceptance.

RANGER RICK—8925 Leesburg Pike, Vienna, VA 22184–0001. Deborah Churchman, Fiction Ed. Action-packed nature- and conservation-related fiction, for 6- to 12-year-olds. Maximum: 900 words. No anthropomorphism. "Multi-cultural stories welcome." Pays to $550, on acceptance. Buys all rights.

REDBOOK—224 W. 57th St., New York, NY 10019. Dawn Raffel, Fiction Ed. Fresh, distinctive short stories, of interest to women, about love and relationships, friendship, careers, parenting, family dilemmas, confronting basic problems of contemporary life. Pays $850 for short-shorts (up to 9 manuscript pages), from $1,000 for short stories (to 20 pages). Allow 6 weeks for reply. Manuscripts without SASE will not be returned. No unsolicited novellas or novels accepted.

ROAD KING—P.O. Box 250, Park Forest, IL 60466. George Friend, Ed. Short stories, 1,200 to 1,500 words, for and/or about truck drivers. Pays to $400, on acceptance.

ST. ANTHONY MESSENGER—1615 Republic St., Cincinnati, OH 45210–1298. Norman Perry, O.F.M., Ed. Barbara Beckwith, Man. Ed. Fiction that makes readers think about issues, lifestyles, and values. Pays 14¢ a word, on acceptance. Queries or manuscripts accepted.

SASSY—230 Park Ave., New York, NY 10169. Christina Kelly, Fiction Ed. Short stories written in the magazine's style, 1,000 to 3,000 words, for girls age 14 to 19. Pays $1,000, on acceptance.

SEA KAYAKER—6327 Seaview Ave. N.W., Seattle, WA 98107–2664. Christopher Cunningham, Ed. Short stories exclusively related to ocean kayaking, 1,000 to 3,000 words. Pays on publication.

SEVENTEEN—850 Third Ave., New York, NY 10022. Adrian LeBlanc, Fiction Ed. High-quality, literary short fiction, to 4,000 words. Pays on acceptance.

SPORTS AFIELD—250 W. 55th St., New York, NY 10019. Tom Paugh, Ed. Occasional fiction, 1,500 words, on hunting, fishing, and related topics. Humor. Pays top rates, on acceptance.

STRAIGHT—8121 Hamilton Ave., Cincinnati, OH 45231. Carla Crane, Ed. Well-constructed fiction, 1,000 to 1,500 words, showing Christian teens using Bible principles in everyday life. Contemporary, realistic teen characters a must. Most interested in school, church, dating, and family life stories. Pays 3¢ to 7¢ a word, on acceptance. Send SASE for guidelines.

SUNDAY DIGEST—850 N. Grove Ave., Elgin, IL 60120. Ronda Oosterhoff, Ed. Short stories, 1,000 to 1,500 words, with evangelical religious slant. Pays 15¢ a word, on acceptance.

SUNSHINE MAGAZINE—Sunshine Press, Litchfield, IL 62056. Peggy Kuethe, Ed. Wholesome fiction, 900 to 1,200 words; short stories for youths, 400 words. Pays $10 to $100, on acceptance. Guidelines. Include SASE.

TAMPA BAY LIFE: THE BAY AREA'S MAGAZINE—6200 Courtney Campbell Causeway, Suite 580, Tampa, FL 33607–1458. Larry Marscheck, Ed. Fiction, 1,200 to 2,000 words. Must have a Tampa Bay region base/flavor. Payment varies, on publication.

'TEEN—8490 Sunset Blvd., Los Angeles, CA 90069. Address Fiction Dept. Short stories, 2,500 to 4,000 words: mystery, teen situations, adventure, romance, humor for teens. Pays from $100, on acceptance.

TQ/TEEN QUEST—Box 82808, Lincoln, NE 68501. Karen Christianson, Man. Ed. Fiction, 1,000 to 2,000 words, for Christian teens. Pays 8¢ to 15¢ a word, on acceptance.

TRUCKERS/USA—P.O. Box 323, Windber, PA 15963. David Adams, Ed. Monthly. Trucking related articles, poetry, and fiction. Payment varies, on acceptance.

VIRTUE—P.O. Box 850, Sisters, OR 97759. Marlee Alex, Ed. Fiction with a Christian slant. Pays 15¢ to 25¢ a word, on acceptance. Query required.

WESTERN PEOPLE—Box 2500, Saskatoon, Sask., Canada S7K 2C4. Short stories, 850 to 1,800 words, on subjects or themes of interest to rural readers in western Canada. Pays $100 to $175, on acceptance. Enclose international reply coupons and SAE.

WILDFIRE—Bear Tribe Publishing, P.O. Box 9167, Spokane, WA 99209–9167. Matthew Ryan, Ed. Fiction, 900 to 4,500 words, with a nature-based focus on spirituality, personal development, alternative lifestyles, natural healings, and ecology. Poetry, to 20 lines. Pays $250, on publication.

WILDFOWL—1901 Bell Ave., Suite #4, Des Moines, IA 50315. R. Sparks, Man. Ed. Occasional fiction, humor, related to duck hunters and wildfowl. Pays $200 to $350, on acceptance.

WOMAN'S WORLD—270 Sylvan Ave., Englewood Cliffs, NJ 07632. Jeanne Muchnick, Fiction Ed. Fast-moving short stories, about 3,200 words, with light romantic theme. (Specify "short story" on outside of envelope.) Mini-mysteries, 1,100 to 1,200 words, with "whodunit" or "howdunit" theme. No science fiction, fantasy, or historical romance and no horror, ghost stories, or gratuitous violence. Pays $1,000 for short stories, $500 for mini-mysteries, on acceptance. Submit manuscript with SASE.

WOMEN'S HOUSEHOLD—306 E. Parr Rd., Berne, IN 46711. Allison Ballard, Ed. Pen pal stories or other stories, 1,000 to 1,500 words, about friendships and family relationships. Pays $40 to $250, on publication.

WOODMEN OF THE WORLD MAGAZINE—1700 Farnam St., Omaha, NE 68102. George M. Herriott, Ed. Family-oriented fiction. Pays 10¢ a word, on acceptance.

YANKEE—Yankee Publishing Co., Dublin, NH 03444. Judson Hale, Ed. Edie Clark, Fiction Ed. High-quality, literary short fiction, to 2,500 words, with setting in or compatible with New England; no sap buckets or lobster pot stereotypes. Pays $1,000, on acceptance.

DETECTIVE AND MYSTERY

ALFRED HITCHCOCK'S MYSTERY MAGAZINE—380 Lexington Ave., New York, NY 10168–0035. Cathleen Jordan, Ed. Well-plotted mystery, detective, suspense, and crime fiction, up to 14,000 words. Submissions by new writers strongly encouraged. Pays 5¢ a word, on acceptance. Guidelines with SASE.

ARMCHAIR DETECTIVE—129 W. 56th St., New York, NY 10019. Kathy Daniel, Ed. Articles on mystery and detective fiction; short stories; biographical sketches, reviews, etc. Pays $10 a printed page for nonfiction; fiction payment varies; reviews are unpaid.

ELLERY QUEEN'S MYSTERY MAGAZINE—380 Lexington Ave., New York, NY 10017. Janet Hutchings, Ed. Detective, crime, and mystery fiction, approximately 4,000 to 6,000 words. No sex, sadism, or sensationalism. Particularly interested in new writers and "first stories." Pays 3¢ to 8¢ a word, on acceptance.

FRONT PAGE DETECTIVE—See *Inside Detective*.

INSIDE DETECTIVE—Reese Communications, Inc., 460 W. 34th St., New York, NY 10001. Rose Mandelsberg, Ed.-in-Chief. Timely, true detective stories, 5,000 to 6,000 words, or 10,000 words. No fiction. Pays $250 to $500, extra for photos, on acceptance. Query. Same address and requirements for *Front Page Detective*.

MASTER DETECTIVE—460 W. 34th St., New York, NY 10001. Rose Mandelsberg, Ed. Detailed articles, 5,000 to 6,000 words, with photos, on current cases, emphasizing human motivation and detective work. No fiction. Pays to $250, on acceptance. Query.

OFFICIAL DETECTIVE STORIES—460 W. 34th St., New York, NY 10001. Rose Mandelsberg, Ed. True detective stories, 5,000 to 6,000 words, on current investigations, strictly from the investigator's point of view. No fiction. Photos. Pays $250, extra for photos, on acceptance. Query.

P.I. MAGAZINE—755 Bronx Ave., Toledo, OH 43609. Bob Mackowiak, Ed. Fiction, 2,500 to 5,000 words, and profiles of professional investigators containing true accounts of their most difficult cases; puzzles. Pays $10 to $25, plus copies, on publication.

TRUE DETECTIVE—460 W. 34th St., New York, NY 10001. Rose Mandelsberg, Ed. Articles, from 5,000 words, with photos, on current police cases, emphasizing detective work and human motivation. No fiction. Pays $250, extra for photos, on acceptance. Query.

SCIENCE FICTION AND FANTASY

ABORIGINAL SF—P.O. Box 2449, Woburn, MA 01888–0849. Charles C. Ryan, Ed. Short stories, 2,500 to 5,500 words, and poetry, one to two typed pages, with strong science content, lively, unique characters, and well-designed plots. No sword and sorcery or fantasy. Pays $250 for fiction, $20 for poetry, $4 for SF jokes, and $20 for cartoons, on publication.

AFTER HOURS—P.O. Box 538, Sunset Beach, CA 90742–0538. William G. Raley, Ed. Quarterly. Fantasy and horror, to 6,000 words, that take place after sundown. "If it's too weird or off the wall for other magazines, send it here." B&W cover art (8 ½" × 11"). Pays 1¢ a word, on acceptance, plus one copy.

AMAZING STORIES—Box 111, Lake Geneva, WI 53147. Mr. Kim Mohan, Ed. Janis Wells, Asst. Ed. Monthly. Original, previously unpublished science fiction, fantasy, and horror, 1,000 to 25,000 words. Pays 6¢ to 10¢ a word, on acceptance.

ANALOG: SCIENCE FICTION/SCIENCE FACT—380 Lexington Ave.,

New York, NY 10168–0035. Stanley Schmidt, Ed. Science fiction with strong characters in believable future or alien setting: short stories, 2,000 to 7,500 words; novelettes, 10,000 to 20,000 words; serials, to 80,000 words. Also uses future-related articles. Pays to 7¢ a word, on acceptance. Query on serials and articles.

THE ASYMPTOTICAL WORLD—P.O. Box 1372, Williamsport, PA 17703. Michael H. Gerardi, Ed. Psychodramas and fantasy, 1,500 to 2,500 words. Illustrations, photographs. Pays 2¢ a word, on acceptance.

BEYOND: SCIENCE FICTION & FANTASY—P.O. Box 1124, Fair Lawn, NJ 07410. Roberta Rogow, Ed. Science fiction and fantasy: original, exciting, thought-provoking fiction, 3,000 to 5,000 words, and poems, 10 to 20 lines. Pays ¼¢ a word, on publication.

DRAGON MAGAZINE—P.O. Box 111, Lake Geneva, WI 53147. Roger E. Moore, Ed. Barbara G. Young, Fiction Ed. Articles, 1,500 to 7,500 words, on fantasy and SF role-playing games. Fantasy, 1,500 to 8,000 words. Pays 6¢ to 8¢ a word for fiction, on acceptance. Pays 4¢ a word for articles, on publication. Guidelines (specify article or fiction).

FANGORIA—475 Park Ave. S., 8th Fl., New York, NY 10016. Anthony Timpone, Ed. Published ten times yearly. Movie previews and interviews, 1,800 to 2,500 words, in connection with upcoming horror films. "A strong love of the genre and an appreciation and understanding of the magazine are essential." Pays $150 to $200, on publication.

FANTASY AND SCIENCE FICTION—Mercury Press, Inc., P.O. Box 11526, Eugene, OR 97440. Kristine K. Rusch, Ed. Monthly. Short stories under 10,000 words. "We have no formula, but you should be familiar with the magazine before submitting"; for sample copies, write to 14 Jewell St., Cornwall, CT 06753. Pays 5¢ to 7¢ a word, on acceptance.

FANTASY MACABRE—P.O. Box 20610, Seattle, WA 98102. Jessica Salmonson, Ed. Fiction, to 3,000 words, including translations. "We look for a tale that is strong in atmosphere, with menace that is suggested and threatening rather than the result of dripping blood and gore." Pays 1¢ a word, to $30 per story, on publication. Also publishes *Fantasy & Terror* for poetry-in-prose pieces.

FIGMENT—Figment Press, P.O. Box 3128, Moscow, ID 83843–0477. Barb and J.C. Hendee, Eds. Science fiction, fantasy, and horror stories, 3,000 to 5,000 words; vignettes, to 3,000 words; novelettes, 7,500 words; and poems. "Science fiction should be character oriented. For horror stories, we prefer deeply emotional work with a haunting sense of mood; must have a SF/fantasy rationale and premise." Pays $17 for stories, $5 for vignettes, $35 for novelettes, $2 to $4 for poems, and $10 to $20 for artwork, within 30 days of acceptance. Send SASE for guidelines.

FOOTSTEPS PRESS—P.O. Box 75, Round Top, NY 12473. Bill Munster, Ed. Horror, mystery, and ghost story chapbooks, 3,000 to 5,000 words. Royalty (usually from $350 to $500).

GRUE MAGAZINE—Box 370, Times Square Sta., New York, NY 10108. Peggy Nadramia, Ed. Fiction, 6,000 words, and macabre/surreal poetry of any length. "We seek very visceral, original horror stories with an emphasis on characterization and motivation." Pays ½¢ a word for fiction, $5 per poem, on publication. Allow three to six months for response.

THE HAUNTED SUN—22000 Mauer, St. Clair Shores, MI 48080. John Habermas, Ed. Horror stories, 1,000 to 3,500 words, and poetry with horror themes, to one page. "We look for strong, compelling openings and satisfying conclusions.

No category horror; be thought-provoking and original." Pays $10 to $20 for fiction, $2 to $5 for poetry, and $5 to $10 for art, on acceptance. Guidelines.

HAUNTS—Nightshade Publications, Box 3342, Providence, RI 02906. Joseph K. Cherkes, Ed. Horror, science/fantasy, and supernatural short stories with strong characters, 1,500 to 8,000 words. No explicit sexual scenes or gratuitous violence. Pays ¼¢ to ½¢ a word, on publication. Submit June 1 to Dec. 1.

ISAAC ASIMOV'S SCIENCE FICTION MAGAZINE—380 Lexington Ave., New York, NY 10168–0035. Gardner Dozois, Ed. Short, character-oriented science fiction and fantasy, to 15,000 words. Pays 5¢ to 8¢ a word, on acceptance. Send SASE for requirements.

THE LEADING EDGE—3163 JKHB, Provo, UT 84602. Eric Lowe, Ed. Short stories, 3,000 to 12,000 words, and some experimental fiction; poems, to 200 lines; and articles, to 8,000 words, on science, scientific speculation, and literary criticism. Fillers and comics. "Do not send originals; manuscripts are marked and critiqued by staff." Pays ½¢ a word with a minimum of $5 for fiction; $4 per published page of poetry; $2 to $4 for fillers, on publication. Guidelines.

THE MAGAZINE OF FANTASY AND SCIENCE FICTION—Box 56, Cornwall, CT 06753. Edward Ferman, Ed. Fantasy and science fiction stories, to 10,000 words. Pays 5¢ to 7¢ a word, on acceptance.

MAGIC REALISM—P.O. Box 620, Orem, UT 84059–0620. C. Darren Butler, Ed. Stories, to 6,000 words (4,000 words preferred), "where the fantastic is treated as if it were reality": fictionalized myth, folktales, fantasy, fables, fairy tales, and literary works with magic realism. Published twice yearly. Pays in one copy.

MARION ZIMMER BRADLEY'S FANTASY MAGAZINE—P.O. Box 245-A, Berkeley, CA 94701. Marion Zimmer Bradley, Ed. Quarterly. Well-plotted stories, 3,500 to 4,000 words. Action and adventure fantasy "with no particular objection to modern settings." Guidelines recommended. Pays 3¢ to 10¢ a word, on acceptance.

NEW DESTINIES—P.O. Box 1403, Riverdale, NY 10471. Jim Baen, Ed. Magazine published in paperback form. Science fiction, 2,000 words, with companion articles, to 40,000 words. Pays competitive rates, on acceptance. No fantasy. Guidelines.

OMNI—1965 Broadway, New York, NY 10023–5965. Ellen Datlow, Ed. Strong, realistic science fiction, 2,000 to 10,000 words, with good characterizations. Some fantasy. No horror, ghost, or sword and sorcery tales. Pays $1,250 to $2,250, on acceptance.

OWLFLIGHT—1025 55th St., Oakland, CA 94608. Millea Kenin, Ed. Science fiction and fantasy, 3,000 to 8,000 words. Science fiction/fantasy poetry, 8 to 100 lines. Photos, illustrations. Pays 1¢ a word, extra for illustrations, on publication. "Often overstocked; query first." Send SASE for guidelines.

QUANTUM: SCIENCE FICTION & FANTASY REVIEW—(formerly *Thrust*) 8217 Langport Terrace, Gaithersburg, MD 20877. D. Douglas Fratz, Ed. Articles, interviews, 2,000 to 6,000 words, for readers familiar with SF and related literary and scientific topics. Book reviews, 100 to 900 words. Pays 1¢ to 2¢ a word, on publication. Query preferred. SASE for guidelines.

SCIENCE FICTION CHRONICLE—P.O. Box 2730, Brooklyn, NY 11202. Andrew Porter, Ed. News items, 200 to 500 words, for SF and fantasy readers, professionals, and booksellers. Photos and short articles on author signings, events, conventions. Pays 3¢ to 5¢ a word, $5 for photos, on publication.

THRUST—See *Quantum: Science Fiction & Fantasy Review.*

TWISTED—22071 Pinewood Dr., Antioch, IL 60002. Christine Hoard, Ed. Fiction and articles, to 5,000 words; poetry, to one page. "No sword and sorcery or hard science fiction. We prefer horror and dark fantasy. Best to query first." Pays in copies.

2 AM—P.O. Box 6754, Rockford, IL 61125–1754. Gretta M. Anderson, Ed. Fiction, of varying lengths. "We prefer dark fantasy/horror; great science fiction and sword and sorcery stories are welcome." Profiles and intelligent commentaries. Poetry, to 50 lines. Pays from ½¢ a word, on acceptance. Guidelines.

WEIRD TALES—P.O. Box 13418, Philadelphia, PA 19101. George Scithers, Pub. Darrell Schweitzer, Ed. Fantasy and horror (no SF), to 20,000 words. Pays 3¢ to 8¢ a word, on acceptance. Guidelines.

CONFESSION AND ROMANCE

BLACK SECRETS—See *Intimacy.*

INTIMACY—355 Lexington Ave., New York, NY 10017. D. Boyd, Ed. Fiction, 5,000 to 5,800 words, for black women ages 18 to 45; must have contemporary plot and contain two romantic and intimate love scenes. Pays $75 to $100, on publication. Same address for *Jive* and *Black Secrets*, geared toward younger women seeking adventure, glamour, and romance. Guidelines.

JIVE—See *Intimacy.*

MODERN ROMANCES—233 Park Ave. S., New York, NY 10003. Cherie Clark King, Ed. Confession stories with reader-identification and strong emotional tone, 2,000 to 10,000 words. Pays 5¢ a word, after publication. Buys all rights.

TRUE EXPERIENCE—233 Park Ave. S., New York, NY 10003. Jean Press Silberg, Ed. Mary Lou Lang, Assoc. Ed. Realistic first-person stories, 4,000 to 10,000 words (short shorts, to 2,000 words), on family life, single life, love, romance, overcoming hardships, psychic/occult occurrences, mysteries. Pays 3¢ a word, after publication.

TRUE LOVE—233 Park Ave. South, New York, NY 10003. Marcia Pomerantz, Ed. Fresh, young, true-to-life romance stories, on love and topics of current interest. Must be written in the first person. Pays 3¢ a word, a month after publication. Buys all rights. Guidelines.

TRUE ROMANCE—233 Park Ave. S., New York, NY 10003. Jean Sharbel, Ed. True, dramatic or romantic first-person stories, 2,000 to 10,000 words. Love poems. Articles, 300 to 700 words, for young wives and singles. Pays 3¢ a word, a month after publication.

POETRY MARKETS

The following list includes markets for both serious and light verse. Although major magazines pay good rates for poetry, the competition to break into print is very stiff, since editors use only a limited number of poems in each issue. On the other hand, college, little, and literary magazines use a great deal of poetry, and though payment is modest—usually in copies—publication in these journals can establish a beginning poet's reputation, and can lead to publication in the major magazines. Poets will also find a number of competitions offering cash awards for unpublished poems in the *Literary Prize Offers* list.

Poets should also consider local newspapers as possible verse markets. Although they may not specifically seek poetry from free lancers, newspaper editors often print verse submitted to them, especially on holidays and for special occasions.

The market for book-length collections of poetry at commercial publishers is extremely limited. There are a number of university presses that publish poetry collections, however (see *University Presses* and *Poetry Series*), and many of them sponsor annual competitions. Consult the *Literary Prize Offers* list for more information.

ALOHA, THE MAGAZINE OF HAWAII—49 South Hotel St., #309, Honolulu, HI 96813. Cheryl Chee Tsutsumi, Ed. Poetry relating to Hawaii. Pays $25 per poem, on publication.

AMERICA—106 W. 56th St., New York, NY 10019. Patrick Samway, S.J., Literary Ed. Serious poetry, preferably in contemporary prose idiom, 10 to 25 lines. Occasional light verse. Submit two or three poems at a time. Pays $1.40 per line, on publication. SASE for guidelines.

THE AMERICAN SCHOLAR—1811 Q St. N.W., Washington, DC 20009. Joseph Epstein, Ed. Highly original poetry, 10 to 32 lines, for college-educated, intellectual readers. Pays $50, on acceptance.

THE ATLANTIC—745 Boylston St., Boston, MA 02116. Peter Davison, Poetry Ed. Previously unpublished poetry of highest quality. Limited market; only two to three poems an issue. Interested in new poets. Occasionally uses light verse. Pays excellent rates, on acceptance.

CAPPER'S—616 Jefferson St., Topeka, KS 66607–1188. Nancy Peavler, Ed. Traditional poetry and free verse, 4 to 16 lines, with simple everyday themes. Submit up to six poems at a time, with SASE. Pays $3 to $6, on acceptance.

CHILDREN'S PLAYMATE—P.O. Box 567, Indianapolis, IN 46206. Elizabeth A. Rinck, Ed. Poetry for children, 6 to 8, on good health, nutrition, exercise, safety, seasonal and humorous subjects. Pays from $15, on publication. Buys all rights.

THE CHRISTIAN SCIENCE MONITOR—One Norway St., Boston, MA 02115. April Austin, The Home Forum. Fresh, vigorous nonreligious poems of high quality, on various subjects. Short poems preferred. Pays varying rates, on acceptance. Submit no more than three poems at a time.

COMMONWEAL—15 Dutch St., New York, NY 10038. Rosemary Deen, Poetry Ed. Catholic. Serious, witty poetry. Pays 50¢ a line, on publication. SASE required.

COMPLETE WOMAN—1165 N. Clark St., Chicago, IL 60610. Address Assoc. Ed. Poetry. Pays $10, on publication. SASE necessary for return of material.

COSMOPOLITAN—224 W. 57th St., New York, NY 10019. Rachel Zalis,

Poetry Ed. Poetry about relationships and other topics of interest to young, active women. Pays from $25, on acceptance. SASE required.

COUNTRY WOMAN—P.O. Box 643, Milwaukee, WI 53201. Kathy Pohl, Man. Ed. Traditional rural poetry and light verse, 4 to 30 lines, on rural experiences and country living. Poems must rhyme. Pays $10 to $40, on acceptance.

EVANGEL—Box 535002, Indianapolis, IN 46253–5002. Vera Bethel, Ed. Free Methodist. Devotional or nature poetry, 8 to 16 lines. Pays $10, on publication.

THE EVANGELICAL BEACON—901 East 78th St., Minneapolis, MN 55420. Carol Madison, Ed. Denominational publication of Evangelical Free Church of America. Some poetry related to Christian faith. Pays 4¢ a word, $5 minimum, on publication.

FAMILY CIRCLE—110 Fifth Ave., New York, NY 10011. No unsolicited poetry.

GOOD HOUSEKEEPING—"Light Housekeeping" Page, 959 8th Ave., New York, NY 10019. Rosemary Leonard, Ed. Light, humorous verses, quips, and poems. Pays $25 for four lines, $50 for six to eight lines, on acceptance. All unused submissions to "Light Housekeeping" page will be returned to author when accompanied by SASE.

JOURNEY—Christian Board of Publication, Box 179, St. Louis, MO 63166. Short poems for 12- to 15-year-olds. Pays 30¢ a line, on publication.

LADIES' HOME JOURNAL—100 Park Ave., New York, NY 10017. Short, humorous poetry for "Last Laughs" page only. Must be accessible to women in general. Pays $50 for accepted poetry.

LEATHERNECK—Box 1775, Quantico, VA 22134–0776. W.V. H. White, Ed. Poetry overstocked at present.

MCCALL'S—110 Fifth Ave., New York, NY 10011. No longer publishing poetry.

MATURE YEARS—201 Eighth Ave. S., P.O. Box 801, Nashville, TN 37202. Donn C. Downall, Ed. United Methodist. Poetry, to 14 lines, on pre-retirement, retirement, seasonal subjects, aging. No saccharine poetry. Pays 50¢ to $1 per line.

MIDSTREAM—110 E. 59th St., New York, NY 10022. Joel Carmichael, Ed. Poetry of Jewish interest. Pays $25, on publication.

THE MIRACULOUS MEDAL—475 E. Chelten Ave., Philadelphia, PA 19144–5785. John W. Gouldrick, C.M., Ed. Catholic. Religious verse, to 20 lines. Pays 50¢ a line, on acceptance.

MODERN BRIDE—475 Park Ave. South, New York, NY 10016. Mary Ann Cavlin, Man. Ed. Short verse of interest to bride and groom. Pays $25 to $35, on acceptance.

THE NATION—72 Fifth Ave., New York, NY 10011. Grace Schulman, Poetry Ed. Poetry of high quality. Pays after publication.

NATIONAL ENQUIRER—Lantana, FL 33464. Michele Cooke, Asst. Ed. Short poems, with traditional rhyming verse, of an amusing, philosophical, or inspirational nature; longer poems of a serious or humorous nature. No experimental poetry. Original epigrams, humorous anecdotes, and "daffynitions." Submit seasonal/holiday material at least two months in advance. Pays $25, after publication. SASE required.

NEW ENGLAND ENTERTAINMENT DIGEST—45 Willard St., West Quincy, MA 02169. Michael R. McCaffrey, Pub. Light verse, of any length, related to the entertainment field. Pays $3, on publication.

THE NEW REPUBLIC—1220 19th St. N.W., Washington, DC 20036. Richard Howard, Poetry Ed. Poetry for liberal, intellectual readers. Pays $75, after publication.

THE NEW YORKER—20 W. 43rd St., New York, NY 10036. First-rate poetry. Pays top rates, on acceptance. Include SASE.

PENTECOSTAL EVANGEL—1445 Boonville, Springfield, MO 65802. Richard G. Champion, Ed. Journal of Assemblies of God. Religious and inspirational verse, 12 to 30 lines. Pays to 50¢ a line, on acceptance.

PURPOSE—616 Walnut Ave., Scottdale, PA 15683–1999. James E. Horsch, Poetry Ed. Poetry, to 8 lines, with challenging Christian discipleship angle. Pays 50¢ to $1 a line, on acceptance.

ST. JOSEPH'S MESSENGER—P.O. Box 288, Jersey City, NJ 07303–0288. Sister Ursula Maphet, Ed. Light verse and traditional poetry, 4 to 40 lines. Pays $5 to $15, on publication.

THE SATURDAY EVENING POST—P.O. Box 567, Indianapolis, IN 46206. Address Post Scripts Ed. Light verse and humor. Pays $15, on publication.

SEVENTEEN—850 Third Ave., New York, NY 10022. Liza DiPrima, Teen Feature Ed. Poetry, to 40 lines, by writers ages 21 and under. Submit up to 5 poems. Pays $15 to $30, after acceptance.

THE UNITED METHODIST REPORTER—P.O. Box 660275, Dallas, TX 75266–0275. Spurgeon M. Dunnam III, Ed. Religious verse, 4 to 16 lines. Pays $2, on acceptance.

YANKEE—Yankee Publishing Co., Dublin, NH 03444. Jean Burden, Poetry Ed. Serious poetry of high quality, to 30 lines. Pays $50 per poem for all rights, $35 for first rights, on publication.

POETRY SERIES

The following university presses publish book-length collections of poetry by writers who have never had a book of poems published. Each has specific rules for submission, so before submitting any material, be sure to write well ahead of the deadline dates for further information. Some organizations sponsor competitions for groups of poems; see *Literary Prize Offers*.

CLEVELAND STATE UNIVERSITY POETRY CENTER—Dept. of English, Rhodes Tower, Room 1815, Cleveland, OH 44115. Best volume of poetry submitted between December 1 and March 1 receives publication in the CSU Poetry Series and $1,000. There is a $10 reading fee. Guidelines recommended before submission.

UNIVERSITY OF GEORGIA PRESS—Contemporary Poetry Series, Athens, GA 30602. Poets who have never had a book of poems published may submit book-length poetry manuscripts for possible publication during the month of September each year. Manuscripts from poets who have published at least one volume of poetry (chapbooks excluded) are considered during the month of January. Send SASE for guidelines before submitting. There is a $10 reading fee. Manuscripts will not be returned.

UNIVERSITY OF PITTSBURGH PRESS—Pitt Poetry Series, Pittsburgh, PA 15260. Poets who have never had a full-length book of poetry published may enter a 48- to 120-page collection of poems to the Agnes Lynch Starrett Poetry Prize between March and April. There is a $10 reading fee. Publication and $2,000 is offered. SASE required.

UNIVERSITY OF WISCONSIN PRESS—Poetry Series, 114 N. Murray St., Madison, WI 53715. Ronald Wallace, Administrator. Manuscripts may be submitted during the month of September to the Brittingham Prize in Poetry competition, which offers $500, plus publication in the poetry series, for an unpublished book-length poetry manuscript. There is a $10 reading fee. Manuscripts will not be returned.

WESLEYAN UNIVERSITY PRESS—110 Mt. Vernon St., Middletown, CT 06457. Considers unpublished book-length poetry manuscripts by poets who have never had a book published, for publication in the Wesleyan New Poets Series. There is no deadline. Submit manuscript, $15 reading fee, and SASE.

YALE UNIVERSITY PRESS—Box 92A, Yale Sta., New Haven, CT 06520. Address Editor, Yale Series of Younger Poets. Conducts Yale Series of Younger Poets Competition, in which the prize is publication of a book-length manuscript of poetry, written by a poet under 40 who has not previously published a volume of poems. Closes in February.

GREETING CARD MARKETS

Greeting card companies often have their own specific requirements for submitting ideas, verse, and artwork. In general, however, each verse or message should be typed, double-space, on a 3x5 or 4x6 card. Use only one side of the card, and be sure to put your name and address in the upper left-hand corner. Keep a copy of every verse or idea you send. (It's also advisable to keep a record of what you've submitted to each publisher.) Always enclose an SASE, and do not send out more than ten verses or ideas in a group to any one publisher. Never send original artwork.

AMBERLEY GREETING CARD COMPANY—11510 Goldcoast Dr., Cincinnati, OH 45249–1695. Ned Stern, Ed. Humorous ideas for birthday, illness, friendship, anniversary, congratulations, "miss you," etc. No seasonal or holiday ideas. Send SASE for market letter before submitting ideas. Pays $50. Buys all rights.

AMERICAN GREETINGS—10500 American Rd., Cleveland, OH 44144. Lynne Shlonsky, Dir., Creative Resources and Development. Study current offerings and query before submitting.

BLUE MOUNTAIN ARTS, INC.—P.O. Box 1007, Boulder, CO 80306. Attn: Editorial Staff, Dept. TW. Poetry and prose about love, friendship, family, philosophies, etc. Also material for special occasions and holidays: birthdays, get well,

Christmas, Valentine's Day, Easter, etc. No artwork or rhymed verse. Pays $200 per poem.

DAYSPRING GREETING CARDS—Outreach Publications, P.O. Box 1010, Siloam Springs, AR 72761. David Taylor, Ed. Inspirational messages that minister love, encouragement, and comfort to the receiver. Holidays, everyday occasions, and special-occasion cards. SASE for guidelines. Allow 4 to 6 weeks for response. Pays $30, on acceptance.

FREEDOM GREETING CARD COMPANY—P.O. Box 715, Bristol, PA 19007. Submit to Jay Levitt. Traditional and humorous verse and love messages. Inspirational poetry for all occasions. Pays negotiable rates, on acceptance. Query with SASE.

HALLMARK CARDS, INC.—2501 McGee, Box 419580, Mail Drop 276, Kansas City, MO 64141. Query Carol King for guidelines and release form; include SASE, no samples. Need conversational prose and humor for everyday and seasonal greeting cards. Mostly staff-written; "free lancers must show a high degree of skill and originality."

KALAN—97 S. Union Ave., Lansdowne, PA 19050. Unique and wildly funny messages for birthday and love greeting cards. Send humorous card ideas for Christmas and Valentine's Day 9 or 10 months before holiday. One-liners (risqué O.K.) about school, dating, money (or lack thereof), life, sex, etc., for key rings. Mark submissions "Attn: Editor." Pays $75 per idea purchased. Very selective; send SASE for guidelines.

MERLYN GRAPHICS CORP.—P.O. Box 9087, Canoga Park, CA 91309. B. Galling, Ed. Humorous, risqué, clever greeting card verse. "Funny, not vulgar or X-rated." Do not submit artwork or photography. Pays $50, on publication. Send SASE for guidelines.

NOBLE WORKS—113 Clinton St., Hoboken, NJ 07030. Christopher Noble, Ed. Humorous greeting card ideas and copy. "No smut, no verse, nothing sweet or sentimental. We like 'Saturday Night Live' style humor." Pays $150 per complete idea against royalties, on publication. (Other deals and licensing agreements dependent on artist and quality of work.) SASE required.

OATMEAL STUDIOS—Box 138 TW, Rochester, VT 05767. Attn: Editor. Humorous, clever, and new ideas needed for all occasions. Query with SASE.

PARAMOUNT CARDS—P.O. Box 6546, Providence, RI 02940–6546. Attn: Editorial Freelance. Humorous and nonhumorous for birthday, relative's birthday, friendship, get well, congratulations, Christmas, Valentine's Day, Easter, Mother's Day, Father's Day, and Graduation. Nonhumorous cards for sympathy and Jewish holidays. Submit each idea (5 to 10 per submission) on 3x5 card with name and address on each. Enclose SASE. Payment varies, on acceptance.

RAINBOW JUNGLE—29 Van Zandt St., Albany, NY 12207. Jonathan Peirce, Ed. Greeting-card text for holidays, birthdays, anniversaries, personal messages, etc. Send #10 SASE for guidelines. Pays to $100, on acceptance.

RED FARM STUDIO—1135 Roosevelt Ave., Pawtucket, RI 02862. Traditional cards for graduation, wedding, birthday, get-well, anniversary, friendship, new baby, sympathy, Christmas, and Valentine's Day. No studio humor. Pays varying rates. SASE required.

SANGAMON COMPANY—Route 48 West, P.O. Box 410, Taylorville, IL 62568. Address Editorial Dept. "We will send writer's guidelines to experienced free lancers before reviewing any submissions. We work on assignment." Pays competitive rates, on acceptance.

SUNRISE PUBLICATIONS, INC.—P.O. Box 4699, Bloomington, IN 47402. Address Editorial Coordinator. Original copy for holiday and everyday cards. "Submit up to 20 verses, one to four lines; simple, to-the-point ideas that could be serious, humorous, or light-hearted, but sincere, without being overly sentimental. Rhymed verse not generally used." SASE required. Allow 2 to 3 months for response. Send #10-size SASE for guidelines. Pays standard rates.

TLC GREETINGS—615 McCall Rd., Manhattan, KS 66502–8512. Michele Johnson, Creative Dir. Humorous and traditional sewing and craft-related cards. General humor cards for women for everyday, Christmas, and Valentine's Day. Very few risqué cards purchased. Pays on acceptance. Guidelines.

VAGABOND CREATIONS, INC.—2560 Lance Dr., Dayton, OH 45409. George F. Stanley, Jr., Ed. Greeting cards with graphics only on cover (no copy) and short tie-in copy punch line on inside page: birthday, everyday, Valentine's Day, Christmas, and graduation. Mildly risqué humor with double entendre acceptable. Ideas for illustrated theme stationery. Pays $15, on acceptance.

WARNER PRESS PUBLISHERS—1200 E. Fifth St., Anderson, IN 46012. Cindy Maddox, Product Ed. Sensitive prose and inspirational verse card ideas for boxed assortments; religious themes. Submit everyday ideas Nov. to Jan.; Christmas material June to Aug. Pays $20 to $35, on acceptance. Also accepts poster verses. Send SASE for guidelines before submitting.

WEST GRAPHICS PUBLISHING—238 Capp St., San Francisco, CA 94110. Attention: Editorial Dept. Outrageous humor concepts, all occasions (especially birthday) and holidays, for photo and illustrated card lines. Submit on 3x5 cards: concept on one side; name, address, and phone number on other. Pays $100, 30 days after publication.

WILLIAMHOUSE-REGENCY, INC.—28 W. 23rd St., New York, NY 10010. Query Nancy Boecker with SASE for writing specs. Captions for wedding invitations only. Pays $25 per caption, on acceptance. SASE required.

CAROL WILSON FINE ARTS, INC.—P.O. Box 17394, Portland, OR 97217. Gary Spector, Ed. Carol Wilson, Ed. Humorous copy for greeting cards. Queries preferred. Pays $75 or negotiated royalties, on publication. Guidelines.

COLLEGE, LITERARY AND LITTLE MAGAZINES

FICTION, NONFICTION, POETRY

The thousands of literary journals, little magazines, and college quarterlies published today welcome work from novices and pros alike; editors are always interested in seeing traditional and experimental fiction, poetry, essays, reviews, short articles, criticism, and satire, and as long as the material is well-written, the fact that a writer is a beginner doesn't adversely affect his or her chances for acceptance.

Most of these smaller publications have small budgets and staffs, so they may be slow in their reporting time—several months is not unusual. In addition, they usually pay only in copies of the issue in which published work appears and some—particularly college magazines—do not read manuscripts during the summer.

Publication in the literary journals can, however, lead to recognition by editors of large-circulation magazines, who read the little magazines in their search for new talent. There is also the possibility of having one's work chosen for reprinting in one of the prestigious annual collections of work from the little magazines.

Because the requirements of these journals differ widely, it is always important to study recent issues before submitting work to one of them. Copies of magazines may be in large libraries, or a writer may send a postcard to the editor and ask the price of a sample copy. When submitting a manuscript, always enclose a self-addressed envelope, with sufficient postage for its return.

For a complete list of literary and college publications and little magazines, writers may consult such reference works as *The International Directory of Little Magazines and Small Presses*, published annually by Dustbooks (P.O. Box 100, Paradise, CA 95967).

AEGEAN REVIEW—220 W. 19th St., Suite 2A, New York, NY 10011. Barbara Fields, Ed. Fiction and nonfiction, to 3,000 words, about Greece or by Greeks in translation. Query for drawings. Semiannual. Pays $50 to $100, on publication.

THE AGNI REVIEW—Dept. TW, Boston University, Creative Writing Program, 236 Bay State Rd., Boston, MA 02215. Askold Melnyczuk, Ed. Short stories, poetry, essays, and artwork. Reading period Oct. 1 to June 1 only. Pays $8 per page.

ALASKA QUARTERLY REVIEW—Dept. of English, Univ. of Alaska, 3211 Providence Dr., Anchorage, AK 99508. Address Eds. Short stories, novel excerpts, poetry (traditional and unconventional forms). Submit manuscripts between August 15 and May 15. Pays in copies.

ALBATROSS—125 Horton Ave., Englewood, FL 34223. Richard Smyth, Richard Brobst, Eds. High-quality poetry; especially interested in ecological and nature poetry written in narrative form. Interviews with well-known poets. Submit 3 to 5 poems at a time with brief bio. Pays in copies.

THE AMARANTH REVIEW—P.O. Box 56235, Phoenix, AZ 85079. Dana L. Yost, Ed. Semiannual journal of fiction (to 5,000 words) and poetry. Query for issue themes and contest information. Pays in copies and subscription.

AMELIA—329 E St., Bakersfield, CA 93304. Frederick A. Raborg, Jr., Ed. Poetry, to 100 lines; critical essays, to 2,000 words; reviews, to 500 words; belles lettres, to 1,000 words; fiction, to 4,500 words; fine pen-and-ink sketches; photos. Pays $35 for fiction and criticism, $10 to $25 for other nonfiction and artwork, $2 to $25 for poetry. Annual contest.

THE AMERICAN BOOK REVIEW—Publications Center, Univ. of Colorado, English Dept., Box 494, Boulder, CO 80309. Don Laing, Man. Ed. John Tytell, Rochelle Ratner, Ronald Sukenick, Eds. Literary book reviews, 700 to 1,200 words. Pays $50 honorarium and copies. Query first to Donald Laing, Man. Ed.

AMERICAN LITERARY REVIEW—University of North Texas, P.O. Box 13615, Denton, TX 76203. J.F. Kobler, Ed. Short stories, to 20 typed, double-spaced pages; submit up to two. Poems; submit up to five. Published in spring and fall. Pays in copies.

THE AMERICAN POETRY REVIEW—1721 Walnut St., Philadelphia, PA 19103. Address Eds. Highest quality contemporary poetry. Responds in 10 weeks. SASE a must.

AMERICAN QUARTERLY—National Museum of American History, Smithsonian Institution, Washington, DC 20560. Gary Kulik, Ed. Scholarly essays, 5,000 to 10,000 words, on any aspect of U.S. culture. Pays in copies.

THE AMERICAN SCHOLAR—1811 Q St. N.W., Washington, DC 20009. Joseph Epstein, Ed. Articles, 3,500 to 4,000 words, on science, politics, literature, the arts, etc. Book reviews. Pays $450 for articles, $100 for reviews, on publication.

AMERICAN WRITING—4343 Manayunk Ave., Philadelphia, PA 19128. Alexandra Grilikhes, Ed. Semiannual that "encourages experimentation in writing." Fiction and nonfiction, to 3,000 words, and poetry. Pays in copies.

AMHERST REVIEW—P.O. Box 1811, Amherst College, Amherst, MA 01002. Colin Hamilton, Ed. Fiction and other prose, to 6,000 words; poetry to 160 lines. Photos, paintings, drawings, and graphic art. Submit material Sept. through March. SASE required.

ANOTHER CHICAGO MAGAZINE—3709 N. Kenmore, Chicago, IL 60613. Fiction, essays on literature, and poetry. Pays $5 to $25, on acceptance.

ANTAEUS—26 W. 17th St., New York, NY 10011. Daniel Halpern, Ed. Short stories, essays, documents, excerpts, translations, poems. Pays on publication.

ANTIETAM REVIEW—82 W. Washington St., Hagerstown, MD 21740. Ann Knox, Ed.-in-Chief. Fiction, to 5,000 words; poetry and photography. Submissions from regional artists only (MD, PA, WV, VA, DE, DC), from Oct. through Feb. Pays from $20 to $100. Guidelines.

THE ANTIGONISH REVIEW—St. Francis Xavier Univ., Antigonish, N.S., Canada. George Sanderson, Ed. Poetry; short stories, essays, book reviews, 1,800 to 2,500 words. Pays in copies.

ANTIOCH REVIEW—P.O. Box 148, Yellow Springs, OH 45387. Robert S. Fogarty, Ed. Timely articles, 2,000 to 8,000 words, on social sciences, literature, and humanities. Quality fiction. Poetry. No inspirational poetry. Pays $15 per printed page, on publication.

APALACHEE QUARTERLY—Apalachee Press, P.O. Box 20106, Tallahassee, FL 32316. Barbara Hamby, Pamela Ball, Mary Jane Ryals, Bruce Boehrer, Paul McCall, Eds. Fiction, to 30 manuscript pages; poems (submit 3 to 5). Pays in copies.

APPALACHIA—299 Gunstock Hill Rd., Gilford, NH 03246. Helen Howe, Poetry Ed. Semiannual publication of the Appalachian Mountain Club. Oldest mountaineering journal in the country covers nature, conservation, climbing, hiking, canoeing, and ecology. Poems, to 30 lines. Pays in copies.

ARACHNE—162 Sturges St., Jamestown, NY 14701-3233. Susan L. Leach, Ed. Fiction, to 1,500 words. Poetry; submit up to 7. "We are looking for rural material and would like first publication rights." No simultaneous submissions. Quarterly. Pays in copies.

THE ARCHER—Pro Poets, 2285 Rogers Ln. N.W., Salem, OR 97304. Winifred Layton, Ed. Contemporary poetry, to 30 lines. Pays in copies. Send SASE for contest information.

ARIZONA QUARTERLY—Univ. of Arizona, Main Library B-541, Tucson, AZ 85721. Edgar A. Dryden, Ed. Criticism of American literature and culture from a theoretical perspective. No poetry or fiction. Pays in copies.

ARTFUL DODGE—College of Wooster, Wooster, OH 44691. Daniel Bourne and Karen Kovacik, Eds. Annual. Fiction, to 20 pages. Literary essays "based on a balance of analysis and insight," to 10 pages. Poetry, including translations of contemporary poets; submit 3 to 6 poems at a time. Long poems encouraged. Pays $5 plus 2 copies, on publication.

AURA LITERARY/ARTS REVIEW—P.O. Box 76, Univ. Center, UAB, Birmingham, AL 35294. Adam Pierce, Stefanie Truelove, Eds. Fiction and essays on literature, to 7,000 words; book reviews, to 4,000 words; poetry; photos. Pays in copies.

BAD HAIRCUT—3115 S.W. Roxbury, Seattle, WA 98126. Ray and Kim Gofroth, Eds. Articles and fiction, to 4,000 words (2,000 words preferred), with a focus on politics, human rights, and environmental themes. Unrhymed poetry, to one page, and drawings also accepted. "We hope that by creating art with these themes we can influence society and help create a better world." Pays in copies.

BELLES LETTRES—11151 Captain's Walk Ct., North Potomac, MD 20878. Janet Mullaney, Ed. Reviews and essays, 250 to 2,000 words, on literature by women. Literary puzzles, interviews, rediscoveries, retrospectives, and fiction. Query required. Pays in copies and subscription.

THE BELLINGHAM REVIEW—The Signpost Press, Inc., 1007 Queen St., Bellingham, WA 98226. Susan Hilton, Ed. Fiction, to 5,000 words, and poetry, any length. Semiannual. Pays in copies and subscription.

BELLOWING ARK—P.O. Box 45637, Seattle, WA 98145. Robert R. Ward, Ed. Short fiction, and poetry and essays of varying lengths, that portray life as a positive, meaningful process. B&W photos; line drawings. Pays in copies.

THE BELOIT FICTION JOURNAL—Box 11, Beloit College, Beloit, WI 53511. Clint McCown, Ed. Short fiction, one to 35 pages, on all themes. (No pornography, political propaganda, religious dogma.) Manuscripts read year round. Pays in copies.

BELOIT POETRY JOURNAL—RFD 2, Box 154, Ellsworth, ME 04605. Strong contemporary poetry, of any length or in any mode. Pays in copies. Send SASE for guidelines.

BLACK BEAR REVIEW—Black Bear Publications, 1916 Lincoln St., Croydon, PA 19021. Ave Jeanne, Ed. Book reviews and contemporary poetry. "We publish poems with social awareness, but any well-written piece is considered." Semiannual. Pays in one copy.

BLACK RIVER REVIEW—855 Mildred Ave., Lorain, OH 44052–1213. Kaye Coller, Ed. Contemporary poetry, fiction, essays, short book reviews, B&W artwork. No greeting card verse or slick magazine prose. Submit between Jan. 1 and May 1. Pays in copies. Guidelines. SASE required.

THE BLACK WARRIOR REVIEW—The Univ. of Alabama, P.O. Box 2936, Tuscaloosa, AL 35486–2936. Glenn Mott, Ed. Fiction; poetry; translations; reviews and essays. Pays per printed page. Annual awards. SASE required.

THE BLOOMSBURY REVIEW—1028 Bannock St., Denver, CO 80204. Tom Auer, Ed. Marilyn Auer, Assoc. Ed. Book reviews, publishing features, interviews, essays, poetry. Pays $5 to $25, on publication.

BLUE UNICORN—22 Avon Rd., Kensington, CA 94707. Address the Editors. Published in Oct., Feb., and June. "We are looking for originality of image, thought, and music; we rarely use poems over a page long." Submit up to 5 poems with SASE. Artwork used occasionally. Pays in one copy.

BLUELINE—English Dept., SUNY, Potsdam, NY 13676. Anthony Tyler, Ed. Reading period Sept. 1 to Dec. 1. Essays, fiction, to 2,500 words, on Adirondack region or similar areas. Poetry, to 44 lines. No more than 5 poems per submission. Pays in copies.

BOSTON REVIEW—33 Harrison Ave., Boston, MA 02111–2008. Josh Cohen, Ed.-in-Chief. Reviews and essays, 800 to 3,000 words, on literature, art, music, film, photography. Original fiction, to 5,000 words. Poetry. Pays $40 to $150.

BOTTOMFISH—21250 Stevens Creek Blvd., Cupertino, CA 95014. Robert Scott, Ed. Annual. Stories, vignettes, and experimental fiction, to 5,000 words. Free verse or traditional poetry, any subject, any length. "Our purpose is to give national exposure to new writers and new styles of creative writing." Pays in copies.

BOULEVARD—2400 Chestnut St., Apt. 2208, Philadelphia, PA 19103. Richard Burgin, Ed. Published three times a year. High-quality fiction and articles, to 30 pages; poetry. Pays to $250, on publication.

THE BRIDGE—14050 Vernon St., Oak Park, MI 48237. Jack Zucker and Helen Zucker, Fiction Eds. Mitzi Alvin, Poetry Ed. Semiannual. Fiction, 7,500 words, and poetry, to 300 lines. Book reviews; query first. Pays $3, on publication.

BUCKNELL REVIEW—Bucknell Univ., Lewisburg, PA 17837. Interdisciplinary journal in book form. Scholarly articles on arts, science, and letters. Pays in copies.

CAESURA—English Dept., Auburn Univ., Auburn, AL 36849. Lex Williford, Ed. R. T. Smith, Man. Ed. Short stories, to 5,000 words; narrative and lyric poetry, to 150 lines. Pays in copies. Contest for poetry and fiction; prizes depend on funding.

CALLALOO—Dept. of English, Univ. of Virginia, Charlottesville, VA 22903. Charles H. Rowell, Ed. Fiction and poetry by, and critical studies on Afro-American, Caribbean, and African artists and writers. Payment varies, on publication.

CALLIOPE—Creative Writing Program, Roger Williams College, Bristol, RI 02809. Martha Christina, Ed. Short stories, to 2,500 words; poetry. Pays in copies and subscription. No submissions April through July.

CALYX, A JOURNAL OF ART & LITERATURE BY WOMEN—P.O. Box B, Corvallis, OR 97339. M. Donnelly, Man. Ed. Fiction, 5,000 words; book reviews, 1,000 words (please query with SASE about reviews); poetry, to 6 poems. Pays in copies. Submissions accepted through 5/92 or 10/1/92 through 11/30/92. Include short bio and SASE. Send for guidelines.

CANADIAN FICTION MAGAZINE—Box 946, Sta. F, Toronto, Ontario, Canada M4Y 2N9. High-quality short stories, novel excerpts, and experimental fiction, to 5,000 words, by Canadians. Interviews with Canadian authors; translations. Pays $10 per page, on publication. Annual prize, $500.

THE CAPE ROCK—Dept. of English, Southeast Missouri State Univ., Cape Girardeau, MO 63701. Harvey E. Hecht, Ed. Poetry, to 70 lines, and B&W photography. (One photographer per issue; pays $100.) Semiannual. Pays in copies and $200 for best poem in each issue.

THE CAPILANO REVIEW—2055 Purcell Way, North Vancouver, B.C.,

Canada V7J 3H5. Pierre Coupey, Ed. Fiction; poetry; visual arts. SASE required. Pays $30 to $120.

THE CARIBBEAN WRITER—Univ. of the Virgin Islands, RR 02, Box 10,000, Kingshill, St. Croix, Virgin Islands, U.S. 00850. Erika J. Smilowitz, Ed. Annual. Fiction (to 15 pages, submit up to 2 stories) and poems (no more than five); the Caribbean should be central to the work. Blind submissions policy: place title only on manuscript; name, address, and title of ms. on separate sheet. Reading period is through Oct. for Spring issue of the following year. Pays in copies.

CAROLINA QUARTERLY—Greenlaw Hall CB#3520, Univ. of North Carolina, Chapel Hill, NC 27599–3520. David Kellogg, Ed. Fiction, to 7,000 words, by new or established writers. Poetry (no restrictions on length, though limited space makes inclusion of works of more than 300 lines impractical). Pays $15 for fiction and poetry, on publication.

CATALYST—Atlanta-Fulton Public Library, 1 Margaret Mitchell Sq., Carnegie & Forsyth Sq., Atlanta, GA 30303–1089. Pearl Cleage, Ed. Biannual. Fiction, to 3,000 words, and poetry by Southern writers, primarily black writers. Pays to $200, on publication. Send SASE for guidelines and themes.

THE CENTENNIAL REVIEW—312 Linton Hall, Michigan State Univ., East Lansing, MI 48824–1044. R.K. Meiners, Ed. Articles, 3,000 to 5,000 words, on sciences, humanities, and interdisciplinary topics. Pays in copies.

THE CHARITON REVIEW—Northeast Missouri State Univ., Kirksville, MO 63501. Jim Barnes, Ed. Highest quality poetry and fiction, to 6,000 words. Modern and contemporary translations. Book reviews. "The only guideline is excellence in all matters."

THE CHICAGO REVIEW—5801 S. Kenwood Ave., Chicago, IL 60637. Anne Myles, David Nicholls, Andy Winston, Eds. Essays, interviews, reviews, fiction, translations, poetry. Pays in copies plus one year's subscription.

CHIRON REVIEW—Rt. 2, Box 111, St. John, KS 67576. Michael Hathaway, Ed. Contemporary fiction, to 4,000 words; articles, 500 to 1,000 words; and poetry, to 30 lines. Photos. Pays in copies.

CICADA—329 E St., Bakersfield, CA 93304. Frederick A. Raborg, Jr., Ed. Single haiku, sequences or garlands, essays about the forms, haibun and fiction related to haiku or Japan. Pays in copies.

CIMARRON REVIEW—205 Morrill Hall, Oklahoma State Univ., Stillwater, OK 74078–0135. Gordon Weaver, Ed. Poetry, fiction, essays, graphics/artwork. Seeks an individual, innovative style that focuses on contemporary themes. Pays in copies.

CINCINNATI POETRY REVIEW—Dept. of English, 069, Cincinnati, OH 45221. Dallas Wiebe, Ed. Published fall and spring. Poetry of all types. Pays in copies.

CLOCKWATCH REVIEW—Dept. of English, Illinois Wesleyan Univ., Bloomington, IL 61702. James Plath, Ed. Semiannual. Fiction, to 4,000 words, and poetry, to 36 lines. "Our preference is for fresh language, a believable voice, a mature style, and a sense of the unusual with the subject matter." Pays in copies and nominal fee, on publication.

COLLAGES & BRICOLAGES—Office of Int'l Programs, 212 Founders Hall, Clarion Univ. of Pennsylvania, Clarion, PA 16212. Marie-José Fortis, Ed. Annual Fiction, nonfiction, and poetry. Surrealistic and expressionistic drawings in ink. "I seek writers who are politically and socially aware and whose writing is not egocentric." Pays in copies.

COLORADO REVIEW—English Dept., 359 Eddy, Colorado State Univ., Fort Collins, CO 80523. Poetry, short fiction, translations, interviews, articles on contemporary themes. Submit from September through May 1.

COLUMBIA: A MAGAZINE OF POETRY & PROSE—404 Dodge, Columbia Univ., New York, NY 10027. Address the Editors. Fiction and nonfiction to 5,000 words; poetry; essays; interviews; visual art. Pays in copies. SASE required. Guidelines and annual awards. Reading period: September 1 to April 1.

THE COMICS JOURNAL—Fantagraphics, Inc. 7563 Lake City Way, Seattle, WA 98115. Address Man. Ed. Monthly journal, 90 percent written by free-lancers with "working knowledge of the diversity and history of the comics medium." Reviews, 2,500 to 5,000 words; domestic and international news, 500 to 7,000 words; "Opening Shots" editorials, 500 to 1,500 words; interviews; and features, 2,500 to 5,000 words. Query for news and interviews. Pays 1 ½¢ a word, on publication. Guidelines.

CONFRONTATION—Dept. of English, C.W. Post of L. I. U., Brookville, NY 11548. Martin Tucker, Ed. Serious fiction, 750 to 6,000 words. Crafted poetry, 10 to 200 lines. Pays $10 to $100, on publication.

THE CONNECTICUT POETRY REVIEW—P.O. Box 3783, New Haven, CT 06525. J. Claire White and James Wm. Chichetto, Eds. Poetry, 5 to 20 lines, and reviews, 700 words. Pays $5 a poem, $10 for a review, on acceptance.

CONNECTICUT RIVER REVIEW—P.O. Box 2171, Bridgeport, CT 06608. Robert Isaacs, Ed. Semiannual poetry journal. Submit 3 to 5 poems, 40 lines or less. Pays in two copies. Guidelines.

CRAB CREEK REVIEW—4462 Whitman N., Seattle, WA 98103. Linda Clifton, Ed. Carol Orlock, Fiction Ed. Published 3 times a year. Clear, dynamic fiction, to 4,000 words, with strong voice and imagery. Nonfiction, to 4,000 words, that "uses image and occasion as a reason to share ideas with an intelligent reader." Poetry, to 80 lines. Pays in copies.

CRAZY QUILT—P.O. Box 632729, San Diego, CA 92163–2729. Address the Editors. Fiction, to 4,000 words, poetry, one-act plays, and literary criticism. Also B&W art, photographs. Pays in copies.

THE CREAM CITY REVIEW—Box 413, Univ. of Wisconsin, Milwaukee, WI 53201. Sandra Nelson and Kathlene Postma, Co-Eds. "We serve a national audience interested in a diversity of writing (in terms of style, subject, genre) and writers (gender, race, class, publishing history, etc.). Both well-known and newly published writers of fiction, poetry, and essays are featured, along with B&W artwork and a debate among 3 or more writers on a contemporary literary issue." Payment varies.

THE CRESCENT REVIEW—Box 15065, Winston-Salem, NC 27113. Guy Nancekeville, Ed. Semiannual. Short stories. "Especially interested in storytellers who have never been published or who have some connection with the South, but all writers are welcome to submit." Pays in copies.

CRITICAL INQUIRY—Univ. of Chicago Press, Wieboldt Hall, 1050 E. 59th St., Chicago, IL 60637. W. J. T. Mitchell, Ed. Critical essays that offer a theoretical perspective on literature, music, visual arts, and popular culture. No fiction, poetry, or autobiography. Pays in copies.

620

CUMBERLAND POETRY REVIEW—P.O. Box 120128, Acklen Sta., Nashville, TN 37212. Address Eds. High-quality poetry and criticism; translations. No restrictions on form, style, or subject matter. Pays in copies.

DENVER QUARTERLY—Univ of Denver, Denver, CO 80208. Donald Revell, Ed. Literary, cultural essays and articles; poetry; book reviews; fiction. Pays $5 per printed page, after publication.

DESCANT—Texas Christian Univ., T.C.U. Sta., Fort Worth, TX 76129. Betsy Colquitt, Stanley Trachtenberg, Eds. Fiction, to 6,000 words. Poetry to 40 lines. No restriction on form or subject. Pays in copies. Submit Sept. through May only.

DEVIANCE—P.O. Box 1706, Pawtucket, RI 02862. Lin Collette, Ed. Published 3 times a year. Fiction, to 2,500 words, and nonfiction essays on political and spiritual issues, to 2,500 words. Poetry, any length, and fillers, 25 to 250 words, on "deviant" subjects. No racist, sexist, homophobic work. Query for nonfiction. Pays in copies.

THE DEVIL'S MILLHOPPER—The Devil's Millhopper Press, College of Humanities, USC/Aiken, 171 University Pkwy., Aiken, SC 29801. Stephen Gardner, Ed. Poetry. Send SASE for guidelines. Pays in copies.

DREAMS & VISIONS—Skysong Press, RR1, Washago, Ontario, Canada L0K 2B0. Wendy Stanton, Manuscript Ed. Eclectic fiction, 2,000 to 7,500 words, that is "in some way unique and relevant to Christian readers today." Pays in copies, with $100 award to best of the year.

EARTH'S DAUGHTERS—Box 622, Station C, Buffalo, NY 14209. Published 3 times per year. Fiction, to 1,000 words; poetry, to 40 lines; and B&W photos or drawings. "Finely crafted work with a feminist theme." Pays in copies. SASE for guidelines.

EMBERS—Box 404, Guilford, CT 06437. Katrina Van Tassel, Mark Johnston, Charlotte Garrett, Eds. Biannual. Poetry. Interested in original new voices as well as published poets.

EOTU, THE MAGAZINE OF EXPERIMENTAL FICTION—#115, 1810 W. State St., Boise, ID 83702. Larry Dennis, Ed. Experimental fiction, to 5,000 words, and experimental poetry, to 2 pages. B&W artwork. "We seek writers working at the edge of their talents and abilities. No taboo, except boring common stuff." Include bio information and SASE. Pays $5 to $25, on acceptance, plus copy.

EVENT—Douglas College, Box 2503, New Westminister, BC, Canada V3L 5B2. Dale Zieroth, Ed. Short fiction, short plays, poetry. Pays $20 per printed page, on publication.

FARMER'S MARKET—P.O. Box 1272, Galesburg, IL 61402. Short stories, essays, and novel excerpts, to 40 pages, and poetry. Pays in copies.

FICTION INTERNATIONAL—English Dept., San Diego State Univ., San Diego, CA 92182. Harold Jaffe, Larry McCaffery, Eds. Post-modernist and politically committed fiction and theory. Manuscripts read from September to December 15. Payment in copies.

THE FIDDLEHEAD—Campus House, Univ. of New Brunswick, Fredericton, N.B., Canada E3B 5A3. Serious fiction, 2,500 words, preferably by Canadians. Pays about $10 per printed page, on publication. SAE with international coupons required.

FIELD—Rice Hall, Oberlin College, Oberlin, OH 44074. Stuart Friebert,

621

David Young, Eds. Serious poetry, any length, by established and unknown poets; essays on poetics by poets. Translations by qualified translators. Pays $20 to $30 per page, on publication.

FINE MADNESS—P.O. Box 31138, Seattle, WA 98103–1138. Poetry, any length; short fiction; essays on poetics; reviews. Pays varying rates. Guidelines.

FIVE FINGERS REVIEW—P.O. Box 15426, San Francisco, CA 94115. Published once or twice a year. Socially aware fiction, nonfiction, and poetry that address concerns of the day in surprising ways. Pays in copies.

FOLIO—Dept. of English, American Univ., Washington, DC 20016. Lisa Norris Stauffer and Keith Custis, Eds. Semiannual. Fiction, poetry, translations, and essays. Photos and drawings. Submissions read Aug. through April. Pays in 2 copies. Contest.

FOOTWORK, THE PATERSON LITERARY REVIEW—Cultural Affairs Dept., Passaic County Comm. College, College Blvd., Paterson, NJ 07509. Maria Mazziotti Gillan, Ed. High quality fiction, to 8 pages, and poetry, to 3 pages, any style. Pays in copies.

FREE INQUIRY—P.O. Box 5, Buffalo, NY 14215–0005. Paul Kurtz, Ed. Tim Madigan, Exec. Ed. Articles, 500 to 5,000 words, for "literate and lively readership. Focus is on criticisms of religious belief systems, and how to lead an ethical life without a supernatural basis." Pays in copies.

THE GAMUT—1218 Fenn Tower, Cleveland State Univ., Cleveland, OH 44115–2440. Louis T. Milic, Ed. Lively articles, 2,000 to 6,000 words, on general-interest topics preferably concerned with the region. Quality fiction and poetry. Photos. Pays $25 to $150, on publication. Send SASE for guidelines.

THE GEORGIA REVIEW—Univ. of Georgia, Athens, GA 30602. Stanley W. Lindberg, Ed. Stephen Corey, Assoc. Ed. Short fiction; interdisciplinary essays on arts, sciences, and the humanities; book reviews; poetry. Novel excerpts discouraged. No submissions in June to September.

THE GETTYSBURG REVIEW—Gettysburg College, Gettysburg, PA 17325. Peter Stitt, Ed. Quarterly. Poetry, fiction, essays, and essay-reviews, 1,000 to 20,000 words. "Review sample copy before submitting." Pays $2 a line for poetry; $25 per printed page for fiction and nonfiction. Allow 3 to 6 months for response.

GRAIN—Box 1154, Regina, Sask., Canada S4P 3B4. Geoffrey Ursell, Ed. Short stories, to 20 typed pages; poems, send up to 8; visual art. Pays $30 to $100 for stories, $100 for cover art, $30 for other art. SAE with international reply coupons required.

GREAT RIVER REVIEW—211 W. 7th St., Winona, MN 55987. Orval Lund, Jr., Ed. Fiction and creative prose, 2,000 to 10,000 words. Quality contemporary poetry; send 4 to 8 poems. Special interest in midwestern writers and themes.

GREEN'S MAGAZINE—P.O. Box 3236, Regina, Sask., Canada S4P 3H1. David Green, Ed. Fiction for family reading, 1,500 to 4,000 words. Poetry, to 40 lines. Pays in copies. International reply coupons must accompany U.S. manuscripts.

THE GREENSBORO REVIEW—Dept. of English, Univ. of North Carolina, Greensboro, NC 27412. Jim Clark, Ed. Semiannual. Poetry and fiction. Submission deadlines: Sept. 15 and Feb. 15. Pays in copies. Guidelines for literary awards issue available on request.

HALF TONES TO JUBILEE—Pensacola Junior College, English Dept.,

622

622

1000 College Blvd., Pensacola, FL 32504. Walter F. Spara, Ed. Fiction, to 1,500 words, and poetry, to 60 lines. Pays in copies.

HAUNTS—Nightshade Publications, Box 3342, Providence, RI 02906. Joseph K. Cherkes, Ed. Short stories, 1,500 to 8,000 words: horror, science-fantasy, and supernatural tales with strong characters. Pays ¼ ¢ to ½ ¢ a word, on publication.

HAWAII REVIEW—Dept. of English, Univ. of Hawaii, 1733 Donagho Rd., Honolulu, HI 96822. Galatea Maman, Ed.-in-Chief. Quality fiction, poetry, interviews, essays, and literary criticism reflecting both regional and universal concerns.

HAYDEN'S FERRY REVIEW—Matthew's Center, Arizona State Univ., Tempe, AZ 85287–1502. Salima Keegan, Ed. Semiannual. Fiction, essays, and poetry (submit up to 6 poems). Photos and drawings (clearly marked slides or B&W prints). Include brief bio and SASE. Deadline for Spring/Summer issue is Sept. 30. Pays in copies.

HERESIES: A FEMINIST PUBLICATION ON ART AND POLITICS— Box 1306, Canal Street Sta., New York, NY 10013. Thematic issues. Fiction, to 20 double-spaced typed pages; nonfiction; poetry; art; photography. SASE required.

THE HIGHLANDER—P.O. Box 397, Barrington, IL 60011. Angus Ray, Ed. Bimonthly. Articles, 1,300 to 1,900 words, related to Scottish history. "We are not concerned with modern Scotland or current problems in Scotland." Pays $100 to $150, on acceptance.

THE HOLLINS CRITIC—P.O. Box 9538, Hollins College, VA 24020. John Rees Moore, Ed. Published 5 times a year. Poetry, to 2 pages. Pays $25, on publication.

HOME LIFE—127 Ninth Ave. N., Nashville, TN 37234. Charlie Warren, Ed. Southern Baptist. Short lyrical verse: humorous, marriage and family, seasonal, and inspirational. Pays to $24 for poetry, 5 ½ ¢ a word for articles, on acceptance.

HOME PLANET NEWS—P.O. Box 415, Stuyvesant Sta., New York, NY 10009. Enid Dame and Donald Lev, Eds. Quarterly art tabloid. Fiction, to 8 typed pages; reviews, 3 to 5 pages; and poetry, any length. "We are looking for quality poetry, fiction and discerning literary and art reviews." Query for nonfiction. Pays in copies and gift subscription.

HOWLING DOG—8419 Rhode, Utica, MI 48317. Mark Donovan, Ed. Semiannual. "Strange" fiction, to 1,000 words. Free verse, avant-garde, wild poetry to 5 pages. "We are looking for pieces with a humorous perspective toward society's problems." Pays in copies.

HURRICANE ALICE: A FEMINIST QUARTERLY—207 Lind Hall, 207 Church St. S.E., Minneapolis, MN 55455. Articles, fiction, essays, interviews, and reviews, 500 to 3,000 words, with feminist perspective. Pays in copies.

ILLINOIS WRITERS REVIEW—P.O. Box 1087, Champaign, IL 61820. Kevin Stein and Jim Elledge, Eds. Semiannual. Critical reviews, essays, and commentary on contemporary writing, 750 to 2,500 words. B&W cover art and photos. Pays $25, on publication.

INDIANA REVIEW—316 N. Jordan Ave., Indiana Univ., Bloomington, IN 47405. Renée Manfredi, Ed. Allison Joseph, Assoc. Ed. Fiction with an emphasis on storytelling and sophistication of language. Poems that are well-executed and ambitious. Pays $5 per page.

INLET—Dept. of English, Virginia Wesleyan College, Norfolk, VA 23502.

Joseph Harkey, Ed. Short fiction, 1,000 to 3,000 words (short lengths preferred). Poems of 4 to 40 lines; all forms and themes. Submit between September and March 1st, each year. Pays in copies.

INTERIM—Dept. of English, Univ. of Nevada, Las Vegas, NV 89154. A. Wilber Stevens, Ed. Semiannual. Fiction, to 6,000 words, and poetry. Pays in copies and 2-year subscription.

INVISIBLE CITY—P.O. Box 2853, San Francisco, CA 94126. John McBride, Paul Vangelisti, Eds. Reviews, translations; especially interested in contemporary European literature. Pays in copies.

THE IOWA REVIEW—EPB 308, Univ. of Iowa, Iowa City, IA 52242. David Hamilton, Ed. Essays, poems, stories, reviews. Pays $10 a page for fiction and nonfiction, $1 a line for poetry, on publication.

JACARANDA REVIEW—Dept. of English, Univ. of California, Los Angeles, CA 90024. Bruce Kijewski, Fiction Ed. Carolie Parker and David Case, Poetry Eds. Semiannual. Fiction, to 50 pages, and poetry (submit up to 3 poems). No payment.

KALEIDOSCOPE—United Cerebral Palsy & Services for the Handicapped, 326 Locust St., Akron, OH 44302. Darshan Perusek, Ph.D., Ed. Semiannual. Fiction, essays, interviews, articles, and biographies relating to the arts, to 5,000 words. Poetry and fillers, any length. Photos a plus. Submissions accepted from disabled or nondisabled writers. Pays $50 for fiction, to $50 for poetry, to $25 for book reviews, to $25 for photos. Guidelines recommended.

KANSAS QUARTERLY—Dept. of English, Denison Hall 122, Kansas State Univ., Manhattan, KS 66506. Literary criticism, art, and history. Fiction and poetry. Pays in copies. Two series of annual awards.

KARAMU—Dept. of English, Eastern Illinois Univ., Charleston, IL 61920. Peggy Brayfield, Ed. Contemporary or experimental fiction. Poetry. Pays in copies.

THE KENYON REVIEW—Kenyon College, Gambier, OH 43022. Marilyn Hacker, Ed. Quarterly. Fiction, poetry, essays, literary criticism, reviews, and humor. Pays $10 a printed page for prose, $15 a printed page for poetry and reviews, on publication. No manuscripts read during summer.

KIOSK—302 Clemens Hall, SUNY Buffalo, Buffalo, NY 14260. N. Gillespie, Ed. "Quirky experimental fiction and poetry." SASE required. Pays in copies.

LAKE EFFECT—Lake County Writers Group, P.O. Box 59, Oswego, NY 13126. Jean O'Connor Fuller, Man. Ed. Short stories, essays, poetry, and humor for a general audience. Pays $25 for fiction and nonfiction, $5 for poems, on publication. Query for nonfiction only.

THE LEADING EDGE—3163 JKHB, Provo, UT 84602. Eric Lowe, Ed. Triannual science fiction and fantasy magazine. Short stories, 3,000 to 12,000 words; poetry, to 200 lines; and articles, to 8,000 words, on science, scientific speculation, and literary criticism. Fillers and comics. "Do not send originals; manuscripts are marked and critiqued by staff." Pays ½¢ per word with $5 minimum for fiction; $4 per published page of poetry; $2 to $4 for fillers; on publication. SASE for guidelines.

LILITH, THE JEWISH WOMEN'S MAGAZINE—250 W. 57th St., New York, NY 10107. Susan Weidman Schneider, Ed. Fiction, 1,500 to 2,000 words, on issues of interest to Jewish women.

THE LION AND THE UNICORN—Ed. Offices, English Dept., Brooklyn

College, Brooklyn, NY 11210. Geraldine DeLuca, Roni Natov, Eds. Articles, from 2,000 words, offering criticism of children's and young-adult books, for teachers, scholars, artists, and parents. Query preferred. Pays in copies.

LITERARY MAGAZINE REVIEW—English Dept., Kansas State Univ., Manhattan, KS 66506. Reviews and articles concerning literary magazines, 1,000 to 1,500 words, for writers and readers of contemporary literature. Pays modest fees and in copies. Query.

THE LITERARY REVIEW—Fairleigh Dickinson Univ., 285 Madison Ave., Madison, NJ 07940. Walter Cummins, Martin Green, Harry Keyishian, William Zander, Eds. Serious fiction; poetry; translations; essays and reviews on contemporary literature. Pays in copies.

LONG SHOT—P.O. Box 6231, Hoboken, NJ 07030. Danny Shot, Jack Wiler, Jessica Chosid, Tom Polhemus, Eds. Fiction, poetry and nonfiction, to 10 pages. B&W drawings. "No taboos." Pays in copies.

THE LONG STORY—11 Kingston St., N. Andover, MA 01845. Stories, 8,000 to 20,000 words; prefer committed fiction. Pays in copies.

LOST CREEK LETTERS—Lost Creek Publications, Box 373A, Rushville, MO 64484. Pamela Montgomery, Ed. Fiction, to 5,000 words, and poetry, any length. "We are looking for shining gems of contemporary literature." Pays $5 for short stories, $2 for poems, or two contributor's copies.

LYRA—P.O. Box 3188, Guttenberg, NJ 07093. Lourdes Gil and Iraida Iturralde, Eds. Fiction, to 12 double-spaced pages. Essays, translations, interviews, and reviews, 3 to 15 pages. Poetry, any length. Quarterly. Pays $25 to $30 per book review, on acceptance, and in copies.

THE MALAHAT REVIEW—Univ. of Victoria, P.O. Box 3045, Victoria, BC, Canada V8W 3P4. Constance Rooke, Ed. Fiction and poetry, including translations. Pays from $20 per page, on acceptance.

THE MANHATTAN REVIEW—440 Riverside Dr., #45, New York, NY 10027. Highest quality poetry. Pays in copies.

MASSACHUSETTS REVIEW—Memorial Hall, Univ. of Massachusetts, Amherst, MA 01003. Literary criticism; articles on public affairs, scholarly disciplines. Short fiction. Poetry. No submissions between June and October. Pays modest rates, on publication. SASE required.

MICHIGAN HISTORICAL REVIEW—Clark Historical Library, Central Michigan Univ., Mt. Pleasant, MI 48859. Address Ed. Scholarly articles related to Michigan's political, social, economic, and cultural history; articles on American, Canadian, and Midwestern history that directly or indirectly explore themes related to Michigan's past. SASE required.

THE MICKLE STREET REVIEW—326 Mickle St., Camden, NJ 08102. Articles, poems, and artwork related to Walt Whitman.

MID-AMERICAN REVIEW—Dept. of English, Bowling Green State Univ., Bowling Green, OH 43403. Ken Letko, Ed. High-quality fiction, poetry, articles, translations, and reviews of contemporary writing. Fiction to 20,000 words. Reviews, articles, 500 to 2,500 words. Pays to $50, on publication. No manuscripts read June through Aug.

MIDWEST QUARTERLY—Pittsburg State Univ., Pittsburg, KS 66762. James B. M. Schick, Ed. Scholarly articles, 2,500 to 5,000 words, on contemporary academic and public issues. Pays in copies.

MINI-MAG—1827 Haight St., #208, San Francisco, CA 94117. Dan Blacharski, Ed. Fiction and nonfiction, to 2,500 words; humor, 1,000 words; and fillers, 500 words. "Broad areas of interest are mystical-metaphysical art, music, interviews/profiles of noteworthy people, education, computers, women's issues, and health." No fictionalized news, but writers should "add their own literary voice to facts." Query with writing samples for nonfiction. Pays $25. Guidelines are available.

THE MINNESOTA REVIEW—English Dept., SUNY-Stony Brook, Stony Brook, NY 11794. Address the Editors. "Politically committed fiction, 3,000 to 6,000 words; nonfiction, 5,000 to 7,500 words; and poetry, up to three pages; for socialist, marxist, or feminist audience." Pays in copies.

MISSISSIPPI REVIEW—Center for Writers, Univ. of Southern Mississippi, Southern Sta., Box 5144, Hattiesburg, MS 39406–5144. Frederick Barthelme, Ed. Serious fiction, poetry, criticism, interviews. Pays in copies.

THE MISSISSIPPI VALLEY REVIEW—Dept. of English, Western Illinois Univ., Macomb, IL 61455. Forrest Robinson, Ed. Short fiction, to 20 typed pages. Poetry; send 3 to 5 poems. Pays in copies.

THE MISSOURI REVIEW—1507 Hillcrest Hall, Univ. of Missouri-Columbia, Columbia, MO 65211. Greg Michalson, Man. Ed. Speer Morgan, Ed. Poems, of any length. Fiction and essays. Pays $20 per printed page, on contract.

MODERN HAIKU—P.O. Box 1752, Madison, WI 53701. Robert Spiess, Ed. Haiku and articles about haiku. Pays $1 per haiku, $5 a page for articles.

MONTHLY REVIEW—122 W. 27th St., New York, NY 10001. Paul M. Sweezy, Harry Magdoff, Eds. Analytical articles, 5,000 words, on politics and economics, from independent socialist viewpoint. Pays $50, on publication.

MOVING OUT—P.O. Box 21249, Detroit, MI 48221. Poetry, fiction, articles, and art by women. Submit 4 to 6 poems at a time. Pays in copies.

NEBO: A LITERARY JOURNAL—Dept. of English and Foreign Languages, Arkansas Tech. Univ., Russellville, AR 72801–2222. Poems (submit up to 5); mainstream fiction, to 3,000 words; critical essays, to 10 pages. Pays in one copy. SASE required. Offices closed May through Aug. SASE for guidelines.

NEGATIVE CAPABILITY—62 Ridgelawn Dr. E., Mobile, AL 36608. Sue Walker, Ed. Poetry, any length; fiction, essays, art. Pays $20 per story. Contests.

NER/BLQ—See *New England Review.*

NEW DELTA REVIEW—c/o Dept. of English, Louisiana State Univ., Baton Rouge, LA 70803–5001. Kathleen Fitzpatrick, Ed. Semiannual. Fiction and nonfiction, 500 to 3,500 words. Submit up to 4 poems, any length. B&W photos or drawings. "We want pieces with raw power behind them." Pays in copies.

NEW ENGLAND REVIEW—(formerly *NER/BLQ*) Middlebury College, Middlebury, VT 05753. T.R. Hummer, Ed. Devon Jersild, Assoc. Ed. Fiction, nonfiction, and poetry of varying lengths. "National, international, literary, political, effectively radical writing." Pays $10 per page, on acceptance, and in copies and subscription.

NEW LAUREL REVIEW—828 Lesseps St., New Orleans, LA 70117. Lee Meitzen Grue, Ed. Annual. Fiction, 20 to 40 pages; nonfiction, to 10 pages; poetry, any length. Library market. No inspirational verse. International readership. Pays in one copy.

NEW LETTERS—5100 Rockhill Rd., Kansas City, MO 64110–2499. James McKinley, Ed. Fiction, 10 to 25 pages. Poetry, submit 3 to 6 at a time. Send SASE for contest guidelines.

NEW MEXICO HUMANITIES REVIEW—Box A, New Mexico Tech, Socorro, NM 87801. Poetry and fiction, to 30 pages, any theme; personal and scholarly essays; articles dealing with southwestern and Native American themes; book reviews. Pays in subscriptions.

NEW ORLEANS REVIEW—Loyola Univ., New Orleans, LA 70118. John Mosier, Ed. Literary or film criticism, to 6,000 words. Serious fiction and poetry.

THE NEW PRESS—87–40 Francis Lewis Blvd. A44, Queens Village, NY 11427. Bob Abramson, Pub. Quarterly. Fiction and nonfiction, to 2,500 words. Poetry to 200 lines. Pays in copies and occasional honorarium.

THE NEW RENAISSANCE—9 Heath Rd., Arlington, MA 02174. Louise T. Reynolds, Ed. An international magazine of ideas and opinions, emphasizing literature and the arts. Query with outline and writing sample for articles; send complete manuscript for essays. SASE required. Payment varies, after publication.

THE NEW YORK QUARTERLY—P.O. Box 693, Old Chelsea Station, New York, NY 100113. William Packard, Ed. Published three times yearly by The National Poetry Foundation. Poems of any style and persuasion, well written and well intentioned. Pays in copies.

NEXUS—Wright State Univ., 006 Univ. Center, Dayton, OH 45435. Ted Cains, Ed. Poetry, hard-hitting fiction, surrealism. Essays on obscure poets, artists, and musicians. Pays in copies.

NIMROD—2210 S. Main St., Tulsa, OK 74114–1190. Publishes two issues annually, one awards and one thematic. Quality poetry and fiction, experimental and traditional. Pays in copies. Annual awards for poetry and fiction. Send #10 SASE for guidelines.

THE NORTH AMERICAN REVIEW—Univ. of Northern Iowa, Cedar Falls, IA 50614. Peter Cooley, Poetry Ed. Poetry of high quality. Pays 50¢ a line, on acceptance.

NORTH ATLANTIC REVIEW—15 Arbutus Lane, Stony Brook, NY 11790–1408. John Gill, Ed. Semiannual. Fiction and nonfiction, to 5,000 words; poetry, any length; fillers, humor, photographs and illustrations. A special section on the 60s will be part of each issue. Pays in copies.

THE NORTH DAKOTA QUARTERLY—Univ. of North Dakota, Grand Forks, ND 58202–8237. Essays in the humanities; fiction, reviews, graphics, and poetry. Limited market. Pays in copies and subscription.

NORTHEASTARTS—Boston Arts Organization, Inc., JFK Station, P.O. Box 6061, Boston, MA 02114. Mr. Leigh Donaldson, Ed. Fiction and nonfiction, to 500 words; poetry, to 30 lines; and brief humor. "Both professional and beginning writers are considered. No obscene or offensive material." Pays in one copy.

NORTHWEST REVIEW—369 PLC, Univ. of Oregon, Eugene, OR 97403. Cecelia Hagen, Fiction Ed. Fiction, commentary, essays, and poetry. Reviews. Pays in copies. Send SASE for guidelines.

THE OHIO REVIEW—Ellis Hall, Ohio Univ., Athens, OH 45701–2979. Wayne Dodd, Ed. Short stories, poetry, essays, reviews. Pays $5 per page for prose, $1 a line for poetry, plus copies, on publication. SASE required. Submissions not read in June, July, or August.

ONIONHEAD—Arts on the Park, Inc., 115 N. Kentucky Ave., Lakeland, FL 33801. Address the Editorial Council. Short stories, to 4,000 words; essays, to 2,500 words; and poetry, to 60 lines; on provocative social, political, and cultural observations and hypotheses. Pays in copies. Send SASE for "Wordart" poetry contest information.

OREGON EAST—Hoke College Center, EOSC, La Grande, OR 97850. Short fiction, nonfiction, to 3,000 words, poetry, to 60 lines, and high-contrast graphics. Pays in copies. Submissions by March 1, notification by June.

ORPHIC LUTE—526 Paul Pl., Los Alamos, NM 87544. Patricia Doherty Hinnebusch, Ed. Brief, structured poems and free verse, to 11 lines. Especially welcome: humorous poetry that is not ribald. Submit 6 to 10 poems at a time. Pays in copies.

OTHER VOICES—820 Ridge Rd., Highland Park, IL 60035. Lois Hauselman, Sharon Fiffer, Eds. Semiannual. Fresh, accessible short stories, one-act plays, and novel excerpts, to 5,000 words. Pays in copies and modest honorarium.

OUTERBRIDGE—College of Staten Island, English Dept. A324, 715 Ocean Terr., Staten Island, NY 10301. Charlotte Alexander, Ed. Annual. Well-crafted stories, to 20 pages, and poetry, to four pages, "directed to a wide audience of literate adult readers." Reading period: September to June. Pays in two copies.

PAINTBRUSH—Language & Literature, Northeast Missouri State Univ., Kirksville, MO 63501. Ben Bennani, Ed. Semiannual. Book reviews, to 1,500 words, and serious, sophisticated poetry (submit 3 to 5). Query preferred for book reviews. Pays in copies.

PAINTED BRIDE QUARTERLY—230 Vine St., Philadelphia, PA 19106. Lee W. Potts and Teresa Leo, Eds. Fiction, nonfiction, and poetry of varying lengths. Pays in subscription.

PANDORA—2844 Grayson, Ferndale, MI 48220. Meg Mac Donald, Ed. Ruth Berman, Poetry Ed. (2809 Drew Ave. S., Minneapolis, MN 55416). Science fiction and speculative fantasy, to 5,000 words; poetry. "Looking for stories about people, not just ideas or futuristic settings. No futile endings, 'It was a dream/joke, etc.' Avoid contemporary fantasy; we want traditional fantasy." Pays to 2¢ a word for fiction, on publication. Payment varies for poetry and artwork.

PANHANDLER—English Dept., Univ. of West Florida, Pensacola, FL 32514. Michael Yots and Stanton Millet, Eds. Semiannual. Fiction, 1,500 to 4,000 words, "that tells a story"; poetry, any length, with a strong sense of colloquial language. Pays in copies.

THE PARIS REVIEW—541 E. 72nd St., New York, NY 10021. Address Fiction and Poetry Eds. Fiction and poetry of high literary quality. Pays on publication.

PARNASSUS—41 Union Sq. W., Rm. 804, New York, NY 10003. Herbert Leibowitz, Ed. Critical essays and reviews on contemporary poetry. International in scope. Pays in cash and copies.

PARTISAN REVIEW—Boston Univ., 236 Bay State Rd., Boston, MA 02215. William Phillips, Ed. Serious fiction, poetry, and essays. Payment varies. No simultaneous submissions.

PASSAGES NORTH—Kalamazoo College, 1200 Academy St., Kalamazoo, MI 49007. Ben Mitchell, Ed. Mark Cox, Poetry Ed. Mary LaChapelle, Fiction Ed.

Published twice a year in December and June. Poetry, fiction, criticism, essays, visual art. Pays in copies. Frequent prizes and honoraria.

THE PENNSYLVANIA REVIEW—Univ. of Pittsburgh, Dept. of English, 526 Cathedral of Learning, Pittsburgh, PA 15260. Fiction, to 5,000 words, book reviews, interviews with authors, and poems (send up to six at once). Submissions not accepted April 1 to Sept. 1. Pays in copies.

PEQUOD—New York University English Dept., 19 University Pl., 2nd Fl., New York, NY 10003. Mark Rudman, Ed. Semiannual. Short stories, essays, and literary criticism, to 10 pages; poetry and translations, to 3 pages. Pays $10 to $25, on publication.

PERMAFROST—English Dept., Univ. of Alaska, Fairbanks, AK 99775. Poetry, short fiction to 7,500 words, creative nonfiction and essays, and B&W photos and graphics. Reading periods: Sept. 1 to Dec. 1 and Jan. 15 to April 1. Pays in copies.

PIEDMONT LITERARY REVIEW—Bluebird Lane, Rt. #1, Box 512, Forest, VA 24551. Evelyn Miles, Man. Ed. Quarterly. Prose, to 2,500 words. Submit prose to Dr. Olga Kronmeyer, 25 West Dale Dr., Lynchburg, VA 24501. Poems, any length and style. Submit up to 5 poems to Gail White, 1017 Spanish Moss Ln., Breaux Bridge, LA 70517. Submit Asian verse to Dorothy McLaughlin, 10 Atlantic Rd., Somerset, NJ 08873. No pornography. Pays in one copy.

PIG IRON—P.O. Box 237, Youngstown, OH 44501. Nate Leslie, Jim Villani, Eds. Fiction and nonfiction, to 8,000 words. Write for upcoming themes. Poetry, to 100 lines. Pays $5 per published page, on publication.

THE PINEHURST JOURNAL—Pinehurst Press, P.O. Box 360747, Milpitas, CA 95036. Michael K. McNamara, Ed. Quarterly. Contemporary fiction, 1,000 to 2,500 words, and 50- to 400-word shorts, gay/lesbian and ageism themes especially welcome; articles and essays, 1,500 to 3,500 words, with historic or nostalgic perspective; opinions, reviews, and personal experience pieces considered. Poetry, under 24 lines. Query for book reviews only. Pays $5 plus nine-month subscription, on publication; $5 plus one copy for poems.

PIVOT—250 Riverside Dr., #23, New York, NY 10025. Martin Mitchell, Ed. Poetry, to 75 lines. Reading period is Jan. 1 to June 1. Annual. Pays two copies.

PLAINS POETRY JOURNAL—Box 2337, Bismarck, ND 58502. Jane Greer, Ed. Poetry using traditional conventions in vigorous, compelling ways; no "greeting card"-type verse or prosaic verse. No subject is taboo. Pays in copies.

PLOUGHSHARES—Emerson College, 100 Beacon St., Boston, MA 02116. Pays $10 to $50, on publication, and 2 copies. Reading periods vary, check recent issue; guidelines.

POEM—c/o English Dept., U.A.H., Huntsville, AL 35899. Nancy Frey Dillard, Ed. Serious lyric poetry. Pays in copies.

POET AND CRITIC—203 Ross Hall, Iowa State Univ., Ames, IA 50011. Neal Bowers, Ed. Poetry, reviews, essays on contemporary poetry. No manuscripts read June through September. Pays in copies.

POET LORE—7815 Old Georgetown Rd., Bethesda, MD 20814. Sunil Freeman, Man. Ed. Original poetry, all kinds. Translations, reviews. Pays in copies. Annual narrative contest.

POETRY—60 West Walton St., Chicago, IL 60610. Joseph Parisi, Ed. Poetry of highest quality. Submit 3 to 4 poems. Allow 8 to 10 weeks for response. Pays $2 a line, on publication.

POETRY EAST—DePaul University, 802 W. Belden Ave., Chicago, IL 60614–3214. Marilyn Woitel, Man. Ed. Published in spring and fall. Poetry, essays, and translations. "Please send a sampling of your best work. Do not send book-length manuscripts without querying first." Pays in copies.

POETRY/LA—P.O. Box 84271, Los Angeles, CA 90073. Helen Friedland, Ed. Semiannual. Quality poems by poets living, working, or attending school within a 100-mile radius of Los Angeles. Pays in copies.

PORTLAND REVIEW—c/o Portland State Univ., P.O. Box 751, Portland, OR 97207. Published 3 times a year. Short fiction, essays, poetry, one-act plays (to 5 pages), photography, and artwork. "Please include a bio." Payment is one copy.

PRAIRIE SCHOONER—201 Andrews Hall, Univ. of Nebraska, Lincoln, NE 68588–0334. Hilda Raz, Ed. Short stories, poetry, essays, book reviews, and translations. Pays in copies. Annual contests. SASE required.

PRISM INTERNATIONAL—E459–1866 Main Mall, Dept. of Creative Writing, Univ. of British Columbia, Vancouver, B.C., Canada V6T 1W5. Blair Rosser, Ed. High-quality fiction, poetry, drama, creative nonfiction, and literature in translation, varying lengths. Include international reply coupons. Pays $20 per published page. Annual short fiction contest.

PROOF ROCK—P.O. Box 607, Halifax, VA 24558. Don Conner, Fiction Ed. Serena Fusek, Poetry Ed. Fiction, to 2,500 words. Poetry, to 32 lines. Reviews. Pays in copies.

PUDDING—60 N. Main St., Johnstown, OH 43031. Jennifer Welch Bosveld, Ed. Poems on popular culture and social concerns, especially free verse and experimental, with fresh language, concrete images, and specific detail. Short articles about poetry in human services.

PUERTO DEL SOL—New Mexico State Univ., Box 3E, Las Cruces, NM 88003–0001. Kevin McIlvoy, Ed. Short stories and personal essays, to 30 pages; novel excerpts, to 65 pages; articles, to 45 pages, and reviews, to 15 pages. Poetry, photos. Pays in copies.

THE QUARTERLY—201 East 50th, New York, NY 10022. Gordon Lish, Ed. "The Magazine of New Writing." Fiction, nonfiction, poetry, and humor, no limits on length. Payment varies, on publication.

QUARTERLY WEST—317 Olpin Union, Univ. of Utah, Salt Lake City, UT 84112. C.F. Pinkerton and Regina Oost, Eds. Short shorts and novellas; nonfiction and criticism. Poetry (submit up to 3 poems at a time). Query for novellas. Pays $15 to $300 for fiction and nonfiction, $1 a line for poetry, on publication.

QUEEN'S QUARTERLY—Queens Univ., Kingston, Ont., Canada K7L 3N6. Articles, to 8,000 words, on a wide range of topics, and fiction, to 5,000 words. Poetry: send no more than 6 poems. B&W art. Pays to $300, on publication.

RAG MAG—P.O. Box 12, Goodhue, MN 55027. Beverly Voldseth, Ed. Semiannual. Fiction and nonfiction, to 1,000 words. Poetry any length. No religious writing. Pays in copies.

RAMBUNCTIOUS REVIEW—1221 W. Pratt Blvd., Chicago, IL 60626. Mary Dellutri, Richard Goldman, Nancy Lennon, Beth Hausler, Eds. Fiction, to 15 pages, poetry (submit up to 5 at a time). Pays in copies. Submit material September through May. Contests.

RED CEDAR REVIEW—Dept. of English, Morrill Hall, Michigan State Univ., East Lansing, MI 48825. Fiction, 10 to 15 pages; poetry (submit up to 5); interviews; book reviews; graphics. Pays in copies.

THE REDNECK REVIEW OF LITERATURE—P.O. Box 730, Twin Falls, ID 83303. Penelope Reedy, Ed. Semiannual. Fiction, to 2,500 words, of the contemporary American West; essays and book reviews, 300 to 1,500 words; poetry. Pays in copies.

RELIGION AND PUBLIC EDUCATION—E262 Lagomarcino Hall, Iowa State Univ., Ames, IA 50011. Charles R. Kniker, Ed.-in-Chief. Paul Blakeley, Poetry Ed. Poems with mythological or religious values or themes. Pays in copies.

RESONANCE—P.O. Box 215, Beacon, NY 12508. Evan Pritchard, Ed. Published three times a year. Fiction, to 1,200 words; thematic nonfiction, to 1,200 words; poetry, to 46 lines. Pays in one copy.

REVIEW: LATIN AMERICAN LITERATURE AND ARTS—Americas Society, 680 Park Ave., New York, NY 10021. Alfred J. MacAdam, Ed. Published twice yearly. Work in English translation by and about young and established Latin American writers; essays and book reviews considered. Send queries for 1,000- to 1,500-word manuscripts, and short poem translations. Payment varies, on acceptance.

RHINO—8403 W. Normal Ave., Niles, IL 60648. Kay Meier and Martha Vertreace, Eds. "Authentic emotion in well-crafted poetry." January to June reading period. Pays in copies.

RIVER CITY—Dept. of English, Memphis State Univ., Memphis, TN 38152. Joe Ranft, Man. Ed. Poems, short stories, essays and interviews. No novel excerpts. Pay varies according to grants. No reading May through Aug. Contests.

RIVERSIDE QUARTERLY—807 Walters #107, Lake Charles, LA 70605. Leland Sapiro, Ed. Science fiction and fantasy, to 3,500 words; reviews, criticism (no maximum length); poetry and letters. "Read magazine before submitting." Send poetry to Sheryl Smith, 515 Saratoga #2, Santa Clara, CA 95050; fiction to Redd Boggs, Box 1111, Berkeley, CA 94701. Buys first rights only. Pays in copies.

ROANOKE REVIEW—Roanoke College, Salem, VA 24153. Robert R. Walter, Ed. Quality short fiction, to 7,500 words, and poetry, to 100 lines. Pays in copies.

ROMANCING THE PAST—17239 S. Oak Park Ave. #207, Tinley Park, IL 60477. Michelle Regan, Ed. Quarterly. Nostalgia and historic material: fiction and nonfiction, to 10 pages, and poetry. Pays in copies.

SAN FERNANDO POETRY JOURNAL—18301 Halstead St., Northridge, CA 91325. Richard Cloke, Ed. Quality poetry, 20 to 100 lines, with social content; scientific, philosophic, and historical themes. Pays in copies.

SAN JOSE STUDIES—San Jose State Univ., San Jose, CA 95192. Fauneil J. Rinn, Ed. Poetry, fiction, and essays on interdisciplinary topics. Occasionally publishes photos and art. Pays in copies. Annual awards.

SANSKRIT LITERARY/ART PUBLICATION—Univ. of North Carolina/Charlotte, Charlotte, NC 28223–0001. Christy Beatty, Ed.-in-Chief. Annual. Poetry, short fiction, photos, and fine art.

SCANDINAVIAN REVIEW—725 Park Ave., New York, NY 10021. Essays on contemporary Scandinavia. Fiction and poetry, translated from Nordic languages. Pays from $100, on publication.

SCRIVENER—McGill Univ., 853 Sherbrooke St. W., Montreal, Quebec, Canada H3A 2T6. Sam Anson, Thea Boyanowsky, Peter Sampson, Eds. Poetry, 5 to 25 lines; prose, to 20 pages; reviews, to 5 pages; essays, to 10 pages. Photography and graphics. Pays in copies.

THE SEATTLE REVIEW—Padelford Hall, GN-30, Univ. of Washington, Seattle, WA 98195. Donna Gerstenberger, Ed. Short stories, to 20 pages, poetry, essays on the craft of writing, and interviews with Northwest writers. Payment varies.

SENECA REVIEW—Hobart & William Smith Colleges, Geneva, NY 14456. Deborah Tall, Ed. Poetry, translations, and essays on contemporary poetry. Pays in copies.

SHOOTING STAR REVIEW—7123 Race St., Pittsburgh, PA 15208. Sandra Gould Ford, Pub. Fiction and folktales, to 3,500 words, essays, to 2,500 words, and poetry, to 50 lines, on the African-American experience. Query for book reviews only. Pays $8 to $30, and in copies. Send SASE for topic deadlines.

SING HEAVENLY MUSE! WOMEN'S POETRY & PROSE—P.O. Box 13320, Minneapolis, MN 55414. Short stories and essays, to 5,000 words. Poetry. Query for themes and reading periods. Pays in copies.

SKYLARK—2233 171st St., Hammond, IN 46323. Pamela Hunter, Ed. The Fine Arts Annual of Purdue Calumet. Fiction and articles, to 5,000 words. Poetry, to 25 lines. B&W prints and drawings. Deadline is May 15th for fall publication. Pays in one copy.

SLIPSTREAM—Box 2071, New Market Sta., Niagara Falls, NY 14301. Contemporary poetry, any length. Pays in copies. Query for themes. (Also accepting cassette tape submissions for audio poetics tape series: spoken word, collaborations, songs, audio experimentation.) Guidelines.

THE SMALL POND MAGAZINE—P.O. Box 664, Stratford, CT 06497. Napoleon St. Cyr, Ed. Published 3 times a year. Fiction, to 2,500 words; poetry, to 100 lines. Query for nonfiction. SASE required. Include short bio. Pays in copies.

SMALL PRESS REVIEW—Box 100, Paradise, CA 95967. Len Fulton, Ed. News pieces and reviews, to 200 words, about small presses and little magazines. Pays in copies.

SNOWY EGRET—R.R. #1, Box 354, Poland, IN 47868. Karl Barnebey and Michael Aycock, Eds. Poetry, fiction, and nonfiction, to 10,000 words. Natural history from artistic, literary, philosophical, and historical perspectives. Pays $2 per page for prose; $2 to $4 for poetry, on publication.

SONORA REVIEW—Dept. of English, Univ. of Arizona, Tucson, AZ 85721. Joan Marcus, Ed.-in-Chief. Fiction, poetry, translations, interviews, literary nonfiction. Pays in copies. Annual prizes for fiction and poetry.

SOUTH COAST POETRY JOURNAL—English Dept., CSUF, Fullerton, CA 92634. John J. Brugaletta, Ed. Semiannual. Poetry, to 40 lines, and B&W line drawings. "We look for excellent poetry, without regard for any other consideration." Pays in one copy. Send SASE for contest information.

SOUTH DAKOTA REVIEW—Box 111, Univ. Exchange, Vermillion, SD 57069. John R. Milton, Ed. Exceptional fiction, 3,000 to 5,000 words, and poetry, 10 to 25 lines. Critical articles, especially on American literature, Western American literature, theory and esthetics, 3,000 to 5,000 words. Pays in copies.

THE SOUTHERN CALIFORNIA ANTHOLOGY—c/o Master of Professional Writing Program, WPH 404, Univ. of Southern California, Los Angeles, CA 90089–4034. Michael Wilds, Ed.-in-Chief. Fiction, to 20 pages, and poetry, to 5 pages. Pays in copies.

SOUTHERN EXPOSURE—P.O. Box 531, Durham, NC 27702. Eric Bates, Ed. Quarterly forum on "Southern movements for social change." Short stories, to 4,500 words, essays, investigative journalism, and oral histories, 500 to 4,500 words. Pays $25 to $200, on publication. Query.

SOUTHERN HUMANITIES REVIEW—9088 Haley Center, Auburn Univ., AL 36849. Thomas L. Wright, Dan R. Latimer, Eds. Short stories, essays, and criticism, 3,500 to 5,000 words; poetry, to 2 pages.

SOUTHERN POETRY REVIEW—Dept. of English, Univ. of North Carolina, Charlotte, NC 28223. Lucinda Grey and Ken McLaurin, Eds. Poems. No restrictions on style, length, or content.

THE SOUTHERN REVIEW—43 Allen Hall, Louisiana State Univ., Baton Rouge, LA 70803. James Olney and Dave Smith, Eds. Emphasis on contemporary literature in United States and abroad with special interest in southern culture and history. Fiction and essays, 4,000 to 8,000 words. Serious poetry of highest quality. Pays $12 a page for prose, $20 a page for poetry, on publication.

SOUTHWEST REVIEW—6410 Airline Rd., Southern Methodist Univ., Dallas, TX 75275. Willard Spiegelman, Ed. "A quarterly that serves the interests of the region but is not bound by them." Fiction, essays, and interviews with well-known writers, 3,000 to 7,500 words. Poetry. Pays varying rates.

SOU'WESTER—Southern Illinois Univ. at Edwardsville, Edwardsville, IL 62026–1438. Fred W. Robbins, Man. Ed. Fiction, to 8,000 words. Poetry, any length. Pays in copies.

SPECTRUM—University of California/Santa Barbara, Box 14800, Santa Barbara, CA 93106. Short stories, essays on literature, memoirs, poetry. Pays in copies. Annual contest.

SPECTRUM JOURNAL—Anna Maria College, Box 72-A, Paxton, MA 01612. Robert H. Goepfert, Ed. Scholarly articles, 3,000 to 15,000 words; short stories, to 10 pages; and poetry, to 2 pages; book reviews, photos and artwork. Pays $20 plus 2 copies. SASE required.

THE SPOON RIVER QUARTERLY—Dept. of English, Stevenson Hall, Illinois State Univ., Normal, IL 61761. Lucia Cordell Getsi, Ed. Poetry, any length. Pays in copies.

SPSM&H—329 E St., Bakersfield, CA 93304. Frederick A. Raborg, Jr., Ed. Single sonnets, sequences, essays about the form, short fiction in which the sonnet plays a part, books, and anthologies. Pays in copies.

STAND MAGAZINE—P.O. Box 5923, Huntsville, AL 35814. Jessie Emerson, Ed. Fiction, 3,500 to 4,000 words, and poetry to 100 lines. No formulaic verse. Pays varying rates, on publication.

STORY QUARTERLY—P.O. Box 1416, Northbrook, IL 60065. Anne Brashler, Diane Williams, Eds. Short stories and interviews. Pays in copies.

STORYTELLING MAGAZINE—P.O. Box 309, Jonesborough, TN 37659. Articles, 500 to 2,500 words, related to storytelling: "Articles can have folkloric, historical, personal, educational, or travel bias, as long as they're related to storytelling." Pays 5¢ a word.

THE SUN—The Sun Publishing Co., 107 N. Roberson St., Chapel Hill, NC 27516. Sy Safransky, Ed. Articles, essays, interviews, and fiction, to 10,000 words; poetry; photos, illustrations, and cartoons. "We're interested in all writing that makes sense and enriches our common space." Pays $100 for fiction and essays, $25 for poetry, on publication.

SWAMP ROOT—Route 2, Box 1098, Hiwassee One, Jacksboro, TN 37757. Al Masarik, Ed. Published 3 times a year. Poetry, any length, any style. Essays, reviews, letters, and interviews related to poetry. Query for artwork. SASE required. Pays in copies and subscription.

SYCAMORE REVIEW—Purdue Univ., Dept. of English, West Lafayette, IN 47907. Henry Hughes, Ed.-in-Chief. Semiannual. Poetry, short fiction (no genre fiction), personal essays, and translations; manuscripts to 10,000 words. Pays in copies. Reading period: September to April.

TAR RIVER POETRY—Dept. of English, East Carolina Univ., Greenville, NC 27834. Luke Whisnant, Ed. Poetry and reviews. "Interested in skillful use of language, vivid imagery. Less academic, more powerful poetry preferred." Submit from Sept. to Nov. or Jan. to April. Pays in copies.

THE TEXAS REVIEW—English Dept., Sam Houston State Univ., Huntsville, TX 77341. Paul Ruffin, Ed. Fiction, poetry, articles, to 20 typed pages. Reviews. Pays in copies and subscription.

THIRTEEN—Box 392, Portlandville, NY 13834–0392. Ken Stone, Ed. Quarterly. Thirteen-line poetry. Pays in one copy.

THE THREEPENNY REVIEW—P.O. Box 9131, Berkeley, CA 94709. Wendy Lesser, Ed. Fiction, to 5,000 words. Poetry, to 100 lines. Essays, on books, theater, film, dance, music, art, television, and politics, 1,500 to 3,000 words. Pays to $100, on acceptance. Limited market. Query first with SASE for guidelines.

TIGHTROPE—323 Pelham Rd., Amherst, MA 01002. Ed Rayher, Ed. Limited-edition, letterpress. Semiannual. Fiction and nonfiction, to 10 pages; poetry, any length. Pays in copies.

TOUCHSTONE—P.O. Box 8308, Spring, TX 77387. Bill Laufer, Pub. Annual. Fiction, 750 to 2,000 words: mainstream, experimental. Interviews, essays, reviews. Poetry, to 40 lines. Pays $2 to $5 for poems; $5 reviews; to $5 per page for prose.

TRANSLATION—The Translation Center, 412 Dodge Hall, Columbia Univ., New York, NY 10027. Frank MacShane, Dir. Semiannual. New translations of contemporary foreign fiction and poetry.

TRIQUARTERLY—Northwestern Univ., 2020 Ridge Ave., Evanston, IL 60208–4302. Serious, aesthetically informed and inventive poetry and prose, for an international and literate audience. Pays $20 per page for prose, $3 per line for poetry. Reading period Oct. 1 to April 30. Allow 8 to 10 weeks for reply.

TRIVIA—P.O. Box 606, N. Amherst, NY 01059. Lise Weil, Ed. Semiannual journal of feminist writing. Literary essays, experimental prose, translations, and reviews. "After readings": essay reviews on books written by women. Submit up to 20 pages. Pays in copies. Guidelines.

2 AM—P.O. Box 6754, Rockford, IL 61125–1754. Gretta Anderson, Ed. Poetry, articles, reviews, and personality profiles, 500 to 2,000 words, as well as fantasy, horror, and some science fiction/sword-and-sorcery short stories, 500 to 5,000 words. Pays ½¢ a word, on acceptance.

THE UNIVERSITY OF PORTLAND REVIEW—Univ. of Portland, Portland, OR 97203. Thompson M. Faller, Ed. Scholarly articles and contemporary fiction, 500 to 2,500 words. Poetry. Book reviews. Pays in copies.

UNIVERSITY OF WINDSOR REVIEW—Dept. of English, Univ. of Windsor, Windsor, Ont., Canada N9B 3P4. Joseph A. Quinn, Ed. Short stories, poetry. Pays $10 to $25, on publication.

THE VILLAGER—135 Midland Ave., Bronxville, NY 10708. Amy Murphy, Ed. Fiction, 900 to 1,500 words: mystery, adventure, humor, romance. Short, preferably seasonal poetry. Pays in copies.

VIRGINIA QUARTERLY REVIEW—One West Range, Charlottesville, VA 22903. Quality fiction and poetry. Serious essays and articles, 3,000 to 6,000 words, on literature, science, politics, economics, etc. Pays $10 per page for prose, $1 per line for poetry, on publication.

VISIONS INTERNATIONAL—1110 Seaton Lane, Falls Church, VA 22046. Bradley R. Strahan, Ed. Published 3 times a year. Poetry, to 40 lines, and B&W drawings. (Query first for artwork.) "Nothing amateurish or previously published." Pays in copies.

WASCANA REVIEW—c/o Dept. of English, Univ. of Regina, Regina, Sask., Canada S4S 0A2. Joan Givner, Ed. Short stories, 2,000 to 6,000 words; critical articles; poetry. Pays $3 per page for prose, $10 for poetry, after publication.

WASHINGTON REVIEW—P.O. Box 50132, Washington, DC 20091–0132. Clarissa Wittenberg, Ed. Poetry; articles on literary, performing and fine arts in the Washington, D.C., area. Fiction, 1,000 to 2,500 words. Area writers preferred. Pays in copies.

WEBSTER REVIEW—Webster Univ., 470 E. Lockwood, Webster Groves, MO 63119. Nancy Schapiro, Ed. Fiction; poetry; interviews; essays; translations. Pays in copies.

WEST BRANCH—Bucknell Hall, Bucknell Univ., Lewisburg, PA 17837. Karl Patten, Robert Taylor, Eds. Poetry and fiction. Pays in copies and subscriptions.

WESTERN HUMANITIES REVIEW—University of Utah, Salt Lake City, UT 84112. Pamela Houston, Man. Ed. Quarterly. Fiction and essays, to 30 pages, and poetry. Pays $50 for poetry, $150 for short stories and essays, on acceptance.

THE WESTMINSTER REVIEW—Dept. of English, Westminster College, New Wilmington, PA 16172. David Swerdlow, Ed. Poetry and fiction. "Interested in writing that explores the frontier between knowledge and mystery." No traditional verse forms, sentimentality, or work that is merely experimental. Submissions accepted Sept. 15 to May 15. Pays in copies. SASE required. Allow 8 to 12 weeks for response.

THE WILLIAM AND MARY REVIEW—Campus Center, College of William and Mary, Williamsburg, VA 23185. William Clark, Ed. Annual. Fiction, critical essays, and interviews, 2,500 to 7,500 words; poetry, all genres (submit five to eight poems). Reading period: September through March. Pays in copies.

WIND—R1-Box 809K, Pikeville, KY 41501. Quentin Howard, Ed. Semiannual. Short stories and poems. Book reviews from small presses, to 250 words. Pays in copies.

WINDFALL—Dept. of English, UW-Whitewater, Whitewater, WI 53190. Ron Ellis, Ed. Semiannual. Intense, highly crafted, lyric poetry. (Occasionally consider poems longer than one page.) No dot matrix or poor copies will be considered. Pays in one copy.

THE WINDLESS ORCHARD—Dept. of English, Indiana-Purdue Univ., Ft. Wayne, IN 46805. Robert Novak, Ed. Contemporary poetry. Pays in copies. SASE required.

WITHOUT HALOS—Ocean County Poets Collective, P.O. Box 1342, Point Pleasant Beach, NJ 08742. Frank Finale, Ed. Submit 3 to 5 poems (to 2 pages) between Jan. 1 and June 30. Pays in copies.

WITNESS—31000 Northwestern Hwy., Suite 200, Farmington Hills, MI 48018. Peter Stine, Ed. Thematic journal. Fiction and essays, 5 to 20 pages, and poems (submit up to 3). Pays $6 per page for prose, $10 per page for poetry, on publication.

WOMAN OF POWER—Box 827, Cambridge, MA 02238–0827. Char McKee, Ed. A magazine of feminism, spirituality, and politics. Fiction and nonfiction, to 3,500 words. Poetry; submit up to 5 poems at a time. Send SASE for issue themes and guidelines. Pays in copies and subscription.

THE WORCESTER REVIEW—6 Chatham St., Worcester, MA 01609. Rodger Martin, Ed. Poetry (submit up to 5 poems at a time), fiction, critical articles about poetry, and articles and reviews with a New England connection. Pays in copies.

THE WORMWOOD REVIEW—P.O. Box 4698, Stockton, CA 95204–0698. Marvin Malone, Ed. Quarterly. Poetry and prose-poetry, 4 to 400 lines. "We encourage wit and conciseness." Pays 3 to 20 copies or cash equivalent.

WRITERS FORUM—Univ. of Colorado, Colorado Springs, CO 80933–7150. Alex Blackburn, Ed. Annual. Mainstream and experimental fiction, 1,000 to 10,000 words. Poetry (one to five poems per submission). Emphasis on western themes and writers. Send material October through May. Pays in copies.

WYOMING, THE HUB OF THE WHEEL—The Willow Bee Publishing House, Box 9, Saratoga, WY 82331. Dawn Senior, Man. Ed. Fiction and nonfiction, to 1,500 words; poetry, to 80 lines. "An international literary/art magazine devoted to peace, the human race, positive relationships, and the human spirit and possibilities." Pays in copies.

XANADU—Box 773, Huntington, NY 11743. Pat Nesbitt, Mildred Jeffrey, Barbara Lucas, Eds. Poetry on a variety of topics; no length restrictions. Pays in copies.

ZYZZYVA—41 Sutter, Suite 1400, San Francisco, CA 94104. Howard Junker, Ed. Publishes work of West Coast writers only: fiction, essays, and poetry. Pays $50 to $250, on acceptance.

HUMOR, FILLERS, SHORT ITEMS

Magazines noted for their excellent filler departments, plus a cross-section of publications using humor, short items, jokes, quizzes, and cartoons, follow. However, almost all magazines use some type of filler material, and writers can find dozens of markets by studying copies of magazines at a library or newsstand.

THE AMERICAN FIELD—542 S. Dearborn, Chicago, IL 60605. B.J. Matthys, Ed. Short fact items and anecdotes on hunting dogs and field trials for bird dogs. Pays varying rates, on acceptance.

THE AMERICAN NEWSPAPER CARRIER—P.O. Box 2225, Kernersville, NC 27285. W.H. Lowry, Ed. Short, humorous pieces, to 1,200 words, for preteen, teenage, and adult newspaper carriers. Pays $25, on publication.

ARMY MAGAZINE—2425 Wilson Blvd., Arlington, VA 22201–3385. L. James Binder, Ed.-in-Chief. True anecdotes on military subjects. Pays $10 to $35, on publication.

THE ATLANTIC—745 Boylston St., Boston, MA 02116. Sophisticated humorous or satirical pieces, 1,000 to 3,000 words. Some light poetry. Pays from $750 for prose, on acceptance.

ATLANTIC SALMON JOURNAL—P.O. Box 289, Guysborough, N.S., Canada B0H 1N0. Harry Bruce, Ed. Fillers, 50 to 100 words, on salmon politics, conservation, and nature. Cartoons. Pays $25 for fillers, $50 for cartoons, on publication.

BICYCLING—33 E. Minor St., Emmaus, PA 18098. Anecdotes, helpful cycling tips, and other items for "Paceline" section, 150 to 250 words. Pays $50, on publication.

BIKEREPORT—Bikecentennial, P.O. Box 8308, Missoula, MT 59807. Daniel D'Ambrosio, Ed. News shorts from the bicycling world for "In Bicycle Circles." Pays $5 to $10, on publication.

CAPPER'S—616 Jefferson St., Topeka, KS 66607–1188. Nancy Peavler, Ed. Household hints, recipes, jokes. Pays varying rates, on publication.

CASCADES EAST—716 N. E. 4th St., P. O. Box 5784, Bend, OR 97708. Geoff Hill, Ed. Fillers related to travel, history, and recreation in central Oregon. Pays 3¢ to 10¢ a word, extra for photos, on publication.

CATHOLIC DIGEST—P.O. Box 64090, St. Paul, MN 55164–0090. No fiction. Articles, 200 to 500 words, on instances of kindness rewarded, for "Hearts Are Trumps." Stories about conversions, for "Open Door." Reports of tactful remarks or actions, for "The Perfect Assist." Accounts of good deeds, for "People Are Like That." Humorous pieces, 50 to 300 words, on parish life, for "In Our Parish." Amusing signs, for "Signs of the Times." Jokes; fillers. Pays $4 to $50, on publication. Manuscripts cannot be acknowledged or returned.

CHICKADEE—56 The Esplanade, Suite 306, Toronto, Ont., Canada M5E 1A7. Humorous juvenile poetry, 10 to 15 lines, about animals and nature. (Also humorous fiction, 800 words.) Pays on acceptance. Enclose international reply coupons.

CHILDREN'S PLAYMATE—1100 Waterway Blvd., P. O. Box 567, Indianapolis, IN 46206. Elizabeth Rinck, Ed. Puzzles, games, mazes for children, ages six to eight, emphasizing health, safety, and nutrition. Pays about 10¢ a word (varies on puzzles), on acceptance.

CHRISTIAN HERALD—40 Overlook Dr., Chappaqua, NY 10514. Bob Chuvala, Ed. Funny or revealing things, 75 to 200 words, that happen in the process of raising, teaching, or working with Christian kids for "Kids of the Kingdom" column. Pay $25, on acceptance.

THE CHURCH MUSICIAN—127 Ninth Ave. N., Nashville, TN 37234. W. M. Anderson, Ed. For Southern Baptist music leaders. Humorous fillers with a music slant. No clippings. Pays around 5¢ a word, on acceptance. Same address and requirements for *Glory Songs* and *The Senior Musician*.

COLUMBIA JOURNALISM REVIEW—Columbia University, 700 Journalism Bldg., New York, NY 10027. Gloria Cooper, Man. Ed. Amusing mistakes in news stories, headlines, photos, etc. (original clippings required), for "Lower Case." Pays $25, on publication.

CORPORATE CASHFLOW—6255 Barfield Rd., Atlanta, GA 30328. Dick Gamble, Ed. Fillers, to 1,000 words, on varied aspects of treasury management and corporate finance, for treasury managers in public and private companies. Pays on publication. Query.

COUNTRY—5400 S. 60th St, Greendale, WI 53129. Fillers, 50 to 200 words, for rural audience. Pays on acceptance. Address Deb Mulvey.

COUNTRY WOMAN—P. O. Box 643, Milwaukee, WI 53201. Kathy Pohl, Man. Ed. Short rhymed verse, 4 to 20 lines, and fillers, to 250 words, on the rural experience. All material must be positive and upbeat. Pays $10 to $50, on acceptance.

CURRENT COMEDY—165 W. 47th St., New York, NY 10036. Gary Apple, Ed. Original, funny, performable one-liners and brief jokes on news, fads, topical subjects, business, etc. Jokes for roasts, retirement dinners, and for speaking engagements. Humorous material specifically geared for public speaking situations such as microphone feedback, hecklers, etc. Also interested in longer original jokes and anecdotes that can be used by public speakers. Pays $12, after publication. SASE for guidelines.

CYCLE WORLD—853 W. 17th St., Costa Mesa, CA 92627. David Edwards, Ed. News items on motorcycle industry, legislation, trends. Pays on acceptance.

THE ELKS MAGAZINE—425 W. Diversey Pkwy., Chicago, IL 60614. Fred D. Oakes, Ed. Informative or humorous pieces, to 2,500 words. No fillers. Pays from $150, on acceptance. Query.

FACES—30 Grove St., Peterborough, NH 03458. Carolyn Yoder, Ed. Puzzles, mazes, crosswords, and picture puzzles, related to monthly themes, for children. Send SASE for list of themes before submitting.

FAMILY CIRCLE—Box 2822, Grand Central Sta., New York, NY 10017. "Between Friends," a column of innovative reader tips on a wide range of topics, including diet, fitness, health, child care, travel, finances, etc. Pays $100. Submit postcards only; unpublished entries cannot be acknowledged or returned.

FARM AND RANCH LIVING—5400 S. 60th St., Greendale, WI 53129. Bob Ottum, Ed. Fillers on rural people and living, 200 words. Pays from $15, on acceptance and publication.

FATE—P.O. Box 64383, St. Paul, MN 55164–0383. Donald Michael Kraig, Ed. Factual fillers, to 300 words, on strange or psychic happenings. True stories, to 300 words, on psychic or mystic personal experiences. Pays 10¢ a word. Send SASE for guidelines.

FIELD & STREAM—2 Park Ave., New York, NY 10016. Duncan Barnes,

Ed. Fillers on hunting, fishing, camping, etc., to 1,000 words. Cartoons. Pays $250 to $750 for fillers, $100 for cartoons, on acceptance.

GALLERY—401 Park Ave. S., New York, NY 10016–8802. Barry Janoff, Ed. Dir. Peter Emshwiller, Man. Ed. Short humor, satire, and short service features for men. Pays varying rates, half on acceptance and half on publication. Query.

GLAMOUR—350 Madison Ave., New York, NY 10017. Articles, 1,000 words, for "Viewpoint" section: opinion pieces for women. Pays $500, on acceptance. Send SASE.

GLORY SONGS—See *The Church Musician*.

GOOD HOUSEKEEPING—959 Eighth Ave., New York, NY 10019. Rosemary Leonard, Ed. Two to eight lines of witty poetry, light verse, and quips with broad appeal, easy to illustrate for "Light Housekeeping" page. Seasonal material welcome. SASE required for return of material. Pays $25 to $50, on acceptance.

GUIDEPOSTS—747 Third Ave., New York, NY 10017. Rick Hamlin, Features Ed. Inspirational anecdotes, to 250 words. Pays $10 to $50, on acceptance.

HEARTH & HOME—P. O. Box 2008, Laconia, NH 03247. Ken Daggett, Ed. Profiles and interviews, 1,000 to 1,800 words, with specialty retailers selling both casual furniture and hearth products (fireplaces, woodstoves, accessories, etc.). Pays $150 to $250, on acceptance.

HUMOR MAGAZINE—Box 41070, Philadelphia, PA 19127. Edward Savaria, Jr., Ed. Quarterly. Fiction, interviews, and profiles, up to 1,000 words; short poetry, jokes, and fillers. "We would edit out all truly gross humor and anything that elicits loud groans. Please, no X-rated jokes or stories." Pays $50 to $300 for stories and articles; $5 to $25 for jokes and fillers, on acceptance.

INDEPENDENT LIVING—44 Broadway, New York, NY 11740. Anne Kelly, Ed. Short humor, to 500 words, and cartoons for magazine addressing lifestyles and home health care of persons who have disabilities. Pays 10¢ a word, on publication. Query.

LADIES' HOME JOURNAL—"Last Laughs," 100 Park Ave., 3rd Fl., New York, NY 10017. Brief, true anecdotes about the amusing things children say for "Out of the Mouths of Babes" column and short poetry about the funny business of being a woman today. All material must be original. Pays $50 for children's anecdotes; $100 for poems and other humor. Due to the volume of mail received, submissions cannot be acknowledged or returned.

MCCALL'S—Child Care Dept., 110 Fifth Ave., New York, NY 10011. Parenting tips and ideas, or words of wisdom on raising children. Pays $10. Include home phone and Social Security number with submission.

MAD MAGAZINE—485 Madison Ave., New York , NY 10022. Address Editors. Humorous pieces on a wide variety of topics. Two- to eight-panel cartoons (not necessary to include sketches with submission). SASE for guidelines strongly recommended. Pays top rates, on acceptance.

MATURE LIVING—127 Ninth Ave. N., MSN 140, Nashville, TN 37234. Brief, humorous, original items; 25-line profiles with action photos; "Grandparents Brag Board" items; Christian inspirational pieces for senior adults, 125 words. Pays $5 to $15.

MATURE YEARS—201 Eighth Ave. S., P.O. Box 801, Nashville, TN 37202. Marvin W. Cropsey, Ed. Poems, cartoons, puzzles, jokes, anecdotes, to 300 words, for older adults. Allow two months for manuscript evaluation. "A Christian magazine that seeks to build faith. We always show older adults in a favorable light." Include name, address, Social Security number with all submissions.

MID-WEST OUTDOORS—111 Shore Dr., Hinsdale, IL 60521. Gene Laulunen, Man. Ed. Where to and how to fish in the Midwest, 400 to 1,500 words, with two photos. Pays $15 to $35, on publication.

MODERN BRIDE—475 Park Ave. S., New York, NY 10016. Mary Ann Cavlin, Man. Ed. Humorous pieces, 500 to 1,000 words, for brides. Pays on acceptance.

MODERN MATURITY—3200 E. Carson St., Lakewood, CA 90712. J. Henry Fenwick, Ed. Money-saving tips; jokes; etc. Submit seasonal material six months in advance. Pays from $50, on acceptance. Query.

NATIONAL ENQUIRER—Lantana, FL 33464. Michele Cooke, Asst. Ed. Short, humorous or philosophical fillers, witticisms, anecdotes, jokes, tart comments. Original items only. Short poetry with traditional rhyming verse, amusing, philosophical, or inspirational in nature. No obscure or artsy poetry. Occasionally uses longer poems of a serious or humorous nature. Submit seasonal/holiday material at least three months in advance. SASE required with all submissions. Pays $25, after publication.

NATIONAL REVIEW—150 E. 35th St., New York, NY 10016. John O'Sullivan, Ed. Satire, to 900 words. Pays to $200, on publication.

NEW CHOICES FOR THE BEST YEARS—28 W. 23rd St., New York, NY 10010. Kate Greer, Ed.-in-Chief. Short humor pieces for lifestyle/service magazine for people ages 45 to 60. Payment varies, on acceptance.

NEW JERSEY MONTHLY—P.O. Box 920, Morristown, NJ 07963–0920. Sarah Fryberger, Assoc. Ed. Short pieces related to life in New Jersey. Pays $400 for about 750 words.

NEW YORK—755 Second Ave., New York, NY 10017. Chris Smith, Assoc. Ed. Short, lively pieces, to 400 words, highlighting events and trends in New York City for "Fast Track." Profiles, to 300 words, for "Brief Lives." Pays $25 to $300, on publication. Include SASE.

THE NEW YORKER—20 West 43rd St., New York, NY 10036. Amusing mistakes in newspapers, books, magazines, etc. Pays from $10, extra for headings and tags, on acceptance. Address Newsbreaks Dept. Material returned only with SASE.

NORTHWEST LIVING!—130 Second Ave. S., Edmonds, WA 98020–3512. Terry W. Sheely, Ed. Shorts, 100 to 400 words, related to the natural resources of the Northwest. Query first with SASE. Pays on publication.

OPTOMETRIC ECOMONICS—American Optometric Assn., 243 N. Lindbergh Blvd., St. Louis, MO 63141. Jack Runninger, Ed. Short humor for monthly magazine on private practice management for optometrists. Payment varies, on acceptance.

PARENTS—685 Third Ave., New York, NY 10017. Ann Pleshette Murphy, Ed. Short items on solutions of child care problems for "Parents Exchange." Pays $50, on publication.

PARISH FAMILY DIGEST—200 Noll Plaza, Huntington, IN 46750. Corine B. Erlandson, Ed. Family- or Catholic parish-oriented humor. Anecdotes, to 250 words, of funny or unusual parish and family experiences. Pays $5, on acceptance.

PLAYBOY—680 N. Lakeshore Dr., Chicago, IL 60611. Address Party Jokes Ed. or After Hours Ed. Jokes; short original material on new trends, lifestyles, personalities; humorous news items. Pays $100 for jokes, on publication; $50 to $350 for "After Hours" items, on publication.

PLAYGIRL—801 Second Ave., New York, NY 10017. Humorous looks at daily life and relationships from male or female perspective, to 800 words, for "The Men's Room" and "The Women's Room." Query Managing Ed. Pays varying rates.

POPULAR MECHANICS—224 W. 57th St., New York, NY 10019. Deborah Frank, Man. Ed. How-to pieces, from 300 words, with photos and sketches, on home improvement and shop and craft projects. Pays $25 to $300, on acceptance. Buys all rights.

READER'S DIGEST—Pleasantville, NY 10570. True, original anecdotes for "Life in These United States," "Humor in Uniform," "Campus Comedy," and "All in a Day's Work." Pays $400, on publication. Original short items for "Toward More Picturesque Speech." Pays $50. Anecdotes, original items, for "Laughter, the Best Medicine," "Personal Glimpses," "Points to Ponder," "Quotable Quotes," etc. Pays $30 per two-column line. No submissions acknowledged or returned. Consult "Contributor's Corner" page for guidelines.

REAL PEOPLE—950 Third Ave., 16th Fl., New York, NY 10022. Alex Polner, Ed. True stories, to 500 words, for "Real Bizarre" column, on the occult, UFOs, strange occurrences, everyday weirdness, etc.; may be funny, sad, or hair-raising.

REDBOOK—"Check Out," 224 West 57th St., New York, NY 10019. Tips about crafts or family-fun ideas, brief anecdotes, and poems. Also witty, warm, and wonderful quotes from children. (Enclose a snapshot of the child.) Include your name, address, and daytime phone number with submissions. Submissions will not be acknowledged or returned. Pays $50.

RHODE ISLAND MONTHLY—18 Imperial Pl., Providence, RI 02903. Vicki Sanders, Man. Ed. Short pieces, to 250 words, on Rhode Island and southeastern Massachusetts: places, customs, people and events; pieces, to 150 words, on products and services; to 200 words on food, chefs, and restaurants. Pays $25 to $50, on publication.

ROAD & TRACK—1499 Monrovia Ave., Newport Beach, CA 92663. Ellida Maki, Man. Ed. Monthly for knowledgeable car enthusiasts. Short automotive articles, to 450 words, of "timeless nature." Pays on publication. Query.

ROAD KING—P. O. Box 250, Park Forest, IL 60466. Address Features Ed. Trucking-related cartoons and anecdotes, to 200 words, for "Trucker's Life." Pays $25 for cartoons, $25 for anecdotes, on publication. SASE required.

THE ROTARIAN—1560 Sherman Ave., Evanston, IL 60201. Willmon L. White, Ed. Occasional humor articles. Payment varies, on acceptance.

RURAL HERITAGE—P. O. Box 516, Albia, IA 52531. Allan Young, Pub. Current articles, 100 to 750 words, related to draft horses, rural events, or crafts. Pays 3¢ to 10¢ a word, on publication.

SACRAMENTO—1021 Second St., Sacramento, CA 95814. "City Lights," interesting and unusual people, places, and behind-the-scenes news items, 75 to 250 words. All material must have Sacramento tie-in. Pays $40 to $100, on publication.

THE SATURDAY EVENING POST—P.O. Box 567, Indianapolis, IN

46206. Steven Pettinga, Post Scripts Ed. Humor and satire, to 100 words; light verse, cartoons, jokes, for "Post Scripts." Pays $15, on publication.

SCHOOL SHOP/TECH DIRECTIONS—Prakken Publishing, Box 8623, 416 Longshore Dr., Ann Arbor, MI 48107. Susanne Peckham, Man. Ed. Cartoons of interest to technology and industrial education teachers and administrators. Pay varies, on publication.

SCORE, CANADA'S GOLF MAGAZINE—287 MacPherson Ave., Toronto, Ont., Canada M4V 1A4. Bob Weeks, Man. Ed. Fillers, 50 to 100 words, related to Canadian golf scene. Rarely uses humor or poems. Pays $10 to $25, on publication. Unused submissions not returned.

THE SENIOR MUSICIAN—See *The Church Musician*.

SKI MAGAZINE—2 Park Ave., New York, NY 10016. Dick Needham, Ed. Short, 100- to 300-word items on events and people in skiing for "Ski Life" department. Humor, 300 to 2,000 words, related to skiing. Pays on acceptance.

SNOWMOBILE—319 Barry Ave. S. Suite 101, Wayzata, MN 55391. Dick Hendricks, Ed. Short humor and cartoons on snowmobiling and winter "Personality Plates" sighted. Pays varying rates, on publication.

SPORTS AFIELD—250 W. 55th St., New York, NY 10019. Unusual, useful tips, anecdotes, 100 to 300 words, for "Almanac" section: hunting, fishing, camping, boating, etc. Photos. Pays 10¢ per column inch, on publication.

SPORTS CARD TRADER—3 Fairchild Ct., Plainview, NY 11803. Douglas Kale, Ed. Monthly. Fillers related to collecting and investing in baseball, football, basketball, and hockey cards. (Also articles on investing in sports cards or memorabilia.) Pays 7¢ a word, on publication.

STAR—660 White Plains Rd., Tarrytown, NY 10591. Topical articles, 50 to 800 words, on human-interest subjects, show business, lifestyles, the sciences, etc., for family audience. Pays varying rates.

TOUCH—Box 7259, Grand Rapids, MI 49510. Carol Smith, Man. Ed. Bible puzzles for Christian girls ages 8 to 14. Pays $5 to $10 per puzzle, on acceptance. Send SASE for theme update.

TRAILER BOATS MAGAZINE—20700 Belshaw Ave., Carson, CA 90746. Wiley Poole, Ed. Fillers and humor, preferably with illustrations, on boating and related activities. Pays $5 per column inch, extra for photos, on publication.

TRAVEL SMART—Dobbs Ferry, NY 10522. Interesting, unusual travel-related tips. Practical information for vacation or business travel. Query for over 250 words. Pays $5 to $100.

VOLKSWAGEN WORLD—Volkswagen of America, 3800 Hamlin Rd., Auburn Hills, MI 48057. Marlene Goldsmith, Ed. Anecdotes, to 100 words, about Volkswagen owners' experiences; humorous photos of current model Volkswagens. Pays $40, on acceptance.

WOMAN'S DAY—1633 Broadway, New York, NY 10019. Address "Neighbors" editor. Heart-warming anecdotes about the public service work of a "good neighbor," creative solutions to community or family problems, true humorous anecdotes. For "Tips to Share": short personal tips, experiences, and practical suggestions for homemakers. Pays $75, on publication.

WOODENBOAT MAGAZINE—Box 78, Brooklin, ME 04616. Jon Wilson, Ed. Address Peter Spectre. News of wooden boat-related activities and projects. Pays $5 to $50, on publication.

JUVENILE, TEENAGE, AND YOUNG ADULT MAGAZINES

JUVENILE MAGAZINES

BEAR ESSENTIAL NEWS FOR KIDS—P.O. Box 26908, Tempe, AZ 85285. Educational and entertaining articles, 300 to 600 words, for children in grades K through 3 and 4 through 8, including: world news in kids' terms; unique school projects; profiles of interesting achievers; family entertainment; science; youth sports and health; bilingual and multicultural topics; hobbies/young careers; pets and pet care; cartoon humor; activities, trivia, or puzzles that are educational. (Also uses 50- to 150-word companion pieces for a Teachers Guide, providing classroom-use ideas related to articles.) Payment is 10¢ a word, on publication; $10 to $35 for photos. Buys all rights. SASE required.

CALLIOPE: WORLD HISTORY FOR YOUNG PEOPLE—Cobblestone Publishing, Inc., 30 Grove St., Peterborough, NH 03458. Carolyn P. Yoder, Ed.-in-Chief. Theme-based magazine, published five times yearly. Articles, 750 words, with lively, original approach to world history (East/West) through the Renaissance. Shorts, 200–750 words, on little-known information related to issue's theme. Fiction, to 1,200 words: historical, biographical, adventure, or retold legends. Activities for children, to 800 words. Poetry, to 100 lines. Puzzles and games. Send SASE for guidelines and themes. Pays 10¢ to 15¢ per word, on publication.

CHICKADEE—The Young Naturalist Foundation, 56 The Esplanade, Suite 306, Toronto, Ont., Canada M5E 1A7. Catherine Ripley, Ed. Animal and adventure stories, 200 to 800 words, for children ages 3 to 8. Also, puzzles, activities, and observation games, 50 to 100 words. Pays varying rates, on acceptance. Send complete manuscript and $1 check or money order for return postage.

CHILD LIFE—1100 Waterway Blvd., P.O. Box 567, Indianapolis, IN 46206. Steve Charles, Ed. Articles, 500 to 1,200 words, for 7- to 9-year-olds. Fiction and humor stories, to 1,200 words, with emphasis on health, fitness, and sports. Puzzles. Photos. Pays about 10¢ a word, extra for photos, on publication. Buys all rights.

CHILDREN'S ALBUM—P.O. Box 6086, Concord, CA 94524. Margo M. Lemas, Ed. Fiction and poetry by children 8 to 14. Workbook and crafts projects, with step-by-step instructions. Guidelines.

CHILDREN'S DIGEST—1100 Waterway Blvd., P.O. Box 567, Indianapolis, IN 46202. Elizabeth Rinck, Ed. Health publication for preteens. Informative articles, 500 to 1,200 words, and fiction (especially realistic, adventure, mystery, and humorous), 500 to 1,500 words, with health, safety, exercise, nutrition, sports, or hygiene as theme. Historical and biographical articles. Poetry activities. Pays 10¢ a word, from $15 for poems, on publication.

CHILDREN'S PLAYMATE—Editorial Office, 1100 Waterway Blvd., P.O. Box 567, Indianapolis, IN 46206. Elizabeth Rinck, Ed. Humorous and health-related short stories, 500 to 700 words, for 6- to 8-year-olds. Simple science articles and how-to crafts pieces with brief instructions. "All About" features, about 500 words, on health, fitness, nutrition, safety, and exercise. Poems, puzzles, dot-to-dots, mazes, hidden pictures. Pays about 10¢ a word, $10 minimum for poetry, on publication.

CHILDREN'S SURPRISES—P.O. Box 236, Chanhassen, MN 55317. Peggy Simenson, Jeanne Palmer, Eds. "Activities for today's kids and parents." Educational activities, puzzles, games in reading, language, math, science, cooking, music, and art. Articles about history, animals, and geography. Pays $15 to $35, on publication.

CLUBHOUSE—Box 15, Berrien Springs, MI 49103. Elaine Trumbo, Ed. Action-oriented Christian stories: features, 800 to 1,200 words. Children in stories should be wise, brave, funny, kind, etc. Pays $30 to $35 for stories.

COBBLESTONE—30 Grove St., Peterborough, NH 03458–1454. Carolyn Yoder, Ed.-in-Chief. Theme-related articles, biographies, fiction, and short accounts of historical events, to 1,000 words, for children ages 8 to 15. Pays 10¢ to 15¢ a word, on publication. Send SASE for editorial guidelines with monthly themes.

CRICKET—Box 300, Peru, IL 61354–0300. Marianne Carus, Pub./Ed.-in-Chief. Articles and fiction, 200 to 1,500 words, for 6- to 14-year-olds. Poetry, to 30 lines. Pays to 25¢ a word, to $3 a line for poetry, on publication. SASE required. Guidelines.

DISCOVERIES—6401 The Paseo, Kansas City, MO 64131. Latta Jo Knapp, Ed. Stories, 500 to 1,000 words, for 3rd to 6th graders, with Christian emphasis. Poetry, 4 to 20 lines. Cartoons and puzzles. Pays 3 ½¢ a word (2¢ a word for reprints), 25¢ a line for poetry (minimum of $2), on acceptance. Send SASE with manuscript.

THE DOLPHIN LOG—The Cousteau Society, 8440 Santa Monica Blvd., Los Angeles, CA 90069. Pam Stacey, Ed. Articles, 500 to 1,000 words, on a variety of topics related to our global water system: marine biology, ecology, natural history, and water-related stories, for children ages 7 to 15. No fiction. Pays $25 to $150, on publication. Query.

FACES—30 Grove St., Peterborough, NH 03458. Carolyn Yoder, Ed.-in-Chief. In-depth feature articles, 800 to 1,200 words, with an anthropology theme. Shorts, 200 to 800 words, related to monthly themes. Fiction, to 1,500 words, on legends, folktales, stories from around the world, etc., related to theme. Activities, to 1,000 words, including recipes, crafts, games, etc., for children. Pays 13¢ to 15¢ a word for features; 10¢ to 12¢ a word for shorts; 10¢ to 15¢ a word for fiction. Send for guidelines and themes.

FAITH 'N STUFF—c/o *Guideposts*, 747 Third Ave., New York, NY 10017. Mary Lou Carney, Ed. Bible-based bimonthly. Problem fiction, 1,500 words; articles, 1,500 words, on issues of interest to kids ages 7 to 12; profiles, 200 to 500 words, of kids doing interesting and unusual activities. "No preachy stories and no Bible games." Pays $100 to $300 for features; $75 to $250 for fiction and fillers; buys all rights, on acceptance. No reprints. Query.

FREE SPIRIT: NEWS & VIEWS ON GROWING UP—Free Spirit Publishing, Inc., 400 First Ave. N., Suite 616, Minneapolis, MN 55401. Judy Galbraith, Ed. Published 5 times a year. Nonfiction, 800 to 1,200 words, related to the lives of teens and preteens (school, peer relationships, family, health, etc.). Annual cartoon and writing contests for kids. Readers are 10 to 14 years old. No fiction. Queries preferred. Pays to $100, on publication.

THE FRIEND—50 E. North Temple, 23rd Floor, Salt Lake City, UT 84150. Vivian Paulsen, Man. Ed. Stories and articles, 1,000 to 1,200 words. Stories, to 250 words, for younger readers and preschool children. Pays from 8¢ a word, from $15 per poem, on acceptance. Prefers completed manuscripts.

HIGHLIGHTS FOR CHILDREN—803 Church St., Honesdale, PA 18431–1824. Kent L. Brown, Ed. Fiction and articles, to 700 words, for 2- to 12-year-olds. Fiction should have strong plot, believable characters, story that holds reader's interest from beginning to end. No crime or violence. For articles, cite references used and qualifications. Easy rebus-form stories. Easy-to-read stories, 300 to 500 words, with strong plots. Pays from 14¢ a word, on acceptance.

HOPSCOTCH—P.O. Box 1292, Saratoga Springs, NY 12866. Donald P. Evans, Ed. Bimonthly. Articles and fiction, 600 to 1,200 words, and short poetry for girls ages 6 to 12. "We believe young girls deserve the right to enjoy a season of childhood before they become young adults; we are not interested in such topics as sex, romance, cosmetics, hairstyles, etc." Pays 6¢ per word; $150 for cover photos, made on acceptance.

HUMPTY DUMPTY'S MAGAZINE—1100 Waterway Blvd., P.O. Box 567, Indianapolis, IN 46206. Christine French Clark, Ed. General-interest publication with an emphasis on health and fitness for children ages 4 to 6. Easy-to-read fiction, to 600 words, some with health and nutrition, safety, exercise, or hygiene as theme; humor and light approach preferred. Creative nonfiction, including photo stories. Crafts with clear, brief instructions. No-cook recipes using healthful ingredients. Short verse, narrative poems. Pays about 10¢ a word, from $15 for poems, on publication. Buys all rights.

JACK AND JILL—Box 567, Indianapolis, IN 46206. Steve Charles, Ed. Articles, 500 to 1,200 words, for 6- to 8-year-olds, on sports, fitness, health, safety, exercise. Features, 1,000 to 1,200 words, on history, biography, life in other countries, etc. Fiction, to 1,500 words. Short poems, games, puzzles, projects, recipes. Photos. Pays about 10¢ a word, extra for photos, varying rates for fillers, on publication.

JUNIOR TRAILS—1445 Boonville Ave., Springfield, MO 65802. Sinda Zinn, Ed. Fiction, 1,000 to 1,200 words, with a Christian focus, believable characters, and moral emphasis. Articles, 500 to 800 words, on science, nature, biography. Pays 2¢ or 3¢ a word, on acceptance.

KID CITY—See *3–2–1 Contact.*

LADYBUG—P.O. Box 300, Peru, IL 61354. Marianne Carus, Pub./Ed.-in-Chief. Theresa Gaffey, Man. Ed. Picture stories, read-aloud stories, fantasy, folk and fairy tales, 300 to 750 words; poetry, to 20 lines; songs and rhymes; crafts, activities, and games, to 4 pages. Pays on publication: 25¢ a word for stories and articles; up to $3 a line for poetry.

LOLLIPOPS—Good Apple, Inc., P.O. Box 299, Carthage, IL 62321–0299. Learning games and activities covering all areas of the curriculum; arts and crafts ideas; stories, for ages 4 to 7. Pays varying rates, on publication. Query first.

MY FRIEND—Daughters of St. Paul, 50 St. Paul's Ave., Boston, MA 02130. Sr. Anne Joan, Ed. "The Catholic Magazine for Kids." Readers are 6 to 12 years old. Fiction, to 400 words, for primary readers; 400 to 600 words for intermediate readers. Nonfiction: general-information articles, lives of saints, etc., 150 to 600 words. Some humorous poetry, 6 to 8 lines. Buys first rights. Pays 3¢ to 7¢ a word (to $45). Query for artwork. Guidelines available.

NATIONAL GEOGRAPHIC WORLD—1145 17th St. N.W., Washington, DC 20036. Pat Robbins, Ed. Picture magazine for young readers, ages 8 and older. Proposals for picture stories only. No unsolicited manuscripts.

ODYSSEY—21027 Crossroads Circle, P.O. Box 1612, Waukesha, WI 53187. Nancy Mack, Ed. Features, 600 to 1,500 words, on astronomy and space science for 8- to 14-year-olds. Short experiments, projects, and games. Pays $100 to $350, on publication.

ON THE LINE—616 Walnut, Scottdale, PA 15683–1999. Mary Clemens Meyer, Ed. Weekly paper for 10- to 14-year-olds. Uses nature and how-to articles, 500 to 650 words; fiction, 900 to 1,200 words; poetry, puzzles, cartoons. Pays to 4¢ a word, on acceptance.

OWL—The Young Naturalist Foundation, 56 The Esplanade, Suite 306, Toronto, Ont., Canada M5E 1A7. Debora Pearson, Ed. Articles, 500 to 1,000 words, for children ages 8 to 12 about animals, science, people, technology, new discoveries, activities. Pays varying rates, on publication. Send for guidelines.

PLAYS, THE DRAMA MAGAZINE FOR YOUNG PEOPLE—120 Boylston St., Boston, MA 02116. Elizabeth Preston, Man. Ed. One-act plays, skits, creative dramatic material, suitable for school productions at junior high, middle, and lower grade levels. Plays with one set preferred. Uses comedies, dramas, satires, farces, melodramas, dramatized classics, folktales and fairy tales, puppet plays. Pays good rates, on acceptance. Buys all rights. Guidelines; send SASE.

POCKETS—1908 Grand Ave., Box 189, Nashville, TN 37202. Janet McNish, Ed. Ecumenical magazine for children ages 6 to 12. Fiction and scripture stories, 600 to 1,500 words; short poems; and articles about the Bible, 400 to 600 words. Pays from 12¢ a word, $25 to $50 for poetry, on acceptance. Guidelines and themes.

RADAR—8121 Hamilton Ave., Cincinnati, OH 45231. Margaret Williams, Ed. Articles, 400 to 650 words, on nature, hobbies, crafts. Short stories, 900 to 1,000 words: mystery, sports, school, family, with 12-year-old as main character; serials of 2,000 words. Christian emphasis. Poems to 12 lines. Pays to 7¢ a word, to 50¢ a line for poetry, on acceptance.

RANGER RICK—1400 16th St. N.W., Washington, DC 20036. Gerald Bishop, Ed. Articles, to 900 words, on wildlife, conservation, natural sciences, and kids in the outdoors, for 6- to 12-year-olds. Nature-related fiction and science fiction welcome. Games, crafts, poems, and puzzles. Pays to $550, on acceptance.

REFLECTIONS—P.O. Box 368, Duncan Falls, OH 43734. Dean Harper, Ed. "A National Magazine Publishing Student Writing." Published twice a year. Fiction and nonfiction, 300 to 2,000 words; poetry, any length. "Our magazine goes into K through 12th grades of schools. The purpose is to encourage writing." Queries not necessary. Pays in copies.

SESAME STREET MAGAZINE—See *3–2–1 Contact.*

SHOE TREE—National Assoc. for Young Writers, 215 Valle del Sol Dr., Santa Fe, NM 87501. Sheila Cowing, Ed.-in-Chief. Fiction, nonfiction, and poetry by writers ages 6 to 14. "We are looking for writing with a strong voice." Pays in copies.

SHOFAR—43 Northcote Dr., Melville, NY 11747. Gerald H. Grayson, Ed. Short stories, 500 to 750 words; articles, 250 to 750 words; poetry, to 50 lines; short fillers, games, puzzles, and cartoons for Jewish children, 8 to 13. All material must have a Jewish theme. Pays 10¢ a word, on publication. Submit holiday pieces at least three months in advance.

SKIPPING STONES—80574 Hazelton Rd., Cottage Grove, OK 97424. Arun N. Toké, Man. Ed. "A Multi-Cultural Children's Quarterly." Articles, of approximately 500 words, relating to cultural celebrations, life in other countries, and traditions for children ages 7 to 13. "Especially invited to submit are children from cultural backgrounds other than European-American and/or those with physical challenges. We print art, poetry, songs, games, stories, and photographs from anywhere in the world and include many different languages." Payment is one copy, on publication. Guidelines.

STONE SOUP, THE MAGAZINE BY CHILDREN—Box 83, Santa Cruz, CA 95063. Gerry Mandel, Ed. Stories, poems, plays, book reviews by children under 14. Pays $10.

STORY FRIENDS—Mennonite Publishing House, Scottdale, PA 15683. Marjorie Waybill, Ed. Stories, 350 to 800 words, for 4- to 9-year-olds, on Christian faith and values in everyday experiences. Poetry. Pays to 5¢ a word, to $10 per poem, on acceptance.

SUPERSCIENCE BLUE—Scholastic, Inc., 730 Broadway, New York, NY 10003. Kathy Burkett, Sr. Ed. Science news, 750 to 1,000 words, for children in grades 4, 5, and 6. Send SASE for editorial calendar of upcoming theme issues. Pays $100 to $500, on acceptance.

3–2–1 CONTACT—Children's Television Workshop, 1 Lincoln Plaza, New York, NY 10023. Jonathan Rosenbloom, Ed. Entertaining and informative articles, 600 to 1,000 words, for 8- to 14-year-olds, on all aspects of science, computers, scientists, and children who are learning about or practicing science. Pays $75 to $500, on acceptance. No fiction. Also publishes *Kid City* and *Sesame Street Magazine*. Query.

TOUCH—Box 7259, Grand Rapids, MI 49510. Carol Smith, Man. Ed. Upbeat fiction and features, 500 to 1,000 words, for Christian girls ages 8 to 14; personal life, nature, crafts. Poetry, puzzles. Pays 2 ½¢ a word, extra for photos, on acceptance. Query with SASE for theme update.

TURTLE MAGAZINE FOR PRESCHOOL KIDS—1100 Waterway Blvd., Box 567, Indianapolis, IN 46206. Christine French Clark, Ed. Stories about safety, exercise, health, and nutrition for preschoolers. Humorous, entertaining fiction, 600 words. Simple poems. Stories-in-rhyme; easy-to-read stories, to 500 words, for beginning readers. Pays about 10¢ a word, on publication. Buys all rights. Send SASE for guidelines.

U.S. KIDS—245 Long Hill Rd., Middletown, CT 06457. Gabriel Davis, Ed. Articles and fiction, 200 to 400 words, on issues related to kids ages 5 to 10, fiction, true-life adventures, science and nature topics. Real-world focus; no fantasy. Pays $100 to $300, on acceptance. Query. Guidelines.

VENTURE—Christian Service Brigade, P.O. Box 150, Wheaton, IL 60189. Deborah Christensen, Man. Ed. Fiction and nonfiction, 1,000 to 1,500 words, for 10- to 15-year-old boys involved in Stockade and Battalion. "Articles and stories should reflect the simple truths of the Gospel and its life-changing power." Humor and fillers and B&W 8x10 photos also accepted. Pays 5¢ to 10¢ a word, on publication.

WONDER TIME—6401 The Paseo, Kansas City, MO 64131. Evelyn J. Beals, Ed. Stories, 200 to 550 words, for 6- to 8-year-olds, with Christian emphasis to correlate with Sunday school curriculum. Poetry, 4 to 12 lines. Pays 3 ½¢ a word, from 25¢ a line for verse, $3 minimum, on acceptance.

YOUNG AMERICAN, AMERICA'S NEWSPAPER FOR KIDS—P.O. Box 12409, Portland, OR 97212. Kristina T. Linden, Ed. Upbeat, positive, sophisticated material for children ages 8 to 14. Fiction, to 1,000 words; articles, to 350 words, on science, humor, history, and newsworthy young people; poetry. Pays from 7¢ a word, from $10 for photos, on publication.

ZILLIONS—Consumers Union of the United States, 256 Washington St., Mt. Vernon, NY 10553. Jeanne Kiefer, Man. Ed. Bimonthly. Articles, 1,000 to 1,500 words, on consumer education (money, product testing, health, etc.), for children, preteens, and young teens. "We are the *Consumer Reports* for kids." Pays $500 to $1,000, on publication. Guidelines.

TEENAGE AND YOUNG ADULT

ALIVE NOW!—P.O. Box 189, Nashville, TN 37202. Mary Ruth Coffman, Ed. Short essays, 250 to 400 words, with Christian emphasis for adults and young adults. Poetry, one page. Photos. Pays $20 to $30, on publication.

BOYS' LIFE—P.O. Box 152079, 1325 Walnut Hill Ln., Irving, TX 75015–2079. William B. McMorris, Ed.-in-Chief. Publication of Boy Scouts of America. Articles and fiction, 500 to 1,200 words, for 8- to 18-year-old boys. Photos. Pays from $350 for major articles, $750 for fiction, on acceptance. Query first.

CHALLENGE—See *Pioneer.*

CHOICES—Scholastic, Inc., 730 Broadway, New York, NY 10003. Laura Galen, Ed. Articles for teenagers on personal development, family relationships, parenting/child care, health and safety, and career concerns. "Article topics should be on the national level and stories should include quotes from real-life teens in real-life situations." Query with published clips and a sample half page (no more) of proposed article. Pays $150 per printed page, on acceptance.

CHRISTIAN LIVING FOR SENIOR HIGH—See *I.D.*

CITY NEWS—2 Park Ave., Suite 2012, New York, NY 10016. Leslie Elgort, Ed. Bimonthly. Articles, 750 to 1,500 words, poetry, fillers, and humor of interest to New York City teenagers; B&W photos. Payment varies, on publication.

EXPLORING—1325 W. Walnut Hill Ln., P.O. Box 152079, Irving, TX 75015–2079. Scott Daniels, Exec. Ed. Publication of Boy Scouts of America. Articles, 500 to 1,500 words, for 14- to 21-year-old boys and girls, on education, careers, Explorer activities (hiking, canoeing, camping) and program ideas for meetings. No controversial subjects. Pays $150 to $500, on acceptance. Query. Send SASE for guidelines.

FREEWAY—Box 632, Glen Ellyn, IL 60138. Kyle Lennart Olund, Ed. First-person true stories, personal experience, how-tos, fillers, humor, fiction, to 1,200 words, for 15- to 22-year-olds. Send photos, if available. Occasionally publishes poetry. Must have Christian emphasis. Pays to 8¢ a word.

GRIT—208 W. Third St., Williamsport, PA 17701. Joanne Decker, Assignment Ed. Articles, 400 to 800 words, with photos, on young people involved in unusual hobbies, occupations, athletic pursuits, and personal adventures. Pays 15¢ a word, extra for photos, on acceptance.

HICALL—1445 Boonville Ave., Springfield, MO 65802–1894. Deanna Harris, Ed. Articles, 500 to 1,000 words, fiction, to 1,500 words, and short poetry, for 12- to 19-year-olds; strong evangelical emphasis. Pays on acceptance.

I.D.—(formerly *Christian Living for Senior High*) 850 N. Grove, Elgin, IL 60120. Douglas C. Schmidt, Ed. Articles and fiction, 750 to 1,000 words, of interest to Christian teens. Don't preach. Pays 10¢ a word, on acceptance.

IN TOUCH—Box 50434, Indianapolis, IN 46250–0434. Angelyn Rodriguez, Ed. Articles, 500 to 1,000 words, on contemporary issues, athletes, and singers from conservative Christian perspective, for 13- to 19-year-olds. Pays 2¢ to 4¢ a word. Send SASE for guidelines.

KEYNOTER—3636 Woodview Trace, Indianapolis, IN 46268. Tamara P. Burley, Exec. Ed. Articles, 1,500 to 2,500 words, for high school leaders: general-interest features; self-help; contemporary teenage problems. No fillers, poetry, or fiction. Photos. Pays $75 to $250, extra for photos, on acceptance. Query preferred.

LISTEN MAGAZINE—Pacific Press Publishing, P.O. Box 7000, Boise, MD 83707. Lincoln Steed, Ed. Articles, 1,200 to 1,500 words, providing teens with "a vigorous, positive, educational approach to the problems arising out of the use of tobacco, alcohol, and other drugs." Pays 5¢ to 7¢ a word, on acceptance.

MERLYN'S PEN, THE NATIONAL MAGAZINE OF STUDENT WRITING—P.O. Box 1058, Dept. WR, East Greenwich, RI 02818. R. James Stahl, Ed. Writing by students in grades 7 through 10 only. Short stories, to 3,500 words; reviews; travel pieces; and poetry, to 100 lines. Pays in copies. Guidelines available.

NEW ERA—50 E. North Temple, Salt Lake City, UT 84150. Richard M. Romney, Ed. Articles, 150 to 3,000 words, and fiction, to 3,000 words, for young Mormons. Poetry. Photos. Pays 5¢ to 20¢ a word, 25¢ a line for poetry, on acceptance. Query.

PIONEER—1548 Poplar Ave., Memphis, TN 38104. Jeno Smith, Ed. Southern Baptist. Articles, to 1,500 words, for 12- and 14-year-old boys, on teen problems, current events. Photo essays on Christian sports personalities. Pays 4 ½¢ a word, extra for photos, on acceptance. Same address and requirements for *Challenge.*

SEVENTEEN—850 Third Ave., New York, NY 10022. Roberta Myers, Articles Ed. Articles, to 2,500 words, on subjects of interest to teenagers. Sophisticated, well-written fiction, 1,500 to 3,500 words, for young adults. Poetry, to 40 lines, by teens. Short news and features, to 750 words, for "Talk." Articles, 1,000 words, by teenagers, for "View." Pays varying rates, on acceptance.

STRAIGHT—8121 Hamilton Ave., Cincinnati, OH 45231. Carla J. Crane, Ed. Articles on current situations and issues, humor, for Christian teens. Well-constructed fiction, 1,000 to 1,200 words, showing teens using Christian principles. Poetry by teenagers. Photos. Pays about 3¢ to 7¢ a word, on acceptance. Guidelines.

SUPERTEEN'S LOUD MOUTH—c/o Sterling's Magazines, 355 Lexington Ave., New York, NY 10017. Louise Barile, Ed. Light celebrity fan pieces and interviews (pop/rock, movies, and TV); occasional serious articles on topics of interest to teens. Query.

TEEN POWER—Box 632, Glen Ellyn, IL 60138. Amy Swanson, Ed. True-to-life fiction or first person (as told to), true teen experience stories with Christian insights and conclusion, 700 to 1,000 words. Include photos. Pays 7¢ to 10¢ a word, extra for photos, on acceptance.

TEENS TODAY—Nazarene Headquarters, 6401 The Paseo, Kansas City, MO 64131. Karen DeSollar, Ed. Short stories, 1,000 to 1,200 words, dealing with teens demonstrating Christian principles in real-life situations. Stories about relationships and ethics. Pays 3 ½¢ a word, on acceptance.

TIGER BEAT—Sterling's Magazines, 355 Lexington Ave., New York, NY 10017. Louise Barile, Ed. Articles, to 4 pages, on young people in show business and music industry. Pays varying rates, on acceptance. Query. Unsolicited manuscripts sent without SASE will not be returned.

TQ/TEEN QUEST—Box 82808, Lincoln, NE 68501. Win Mumma, Ed.

Articles, to 1,800 words, and well-crafted fiction, to 2,500 words, for conservative Christian teens. Cartoons. B&W photos and color slides. Pays 10¢ to 15¢ a word, on publication.

WRITING!—60 Revere Dr., Northbrook, IL 60062–1563. Alan Lenhoff, Ed. Interviews, 1,200 words, for "Writers at Work" department, for high school students. Pays $200, on publication. Query.

YM—685 Third Ave., New York, NY 10017. Peter McQuaid, Entertainment Ed. Cathy Cavender, Man. Ed. Articles, to 1,500 words, on entertainment, lifestyle, fashion, beauty, relationships, health, for women ages 14 to 22. Query with clips. SASE. Payment varies, on acceptance.

YOUNG AND ALIVE—4444 S. 52nd St., Lincoln, NE 68506. Richard Kaiser, Ed. Feature articles, 800 to 1,400 words, for blind and visually impaired young adults, on adventure, biography, camping, health, hobbies, and travel. Photos. Pays 3¢ to 5¢ a word, extra for photos, on acceptance. Write for guidelines.

YOUNG SALVATIONIST—The Salvation Army, 799 Bloomfield Ave., Verona, NJ 07044. Capt. Robert R. Hostetler, Ed. Articles for teens, 800 to 1,200 words, with Christian perspective; fiction, 800 to 1,200 words; short fillers. Pays 4¢ to 6¢ a word, on acceptance.

THE DRAMA MARKET

Community, regional, and civic theaters and college dramatic groups offer the best opportunities today for playwrights to see their plays produced, whether for staged production or for dramatic readings. Indeed, aspiring playwrights who can get their work produced by any of these have taken an important step toward breaking into the competitive dramatic field—many well-known playwrights received their first recognition in the regional theaters. Payment is generally nominal, but regional and university theaters usually buy only the right to produce a play, and all further rights revert to the author. Since most directors like to work closely with the authors on any revisions necessary, theaters will often pay the playwright's expenses while in residence during rehearsals. The thrill of seeing your play come to life on the stage is one of the pleasures of being on hand for rehearsals and performances.

Aspiring playwrights should query college and community theaters in their region to find out which ones are interested in seeing original scripts. Dramatic associations of interest to playwrights include The Foundation of the Dramatists Guild (234 W. 44th St., New York, NY 10036) and Theatre Communications Group, Inc. (355 Lexington Ave., New York, NY 10017), which publishes the annual *Dramatists Sourcebook*. *The Playwright's Companion*, published by Feedback Theatrebooks, P.O. Box 5187, Bloomington, IN 47402–5187, is an annual directory of theatres and prize contests seeking scripts.

Some of the theaters on the following list require that playwrights submit all or some of the following with scripts—cast list, synopsis, resumé, recommendations, return postcard—and with scripts and queries, SASEs must always be enclosed. Playwrights may also wish to register their material with the U.S. Copyright Office. For additional information about this, write Register of Copyrights, Library of Congress, Washington, DC 20559.

REGIONAL AND UNIVERSITY THEATERS

ACADEMY THEATRE—P.O. Box 10306, Atlanta, GA 30319. Elliott J. Berman, Lit. Mgr. Comedies and dramas that "stretch the boundaries of imagination, with poetic language, and imagery." Prefers local and regional playwrights or subjects relating to the Southeast. Considers regional and national playwrights for new play premieres. Royalty is negotiable.

ACTORS THEATRE OF LOUISVILLE—316 W. Main St., Louisville, KY 40202. Michael Bigelow Dixon, Lit. Mgr. Ten-minute comedies and dramas, to 10 pages; include SASE. Annual contest. Guidelines.

A. D. PLAYERS—2710 W. Alabama, Houston, TX 77098. Jeannette Clift George, Artistic Dir. Ragan Courtney, Lit. Mgr. Full-length or one-act comedies, dramas, musicals, children's plays, and adaptations with Christian world view. Submit script with SAS postcard, resumé, cast list, and synopsis. (Christmas plays should be submitted before Oct.) Readings. Pays negotiable rates.

ALABAMA SHAKESPEARE FESTIVAL—The State Theatre, #1 Festival Drive, Montgomery, AL 36117–4605. Kent Thompson, Art. Dir. Full-length adaptations and plays dealing with southern or black issues. Send resumé and synopsis in June.

ALLEY THEATRE—615 Texas Ave., Houston, TX 77002. Christopher Baker, Lit. Dir. Full-length plays and musicals, including translations and adaptations, plays for young audiences. Query with synopsis, 10 sample pages, and resumé. No unsolicited scripts.

ALLIANCE THEATRE COMPANY—1280 Peachtree St. N.E., Atlanta, GA 30309. Sandra Deer, Lit. Mgr. Full-length comedies and dramas. Query with synopsis and cast list. Pay varies.

AMERICAN LIVING HISTORY THEATER—P.O. Box 2677, Hollywood, CA 90078. Dorene Ludwig, Art. Dir. One-act, historically accurate (primary source materials only) dramas. Submit script with SASE. Reports in 1 to 6 months. Pays varying rates.

AMERICAN REPERTORY THEATRE—64 Brattle St., Cambridge, MA 02138. Robert Scanlan, Lit. Dir. No unsolicited manuscripts. Submit one-page description of play, 10-page sample; nothing returned without SASE; 3 to 4 months for response.

AMERICAN STAGE COMPANY—FDU, Box 336, Teaneck, NJ 07666. James Vagias, Exec. Prod. Full-length comedies, dramas, and musicals for cast of 5 or 6 and single set. Submit synopsis with resumé, cast list, and return postcard. Read in spring, reports in 3 to 4 months. No unsolicited scripts.

AMERICAN STANISLAVSKI THEATRE—485 Park Ave., #6A, New York, NY 10022. Sonia Moore, Art. Dir. Full-length or one-act dramas with important message. No offensive language. For cast ages 16 to 45. Submit script with SAS postcard in April and May; reports in Sept. No payment.

AMERICAN THEATRE OF ACTORS—314 W. 54th St., New York, NY 10019. James Jennings, Art. Dir. Full-length dramas for a cast of 2 to 6. Submit complete play and SASE. Reports in one to 2 months.

ARENA STAGE—Sixth and Maine Ave. S.W., Washington, DC 20024. Laurence Maslon, Lit. Mgr./Dramaturg. No unsolicited manuscripts. Allow 3 months for reply.

ARKANSAS ARTS CENTER CHILDREN'S THEATRE—Box 2137, Little Rock, AR 72203. Bradley Anderson, Art. Dir. Seeks solid, professional full-length or one-act scripts, especially work adapted from contemporary and classic literature. Some original work.

ARKANSAS REPERTORY THEATRE COMPANY—601 S. Main, P.O. Box 110, Little Rock, AR 72203–0110. Brad Mooy, Lit. Mgr. Full-length comedies, dramas, and musicals; prefer up to 8 characters. Send synopsis, cast list, resumé, and return postage. Reports in 5 to 6 months.

ARTREACH TOURING THEATRE—3074 Madison Rd., Cincinnati, OH 45209. Kathryn Schultz Miller, Art. Dir. One-act dramas and adaptations for touring children's theater; cast to 3, simple sets. Submit script with synopsis, cast list, resumé, recommendations, and SASE. Payment varies.

BAILIWICK REPERTORY—3212 N. Broadway, Chicago, IL 60657–3515. David Zak, Exec. Dir. Produces Main Stage Series of 5 plays; Director's Festival of 50 one-act plays; Pride Performance Series (gay and lesbian works); and New Directors Series of experimental work. Large casts or musicals are O.K. Plays are highly theatrical and politically aware. "Know the rules, then break them creatively and boldly. Creative staging is a must." Send SASE for guidelines before submitting. Submit one-act plays before Dec. 1. (One-act-play festival runs March through April.) Reports in 3 months. Pays 6% to 8% royalty.

BARTER THEATER—P.O. Box 867, Abingdon, VA 24210. Rex Partington, Producing Dir. Full-length dramas, comedies, adaptations, musicals, and children's plays. Full workshop and reading productions. Allow 6 to 8 months for report. Payment rates negotiable.

BERKELEY REPERTORY THEATRE—2025 Addison St., Berkeley, CA 94704. Sharon Ott, Art. Dir. No unsolicited manuscripts; agent submissions or professional recommendations only. Reporting time: 3 to 4 months.

BERKSHIRE THEATRE FESTIVAL—Box 797, Stockbridge, MA 01262. Richard Dunlap, Art. Dir. Full-length comedies, musicals, and dramas; cast to 8. Submit through agent only.

BOARSHEAD THEATER—425 S. Grand Ave., Lansing, MI 48933. John Peakes, Art. Dir. Full-length comedies and dramas with simple sets and cast to 10. Send precis, 5 to 10 pages of dialogue, cast list with descriptions, and resumé. SAS postcard for reply.

BRISTOL RIVERSIDE THEATRE—Box 1250, Bristol, PA 19007. Susan D. Atkinson, Producing/Art. Dir. Full-length and one-act plays with up to 10 actors on simple set. Submit synopsis with return postcard in summer. Pays a percentage of box office proceeds. Offers workshops and readings.

CALIFORNIA UNIVERSITY THEATRE—California, PA 15419. Dr. Roger C. Emelson, Chairman. Unusual, avant-garde, and experimental one-act and full-length comedies and dramas, children's plays, and adaptations. Cast size varies. Submit synopsis with short, sample scene(s). Payment available.

CENTER STAGE—700 N. Calvert St., Baltimore, MD 21202. Rick Davis, Assoc. Art. Dir. Full-length and one-act comedies, dramas, translations, adaptations. No unsolicited manuscripts. Send synopsis, a few sample pages, resumé, cast list, and production history. Pays varying rates. Allow 4 to 8 weeks for reply.

CHILDSPLAY, INC.—Box 517, Tempe, AZ 85280. David Saar, Art. Dir. Plays running 45 to 90 minutes: dramas, musicals, children's plays, and adaptations. Sets must travel. Cast size, 4 to 8. Submissions accepted July through November. Reports in 2 to 6 months. Payment varies.

CIRCLE IN THE SQUARE/UPTOWN—1633 Broadway, New York, NY 10019–6795. Theodore Mann, Art. Dir. Full-length comedies, dramas, and adaptations. Send synopsis with resumé, cast list, and 10-page dialogue sample to Nancy Bosco, Lit. Advisor. No unsolicited scripts. SASE required.

CITY THEATRE COMPANY—57 S. 13th St., Pittsburgh, PA 15203. Scott Cummings, Lit. Dir. Full-length comedies and dramas; query Sept. to May. Cast to 12; simple sets. Readings. Royalty.

CLASSIC STAGE COMPANY—136 E. 13th St., New York, NY 10003. Patricia Taylor, Managing Dir. Carey Perloff, Artistic Dir. Full-length adaptations and translations of existing classic literature. Submit synopsis with cast list and SASE, Sept. to May. Offers readings. Pays on royalty basis.

CREATIVE THEATRE—102 Witherspoon St., Princeton, NJ 08540. Eloise Bruce, Art. Dir. Participatory plays for children, grades K through 6; cast of 4 to 6; arena or thrust stage. Submit manuscript with synopsis and cast list. Pay varies.

THE CRICKET THEATRE—1407 Nicollet Ave., Minneapolis, MN 55403. William Partlan, Art. Dir. Send synopsis, resumé, and 10-page sample of work; "prefer contemporary plays." Cast to 8. Reports in 6 months.

CROSSROADS THEATRE CO.—320 Memorial Pkwy., New Brunswick, NJ 08901. Ricardo Khan, Art. Dir. Sydné Mahone, Lit. Mgr. Full-length and one-act dramas, comedies, musicals, and adaptations; issue-oriented experimental pieces that offer honest, imaginative, and insightful examinations of the African-American experience. Also interested in African, Caribbean, and interracial plays. Queries only, with synopsis, cast list, resumé, and SASE.

DELAWARE THEATRE COMPANY—P.O. Box 516, Wilmington, DE 19899. Cleveland Morris, Art. Dir. Full-length comedies, dramas, musicals, and adaptations, with cast to 10; prefer single set. Send cast list, synopsis, and SASE. Reports in 6 months. Pays royalty.

DENVER CENTER THEATRE COMPANY—1050 13th St., Denver, CO 80204. Send full-length, previously unproduced scripts with cast to 12, June through December. Stipend and housing. Annual New Play Festival, "U.S. West Fest."

DETROIT REPERTORY THEATRE—13103 Woodrow Wilson Ave., Detroit, MI 48238. Barbara Busby, Lit. Mgr. Full-length comedies and dramas. Enclose SASE. Pays royalty.

DOBBINS PRODUCTIONS, STEVE—25 Van Ness Ave., Lower Level, San Francisco, CA 94102. Michelle Hickey, Lit. Dir. Full-length comedies, dramas, and musicals. Cast to 12. Query with synopsis and resumé. No unsolicited manuscripts. Reports in 6 months. Offers workshops and readings. Pays 6% of gross.

DORSET THEATRE FESTIVAL—Box 519, Dorset, VT 05251. Jill Charles, Art. Dir. Full-length comedies, musicals, dramas, and adaptations; cast to 8; simple set preferred. Agent submissions and professional recommendations only. Pays varying rates. Residencies at Dorset Colony House for Writers available Oct. to June. See "Writers Colonies" listing.

DRIFTWOOD SHOWBOAT—Box 1032, Kingston, NY 12401. Fred Hall, Resident Company Art. Dir. Full-length family comedies for 2- to 6-person cast, single setting. No profanity. Submit cast list, synopsis, and return postcard Sept. to June.

EAST WEST PLAYERS—4424 Santa Monica Blvd., Los Angeles, CA 90029. Nobu McCarthy, Art. Dir. Dick Dotterer, Dramaturg. Produces 2 to 3 new plays annually. Original plays, translations, adaptations, musicals, and youth theater. Readings. Prefer to see query letter with synopsis and 10 pages of dialogue; complete scripts also considered. Reports in 5 to 6 weeks for query; 6 months for complete script.

ECCENTRIC CIRCLES THEATRE—400 W. 43rd St., #4N, New York, NY 10036. Rosemary Hopkins, Art. Dir. Full-length and one-act comedies and dramas with simple sets and a cast size to 10. Submit manuscript with resumé and SASE. Reports in 6 weeks.

EMPIRE STATE INSTITUTE FOR THE PERFORMING ARTS—See New York State Theatre Institute.

THE EMPTY SPACE THEATRE—P.O. Box 1748, Seattle, WA 98111–1748. Kurt Beattie, Art. Dir. Unsolicited scripts accepted only from WA, OR, WY, MT, and ID. Outside five-state N.W. region: scripts accepted through agents or established theater groups only.

ENSEMBLE STUDIO THEATRE—549 W. 52nd St., New York, NY 10019. Address Lit. Mgr. Send full-length or one-act comedies and dramas, with resumé and SASE, Sept. to April. Pay varies. Readings.

FLORIDA STUDIO THEATRE—1241 N. Palm Ave., Sarasota, FL 33577. Steve Ramay, New Play Development. Innovative smaller cast plays that are pertinent and contemporary. Query first with synopsis and SASE. Also accepting musicals.

GE VA THEATRE—75 Woodbury Blvd., Rochester, NY 14607. Ann Patrice Carrigan, Lit. Dir. Query for comedies and dramas with synopsis and cast list. Readings.

GEER THEATRICUM BOTANICUM, WILL—Box 1222, Topanga, CA 90290. All types of scripts for outdoor theater, with large playing area. Submit synopsis with SASE. Pays varing rates.

GIFFORD CHILDREN'S THEATER, EMMY—3504 Center St., Omaha, NE 68105. James Larson, Art. Dir. Unsolicited scripts accepted with SASE.

THE GOODMAN THEATRE—200 S. Columbus Dr., Chicago, IL 60603. Tom Creamer, Dramaturg. Queries required for full-length comedies or dramas and must come through recognized literary agents or producing organizations. No unsolicited scripts or synopses accepted.

THE GUTHRIE THEATER—725 Vineland Pl., Minneapolis, MN 55403. Full-length comedies, dramas, and adaptations. Manuscripts accepted only from recognized theatrical agents. Query with detailed synopsis and cast size. Reports in one to 2 months.

HARRISBURG COMMUNITY THEATRE—513 Hurlock St., Harrisburg, PA 17110. Thomas G. Hostetter, Art. Dir. Full-length comedies, dramas, musicals, and adaptations; cast to 20; prefers simple set. Submit script with cast list, resumé, synopsis, and SAS postcard. Best time to submit: June to August. Reporting time: 6 months. Pays negotiable rates.

HIPPODROME STATE THEATRE—25 S.E. Second Pl., Gainesville, FL 32601. Mary Hausch, Producing Art. Dir. Full-length plays with unit sets and casts up to 15. Submit in summer and fall. Enclose return postcard and synopsis.

HOLLYWOOD THEATER COMPANY—12838 Kling St., Studio City, CA 91604–1127. Rai Tasco, Art. Dir. Full-length comedies and dramas for integrated cast. Include cast list and stamped return postcard with submission.

HONOLULU THEATRE FOR YOUTH—2846 Ualena St., Honolulu, HI 96819. Pam Sterling, Art. Dir. Plays, 60 to 90 minutes playing time, for young people/family audiences. Adult casts. Contemporary issues, Pacific themes, etc. Unit sets, small cast. Query or send cover letter with synopsis, cast list, and SASE. Royalties negotiable.

HORIZON THEATRE COMPANY—P. O. Box 5376, Station E, Atlanta, GA 30307. Jeffrey and Lisa Adler, Co-Artistic Directors. Full-length comedies, dramas, and satires that use "heightened" realism and other highly theatrical forms. Cast to 10. Submit synopsis with cast list, resumé, and recommendations. Pays percentage. Readings. Reports in 6 months.

ILLINOIS THEATRE CENTER—400 Lakewood Blvd., Park Forest, IL 60466. Steve S. Billig, Art. Dir. Full-length comedies, dramas, musicals, and adaptations, for unit/fragmentary sets, and cast to 8. Send summary and return postcard. No unsolicited manuscripts. Pays negotiable rates. Workshops and readings offered.

ILLUSTRATED STAGE COMPANY—Box 640063, San Francisco, CA 94164–0063. Steve Dobbins, Art. Dir. Full-length comedies, dramas, and musicals for a cast to 18. Query with synopsis and SASE. No unsolicited manuscripts. Offers workshops and readings.

INVISIBLE THEATRE—1400 N. First Ave, Tucson, AZ 85719. Deborah Dickey, Lit. Mgr. Reads queries for full-length comedies, dramas, musicals, adaptations, Jan. to May. Cast to 10; simple set. Pays royalty.

JEWISH REPERTORY THEATRE—344 E. 14th St., New York, NY 10003. Ran Avni, Art. Dir. Full-length comedies, dramas, musicals, and adaptations, with cast to 10, relating to the Jewish experience. Pays varying rates. Enclose SASE.

KUMU KAHUA—Kennedy Theatre, Univ. of Hawaii at Manoa, 1770 East-West Rd., Honolulu, HI 96822. Dennis Carroll, Man. Dir. Full-length plays specially relevant to life in Hawaii. Prefer simple sets for arena and in-the-round productions. Submit resumé and synopsis January through April. Pays $35 per performance. Readings. Contests.

LIVE OAK THEATRE—311 Nueces, Austin, TX 78701. Mari Marchbanks, Lit. Mgr. Full-length plays, one-acts, translations, adaptations, musicals, and plays for young audiences. "Special interest in producing works of Texas and southern topics and new American plays." No unsolicited scripts; send synopsis, letter of inquiry, and 10 pages of dialogue. Contest. Guidelines.

LONG ISLAND STAGE—P. O. Box 9001, Rockville Centre, New York, NY 11571–9001. Clinton J. Atkinson, Art. Dir. Full-length dramas and adaptations. Query with SASE in late spring/early summer. Pays varying rates.

LOS ANGELES DESIGNERS' THEATRE—P. O. Box 1883, Studio City, CA 91614–0883. Richard Niederberg, Art. Dir. Full-length comedies, dramas, musicals, fantasies, or adaptations. Religious, political, social, and controversial themes encouraged. Nudity, "adult" language, etc., O.K. "Please detail in the cover letter what the writer's proposed involvement with the production would be." Payment varies.

THE MAGIC THEATRE—Bldg. D, Fort Mason, San Francisco, CA 94123. Eugenie Chan, Lit. Mgr. Comedies and dramas, ethnic-American, workshop productions. Query with synopsis, resumé, and 3 to 5 pages of sample dialogue. Pays varying rates.

MANHATTAN THEATRE CLUB—453 W. 16th, New York, NY 10011. Address Kate Loewald. Full-length and one-act comedies, dramas, and musicals. No unsolicited manuscripts. Send synopsis with 10 to 15 pages of dialogue, cast list, resumé, recommendations, and SASE. Pays negotiable rates. Allow 6 months for reply.

MAXWELL ANDERSON PLAYWRIGHTS SERIES, INC.—6 Sagamore Rd., Stamford, CT 06902. Philip Devine, Pres. Produces 6 to 8 staged readings of new plays each year. Send complete script with SASE.

MILL MOUNTAIN THEATRE—Center in the Sq., One Market Square, Roanoke, VA 24011. Jo Weinstein, Lit. Mgr. Full-length or one-act comedies, dramas, musicals; include publicity, resumé. One-act plays limited to 25 to 40 minutes. Payment varies.

MISSOURI REPERTORY THEATRE—4949 Cherry St., Kansas City, MO 64110. Felicia Londré, Dramaturg. Full-length comedies and dramas. Query with synopsis, cast list, resumé, and return postcard. Pays standard royalty.

MUSICAL THEATRE WORKS—440 Lafayette St., New York, NY 10003. Gary Littman, Lit. Mgr. Full-length musicals, cast to 10; simple sets. Submit manuscript with SASE and cassette score. No payment.

NATIONAL BLACK THEATRE—2033 Fifth Ave., Harlem, NY 10035. Submit to Tunde Samuel. Drama, musicals, and children's plays. "Scripts should reflect African and African-American lifestyle. Historical, inspirational, and ritualistic forms appreciated." Workshops and readings.

NATIONAL PLAYWRIGHTS CONFERENCE, EUGENE O'NEILL THEATRE CENTER—234 W. 44th St., Suite 901, New York, NY 10036. Annual competition to select new stage and television plays for development during the summer at organization's Waterford, CT, location. Submission deadline: Dec. 1. Send #10-size SASE in the fall for guidelines to National Playwright's Conference, c/o above address. Pays stipend, plus travel/living expenses during conference.

NEW EHRLICH THEATRE—Boston Center for the Arts, 539 Tremont St., Boston, MA 02116. New full-length scripts (no musicals) by Massachusetts playwrights for readings and workshop productions. Include SASE. Address to NE-Works Submissions Program.

NEW TUNERS/PERFORMANCE COMMUNITY—1225 W. Belmont Ave., Chicago, IL 60657. Allan Chambers, Dramaturg. Full-length musicals only, for cast to 15; no wing/fly space. Send manuscript with cassette tape of score, cast list, resumé, SASE, and return postcard. Pays on royalty basis.

NEW YORK SHAKESPEARE FESTIVAL/PUBLIC THEATER—425 Lafayette St., New York, NY 10003. Gail Merrifield, Dir. of Plays and Musicals. Plays and musical works for the theater, translations, and adaptations. Submit manuscript, cassette (with musicals), and SASE. Allow 3 to 4 months for response.

656

NEW YORK STATE THEATRE INSTITUTE—(formerly Empire State Institute for the Performing Arts) PAC 266, 1400 Washington Ave., Albany, NY 12222. Query for new musicals and plays for family audiences, with synopsis, cast list. Submit between June and August. Payment varies.

ODYSSEY THEATRE ENSEMBLE—2055 South Sepulveda Blvd., Los Angeles, CA 90025. Ron Sossi, Art. Dir. Full-length comedies, dramas, musicals, and adaptations: provocative subject matter, or plays that stretch and explore the possibilities of theater. Query Jan Lewis, Lit. Mgr., with synopsis and return postcard. Pays variable rates. Allow 2 to 6 months for reply. Workshops and readings.

OLD GLOBE THEATRE—Simon Edison Center for the Performing Arts, Box 2171, San Diego, CA 92112. Address Mark Hofflund. Full-length comedies, dramas, and musicals. No unsolicited manuscripts. Submit through agent, or query with synopsis.

OLDCASTLE THEATRE COMPANY—Southern Vermont College, Box 1555, Bennington, VT 05201. Eric Peterson, Dir. Full-length comedies, dramas, and musicals for a small cast (up to 10) and a single stage set. Submit synopsis and cast list in the winter. Reports in 2 months. Offers workshops and readings. Pays expenses for playwright to attend rehearsals. Royalty.

PAPER MILL PLAYHOUSE—Brookside Dr., Millburn, NJ 07041. Maryan F. Stephens, Lit. Advisor. Full-length plays and musicals. Submit synopsis, resumé, and tape for musicals; reporting time, 4 to 6 months.

PENGUIN REPERTORY COMPANY—Box 91, Stony Point, Rockland County, NY 10980. Joe Brancato, Art. Dir. Full-length comedies and dramas with cast size to 5. Submit script, resumé, and SASE. Payment varies.

PENNSYLVANIA STAGE COMPANY—837 Linden St., Allentown, PA 18101. Full-length plays with cast to 8; one set. Send synopsis, cast list, and SASE to Literary Dept. Pays negotiable rates. Allow 6 months for reply. Readings.

PEOPLE'S LIGHT AND THEATRE COMPANY—39 Conestoga Rd., Malvern, PA 19355. Alda Cortese, Lit. Mgr. One-act or full-length comedies, dramas, adaptations. Query with synopsis, 10 pages of script required. Reports in 6 months. Payment negotiable.

PIER ONE THEATRE—Box 894, Homer, AK 99603. Lance Petersen, Lit. Dir. Full-length and one-act comedies, dramas, musicals, children's plays, and adaptations. Submit complete script; include piano score with musicals. New works given staged readings. "We think new works in the theater are extremely important!" Pays 8% of ticket sales for mainstage musicals; other payment varies.

PLAYHOUSE ON THE SQUARE—51 S. Cooper in Overton Sq., Memphis, TN 38104. Jackie Nichols, Art. Dir. Full-length comedies, dramas; cast to 15. Southern playwrights given preference. Contest deadline is April for fall production. Pays $500.

PLAYWRIGHTS HORIZONS—416 W. 42nd St., New York, NY 10036. Address Lit. Dept. Full-length, original comedies, dramas, and musicals by American authors. Send resumé and SASE. Pays varying rates.

PLAYWRIGHTS' PLATFORM—164 Brayton Rd., Boston, MA 02135. Script development workshops and public readings for New England playwrights only. Full-length and one-act plays of all kinds. No sexist or racist material accepted. Residents of New England send scripts with short synopsis, resumé, return postcard, and SASE.

657

POPLAR PIKE PLAYHOUSE—7653 Old Poplar Pike, Germantown, TN 38138. Frank Bluestein, Art. Dir. Full-length and one-act comedies, dramas, musicals, and children's plays. Submit synopsis with return postcard and resumé. Pays $300.

PORTLAND STAGE COMPANY—Box 1458, Portland, ME 04104. Richard Hamburger, Art. Dir. Full-length plays for cast to 8. Send synopsis and sample dialogue with return postcard. Pays fee, travel, and living arrangements if play is produced on mainstage.

PRINCETON REPERTORY COMPANY—13 Witherspoon St., Princeton, NJ 08542. Victoria Liberatori, Art. Dir. Full-length comedies and dramas for a cast to 8. One set. Submit synopsis with resumé and cast list, or complete manuscript. "Scripts with socially relevant themes that move beyond domestic drama preferred. The treatment of these themes might be lyrical, surreal, realistic, or high concept." Workshops and readings offered. Response within one year.

THE PUERTO RICAN TRAVELING THEATRE—141 W. 94th St., New York, NY 10025. Miriam Colon Valle, Art. Dir. Full-length and one-act comedies, dramas, and musicals; cast to 8; simple sets. "We prefer plays based on the contemporary Hispanic experience, material with social, cultural, or psychological content." Payment negotiable.

THE REPERTORY THEATRE OF ST. LOUIS—Box 191730, St. Louis, MO 63119. Agent submissions only.

THE ROAD COMPANY—Box 5278 EKS, John City, TN 37603. Robert H. Leonard, Art. Dir. Christine Murdock, Lit. Mgr. Full-length and one-act comedies, dramas with social/political relevance to small-town audiences. Send synopsis, cast list, and production history, if any. Pays negotiable rates. Reports in 6 to 12 months.

ROUND HOUSE THEATRE—12210 Bushey Dr., Silver Spring, MD 20902. Address Production Office Mgr. Full-length comedies, dramas, adaptations, and musicals; cast to 10; prefer simple set. Send one page synopsis. No unsolicited manuscripts.

SALT AND PEPPER MIME COMPANY/NEW ENSEMBLE ACTORS THEATRE—320 E. 90th St., #1B, New York, NY 10128. Ms. Scottie Davis, Art. Prod. One-acts, all types, especially those conducive to "nontraditional" casting. "Very interested in pieces suitable to surrealistic or mimetic concept in philosophy or visual style." Cast size to 8. Send resumé, return postcard, cast list, and synopsis. Scripts reviewed from May to September. Payment of royalties based on rates established at beginning of run. Works also considered for readings, storyplayers, experimental development, and readers theater.

SEATTLE GROUP THEATRE—3940 Brooklyn Ave. N.E., Seattle, WA 98105. Full-length satires, dramas, musicals, and translations, cast to 10; simple set. Special interest in plays suitable for multi-ethnic cast; serious plays on social/cultural issues; satires. Query with synopsis, self-addressed postcard, sample dialogue, and resumé required. Reporting time: 6 weeks.

SOCIETY HILL PLAYHOUSE—507 S. 8th St., Philadelphia, PA 19147. Walter Vail, Dramaturg. Full-length dramas and comedies; cast to 6; simple set. Submit synopsis and SASE. Reports in 6 months. Nominal payment.

SOUTH COAST REPERTORY—P. O. Box 2197, Costa Mesa, CA 92628. John Glore, Lit. Mgr. Full-length comedies, dramas, musicals, juveniles. Query first with synopsis and resumé. Payment varies.

SOUTHERN APPALACHIAN REPERTORY THEATRE—P.O. Box 620,

Mars Hill, NC 28754. James W. Thomas, Art. Dir. Full-length comedies, dramas, musicals, and plays with Appalachian theme. Submit resumé, recommendations, full script, and SASE to Jan W. Blalock, Asst. Man. Dir. Send SASE for information on Southern Appalachian Playwright's Conference (held in January each year). Pays $500 royalty if play is selected for production during the summer season. Deadline for submissions is Dec. 15 each year.

STAGE LEFT THEATRE—3244 N. Clark, Chicago, IL 60657. Dennis McCullough, Art. Dir. Full-length comedies, dramas, and adaptations for cast of 3 to 12. "We are committed to producing material that is politically and socially conscious." Offers workshops and readings. No unsolicited scripts. Payment varies.

STAGE ONE: THE LOUISVILLE CHILDREN'S THEATRE—425 W. Market St., Louisville, KY 40202. Adaptations of classics and original plays for children ages 4 to 18. Submit script with resumé and SASE. Reports in 4 months.

STAGES REPERTORY THEATRE—3201 Allen Pkwy., #101, Houston, TX 77019. Jim Bernhard, Acting Art. Dir. Unproduced new works: full-length dramas, comedies, translations, and adaptations, with small casts and simple sets. Texas playwrights' festival held in the spring. Send script with synopsis, resumé, and SASE.

STUDIO ARENA THEATRE—710 Main St., Buffalo, NY 14202. Comedies, dramas; cast to 8. Particular interest in plays by and about women or minorities. Include synopsis, resumé, cast list, sample dialogue.

TAKOMA PLAYERS, INC.—Box 56512, Washington, DC 20012. Realistic, full-length dramas, comedies, and musicals. Special interest in plays suitable to multi-ethnic casts. Submit manuscript with SASE to Gaynelle Reed Lewis; report, in 3 months. Payment negotiable.

MARK TAPER FORUM—135 N. Grand Ave., Los Angeles, CA 90012. Oliver Mayer, Lit. Assoc. Full-length comedies, dramas, musicals, juveniles, adaptations. Query first.

THE TEN MINUTE MUSICALS PROJECT—Box 461194, West Hollywood, CA 90046. Michael Koppy, Prod. One-act musicals. Include audio cassette, libretto, and lead sheets with submission. "We are looking for complete short musicals." Pays $250.

THEATER ARTISTS OF MARIN—Box 150473, San Rafael, CA 94915. Charles Brousse, Art. Dir. Full-length comedies, dramas, and musicals for a cast of 2 to 8. Submit complete script with SASE. Reports in 4 to 6 months. Three showcase productions each year.

THEATRE AMERICANA—Box 245, Altadena, CA 91001. Full-length comedies and dramas, preferably with American theme. No children's plays. Language and subject matter should be suitable for a community audience. Send bound manuscript with cast list, resumé, and SASE, by January 1. No payment. Allow 3 to 6 months for reply. Submit no more than two entries per season.

THEATRE ON THE SQUARE—450 Post St., San Francisco, CA 94102. Jonathan Reinis, Art. Dir. Full-length comedies, dramas, and musicals for 15-person cast. Submit cast list and script with SASE. Reports in 30 days.

THEATRE/TEATRO—Bilingual Foundation for the Arts, 421 N. Ave., #19, Los Angeles, CA 90031. Margarita Galban, Art. Dir. Full-length plays about Hispanic experience; small casts. Submit manuscript with SASE. Pays negotiable rates.

659

THEATREWORKS/USA—890 Broadway, 7th Fl., New York, NY 10003. Barbara Pasternack, Lit. Mgr. One-hour children's musicals for 5-person cast. Playwrights must be within commutable distance to New York City. Submit outline or treatment, sample scenes, and songs in spring, summer. Pays royalty.

WALNUT STREET THEATRE COMPANY—9th and Walnut Sts., Philadelphia, PA 19107. Alexa Kelly, Lit. Mgr. Full-length comedies, dramas, musicals, and adaptations; also, 1- to 5- character plays for studio stage. Submit 20 sample pages with return postcard, cast list, and synopsis. Musical submissions must include an audio tape. Reports in 5 months. Payment varies.

THE WESTERN STAGE—156 Homestead Ave., Salinas, CA 93901. Tom Humphrey, Art. Dir. The Steinbeck Playwriting Prize. Submissions June 1 to August 31 to Joyce Lower, Dramaturg. Full-length plays in the spirit of John Steinbeck. No one-acts or adaptations. Prize includes readings, workshops, residency, a full-scale production, royalties, and support during reworking (up to $4,000).

WISDOM BRIDGE THEATRE—1559 W. Howard St., Chicago, IL 60626. Jeffrey Ortmann, Prod. Dir. Jose Calleja, Lit. Mgr. Plays dealing with contemporary social/political issues; small-scale musicals, literary adaptations; cast to 12. Synopsis only. No unsolicited scripts.

WOOLLY MAMMOTH THEATRE COMPANY—1401 Church St. N.W., Washington, DC 20005. Greg Tillman, Lit. Mgr. Looking for offbeat material, unusual writing. Unsolicited scripts accepted. Pay negotiable.

GARY YOUNG MIME THEATRE—23724 Park Madrid, Calabasas, CA 91302. Gary Young, Art. Dir. Comedy monologues and two-person vignettes, for children and adults, one minute to 90 minutes in length; casts of one or 2, and portable set. Pays varying rates. Enclose return postcard, resumé, recommendations, cast list, and synopsis.

PLAY PUBLISHERS

ART CRAFT PLAY COMPANY—Box 1058, Cedar Rapids, IA 52406. Three-act comedies, mysteries, musicals, and farces, and one-act comedies or dramas, with one set, for production by junior or senior high schools. Pays on royalty basis or by outright purchase.

BAKER'S PLAYS—100 Chauncy St., Boston, MA 02111. Scripts for amateur production: one-act plays for competition, children's plays, musicals, religious drama, full-length plays for high school production. Three- to four-month reading period. Include SASE.

CHILDREN'S PLAYMATE—1100 Waterway Blvd., P. O. Box 567, Indianapolis, IN 46206. Elizabeth A. Rinck, Ed. Plays, 200 to 600 words, for children ages 6 to 8: special emphasis on health, nutrition, exercise, and safety. Pays about 10¢ a word, on publication.

CONTEMPORARY DRAMA SERVICE—Meriwether Publishing Co., Box 7710, 885 Elkton Dr., Colorado Springs, CO 80903. Arthur Zapel, Ed. Books on theater arts subjects and anthologies. Textbooks for speech and drama. Easy-to-stage comedies, skits, one-acts, musicals, puppet scripts, full-length plays for schools and churches. (Jr. high through college level; no elementary level material.) Adaptations of classics and improvised material for classroom use. Comedy monologues and duets. Chancel drama for Christmas and Easter church use. Enclose synopsis. Pays by fee arrangement or on royalty basis.

THE DRAMATIC PUBLISHING CO.—311 Washington St., Woodstock, IL 60098. Full-length and one-act plays and musicals for the stock, amateur, and children's theater market. Pays on royalty basis. Address Sarah Clark. Reports within 12 to 16 weeks.

DRAMATICS—Educational Theatre Assoc., 3368 Central Pkwy., Cincinnati, OH 45225–2392. Don Corathers, Ed. One-act and full-length plays for high school production. Pays $100 to $400, on acceptance.

ELDRIDGE PUBLISHING COMPANY—P. O. Drawer 216, Franklin, OH 45005. Nancy Vorhis, Ed. Dept. One-, two-, and three-act plays and operettas for schools, churches, community groups, etc. Special interest in comedies and Christmas plays. Include cassette for operettas. Pays varying rates. Responds in 2 to 3 months.

FRENCH, INC., SAMUEL—45 W. 25th St., New York, NY 10010. Lawrence R. Harbison, Ed. Full-length plays for dinner, community, stock, college, and high school theaters. One-act plays (30 to 45 minutes). Children's plays, 45 to 60 minutes. Pays on royalty basis.

HEUER PUBLISHING COMPANY—Drawer 248, Cedar Rapids, IA 52406. C. Emmett McMullen, Ed. One-act comedies and dramas for contest work; three-act comedies, mysteries, or farces, and musicals, with one interior setting, for high school production. Pays royalty or flat fee.

PIONEER DRAMA SERVICE—P. O. Box 22555, Denver, CO 80222. Full-length and one-act plays; plays for young audiences; musicals, melodramas, and Christmas plays. No unproduced plays, plays with largely male casts or multiple sets. Query. Outright purchase or royalty.

PLAYS, THE DRAMA MAGAZINE FOR YOUNG PEOPLE—120 Boylston St., Boston, MA 02116. Elizabeth Preston, Man. Ed. One-act plays, with simple settings, for production by young people, 7 to 17: holiday plays, comedies, dramas, farces, skits, adaptations of classics and folktales, puppet plays, melodramas, and creative dramatics. Maximum lengths: lower grades, 10 double-spaced pages; middle grades, 15 pages; junior and senior high, 20 pages. Send SASE for manuscript specification sheet. Query first for adaptations. Pays good rates, on acceptance. Buys all rights.

SCHOLASTIC VOICE—730 Broadway, New York, NY 10003. Forrest Stone, Ed. For ages 14 to 18 with at least an 8th-grade reading level. Plays, 1,000 to 3,000 words, on any subject. Magazine is distributed though schools. Pays good rates, on acceptance.

THE TELEVISION MARKET

The almost round-the-clock television offerings on commercial, educational, and cable TV stations may lead free-lance writers to believe that opportunities to sell scripts or program ideas are infinite. Unfortunately, this is not true. With few exceptions, producers and programmers do not consider scripts submitted directly to them, no matter how good they are. In general, free lancers can achieve success in this nearly closed field by concentrating on getting their fiction (short and in novel form) and nonfiction published in magazines or books, combed diligently by television producers for possible adaptations. A large percentage of the material offered over all types of networks (in addition to the motion pictures made in

661

Hollywood or especially for TV) is in the form of adaptations of published material.

Writers who want to try their hand at writing directly for this very limited market should be prepared to learn the special techniques and acceptable format of script writing. Also, experience in playwriting and a knowledge of dramatic structure gained through working in amateur, community, or professional theaters can be helpful.

Since virtually all TV producers will read scripts and queries submitted only through recognized agents, we've included a list of agents who have indicated to us that they are willing to read queries for TV scripts. The Association of Authors' Representatives (10 Astor Pl., 3rd Floor, New York, NY 10003) will send out a listing of agents upon receipt of an SASE, and *Literary Market Place* (Bowker), available in most libraries, also has a list of agents. Before submitting scripts to producers or to agents, authors should query to learn whether they prefer to see the material in script form, or as an outline or summary. A list of network (ABC, NBC, CBS, FOX) shows and production companies may be found in *Ross Reports Television*, published monthly by Television Index, Inc., (40–29 27th St., Long Island City, NY 11101).

Writers may wish to register their story, treatment, series format, or script with the Writers Guild of America. This registration does not confer statutory rights, but it does supply evidence of authorship and date of authorship. Registration is effective for five years (and is renewable after that). The WGA's registration service is available to guild members and non-members for a reasonable fee. For more information, write the Writers Guild of America Registration Service East, Inc., 555 W. 57th St., New York, NY 10019. Dramatic material can also be registered with the U.S. Copyright Office (Register of Copyrights, Library of Congress, Washington, DC 20559). Finally, those interested in writing for television may want to read such daily trade newspapers as *Daily Variety* (5700 Wilshire Blvd., Suite 120, Los Angeles, CA 90036) and *Hollywood Reporter* (6715 Sunset Blvd., Hollywood, CA 90028).

TELEVISION SCRIPT AGENTS

MARCIA AMSTERDAM AGENCY—41 W. 82nd St., #9A, New York, NY 10024. Query with SASE.

ANN ELMO AGENCY, INC.—60 E. 42nd St., New York, NY 10165. Prefer queries on TV or screen feature material. Writers with screen credits only.

ROBERT A. FREEDMAN—Dramatic Agency, Inc., 1501 Broadway, #2310, New York, NY 10036. Two-hour teleplays. Query with SASE.

OTTO R. KOZAK LITERARY AGENCY—P.O. Box 152, Long Beach, NY 11561. Query with SASE.

THE LANTZ OFFICE—888 Seventh Ave., New York, NY 10106. Limited market. Query.

HAROLD OBER ASSOCIATES, INC.—425 Madison Ave., New York, NY 10017. Query with SASE.

RAINES & RAINES—71 Park Ave., New York, NY 10016. Screenplays and teleplays. Query.

THE SHUKAT COMPANY, LTD.—340 W. 55th St., #1A, New York, NY 10036. Query.

ANN WRIGHT REPRESENTATIVES, INC.—136 E. 56th St., New York, NY 10022–3615. Screenplays and teleplays. Query with SASE.

WRITERS AND ARTISTS AGENCY—19 West 44th St., Suite 1000, New York, NY 10036. Reads queries with SASEs. Considers screenplays, teleplays, and plays. Send bio and resumé.

BOOK PUBLISHERS

The following list includes the major publishers of trade books (adult and juvenile fiction and nonfiction) and a representative number of small publishers from across the country. All companies in the list publish both hardcover and paperback books, unless otherwise indicated.

Before sending a complete manuscript to an editor, it is advisable to send a brief query letter describing the proposed book. The letter should also include information about the author's special qualifications for dealing with a particular topic and any previous publication credits. An outline of the book (or a synopsis for fiction) and a sample chapter may also be included.

It is common practice to submit a book manuscript to only one publisher at a time, although it is becoming more and more acceptable for writers, even those without agents, to submit the same query or proposal to more than one editor at the same time.

Book manuscripts may be sent in typing paper boxes (available from a stationer) and sent by first-class mail, or, more common and less expensive, by "Special Fourth Class Rate—Manuscript." For rates, details of insurance, and so forth, inquire at your local post office. With any submission to a publisher, be sure to enclose sufficient postage for the manuscript's return.

Royalty rates for hardcover books usually start at 10% of the retail price of the book and increase after a certain number of copies have been sold. Paperbacks generally have a somewhat lower rate, about 5% to 8%. It is customary for the publishing company to pay the author a cash advance against royalties when the book contract is signed or when the finished manuscript is received. Some publishers pay on a flat fee basis.

ABBEY PRESS—St. Meinrad, IN 47577. Keith McClellan, O.S.B., Pub. Nonfiction books on marriage, family, pastoral care, and spiritual growth with a mainline Judeo-Christian religious slant. Query with table of contents, writing sample, and SASE.

ABINGDON PRESS—201 Eighth Ave. S., Nashville, TN 37202. Mary Catherine Dean, Ed. Religious books: mainline, social issues, marriage/family, self-help, exceptional persons. Query with outline and one or two sample chapters. Guidelines.

ACADEMIC PRESS—Harcourt, Brace, Jovanovich, Inc., 1250 Sixth St., San Diego, CA 92101. Scientific books for professionals; upper-level undergraduate and graduate science texts. Query.

ACCENT BOOKS—Box 15337, 12100 W. 6th Ave., Denver, CO 80215. Mary Nelson, Exec. Ed. Fiction and nonfiction from evangelical Christian perspective. "Request guidelines before querying." Query with sample chapters and SASE. Royalty. Paperback only.

ACE BOOKS—Imprint of Berkley Publishing Group, 200 Madison Ave., New York, NY 10016. Susan Allison, V.P., Ed.-in-Chief. Science fiction and fantasy. Royalty. Query with first three chapters and outline.

ADAMA BOOKS—See Modan Publishing.

ADDISON-WESLEY PUBLISHING CO.—Rt. 128, Reading, MA 01867. General Publishing Group: Adult nonfiction on current topics: education, health, psychology, computers, software, business, biography, child care, etc. Specializing in literary nonfiction. Royalty.

ALASKA NORTHWEST BOOKS—A Div. of GT/E Discovery Publications, 22026 20th Ave. S.E., Bothell, WA 98021. Maureen Zimmerman, Mgr. Nonfiction, 50,000 to 100,000 words, with an emphasis on natural world and history of Alaska, Western Canada, Pacific Northwest, and Pacific Rim: travel books; cookbooks; field guides; children's books; outdoor recreation; native culture; lifestyle. Send query or sample chapters with outline.

ALGONQUIN BOOKS OF CHAPEL HILL—Div. of Workman Publishing Co., Inc., Box 2225, Chapel Hill, NC 27515. Shannon Ravenel, Ed. Dir. Trade books, fiction and nonfiction, for adults.

THE AMERICAN PSYCHIATRIC PRESS—1400 K St. N.W., Washington, DC 20005. Carol C. Nadelson, M.D., Ed.-in-Chief. Books that interpret scientific and medical aspects of psychiatry for a lay audience and that address specific psychiatric problems. Authors must have appropriate credentials to write on medical topics. Query required. Royalty.

ANCHOR BOOKS—Imprint of Doubleday and Co., 666 Fifth Ave., New York, NY 10103. Martha K. Levin, Pub. Adult trade paperbacks. General fiction and nonfiction, sociology, psychology, philosophy, women's interest, etc. No unsolicited manuscripts.

AND BOOKS—702 S. Michigan, South Bend, IN 46618. Janos Szebedinsky, Ed. Adult nonfiction. Topics include computers, fine arts, health, philosophy, sports and recreation, regional subjects, and social justice.

APPALACHIAN MOUNTAIN CLUB BOOKS—5 Joy St., Boston, MA 02108. Regional (New England) and national nonfiction titles (250 to 400 pages) for adult audience; juvenile and young-adult nonfiction. Topics include guidebooks on backcountry (non-motorized) recreation, nature, mountain history/biography, search and rescue, and environmental management. Send queries with outline and sample chapters to the editor. Multiple queries considered. Royalty.

APPLE BOOKS—See Scholastic, Inc.

ARCADE PUBLISHING—Subsidiary of Little, Brown, and Co., 141 Fifth

Ave., New York, NY 10010. Richard Seaver, Pub./Ed. Fiction, nonfiction, and children's books. Query first.

ARCHWAY PAPERBACKS—Pocket Books, 1230 Ave. of the Americas, New York, NY 10020. Patricia MacDonald, Exec. Ed. Young-adult contemporary fiction (suspense thrillers, survival adventure, strong boy/girl stories) and nonfiction (popular current topics), for ages 11 and up. Query and SASE required; include outline and sample chapter.

ARCO PUBLISHING—Div. of Simon & Schuster, Gulf & Western Bldg., One Gulf & Western Plaza, 16th Fl., New York, NY 10023. Charles Wall, Assoc. Pub. Nonfiction, originals and reprints, from 50,000 words. Career guides, test preparation. Royalty. Unsolicited manuscripts not accepted.

ARCSOFT PUBLISHERS—P.O. Box 132, Woodsboro, MD 21798. Anthony Curtis, Pres. Nonfiction hobby books for beginners: personal computing, space science, desktop publishing, journalism. Hobby electronics for laymen and consumers, beginners and novices. Outright purchase and royalty basis. Query. Paper only.

ATHENEUM PUBLISHERS—Subsidiary of Macmillan Publishing Co., 866 Third Ave., New York, NY 10022. Mr. Lee Goerner, Pub. General nonfiction, biography, history, current affairs, fiction, belles lettres. Query with sample chapters and outline.

THE ATLANTIC MONTHLY PRESS—19 Union Square West, New York, NY 10003. Morgan Entrekin, Pub. Fiction, general nonfiction. Hardcover and trade paperback. Royalty. SASE required.

AVALON BOOKS—Imprint of Thomas Bouregy & Co., Inc., 401 Lafayette St., New York, NY 10003. Barbara J. Brett, Ed. Hardcover library books. Wholesome contemporary romances and mystery romances about young single (never married) women. Wholesome westerns. Length: 40,000 to 50,000 words. Query with first chapter and outline. SASE required. Guidelines for SASE.

AVERY PUBLISHING GROUP—120 Old Broadway, Garden City Park, NY 11040. Nonfiction, from 40,000 words, on health, childbirth, child care, healthful cooking. Query first with SASE. Royalty.

AVIATION PUBLISHERS—Ultralight Publications, Inc., One Aviation Way, Lock Box 234, Hummelstown, PA 17036. Michael A. Markowski, Ed. Nonfiction, from 30,000 words, on aviation, cars, model cars and planes, boats, trains, health, self-help, success, motivation, and inspiration. Query with outline and sample chapters. Royalty.

AVON BOOKS—1350 Ave. of the Americas, New York, NY 10019. Carolyn Reidy, Pres./Pub. Robert Mecoy, Ed.-in-Chief. Genre fiction, general nonfiction, historical romance, 60,000 to 200,000 words. Science fiction, 75,000 to 100,000 words. Query with synopsis and sample chapters. Ellen Edwards, Historical Romance; John Douglas, Science Fiction; Chris Miller, Fantasy. Camelot Books: Ellen Krieger, Ed. Fiction and nonfiction for 7- to 10-year-olds. Query. Flare Books: Ellen Krieger, Ed. Fiction and nonfiction for 12-year-olds and up. Query. Royalty. Paperback only.

BACKCOUNTRY PUBLICATIONS—Div. of The Countryman Press, Inc., P. O. Box 175, Woodstock, VT 05091. Carl Taylor, Ed. Regional guidebooks, 150 to 250 pages, on hiking, walking, canoeing, bicycling, mountain biking, cross-country skiing, and fishing covering New England, the mid-Atlantic states, and the Midwest. Send outline and sample chapter. Royalty.

BAEN BOOKS—Baen Enterprises, P.O. Box 1403, Riverdale, NY 10471–1403. Jim Baen, Pres. and Ed.-in-Chief. Strongly plotted science fiction; innovative fantasy. Query with synopsis and manuscript. Advance and royalty. Guidelines available for letter-sized SASE.

BAKER BOOK HOUSE—P. O. Box 6287, Grand Rapids, MI 49516–6287. Allan Fisher, Dir. of Publications. Religious nonfiction: books for trade, clergy, seminarians, collegians. Religious fiction. Royalty.

BALLANTINE BOOKS—201 E. 50th St., New York, NY 10022. Robert Wyatt, Ed.-in-Chief. General fiction and nonfiction. Query.

BANTAM BOOKS—Div. of Bantam, Doubleday, Dell, 666 Fifth Ave., New York, NY 10103. Linda Grey, Pres. Jeff Stone, Pub. Adult Fiction and Nonfiction. Mass-market titles, submit queries to the following imprints: Crime Line, crime and mystery fiction; Domain, frontier fiction, historical sagas, traditional westerns; Fanfare, women's fiction (historical novels and regency romance to contemporary and romantic suspense); Falcon, high-tech action, suspense, espionage, adventure; Bantam Nonfiction, wide variety of commercial nonfiction, including true crime, health and nutrition, sports, reference; Spectra, science fiction, reference. Judy Gitenstein, Ed. Dir., Books for Young Readers: fiction and science fiction, ages 6 to 12. Beverly Horowitz, Ed. Dir., Books for Young Adults: fiction and non-formula romance for teens. Only agented queries and manuscripts.

BARRICADE/DEMBNER BOOKS—61 4th Ave., New York, NY 10003. Larry Alson, Pub. Popular reference books, popular medicine, mystery fiction. No first-person tragedy, no romance or pornography, no fads. Send synopsis and two sample chapters with SASE. Modest advances against royalties.

BARRON'S—250 Wireless Blvd., Hauppauge, NY 11788. Grace Freedson, Acquisitions Ed. Nonfiction for juveniles (science, nature, history, hobbies, and how-to) and picture books for ages 3 to 6. Nonfiction for adults (business, childcare, sports). Queries required. Guidelines.

BAUHAN, PUBLISHER, WILLIAM L.—Dublin, NH 03444. William L. Bauhan, Ed. Biographies, fine arts, gardening, and history books with an emphasis on New England. Submit query with outline and sample chapter.

BEACH BOOKS—See National Press.

BEACON PRESS—25 Beacon St., Boston, MA 02108. Wendy Strothman, Dir. Lauren Bryant, Sr. Ed. General nonfiction: world affairs, women's studies, anthropology, history, philosophy, religion, gay and lesbian studies, environment, nature writing, African-American studies, Asian-American studies, Native-American studies. Series: Concord Library (nature writing); Asian Voices (fiction and nonfiction); Barnard New Women Poets; Black Women Writers (fiction); Men and Masculinity (nonfiction); Night Lights (juveniles). Query first. SASE required.

BEAR & COMPANY, INC.—P.O. Drawer 2860, Santa Fe, NM 87504. Barbara Clow, Ed. Nonfiction "that will help transform our culture philosophically, environmentally, and spiritually." Query with outline and sample chapters. SASE required. Royalty.

BERKLEY PUBLISHING GROUP—200 Madison Ave., New York, NY 10016. Roger Cooper, Pub. Leslie Gelbman, Ed.-in-Chief. General-interest fiction and nonfiction: science fiction, suspense and espionage novels; romance. Submit through agent only. Publishes both reprints and originals. Paper only.

BETHANY HOUSE PUBLISHERS—6820 Auto Club Rd., Minneapolis,

MN 55438. Address Editorial Dept. Fiction, nonfiction. Religious. Query with SASE required. Royalty.

BETTER HOMES AND GARDENS BOOKS—See Meredith Corporation.

BINFORD & MORT PUBLISHING—1202 N.W. 17th Ave., Portland, OR 97209. J. F. Roberts, Ed. Books on subjects related to the Pacific Coast and the Northwest. Lengths vary. Query first. Royalty.

BLAIR, PUBLISHER, JOHN F.—1406 Plaza Dr., Winston-Salem, NC 27103. Stephen D. Kirk, Ed. Dept. Biography, history, fiction, folklore, and guidebooks, with Southeastern tie-in. Length: at least 50,000 words. Query. Royalty.

BLAZER BOOKS—P.O. Box 1153, Scarsdale, NY 10583. Bruce J. Bloom, Pub. How-to titles, 50,000 to 70,000 words, on mainstream subjects; ideas for books geared to smaller, niche markets. "No advances, but we pay highly competitive royalties." Send synopsis or outline, with up to 20 sample pages.

BOLCHAZY-CARDUCCI PUBLISHERS—1000 Brown St., Unit 101, Wauconda, IL 60084. Casey Fredericks, Ed. Nonfiction for classroom, university, library, or trade markets. Adult books from 25,000 words in any subject category, including English translations or foreign classics. Multiple queries considered. Royalty.

BONUS BOOKS—160 E. Illinois St., Chicago, IL 60611. Larry Razbadouski, Ed. Nonfiction; topics vary widely. Query with sample chapters and SASE. Royalty.

BOOKS FOR PROFESSIONALS—See Harcourt Brace Jovanovich, Publishers.

BOYDS MILL PRESS—*Highlights for Children*, 910 Church St., Honesdale, PA 18431. Juanita Galuska, Manuscript Coordinator. Hardcover and paperback trade books for children. Fiction: picture books; middle-grade fiction with fresh ideas and involving story; young-adult novels of literary merit. Nonfiction should be "fun, entertaining, and informative." Send outline and sample chapters for young-adult nonfiction, complete manuscripts for all other categories. Royalty.

BRADBURY PRESS—866 Third Ave., New York, NY 10022. Barbara Lalicki, Ed. Hardcover: fiction (general, humor, science fiction), grades 4 to 12; nonfiction (science, sports, history) up to grade 6; picture books, to age 8. Submit complete manuscript. Royalty.

BRANDEN PUBLISHING COMPANY—17 Station St., Box 843, Brookline Village, MA 02147. Novels, biographies, and autobiographies. Especially books by or on women, 250 to 350 pages. Also considers queries on history, computers, business, performance arts, and translations. Query only with SASE. Royalty.

BRICK HOUSE PUBLISHING—Box 2134, 11 Thoreau Rd., Acton, MA 01720. Robert Runck, Ed. Books on business, personal finance, careers, travel, and home design and maintenance. Query with outline and sample chapters. Royalty.

BRISTOL PUBLISHING ENTERPRISES—P.O. Box 1737, San Leandro, CA 94577. Patricia J. Hall, Ed. Mature reader series: nonfiction for 50+ population, approximately 40,000 words. Nitty Gritty Cookbooks: 120-recipe manuscripts. Query with outline, sample chapters, SASE. Royalty.

BROADMAN PRESS—127 Ninth Ave. N., Nashville, TN 37234. Harold S. Smith, Mgr. Religious and inspirational fiction and nonfiction. Query. Royalty.

BUCKNELL UNIVERSITY PRESS—Bucknell University, Lewisburg, PA 17837. Mills F. Edgerton, Jr., Dir. Scholarly nonfiction. Query. Royalty.

BULFINCH PRESS—Div. of Little, Brown and Co., 34 Beacon St., Boston, MA 02108. Books on fine arts and photography. Query with outline or proposal and vita.

C&T PUBLISHING—5021 Blum Rd., #1, Martinez, CA 94553. Diane Pedersen, Ed. Quilting books, 72 to 200 finished pages. "Our focus is how-to, although we will consider picture, inspirational, or history books on quilting." Send query, outline, or sample chapters. Multiple queries considered. Royalty.

CAMELOT BOOKS—See Avon Books.

CANDLEWICK PRESS—1067 Massachusetts Ave., Cambridge, MA 02140. Address Editors. Children's books: baby books, picture books, Easy-to-Reads and Read Alouds, middle-grade fiction and nonfiction, and young-adult novels. Poetry and all genres of fiction and nonfiction considered. Query or send complete manuscript. Royalty.

CAROLRHODA BOOKS—241 First Ave. N., Minneapolis, MN 55401. Rebecca Poole, Ed. Complete manuscripts for ages 7 to 12: biography, science, nature, history, photo essays; historical fiction, 10 to 15 pages, for ages 6 to 10. Guidelines. Hardcover.

CARROLL AND GRAF PUBLISHERS, INC.—260 Fifth Ave., New York, NY 10001. Kent E. Carroll, Exec. Ed. General fiction and nonfiction. Query with SASE. Royalty.

CASSANDRA PRESS—P.O. Box 868, San Rafael, CA 94915. New Age, holistic health, metaphysical, and psychological books. Query with outline and sample chapters, or complete manuscript. Royalty.

THE CATHOLIC UNIVERSITY OF AMERICA PRESS—620 Michigan Ave. N.E., Washington, DC 20064. David J. McGonagle, Dir. Scholarly nonfiction: American and European history (both ecclesiastical and secular); Irish studies; American and European literature; philosophy; political theory; theology. Query with prospectus, annotated table of contents, or introduction and author's resumé. Royalty.

CHARTER/DIAMOND BOOKS—Imprint of Berkley Publishing Co., 200 Madison Ave., New York, NY 10012. Leslie Gelbman, Ed.-in-Chief. Adventure, suspense fiction, horror, historical romances, regencies, women's contemporary fiction, family sagas, and historical novels. Westerns, male action/adventure. Paperback.

CHATHAM PRESS—P. O. Box A, Old Greenwich, CT 06870. Roger H. Lourie, Man. Dir. Books on the Northeast coast, New England maritime subjects, and the ocean. Large photography volumes. Query with outline, sample chapters, illustrations, and SASE large enough for the return of material. Royalty.

CHELSEA GREEN PUBLISHING CO.—Route 113, P.O. Box 130, Post Mills, VT 05058–0130. Ian Baldwin, Jr., Ed. Primarily nonfiction: natural history, environmental issues, outdoor recreation, and travel. Occasional fiction with northern New England or environmental focus. Query with outline and SASE. Royalty.

CHICAGO REVIEW PRESS—814 N. Franklin St., Chicago, IL 60610. Linda Matthews, Ed. Nonfiction: project books for young people ages 10 to 18, anthropology, travel, nature, and regional topics. Query with outline and sample chapters.

CHILTON BOOK CO.—One Chilton Way, Radnor, PA 19089. Christopher J. Kuppig, Gen. Mgr. Antiques and collectibles, sewing and crafts, and automotive topics. Query with outline, sample chapter, and return postage. Wallace-Homestead Books.

CHRONICLE BOOKS—275 Fifth St., San Francisco, CA 94103. Topical nonfiction, history, biography, fiction, art, photography, architecture, nature, food, regional, and children's books. Send proposal with SASE.

CLARION BOOKS—215 Park Ave. S., New York, NY 10003. Dorothy Briley, Ed.-in-Chief/Pub. Fiction, nonfiction, and picture books: short novels and lively stories for ages 8 to 12, historical fiction, humor; picture books for infants to age 7; biography, natural history, social studies, American and world history for readers 5 to 8 and 9 and up. Royalty. Hardcover.

CLIFFHANGER PRESS—P.O. Box 29527, Oakland, CA 94604-9527. Nancy Chirich, Ed. Mystery and suspense. Unagented manuscripts only. Query with first three chapters, outline, and SASE. Quality trade paperbacks. Royalty. Guidelines.

CLOVERDALE PRESS—96 Morton St., New York, NY 10014. Book packager. Adult nonfiction; YA, middle- and lower-grade fiction and nonfiction. "Since our requirements vary considerably and frequently according to our publishers' needs, please send query letter before submitting material." Address YA and juvenile to Marion Vaarn; adult to Lisa Howell.

COBBLEHILL BOOKS—375 Hudson St., New York, NY 10014. Joe Ann Daly, Ed. Dir. Rosanne Lauer, Sr. Ed. Fiction and nonfiction for preschoolers through junior high school. Query with outline and sample chapters. For picture books send complete manuscript. Royalty.

COFFEE HOUSE PRESS—27 N. 4th St., Suite 400, Minneapolis, MN 55401. Address W. Wiegers. Fiction (no genres), and essays. Query or send complete manuscript. Allow three months for response. Royalty.

COLLIER BOOKS—See Macmillan Publishing Co.

COMPCARE PUBLISHERS—2415 Annapolis Ln., Minneapolis, MN 55441. Margaret Marsh, Man. Ed. Adult nonfiction; young-adult nonfiction: books on recovery from addictive/compulsive behavior; emotional health; growth in personal, couple, and family relationships. Submit complete manuscript. Royalty.

COMPUTE BOOKS—324 West Wendover Ave., Greensboro, NC 27408. PC games books, video game books. Also specializes in Amiga and PC application books.

CONCORDIA PUBLISHING HOUSE—3558 S. Jefferson Ave., St. Louis, MO 63118. Practical nonfiction with explicit religious content, conservative Lutheran doctrine. Children's fiction with explicit Christian content. No poetry. Query. Royalty.

CONSUMER REPORTS BOOKS—101 Truman Ave., Yonkers, NY 10703. Address Exec. Ed. Medicine/health, finances, automotive, homeowners, food and cooking topics. Submit complete manuscript, or send contents, outline, three chapters, and resumé.

CONTEMPORARY BOOKS, INC.—180 N. Michigan Ave., Chicago, IL 60601. Nancy Crossman, Ed. Dir. Trade nonfiction, 100 to 400 pages, on health, fitness, sports, cooking, humor, business, popular culture, biography, real estate, finance, women's issues. Query with outline and sample chapters. Royalty.

COOK PUBLISHING CO., DAVID C.—850 N. Grove Ave., Elgin, IL 60120. Catherine Davis, Man. Ed., Chariot Children's Books: fiction that "helps children better understand themselves and their relationship with God"; nonfiction that illuminates the Bible; picture books, ages 1 to 7; fiction for ages 8 to 10, 10 to 12, and 12 to 14. Life Journey General Titles: fiction with underlying spiritual theme; books on parenting from a Christian perspective. Lengths and payment vary. Query required. Guidelines.

CRAFTSMAN BOOK COMPANY—6058 Corte del Cedro, P.O. Box 6500, Carlsbad, CA 92008. Laurence D. Jacobs, Ed. How-to construction and estimating manuals and software for builders, 450 pages. Query. Royalty. Softcover.

CREATIVE ARTS BOOK CO.—833 Bancroft Way, Berkeley, CA 94710. Donald S. Ellis, Pub. Adult nonfiction, women, music, and California topics. Query with outline and sample chapters. Include SASE. Royalty.

THE CROSSING PRESS—97 Hangar Way, Watsonville, CA 95076. Elaine Goldman Gill, John Gill, Pubs. Fiction, health, men's studies, feminist studies, science fiction, mysteries, gay topics, cookbooks. Royalty.

CROWELL, THOMAS Y.—See HarperCollins Childrens Books.

CROWN BOOKS FOR YOUNG READERS—225 Park Ave. S., New York, NY 10003. Simon Boughton, Exec. Ed. Children's fiction (including humor and mystery), nonfiction (biography, science, sports, nature, music, and history), and picture books for ages 3 and up. Query with outline and sample chapter; send manuscript for picture books. Guidelines.

DANIEL AND COMPANY, JOHN—P.O. Box 21922, Santa Barbara, CA 93121. John Daniel, Pub. Books (under 200 pages) in the field of belles lettres and literary memoirs; stylish and elegant writing; essays and short fiction dealing with social issues; one poetry title per year. Send synopsis or outline with no more that 50 sample pages and SASE. Allow 6 to 8 weeks for response. Royalty.

DAW BOOKS, INC.—375 Hudson St., New York, NY 10014–3658. Elizabeth R. Wollheim, Ed.-in-Chief. Sheila Gilbert, Sr. Ed. Peter Stampfel, Submissions Ed. Science fiction and fantasy, 60,000 to 120,000 words. Royalty.

DEARBORN FINANCIAL PUBLISHING, INC.—(formerly Longman Financial Services Publishing) Div. of Dearborn Group USA, 520 N. Dearborn St., Chicago, IL 60610. Anita A. Constant, Sr. V.P. Books on financial services, real estate, banking, etc. Query with outline and sample chapters. Royalty and flat fee.

DEL REY BOOKS—201 E. 50th St., New York, NY 10022. Shelly Shapiro, SF Ed. Lester del Rey, V.P. and Fantasy Ed. Science fiction and fantasy; first novelists welcome. Material must be well paced with logical resolutions. Fantasy with magic basic to plotline. Length, 60,000 to 120,000 words. Complete manuscripts preferred, or send outline with three sample chapters. Royalty.

DELACORTE PRESS—666 Fifth Ave., New York, NY 10103. Brian DeFiore, Jackie Farber, Emily Reichert, Eds. Adult fiction and nonfiction. Juvenile and YA fiction (George Nicholson, Ed.). Accepts fiction (mystery, YA, romance, fantasy, etc.) from agents only.

DELL BOOKS—666 Fifth Ave., New York, NY 10103. Family sagas, historical romances, war action, general fiction, occult/horror/psychological suspense, true crime, men's adventure. Send four-page narrative synopsis for fiction, or an outline for nonfiction. Enclose SASE. Address submissions to Dell Books, Editorial Dept., Book Proposal.

DELTA BOOKS AND DELTA TRADE PAPERBACKS—666 Fifth Ave., New York, NY 10103. Address Editors. Delta Books: General-interest nonfiction, psychology, feminism, health, nutrition, child care, science. Delta Trade Paperbacks: nonfiction, self-help, and how-to. Send an outline with SASE. Address submissions to appropriate imprint, Editorial Dept., Book Proposal.

DEVIN-ADAIR PUBLISHERS, INC.—6 N. Water St., Greenwich, CT 06830. C. de la Belle Issue, Pub. J. Andrassi, Ed. Books on conservative affairs, Irish topics, photography, Americana, self-help, health, gardening, cooking, and ecology. Send outline, sample chapters, and SASE. Royalty.

DIAL BOOKS FOR YOUNG READERS—375 Hudson St., New York, NY 10014. Phyllis Fogelman, Pub./Ed.in-Chief. Picture books; Easy-to-Read Books; middle-grade readers; young-adult fiction and some nonfiction. Submit complete manuscript for picture books and Easy-to-Reads; outline and sample chapters for nonfiction and novels. Enclose SASE. Royalty. Hardcover only.

DILLON PRESS—Macmillan Publishing Co. 866 Third Ave., New York, NY 10022. Frank Sloan, Ed. Dir. Juvenile nonfiction: international festivals and foods, unusual animals, Third World countries and U.S. states, major world cities, world geography/places of interest, environmental topics, contemporary and historical biographies for elementary and middle-grade levels. Length, 10 to 90 pages. Royalty and outright purchase. Query.

DOUBLEDAY AND CO.—666 Fifth Ave., New York, NY 10103. Steve Rubin, Pub./Pres. David Gernert, Ed.-in-Chief. Hardcover for Perfect Crime or Science Fiction: mystery/suspense fiction, science fiction, 70,000 to 80,000 words. Send query and outline. Paperback: Currency line, business books for a general audience on "the art of getting things done." No unsolicited manuscripts.

DUNNE BOOKS, THOMAS—Imprint of St. Martin's Press, 175 Fifth Ave., New York, NY 10010. Thomas L. Dunne, Ed. Adult fiction (mysteries, trade, SF, etc.) and nonfiction (history, biographies, science, politics, etc.). Query with outline and sample chapters and SASE. Royalty.

DUQUESNE UNIVERSITY PRESS—600 Forbes Ave., Pittsburgh, PA 15282–0101. Scholarly publications in the humanities and social sciences.

DUTTON CHILDREN'S BOOKS—Div. of Penguin USA, 375 Hudson St., New York, NY 10014. Lucia Monfried, Ed.-in-Chief. Picture books, easy-to-read books; fiction and nonfiction for preschoolers to young adults. Submit outline and sample chapters with query for fiction and nonfiction, complete manuscripts for picture books and easy-to-read books. Manuscripts should be well-written with fresh ideas and child appeal.

DUTTON ADULT—Div. of Penguin USA, 375 Hudson St., New York, NY 10014. Kevin Mulroy, Ed. Dir. Fiction and nonfiction books. Manuscripts accepted only from agents or on personal recommendation.

EERDMANS PUBLISHING COMPANY, INC., WM. B—255 Jefferson Ave. S.E., Grand Rapids, MI 49503. Jon Pott, Ed.-in-Chief. Protestant, Roman Catholic, and Orthodox theological nonfiction; American religious history; some fiction. Royalty.

ENSLOW PUBLISHERS, INC.—Bloy St. & Ramsey Ave., Box 777, Hillside, NJ 07205. R. M. Enslow, Jr., Ed/Pub. Nonfiction books for young people. Areas of emphasis are children's and young-adult books for ages 10 to 16 in the fields of science, social studies, and biography. Other specialties for young people are reference books for all ages and easy reading books for teenagers.

ERIKSSON, PUBLISHER, PAUL S.—208 Battell Bldg., Middlebury, VT

05753. General nonfiction (send outline and cover letter); some fiction (send three chapters with query). Royalty.

EVANS & CO., INC., M.—216 E. 49th St., New York, NY 10017. Books on humor, health, self-help, popular psychology, and cookbooks. Western and romance fiction for adults; fiction and nonfiction for young adults. Query with outline, sample chapter, and SASE. Royalty.

FACTS ON FILE PUBLICATIONS—460 Park Ave. S., New York, NY 10016. Gerard Helferich, V.P./Assoc. Pub. Reference and trade books on nature, business, science, health, language, history, the performing arts, etc. (No fiction, poetry, computer books, technical books or cookbooks, etc.) Query with outline, sample chapter, and SASE. Royalty. Hardcover.

FANFARE—Imprint of Bantam Books, 666 Fifth Ave., New York, NY 10103. Nita Taublib, Publishing Assoc. Women's popular fiction, historical or contemporary. Over 90,000 words. Query required. Paperback only.

FARRAR, STRAUS & GIROUX—19 Union Sq. West, New York, NY 10003. Adult and juvenile fiction and nonfiction.

FELL PUBLISHERS, INC.—2131 Hollywood Blvd., Hollywood, FL 33020. Allen Etling, Ed. Nonfiction (100 to 300 pages): general interest, how-tos, business, health, and inspirational. Query with letter or outline and sample chapter, include SASE. Royalty.

THE FEMINIST PRESS AT THE CITY UNIVERSITY OF NEW YORK —311 E. 94th St., New York, NY 10128. Florence Howe, Pub. Reprints of significant "lost" fiction, memoirs, autobiographies, or other feminist work from the past; biography; intercultural anthologies; handbooks; bibliographies. "We are especially interested in international literature, women and peace, women and music, and women of color." Royalty.

FINE, INC., DONALD I.—19 West 21st St., New York, NY 10010. Literary and commercial fiction. General nonfiction. No queries or unsolicited manuscripts. Submit through agent only.

FIREBRAND BOOKS—141 The Commons, Ithaca, NY 14850. Nancy K. Bereano, Ed. Feminist and lesbian fiction and nonfiction. Royalty. Paperback.

FLARE BOOKS—See Avon Books.

FODOR'S TRAVEL GUIDES—201 E. 50th St., New York, NY 10022. Michael Spring, Ed. Travel guides for both foreign and US destinations. "We hire writers who live in the area they will write about." Books follow established format; send writing sample and details about your familiarity with a given area.

FORTRESS PRESS—426 S. Fifth St., Box 1209, Minneapolis, MN 55440. Dr. Marshall D. Johnson, Dir. Books in the areas of biblical studies, theology, ethics, and church history for academic and professional markets, including libraries. Query first.

FOUR WINDS PRESS—Imprint of Macmillan Publishing Co., 866 Third Ave., New York, NY 10022. Cindy Kane, Ed.-in-Chief. Juveniles: picture books, nonfiction for all ages. Fiction for young children. Query with SASE required for nonfiction. No simultaneous submissions. Hardcover only.

THE FREE PRESS—See Macmillan Publishing Co.

FRIENDS UNITED PRESS—101 Quaker Hill Dr., Richmond, IN 47374.

Ardith Talbot, Ed. Nonfiction and fiction, 200 pages, on Quaker history, biography, and Quaker faith experience. Query with outline and sample chapters. Royalty.

GARDEN WAY PUBLISHING COMPANY—Storey Communications, Schoolhouse Rd., Pownal, VT 05261. Kim Foster, Assoc. Ed. How-to books on gardening, cooking, crafts, building, animals, country living. Royalty or outright purchase. Query with outline and sample chapter.

GARRETT PARK PRESS—P.O. Box 190, Garrett Park, MD 20896. Robert Calvert, Jr., Pub. Reference books on career education, occupational guidance, and financial aid only. Query required. Multiple queries considered but not encouraged. Royalty.

GEORGIA STATE UNIVERSITY BUSINESS PRESS—University Plaza, Atlanta, GA 30303-3093. Books, software, research monographs, and directories in the business sciences and related disciplines.

GERINGER BOOKS, LAURA—See HarperCollins Childrens Books.

GIBBS SMITH PUBLISHER/PEREGRINE SMITH BOOKS—P. O. Box 667, Layton, UT 84401. Steve Chapman, Fiction Ed. Madge Baird, Nonfiction Ed. Adult fiction and nonfiction. Query. Royalty.

GINIGER CO. INC., THE K.S.—250 W. 57th St., Suite 519, New York, NY 10107. General nonfiction. Query with SASE; no unsolicited manuscripts. Royalty.

GLOBE PEQUOT PRESS, THE—138 W. Main St., Chester, CT 06412. Laura Strom, Assoc. Ed. Nonfiction with national and regional focus; nature and outdoor guides; environment and natural sciences; how-tos; gardening; journalism and media; biographies. Query with sample chapter, contents, and one-page synopsis. SASE required. Royalty.

GOLD EAGLE BOOKS—See Worldwide Library.

GOLDEN PRESS—See Western Publishing Co., Inc.

GOLDEN WEST PUBLISHERS—4113 N. Longview, Phoenix, AZ 85014. Hal Mitchell, Ed. Cookbooks and Western history and travel books. Query first. Pays royalty or flat fee.

GRAYWOLF PRESS—2402 University Ave., Suite 203, St. Paul, MN 55114. Scott M. Walker, Ed. Literary fiction (short story collections and novels), poetry, and essays. Query with sample chapters.

GREENWILLOW BOOKS—Imprint of William Morrow and Co., Inc., 1350 Ave. of the Americas, New York, NY 10019. Susan Hirschman, Ed.-in-Chief. Children's books for all ages. Picture books.

GROLIER PRESS—See Franklin Watts, Inc.

GROSSET AND DUNLAP, INC.—Div. of Putnam & Grosset Books, 200 Madison Ave., New York, NY 10016. Craig Walker, Ed.-in-Chief. Material accepted through agents only.

GULLIVER BOOKS—See Harcourt Brace Jovanovich.

HAMMOND INC.—Maplewood, NJ 07040. Charles Lees, Ed. Nonfiction: cartographic reference, travel. Payment varies. Query with outline and sample chapters. SASE required.

HANCOCK HOUSE PUBLISHERS—1431 Harrison Ave., Blaine, WA 98230. David Hancock, Ed. Nonfiction: gardening, outdoor guides, Western history, Native Americans, aviculture, and conservation. Royalty.

HARBINGER HOUSE—2802 N. Alvernon Way, Tucson, AZ 85712. Zdenek Gerych, Ed.-in-Chief. Jeffrey H. Lockridge, Children's Books Ed. Adult nonfiction focusing on social issues and personal growth; very little adult fiction. Children's picture books; stories for middle readers; nonfiction (Natural History Series). Submit resumé, outline/synopsis, two sample chapters, and SASE. For short children's book, submit entire manuscript with SASE. Royalty.

HARCOURT BRACE JOVANOVICH—1250 Sixth Ave., San Diego, CA 92101. Adult trade nonfiction and fiction. Books for Professionals: test preparation guides and other student self-help materials. Juvenile fiction and nonfiction for beginning readers through young adults under imprints: HBJ Children's Books, Gulliver Books, and Voyager Paperbacks. Adult books: no unsolicited manuscripts or queries. Children's books: unsolicited manuscripts accepted by HBJ Children's Books only. No simultaneous submissions. Send query or manuscript to Manuscript Submissions, Children's Book Division.

HARLEQUIN BOOKS/CANADA—225 Duncan Mill Rd., Don Mills, Ont., Canada M3B 3K9. Harlequin Romance: Paula Eykelhof, Ed. Contemporary romance novels, 50,000 to 55,000 words, any setting, ranging in plot from the traditional and gentle to the more sophisticated. Query first. Harlequin Regency: Marmie Charndoff, Ed. Short traditional novels set in 19th century Europe, 50,000 to 60,000 words. Query first. Harlequin Superromance: Marsha Zinberg, Sr. Ed. Romance contemporary, 85,000 words, with North American or foreign setting. Query first. Harlequin Temptation: Birgit Davis-Todd, Sr. Ed. Sensually charged contemporary romantic fantasies, 60,000 to 65,000 words. Query first.

HARLEQUIN BOOKS/U.S.—300 E. 42nd St., 6th Fl., New York, NY 10017. Debra Matteucci, Sr. Ed. Contemporary romances, 70,000 to 75,000 words. Send for tip sheets. Paperback. Harlequin American Romance: Contemporary believable situations, set in the U.S. Harlequin Intrigue: Set against backdrop of suspense and adventure. Worldwide locales. Query.

HARPER PAPERBACKS—HarperCollins, 10 E. 53rd St., New York, NY 10022. Ed Breslin, Pub. Karen Solem, Ed.-in-Chief. Jessica Kovar, Ed. Carolyn Marino, Ed. Katie Smith, Ed. Agent submissions only.

HARPERCOLLINS CHILDRENS BOOKS—10 East 53rd St., New York, NY 10022–5299. Katrin Magnusson, Admin. Coord. West Coast: 8948 S.W. Barbur Blvd., Suite 154, Portland, OR 92719. Linda Zuckerman, Exec. Ed. (Query one address only.) Juvenile fiction, nonfiction, and picture books imprints include Thomas Y. Crowell Co., Publishers: juveniles, etc.; J. B. Lippincott Co.: juveniles, picture books, etc.; Harper & Row: juveniles, picture books, etc.; HarperTrophy Books: paperback juveniles; Laura Geringer, juvenile books. All publish from preschool to young-adult titles. Guidelines available. Query, send sample chapters, or complete manuscript. Royalty.

HARPERCOLLINS PUBLISHERS—(formerly Harper & Row) 10 E. 53rd St., New York, NY 10022–5299. Fiction, nonfiction (biography, economics, history,etc.), reference. Adult Trade Dept.: Agents only, Tracy Behar, Man. Ed., Gen. Books. College texts: address College Dept. Children's books: address Junior Books Dept., Attn. Sedora Belin, 9th Floor. Unsolicited material accepted. Religion, theology, etc.: address Harper San Francisco, Ice House One-401, 151 Union St., San Francisco, CA 94111–1299. No unsolicited manuscripts; query only.

HARVARD COMMON PRESS—535 Albany St., Boston, MA 02118. Bruce Shaw, Ed. Adult nonfiction: cookbooks, travel guides, books on family matters, small business, etc. Send outline and sample chapters or complete manuscript. Royalty.

HARVEST HOUSE PUBLISHERS—1075 Arrowsmith, Eugene, OR 97402. Eileen L. Mason, V.P. Editorial. Nonfiction with evangelical theme: how-tos, educational, counseling, marriage, women, contemporary issues. No biographies, history, fiction, children's books, or poetry. Query first. SASE required.

HEALTH COMMUNICATIONS, INC.—3201 S.W. 15th St., Deerfield Beach, FL 33442. Marie Stilkind, Ed. Books on self-help recovery for adults (250 pages) and juveniles (100 pages). "Looking for children's books (ages 8 to 13) stressing good self-esteem and healthy feelings, 40 to 60 pages." Query with outline and sample chapter, or send manuscript. Royalty.

HEALTH PLUS PUBLISHERS—P.O. Box 1027, Sherwood, OR 97140. Paula E. Clure, Ed. Books on health and fitness. Query with outline and sample chapters.

HEALTH PRESS—P.O. Box 1388, Santa Fe, NM 87501. Kathleen Schwartz, Ed. Health-related adult books, 100 to 300 finished pages. "We're seeking cutting-edge, original manuscripts that will excite and help readers. Author must have credentials, or preface/intro must be written by MD, Ph.D., etc. Controversial topics are desired; must be well researched and documented." Prefer completed manuscript, but will consider queries with outline and sample chapters. Multiple queries considered. Royalty.

HEARST BOOKS AND HEARST MARINE BOOKS—See William Morrow and Co.

HEARTFIRE ROMANCES—See Zebra Books.

HEATH & COMPANY, D. C.—125 Spring St., Lexington, MA 02173. Textbooks for school and college. Query Vince Duggan.

HEMINGWAY WESTERN STUDIES SERIES—Boise State University, 1910 University Dr., Boise, ID 83725. Tom Trusky, Ed. Nonfiction relating to the Inter-Mountain West (Rockies) in areas of history, political science, anthropology, natural sciences, film, fine arts, literary history or criticism. Publishes up to two books annually.

HERALD PRESS—616 Walnut Ave., Scottdale, PA 15683. Christian books for adults and children: inspiration, Bible study, self-help, devotionals, current issues, peace studies, church history, missions, evangelism, family life, fiction, and personal experience. Send one-page summary and two sample chapters. Royalty.

HIPPOCRENE BOOKS—171 Madison Ave., New York, NY 10016. George Blagowidow, Ed. Dir. Language instruction books and foreign language dictionaries, travel guides, and military history. Send outline and sample chapters. Multiple queries considered. Royalty.

HOLIDAY HOUSE, INC.—425 Madison Ave., New York, NY 10017. Margery S. Cuyler, Vice Pres. Alyssa Chase, Asst. Ed. General juvenile and young adult fiction and nonfiction. Submit complete manuscript for picture books; three sample chapters and summary for novels and nonfiction. Hardcover only. Royalty.

HOLT AND CO., HENRY—115 W. 18th St., New York, NY 10011. William Strachan, Ed.-in-Chief. Fiction and nonfiction (mysteries, history, autobiographies, natural history, travel, art, and how-to) of highest literary quality. Query with SASE required. Royalty.

HOUGHTON MIFFLIN COMPANY—2 Park St., Boston, MA 02108. Fiction: literary, historical, suspense. Nonfiction: history, biography, psychology. No unsolicited manuscripts. Query Submissions Dept. with SASE. Children's Book Division, address Children's Trade Books: picture books, fiction, and nonfiction for all ages. Query. Royalty.

H. P. BOOKS—Div. of Price Stern Sloan, 11150 Olympic Blvd., Suite 650, Los Angeles, CA 90064. Illustrated how-tos on cooking, gardening, photography, health and fitness, automotive, etc. Query with SASE. Royalty.

HUNTER PUBLISHING, INC.—300 Raritan Center Pkwy., Edison, NJ 08818. Michael Hunter, Ed. Travel guides. Query with outline.

INDIANA UNIVERSITY PRESS—601 N. Morton St., Bloomington, IN 47404–3797. Scholarly nonfiction, especially cultural studies, literary criticism, music, history, women's studies, archaeology, anthropology, etc. Query with outline and sample chapters. Royalty.

ISLAND PRESS—1718 Connecticut Ave. N.W., Suite 300, Washington, DC 20009. Charles C. Savitt, Pub. Fiction and nonfiction focusing on the west, and on natural history. "We don't do much first fiction." Query with SASE.

JAMES BOOKS, ALICE—33 Richdale Ave., Cambridge, MA 02140. Marjorie Fletcher, Pres. "Shared-work cooperative" publishes books of poetry, 60 to 70 pages, by writers living in New England. Manuscripts read in September and February. "We emphasize the publication of poetry by women, but also welcome and publish manuscripts by men." Authors paid with 100 copies of their books. Guidelines available.

JOHNSON BOOKS, INC.—1880 S. 57th Court, Boulder, CO 80301. Rebecca Herr, Ed. Dir. Nonfiction: environmental subjects, archaeology, geology, natural history, astronomy, travel guides, outdoor guidebooks, fly fishing, regional. Query. Royalty.

JONATHAN DAVID PUBLISHERS, INC.—68–22 Eliot Ave., Middle Village, NY 11379. Alfred J. Kolatch, Ed.-in-Chief. General nonfiction (how-to, sports, cooking and food, self-help, etc.) and specializing in Judaica. Query with outline, sample chapter, and resumé required. SASE. Royalty or outright purchase.

JOVE BOOKS—200 Madison Ave., New York, NY 10016. Fiction and nonfiction. No unsolicited manuscripts.

JOY STREET BOOKS—Imprint of Little, Brown & Co., 34 Beacon St., Boston, MA 02108. Melanie Kroupa, Ed.-in-Chief. Juvenile picture books; fiction and nonfiction for middle readers and young adults. Especially interested in fiction for 8- to 12-year-olds and innovative nonfiction. Query with outline and sample chapters for nonfiction; send complete manuscript for fiction. Royalty.

KAR-BEN COPIES—6800 Tildenwood Lane, Rockville, MD 20852. Judye Groner, Ed. Books on Jewish themes for pre-school and elementary-age children (to age 9): picture books, fiction, and nonfiction. Complete manuscript preferred. Flat fee and royalty.

KEATS PUBLISHING, INC.—27 Pine St., Box 876, New Canaan, CT 06840. Nathan Keats, Pub. Nonfiction: health, inspiration, how-to. Query. Royalty.

KENT STATE UNIVERSITY PRESS—Kent State University, Kent, OH 44242. John T. Hubbel, Dir. Julia Morton, Sr. Ed. Publishes hardcover and paperback originals and some reprints. Especially interested in scholarly works in history and literary studies of high quality, any titles of regional interest for Ohio, scholarly biographies, archaeological research, the arts, and general nonfiction.

KESTRAL BOOKS—Imprint of Penguin USA, 375 Hudson St., New York, NY 10014. Address Editors. Fiction and nonfiction, including biography, history, and sports, for ages 7 to 14. Humor and picture books for ages 2 to 6. Query Children's Book Dept. with outline and sample chapter. SASE required. Also publishes adult fiction and nonfiction hardcovers. Royalty.

KNOPF BOOKS FOR YOUNG READERS, ALFRED A.—225 Park Ave. S., New York, NY 10003. Janet Schulman, Pub. Stephanie Spinner, Assoc. Pub. Frances Foster, Ed. at Large. Anne Schwartz, Exec. Ed. Reg Kahney, Sr. Ed., Nonfiction. Sherry Gerstein, Paperback Ed. Distinguished juvenile fiction and nonfiction; query. Royalty. Guidelines.

KNOPF, INC., ALFRED A.—201 E. 50th St., New York, NY 10022. Stephanie Spinner, Assoc. Pub. Frances Foster and Anne Schwartz, Sr. Eds. Reg Kahney, Sr. Ed., Nonfiction. Sherry Gerstein, Paperback Ed. Ashbel Green, V.P. and Sr. Ed. Distinguished adult fiction and general nonfiction; query. Royalty. Guidelines.

KODANSHA INTERNATIONAL—114 Fifth Ave., New York, NY 10011. Attn: Editorial Dept. Books, 50,000 to 200,000 words, on popular science, sports, business management, travel, biography, gardening, health, history, and cooking, for an international adult audience. Query with outline and sample chapters. Royalty.

LARK BOOKS—50 College St., Asheville, NC 28801. Rob Pulleyn, Pub. Publishes "distinctive books for creative people" in crafts, how-to, leisure activities, and "coffee table" categories. Query with outline. Royalty.

LAUREL BOOKS—Imprint of Bantam, Doubleday, Dell Publishing, Co., 666 Fifth Ave., New York, NY 10103. Address Editors. Nonfiction. History, politics, language, reference. Submissions accepted from agents only.

LAUREL-LEAF—Imprint of Bantam, Doubleday, Dell Publishing Co., 666 Fifth Ave., New York, NY 10103. Address Editors. Books for children grades 7 through 12. Submissions accepted from agents only.

LEISURE BOOKS—Div. of Dorchester Publishing Co., 276 Fifth Ave., New York, NY 10001. Frank Walgren, Sub. Ed. Historical romance novels, from 100,000 words; gothic, futurisitic, and time-travel romances, from 85,000 words; regency romances from 75,000 words. Query with synopsis, sample chapters, and SASE. Royalty.

LION PUBLISHING—1705 Hubbard Ave., Batavia, IL 60510. Robert Bittner, Ed. Fiction and nonfiction written from a Christian viewpoint for a general audience. Guidelines. Royalty.

LIPPINCOTT COMPANY, J.B.—See HarperCollins Childrens Books.

LITTLE, BROWN & CO.—1271 Ave. of the Americas, New York, NY 10020. Maria Modugno, Ed.-in-Chief. Fiction, general nonfiction, sports books; divisions for law and medical texts. Royalty. Query Children's Book Dept. (34 Beacon St., Boston, MA 02106) for juvenile fiction and nonfiction (science, history, and nature) and picture books (ages 3 to 8). Guidelines.

LITTLE ROOSTER BOOKS—Imprint of Bantam Doubleday Dell, 666 Fifth Ave., New York, NY 10103. Sally Doherty, Sr. Ed. Hardcover and paperback picture books for ages 4 to 8. Send complete manuscript; indicate multiple submissions. Royalty.

LODESTAR—An affiliate of Dutton Children's Books, a Div. of Penguin Books USA, Inc., 375 Hudson St., New York, NY 10014. Virginia Buckley, Ed. Dir.

Fiction (YA, mystery, fantasy, science fiction, western) and nonfiction (science, contemporary issues, nature, history) considered for ages 9 to 11, 10 to 14, and 12 and up. Also fiction and nonfiction picture books for ages 4 to 8. Send manuscript for fiction; query for nonfiction.

LONGMAN FINANCIAL SERVICES PUBLISHING—See Dearborn Financial Publishing, Inc.

LOTHROP, LEE & SHEPARD BOOKS—Imprint of William Morrow & Co., Inc., 105 Madison Ave., New York, NY 10016. Susan Pearson, Ed.-in-Chief. Juvenile, picture books, fiction, and nonfiction. Does not review unsolicited material. Royalty.

LOVEGRAM ROMANCES—See Zebra Books.

LOVESWEPT—Imprint of Bantam Books, 666 Fifth Ave., New York, NY 10103. Nita Taublib, Publishing Assoc. Highly sensual, adult contemporary romances, approximately 55,000 words. Study field before submitting. Query required. Paperback only.

LOYOLA UNIVERSITY PRESS—3441 N. Ashland Ave., Chicago, IL 60657–1397. Joseph Downey, S. J., Ed. Religious material for college-educated Catholic readers. Campion Book Series: art, literature, and religion; contemporary Christian concerns; Jesuit studies; Chicago books. Nonfiction, 200 to 400 pages. Query with outline. Royalty.

LYONS & BURFORD, PUBLISHERS—31 W. 21st St., New York, NY 10010. Peter Burford, Ed. Books, 100 to 300 pages, related to the outdoors (camping, natural history, etc.). Query with outline. Royalty.

MCELDERRY BOOKS, MARGARET K.—Macmillan Children's Book Group, 866 Third Ave., New York, NY 10022. Margaret K. McElderry, Ed. Picture books; quality fiction, including fantasy, science fiction, beginning chapter books, humor, and realism; nonfiction. For ages 3 to 5, 6 to 9, 8 to 12, 10 to 14, and 12 and up.

MCFARLAND & COMPANY, INC.—Box 611, Jefferson, NC 28640. Robert Franklin, Ed. Scholarly and reference books in many fields, except mathematical sciences, New Age, inspirational, children's, poetry, fiction, exposés. Submit manuscripts, 225 pages and up, double-spaced, or query with outline and sample chapters. Royalty.

MCKAY COMPANY, DAVID—201 E. 50th St., New York, NY 10022. Nonfiction. Unsolicited manuscripts neither acknowledged nor returned.

MACMILLAN CHILDREN'S BOOK GROUP—866 Third Ave., New York, NY 10022. Sarah Lehman Schwartz, Ed. Aladdin Books paperback imprint: Fiction (except for problem novels) for middle grades (age 8 to 12) and young adults (age 12 and up). Collier Books for Young Adults: young-adult novels. Query with outline; no multiple queries. Royalty.

MACMILLAN PUBLISHING CO., INC.—866 Third Ave., New York, NY 10022. General Books Division: Religious, sports, science, and reference books. No fiction. Paperbacks, Collier Books. College texts and professional books in social sciences, humanities, address The Free Press. Royalty.

MADISON BOOKS—4720 Boston Way, Lanham, MD 20706. Full-length, nonfiction manuscripts on history, biography, contemporary affairs, trade reference. Query required. Royalty.

MEADOWBROOK PRESS—18318 Minnetonka Blvd., Deephaven, MN

55391. Upbeat, useful books on pregnancy, childbirth and parenting, travel, humor, children's activities, 60,000 words. Query with outline, sample chapters, and qualifications. Royalty or flat fee.

MENTOR BOOKS—Imprint of Penguin USA, 375 Hudson St., New York, NY 10014. Address Editors. Nonfiction originals for the college and high school market. Query required. Royalty.

MERCURY HOUSE—201 Filbert St., Suite 400, San Francisco, CA 94133. Mr. Thomas Christenson, Exec. Ed. Quality fiction and nonfiction. Nonfiction subjects include international politics, literary travel, environment, philosophy/ personal growth, and performing arts. Query with outline, sample chapters, and SASE.

MEREDITH CORP. BOOK GROUP—(Better Homes and Gardens Books) 1716 Locust St., Des Moines, IA 50336. David A. Kirchner, Man. Ed. Books on gardening, crafts, health, decorating, etc., mostly staff written. "Interested in free-lance writers with expertise in these areas rather than in queries for book-length manuscripts." Limited market. Query with SASE.

MESSNER, JULIAN—Div. of Simon & Schuster, Prentice Hall Bldg., Rt. 9W, Englewood Cliffs, NJ 07632. Bonnie Brook, Ed.-in-Chief. Curriculum-oriented nonfiction. General nonfiction, ages 8 to 14, includes science, nature, biography, history, and hobbies. Lengths vary. Royalty.

METAMORPHOUS PRESS—P.O. Box 10616, Portland, OR 97210. Gene Radeka, Acquisitions Ed. Business, education, health, how-to, humor, performance arts, psychology, sports and recreation, and women's topics. Also children's books that promote self-esteem and self-reliance. "We select books that provide the tools to help people improve their lives and the lives of those around them." Query with sample chapter and outline.

METEOR PUBLISHING—3369 Progress Dr., Bensalem, PA 19020. Kate Duffy, Ed.-in-Chief. Contemporary romance novels, 65,000 words, sold through direct mail only. Royalty.

THE MICHIGAN STATE UNIVERSITY PRESS—1405 S. Harrison Rd., Suite 25, Manly Miles Bldg., E. Lansing, MI 48823–5202. Scholarly nonfiction. Submit prospectus, table of contents, and sample chapter. Authors should refer to *The Chicago Manual of Style, 13th Edition*, for formats and styles.

MILKWEED EDITIONS—528 Hennepin Ave., Suite 505, Minneapolis, MN 55403. Emilie Buchwald, Ed. "We publish excellent fiction, poetry, essays, and collaborative books—the kind of writing that makes for good reading." This small press publishes about 12 books a year. Writers are encouraged to query first with sample chapters. Royalty.

THE MILLBROOK PRESS—2 Old New Milford Rd., Brookfield, CT 06804. Susan Misselbeck, Manuscript Coord. Nonfiction for early elementary grades through grades seven and up, appropriate for the school and public library market, encompassing curriculum-related topics and extracurricular interests. Send query with outline and sample chapter. Royalty.

MILLER ACCOUNTING PUBLICATIONS, INC.—Imprint of Harcourt Brace Jovanovich, 1250 Sixth Ave., San Diego, CA 92101. Professional books for practitioners in accounting and finance. College accounting texts. Query required. Royalty.

MILLS & SANDERSON, PUBLISHERS—41 North Rd., #201, Bedford,

MA 01730. Georgia Mills, Pub. Books, 250 pages, on travel and fitness. Query. Royalty.

MINSTREL BOOKS—Imprint of Pocket Books, 1230 Ave. of the Americas, New York, NY 10020. Patricia MacDonald, Exec. Ed. Fiction for girls and boys ages 6 to 11: scary stories, fantasies, funny stories, school stories, adventures, animal stories. No picture books. Query first with detailed plot outline, sample chapter, and SASE. Royalty.

THE MIT PRESS—Acquisitions Dept., 55 Hayward St., Cambridge, MA 02142. Books on computer science/artificial intelligence; cognitive sciences; economics; architecture; aesthetic and social theory; linguistics; technology studies; environmental studies; and neuroscience.

MODAN PUBLISHING—P.O. Box 1202, Bellmore, NY 11710. Bennett Shelkowitz, Man. Dir. Adult nonfiction. Young-adult fiction and nonfiction. Children's picture books. Books with international focus or related to political or social issues. Judaica and Hebrew books from Israel. Adama Books.

MOON HANDBOOKS—Moon Publications, Inc., 722 Wall St., Chico, CA 95928. Mark Morris, Ed. Travel guides of varying lengths. Will consider multiple submissions. Query. Royalty.

MOREHOUSE PUBLISHING—78 Danbury Rd., Wilton, CT 06897. E. Allen Kelley, Pub. Theology, pastoral care, church administration, spirituality, Anglican studies, history of religion, books for children, youth, elders, etc. Query with outline, contents, and sample chapter. Royalty.

MORROW AND CO., INC., WILLIAM—1350 Avenue of the Americas, New York, NY 10019. James Landis, Pub./Ed.-in-Chief. Adult fiction and nonfiction: no unsolicited manuscripts. Morrow Junior Books: David Reuther, Ed.-in-Chief. Children's books for all ages. Hearst Marine Books and Hearst Books: Ann Bramson, Ed. Dir. General nonfiction. Submit through agent only.

MOUNTAIN PRESS PUBLISHING—2016 Strand Ave., P.O. Box 2399, Missoula, MT 59806. Address John Rimel. Nonfiction, 300 pages, in the areas of natural history, horses and cowboys, Montana history, and fur trading lore. Query with outline and sample chapters; multiple queries considered. Royalty.

THE MOUNTAINEERS BOOKS—1011 S.W. Klickitat Way, Suite 107, Seattle, WA 98134. Margaret Foster-Finan, Ed. Mgr. Nonfiction books on noncompetitive aspects of outdoor sports such as mountaineering, backpacking, canoeing, kayaking, bicycling, skiing. Field guides, regional histories, biographies of outdoor people; accounts of expeditions. Nature books. Submit sample chapters and outline. Royalty.

MUIR PUBLICATIONS, JOHN—P.O. Box 613, Santa Fe, NM 87504–0613. Ken Luboff, Ed. Books for children and adults on travel and other cultural and environmental topics; easy-to-use car repair manuals. Send manuscript or query with sample chapters. Royalty.

MULTNOMAH PRESS—10209 S.E. Division St., Portland, OR 97266. Conservative, evangelical nonfiction. Some juvenile fiction with Christian world view. Request guidelines and manuscript questionnaire. Royalty.

MUSTANG PUBLISHING CO., INC.—Box 3004, Memphis, TN 38173. Rollin A. Riggs, Pres. Nonfiction for 18- to 40-year-olds. Send queries for 100- to 300-page books, with outlines and sample chapters. Royalty. SASE required.

THE MYSTERIOUS PRESS—129 W. 56th St., New York, NY 10019. William Malloy, Ed.-in-Chief. Mystery/suspense novels. Agented manuscripts only.

NAIAD PRESS, INC.—Box 10543, Tallahassee, FL 32302. Barbara Grier, Ed. Adult fiction, 52,000 to 60,000 words, with lesbian themes and characters: mysteries, romances, gothics, ghost stories, westerns, regencies, spy novels, etc. Query with letter and one-page précis only. Royalty.

NATIONAL PRESS—7200 Wisconsin Ave., Suite 212, Bethesda, MD 20814. G. Edward Smith, Ed. Fiction for Beach Books imprint. Nonfiction: history, criminology, reference, and health (Zenith Editions); cookbooks; sports and parenting; business, management, and automotive titles (Plain English Press). Royalty. Query with outline and sample chapters.

NATUREGRAPH PUBLISHERS—P. O. Box 1075, Happy Camp, CA 96039. Barbara Brown, Ed. Nonfiction: Native American culture, natural history, outdoor living, land and gardening, holistic learning and health, Indian lore, crafts, and how-to. Query. Royalty.

THE NAVAL INSTITUTE PRESS—Annapolis, MD 21402. Nonfiction (60,000 to 100,000 words): how-tos on boating and navigation; battle histories; biography; ship guides. Occasional fiction (75,000 to 110,000 words). Query with outline and sample chapters. Royalty.

NELSON, INC., THOMAS—Nelson Place at Elm Hill Pike, P. O. Box 141000, Nashville, TN 37214–1000. Religious adult nonfiction. Teen and adult nonfiction. Query with outline and sample chapter.

NEW SOCIETY PUBLISHERS—4527 Springfield Ave., Philadelphia, PA 19143. Books on fundamental social change through nonviolent social action. Nonfiction only. Request guidelines before submitting proposal. SASE required.

NEW WORLD LIBRARY—58 Paul Dr., San Rafael, CA 94903. Submissions Ed. Nonfiction to 300 pages, especially high quality, inspirational/self-help books, environmental awareness. "Aim for intelligent, aware audience, interested in personal and planetary transformation." Query with outline. Multiple queries accepted. Royalty.

NEWCASTLE PUBLISHING—13419 Saticoy St., N. Hollywood, CA 91605. Al Saunders, Pub. Nonfiction manuscripts (200 to 250 pages) for older adults on personal health, health care issues, and relationships. "We are not looking for fads or trends. We want books with a long shelf life." Multiple queries considered. Royalty.

NEWMARKET PRESS—18 E. 48th St., New York, NY 10017. Keith Hollaman, Man. Ed. Nonfiction on health, self-help, child care, parenting, and music. Query first. Royalty.

NORTH COUNTRY PRESS—P.O. Box 440, Belfast, ME 04915. William M. Johnson, Pub. Nonfiction with a Maine and/or New England tie-in. "Our goal is to publish high-quality books for people who love New England." Query with SASE, outline, and sample chapters. Royalty.

NORTHWORD PRESS, INC.—Box 1360, 7520 Highway 51, Minocqua, WI 54548. Tom Klein, Ed. Natural history and natural heritage books, from 25,000 words. Send outline with sample chapters, or complete manuscript. Royalty or flat fee.

NORTON AND CO., INC., W.W.—500 Fifth Ave., New York, NY 10110. Liz Malcolm, Ed. High-quality fiction and nonfiction. No occult, paranormal, religious, genre fiction (formula romance, SF, westerns), cookbooks, arts and crafts, YA, or children's books. Query with synopsis, two to three chapters, and resumé. Return postage and packaging required. Royalty.

ONEWORLD PUBLICATIONS, INC.—Country Route 9, P.O. Box 357, Chatham, NY 12037. Leo Hallen, Sales and Marketing Dir., Books for Thoughtful People. "We deal with issues bearing on the collective life of humanity and its changing needs as we approach the 21st century. As a broad guide, all works should be in tune with Baha'i ideals." Queries required.

OPEN COURT PUBLISHING COMPANY—Box 599, Peru, IL 61354. Scholarly books on philosophy, psychology, religion, oriental thought, history, public policy, and related topics. Send sample chapters with outline and resumé. Royalty.

ORCHARD BOOKS—Div. of Franklin Watts, 387 Park Ave., New York, NY 10016. Norma Jean Sawicki, Pub. Hardcover picture books. Fiction for middle grades and young adults. Nonfiction and photo essays for young children. Submit complete manuscript. Royalty.

OREGON STATE UNIVERSITY PRESS—101 Waldo Hall, Corvallis, OR 97331. Scholarly books in a limited range of disciplines and books of particular importance to the Pacific Northwest. Query with summary of manuscript.

OSBORNE/MCGRAW HILL—2600 Tenth St., Berkeley, CA 94710. Jeffrey M. Pepper, Ed.-in-Chief. Microcomputer books for general audience. Query. Royalty.

THE OVERLOOK PRESS—149 Wooster St., New York, NY 10012. Jessika Hegewisch, Ed. Dir. General nonfiction, including biography, carpentry, architecture, how-to, crafts, martial arts, Hudson Valley regionals, and gardening. Query with outline and sample chapters. Royalty.

OWEN PUBLISHERS, INC., RICHARD C.—135 Katonah Ave., Katonah, NY 10536. Janice Boland, Ed. Fiction, nonfiction, and poetry books of 8, 12, and 16 pages (including illustration) suitable for five-, six-, and seven-year-old beginning readers for the "Ready to Read" program. Royalties for writers. Flat fee for illustrators. Guidelines.

OXFORD UNIVERSITY PRESS—200 Madison Ave., New York, NY 10016. Authoritative books on literature, history, philosophy, etc.; college textbooks, medical, and reference books. Query. Royalty.

OXMOOR HOUSE, INC.—Box 2262, Birmingham, AL 35201. Nancy Fitzpatrick, Ed. Nonfiction: art, photography, gardening, decorating, cooking, sports, and crafts. Royalty.

PACER BOOKS FOR YOUNG ADULTS—Imprint of Berkley Publishing Group, 200 Madison Ave., New York, NY 10016. Fiction: adventure, fantasy, and role-playing fantasy gamebooks. No unsolicited manuscripts; queries only. Address Melinda Metz. Paperback only.

PANTHEON BOOKS—Div. of Random House, 201 E. 50th St., New York, NY 10022. Quality fiction and nonfiction. Query required. Royalty.

PARA PUBLISHING—P.O. Box 4232, Santa Barbara, CA 93140–4232. Dan Poynter, Ed. Adult nonfiction books on parachutes and skydiving only. Author must present evidence of having made at least 1,000 jumps. Company publishes an average of five new books each year. Query. Royalty.

PARAGON HOUSE—90 Fifth Ave., New York, NY 10011. Ken Stuart,

Ed.-in-Chief. Serious nonfiction, including biography, history, reference, parenting, self help, military history, politics and current affairs, and how-to. Query or send manuscript. Royalty.

PASSPORT BOOKS—4255 W. Touhy Ave., Lincolnwood, IL 60646–1975. Michael Ross, Ed. Dir. Adult nonfiction, 200 to 400 pages, picture books up to 120 pages, and juvenile nonfiction. Send outline and sample chapters for books on foreign language, travel, and culture. Multiple queries considered. Royalty and flat fee.

PATH PRESS—53 W. Jackson Blvd., Chicago, IL 60604. Bennett Johnson, Pres. Herman C. Gilbert, Ed. Quality books by and about African-Americans and Third-World peoples. Submit outline and sample chapters. Royalty.

PEACHTREE PUBLISHERS, LTD.—494 Armour Circle N.E., Atlanta, GA 30324. Wide variety of fiction and nonfiction. No religious material, SF/fantasy, romance, mystery/detective, historical fiction; no business, scientific, or technical books. Send outline and sample chapters for fiction and nonfiction. SASE required. Royalty.

PELICAN PUBLISHING CO., INC.—1101 Monroe St., Gretna, LA 70053. Nina Kooij, Ed. General nonfiction: Americana, regional, architecture, how-to, travel, cookbooks, inspirational, motivational, music, parenting, etc. Juvenile fiction. Royalty.

PENGUIN BOOKS—375 Hudson St., New York, NY 10014. Address Editors. Adult fiction and nonfiction paperbacks. Royalty.

THE PERMANENT PRESS—R.D. 2, Noyac Rd., Sag Harbor, NY 11963. Judith Shepard, Ed. Seeks original and arresting novels, trade books, biographies. Query. Royalty.

PHAROS BOOKS—200 Park Ave., New York, NY 10166. Hana Umlauf Lane, Ed. Current issues, personal finance, food, health, history, true crime, how-to, humor, politics, reference, and sports. Reference books for children, ages 6 and up. Query with sample chapter and outline. Royalty.

PHILOMEL BOOKS—Div. of The Putnam & Grosset Group, 200 Madison Ave., New York, NY 10016. Patricia Lee Gauch, Ed. Dir. Paula Wiseman, Ed.-in-Chief. Picture books, young-adult fiction, and some biographies. Fresh, original work with compelling characters and "a truly childlike spirit." Query required.

PINEAPPLE PRESS—P.O. Drawer 16008, Southside Sta., Sarasota, FL 34239. June Cussen, Ed. Serious fiction and nonfiction, 60,000 to 125,000 words. Query with outline, sample chapters, and SASE. Royalty.

PIPPIN PRESS—229 E. 85th St., Gracie Sta., Box 92, New York, NY 10028. Barbara Francis, Pub. High-quality picture books for pre-schoolers; middle-group fiction, humor and mysteries; imaginative nonfiction for children of all ages. Query with outline. Royalty.

PLAIN ENGLISH PRESS—See National Press.

PLENUM PUBLISHING CORP.—233 Spring St., New York, NY 10013. Linda Greenspan Regan, Sr. Ed. Trade nonfiction, approximately 300 pages, on science, criminology, psychology, sociology, and health. Query required. Royalty. Hardcover.

PLUME BOOKS—Imprint of Penguin USA, 375 Hudson St., New York, NY 10014. Address Editors. Nonfiction: on hobbies, business, health, cooking, child care, psychology, history, popular culture, biography, and politics. Fiction: serious literary and gay.

POCKET BOOKS—Div. of Simon and Schuster, 1230 Ave. of the Americas, New York, NY 10020. William R. Grose, Ed. Dir. Original fiction and nonfiction. Mystery line: police procedurals, private eye, and amateur sleuth novels; query with outline and sample chapters to Jane Chelius, Sr. Ed. Royalty.

POINT—See Scholastic, Inc.

POPULAR PRESS—Bowling Green State University, Bowling Green, OH 43403. Ms. Pat Browne, Ed. Nonfiction, 250 to 400 pages, examining some aspect of popular culture. Query with outline. Flat fee or royalty.

POSEIDON PRESS—Imprint of Simon & Schuster, 1230 Ave. of the Americas, New York, NY 10020. Ann Patty, V.P./Pub. General fiction and nonfiction. No unsolicited material. Royalty.

POTTER, CLARKSON—201 E. 50th St., New York, NY 10022. Carol Southern, Assoc. Pub./Ed.-in-Chief. General trade books. Submissions accepted through agents only.

PRAEGER PUBLISHERS—Imprint of Greenwood Publishing Group, 1 Madison Ave., New York, NY 10010. Ron Chambers, Pub. General nonfiction; scholarly and reference books. Query with outline. Royalty.

PREISS VISUAL PUBLICATIONS, BYRON—24 W. 25th St., New York, NY 10010. Creates series to sell to publishers. Adult books, 60,000 words: science fiction, fantasy, mystery. Produces juvenile fiction and nonfiction (science and wildlife) and young adult fiction and nonfiction. "We need people who can write well and are willing to write to our specifications." Submit writing samples rather than specific manuscripts. Royalty.

PRESIDIO PRESS—31 Pamaron Way, Novato, CA 94949. Nonfiction: contemporary military history, from 80,000 words. Selected military and action-adventure fiction. Query. Royalty.

PRICE STERN SLOAN PUBLISHERS, INC.—11150 Olympic Blvd., Suite 650, Los Angeles, CA 90064. Children's books; adult trade nonfiction, including humor. Query with SASE required. Royalty.

PRIMA PUBLISHING—P.O. Box 1260, Rocklin, CA 95677. Ben Dominitz, Pub. Nonfiction on variety of subjects, including business, health, and cookbooks. "We want books with originality, written by highly qualified individuals." Royalty.

PRUETT PUBLISHING COMPANY—2928 Pearl, Boulder, CO 80301. Jim Pruett, Pres. Nonfiction: outdoors and recreation, western U.S. history and travel, adventure travel and railroadiana. Query. Royalty.

PUFFIN BOOKS—Imprint of Penguin USA, 375 Hudson St., New York, NY 10014. Address Editors. Children's fiction and nonfiction paperbacks. Query required. Royalty.

PUTNAM'S SONS, G.P.(BOOKS FOR YOUNG READERS)—Div. of The Putnam & Grosset Book Group, 200 Madison Ave., New York, NY 10016. Margaret Frith, Ed.-in-Chief. Picture books, fiction and nonfiction. No unsolicited manuscripts. Query with sample pages.

QUEST BOOKS—Imprint of The Theosophical Publishing House, 306 W. Geneva Rd., P. O. Box 270, Wheaton, IL 60189–0270. Shirley Nicholson, Sr. Ed.

Nonfiction books on Eastern and Western religion and philosophy, holism, healing, meditation, yoga, ancient wisdom. Query. Royalty.

QUILL—Imprint of William Morrow and Co., Inc., 105 Madison Ave., New York, NY 10016. Andrew Dutter, Ed. Trade paperback adult nonfiction. Submit through agent only.

RANDOM HOUSE JUVENILE DIV.—225 Park Ave. S., New York, NY 10003. Kate Klimo, Ed.-in-Chief. Fiction and nonfiction for beginning readers; paperback fiction line for 7- to 9-year-olds; 35 pages maximum. Query with three chapters and outline for nonfiction; complete manuscript for fiction. SASE for all correspondence. Royalty.

RANDOM HOUSE, INC.—201 E. 50th St., New York, NY 10022. General fiction and nonfiction. Query with three chapters and outline for nonfiction; complete manuscript for fiction. SASE required. Royalty.

REGNERY GATEWAY—1130 17th St. N.W., Suite 600, Washington, DC 20036. Nonfiction books on public policy. Query. Royalty.

RENAISSANCE HOUSE—541 Oak St., P. O. Box 177, Frederick, CO 80530. Eleanor H. Ayer, Ed. Regional guidebooks in series. Currently publishing guidebooks on Colorado, Arizona, California, and the Southwest. "We use only manuscripts written to our specifications for new or ongoing series." Submit outline and short bio. Royalty.

RODALE PRESS—33 E. Minor St., Emmaus, PA 18098. Pat Corpora, Pub. Books on health, gardening, homeowner projects, cookbooks, inspirational topics, pop psychology, woodworking, natural history. Query with outline and sample chapter. Royalty and outright purchase. In addition: "We're always looking for truly competent free lancers to write chapters for books conceived and developed in-house"; payment on a "writer-for-hire" basis; address Bill Gottlieb, V.P.

RUTGERS UNIVERSITY PRESS—109 Church St., New Brunswick, NJ 08901. Literary fiction.

RUTLEDGE HILL PRESS—513 Third Ave. S., Nashville, TN 37210. Ronald E. Pitkin, V.P. Southern-interest fiction and market-specific nonfiction. Query with outline and sample chapters. Royalty.

ST. ANTHONY MESSENGER PRESS—1615 Republic St., Cincinnati, OH 45210–1298. Lisa Biedenbach, Man. Ed. Inspirational nonfiction for Catholics, supporting a Christian lifestyle in our culture; prayer aids, education, practical spirituality, parish ministry, liturgy resources. Query with 500-word summary. Royalty.

ST. MARTIN'S PRESS—175 Fifth Ave., New York, NY 10010. General adult fiction and nonfiction. Query first. Royalty.

SANDLAPPER PUBLISHING, INC.—P.O. Drawer 730, Orangeburg, SC 29116–0730. Frank N. Handal, Book Ed. Books on South Carolina history, culture, cuisine. Nonfiction about South Carolina or fiction set in South Carolina. Submit query with outline and sample chapters.

SASQUATCH BOOKS—1931 Second Ave., Seattle, WA 98101. Books by local authors on a wide range of nonfiction topics related to the Pacific Northwest: travel, natural history, gardening, cooking, history, and public affairs. Books must have a Pacific Northwest angle; length is 60,000 to 80,000 words. Query with SASE. Royalty.

SCARECROW PRESS—P.O. Box 4167, Metuchen, NJ 08840. Norman Horrocks, V.P./Editorial. Reference works and bibliographies, 150 pages and up, especially in the areas of cinema, TV, radio, and theater, mainly for use by libraries. Query or send complete manuscript; multiple queries considered. Royalty.

SCHOCKEN BOOKS—Div. of Pantheon Books, 201 E. 50th St., New York, NY 10022. General nonfiction: Judaica, women's studies, education, art history. Query with outline and sample chapter. Royalty.

SCHOLASTIC, INC.—730 Broadway, New York, NY 10003. Point: Regina Griffin, Sr. Ed. Young-adult fiction for readers 12 and up. Apple Books: Regina Griffin, Sr. Ed. Fiction for readers ages 8 to 12. Submit complete manuscript with cover letter and SASE. Royalty. Sunfire: Ann Reit, Ed. American historical romances, for girls 12 and up, 55,000 words. Query with outline and three sample chapters. Write for tip sheets.

SCOTT, FORESMAN AND CO.—1900 E. Lake Ave., Glenview, IL 60025. Richard E. Peterson, Pres. Elementary and secondary textbooks. Royalty or flat fee.

SCRIBNER'S SONS, CHARLES—866 Third Ave., New York, NY 10022. Barbara Grossman, Pub. Fiction, general nonfiction, science, history, and biography; query first. Clare Costello, Ed., Books for Young Readers: fantasy, mystery, SF, and problem novels; picture books, ages 5 and up; and nonfiction (science and how-tos). Query with outline and sample chapter.

SEVEN SEAS PRESS—International Marine, Box 220, Camden, ME 04843. Jonathan Eaton, VP/Ed. James Babb, Acquisitions Ed. Books on boating (sailing and power) and outdoor recreation.

SHAW PUBLISHERS, HAROLD—388 Gunderson Dr., Box 567, Wheaton, IL 60189. Ramona Cramer Tucker, Dir. of Ed. Services. Nonfiction, 120 to 220 pages, with an evangelical Christian perspective. Teen and adult fiction and literary books. Query. Flat fee.

SIERRA CLUB BOOKS—100 Bush St., San Francisco, CA 94104. Nonfiction: environment, natural history, the sciences, outdoors and regional guidebooks, nature photography; juvenile fiction and nonfiction. Query with SASE. Royalty.

SIGNET BOOKS AND SIGNET CLASSIC—Imprint of Penguin USA, 375 Hudson St., New York, NY 10014. Address Editors. Commercial fiction (historicals, sagas, thrillers, action/adventure novels, westerns, horror, science fiction and fantasy) and nonfiction (self-help, how-to, etc.). Royalty.

SILHOUETTE BOOKS—300 E. 42nd St., New York, NY 10017. Isabel Swift, Ed. Mgr. Silhouette Romances: Valerie Hayward, Sr. Ed. Contemporary romances, 53,000 to 58,000 words. Special Edition: Tara Gavin, Sr. Ed. Sophisticated contemporary romances, 75,000 to 80,000 words. Silhouette Desire: Lucia Macro, Sr. Ed. Sensuous contemporary romances, 53,000 to 60,000 words. Intimate Moments: Leslie Wainger, Sr. Ed./Ed. Coord. Sensuous, exciting contemporary romances, 80,000 to 85,000 words. Historical romance: 95,000 to 105,000 words, set in England, France, and North America between 1700 and 1900; query with synopsis and three sample chapters to Tracy Farrell, Sr. Ed. Query with synopsis and SASE to appropriate editor. Tipsheets available.

SIMON & SCHUSTER—1230 Ave. of the Americas, New York, NY 10020. Adult books: No unsolicited material. Children's Book Division: 15 Columbus Cir., New York, NY 10023. Olga Litowinsky, Ed. Material for middle-grade readers only. "Everything from chapter books for 7-year-olds up to novels for 10- to 14-year-olds."

SLAWSON COMMUNICATIONS, INC.—165 Vallecitos de Oro, San Marcos, CA 92069–1436. Ron Tucker, Asst. to the Pub. High-level computer books, 160 to 256 pages, for Microtrend imprint. Business titles for Avant imprint. Query with sample chapters. Royalty.

SOHO PRESS—853 Broadway, New York, NY 10003. Juris Jurjevics, Ed. Adult fiction, mysteries, thrillers, and nonfiction, from 75,000 words. Send SASE and complete manuscript. Royalty.

SOUTHERN ILLINOIS UNIVERSITY PRESS—Box 3697, Carbondale, IL 62902–3697. Curtis L. Clark, Ed. Nonfiction in the humanities, 200 to 400 pages. Query with outline and sample chapters. Royalty.

SOUTHERN METHODIST UNIVERSITY PRESS—Box 415, Dallas, TX 75275. Kathryn Lang, Sr. Ed. Fiction: serious literary fiction, short story collections, set in Texas or the Southwest, 150 to 400 pages. Nonfiction: scholarly studies in ethics, composition/rhetoric, theater, film, North African archaeology, belles lettres, scholarly writing about Texas or Southwest, 150 to 400 pages. No juvenile material or poetry. Query. Royalty or flat fee.

SPECTRA BOOKS—Imprint of Bantam Books, 666 Fifth Ave., New York, NY 10103. Lou Aronica, Pub. Science fiction and fantasy, with emphasis on storytelling and characterization. Query with SASE; no unsolicited manuscripts. Royalty.

STANDARD PUBLISHING—8121 Hamilton Ave., Cincinnati, OH 45231. Address Mark Plunkett. Fiction: juveniles, based on Bible or with moral tone. Nonfiction: biblical, Christian education. Conservative evangelical. Query preferred.

STANFORD UNIVERSITY PRESS—Stanford University, Stanford, CA 94305–2235. Norris Pope, Ed. "For the most part, we publish academic scholarship." No original fiction or poetry. Query with outline and sample chapters. Royalty.

STECK-VAUGHN COMPANY—National Education Corp., 11 Prospect St., Madison, NJ 07940. Walter Kossmann, Ed. Nonfiction books, 5,000 to 30,000 words, for school and library market: biographies for grades 6 and up; and science, social studies, and history books for primary grades through high school. Query with outline and sample chapters; SASE required. Flat fee and royalty.

STEMMER HOUSE PUBLISHERS, INC.—2627 Caves Rd., Owings Mills, MD 21117. Barbara Holdridge, Ed. Juvenile fiction and adult fiction and nonfiction. Specialize in art, design, cookbooks, and horticultural titles. Query with SASE. Royalty.

STERLING PUBLISHING CO., INC.—387 Park Ave. S., New York, NY 10016. Sheila Anne Barry, Acquisitions Mgr. How-to, hobby, woodworking, health, fiber arts, craft, wine, nature, oddities, New Age, puzzles, juvenile humor and activities, juvenile science, sports and games books, and military topics. Query with outline, sample chapter, and sample illustrations. Royalty.

STONE WALL PRESS, INC.—1241 30th St. N.W., Washington, DC 20007. Nonfiction on natural history, outdoors, conservation, 200 to 300 manuscript pages. Query first. Royalty.

STONEYDALE PRESS—205 Main St., Drawer B, Stevensville, MT 59870. Dale A. Burk, Ed. Adult nonfiction, primarily how-to on outdoor recreation with emphasis on big game hunting. "We're a very specialized market. Query with outline and sample chapters essential." Royalty.

STORMLINE PRESS—P.O. Box 593, Urbana, IL 61801. Linda Bial, Ed. Literary fiction and nonfiction having to do with rural and small town life. Query. Royalty.

STORY LINE PRESS—Three Oaks Farm, Brownsville, OR 97327–9718. Robert McDowell, Ed. Fiction, nonfiction, and poetry of varying lengths. Query. Royalty.

STRAWBERRY HILL PRESS—3848 S.E. Division St., Portland, OR 97202–1641. Carolyn Soto, Ed. Nonfiction: biography, autobiography, history, cooking, health, how-to, philosophy, performance arts, and Third World. Query first with sample chapters, outline, and SASE. Royalty.

SUMMIT BOOKS—1230 Ave. of the Americas, New York, NY 10020. General-interest fiction and nonfiction of high literary quality. No category books. Query through agents only. Royalty.

SUNFIRE—See Scholastic, Inc.

TAB BOOKS—A Div. of McGraw-Hill, Inc., Blue Ridge Summit, PA 17294. Ron Powers, Dir. of Acquisitions, Ed. Dept. Nonfiction: electronics, computers, how-to, aviation, science fair projects, self-help, business, solar and energy, science and technology, back to basics, automotive, marine and outdoor life, hobby and craft, military history, graphic design, and engineering. Fiction: military. Royalty or flat fee.

TAMBOURINE BOOKS—Imprint of William Morrow & Co., Inc., 1350 Ave. of the Americas, New York, NY 10019. Paulette C. Kaufmann, V.P./Ed.-in-Chief. Picture books, fiction, and nonfiction for all ages in general trade market. "We hope to find new talented writers and illustrators who are working outside the New York area."

TAYLOR PUBLISHING CO.—1550 W. Mockingbird Ln., Dallas, TX 75235. Adult nonfiction: cooking, gardening, sports and recreation, health, self-help, humor, parenting, home improvement, nature/outdoors. Query with outline, sample chapters, relevant author bio, and SASE. Royalty.

TEMPLE UNIVERSITY PRESS—Broad and Oxford Sts., Philadelphia, PA 19122. Michael Ames, Ed. Adult nonfiction. Query with outline and sample chapters. Royalty.

TEN SPEED PRESS—P.O. Box 7123, Berkeley, CA 94707. Mariah Bear, Ed. Self-help and how-to on careers, recreation, etc.; natural science, history, cookbooks. Query with outline and sample chapters. Royalty. Paperback.

THUNDER'S MOUTH PRESS—54 Greene St., Suite 4S, New York, NY 10013. Neil Ortenberg, Ed. Mainly nonfiction: popular culture, current affairs, memoir, and biography, to 200 pages. Royalty.

TICKNOR & FIELDS—Subsidiary of Houghton Mifflin Company, 215 Park Ave. S., New York, NY 10003. John Herman, Ed. Dir. General nonfiction and fiction. Royalty.

TIMES BOOKS—Div. of Random House, Inc., 201 E. 50th St., New York, NY 10022. Steve Wasserman, Ed. Dir. General nonfiction specializing in business, science, and current affairs. No unsolicited manuscripts or queries accepted.

TOR BOOKS—49 W. 24th St., New York, NY 10010. Patrick Nielsen Hayden, Sr. Ed., science fiction and fantasy. Melissa Ann Singer, Sr. Ed., general fiction. Length: from 60,000 words. Query with outline and sample chapters. Royalty.

TROLL ASSOCIATES—100 Corporate Dr., Mahwah, NJ 07430. M. Francis, Ed. Juvenile fiction and nonfiction. Query preferred. Royalty or flat fee.

TROPHY BOOKS—See HarperCollins Children's Books.

TROUBADOR PRESS—Imprint of Price Stern Sloan, 11150 Olympic Blvd., Suite 650, Los Angeles, CA 90064. Juvenile illustrated game, activity, paper doll, coloring, and cut-out books. Query with outline and SASE. Royalty or flat fee.

TSR, INC.—P.O. Box 756, Lake Geneva, WI 53147. Address Manuscript Ed. "Seeking highly original works of fantasy, science fiction or horror or mystery related to those genres," 100,000 words. Query required.

TUDOR PUBLISHERS, INC.—P.O. Box 38366, Greensboro, NC 27438. Eugene E. Pfaff, Jr., Ed. Helpful nonfiction books for senior citizens, teenagers, and minorities. Reference library titles. Occasional high-quality fiction. Send proposal or query with sample chapters. Royalty.

TYNDALE HOUSE—351 Executive Dr., Box 80, Wheaton, IL 60189. Ron Beers, Ed. Dir. Christian. Juvenile and adult fiction and nonfiction on subjects of concern to Christians. Picture books with religious focus for third-grade readers. Submit complete manuscripts. Guidelines.

UNIVERSE BOOKS—300 Park Ave. S., New York, NY 10010. Adele J. Ursone, Ed. Dir. Fine arts and art history, photography, design, art calendars. Query with SASE. Royalty.

UNIVERSITY OF ALABAMA PRESS—P.O. Box 870380, Tuscaloosa, AL 35487–0380. Scholarly and general regional nonfiction. Submit to appropriate editor: Malcolm MacDonald, Ed. (history, public administration, political science); Nicole Mitchell, Ed. (English, rhetoric and communication, Judaic studies, women's studies); Judith Knight, Ed. (archaeology, anthropology). Send complete manuscript. Royalty.

UNIVERSITY OF ARIZONA PRESS—1230 N. Park Ave., Suite 102, Tucson, AZ 85719. Joanne O'Hare, Sr. Ed. Jennifer Shopland, Acquiring Ed. Scholarly nonfiction, to 100,000 words: Arizona, American West, anthropology, archaeology, environmental science, global change, Latin America, Native Americans, natural history, space sciences, women's studies. Query with outline and sample chapters or send complete manuscript. Royalty.

UNIVERSITY OF CALIFORNIA PRESS—2120 Berkeley Way, Berkeley, CA 94720. Address Acquisitions Department. Scholarly nonfiction. Query with outline and sample chapters.

UNIVERSITY OF GEORGIA PRESS—University of Georgia, Athens, GA 30602. Karen Orchard, Ed. Short story collections and poetry, scholarly nonfiction and literary criticism, Southern and American history, regional studies, biography and autobiography. For nonfiction, query with outline and sample chapters. Poetry collections considered in Sept. and Jan. only; short fiction in June and July only. A $10 fee is required for all poetry and fiction submissions. Royalty. SASE for competition guidelines.

UNIVERSITY OF ILLINOIS PRESS—54 E. Gregory Dr., Champaign, IL 61820. Richard L. Wentworth, Ed.-in-Chief. Short story collections, 140 to 180 pages; nonfiction; and poetry, 70 to 100 pages. Rarely considers multiple submissions. Query. Royalty.

UNIVERSITY OF MINNESOTA PRESS—2037 University Ave. S.E., Minneapolis, MN 55414. Biodun Iginla, Ed. Janaki Bakhlé, Ed. Nonfiction: media

689

studies, literary theory, philosophy, cultural criticism, regional titles, 50,000 to 225,000 words. Query with detailed prospectus or introduction, table of contents, sample chapter, and recent resumé. Royalty.

UNIVERSITY OF MISSOURI PRESS—2910 LeMone Blvd., Columbia, MO 65201–8227. Scholarly books on American and European history; American, British, and Latin American literary criticism; political philosophy; intellectual history; regional studies; and poetry and short fiction. Query Beverly Jarrett, Dir. and Ed.-in-Chief, for scholarly studies and creative nonfiction. Query Mr. Clair Willcox, Poetry and Fiction Editor, with four to six sample poems or one short story, table of contents for entire manuscript, and cover letter describing the work and author's professional background.

UNIVERSITY OF NEBRASKA PRESS—901 N. 17th St., Lincoln, NE 68588–0520. Address the Editors. Specializes in the history of the American West. Send proposals with summary, two sample chapters, and resumé.

UNIVERSITY OF NEW MEXICO PRESS—University of New Mexico Press, Albuquerque, NM 87131. Elizabeth C. Hadas, Ed. Dir. David V. Holtby, Jeffrey Grathwohl, Dana Asbury, and Barbara Guth, Eds. Scholarly nonfiction on social and cultural anthropology, archaeology, Western history, art, and photography. Query. Royalty.

UNIVERSITY OF NORTH CAROLINA PRESS—P.O. Box 2288, Chapel Hill, NC 27515–2288. David Perry, Ed. General-interest books (75,000 to 125,000 words) on the lore, crafts, cooking, gardening, travel, and natural history of the southeast. No fiction or poetry. Query preferred. Royalty.

UNIVERSITY OF OKLAHOMA PRESS—1005 Asp Ave., Norman, OK 73019–0445. John Drayton, Asst. Dir. Books, to 300 pages, on the history of the American West, Indians of the Americas, congressional studies, classical studies, literary criticism, and natural history. Query. Royalty.

UNIVERSITY OF TENNESSEE PRESS—293 Communications Bldg., Knoxville, TN 37996–0325. Nonfiction, 200 to 300 pages. Query with outline and sample chapters. Royalty.

UNIVERSITY OF UTAH PRESS—101 U.S.B., Salt Lake City, UT 84112. Norma Mikkelsen, Ed. Nonfiction from 200 pages and poetry from 60 pages. (Submit poetry during March only.) Query. Royalty.

UNIVERSITY PRESS OF MISSISSIPPI—3825 Ridgewood Rd., Jackson, MS 39211–6492. Seetha Srinivasan, Ed.-in-Chief. Scholarly and trade titles in American literature, history, and culture; southern studies; African-American, women's and American studies; social sciences; popular culture; folklife; art and architecture; natural sciences; reference; and other liberal arts.

UNIVERSITY PRESS OF NEW ENGLAND—17 ½ Lebanon St., Hanover, NH 03755. General and scholarly nonfiction. American, British, and European history, literature, literary criticism, and cultural studies. Jewish studies, women's studies, and studies of the New England region.

UNIVERSITY PRESSES OF FLORIDA—15 N.W. 15th St., Gainesville, FL 32611–2079. Walda Metcalf, Sr. Ed. and Asst. Dir. Nonfiction, 150 to 450 manuscript pages, on regional studies, Native Americans, folklore, women's studies, Latin American studies, contemporary literary criticism, sociology, anthropology, archaeology, international affairs, labor studies, and history. Poetry. Royalty.

VAN NOSTRAND REINHOLD—115 Fifth Ave., New York, NY 10003. Judith R. Joseph, Pres./C.E.O. Business, professional, scientific, and technical publishers of applied reference works: hospitality; architecture; graphic and interior design; gemology; chemistry; industrial and environmental health and safety; food science and technology; computer science and engineering. Royalty.

VANDAMERE PRESS—P.O. Box 5243, Arlington, VA 22205. Arthur F. Brown, Ed. Adult nonfiction, any length. Areas of special interest: history; Washington, DC area; career guides; parenting; mid-Atlantic area; and travel. Prefer outline with sample chapter for first submission. Multiple queries considered. Royalty.

VIKING BOOKS—Imprint of Penguin USA, 375 Hudson St., New York, NY 10014. No unagented manuscripts.

VILLARD BOOKS—Div. of Random House, 201 E. 50th St. , New York, NY 10022. Peter Gethers, V.P./Ed. Dir. "We look for good books we can sell: fiction, sports, inspiration, how-to, biography, humor, etc. We do look for authors who are promotable and books we feel we can market well." Royalty.

VOYAGER PAPERBACKS—See Harcourt Brace Jovanovich.

WALKER AND COMPANY—720 Fifth Ave., New York, NY 10019. Fiction: mysteries, suspense, westerns, regency romance, and espionage. Nonfiction: Americana, biography, history, science, natural history, medicine, psychology, parenting, sports, outdoors, reference, popular science, self-help, business, and music. Juvenile nonfiction, including biography, science, history, music, and nature. Fiction and young-adult problem novels. Query with synopsis and SASE. Royalty.

WALLACE-HOMESTEAD—See Chilton Book Co.

WARNE, FREDERICK—Imprint of Penguin USA, 375 Hudson St., New York, NY 10014. Address Editors. Children's hardcovers and paperbacks. Royalty.

WARNER BOOKS—666 Fifth Ave., New York, NY 10103. Mel Parker, Ed.-in-Chief. Fiction: historical romance, contemporary women's fiction, unusual big-scale horror and suspense. Nonfiction: business books, health and nutrition, self-help. Query with sample chapters.

WATTS, INC., FRANKLIN—387 Park Ave. S., New York, NY 10016. Philippe Gray, Asst. to Ed. Dir. Nonfiction for grades 5 to 12, including science, history, and biography. Adult nonfiction dealing with family life, submit to Judith Rothman, Pub., Grolier Press. Query with SASE required.

WESLEYAN UNIVERSITY PRESS—110 Mt. Vernon St., Middletown, CT 06459–6050. Terry Cochran, Dir. Wesleyan Poetry: new poets, 64 pages; published poets, 64 to 80 pages. Send query. Royalty.

WESTERN PUBLISHING CO., INC.—850 Third Ave., New York, NY 10022. Robin Warner, V.P./Pub., Children's Books; Margo Lundell, Selma Lanes, Ed. Dirs., Children's Books. Children's books, fiction and nonfiction: picture books, storybooks, concept books, novelty books. Adult nonfiction: field guides. No unsolicited manuscripts. Same address and requirements for Golden Press. Royalty or flat fee.

WHITMAN, ALBERT—6340 Oakton, Morton Grove, IL 60053. Kathleen Tucker, Ed. Picture books; novels, biographies, mysteries, and general nonfiction for middle-grade readers. Submit complete manuscript for picture books, three chapters and outline for longer fiction; query for nonfiction. Royalty.

WILDERNESS PRESS—2440 Bancroft Way, Berkeley, CA 94704. Thomas Winnett, Ed. Nonfiction: sports, recreation, and travel in the western U.S. Royalty.

WILEY & SONS, JOHN—605 Third Ave., New York, NY 10158–0012. David Sobel, Pub. Nonfiction manuscripts, 250 to 350 pages: science/nature; business/management; real estate; travel; cooking; biography; psychology; microcomputers; language; history; current affairs; health; finance. Send proposals with outline, author vita, market information, and sample chapter. Royalty.

WILSHIRE BOOK COMPANY—12015 Sherman Rd., N. Hollywood, CA 91605. Melvin Powers, Ed. Dir. Psychological self-help with strong motivational messages. Adult fables. Query or send synopsis. Royalty.

WINDSWEPT HOUSE PUBLISHERS—Mt. Desert, ME 04660. Jane Weinberger, Ed. Children's picture books, 150 words, with illustrations. Query first for how-to and teenage novels.

WINGBOW PRESS—2929 Fifth St., Berkeley, CA 94710. Randy Fingland, Ed. Nonfiction: women's interests, health, psychology. Query preferred. Royalty.

WOODBINE HOUSE—5615 Fishers Lane, Rockville, MD 20852. Susan Stokes, Ed. Nonfiction of all types; especially interested in science, history, special education, travel, natural history, and general reference. "No personal accounts or books that can be marketed only through bookstores." Query or submit complete manuscript with SASE. Guidelines for SASE. Royalty.

WORDWARE PUBLISHING—1506 Capital Ave., Plano, TX 75074. Russell A. Stultz, Ed. Computer reference books and business/professional books. Query with outline and sample chapters. Flat fee.

WORKMAN PUBLISHING CO., INC.—708 Broadway, New York, NY 10003. Address Editors. General nonfiction. Normal contractual terms based on agreement.

WORLDWIDE LIBRARY—Div. of Harlequin Books, 225 Duncan Mill Rd., Don Mills, Ont., Canada M3B 3K9. Randall Toye, Ed. Dir. Action adventure series and futuristic fiction for Gold Eagle imprint; mystery fiction. Query. Paperback only.

YANKEE BOOKS—33 E. Minor St., Emmaus, PA 18098. Books relating specifically to New England: cooking, crafts, travel guides, environmental issues, gardening, nature, humor, popular history. No fiction. Query or send proposal. Royalty.

YEARLING BOOKS—Imprint of Dell Publishing Co., 666 Fifth Ave., New York, NY 10103. Address Editors. Books for kindergarten through 6th grade. Manuscripts accepted from agents only.

ZEBRA BOOKS—475 Park Ave. S., New York, NY 10016. Ann LaFarge, Sr. Ed. Carin Cohen Ritter, Sr. Ed. Popular fiction: horror; historical romance (Heartfire Romances, 107,000 words, and Lovegram Romances, 130,000 words); traditional gothics (first person, 100,000 words); regencies (80,000 to 120,000 words); sagas (150,000 words); glitz (100,000 words); men's adventure; westerns; thrillers, etc. Query with synopsis and sample chapters preferred.

ZENITH EDITIONS—See National Press.

ZONDERVAN PUBLISHING HOUSE—1415 Lake Dr. S.E., Grand Rapids, MI 49506. Christian titles. General fiction and nonfiction; academic and professional books. Address Manuscript Review. Query with outline, sample chapter, and SASE. Royalty. Guidelines.

UNIVERSITY PRESSES

University presses generally publish books of a scholarly nature or of specialized interest by authorities in a given field. A few publish fiction and poetry. Many publish only a handful of titles a year. Always query first. Do not send a manuscript until you have been invited to do so by the editor. Several of the following presses and their detailed editorial submission requirements are included in the *Book Publishers* list.

BRIGHAM YOUNG UNIVERSITY PRESS—205 University Press Bldg., Provo, UT 84602.

BUCKNELL UNIVERSITY PRESS—Bucknell University, Lewisburg, PA 17837.

CAMBRIDGE UNIVERSITY PRESS—40 W. 20th St., New York, NY 10011–4211.

THE CATHOLIC UNIVERSITY OF AMERICA PRESS—620 Michigan Ave. N.E., Washington, DC 20064.

COLUMBIA UNIVERSITY PRESS—562 West 113th St., New York, NY 10025.

DUKE UNIVERSITY PRESS—Box 6697, College Station, Durham, NC 27708.

DUQUESNE UNIVERSITY PRESS—600 Forbes Ave., Pittsburgh, PA 15282–0101.

GEORGIA STATE UNIVERSITY BUSINESS PRESS—University Plaza, Atlanta, GA 30303–3093.

HARVARD UNIVERSITY PRESS—79 Garden St., Cambridge, MA 02138.

INDIANA UNIVERSITY PRESS—601 N. Morton St., Bloomington, IN 47404–3797.

THE JOHNS HOPKINS UNIVERSITY PRESS—701 W. 40th St., Suite 275, Baltimore, MD 21211–2190.

KENT STATE UNIVERSITY PRESS—Kent State Univ., Kent, OH 44242.

LOUISIANA STATE UNIVERSITY PRESS—LSU, Baton Rouge, LA 70893.

LOYOLA UNIVERSITY PRESS—3441 N. Ashland Ave., Chicago, IL 60657–1397.

MICHIGAN STATE UNIVERSITY PRESS—1405 S. Harrison Rd., Suite 25, East Lansing, MI 48823–5202.

THE MIT PRESS—Acquisitions Dept., 55 Hayward St., Cambridge, MA 02142.

NEW YORK UNIVERSITY PRESS—Washington Sq., New York, NY 10003.

OHIO STATE UNIVERSITY PRESS—180 Pressey Hall, 1070 Carmack Rd., Columbus, OH 43210.

OREGON STATE UNIVERSITY PRESS—101 Waldo Hall, Corvallis, OR 97331.

THE PENNSYLVANIA STATE UNIVERSITY PRESS—Barbara Bldg., Suite C, 820 N. University Dr., University Park, PA 16802.

PRINCETON UNIVERSITY PRESS—41 William St., Princeton, NJ 08540.

RUTGERS UNIVERSITY PRESS—109 Church St., New Brunswick, NJ 08901.

SOUTHERN ILLINOIS UNIVERSITY PRESS—Box 3697, Carbondale, IL 62902–3697.

SOUTHERN METHODIST UNIVERSITY PRESS—Box 415, Dallas, TX 75275.

STANFORD UNIVERSITY PRESS—Stanford University, Stanford, CA 94305–2235.

STATE UNIVERSITY OF NEW YORK PRESS—State University Plaza, Albany, NY 12246–0001.

TEMPLE UNIVERSITY PRESS—Broad and Oxford Sts., Philadelphia, PA 19122.

UNIVERSITY OF ALABAMA PRESS—P.O. Box 870380, Tuscaloosa, AL 35487–0380.

UNIVERSITY OF ARIZONA PRESS—1230 N. Park Ave., Suite 102, Tucson, AZ 85719.

UNIVERSITY OF CALIFORNIA PRESS—2120 Berkeley Way, Berkeley, CA 94720.

UNIVERSITY OF CHICAGO PRESS—5801 Ellis Ave., Chicago, IL 60637–1496.

UNIVERSITY OF GEORGIA PRESS—University of Georgia, Athens, GA 30602.

UNIVERSITY OF ILLINOIS PRESS—54 E. Gregory Dr., Champaign, IL 61820.

UNIVERSITY OF MASSACHUSETTS PRESS—Box 429, Amherst, MA 01004.

UNIVERSITY OF MICHIGAN PRESS—839 Greene St., P.O. Box 1104, Ann Arbor, MI 48106–1104.

UNIVERSITY OF MINNESOTA PRESS—2037 University Ave. S.E., Minneapolis, MN 55414.

UNIVERSITY OF MISSOURI PRESS—2910 LeMone Blvd., Columbia, MO 65201–8227.

UNIVERSITY OF NEBRASKA PRESS—901 North 17th St., Lincoln, NE 68588–0520.

UNIVERSITY OF NEW MEXICO PRESS—UNM, Albuquerque, NM 87131.

UNIVERSITY OF NORTH CAROLINA PRESS—P.O. Box 2288, Chapel Hill, NC 27515–2288.

694

UNIVERSITY OF OKLAHOMA PRESS—1005 Asp Ave., Norman, OK 73019–0445.

UNIVERSITY OF PITTSBURGH PRESS—127 North Bellefield Ave., Pittsburgh, PA 15260.

UNIVERSITY OF SOUTH CAROLINA PRESS—1716 College St., Columbia, SC 29208.

UNIVERSITY OF TENNESSEE PRESS—293 Communications Bldg., Knoxville, TN 37996–0325.

UNIVERSITY OF UTAH PRESS—101 U.S.B., Salt Lake City, UT 84112.

UNIVERSITY OF WASHINGTON PRESS—P.O. Box 50096, Seattle, WA 98145–5096.

UNIVERSITY OF WISCONSIN PRESS—114 N. Murray St., Madison, WI 53715–1199.

UNIVERSITY PRESS OF COLORADO—P.O. Box 849, Niwot, CO 80544.

UNIVERSITY PRESS OF KENTUCKY—663 S. Limestone St., Lexington, KY 40506–0336.

UNIVERSITY PRESS OF MISSISSIPPI—3825 Ridgewood Rd., Jackson, MS 39211–6492.

UNIVERSITY PRESS OF NEW ENGLAND—17 ½ Lebanon St., Hanover, NH 03755.

THE UNIVERSITY PRESS OF VIRGINIA—Box 3608, University Sta., Charlottesville, VA 22903.

UNIVERSITY PRESSES OF FLORIDA—15 N.W. 15th St., Gainesville, FL 32611–2079.

WAYNE STATE UNIVERSITY PRESS—5959 Woodward Ave., Detroit, MI 48202.

WESLEYAN UNIVERSITY PRESS—110 Mt.Vernon St., Middletown, CT 06459–0049.

YALE UNIVERSITY PRESS—92A Yale Sta., New Haven, CT 06520.

SYNDICATES

Syndicates are business organizations that buy material from writers and artists to sell to newspapers all over the country and the world. Authors are paid either a percentage of the gross proceeds or an outright fee.

Of course, features by people well known in their fields have the best chance of being syndicated. In general, syndicates want columns that have been popular in a local newspaper, perhaps, or magazine. Since most syndicated fiction has been published previously in magazines or books, beginning fiction writers should try to sell their stories to magazines before submitting them to syndicates.

Always query syndicates before sending manuscripts, since their needs change frequently, and be sure to enclose SASEs with queries and manuscripts.

ARKIN MAGAZINE SYNDICATE—1817 N.E. 164th St., N. Miami Beach, FL 33162. Joseph Arkin, Ed. Dir. Articles, 750 to 2,200 words, for trade and professional magazines. Must have small-business slant, written in layman's language, and offer solutions to business problems. Articles should apply to many businesses, not just a specific industry. No columns. Pays 3¢ to 10¢ a word, on acceptance. Query not necessary.

BUSINESS FEATURES SYNDICATE—P.O. Box 9844, Ft. Lauderdale, FL 33310. Dana K. Cassell, Ed. Articles, 1,500 to 2,000 words, for the independent retailer or small service business owner, on marketing, security, personnel, merchandising, general management. Pays 50% of sales.

CONTEMPORARY FEATURES SYNDICATE—P. O. Box 1258, Jackson, TN 38302–1258. Lloyd Russell, Ed. Articles, 1,000 to 10,000 words: how-to, money savers, business, etc. Self-help pieces for small business. Pays from $25, on acceptance.

HARRIS & ASSOCIATES FEATURES—12084 Caminito Campana, San Diego, CA 92128. Dick Harris, Ed. Sports and family-oriented features, to 1,200 words; fillers and short humor, 500 to 800 words. Queries preferred. Pays varying rates.

HISPANIC LINK NEWS SERVICE—1420 N St. N.W., Washington, DC 20005. Charles A. Ericksen, Ed. Trend articles, opinion and personal experience pieces, and general features with Hispanic focus, 650 to 700 words; editorial cartoons. Pays $25 for op-ed columns and cartoons, on acceptance. Send SASE for guidelines.

THE HOLLYWOOD INSIDE SYNDICATE—Box 49957, Los Angeles, CA 90049. John Austin, Dir. Feature articles, 750 to 2,500 words, on TV and film personalities with B&W photo(s). Story suggestions for three-part series. Pieces on unusual medical and scientific breakthroughs. Pays on percentage basis for features, negotiated rates for ideas, on acceptance.

KING FEATURES SYNDICATE—235 E. 45th St., New York, NY 10017. Merry Clark, Dir. of Ed. Projects. Columns, comics; all contributions on contract for regular columns. "We do not consider or buy individual articles. We are interested in ideas for nationally syndicated columns." Submit cover letter, six sample columns of 650 words each, bio sheet and any additional clips, and SASE. No simultaneous submissions. Query with SASE for guidelines.

LOS ANGELES TIMES SYNDICATE—Times Mirror Sq., Los Angeles, CA 90053. Commentary, features, columns, editorial cartoons, comics, puzzles and games; news services. Send SASE for submission guidelines.

NATIONAL NEWS BUREAU—P.O. Box 5628, Philadelphia, PA 19129. Harry Jay Katz, Ed. Articles, 500 to 1,500 words, interviews, consumer news, how-tos, travel pieces, reviews, entertainment pieces, features, etc. Pays on publication.

NEW YORK TIMES SYNDICATION SALES—130 Fifth Ave., New York,

NY 10011. Barbara Gaynes, Man. Ed. Previously published health, lifestyle, and entertainment articles only, to 2,000 words. Query with published article or tear sheet and SASE. Pays varying rates, on publication.

NEWSPAPER ENTERPRISE ASSOCIATION—200 Park Ave., New York, NY 10166. Howard Siner, Man. Ed. Ideas for new concepts in syndicated columns. No single stories or stringers. Payment by contractual arrangement.

OCEANIC PRESS SERVICE—P. O. Box 6538, Buena Park, CA 90622–6538. Peter Carbone, General Mgr. Buys reprint rights for foreign markets, on previously published novels, self-help, and how-to books; interviews with celebrities; illustrated features on celebrities, family, health, beauty, personal relations, etc.; cartoons, comic strips. Pays on acceptance or 50:50 syndication. Query.

SINGER MEDIA CORP.—3164 W. Tyler Ave., Anaheim, CA 92801. Kurt D. Singer, Ed. U.S. and/or foreign reprint rights to romantic short stories, historical and romantic novels, gothics, westerns, and mysteries published during last 25 years; business management titles. Biography, women's-interest material, all lengths. Home repair, real estate, crosswords, psychological quizzes. Interviews with celebrities. Illustrated columns, humor, cartoons, comic strips. Pays on percentage basis or by outright purchase.

TRIBUNE MEDIA SERVICES—64 E. Concord St., Orlando, FL 32801. Michael Argirion, Ed. Continuing columns, comic strips, features, electronic data bases.

UNITED FEATURE SYNDICATE—200 Park Ave., New York, NY 10166. Diana Loevy, Deputy Editorial Dir. Syndicated columns; no one-shots or series. Payment by contractual arrangement. Send samples with SASE.

UNITED PRESS INTERNATIONAL—1400 Eye St. N.W., Washington, DC 20005. Bill G. Ferguson, Man. Ed. Seldom accepts free-lance material.

LITERARY PRIZE OFFERS

Each year many important literary contests are open to free-lance writers. The short summaries given below are intended merely as guides. Closing dates, requirements, and rules are tentative. Every effort has been made to ensure the accuracy of information provided here. However, due to the ever-changing nature of literary competitions, writers are advised to check the monthly "Prize Offers" column of *The Writer* Magazine (120 Boylston St., Boston, MA 02116–4615) for the most up-to-date contest requirements. Writers should send SASE for guidelines before submitting to any contest.

ACADEMY OF AMERICAN POETS—177 E. 87th St., New York, NY 10128. Offers Walt Whitman Award: publication and $1,000 cash prize for a book-length poetry manuscript by a poet who has not yet published a volume of poetry. Closes in November.

697

ACTORS THEATRE OF LOUISVILLE—316 W. Main St., Louisville, KY 40202. Conducts Ten-Minute Play Contest. Offers $1,000 for previously unproduced ten-page script. Closes in December.

AMERICAN ACADEMY OF ARTS AND LETTERS—633 W. 155th St., New York, NY 10032. Offers Richard Rodgers Production Award, which consists of subsidized production in New York City by a non-profit theater for a musical, play with music, thematic review, or any comparable work other than opera. Closes in November.

AMERICAN FICTION—English Dept., Springfield College, Springfield, MA 01109. Michael C. White, Ed. A $1,000 first prize, $500 second prize, and $250 third prize are awarded for short stories, to 10,000 words. Birch Lane Press publishes anthology of 25 finalists. Closes in April.

THE ASSOCIATED WRITING PROGRAMS ANNUAL AWARDS SERIES—Old Dominion University, Norfolk, VA 23529–0079. Conducts Annual Awards Series in poetry, short fiction, the novel, and nonfiction. In each category the prize is book publication and a $1,500 honorarium. Closes in February.

ASSOCIATION OF JEWISH LIBRARIES—15 Goldsmith St., Providence, RI 02906. Address Lillian Schwartz, Secretary. Conducts Sydney Taylor Manuscript Competition for best fiction manuscript for readers 8 to 12. Prize is $1,000. Closes in January.

BARNARD COLLEGE—Women Poets at Barnard, Columbia University, 3009 Broadway, New York, NY 10027–6598. The Barnard New Women Poets Prize offers $1,500 and publication by Beacon Press for an unpublished poetry manuscript, 50 to 100 pages, by a female poet who has never published a book of poetry. Closes in September.

BEVERLY HILLS THEATRE GUILD/JULIE HARRIS PLAYWRIGHT AWARD—2815 N. Beachwood Dr., Los Angeles, CA 90068. Address Marcella Meharg. Offers prize of $5,000, plus possible $2,000 for production in Los Angeles area, for previously unproduced and unpublished full-length play. A $1,000 second prize and $500 third prize are also offered. Closes in November.

THE CHICAGO TRIBUNE/NELSON ALGREN AWARDS FOR SHORT FICTION—425 N. Michigan Ave., Chicago, IL 60611. Sponsors Nelson Algren Awards for Short Fiction, with a first prize of $5,000 and three runner-up prizes of $1,000 for outstanding unpublished short stories, 2,500 to 10,000 words, by American writers. Closes in February.

EUGENE V. DEBS FOUNDATION—Dept. of History, Indiana State Univ., Terre Haute, IN 47809. Offers Bryant Spann Memorial Prize of $1,000 for published or unpublished article or essay on themes relating to social protest or human equality. Closes in April.

DELACORTE PRESS—Dept. BFYR, 666 Fifth Ave., New York, NY 10103. Sponsors Delacorte Press Prize for outstanding first young adult novel. The prize consists of one Delacorte hardcover and one Dell paperback contract, an advance of $6,000 on royalties, and a $1,500 cash prize. Closes in December.

HELICON NINE EDITIONS—9000 W. 64th Terrace, Merriam, KS 66202. Attn: Gloria Hickok. Offers the Marianne Moore Poetry Prize of $1,000 for an original unpublished poetry manuscript of at least 50 pages, as well as the Willa Cather Fiction Prize of $1,000 for an original full-length fiction manuscript (novel, novella, short stories) from 150 to 350 pages. Both close in January.

HIGHLIGHTS FOR CHILDREN—803 Church St., Honesdale, PA 18431.

Conducts children's short fiction contest, with three $1,000 prizes and publication offered for stories to 900 words. Closes in February.

HONOLULU MAGAZINE/PARKER PEN—36 Merchant St., Honolulu, HI 96813. Sponsors annual fiction contest, with cash prize of $1,000, plus publication in *Honolulu*, for unpublished short story with Hawaiian theme, setting, and/or characters. Closes in November.

HUMBOLDT STATE UNIVERSITY—English Dept., Arcata, CA 95521–4957. Sponsors Raymond Carver Short Story Contest, with a prize of $500, plus publication in the literary journal *Toyon*, and a $250 second prize for an unpublished short story by a writer living in the U.S. Closes in November.

INTERNATIONAL SOCIETY OF DRAMATISTS—ISD Fulfillment Center, P. O. Box 1310, Miami, FL 33153. Sponsors Adriatic Award: a prize of $250 for a full-length play. Closes in November.

IUPUI CHILDREN'S THEATRE PLAYWRITING COMPETITION—Indiana University-Purdue University at Indianapolis, 525 N. Blackford St., Indianapolis, IN 46202–3120. Offers four $1,000 prizes plus staged readings for plays for young people. Closes in September of even-numbered years.

JEROME PLAYWRIGHT-IN-RESIDENCE FELLOWSHIPS—The Playwrights' Center, 2301 Franklin Ave. East, Minneapolis, MN 55406. Annually awards six emerging playwrights a $5,000 stipend and 12-month residency; housing and travel are not provided. Closes in January.

JEWISH COMMUNITY CENTER THEATRE IN CLEVELAND—3505 Mayfield Rd., Cleveland Heights, OH 44118. Elaine Rembrandt, Dir. of Cultural Arts. Offers cash award of $1,000 and a staged reading in the Dorothy Silver Playwriting Competition for an original, previously unproduced full-length play, on some aspect of the Jewish experience. Closes in December.

CHESTER H. JONES FOUNDATION—P. O. Box 498, Chardon, OH 44024. Conducts the National Poetry Competition, with more than $1,900 in cash prizes (including a $1,000 first prize) for original, unpublished first poems. Closes in March.

THE JOURNAL: THE LITERARY MAGAZINE OF O.S.U.—The Ohio State University Press, 180 Pressey Hall, 1070 Carmack Rd., Columbus, OH 43210–1002. Attn: David Citino, Poetry Editor. Awards $1,000 plus publication for at least 48 pages of original, unpublished poetry. Closes in September.

LINCOLN COLLEGE—Lincoln, IL 62656. Address Janet Overton. Offers the Billee Murray Denny Poetry Award for original poem by poet who has not previously published a volume of poetry. A first prize of $1,000, 2nd prize of $500, and 3rd prize of $250 are offered. Closes in May.

LIVE OAK THEATRE NEW PLAY AWARDS—311 Nueces St., Austin, TX 78701. Offers $1,000 each plus possible production for Best American Play and Best Play by a Texas Playwright for unproduced, unpublished, full-length scripts. Closes in November.

MADEMOISELLE MAGAZINE—350 Madison Ave., New York, NY 10017. Sponsors Fiction Writers Contest, with first prize of $2,500, plus publication, and second prize of $500, for short fiction by unpublished writers (female or male) ages 18 to 30. Closes in March.

MILL MOUNTAIN THEATRE NEW PLAY COMPETITION—Center in the Square, One Market Square, Roanoke, VA 24011. Jo Weinstein, Lit. Mgr.

Sponsors New Play Competition with a $1,000 prize and staged reading, with possible full production, for unpublished, unproduced, full-length or one-act play. Cast size to ten. Closes in January.

THE MOUNTAINEERS BOOKS—1011 S. W. Klickitat Way, Seattle, WA 98134. Address Donna DeShazo, Dir. Offers The Barbara Savage/"Miles From Nowhere" Memorial Award for a book-length, nonfiction personal-adventure narrative. The prize consists of a $3,000 cash award, plus publication and a $12,000 guaranteed advance against royalties. Closes in February of even-numbered years.

MULTICULTURAL PLAYWRIGHTS' FESTIVAL—The Group Theatre, 3940 Brooklyn Ave. N.E., Seattle, WA 98105. Awards two American citizens of Asian, African American, Chicano/Hispanic, or Native American ethnicity $1,000 plus production for a previously unproduced one-act or full-length play. Closes in November.

NATIONAL ENDOWMENT FOR THE ARTS—Nancy Hanks Center, 1100 Pennsylvania Ave. N.W., Washington, DC 20506. Address Director, Literature Program. Offers fellowships to writers of poetry, fiction, and creative nonfiction. Deadlines vary; write for guidelines.

NATIONAL PLAY AWARD—630 N. Grand Ave., Suite 405, Los Angeles, CA 90012. National Play Award consists of $7,500 cash prize, plus $5,000 for production, for an original, previously unproduced play. Sponsored by National Repertory Theatre Foundation. Closes in June of even-numbered years.

NATIONAL POETRY SERIES—26 W. 17th St., New York, NY 10011. Sponsors Annual Open Competition for unpublished book-length poetry manuscripts. The prize is publication. Closes in February.

NEGATIVE CAPABILITY SHORT FICTION CONTEST—62 Ridgelawn Dr. East, Mobile, AL 36608. Attn: Sue Walker. Sponsors the $1,000 Short Fiction Award for previously unpublished stories. Closes in December.

NEW DRAMATISTS—L. Arnold Weissburger Playwriting Competition, 424 W. 44th St., New York, NY 10036. Sponsors competition for full-length, unpublished, unproduced scripts; $5,000 is awarded the winning playwright. Closes in January.

NEW ENGLAND THEATRE CONFERENCE—50 Exchange St., Waltham, MA 02154. First prize of $500 and second prize of $250 are offered for unpublished and unproduced one-act plays in the John Gassner Memorial Playwriting Award Competition. Closes in April.

NILON AWARD FOR MINORITY FICTION—Fiction Collective Two, English Dept. Publications Ctr., University of Colorado, Campus Box 494, Boulder, CO 80309–0494. Awards $1,000 plus joint publication by Fiction Collective Two and CU-Boulder for original, unpublished, English Language, book-length fiction (novels, novellas, short story collections) by U.S. citizens of the following ethnic minorities: African-American, Hispanic, Asian, Native American or Alaskan Native, and Pacific Islander. Closes in November.

NIMROD/HARDMAN AWARDS—Arts and Humanities Council of Tulsa, 2210 S. Main St., Tulsa, OK 74114. Awards a $1,000 first prize and $500 second prize to winners of the Katherine Anne Porter Prize for Fiction (to 7,500 words) and the Pablo Neruda Prize for Poetry (one long poem, or a selection of poems). Closes in April.

NORTHEASTERN UNIVERSITY PRESS—English Dept., 406 Holmes, Northeastern Univ., Boston, MA 02115. Guy Rotella, Chairman. Offers Samuel

French Morse Poetry Prize: $500 plus publication of full-length poetry manuscript by U.S. poet who has published no more than one book of poems. August is deadline for inquiries; contest closes in September.

O'NEILL THEATER CENTER—234 W. 44th St., Suite 901, New York, NY 10036. Offers stipend, staged readings, and room and board at the National Playwrights Conference, for new stage and television plays. Send SASE for guidelines. Closes in December.

THE PARIS REVIEW—541 E. 72nd St., New York, NY 10021. Sponsors the Aga Khan Prize for Fiction: $1,000, plus publication, for previously unpublished short story; closes in June. Offers Bernard F. Connors Prize: $1,000, plus publication, for previously unpublished poem; closes in May. Offers John Train Humor Prize: $1,500, plus publication, for unpublished work of humorous fiction, nonfiction, or poetry; closes in March.

PEN/JERARD FUND AWARD—568 Broadway, New York, NY 10012. Address John Morrone, Programs & Publications. Offers $3,000 to beginning female writers for a work-in-progress of general nonfiction. Applicants must have published at least one article in a national magazine or major literary magazine, but not more than one book of any kind. Submissions accepted in September of even-numbered years.

PEN SYNDICATED FICTION PROJECT—P.O. Box 15650, Washington, DC 20003. For previously unpublished short fiction, to 2,500 words. Offers $500 for rights to each story selected and $100 each time it is published by a newspaper. All selected stories are used on the Project's radio show, "The Sound of Writing." Closes in January.

PLAYBOY MAGAZINE COLLEGE FICTION CONTEST—680 N. Lakeshore Dr., Chicago, IL 60611. Sponsors college fiction contest, with first prize of $3,000 and publication in *Playboy*, for a short story by a college student; second prize is $500. Closes in January.

POETRY SOCIETY OF AMERICA—15 Gramercy Park, New York, NY 10003. Conducts annual contests (The Celia B. Wagner Memorial Award, the John Masefield Memorial Award, the Elias Lieberman Student Poetry Award, the George Bogin Memorial award, the Robert H. Winner Memorial Award, and the Ruth Lake Memorial Award) in which cash prizes are offered for unpublished poems. All contests close in December.

PRIVATE EYE WRITERS OF AMERICA—PWA/St. Martin's Press, 175 Fifth Ave., New York, NY 10010. Winner of the Best First Private Eye Novel Contest receives publication with St. Martin's Press plus $10,000 against royalties; open to previously unpublished writers of private eye novels. Closes in August.

PURDUE UNIVERSITY PRESS—South Campus Courts-B, W. Lafayette, IN 47907–1131. Attn: Managing Editor. The Verna Emery Poetry Competition for an unpublished collection of poetry (65 pages) awards $500 plus publication for original poems. Closes in January.

REGARDIE'S MAGAZINE—1010 Wisconsin Ave., Suite 600, Washington, DC 20007. Sponsors the annual Money, Power, Greed Fiction Contest for short stories, 2,000 to 10,000 words, about the world of movers and shakers in and around Washington. Publication and a $3,000 first prize, $2,000 second prize, and $1,000 third prize are offered. Closes in May.

RIVER CITY WRITING AWARDS—River City, Dept. of English, Memphis State University, Memphis, TN 38152. Sharon Bryan, Ed. Awards $2,000 first prize, plus publication, $500 second prize, and $300 third prize, for previously unpublished short stories, to 7,500 words. Closes in December.

ST. MARTIN'S PRESS/MALICE DOMESTIC CONTEST—Thomas Dunne Books, 175 Fifth Ave., New York, NY 10010. Co-sponsored by Macmillan London, offers publication plus a $10,000 advance against royalties, for Best First Traditional Mystery Novel. Closes in November.

SHIRAS INSTITUTE—Playwriting Award Information, Forest Roberts Theatre, Northern Michigan Univ., Marquette, MI 49855. Conducts annual Shiras Institute/Albert & Mildred Panowski Playwriting Competition, with prize of $2,000, plus production, for original, full-length, previously unproduced and unpublished play. Closes in November.

SIERRA REPERTORY THEATRE—P. O. Box 3030, Sonora, CA 95370. Attn: Dennis Jones, Producing Dir. Offers annual playwriting award of $500, plus possible production, for full-length plays or musicals that have received no more than two productions or staged readings. Closes in August.

SOCIETY OF AMERICAN TRAVEL WRITERS—1155 Connecticut Ave. N.W., Suite 500, Washington, DC 20036. Sponsors Lowell Thomas Travel Journalism Award for published and broadcast work by U.S. and Canadian travel journalists. Prizes total $11,000. Closes in February.

STANLEY DRAMA AWARD—Wagner College, Dept. of Humanities, 631 Howard Ave., Staten Island, NY 10301. Awards $2,000 for an original, previously unpublished and unproduced full-length play. Closes in September.

STORY LINE PRESS—27006 Gap Rd., Three Oaks Farm, Brownsville, OR 97327–9718. Sponsors the Nicholas Roerich Prize of $1,000 plus publication for an original, unpublished book of poetry by a poet who has never been published in book form. Closes in October.

SYRACUSE UNIVERSITY PRESS—1600 Jamesville Ave., Syracuse, NY 13244–5160. Address Director. Sponsors John Ben Snow Prize: $1,500, plus publication, for an unpublished book-length nonfiction manuscript about New York State, especially upstate or central New York. Closes in December.

THEATERWORKS, INC.—P.O. Box 635, Boston, MA 02117. Conducts Clauder Competition for a full-length play by a New England writer. The prize is $3,000 and workshop production. Closes in June of even-numbered years.

THEATRE AMERICANA—P.O. Box 245, Altadena, CA 91001. Sponsors the $500 David James Ellis Memorial Award for an original, unproduced full-length play in two or three acts (no musicals or children's plays). Preference is given to American authors and to plays of the American scene. Closes in January.

U.S. NAVAL INSTITUTE—Membership Dept., A.B.E.C., Annapolis, MD 21402. Conducts the Arleigh Burke Essay Contest, with prizes of $2,000, $1,000, and $750, plus publication, for essays on the advancement of professional, literary, or scientific knowledge in the naval or maritime services, and the advancement of the knowledge of sea power. Closes in December.

UNIVERSITY OF ARKANSAS PRESS—Arkansas Poetry Award, Fayetteville, AR 72701. Awards publication of a 50- to 80-page poetry manuscript to a writer who has never had a book of poetry published. Closes in May.

UNIVERSITY OF GEORGIA PRESS—Athens, GA 30602. Offers Flannery O'Connor Award for Short Fiction: Two prizes of $1,000, plus publication, for a book-length collection of short fiction. Closes in July.

UNIVERSITY OF HAWAII AT MANOA—Dept. of Drama and Theatre, 1770 East-West Rd., Honolulu, HI 96822. Conducts annual Kumu Kahua Playwriting Contest with $500 prize for a full-length play, and $200 for a one-act, set in Hawaii and dealing with some aspect of the Hawaiian experience. Also conducts contest for plays written by Hawaiian residents. Write for conditions-of-entry brochure. Closes in January.

UNIVERSITY OF IOWA—Dept. of English, English-Philosophy Bldg., University of Iowa, Iowa City, IA 52242. Offers the John Simmons Short Fiction Award and the Iowa Short Fiction Award, each offering $1,000, plus publication, for an unpublished full-length collection of short stories (150 pages or more). Closes in September.

UNIVERSITY OF MASSACHUSETTS PRESS—Juniper Prize, Univ. of Massachusetts Press, c/o Mail Office, Amherst, MA 01003. Offers the annual Juniper Prize of $1,000, plus publication, for a book-length manuscript of poetry; awarded in odd-numbered years to writers who have never published a book of poetry, and in even-numbered years to writers who have published a book of poetry. Closes in September.

UNIVERSITY OF PITTSBURGH PRESS—127 N. Bellefield Ave., Pittsburgh, PA 15260. Sponsors Drue Heinz Literature Prize of $7,500, plus publication and royalty contract, for unpublished collection of short stories. Closes in August. Also sponsors the Agnes Lynch Starrett Poetry Prize of $2,000, plus publication in the Pitt Poetry Series, for a book-length collection of poems by a poet who has not yet published a volume of poetry. Closes in April.

TENNESSEE WILLIAMS/NEW ORLEANS LITERARY FESTIVAL— Suite 217, 5500 Prytania St., New Orleans, LA 70115. A $1,000 prize plus a reading at the festival is offered for an original, unpublished one-act play on an American subject. Closes in February.

WRITERS COLONIES

Writers colonies offer isolation and freedom from everyday distractions and a quiet place for writers to concentrate on their work. Though some colonies are quite small, with space for just three or four writers at a time, others can provide accommodations for as many as thirty or forty. The length of a residency may vary, too, from a couple of weeks to five or six months. These programs have strict admissions policies, and writers must submit a formal application or letter of intent, a resumé, writing samples, and letters of recommendation. Write for application information first, enclosing a stamped, self-addressed envelope. Residency fees listed are subject to change.

THE EDWARD F. ALBEE FOUNDATION, INC.—"The Barn," or the William Flanagan Memorial Creative Persons Center, on Long Island, is maintained by the Foundation. "The standards for admission are, simply, talent and need." Sixteen writers are accepted each season for one-month residencies, available from June 1st to October 1st; applications, including writing samples, project description, and resumé, are accepted from January 1st to April 1st. There is no fee, though residents are responsible for their own food and travel expenses. Write to: David Briggs, Foundation Secretary, The Edward F. Albee Foundation, Inc., 14 Harrison St., New York, NY 10013.

BLUE MOUNTAIN CENTER—Hosts month-long residencies for artists and writers from mid-June to mid-October. Fiction and nonfiction writers of "fine work which evinces social and ecological conern" are among the 14 residents accepted per session. Apply by sending a brief biographical sketch, a statement of your plan for work at Blue Mountain, names and phone numbers of three references, five slides or approximately 10 pages of work, an indication of your preference for an early summer, late summer, or fall residence, and a $20 application fee (due no later than February 1), to Harriet Barlow, Director, Blue Mountain Center, Blue Mountain Lake, NY 12812. There is no charge to residents for their time at Blue Mountain, although all visitors are invited to contribute to the studio construction fund. Brochure available upon request.

CENTRUM—Centrum sponsors month-long residencies at Fort Worden State Park, a Victorian fort on the Strait of Juan De Fuca in Washington. The program "provides a working retreat for selected artists to create, without distractions, in a beautiful setting." Nonfiction, fiction, and poetry writers may apply for residency awards, which include housing and a $75 a week stipend. Families are welcome, but no separate working space is provided. Application deadlines: October 1 and April 1. For details, send SASE to Sarah Muirhead, Centrum, P.O. Box 1158, Port Townsend, WA 98368.

COTTAGES AT HEDGEBROOK—"This is a retreat setting for women writers of all ages and all cultural backgrounds. Our total program is to support that activity by providing homey living space, nutritious meals, and a dedicated staff." Writers stay in single-occupancy cottages; dinner is eaten together. There are no fees, and limited travel subsidies are available. Applicants may request residencies ranging from one week to three months. April 1 is the application deadline for residencies from July 1 to December 10; October 1 for the period from January 10 to June 19; 25 writers are accepted each period. Write to: Nancy Nordhoff, Cottages at Hedgebrook, 2197 E. Millman Rd., Langley, WA 98260.

CUMMINGTON COMMUNITY OF THE ARTS—Residencies for artists of all disciplines. Living/studio space in individual cottages or in two main houses on 100 acres in the Berkshires. Work exchange available. During July and August, artists with children are encouraged to apply; there is a children's program with supervised activities. Fees are about $400 to $500 per month (children extra); financial aid available. Application deadlines: February 1st for April, May, June; March 15th for July, August; June 1st for September and October; and August 1st for November, December. Contact Lucius Parshall, Exec. Dir., Cummington Community of the Arts, RR#1, Box 145, Cummington, MA 01026.

CURRY HILL—Retreat for eight fiction and nonfiction writers, offered by writer/teacher Elizabeth Bowne each spring, usually the last week in April. "I care about writers and am delighted and enthusiastic when I can help develop talent." A $400 fee covers meals and lodging at Curry Hill, a family plantation home near Bainbridge, Georgia. Applications should be sent in early January; qualified applicants accepted on a first-come basis. Write to Mrs. Elizabeth Bowne, Curry Hill/ Georgia, c/o 404 Crestmont Ave., Hattiesburg, MS 39401.

DORLAND MOUNTAIN ARTS COLONY—Novelists, playwrights, poets, nonfiction writers, composers, and visual artists are encouraged to apply for residencies of two weeks to three months. Dorland is a nature preserve located in the Palomar Mountains of Southern California. "A primitive retreat for creative people. Without electricity, residents find a new, natural rhythm for their work." Fee of $150 a month includes cottage, fuel, and firewood. Application deadlines are March 1 and September 1. Send SASE to Admissions Committee, Dorland Mt. Arts Colony, Box 6, Temecula, CA 92593.

DORSET COLONY HOUSE—Writers and playwrights are offered low-cost room with kitchen facilities at the historic Colony House in Dorset, Vermont. Residencies are one week to 2 months, and are available between October 1st and June 1st. Applications are accepted year round, and up to eight writers stay at a time. The fee is $75 per week; financial aid is limited. For more information, send SASE to John Nassivera, Director, Dorset Colony House, Dorset, VT 05251.

FINE ARTS WORK CENTER IN PROVINCETOWN—Fellowships, including living and studio space and monthly stipends, are available at the Fine Arts Work Center on Cape Cod, for writers to work independently. Residencies are for seven months long (October to May); apply before February 1 deadline. Eight first-year fellows and two second-year fellows are accepted. For details, send SASE to Susan Slocum, Exec. Dir., Fine Arts Work Center, P.O. Box 565, 24 Pearl St., Provincetown, MA 02657.

THE HAMBIDGE CENTER—"An environment for those in search of creative excellence in the arts, humanities, and sciences." Six private cottages are available for fellows, who are asked to contribute about $125 per week. Two-week to two-month residencies, from May to October, are offered to writers, artists, composers, historians, humanists, and scientists at the Hambidge Center for Creative Arts and Sciences located on 600 acres of quiet woods in the north Georgia mountains. Send SASE for application form to Judy Barber, Director, The Hambidge Center, P.O. Box 339, Rabun Gap, GA 30568. Application reviews begin March 25.

KALANI HONUA—Located in a country, coastal setting of 20 botanical acres, Kalani Honua "provides participants with quality educational programs and the aloha experience that is its namesake: harmony of heaven and earth." Residencies range from two weeks to two months and are available throughout the year. Fees range from $20 to $80 per day, depending on accommodations; fee subsidies are available. Applications accepted year round. Write to: Richard Koob, Program Coordinator, Kalani Honua, Artist-in-Residence Program, RR2, Box 4500, Kalapana, HI 96778.

THE MACDOWELL COLONY—Studios, room and board at the Mac-Dowell Colony of Peterborough, New Hampshire, are available for writers to work without interruption in semi-rural woodland setting. Selection is competitive. Apply by January 15 for stays May through August; April 15 for September through December; and September 15 for January through April. Residencies last up to eight weeks, and 80 to 90 writers are accepted each year. The suggested residency fee is $15 per day. For details and application forms, send SASE to Admissions Coordinator, The MacDowell Colony, 100 High St., Peterborough, NH 03458.

THE MILLAY COLONY FOR THE ARTS—At Steepletop in Austerlitz, New York (former home of Edna St. Vincent Millay), studios, living quarters, and meals are provided to writers at no cost. Residencies are for one month. Application deadlines are February 1, May 1, and September 1. For information and an application form, write to Gail Giles, Asst. Dir., Millay Colony for the Arts, Inc., Steepletop, P.O. Box 3, Austerlitz, NY 12017–0003.

MONTALVO CENTER FOR THE ARTS—One- to three-month, low-cost residencies at the Villa Montalvo in the foothills of the Santa Cruz Mountains south of San Francisco, for writers working on specific projects. There are a few small fellowships available to writers with demonstrable financial need. September 1st and April 1st are the application deadlines. Send self-addressed envelope and 98¢ stamp for application forms to Admissions Dir., Montalvo Residency Program, P.O. Box 158, Saratoga, CA 95071.

THE NORTHWOOD INSTITUTE—"The Fellowship Program allows individuals time away from their ongoing daily routines to pursue their project ideas without interruption. A project idea should be innovative, creative, and have potential for impact in its field." Four ten-week residencies, lasting from mid-June to mid-August, are awarded yearly. There are no fees and a modest stipend is provided. Applications are due December 31st. Send SASE to Carol B. Coppage, Dir., The Northwood Institute, Alden B. Dow Creativity Center, Midland, MI 48640–2398.

PALENVILLE INTERARTS COLONY—Support is provided for "artists of the highest calibre in all disciplines, either working alone or in groups. The admissions panel is interested in interartistic collaboration and intercultural projects." Residencies last from one to eight weeks, and fees range from $125 to $260 per week; scholarships are available. About 50 applicants are accepted for May through October season. April 1st is the deadline for writers seeking grants and financial aid; otherwise deadline is July 1st. Send SASE to: Palenville Interarts Colony, 2 Bond St., New York, NY 10012.

RAGDALE FOUNDATION—Residencies from two weeks to two months are available for writers, artists, and composers. "Uninterrupted time and peaceful space allow writers a chance to finish works in progress, to begin new works, to solve thorny creative problems, and to experiment in new genres." Located in Lake Forest, Illinois, 30 miles north of Chicago, on 40 acres of prairie. Low fees; some full and partial fee waivers available. Deadlines are January 15 for May-August; April 15 for September-December; and September 15 for January-April. Late applications considered when space is available. For application, send SASE to Ragdale Foundation, 1260 N. Green Bay Rd., Lake Forest, IL 60045.

MILDRED I. REID WRITERS COLONY—A country setting with pine groves, a brook, and a village on the Contoocook River. Much of the day is spent writing or revising. Two mornings a week are set aside for private writing consultations, and in the two evening classes, work is read and analyzed, and Ms. Reid lectures on various writing techniques. Residents may stay from one to six weeks during July and August. Ten writers stay each week, at the rate of $125 to $170 per week. Work exchange fee subsidies are available. Write to: Mildred I. Reid, Mildred I. Reid Writers Colony, Penacook Rd., RR5, Box 51, Contoocook, NH 03229.

THE TYRONE GUTHRIE CENTRE—"The mansion is set on a 400-acre country estate. The Guthrie Centre offers peace and seclusion to writers and other artists to enable them to get on with their work. All art forms are represented." One- to three-month residencies are offered throughout the year, at the rate of 1,200 Irish pounds per month; financial assistance available to Irish citizens only. Writers may apply for acceptance year round. Write to: Bernard Loughlin, Dir., The Tyrone Guthrie Centre, Annaghmakerrig, Newbliss, County Monaghan, Ireland.

UCROSS FOUNDATION—Residencies, two weeks to four months, at the Ucross Foundation in the foothills of the Big Horn Mountains in Wyoming, "with lots of open spaces," for writers, artists, and scholars to concentrate on their work without interruptions. Two residency sessions are scheduled annually: January-May

706

and August-November. There is no charge for room, board, or studio space. Application deadlines are March 1 for fall session and October 1 for spring session. For more information, send SASE to Director, Residency Program, Ucross Foundation, 2836 US Hwy 14–16 East, Clearmont, WY 82835.

VERMONT STUDIO CENTER—Four- and eight-week residencies are available January through April. Fellowships are awarded. Applications may be submitted at any time up to a year in advance and are reviewed on a monthly basis. Write to: Susan Kowalsky, Vermont Studio Center, P.O. Box 613, Johnson, VT 05656.

VIRGINIA CENTER FOR THE CREATIVE ARTS—"Rural and bucolic. Our philosophy is to give artists the opportunity to work without invasion or interruption, as long as they want." Residencies are up to three months, available all year. Application deadlines are the 25th of January, May, and September; about 300 residents are accepted each year. A limited amount of financial assistance is available. For more information, send SASE to Admissions Committee, Virginia Center for the Creative Arts, Sweet Briar, VA 24595.

HELENE WURLITZER FOUNDATION OF NEW MEXICO—Rent-free and utility-free studios at the Helene Wurlitzer Foundation in Taos, New Mexico, are offered to creative writers and artists in all media. All artists are given the "opportunity to be free of the shackles of a nine-to-five routine." Length of residency varies from three to six months. The Foundation is closed from October 1 through March 31 annually. For details, write to Henry A. Sauerwein, Jr., Exec. Dir., The Helene Wurlitzer Foundation of New Mexico, Box 545, Taos, NM 87571.

YADDO—Artists, writers, and composers are invited for stays from two weeks to two months at Yaddo in Saratoga Springs, New York. Voluntary payment of $20 a day is requested. No artist deemed worthy of admission by the judging panels will be denied admission on the basis of an inability to contribute. Deadlines are January 15 and August 1. Send SASE for application to Myra Sklarew, President, Yaddo, Box 395, Saratoga Springs, NY 12866. An application fee of $20 is required.

WRITERS CONFERENCES

Each year, hundreds of writers conferences are held across the country. The following list, arranged geographically, represents a sampling of conferences; each listing includes the location of the conference, the month during which it is usually held, and the name of the person from whom specific information may be received. Additional conferences are listed annually in the May issue of *The Writer* Magazine (120 Boylston St., Boston, MA 02116–4615).

ALASKA

SITKA SUMMER WRITERS SYMPOSIUM—Sitka, AK. June. Write Box 2420, Sitka, AK 99835.

ANNUAL TRAVEL WRITING CONFERENCE—Juneau, AK. June. Write Tony Soltys, UAS Cont. Ed., 11120-W Glacier Hwy., Juneau, AK 99801–8682.

ARIZONA

PIMA WRITERS' WORKSHOP—Tucson, AZ. May. Write Peg Files, Dir., Pima College, 2202 W. Anklam Rd., Tucson, AZ 85709.

ANNUAL ARIZONA CHRISTIAN WRITER'S CONFERENCE—Phoenix, AZ. October. Write Reg Forder, Dir., P.O. Box 5168, Phoenix, AZ 85010.

ARKANSAS

ARKANSAS WRITER'S CONFERENCE—Little Rock, AR. June. Write Clovita Rice, Dir., 1115 Gillette Dr., Little Rock, AR 72207.

OZARK CREATIVE WRITERS, INC.—Eureka Springs, AR. October. Write Peggy Vining, Dir., 6817 Gingerbread Ln., Little Rock, AR 72204.

CALIFORNIA

SAN DIEGO STATE UNIVERSITY WRITERS CONFERENCE—San Diego, CA. January. Write SDSU Extended Studies, San Diego, CA 92182.

BAY AREA WRITERS' WORKSHOP—Oakland, CA. Weekend dates June-August. Write Laura Jason, Dir., P.O. Box 620327, Woodside, CA 94062.

CALIFORNIA WRITERS' CONFERENCE—Pacific Grove, CA. July. Write Dorothy V. Benson, 2214 Derby St., Berkeley, CA 94705.

ANNUAL BLACK WRITERS CONFERENCE—San Francisco, CA. July. Write E. Crutchfield, International Black Writers & Artists, Inc., 5312 Normandie, Oakland, CA 94619.

ANNUAL WRITERS CONFERENCE IN CHILDREN'S LITERATURE—Los Angeles, CA. August. Write Lin Oliver, Dir., SCBW, P.O. Box 66296, Mar Vista Station, Los Angeles, CA 90066.

ANNUAL WOMEN'S NATIONAL BOOK ASSOCIATION CONFERENCE—Culver City, CA. October. Send SASE to Sue Mac Laurin, Dir., Women's National Book Association, 3554 Crownridge Dr., Sherman Oaks, CA 91403.

COLORADO

WRITERS IN THE ROCKIES—Denver, Boulder, and Ft. Collins, CO. June-August. Write James D. Hutchinson, Dir., The Writers Studio, 837 15th St.,Boulder, CO 80302.

ASPEN WRITERS' CONFERENCE—Aspen, CO. July. Write Kurt Brown and Laure-Anne Bosselaar, Dirs., Box 5840, Snowmass Village, CO 81615.

SCBW ANNUAL ROCKY MOUNTAIN WRITERS RETREAT—Colorado Springs, CO. July. Write Mary Fritt, Society of Children's Book Writers, 807 Hercules Pl., Colorado Springs, CO 80906.

STEAMBOAT SPRINGS WRITERS CONFERENCE—Steamboat Springs, CO. August. Write Harriet Freiberger, Dir., P.O. Box 774284, Steamboat Springs CO 80477.

NATIONAL WRITERS CLUB INTERNATIONAL CONFERENCE—Denver, CO. October. Write James L. Young, Dir., National Writers Club, 1450 S. Havana, Suite 620, Aurora, CO 80012.

CONNECTICUT

WESLEYAN WRITERS CONFERENCE—Middletown, CT. June. Write Anne Greene, Dir., Wesleyan Writers Conf., Wesleyan Univ., Middletown, CT 06457.

WRITERS RETREAT WORKSHOP—Bristol, CT. October. Write Gary Provost, Dir., WRW, P.O. Box 139, S. Lancaster, MA 01561.

WASHINGTON, DC

WIW SPRING CONFERENCE—Washington, DC. May. Write Isolde Chapin, Dir., Washington Independent Writers, 220 Woodward Bldg., 733 15th St. N.W., Washington, D.C. 20005.

FLORIDA

KEY WEST LITERARY SEMINAR—Key West, FL. January. Write Key West Literary Seminars, P.O. Box 391, Sugarloaf Shores, FL 33044.

FLORIDA SPACE COAST WRITERS CONFERENCE—Melbourne, FL. March. Write Dr. Edwin J. Kirschner, F.S.C.W.C., Box 804, Melbourne, FL 32902.

ANNUAL FLORIDA STATE WRITERS CONFERENCE—Ft. Lauderdale, FL. May. Write Dana K. Cassell, Dir., Florida Freelance Writers Assoc., P.O. Box 9844, Ft. Lauderdale, FL 33310.

GEORGIA

ANNUAL COUNCIL OF AUTHORS AND JOURNALISTS CONFERENCE—St. Simmons Island, GA. June. Write Tamela Thomas, Dir., 1214 Laurel Hill Dr., Decatur, GA 30033.

HAWAII

1991 LDS WRITER'S CONFERENCE—Laie, HI. June. Write Dr. Chris Crowe, Dir., Div. of Cont. Ed., Brigham Young University, Laie, HI 96762.

ILLINOIS

INTERNATIONAL WOMEN'S WRITING GUILD MIDWEST CONFERENCE—New York, NY. May. Write Hannelore Hahn, IWWG, P.O. Box 810, Gracie Station, New York, NY 10028.

ANNUAL CHRISTIAN WRITERS INSTITUTE CONFERENCE—Wheaton, IL. June. Write June Eaton, Dir., Christian Writers Inst., 388 E. Gundersen Dr., Carol Stream, IL 60188.

OF DARK AND STORMY NIGHTS ANNUAL CONFERENCE—Evanston, IL. June. Write Betty Nicholas, Dir., Mystery Writers of America-Midwest Chapter, Box 8, Techny, IL 60082.

MOODY WRITE-TO-PUBLISH CONFERENCE—Chicago, IL. June. Write Lin Johnson, Dir., Moody Bible Institute, 820 N. LaSalle Dr., Chicago, IL 60610.

ILLINOIS WESLEYAN UNIVERSITY WRITERS' CONFERENCE—Bloomington, IL. August. Write Bettie Wilson Story, Dir., IWUWC, P.O. Box 2900, Bloomington, IL 61702.

INDIANA

WRITERS, ILLUSTRATORS CONFERENCE IN CHILDREN'S LITERATURE—Indianapolis, IN. June. Write Betsy Storey, Dir., Indiana Society Of Children's Book Writers, 4810 Illinois Rd, Ft. Wayne, IN 46804.

MIDWEST WRITERS WORKSHOP—Muncie, IN. August. Write Earl L. Conn, Dept. of Journalism, Ball State Univ., Muncie, IN 47306.

IOWA

IOWA SUMMER WRITING FESTIVAL—Iowa City, IA. June, July. Write Peggy Houston, Dir., Cont. Ed., 116 International Center, Univ. of Iowa, Iowa City, IA 52242.

EXPLORING MYSTERY FOR NON-MYSTERY WRITERS—Cedar Rapids, IA. October. Write Marvin E. Ceynar, Dir., 300 Cherry Hill Rd. N.W., Cedar Rapids, IA 52405.

KANSAS

NATIONAL LAMPLIGHTERS WRITERS CONFERENCE—North Newton, KS. July. Write Sharon Stanhope, Dir., Box 415, Benton, KS 67017–0415.

KENTUCKY

CARTER CAVES WRITER'S WORKSHOP—Olive Hill, KY. June. Write Lee Pennington, Dir., Carter Caves State Resort Park, Olive Hill, KY 41164.

ANNUAL WRITING WORKSHOP FOR PEOPLE OVER 57—Lexington, KY. June. Write Roberta James, Donovan Scholars Program, Univ. of Kentucky, Ligon House, 658 S. Limestone St., Lexington, KY 40506–0442.

ANNUAL GREEN RIVER WRITERS' RETREAT—Louisville, KY. July, August. Write Deborah Spears, Dir., 403 S. Sixth St., Ironton, OH 45638.

APPALACHIAN WRITERS WORKSHOP—Hindman, KY. August. Write Mike Mullins, Dir., Box 844, Hindman, KY 41822.

LOUISIANA

ANNUAL ROMANCE WRITERS OF AMERICA CONFERENCE—New Orleans, LA. July. Write Darlene Layman, Coord., 13700 Veterans Memorial, Suite 315, Houston TX 77014.

DEEP SOUTH WRITERS CONFERENCE—Lafayette, LA. September. Write John Fiero, Dir., DSWC, P.O. Drawer 44691, USL Sta., Lafayette, LA 70504–4691.

MAINE

ANNUAL STONECOAST WRITERS' CONFERENCE—Portland, ME. July, August. Write Univ. of Southern Maine, Summer Session, 96 Falmouth St., Portland, ME 04103.

ANNUAL STATE OF MAINE WRITERS' CONFERENCE—Ocean Park, ME. August. Write Richard F. Burns, Dir., P.O. Box 296, Ocean Park, ME 04063.

MARYLAND

WESTERN MARYLAND WRITERS' WORKSHOP—Frostburg, MD. June. Write Barbara Wilson, Dir., Frostburg State Univ., Dept. of English, Frostburg, MD 21532.

MASSACHUSETTS

NEW ENGLAND WRITERS' WORKSHOP AT SIMMONS COLLEGE—Boston, MA. June. Write Theodore Vrettos, Dir., Simmons College, 300 The Fenway, Boston, MA 02115.

HARVARD SUMMER WRITING PROGRAM—Cambridge, MA. June-August. Write Harvard Summer School, Dept. 457, 20 Garden St., Cambridge, MA 02138.

CAPE COD WRITERS CONFERENCE—Craigville, MA. August. Write Marion Vuilleumier, Dir., CCWC c/o Cape Cod Conservatory of Music & Arts, Route 132, West Barnstable, MA 02668.

ANNUAL CHRISTIAN WRITERS CONFERENCE—Orleans, MA. October. Write Kathie Fetveit, P.O. Box 443, Cornville, AZ 86325.

MICHIGAN

INTERNATIONAL CHRISTIAN WRITERS WORKSHOP—Berrien Springs, MI. June. Write Ronald W. Bowes, Dir., ICWW-Lifelong Learning, Andrews University, Berrien Springs, MI 49104–0050.

MIDLAND WRITERS CONFERENCE—Midland, MI. June. Write Eileen Finzel and Margaret Allen, Dirs., Grace A. Dow Memorial Library, 1710 W. St. Andrews, Midland, MI 48640.

MINNESOTA

YOUNG PLAYWRIGHTS' SUMMER CONFERENCE—St. Paul, MN. June. Write Sally MacDonald, Outreach Dir., The Playwrights' Center, Franklin Ave. E., Minneapolis, MN 55406.

MISSOURI

ANNUAL MARK TWAIN WRITER'S CONFERENCE—Hannibal, MO. June. Write Dr. James C. Hefley, Dir., Hannibal-LaGrange College, 921 Center St., Hannibal, MO 63401.

WRITING FOR CHILDREN WORKSHOP—Springfield, MO. July. Write Sandy Asher, Dir., 900 N. Benton, Springfield, MO 65802.

MONTANA

ANNUAL "GATHERING AT BIGFORK"—Bigfork, MT. May. Write Malcolm Hillgartner, Dir., P.O. Box 1230, Bigfork, MT 59911.

YELLOW BAY WRITERS' WORKSHOP—Flathead Lake, MT. August. Write Annick Smith and Judy Jones, Dirs., Center for Cont. Ed., Univ. of Montana, Missoula, MT 59812.

NEBRASKA

ANNUAL MIDWEST MYSTERY AND SUSPENSE CONVENTION—Omaha, NE. May. Write Baker Square Little Professor Book Center, 13455 W. Center Rd., Omaha, NE 68144.

NEW HAMPSHIRE

SCBW NEW ENGLAND CONFERENCE—Concord, NH. May. Write Jane H. Mruczek, Regional Advisor, Society Of Children's Book Writers, 188 Amherst St., Wethersfield, CT 06109.

MILDRED I. REID WRITERS COLONY—Contoocook, NH. July, August. Write Mildred I. Reid, Dir., Penacook Rd., Contoocook, NH 03229.

ANNUAL SEACOAST WRITERS CONFERENCE—Portsmouth, NH. September. Write Urban Forestry Center, P.O. Box 6553, Portsmouth, NH 03802–6553.

NEW JERSEY

ANNUAL NEW JERSEY WRITING CONFRENCE—Morristown,NJ. November. Write Hannelore Hahn, Dir., International Women's Writing Guild, P.O.-Box 810, Gracie Station, NY 10028.

NEW MEXICO

WRITERS' CONFERENCE AT SANTA FE—Santa Fe, NM. June. Write Ruth Crowley, Dir., Santa Fe Community College, P.O. Box 4187, Santa Fe, NM 87502–4187.

SOUTHWEST CHRISTIAN WRITERS ASSOCIATION—Farmington, NM. August. Write Patricia A. Burke, Dir., P.O. Box 2635, Farmington, NM 87499.

SOUTHWEST WRITERS WORKSHOP—Albuquerque, NM. September. Write Paula Paul and Eileen Stanton, Dirs., P.O. Box 14632, Albuquerque, NM 87191.

NEW YORK

ANNUAL ASJA WRITER'S CONFERENCE—New York, NY. May. Write Ruth Winter, Dir., American Society Of Journalists & Authors, Inc., 1501 Broadway, #1907, New York, NY 10036.

HIGHLIGHTS FOUNDATION WRITERS WORKSHOP AT CHAUTAUQUA—Chautauqua, NY. July. Write Jan Keen, Dir., Dept WC, 711 Court St., Honesdale, PA 18431.

FEMINIST WOMEN'S WRITING WORKSHOPS, INC.—Aurora, NY. July. Write Rachel Guido deVries,Dir., FWWW, P.O. Box 6583, Ithaca, NY 14851.

ANNUAL IWWG SUMMER CONFERENCE—Saratoga Springs, NY. July, August. Write Hannelore Hahn, Exec. Dir., International Women's Writing Guild, P.O. Box 810, Gracie Station, NY 10028.

HOFSTRA UNIVERSITY SUMMER WRITERS' CONFERENCE—Hempstead, NY. August. Write Lewis Shena, U.C.C.E., Davison Hall, 205, Hempstead, NY 11550.

NORTH CAROLINA

BLUE RIDGE WRITERS CONFERENCE—Montreat, NC. June. Write Yvonne Lehman, P.O. Box 188, Black Mountain, NC 28711.

NORTH DAKOTA

WRITERS CONFERENCE IN CHILDREN'S LITERATURE—Grand Forks, ND. October. Write Faythe Thureen, Dir., English Dept., Univ. of North Dakota, Grand Forks, ND 58202.

OHIO

ANTIOCH WRITERS' WORKSHOP—Yellow Springs, OH. July. Write Sandra Love, Dir., 135 N. Walnut St., Yellow Springs, OH 45387.

ANNUAL SKYLINE WRITERS' CONFERENCE—North Royalton, OH. August. Write Linda Buchsbaum,Dir., 737 Bridle Ln., Berea, OH 44017.

ANNUAL MIDWEST WRITERS' CONFERENCE—Canton, OH. October. Write Gregg L. Andrews, Dir., 6000 Frank Ave. N.W., Canton, OH 44720.

OKLAHOMA

OKLAHOMA WRITER'S FEDERATION CONFERENCE—Oklahoma City, OK. May. Write Nancy Salisbury, Pres., Rt. 2, Box 109, Vici, OK 73859.

ANNUAL WRITERS OF CHILDREN'S LITERATURE CONFERENCE—Lawton, OK. June. Write Dr. George E. Stanley, P.O. Box 16355, Cameron Univ. Station, Lawton, OK 73505.

OREGON

HAYSTACK PROGRAM IN THE ARTS AND SCIENCES—Cannon Beach, OR. July, August. Portland State Univ., Summer Session, P.O. Box 751, Portland, OR 97207.

OREGON ASSOCIATION OF CHRISTIAN WRITERS CONFERENCE—Turner, OR. August. Write Kristen Johnson Ingram, Dir., 1831 Menlo Loop, Springfield, OR 97477.

PENNSYLVANIA

ANNUAL PENNWRITERS' CONFERENCE—Pittsburgh, PA. May. Write Polly Moran, Dir., 775 Cottonwood Dr., Monroeville, PA 15146.

ST. DAVIDS CHRISTIAN WRITERS' CONFERENCE—St. Davids, PA. June. Write S. Eaby, Registrar, 1775 Eden Rd., Lancaster, PA 17601–3523.

SOUTH CAROLINA

FRANCIS MARION WRITERS' RETREAT—Florence, SC. May. Write Robert Parham, Dir., Francis Marion College,P.O. Box 7500, Florence, SC 29501.

SOUTH DAKOTA

BLACK HILLS WRITERS CONFERENCE—Hill City, SD. July. Write Paul Lippman, Dir., Authors and Artists Agency, 4444 Lakeside Dr., Burbank, CA 91505.

TENNESSEE

WRITING FOR CHILDREN—Memphis, TN. June-August. Write Renee Cooley, Dir., Rhodes College, 2000 N. Parkway, Memphis, TN 38112.

TEXAS

WRITERS INFORMATION NETWORK—Houston, TX. May, October. Write Elaine Wright Colvin, Dir., P.O. Box 11337, Bainbridge Island, WA 98110.

SOCIETY OF CHILDREN'S BOOK WRITERS CONFERENCE—Arlington, TX. July. Write Marilyn Yates, Dir., 3909 Allendale, Colleyville, TX 76034.

ANNUAL CRAFT OF WRITING CONFERENCE—Dallas, TX. September. Write Janet Harris, Dir., UTD Center for Cont. Ed., P.O. Box 830688, M/S, CN1.1, Richardson, TX 75083–0688.

UTAH

WRITERS AT WORK—Park City, UT. June. Write Dave Bean, Dir., Writers at Work, P.O. Box 3182, Park City, UT 84060.

VERMONT

BENNINGTON WRITING WORKSHOPS—Bennington, VT. July. Write Sally Cahill, Bennington Writing Workshops, Bennington College, Bennington, VT 05201.

ANNUAL BREAD LOAF WRITERS' CONFERENCE—Ripton, VT. August. Write Bread Loaf Writers' Conference, Middlebury College, W. Middlebury, VT 05753.

VIRGINIA

ANNUAL HIGHLAND SUMMER CONFERENCE—Radford, VA. June.

Write Dr. Grace Toney Edwards, Dir., Box 5917, Radford Univ., Radford, VA 24142.

SCBW WRITING FOR THE JUVENILE MARKET CONFERENCE— Richmond, VA. June. Write T.R. Hollingsworth, Society of Children's Book Writers, P.O. Box 1707, Midlothian, VA 23112.

BLUE RIDGE WRITERS CONFERENCE—Salem, VA. October. Write Mary Jo Shannon, Dir., 2824 Northview Drive, Roanoke, VA 24015.

WASHINGTON

SEATTLE PACIFIC CHRISTIAN WRITERS' CONFERENCE—Seattle, WA. June. Write Linda Wagner, Dir., Humanities Dept., Seattle Pacific Univ., Seattle, WA 98119.

CLARION WEST WRITERS' WORKSHOP—Seattle, WA. June, July. Write Donna Davis, Clarion West Writers' Workshop, 340 15th Ave., East, Suite 350, Seattle, WA 98112.

PORT TOWNSEND WRITERS' CONFERENCE—Port Townsend, WA. July. Write Carol Jane Bangs, Dir., CENTRUM, Box 1158, Port Townsend, WA 98368.

WEST VIRGINIA

ANNUAL GOLDEN ROD WRITERS CONFERENCE—Morgantown, WV. October. Write George M. Lies, P.O. Box 239, Morgantown, WV 26505.

WISCONSIN

WRITE TOUCH CONFERENCE—Milwaukee, WI. May. Send SASE to Susie M. Just, Wisconsin Romance Writers Of America, P.O. Box 1015, Brookfield, WI 53008.

WYOMING

WYOMING WRITER'S CONFERENCE—Rock Springs, WY. May. Write Kathy Zumpfe, Dir., 404 Cook Dr., Rock Springs, WY 82901.

CANADA

AMERICAN MEDICAL WRITERS ASSOCIATION CONFERENCE— Toronto, Canada. October. Write AMWA, 9650 Rockville Pike, Bethesda, MD 20814.

MARITIME WRITERS' WORKSHOP—Fredericton, New Brunswick. July. Write Glenda Turner, Dir., Dept. of Extension, Univ. of New Brunswick, P.O. Box 4400, Fredericton, NB, Canada E3B 5A3.

INTERNATIONAL

"MAGIC WORDS," WRITING WITH D.M. THOMAS—Cornwall, England. September, October. Write D.M. Thomas, Coach House, Rashleigh Vale, Truro, Cornwall, TR1 1TJ, England.

STATE ARTS COUNCILS

State arts councils sponsor grants, fellowships, and other programs for writers. To be eligible for funding, a writer *must* be a resident of the state in which he is applying. For more information, write to the addresses below.

ALABAMA STATE COUNCIL ON THE ARTS
Albert B. Head, Executive Director
One Dexter Ave.
Montgomery, AL 36130

ALASKA STATE COUNCIL ON THE ARTS
Christine D'Arcy, Director
411 W. 4th Ave., Suite 1E
Anchorage, AK 99501–2343

ARIZONA COMMISSION ON THE ARTS
Shelley Cohn, Executive Director
417 W. Roosevelt
Phoenix, AZ 85003

ARKANSAS ARTS COUNCIL
The Heritage Center, Suite 200
225 E. Markham
Little Rock, AR 72201

CALIFORNIA ARTS COUNCIL
Public Information Office
2411 Alhambra Blvd.
Sacramento, CA 95817

COLORADO COUNCIL ON THE ARTS AND HUMANITIES
Barbara Neal, Executive Director
750 Pennsylvania St.
Denver, CO 80203–3699

CONNECTICUT COMMISSION ON THE ARTS
John Ostrout, Acting Executive Director
227 Lawrence St.
Hartford, CT 06106

DELAWARE DIVISION OF THE ARTS
Cecelia Fitzgibbon, Director
Carvel State Building
820 N. French St.
Wilmington, DE 19801

FLORIDA ARTS COUNCIL
Ms. Peyton Fearington
Dept. of State
Div. of Cultural Affairs
The Capitol
Tallahassee, FL 32399–0250

GEORGIA COUNCIL FOR THE ARTS
Literary Coordinator
2082 E. Exchange Pl., Suite 100
Tucker, GA 30084

HAWAII STATE FOUNDATION ON CULTURE AND THE ARTS
Wendell P.K. Silva, Executive Director
335 Merchant St., Room 202
Honolulu, HI 96813

IDAHO COMMISSION ON THE ARTS
304 W. State St.
Boise, ID 83720

ILLINOIS ARTS COUNCIL
Richard Gage, Communication Arts Program Director
State of Illinois Center
100 W. Randolph, Suite 10–500
Chicago, IL 60601

INDIANA ARTS COMMISSION
402 W. Washington St., Rm. 072
Indianapolis, IN 46204–2741

IOWA STATE ARTS COUNCIL
Iowa Literary Awards
Capitol Complex
Des Moines, IA 50319

KANSAS ARTS COMMISSION
Robert T. Burtch, Information Coordinator
700 Jackson, Suite 1004
Topeka, KS 66603–3731

KENTUCKY ARTS COUNCIL
31 Fountain Pl.
Frankfort, KY 40601

LOUISIANA COUNCIL FOR MUSIC AND PERFORMING ARTS
Literature Program Associate
7524 St. Charles Ave.
New Orleans, LA 70118

MAINE ARTS COMMISSION
David Cadigan
State House, Station 25
Augusta, ME 04333

MARYLAND STATE ARTS COUNCIL
Linda Vlasak, Program Director
Artists-in-Education
15 W. Mulberry St.
Baltimore, MD 21201

MASSACHUSETTS CULTURAL COUNCIL
Tesair Lauve, Literature Coordinator
80 Boylston St., 10th Fl.
Boston, MA 02116

MICHIGAN COUNCIL FOR THE ARTS
Barbara K. Goldman, Executive Director
1200 Sixth Ave., Suite 1180
Detroit, MI 48226–2461

717

MINNESOTA STATE ARTS BOARD
Karen Mueller
Artist Assistance Program Associate
432 Summit Ave.
St. Paul, MN 55102

COMPAS: WRITERS AND ARTISTS IN THE SCHOOLS
Molly LaBerge, Executive Director
Daniel Gabriel, Director
305 Landmark Center
75 W. 5th St.
St. Paul, MN 55102

MISSISSIPPI ARTS COMMISSION
Jane Crater Hiatt, Executive Director
239 N. Lamar St., Suite 207
Jackson, MS 39201

MISSOURI ARTS COUNCIL
Autry Jackson, Program Administrator for Literature
Wainwright Office Complex
111 N. 7th St., Suite 105
St. Louis, MO 63101–2188

MONTANA ARTS COUNCIL
Julia A. Smith, Director, Artist Services
New York Block
48 North Last Chance Gulch
Helena, MT 59620

NEBRASKA ARTS COUNCIL
Jennifer S. Clark, Executive Director
1313 Farnam On-the-Mall
Omaha, NE 68102–1873

NEVADA STATE COUNCIL ON THE ARTS
William L. Fox, Executive Director
329 Flint St.
Reno, NV 89501

NEW HAMPSHIRE STATE COUNCIL ON THE ARTS
Phenix Hall, 40 N. Main St.
Concord, NH 03301–4974

NEW JERSEY STATE COUNCIL ON THE ARTS
Grants Office
4 N. Broad St. CN-306
Trenton, NJ 08625

NEW MEXICO ARTS DIVISION
Artists Residency Program
228 E. Palace Ave.
Santa Fe, NM 87501

NEW YORK STATE COUNCIL ON THE ARTS
Jewelle L. Gomez, Director, Literature Program
915 Broadway
New York, NY 10010

NORTH CAROLINA ARTS COUNCIL
Deborah McGill, Literature Director
Dept. of Cultural Resources
Raleigh, NC 27601–2807

NORTH DAKOTA COUNCIL ON THE ARTS
Vern Goodin, Executive Director
Black Building, Suite 606
Fargo, ND 58102

OHIO ARTS COUNCIL
727 E. Main St.
Columbus, OH 43205–1796

STATE ARTS COUNCIL OF OKLAHOMA
Laurie Foor, Assistant Director
Jim Thorpe Bldg., Room 640
Oklahoma City, OK 73105

OREGON ARTS COMMISSION
835 Summer St., N.E.
Salem, OR 97301

PENNSYLVANIA COUNCIL ON THE ARTS
Derek Gordon, Literature and Theatre Programs
Diane Young, Artists-in-Education Program
Room 216, Finance Bldg.
Harrisburg, PA 17120

RHODE ISLAND STATE COUNCIL ON THE ARTS
Iona B. Dobbins, Executive Director
95 Cedar St., Suite 103
Providence, RI 02903

SOUTH CAROLINA ARTS COMMISSION
Steve Lewis, Director, Literary Arts Program
1800 Gervais St.
Columbia, SC 29201

SOUTH DAKOTA ARTS COUNCIL
108 W. 11th St.
Sioux Falls, SD 57102–0788

TENNESSEE ARTS COMMISSION
320 Sixth Ave., N., Suite 100
Nashville, TN 37243–0780

TEXAS COMMISSION ON THE ARTS
P.O. Box 13406
Austin, TX 78711–3406

UTAH ARTS COUNCIL
G. Barnes, Literary Arts Coordinator
617 East South Temple
Salt Lake City, UT 84102

VERMONT COUNCIL ON THE ARTS
Cornelia Carey, Grants Officer
136 State St.
Montpelier, VT 05602

719

VIRGINIA COMMISSION FOR THE ARTS
Peggy J. Baggett, Executive Director
223 Governor St.
Richmond, VA 23219

WASHINGTON STATE ARTS COMMISSION
110 9th and Columbia Bldg., MS GH-11
Olympia, WA 98504–4111

WEST VIRGINIA DEPT. OF EDUCATION AND THE ARTS
Culture and History Division
Arts and Humanities Section
The Cultural Center, Capitol Complex
Charleston, WV 25305

WISCONSIN ARTS BOARD
Dean Amhaus, Executive Director
131 W. Wilson St., Suite 301
Madison, WI 53703

WYOMING ARTS COUNCIL
Joy Thompson, Director
2320 Capitol Ave.
Cheyenne, WY 82002

ORGANIZATIONS FOR WRITERS

THE ACADEMY OF AMERICAN POETS
177 E. 87th St.
New York, NY 10128
Mrs. Edward T. Chase, *President*
    The Academy of American Poets was founded in 1934 to promote American poetry through fellowships, awards programs, public programs, and publications. The Academy offers an annual fellowship for distinguished poetic achievement, the Peter I. B. Lavan Younger Poet Awards, three major book awards, and sponsors prizes for poetry at 178 universities and colleges nationwide. The Academy's readings, lectures, and regional symposia take place at various New York City locations and other locations in the United States. Membership is open to all: $45 annual fee includes subscription to the bimonthly newsletter, *Poetry Pilot*, and complimentary copies of prize book selections.

AMERICAN CRIME WRITERS LEAGUE
12 St. Ann Dr.
Santa Barbara, CA 93109
Barbara Mertz, *President*
Michael Collins, *Membership Chair*
    A national organization of working professional mystery authors. To be eligible for membership in ACWL you must have published a minimum of one

full-length work of fiction, or three short stories, or three nonfiction crime articles. The bimonthly ACWL BULLETin features articles by reliable experts and an exchange of information and advice among professional writers. Annual dues: $35.

AMERICAN MEDICAL WRITERS ASSOCIATION
9650 Rockville Pike
Bethesda, MD 20814
Lillian Sablack, *Executive Director*
Members of this association are engaged in biomedical communications. Any person actively interested in or professionally associated with any medium of medical communication is eligible for membership. The annual dues are $65.

AMERICAN SOCIETY OF JOURNALISTS AND AUTHORS, INC.
1501 Broadway, Suite 302
New York, NY 10036
Alexandra Cantor, *Executive Director*
This nationwide organization of independent writers of nonfiction is dedicated to promoting high standards of nonfiction writing through monthly meetings, annual writers' conferences, etc. ASJA offers extensive benefits and services including referral services, numerous discount services, and the opportunity to explore professional issues and concerns with other writers. Members also receive a monthly newsletter with confidential market information. Membership is open to professional free-lance writers of nonfiction; qualifications are judged by Membership Committee. Call or write for application details. Phone number: (212) 997-0947; fax number (212) 768-7414.

THE AUTHORS LEAGUE OF AMERICA, INC.
(The Authors Guild and The Dramatists Guild)
330 W. 42nd St.
New York, NY 10036-6902
The Authors League of America is a national organization of over 14,000 authors and dramatists, representing them on matters of joint concern, such as copyright, taxes, and freedom of expression. Membership in the league is restricted to authors and dramatists who are members of The Authors Guild and The Dramatists Guild. Matters such as contract terms and subsidiary rights are in the province of the two guilds.

A writer who has published a book in the last seven years with an established publisher, or one who has published several magazine pieces with periodicals of general circulation within the last eighteen months, may be eligible for active voting membership in The Authors Guild. A new writer may be eligible for associate membership; write to the Membership Committee. Dues: $90 a year.

The Dramatists Guild is a professional association of playwrights, composers, and lyricists, established to protect dramatists' rights and to improve working conditions. Services include use of the Guild's contracts, business counseling, publications, and symposia in major cities. All playwrights (produced or not) are eligible for membership.

THE INTERNATIONAL SOCIETY OF DRAMATISTS
Box 1310
Miami, FL 33153
Open to playwrights, agents, producers, screenwriters, and others involved in the theater. Publishes *Dramatist's Bible*, a directory of script opportunities, and *The Globe*, a newsletter with information and news of theaters across the country. Also provides free referral service for playwrights.

MYSTERY WRITERS OF AMERICA, INC.
17 E. 47th St., 6th Floor
New York, NY 10017
Priscilla Ridgway, *Executive Secretary*

The MWA exists for the purpose of raising the prestige of mystery and detective writing, and of defending the rights and increasing the income of all writers in the field of mystery, detection, and fact crime writing. Each year, the MWA presents the Edgar Allan Poe Awards for the best mystery writing in a variety of fields. The four classifications of membership are: *active* (open to any writer who has made a sale in the field of mystery, suspense, or crime writing); *associate* (for professionals in allied fields/writers in other fields); *corresponding* (for writers living outside the U.S.); *affiliate* (for unpublished writers and mystery enthusiasts). Annual dues: $65; $32.50 for corresponding members.

NATIONAL ASSOCIATION OF SCIENCE WRITERS, INC.
P.O. Box 294
Greenlawn, NY 11740

The NASW promotes the dissemination of accurate information regarding science through all media, and conducts a varied program to increase the flow of news from scientists, to improve the quality of its presentation, and to communicate its meaning to the reading public.

Anyone who has been actively engaged in the dissemination of science information is eligible to apply for membership. Active members must be principally involved in reporting on science through newspapers, magazines, TV, or other media that reach the public directly. Associate members report on science through limited-circulation publications and other media. Annual dues: $45.

THE NATIONAL WRITERS CLUB
1450 S. Havana, Suite 620
Aurora, CO 80012
James Lee Young, *Executive Director*

New and established writers, poets, and playwrights throughout the U.S. and Canada may become members of The National Writers Club, a full-time, customer-service-oriented association founded in 1937. Membership includes bimonthly newsletter, *Authorship*. Annual dues: $60 (Professionals), $50 (Regulars), plus a $15 one-time initiation fee; add $20 outside the USA, Canada, and Mexico. Phone: (303) 751-7844; fax: (303) 751-8593.

NATIONAL WRITERS UNION
13 Astor Pl., 7th Fl.
New York, NY 10003

The National Writers Union, a new labor organization dedicated to bringing about equitable payment and fair treatment of free-lance writers through collective action, has over 3,000 members, including book authors, poets, free-lance journalists, and technical writers in eleven chapters nationwide. The NWU offers its members contract and agent information, health insurance plans, press credentials, grievance handling, a union newspaper, and sponsors events across the country. Membership is open to writers who have published a book, play, three articles, five poems, one short story or an equivalent amount of newsletter, publicity, technical, commercial, government or institutional copy, or have written an equivalent amount of unpublished material and are actively seeking publication. Dues range from $55 to $135.

OUTDOOR WRITERS ASSOCIATION OF AMERICA, INC.
2017 Cato Ave., Suite 101
State College, PA 16801
Sylvia G. Bashline, *Executive Director*

The OWAA is a non-profit, international organization representing professional communicators who report and reflect upon America's diverse interests in the outdoors. Membership (by nomination only) includes a monthly publication, *Outdoors Unlimited*; annual conference; annual membership directory; contests. OWAA also provides scholarships to qualified students.

PEN AMERICAN CENTER
568 Broadway
New York, NY 10012

PEN American Center is one of more than 104 centers in 69 countries that make up International PEN, a worldwide association of literary writers, offering conferences, writing programs, and financial and educational assistance. Membership is open to writers who have published two books of literary merit, as well as editors, agents, playwrights, and translators who meet specific standards. (Apply to nomination committee.) PEN sponsors annual awards and grants and publishes the quarterly *PEN Newsletter* and the biennial directory, *Grants and Awards Available to American Writers*.

THE POETRY SOCIETY OF AMERICA
15 Gramercy Park
New York, NY 10003
Elise Paschen, *Executive Director*

Founded in 1910, The Poetry Society of America seeks through a variety of programs to gain a wider audience for American poetry. The Society offers 19 annual prizes for poetry (with many contests open to non-members as well as members), and sponsors workshops, poetry readings, and publications. Maintains the Van Vooris Library of American Poetry. Dues: $35 annually.

POETS AND WRITERS, INC.
72 Spring St.
New York, NY 10012
Elliot Figman, *Executive Director*

Poets & Writers, Inc., was founded in 1970 to foster the development of poets and fiction writers and to promote communication throughout the literary community. A non-membership organization, it offers a nationwide information center for writers; *Poets & Writers Magazine* and other publications; as well as sponsored readings and workshops.

PRIVATE EYE WRITERS OF AMERICA
1830 Haring St.
Brooklyn, NY 11229
Robert J. Randisi, *Executive Director*

Private Eye Writers of America is a national organization that seeks to promote a wider recognition and appreciation of private eye literature. Writers who have published a work of fiction (short story, novel, TV script, or movie screen play) with a private eye as the central character are eligible to join as active members. Serious devotees of the P.I. story may become associate members. Dues: $30 (Active), $24 (Associate), $36 (International). Annual Shamus Award for the best in P.I. fiction.

ROMANCE WRITERS OF AMERICA
13700 Veterans Memorial Dr., Suite 315
Houston, TX 77014
Bobbi Stinson, *Office Supervisor*

The RWA is an international organization with over 80 local chapters across the U.S. and Canada, open to any writer, published or unpublished, interested in the field of romantic fiction. Annual dues of $45, plus $10 application fee for new members; benefits include annual conference, contest, market information, and bimonthly newsmagazine, *Romance Writers' Report*.

SCIENCE FICTION WRITERS OF AMERICA, INC.
P.O. Box 4335
Spartanburg, SC 29305
Peter Dennis Pautz, *Executive Secretary*

The purpose of the SFWA, a professional organization of science fiction and fantasy writers, is to foster and further the interests of writers of fantasy and science fiction. SFWA presents the Nebula Award annually for excellence in the field and publishes the *Bulletin* for its members.

Any writer who has sold a work of science fiction or fantasy is eligible for membership. Dues: $60 per year for active members, $42 for affiliates, plus $10 installation fee; send for application and information. The *Bulletin* is available to nonmembers for $15 (four issues) within the U.S.; $18.50 overseas.

SMALL PRESS WRITERS AND ARTISTS ORGANIZATION
5116 S.143rd St.
Omaha, NE 68137
Marthayn Pelegrimas, *Secretary*

Founded in 1977, the SPWAO is an international service organization of 400 writers, artists, poets, and publishers dedicated to the promotion of excellence in the small press fields of science fiction, fantasy, and horror. Members receive the bimonthly *SPWAO Newsletter*, critiques by fellow members, grievance arbitration, and research assistance. Initial dues: $17.50; annual renewal is $15.

SOCIETY FOR TECHNICAL COMMUNICATION
901 N. Stuart St., #304
Arlington, VA 22203
William C. Stolgitis, *Executive Director*

The Society for Technical Communication is a professional organization dedicated to the advancement of the theory and practice of technical communication in all media. The 15,000 members in the U.S. and other countries include technical writers and editors, publishers, artists and draftsmen, researchers, educators, and audiovisual specialists.

SOCIETY OF AMERICAN TRAVEL WRITERS
1155 Connecticut Ave. N.W., Suite 500
Washington, D.C. 20036
Ken Fischer, *Administrative Coordinator*

The Society of American Travel Writers represents writers and other professionals who strive to provide travelers with accurate reports on destinations, facilities, and services.

Membership is by invitation. Active membership is limited to salaried travel writers and freelancers who have a steady volume of published or distributed work about travel. Initiation fee for active members is $200, for associate members $400. Annual dues: $120 (Active); $240 (Associate).

724

SOCIETY OF CHILDREN'S BOOK WRITERS

P.O. Box 66296
Mar Vista Station
Los Angeles, CA 90066
Lin Oliver, *Executive Director*

This national organization of authors, editors, publishers, illustrators, filmmakers, librarians, and educators offers a variety of services to people who write, illustrate for or share an interest in children's literature. Full memberships are open to those who have had at least one children's book or story published. Associate memberships are open to all those with an interest in children's literature. Yearly dues are $40.

SOCIETY OF PROFESSIONAL JOURNALISTS

16 S. Jackson St.
Greencastle, IN 46135
Ira D. Perry, *Executive Director*

With over 16,000 members and 300 chapters, the SPJ serves the interests of print, broadcast, and wire journalists. Services include legal counsel on journalism issues, jobs-for-journalists career search program, professional development seminars, and awards that encourage journalism. Members receive *The Quill*, a monthly magazine that explores current issues in the field. SPJ promotes ethics and freedom of information programs.

Members must spend at least 50 percent of their working hours in journalism. National dues: $55 for professionals; $27.50 for students.

WESTERN WRITERS OF AMERICA

P.O. Box 823
Sheridan, WY 82801
Barbara Ketcham, *Secretary/Treasurer*

Published writers of fiction, nonfiction, and poetry pertaining to the traditions, legends, development, and history of the American West may join the nonprofit Western Writers of America. Its chief purpose is to promote a more widespread distribution, readership, and appreciation of the West and its literature. Dues are $60 a year. Sponsors annual Spur Awards, Owen Wister Award, and Medicine Pipe Bearer's Award for Published Work.

WRITERS GUILD OF AMERICA, EAST, INC.

555 W. 57th St.
New York, NY 10019
Mona Mangan, *Executive Director*

WRITERS GUILD OF AMERICA, WEST, INC.

8955 Beverly Blvd.
West Hollywood, CA 90048
Brian Walton, *Executive Director*

The Writers Guild of America (East and West) represents writers in the fields of radio, television, and motion pictures in both news and entertainment. In order to qualify for membership, a writer must fulfill current requirements for employment or sale of material in one of these three fields.

The basic dues are $25 per quarter for the Writers Guild West and $12.50 per quarter for Writers Guild East. In addition, there are quarterly dues based on percentage of the member's earnings in any of the fields over which the Guild has jurisdiction. The initiation fee is $1,000 for Writers Guild East and $1,500 for Writers Guild West. (Writers living east of the Mississippi join Writers Guild East, and those living west of the Mississippi, Writers Guild West.)

AMERICAN LITERARY AGENTS

The following is a sampling of agents that handle literary and/or dramatic material. Most literary agents do not accept new writers as clients; since their income is a percentage (10% to 20%) of the sales made from their clients, the writers they represent must be selling fairly regularly to good markets. Always query an agent first. Do not send any manuscripts until the agent has asked you to do so; and be wary of agents who charge fees for reading manuscripts.

The Association of Authors Representatives represents the recent merger of the Society of Authors' Representatives (10 Astor Pl., 3rd Floor, New York, NY 10003) and the Independent Literary Agents Association, Inc. (15 E. 26th St., Suite 1801, New York, NY 10010); for their most up-to-date list of members and code of ethics, send a 52¢ legal-size SASE to either address.

Addresses that include zip codes in parentheses are located in New York City. An extensive list of agents and their policies can be found in *Literary Market Place*, a directory found in most libraries, and in *Literary Agents of North America* (Author Aid/Research Associates International, 340 E. 52nd St., New York, NY 10022).

CAROLE ABEL Carole Abel Literary Agent, 160 W. 87th St. (10024)

DOMINICK ABEL Dominick Abel Literary Agency, 498 West End Ave. (10024)

EDWARD J. ACTON Edward J. Acton, Inc., 928 Broadway, Suite 301 (10010)

BRET ADAMS, LTD. 448 W. 44th St. (10036)

MARCIA AMSTERDAM AGENCY 41 W. 82nd St., #9A (10024)

STEVE AXELROD The Axelrod Agency, 66 Church St., Lenox, MA 02140

JULIAN BACH LITERARY AGENCY, INC. 747 Third Ave. (10017)

RICHARD BALKIN The Balkin Agency, P.O. Box 222, Amherst, MA 01004

VIRGINIA BARBER Virginia Barber Agency, Inc., 353 W. 21st St. (10011)

LORETTA BARRETT 121 W. 27th St., #601 (10001)

AMY BERKOWER Writers House, 21 W. 26th St. (10010)

LOIS BERMAN The Little Theatre Bldg., 240 W. 44th St. (10036)

MEREDITH G. BERNSTEIN 2112 Broadway, Suite 503A (10023)

VICKY BIJUR 333 West End Ave. (10023)

DAVID BLACK David Black Literary Agency, 220 Fifth Ave., Suite 1400 (10001)

GEORGES BORCHARDT, INC. 136 E. 57th St. (10022)

BRANDT & BRANDT LITERARY AGENTS, INC. 1501 Broadway (10036)

THE HELEN BRANN AGENCY, INC. 94 Curtis Rd., Bridgewater, CT 06752

BROADWAY PLAY PUBLISHING 357 W. 20th St. (10011)

ANDREA BROWN 1081 Alameda, Suite 71, Belmont, CA 94002

CURTIS BROWN, LTD. 10 Astor Pl. (10003)

JANE JORDAN BROWNE Multimedia Product Development, Inc., 410 S. Michigan Ave., Rm. 724, Chicago, IL 60605

KNOX BURGER ASSOCIATES, LTD. 39 ½ Washington Square S. (10012)

MARIA CARVAINIS Maria Carvainis Agency, Inc., 235 West End Ave. (10023)

MARTHA CASSELMAN Box 342, Calistoga, CA 94515–0342

JULIE CASTIGLIA Waterside Productions, 191 San Elijo Ave., Cardiff, CA 92007

RUTH COHEN Ruth Cohen Inc. Literary Agency, Box 7626, Menlo Park, CA 94025

SUSAN B. COHEN Writers House, 21 W. 26th St. (10010)

OSCAR COLLIER Collier Associates, 2000 Flat Run Rd., Seaman, OH 45679

FRANCES COLLIN LITERARY AGENCY 110 W. 40th St., Suite 1403 (10018)

DON CONGDON ASSOCIATES, INC. 156 Fifth Ave., Suite 625 (10010)

ROBERT CORNFIELD Robert Cornfield Literary Agency, 145 W. 79th St. (10024)

WILLIAM CRAVER Writers and Artists Agency, 19 W. 44th St., Suite 1000 (10036)

RICHARD CURTIS Richard Curtis Associates, Inc., 171 E. 74th St. (10021)

LIZ DARHANSOFF 1220 Park Ave. (10028)

JOAN DAVES 21 W. 26th St. (10010–1003)

ANITA DIAMANT 310 Madison Ave., #1508 (10017)

SANDRA DIJKSTRA Sandra Dijkstra Literary Agency, 1237 Camino Del Mar, Suite 515C, Del Mar, CA 92014

CANDIDA DONADIO & ASSOCIATES, INC. 231 W. 22nd St. (10011)

ANNE EDELSTEIN Anne Edelstein Literary Agency, 510 W. 110th St., #7E (10025)

JOSEPH ELDER Joseph Elder Agency, 150 W. 87th St., Apt. 6D (10024)

ANN ELMO AGENCY, INC. 60 E. 42nd St. (10165)

FELICIA ETH 140 University Ave., Suite 62, Palo Alto, CA 94301

EILEEN FALLON Fallon Literary Agency, 1456 Second Ave., #108 (10021)

JOHN FARQUHARSON, LTD. 250 W. 57th St., Suite 1007 (10107)

MARJE FIELDS 165 W. 46th St., Suite 1205 (10036)

DIANA FINCH Ellen Levine Literary Agency, 15 E. 26th St., Suite 1801 (10010)

JOYCE FLAHERTY 816 Lynda Ct., St. Louis, MO 63122

THE FOX CHASE AGENCY, INC. Public Ledger Bldg. #930, Independence Sq., Philadelphia, PA 19106

ROBERT A. FREEDMAN DRAMATIC AGENCY, INC. 1501 Broadway, #2310 (10036)

SAMUEL FRENCH, INC. 45 W. 25th St. (10010)

SARA JANE FREYMANN Stepping Stone Literary Agency, 58 W. 71st St. (10023)

JAY GARON Jay Garon-Brooke Associates, 415 Central Park West (10025)

JANE GELFMAN John Farquharson Ltd., 250 W. 57th St., Suite 1007 (10107)

PETER GINSBERG Curtis Brown, Ltd., 10 Astor Pl. (10003)

FRANCIS GOLDIN 305 E. 11th St. (10003)

ARNOLD P. GOODMAN Goodman Associates, 500 West End Ave. (10024)

ELISE SIMON GOODMAN Goodman Associates, 500 West End Ave. (10024)

IRENE GOODMAN Irene Goodman Literary Agency, 521 Fifth Ave., 17th Fl. (10017)

GRAHAM AGENCY 311 W. 43rd St. (10036)

FRANCIS GREENBURGER Sanford J. Greenburger Associates, 55 Fifth Ave., 15th Fl. (10003)

MAXINE GROFFSKY Maxine Groffsky Literary Agency, 2 Fifth Ave. (10011)

FAITH HORNBY HAMLIN Sanford J. Greenburger Associates, 55 Fifth Ave., 15th Fl. (10003)

JEANNE K. HANSON Jeanne K. Hanson Literary Agency, 511 Wooddale Ave. S., Edina, MN 55424

HELEN HARVEY 410 W. 24th St., (10011)

JOHN HAWKINS & ASSOCIATES, INC. 71 W. 23rd St., Suite 1600 (10010)

LINDA HAYES Columbia Literary Associates, 7902 Nottingham Way, Ellicott City, MD 21403

JAMES B. HEACOCK Heacock Literary Agency, 1523 Sixth Ave., Suite 14, Santa Monica, CA 90401

MERILEE HEIFETZ Writers House, 21 W. 26th St. (10010)

JEFF HERMAN The Jeff Herman Agency, Inc., 500 Greenwich St., Suite 501C (10013)

JOHN L. HOCHMAN John L. Hochman Books, 320 E. 58th St. (10022)

BERENICE HOFFMAN Berenice Hoffman Literary Agency, 215 W. 75th St. (10023)

BERT HOLTJE James Peters Associates, Box 772, Tenafly, NJ 07670

INTERNATIONAL CREATIVE MANAGEMENT, INC. 40 W. 57th St. (10019)

SHARON JARVIS Sharon Jarvis & Co., 260 Willard Ave., Staten Island, NY 10314

JCA LITERARY AGENCY, INC. 27 W. 20th St., Suite 1103 (10011)

NATASHA KERN Natasha Kern Literary Agency, P.O. Box 2908, Portland, OR 97208–2908

KIDDE, HOYT & PICARD 335 E. 51st St. (10022)

ELIZABETH FROST KNAPPMAN New England Publishing Associates, P.O. Box 5, Chester, CT 06412

BARBARA S. KOUTS P.O. Box 558, Bellport, NY 11713

OTTO R. KOZAK LITERARY AGENCY P.O. Box 152, Long Beach, NY 11561

LUCY KROLL AGENCY 390 West End Ave. (10024)

PINDER LANE PRODUCTIONS, LTD. 159 W. 53rd St. (10019)

HEIDE LANGE Sanford J. Greenburger Associates, 55 Fifth Ave., 15th Fl. (10003)

VICKI LANSKY The Book Peddlers, 18326 Minnetonka Blvd., Deephaven, MN 55391

THE ROBERT LANTZ-JOY HARRIS LITERARY AGENCY 888 Seventh Ave. (10106)

MICHAEL LARSEN Michael Larsen/Elizabeth Pomada, 1029 Jones St., San Francisco, CA 94109

LESCHER & LESCHER, LTD. 67 Irving Pl. (10003)

ELLEN LEVINE Ellen Levine Literary Agency, 15 E. 26th St., Suite 1801 (10010)

WENDY LIPKIND Wendy Lipkind Agency, 165 E. 66th St. (10021)

LONDON STAR PROMOTIONS 21704 Devonshire St., Suite 200, Chatsworth, CA 91311–2903

NANCY LOVE Nancy Love Literary Agency, 250 E. 65th St. (10021)

BARBARA LOWENSTEIN Barbara Lowenstein Associates, 121 W. 27th St., Suite 601 (10001)

DONALD MAASS Donald Maass Literary Agency, 8P, 304 W. 92nd St. (10025)

MARGARET MCBRIDE Margaret McBride Literary Agency, 4350 Executive Dr., Suite 225, San Diego, CA 92121

GERARD MCCAULEY AGENCY, INC. P.O. Box AE, Katonah, NY 10536

ANITA D. MCCLELLAN Anita D. McClellan Associates, 50 Stearns St., Cambridge, MA 02138

MCINTOSH & OTIS, INC. 310 Madison Ave. (10017)

CAROL MANN Carol Mann Literary Agency, 55 Fifth Ave. (10003)

JANET WILKENS MANUS Janet Wilkens Manus Literary Agency, 417 E. 57th St., Suite 5D (10022)

DENISE MARCIL Denise Marcil Literary Agency, 685 West End Ave. (10025)

BETTY MARKS 176 E. 77th St., Apt. 9F (10021)

ELAINE MARKSON Elaine Markson Literary Agency, 44 Greenwich Ave. (10011)

MILDRED MARMUR 310 Madison Ave., Rm. 607 (10017)

EVAN MARSHALL Evan Marshall Literary Agency, 228 Watchung Ave., Upper Montclair, NJ 07043

ELISABETH MARTON 96 Fifth Ave. (10011)

HAROLD MATSON COMPANY, INC. 276 Fifth Ave. (10001)

CLAUDIA MENZA 237 W. 11th St. (10014)

HELEN MERRILL, LTD. 435 W. 23rd St., #1A (10011)

MARTHA MILLARD Martha Millard Literary Agency, 204 Park Ave., Madison, NJ 07940

HOWARD MORHAIM Howard Morhaim Literary Agency, 175 Fifth Ave., Rm. 709 (10010)

WILLIAM MORRIS AGENCY, INC. 1350 Ave. of the Americas (10019)

JEAN V. NAGGAR Jean V. Naggar Literary Agency, Inc., 216 E. 75th St. (10021)

RUTH NATHAN Ruth Nathan Agency, 658 Broadway, Suite 402B (10012)

BETSY NOLAN The Betsy Nolan Literary Agency, 50 W. 29th St., 9W (10001)

HAROLD OBER ASSOCIATES, INC. 425 Madison Ave. (10017)

FIFI OSCARD ASSOCIATES, INC. 19 W. 44th St. (10036)

RICHARD PARKS 138 E. 16th St., 5B (10003)

LORI PERKINS L. Perkins & Associates, 330 Haven Ave., Apt. E (10033)

BELA POMER Bela Pomer Agency, Inc., 22 Shalimar Blvd., PH2, Toronto, Ont. M5N 2Z8, Canada

SUSAN ANN PROTTER 110 W. 40th St. (10018)

ROBERTA PRYOR Roberta Pryor, Inc., 24 W. 55th St. (10019)

VICTORIA PRYOR Arcadia, Ltd., 221 W. 82nd St., Suite 7D (10024)

RAINES & RAINES 71 Park Ave. (10016)

HELEN REES Helen Rees Literary Agency, 308 Commonwealth Ave., Boston, MA 02116

JOSEPH RHODES Rhodes Literary Agency, 140 West End Ave. (10023)

FLORA ROBERTS, INC. Penthouse A, 157 W. 57th St. (10019)

ROSENSTONE/WENDER 3 E. 48th St. (10017)

JANE ROTROSEN Jane Rotrosen Agency, 318 E. 51st St. (10022)

RUSSELL & VOLKENING, INC. 50 W. 29th St. (10001)

RAPHAEL SAGALYN Raphael Sagalyn, Inc., Literary Agency, 2813 Bellevue Terr. N.W., Washington, DC 20007

HAROLD SCHMIDT 668 Greenwich St., Apt. 1005 (10014)

DEBORAH SCHNEIDER John Farquharson Ltd., 250 W. 57th St. (10107)

SUSAN SCHULMAN Susan Schulman Literary Agency, 454 W. 44th St. (10036)

EDYTHEA GINIS SELMAN 14 Washington Pl. (10003)

CHARLOTTE SHEEDY Charlotte Sheedy Literary Agency, 41 King St. (10014)

THE SHUKAT COMPANY, LTD. 340 W. 55th St., #1A (10019)

ROSALIE SIEGEL 111 Murphy Dr., Pennington, NJ 10014

IRENE SKOLNIK Curtis Brown, Ltd., 10 Astor Pl. (10003)

NICKI SMITH Smith-Skolnik Literary Agency, 23 E. 10th St. (10003)

ELYSE SOMMER Elyse Sommer, Inc., 110–34 73rd Rd., P.O. Box 1133, Forest Hills, NY 11375

PHILIP G. SPITZER LITERARY AGENCY 788 Ninth Ave. (10019)

STERLING LORD LITERISTIC, INC. 1 Madison Ave. (10010)

GLORIA STERN 1230 Park Ave. (10028)

ROBIN STRAUS Robin Straus Agency, Inc. 229 E. 79th St. (10021)

TAMS-WITMARK MUSIC LIBRARY, INC. 560 Lexington Ave. (10022)

ROSLYN TARG Roslyn Targ Literary Agency, 105 W. 13th St., #15E (10011)

PATRICIA TEAL Teal & Watt Literary Agency, 2036 Vista del Rosa, Fullerton, CA 92631

SUSAN P. URSTADT 103 Brushy Ridge Rd., New Canaan, CT 06840

RALPH VICINANZA Ralph Vicinanza Ltd., 432 Park Ave. S., Suite 1205 (10016)

THE WALLACE AGENCY 177 E. 70th St. (10021)

MAUREEN WALTERS Curtis Brown, Ltd., 10 Astor Pl. (10003)

THE WENDY WEIL AGENCY, INC. 747 Third Ave. (10017)

RHODA WEYR Rhoda Weyr Agency, 151 Bergen St., Brooklyn, NY 11217

AUDREY R. WOLF Audrey R. Wolf Literary Agency, 1001 Connecticut Ave. N.W., Suite 1210, Washington, DC 20036

ANN WRIGHT REPRESENTATIVES, INC. 136 E. 56th St. (10022–3615)

MARY YOST ASSOCIATES, INC. 59 E. 54th St., #72 (10022)

SUSAN ZECKENDORF Susan Zeckendorf Associates, 171 W. 57th St. (10019)

ALBERT ZUCKERMAN Writers House, 21 W. 26th St. (10010)

INDEX TO MARKETS

733